CRITICAL
MEDIA
STUDIES

About the Authors

Elinor Christopher Light

Brian L. Ott (right) is Associate Professor of Media Studies at the University of Colorado Denver. He is the author of *The Small Screen: How Television Equips Us to Live in the Information Age* (Wiley Blackwell, 2007) and co-editor of *It's Not TV: Watching HBO in the Post-Television Era* (Routledge, 2008). Brian enjoys all things sci-fi and was a huge fan of *Breaking Bad*. His favorite film is *Lost in Translation*, which he believes perfectly captures life in the contemporary moment and, as such, provides the inspiration for the book's cover art.

Robert L. Mack (left) is a Ph.D. candidate in Communication Studies at the University of Texas, Austin. His scholarship concerns the text-audience interface with a focus on the medium of television. Rob enjoys tabletop board games and passionately believes that Janeway was the best *Star Trek* captain. His favorite subgenres of film include class warfare period pieces, films that attempted to introduce computers to the masses before the technology was widely available, and movies where Whoopi Goldberg evades danger in large, metropolitan cities.

**Brian L. Ott and
Robert L. Mack**

CRITICAL MEDIA STUDIES
AN INTRODUCTION

Second Edition

WILEY Blackwell

This second edition first published 2014
© 2014 John Wiley & Sons, Inc

Edition history: John Wiley & Sons, Inc. (1e, 2010)

Registered Office
John Wiley & Sons, Ltd, The Atrium, Southern Gate, Chichester, West Sussex, PO19 8SQ, UK

Editorial Offices
350 Main Street, Malden, MA 02148-5020, USA
9600 Garsington Road, Oxford, OX4 2DQ, UK
The Atrium, Southern Gate, Chichester, West Sussex, PO19 8SQ, UK

For details of our global editorial offices, for customer services, and for information about how
to apply for permission to reuse the copyright material in this book please see our website at
www.wiley.com/wiley-blackwell.

The right of Brian L. Ott and Robert L. Mack to be identified as the authors of this work has been
asserted in accordance with the UK Copyright, Designs and Patents Act 1988.

Library of Congress Cataloging-in-Publication data is available for this book.

9781118553978 (paperback)

A catalogue record for this book is available from the British Library.

Cover image: Wet evening in Shinjuku © Jon Hicks / Corbis
Cover design by RBDA Studio

Set in 10.5/13pt Minion by SPi Publisher Services, Pondicherry, India

Printed in the USA by Strategic Content Imaging

5   2015

Contents

Preface

To our billions of readers, welcome to the second edition of *Critical Media Studies: An Introduction*! Okay, we recognize that is an optimistic first sentence, but it sounds more impressive than, "Hey, Ian, Gordana, and crazy Uncle Carl, thanks for reading our book." Besides, who knows how many readers we have on Kobol (hello, fellow fans of *Battlestar Galactica*!).

When we began work on the first edition of the book nearly five years ago, it was tentatively titled *Critical Media Studies: An Interstellar Guide to Fabulous Dinner Conversation*. In the ensuing time, the book has undergone numerous changes, not least of which was a rethinking of its title. Apparently, "some" (who shall remain nameless, Elizabeth!) thought that the reference to *dinner conversation* might be confusing and misleading. We remain convinced, however, that it would have been an effective way to target fans of the *Food Network* – a demographic that has, in our opinion, been ignored by academic publishers for far too long (hello, fellow fans of *Iron Chef America*!). Although we harbor no hard feelings about this change, we nevertheless hope that readers *will* discuss the book over dinner (or any meal-like activity, including tea time: hello, British readers!) and that the ensuing conversation *will* be fabulous.

Another significant development has been the book's cover art. Initially we wanted an image of two squirrels "doing it" . . . a metaphor, of course, for the frenzied but emotionally hollow exchange that occurs between media producers and consumers. But as with the title, more sensible heads prevailed, resulting in the equally enticing image of Tokyo at night. We, nevertheless, would like to thank our friend, Greg, for bravely approaching said squirrels, snapping a picture, and almost losing a finger in the process (hello and apologies, Greg!). Despite our disappointment that the squirrel-on-squirrel image was not selected, we believe that the existing cover is equally appropriate to the themes raised in the book. The rain symbolizes the steady stream of media messages that relentlessly pour down upon us each day. Meanwhile, the unfamiliar signs of the cityscape invite readers to wonder about their meanings just as *Critical Media Studies* asks readers to wonder about the role of media in their lives. Finally, the array of brilliant colors that comprise the image reflects the array of critical perspectives contained in the book, each shedding its own light on the media.

In closing, we wish to acknowledge our debt to the sensible heads mentioned above. In particular, we would like to express our gratitude to the team at Wiley Blackwell, especially Elizabeth P. Swayze, Senior Editor, and Julia Kirk, Senior Project Editor. Their guidance and support has been invaluable. We feel fortunate to have had such a dynamic, creative, and thoughtful team guiding us. We also wish to thank Dave Nash for his persistence and good humor in securing various copyright permissions. Finally, we extend a very special thanks to Kathleen McCully, who copy-edited the manuscript, and Nora Naughton, who oversaw the manuscript through its copy-editing, typesetting, proofreading and indexing stages (Kathleen and Nora, thank you for your tireless efforts to correct our many mistakes!). Since it is cliché to say that any remaining mistakes are solely our own, we instead locate the blame squarely with the Illuminati (hello, Illuminati!).

Cheers,
Brian and Rob
October 14, 2013

1 Introducing Critical Media Studies

KEY CONCEPTS

CONVERGENCE
CRITICAL MEDIA STUDIES
FRAGMENTATION
GLOBALIZATION
MASS MEDIA
MEDIUM
MOBILITY
POSTMODERNITY
SOCIALIZATION
THEORY
SIMULATION

How We Know What We Know

Everything we know is learned in one of two ways.[1] The first way is *somatically*. These are the things we know through direct sensory perception of our environment. We know what some things look, smell, feel, sound, or taste like because we personally have seen, smelled, felt, heard, or tasted them. One of the authors of this text knows, for example, that "Rocky Mountain oysters" (bull testicles) are especially chewy because he tried them once at a country and western bar. In short, some of what we know is based on first-hand, unmediated experience. But the things we know through direct sensory perception make up a very small percentage of the total things we know. The vast majority of what we know comes to us a second way, *symbolically*. These are the things we know *through* someone or something such as a parent, friend, teacher, museum, textbook, photograph, radio, film, television, or the internet. This type of information is mediated, meaning that it came to us via some indirect channel or **medium**. The word medium is derived from the Latin word *medius*, which means "middle" or that which comes between two things: the way that television and the Discovery Channel might come between us and the animals of the Serengeti, for instance.

Critical Media Studies: An Introduction, Second Edition. Brian L. Ott and Robert L. Mack.
© 2014 John Wiley & Sons, Inc. Published 2014 by John Wiley & Sons, Inc.

In the past 30 seconds, those readers who have never eaten Rocky Mountain oysters now know they are chewy, as that information has been communicated to them through, or mediated by, this book. When we stop to think about all the things we know, we suddenly realize that the vast majority of what we know is mediated. We may know something about China even if we have never been there thanks to Wikipedia; we may know something about King George VI even though he died long before we were born thanks to *The King's Speech* (2010); we may even know something about the particulars of conducting a homicide investigation even though we have likely never conducted one thanks to the crime drama *CSI*. The mass media account, it would seem, for much of what we know (and do not know) today. But this has not always been the case.

Before the invention of mass media, the spoken or written word was the primary medium for conveying information and ideas. This method of communication had several significant and interrelated limitations. First, as the transmission of information was tied to the available means of transportation (foot, horse, buggy, boat, locomotive, or automobile depending upon the time period), its dissemination was extraordinarily slow, especially over great distances like continents and oceans. Second, because information could not easily be reproduced and distributed, its scope was extremely limited. Third, since information often passed through multiple channels (people), each of which altered it, if only slightly, there was a high probability of message distortion. Simply put, there was no way to communicate a uniform message to a large group of people in distant places quickly prior to the advent of the modern mass media. What distinguishes mass media like print, radio, and television from individual media like human speech and hand-written letters, then, is precisely their unique capacity to address large audiences in remote locations with relative efficiency.

Critical Media Studies is about the social and cultural consequences of that revolutionary capability. Recognizing that mass media are, first and foremost, communication technologies that increasingly mediate both what we know and how we know, this book surveys a variety of perspectives for evaluating and assessing the role of mass media in our daily lives. Whether listening to an iPod while walking across campus, sharing pictures with friends on Facebook, receiving the latest sports scores via your smartphone, sharing your favorite YouTube video over email, or settling in for the most recent episode of *The Big Bang Theory* or *Downton Abbey*, the mass media are regular fixtures of everyday life. But before beginning to explore the specific and complex roles that mass media play in our lives, it is worth looking, first, at who they are, when they originated, and how they have developed.

Categorizing Mass Media

As is perhaps already evident, *media* is a very broad term that includes a diverse array of communication technologies such as cave drawings, speech, smoke signals, letters, books, telegraphy, telephony, magazines, newspapers, radio, film, television, smartphones, video games, and networked computers to name just a few. But this book is principally concerned with **mass media** or those communication technologies that have the *potential* to reach a large audience in remote locations. What distinguishes mass media from individual media, then, is not merely audience size. While a graduation speaker or musician may address as many as 40,000 people at once in a stadium, for instance, neither one is mass mediated because the audience is not remote. Now, of course, if a Lady Gaga concert is being broadcast live via satellite, those watching at home on their televisions or streaming it live over the internet are experiencing it through mass media. Mass media collapse the distance between artist and audience, then. Working from this definition, we have organized the mass media into four sub-categories: print media, motion picture and sound recording, broadcast media, and new media. These categories, like all acts of classification, are arbitrary, meaning that they emphasize certain features of the media they group together at the expense of others. Nonetheless, we offer these categories as one way of conceptually organizing mass communication technologies.

Print media

In an electronically saturated world like the one in which we live today, it is easy to overlook the historical legacy and contemporary transformations of print media, the first mass medium. German printer Johannes Gutenberg invented the movable-type printing press in 1450, sparking a revolution in the ways that human beings could disseminate, preserve, and ultimately relate to knowledge. Printed materials before the advent of the press were costly and rare, but the invention of movable type allowed for the (relatively) cheap production of a diverse array of pamphlets, books, and other items. This flourishing of printed materials touched almost every aspect of human life. Suddenly knowledge could be recorded for future generations in libraries or religious texts, and social power increasingly hinged upon literacy and ownership of printed materials. Most importantly, the press allowed for an unprecedented circulation of knowledge to far-flung cities across Europe. Although still limited by class distinctions, access to information from outside of one's immediate context was a real possibility. Mass media was born.

Not long after the settlement of Jamestown in the USA in 1607, the colonies established their first printing press. Located in Cambridge, Massachusetts, the press was printing popular religious tracts such as the *Bay Psalm Book*, a 148-page collection of English translations of Hebrew, by 1640.[2] Although much of the early printing in the colonies was religion-oriented, novels such as *Robinson Crusoe* (1719) and *Tom Jones* (1749), imported from England, were also popular. Religious tracts were eventually followed by almanacs, newspapers, and magazines. The most well-known early almanac, *Poor Richard's Almanac*, which included information on the weather along with some political opinions, was printed from 1733 to 1757 by Benjamin Franklin in Philadelphia. Although various cities had short-lived or local non-daily newspapers in the 1700s, the New York *Sun*, which is considered the first

Table 1.1   Number of consumer magazine titles in the USA

	1990	1995	2000	2005	2010
Number of titles	587	668	836	718	628

Source: Audit Bureau of Circulations.

successful mass-circulation newspaper, did not begin operations until 1833.[3] The failure of earlier newspapers is often attributed to the fact that they were small operations run by local printers. It was not until newspapers began using editors and receiving substantial financial backing – first from political parties and later from wealthy elites like Joseph Pulitzer and William Randolph Hearst – that the newspaper industry mushroomed.

During the nineteenth and twentieth centuries, the newspaper industry experienced rapid growth. This trend continued until 1973, at which point there were 1,774 daily newspapers with a combined circulation of 63.1 million copies.[4] This meant that about 92 percent of US households were subscribing to a daily newspaper in 1973. Since then, however, newspaper production and circulation has steadily declined. In 2011, the total number of daily newspapers printed in the USA was 1,382 and they had a combined circulation of 44.4 million copies or less than 40 percent of US households.

In many ways, the history of the magazine industry in the USA closely mirrors that of the newspaper industry. It began somewhat unsteadily, underwent tremendous growth, and is currently experiencing a period of considerable instability. The first US magazine, *American Magazine*, was published in 1741. But the magazine boom did not really begin until the mid-nineteenth century. And though the industry continued to experience growth throughout the twentieth century, more recently it has suffered a decline in both the total number of titles (Table 1.1) and paid circulation (Table 1.2). Table 1.1 illustrates that the number of consumer magazine titles in the USA grew by 30 percent from 1990 to 2000 before declining by nearly 25 percent from 2000 to 2010.

Moreover, as Table 1.2 shows, the total paid circulation of the top 10 magazines in 2012 is more than 30 million less than the total paid circulation of the top 10 magazines 20 years earlier. Interestingly, the highest circulating magazine in 2012, *Game Informer Magazine*, had existed for only 1 year in 1992, while the second highest circulating magazine in 1992, *TV Guide*, no longer exists. The book publishing industry has, until very recently, not experienced the deep losses occurring in the newspaper and magazine industries over the past two decades. But in 2012, unit sales of traditional paper books fell by about 9 percent for the third year in a row; adult non-fiction was the hardest hit, falling 13 percent.[5] Despite declining circulation and unit sales in the newspaper, magazine, and book industries, Americans are still reading. But how they are reading – thanks to e-books and online newspapers and magazines – is changing both rapidly and dramatically.

Table 1.2 Top 10 US consumer magazines by paid circulation in 1992 and 2012*

1992		2012	
Rank/Publication	Circulation	Rank/Publication	Circulation
1. *Reader's Digest*	16,258,476	1. *Game Informer Magazine*	7,864,326
2. *TV Guide*	14,498,341	2. *Better Homes and Gardens*	7,621,456
3. *National Geographic*	9,708,254	3. *Reader's Digest*	5,527,183
4. *Better Homes and Gardens*	8,002,585	4. *Good Housekeeping*	4,354,740
5. *The Cable Guide*	5,889,947	5. *Family Circle*	4,143,942
6. *Family Circle*	5,283,660	6. *National Geographic*	4,125,152
7. *Good Housekeeping*	5,139,355	7. *People*	3,637,633
8. *Ladies' Home Journal*	5,041,143	8. *Woman's Day*	3,374,479
9. *Woman's Day*	4,810,445	9. *Time*	3,281,175
10. *McCall's*	4,704,772	10. *Taste of Home*	3,268,549
Total circulation of top 10	**79,336,978**	**Total circulation of top 10**	**47,198,635**

Source: *Adweek*, March 29, 1993; Alliance for Audited Media, February 7, 2013. *Data exclude magazines whose circulation is tied to membership benefits (i.e. *AARP The Magazine* [formerly *Modern Maturity*] and *AARP Bulletin*).

Motion picture and sound recording

Sound recording and motion pictures may seem like an odd pairing at first, but their histories are deeply intertwined thanks in large part to Thomas Edison. In the span of 15 years, Edison and his assistant, William Kennedy Laurie Dickson, created what would later develop into the first two new mass media since print. Edison's first invention, of the phonograph in 1877, was a device that played recorded sound, and his second, the kinetoscope in 1892, was an early motion picture device that showed short, silent films in peep-show fashion to individual viewers. But Edison's goal was to synchronize audio and visual images into a film projector that would allow for more than one viewer at a time. Although sound film did not become possible until the early 1920s, improvements in film projection, namely the development of the vitascope, gave rise to the silent film era in the meantime. The eventual synchronization of sound and film launched talking pictures, or "talkies." The first commercially successful, feature-length talkie was a musical film, *The Jazz Singer*, in 1927. Hollywood was about to enter its Golden Age of the 1930s and 1940s, in which "the studios were geared to produce a singular commodity, the feature film."[6]

With the motion picture industry firmly established, sound recording was now receiving independent attention and the record industry began to dominate the music industry, which had previously been involved primarily in the production of sheet music. By the start of the twentieth century, profits from the sale of sound recordings quickly eclipsed profits from the sale of sheet music.

This shift was fueled in large part by the continuous development of cheap and easily reproducible formats such as magnetic tape in 1926, long-playing (LP) records in 1948, compact or audio cassettes in 1963, optical or compact discs (CDs) in 1982, and lossy bitcompression technologies such as MPEG-1 Audio Layer 3 (MP3s) in 1995. With the exception of magnetic tape for sound recording, which was invented by German engineer Fritz Pfleumer, and Columbia Records' LP, Sony and Philips are responsible for the previously mentioned recording formats, as well as the Betamax (1975), LaserDisc (1978), Video2000 (1980), Betacam (1982), Video8 (1985), Digital Audio Tape (1987), Hi8 (1989), CD-i (1991), MiniDisc (1992), Digital Compact Disc (1992), Universal Media Disc (2005), Blu-ray Disc (2006), and DVD (as part of the 1995 DVD Consortium) formats. Several of these more recent formats have had implications for the motion picture industry, as they allow for the playback and recording of movies on DVD players and computers at home.

Broadcast media

The development of broadcast technologies changed the media landscape once again. Instead of media physically having to be distributed to stores or shipped to audiences as books, magazines, and newspapers are, or audiences physically having to travel to the media as in the case of film, media could now be brought directly to audiences over public airwaves. This was an important development because it freed mass media from transportation for the first time in history. We have excluded the electrical telegraph (1830s) because, like the telephone (1870s), it is better classified as a personal medium than a mass medium. Radio came on the scene first, experimenting with transmissions as early as the 1890s and making scheduled broadcasts in the 1920s. But television followed shortly thereafter with Philo T. Farnsworth, a Mormon from the small farm community of Rigby, Idaho, applying for the first television patent in 1927 and CBS launching the first television schedule in 1941. Not only do radio and television share an overlapping technological history, but they also share an overlapping professional history, as many of television's early stars came from radio. After the Federal Communications Commission (FCC) sorted out broadcast frequencies for radio in 1945 and television in 1952, commercial broadcast stations spread rapidly (see Table 1.3).

The tremendous growth in the number of commercial radio and television stations since 1950 suggests strong consumer demand for their content. This perception is confirmed by the data on radio and television ownership and usage. As of 2011, 99 percent of US households had at least one radio and 96.7 percent of US households had at least one television set (the lowest percentage since 1975 and down from 98.9 percent at the height of television's penetration).[7] The average US home, however, is equipped with 8 radios and 2.93 television sets.[8] And by all accounts, these devices garner substantial use. While radio usage is difficult to

Table 1.3   Number of commercial broadcast stations in the USA*

	1950	1960	1970	1980	1990	2000	2009
AM radio stations	2,118	3,539	4,323	4,589	4,987	4,685	4,790
FM radio stations	493	815	2,196	3,282	4,392	5,892	6,479
Television stations: UHF and VHF	47	515	677	734	1,092	1,288	1,392

Source: The Federal Communications Commission; US Census Bureau, Statistical Abstract of the United States: 2001, Table 1126; and US Census Bureau, Statistical Abstract of the United States: 2012, Table 1132. *Data exclude educational broadcast stations.

measure, as we listen to the radio at work, at home, in cars, and in a variety of other contexts, industry experts estimate that the typical American listens to about 1 hour and 30 minutes of radio per day. But television is still, far and away, the dominant medium in terms of usage. The Nielsen Company estimates that, in 2010, the average American watched more than 35½ hours of television per week.[9] Suffice to say, Americans spend a significant amount of time with radio and television.

Before turning to the fourth and final category of mass media, two recent developments with regard to radio and television need to be addressed: satellite radio and cable and satellite television. In many ways, these developments are analogous. Both technologies charge for content, include some content that cannot be broadcast over public airwaves, and trouble the traditional understanding of broadcast media. Satellite radio and television and, increasingly, cable television employ a digital signal, which qualifies them for inclusion in the category of new media. That having been said, not all cable television is digital, and satellite radio and television, which use a digital signal, are broadcast. As such, neither cable nor satellite technology fits neatly into the category of broadcast *or* new media. Confusion over how to categorize satellite radio and cable and satellite television has not stopped either one from being successful, however. Sirius XM Radio Inc, the sole satellite radio provider in the USA, has 21 million paying subscribers and made $763 million in 2011.[10] Meanwhile, from 1970 to 2011, the number of US households with either cable or satellite television has grown from 7 to over 85 percent.[11] As these data suggest, satellite radio and cable and satellite television are growing rapidly, though even their success is threatened by the proliferation of new media.

New media

New media is the broadest and, hence, the most difficult of the four categories of mass media to delimit and define. Though we offer a definition from Lev Manovich, even he is aware of its problematic nature: "new media are the cultural objects which use digital computer technology for distribution and circulation."[12] One difficulty with this definition is that what it includes must continuously be revised as computing technology becomes a more common mode of distribution. The development of digital television, film, photography, and e-books, for instance, would place them in the category of new media along with the internet, websites, online computer games, and internet capable mobile telephony. The ever-expanding character of this category raises a second problem, which can be posed as a question; will it eventually come to include all media and therefore be a meaningless category? The likely answer is yes, for reasons we will discuss later under the topic of convergence. But for the time being, it remains a helpful way to differentiate it from traditional print, celluloid film, and broadcast radio and television. As long as there are mass media that exist as something other than 0s and 1s, new media will remain a useful and meaningful category.

The history of new media begins with the development of the microprocessor or computer chip. Introduced in 1971, the world's first commercial microprocessor, the 4-bit Intel 4004, executed about 60,000 calculations a second. By the early 1990s, the 486 microprocessor, which was typical of computers at the time, could perform 54 million calculations per second. Intel's Pentium Pro, introduced in 1995, increased performance yet again to roughly 250 million calculations per second. But computers were not only rapidly becoming more powerful, they were also rapidly becoming more connected. Developed initially as a communication technology for the US Department of Defense, the internet began to catch the public's attention in the 1970s when its potential for sending personal electronic messages (emails) became evident. But it was the development of a graphic-based user interface and common network protocols in the early 1990s that popularized the internet by transforming it into the hypertextual platform we know now as the World Wide Web. At the turn of the millennium, experts estimated that there were more than 8 billion web pages, a number that was doubling at the time every 6 months.[13] With the infrastructure in place, the cost of computing technology declining, and the ability of ordinary people to become mass producers of information, the adoption of new media in the USA is growing exponentially.

Let us consider the rate at which a few of these technologies have invaded our lives. The Pew Internet and American Life Project reports that only 10 percent of American adults were using the internet in 1995. By August 2011, however, that number had grown to 78 percent of adults and 95 percent of teenagers.[14] Today, millions of people use the internet for everything from online banking and bill paying to job searching and social networking. Indeed, the social networking site Facebook, which did not even exist until 2004, attracted more than a billion active users worldwide in less than a decade. Other new media technologies, like cell phones, MP3 players, and digital games, have also experienced staggering adoption rates. Though cell phone adoption in the USA lags behind many European countries, mobile telephony still boasts one of the fastest penetration rates of any communication technology in history. In 2004, only about 39 percent of youth (8- to 18-year-olds) owned a cell phone, but that number jumped to 66 percent in just 5 years. In that same time span (2004 to 2009), the percentage of youth who owned an MP3 player skyrocketed from 18 percent to 76 percent.[15] As of 2012, 46 percent of US households (roughly 162 million people) owned a gaming console

Table 1.4   Projected use of select new media for 2013 in the USA

	Users in millions 2013	% increase over 2012	% of US population
Internet use			
Internet users	245.2	2.6%	77.6%
Social network users	146.7	3.9%	46.4%
Online video viewers	178.7	5.6%	56.6%
Online television viewers	110.4	12.8%	35.0%
Online casual gamers	87.6	15.8%	27.7%
Online movie viewers	97.3	3.9%	30.8%
Online console gamers	44.0	9.7%	14.0%
Mobile phone use			
Mobile phone users	247.5	2.0%	78.3%
Mobile internet users	143.8	18.0%	45.5%
Smartphone users	137.5	18.8%	43.5%
Mobile gamers	121.3	19.0%	38.4%
Smartphone gamers	97.6	27.8%	30.9%

Source: eMarketer, *US Digital Media Usage: A Snapshot of 2013*, November 2012.

and 39 percent owned a 7th generation console (Wii, PS3, or Xbox 360).[16] Table 1.4 shows the projected use of select new media technologies in 2013.

Living in Postmodernity

As the previous section illustrates, the mass media develop and change over time. It is important, therefore, to study them in historical context. Since the focus of this book is on *contemporary* mass media, this section reflects on the character of the contemporary historical moment. The present moment has variously been described as the information age, the network era, the third wave, post-industrial society, the digital age, and postmodernity. While none of these labels is without its shortcomings, we prefer the term postmodernity to refer to the contemporary moment given its widespread adoption by media scholars. **Postmodernity** describes the historical epoch that began to emerge in the 1960s as the economic mode of production in most Western societies gradually shifted from commodity-based manufacturing to information-based services. Postmodernity should not be confused with *postmodernism*, an aesthetic sensibility or "style of culture which reflects something of this epochal change, in a . . . self-reflexive, playful, derivative, eclectic, pluralistic art."[17] In the transition from modernity to postmodernity, the mass production of standardized, durable goods such as automobiles and toasters has steadily given way to the reproduction of highly customizable soft goods such as iTunes libraries and cell phone plans. Table 1.5 highlights some of the key differences between modernity

Table 1.5   Comparison of modernity and postmodernity

Modernity	Postmodernity
~1850s to 1960s	~1960s to present
Monopoly (imperial) capitalism	Multinational (global) capitalism
Industrialism	Informationalism
Fordism	Flexible accumulation
Manufacturing and production	Marketing and public relations
Mechanization	Computerization
Standardization	Customization
Heavy industries	Image industries
Durable goods	Information and ideas
Product-based	Service-oriented
Mass markets	Niche markets
Economies of scale	Economies of speed
Nation-state	Global corporation
State macro-economic regulation	Free-market neoliberalism

and postmodernity. As the mass media have both contributed to and been transformed by this historical transition, the remainder of this section explores five key trends driving the mass media in postmodernity: convergence, mobility, fragmentation, globalization, and simulation.

Convergence

The previous section organizes the media into four categories as a way of sketching a brief history of mass communication technologies. Ironically, the first major trend in the mass media today involves the erasure of such boundaries. Increasingly, contemporary media reflect **convergence**, the tendency of formerly diverse media to share a common, integrated platform. As strange as it may seem today in light of the prevalence of streaming video, internet radio, and online newspapers, convergence is a relatively recent phenomenon that was considered visionary in the early 1980s when Nicholas Negroponte and others at the MIT Media Lab began exploring multimedia systems. Before media convergence could become a reality, it had to overcome two major obstacles. First, the noise associated with analog signals such as those used in television and radio broadcasting generated message distortion and decay over long distances. This problem was solved through digitization, which reduces distortion by relying on bits rather than a continuous signal. Second, bandwidth limitations prevented large data packets involving images and video from being transmitted quickly and easily over a communication channel. But improved data-compression techniques along with bandwidth expansions have made possible the real-time transmission of large data packets over communication channels. As these technical hurdles have been overcome, convergence has accelerated.

Mobility

Historically, mass media have not been very portable. If you wanted to see a film, you had to go to the theater. If you wanted to watch your favorite television show, you had to do so in the privacy of your own home. Even print media such as books, magazines, and newspapers were limited in their mobility, as their size and weight significantly restricted the amount of printed material one was likely to carry around. But the development of powerful microprocessors and wireless technology is rapidly changing all this, and today, instead of us going *to* places for media, media can increasingly go places *with* us. **Mobility** refers to the ease with which an object can be moved from place to place. As one of the book's authors typed this paragraph, for instance, he was sitting in his favorite café, listening to music on his iPhone, and working on his laptop. In addition to being able to take his whole music library with him, much of the research for this book is stored on his computer. When he needed to locate information not on his computer, he simply connected wirelessly to the University library and downloaded the necessary research. In fact, in the past few years, this author has pretty much stopped going to the library altogether. Even when he requires a book that does not exist electronically (yet!), he simply logs into the library website and arranges for delivery to his office. As technology becomes more and more mobile, media are being transformed from generic home appliances into highly personal (often fashion) accessories. In light of the drive toward mobility, the next evolutionary stage is likely to see media go from being something we carry around or wear to something we embody or become in the form of cybernetic implants.

Fragmentation

Despite its continued use, the phrase mass media is rapidly becoming a misnomer. The *mass* in mass media has traditionally referred to the large, undifferentiated, anonymous, and passive audience addressed by television, radio, and print's standardized messages. But the explosion of information in postmodernity has given way to cultural **fragmentation**, a splintering of the consuming public into ever more specialized taste cultures. This, in turn, has resulted in a tremendous proliferation of media content, if not media ownership, along with niche marketing. What Alvin Toffler has called the "de-massification" of media has been underway since at least the early 1970s.[18] Decreasing production costs have greatly altered the economics of the media industry, reducing the necessity for standardization. The result has been a dramatic increase in media output that caters to specific interests and tastes. Long gone are the days of only three television networks, which could not fill 24 hours of programming. Today, there are hundreds of networks, as well as premium cable services, with around-the-clock programming. Nor is television unique; the print media and radio have witnessed a similar proliferation of specialty outlets. General-purpose magazines such as *The Saturday Evening Post* and *Life* that dominated the magazine industry in the 1960s had been replaced by 4,000 special-interest magazines by 1980.[19]

The internet, of course, reflects the most diversified medium, delivering a dizzying array of content. Even an online bazaar like Amazon.com has country-specific portals and employs tracking software, or so-called cookies, that record user preferences to create a highly customized shopping experience. As this technology improves, we can count on media becoming more and more tailored to individual tastes.

Globalization

Globalization is *the* buzzword of the moment, having captured the attention of academics, business leaders, and politicians alike.[20] Even as the world has become increasingly fragmented by specialized interests, it has simultaneously become more global as well. **Globalization** is a complex set of social, political, and economic processes in which the physical boundaries and structural policies that previously reinforced the autonomy of the nation state are collapsing in favor of instantaneous and flexible worldwide social relations. While globalization is multidimensional, we wish to focus chiefly on economic globalization. In the past few decades, the spread of capitalism has fueled the rise of multinational corporations that wish to profit from untapped "global markets." Hence, these corporations aggressively support free-trade policies that eliminate barriers such as trade tariffs between national and international markets. For the mass media, which are owned and controlled almost exclusively today by multinational corporations, globalization creates opportunities to bring their cultural products to distant local markets. This fact has raised fears about *cultural imperialism*, the imposition of one set of cultural values on other cultures. The process is dialectical or bidirectional, however. Local markets are influencing the products and thinking of the very companies targeting them, leading to concern that cultural difference is being eradicated in favor of one large hybridized culture.

Simulation

Although the concept of simulation can be traced back to the ancient Greeks, its current cultural cachet is due principally to the French theorist Jean Baudrillard and his book *Simulacra and Simulation*. "Simulation," Baudrillard writes, "is the generation by models of a real without origin or reality: a hyperreal."[21] According to Baudrillard, Western societies, and "America" in particular, are increasingly characterized by **simulation**, an implosion of the image (i.e. representations) and the real. This argument is premised on, in Baudrillard's words, the *precession* of simulacra, which suggests that the image has evolved from being a good representation of an external reality, to a distorted representation of an external reality, to a mask that conceals the absence of a basic reality, to bearing no relation to any reality at all.[22] The matter of simulation is an important one, as the mass media are the key social institutions fueling this social phenomenon. The media, for instance, endlessly produce and reproduce images of love, violence, and family (to name only a few) that no longer point or refer to some external reality. Rather, they exist only as images of images for which there is no original. Simulation suggests that the media no longer represent, if they ever did, our social world; they construct a realer-than-real space that *is* our social world.

Why Study the Media?

Perhaps the most important reason to study mass media today is because of their sheer ubiquity. In the transition to postmodernity, mass media have gone from being one institution among many within our cultural environment to being the very basis of our cultural environment. The further back in history one travels, the less central mass media are to social life and the more central are other social institutions such as the family, the church, the school, and the state. But today, these social institutions have been subsumed by, and are largely filtered through, the mass media. More than ever before, the mass media have replaced families as caretakers, churches as arbiters of cultural values, schools as sites of education, and the state as public agenda-setters. In this introduction, we explored the two ways we know things, somatically and symbolically (i.e. directly and indirectly). Not only do we know most things symbolically, but the media represent an ever-expanding piece of the total symbolic pie of social mediators. Table 1.6 illustrates the expanding number of hours the average American spends per day with select media.

As Table 1.6 indicates, though we may gradually be changing which media we use, the mass media remain a significant socializing force in contemporary society. **Socialization** describes the process by which persons – both individually and collectively – learn, adopt, and internalize the prevailing cultural beliefs, values, and norms of a society. Because all social institutions are mediators, they all contribute to socialization. When information passes through a channel or medium, it is translated from direct sensory experience into a set of symbols. Since symbols are selective, privileging some aspects of

Table 1.6   Average time (in hours) spent per day with select media in the USA

Medium	2008	2009	2010	2011
Television and video	4:14	4:27	4:24	4:34
Internet	2:17	2:26	2:35	2:47
Radio	1:42	1:38	1:36	1:34
Mobile	0:32	0:39	0:55	1:05
Newspapers	0:38	0:33	0:32	0:26
Magazines	0:25	0:22	0:20	0:18
Other	0:48	0:46	0:46	0:48
Total hours	**10:35**	**10:50**	**11:00**	**11:33**

Source: eMarketer, *Time Spent with Media: Consumer Behavior in the Age of Multitasking*, 2012. Note: many of these hours are spent multitasking; numbers may not add up to total due to rounding.

the thing being represented at the expense of others, they function as filters. Language is perhaps the most obvious example of how symbols operate as filters. When you listen to a friend tell a story or read about history in a textbook, you are not experiencing the events being described directly. You are only experiencing them symbolically. The words you hear or read are representations of the event you are learning about, not the actual event itself. This is why two accounts of the same event, while potentially very similar, are never identical. Stories are inevitably filtered through the symbols, and therefore the perspective, of the storyteller. As society's main storytellers, the mass media filter virtually every aspect of our world, shaping both *what* we learn and *how* we learn.

What we learn

Mediated messages are comprised of content and form. Broadly speaking, the content influences what we learn and the form influences how we learn. Both content and form are central to the socializing function of the mass media, though content has typically been given more attention. *Content* refers to the informational component of a message, to the specific details, facts, ideas, and opinions communicated through mass media. Audiences are often consciously aware of the content of mediated messages. We know, for instance, that when we read the news we are learning specifics about our world. After just briefly scanning *USA Today* online, one author learned that the American Civil Liberties Union is suing to prevent an Iowa law that would make it easier for the state to remove voters from its voter registration lists, that Facebook is launching a smartphone that showcases its social networking site, and that Justin Bieber is facing fines in Germany for sneaking a monkey named Mally onto a private jet without the proper documentation. It should probably be noted at this point that the content of a message need not have use-value or truth-value to be classified as informational. As both misinformation and disinformation would suggest, fairness and accuracy are not defining attributes of information. Information need only be *meaningful*, as opposed to gibberish, to count as information.

The content of the mass media matters for several reasons. First, by choosing to include or cover some topics and to exclude or ignore others, the media establish which social issues are considered important and which are considered unimportant. Simply put, the mass media largely determine what we talk and care about. Second, content lacking a diversity of views and opinions significantly limits the scope of public debate and deliberation on matters of social importance. Unpopular and dissenting viewpoints are essential to a healthy democracy, however, as they often reframe issues in fresh, productive ways. Third, because media content is communicated using symbols and all symbols are selective, media content is necessarily biased. The language and images used to inform, educate, and entertain you also convey selective attitudes and beliefs. In short, the content of the mass media socializes us to care about some issues and not others, to see those issues from some perspectives and not others, and to adopt particular attitudes toward the perspectives it presents.

How we learn

Whereas content refers to the informational component of a message, *form* describes the cognitive component of a message. Form can be thought of as the way a message is packaged and delivered. The packaging of a message is a consequence, first, of the medium and, second, of the genre or class. Every medium or communication technology packages messages differently.[23] The unique ways that a message is packaged influence how we process it. In other words, communication mediums train our conscious to think in particular ways, not *what* to think, but *how* to think. Media scholars generally agree, for instance, that the way we interpret and make sense of language differs radically from the way we interpret and make sense of images. Whereas language is highly temporal and thus favors a sequential or linear way of knowing,[24] images are decidedly spatial and hence privilege an associative or non-linear way of knowing. A simple way to confirm this difference is to place a page of printed text next to an image. While the printed text only makes sense when the words are read in succession, the elements within the image can be processed simultaneously.

Because the medium of a message conditions how one processes the informational elements within a message, some media scholars contend that message form is a more fundamental and important socializing force than message content. This position is most famously associated with Marshall McLuhan, who succinctly claimed, "The medium is the message." Given the transition to postmodernity, in which the image has steadily replaced the word as the prevailing form in mass media (even print media such as magazines and newspapers are increasingly filled with pictures), the belief that young people today are cognitively different than their parents is rapidly gaining adherents. If media guru Douglas Rushkoff is correct, then television and MTV along with video games and the internet may account for everything from the invention and popularity of snowboarding to the emergence and spread of attention deficit disorder. As such, critical media scholars must attend not only to what the mass media socialize us to think, but also to how they socialize us to think.

Doing Critical Media Studies

As powerful socializing agents that shape what and how we know ourselves and our world, it is vital that we analyze and evaluate the mass media critically. **Critical media studies** is an umbrella term used to describe an array of theoretical perspectives which, though diverse, are united by their skeptical attitude, humanistic approach, political assessment, and commitment to social justice. Before turning to the individual perspectives that comprise critical studies, let us examine the four key characteristics they share in greater detail.

Attitude: skeptical

The theoretical perspectives that comprise critical studies all begin with the assumption that there is more at stake in mass media than initially meets the eye. To a lay-person, for instance, what gets reported on the evening news may appear to be an objective retelling of the day's major events. But to the critical scholar, the production of news is a complex process shaped by the pragmatic need to fill a one-hour time block every day, as well as to garner high ratings. These factors, in large part, determine what counts as news, how the news is produced, and what the news looks like. Just as there is value in looking more closely at the news, there is value in looking more closely at all media. Thus, the various perspectives within the field of critical media studies adopt an attitude of *skepticism*, not as a way of rejecting media, but as a way of understanding how they work and what they do. Some critics refer to this skeptical attitude as a "hermeneutics of suspicion."[25] Hermeneutics describes a mode of interpretation grounded in close analysis. So, a hermeneutics of suspicion would be a mode of close analysis with a deep distrust of surface appearances and "common-sense" explanations.

Approach: humanistic

Universities, like many other cultural institutions, are divided into various departments and units. Though the precise character of such divisions varies from one institution to the next, one common way of organizing disciplines and departments is according to the categories of natural sciences, social sciences, and humanities. These categories, while neither rigid nor entirely discrete, reflect a set of general distinctions concerning subject matter, outlook, and method (i.e. procedure of investigation). Whereas the natural sciences seek to understand the physical world by empirical and "objective" means, for instance, the humanities aim to understand cultural and social phenomena by interpretive and analytical means. To say that critical media studies is humanistic, then, is to associate it with a particular set of intellectual concerns and approaches to the discovery of knowledge. Adopting a humanistic approach to the social world and our place in it, critical media studies emphasizes self-reflection, critical citizenship, democratic principles, and humane education.[26] It is an approach that entails "thinking about freedom and responsibility and the contribution that intellectual pursuit can make to the welfare of society."[27] Because of the subjective element of humanistic criticism, the knowledge it creates is never complete, fixed, or finished.[28]

Assessment: political

In many scholarly arenas, the final step in research is the objective reporting of one's findings (usually in an academic journal). But critical media studies is interested in the practical and political implications of those findings and, thus, entails judgment.

Although there is no universal criterion for leveling political judgments across individual studies of the mass media, critical studies are generally concerned with determining whose interests are served by the media, and how those interests contribute to domination, exploitation, and/or asymmetrical relations of power. Research in this tradition interrogates how media create, maintain, or subvert particular social structures, and whether or not such structures are just and egalitarian. A Feminist study of television sitcoms, for instance, would examine how the representation of male and female characters in such programs functions to reinforce or challenge gender and sexual stereotypes. Critical studies view society as a complex network of interrelated power relations that symbolically privilege and materially benefit some individuals and groups over others. The central aim of critical scholarship is to evaluate the media's role in constructing and maintaining particular relationships of power.

Ambition: social justice

One of the most unique and, at times, controversial characteristics of critical media studies is its desire to better our social world. While scholars in many fields believe that research should be neutral and non-interventionist, critical media studies aims not only to identify political injustices but also to confront and challenge them. Critical media studies is premised on a commitment to social justice and maintains that scholars should "have as their determinate goal the improvement of society."[29] Many media scholars who work within the critical media studies paradigm belong to media-reform organizations such as Fairness and Accuracy in Reporting (FAIR), the Media Education Foundation, Media Democracy in Action, Free Press, the Action Coalition for Media Education, the Center for Creative Voices in Media, and countless others. Critical media studies scholars believe that it is incumbent upon citizens and not just their governments to hold big corporate media accountable. Social activism can take many forms, from boycotts and culture jamming to producing alternative media and supporting independent media outlets.

Key Critical Perspectives

In an effort to assist students in evaluating the media critically, this book examines, explains, and demonstrates 12 critical perspectives, each of which is rooted in a different social theory. **Theory** is an explanatory and interpretive tool that simultaneously enables and limits our understanding of the particular social product, practice, or process under investigation. The term theory derives from the Greek word *theoria*, which refers to vision, optics, or a way of seeing. Since, as Kenneth Burke notes in *Permanence and Change*, "Every way of seeing is also a way of not seeing,"[30] no theory is without limitations. We believe that since every theory has biases and blind spots, no theory ought to be treated as the final word on any subject.

Theory is most useful when it is used and understood as a partial explanation of the phenomenon being studied. Students are strongly encouraged to take each perspective seriously, but none as infallible or universal. We have grouped the 12 critical perspectives in this book into three clusters based upon whether their primary focus is on media industries, messages, or audiences. A brief examination of those three theory clusters provides a chapter overview of the book.

Media industries: Marxist, Organizational, and Pragmatic

Part I of *Critical Media Studies* examines media industries and their practices of production, paying particular attention to the economic, corporate, and governmental structures that enable and constrain how mass media operate. Chapter 2 explores the media from a Marxist theoretical perspective by examining the ways that capitalism and the profit-motive influence media-ownership patterns and corporate practices. Chapter 3 approaches the media from an Organizational perspective by focusing on the work routines and professional conventions within media industries. Chapter 4, the final chapter in the first part, investigates media industries from a Pragmatic perspective, exploring how government laws and regulations impact media products.

Media messages: Rhetorical, Cultural, Psychoanalytic, Feminist, and Queer

Part II of the book centers on media messages, and concerns how the mass media convey information, ideas, and ideologies. Chapter 5 utilizes a Rhetorical perspective to illuminate how the various structures within media texts work to influence and move audiences. Chapter 6 reflects a Cultural perspective and investigates how the media convey ideologies about matters such as class and race that, in turn, shape cultural attitudes toward various social groups. Chapter 7 adopts a Psychoanalytic perspective, considering parallels between media messages and the unconscious structures of the human psyche. Chapter 8 approaches media from a Feminist perspective, highlighting the complex ways that media influence our cultural performances of gender, whereas Chapter 9 adopts a Queer perspective to illustrate how media contribute to our attitudes about sexuality.

Media audiences: Reception, Sociological, Erotic, and Ecological

In Part III, *Critical Media Studies* turns to media audiences, attending to the diverse ways that audiences interpret, negotiate, and use media to create meanings, pleasures, and identities. Employing a Reception approach, Chapter 10 explores the various meaning-making practices in which audiences engage. Chapter 11 adopts a Sociological approach to media, exploring how audiences use media to negotiate the symbolic and material demands of their everyday lives. Chapter 12 employs an Erotic perspective to understand the transgressive pleasures that audiences experience as they increasingly become active producers as well as consumers of media. Chapter 13 concludes Part III by offering an Ecological perspective, which concerns the ways media technologies dominate our social environment and shape human consciousness.

SUGGESTED READING

Allen, R.C. (ed.) *Channels of Discourse, Reassembled: Television and Contemporary Criticism*, 2nd edn. Chapel Hill, NC: University of North Carolina Press, 1992.

Berger, A.A. *Media Analysis Techniques*, 4th edn. Thousand Oaks, CA: Sage Publications, 2012.

Berger, A.A. *Media and Society: a Critical Perspective*, 3rd edn. Lanham, MD: Rowman & Littlefield Publishers, Inc., 2012.

Devereux, E. *Understanding the Media*, 2nd edn. Thousand Oaks, CA: Sage Publications, 2007.

Durham, M.G. and Kellner, D.M. (eds) *Media and Cultural Studies: KeyWorks*, revised edn. Oxford: Blackwell, 2006.

Gripsrud, J. *Understanding Media Culture*. London: Arnold, 2002.

Grossberg, L., Wartella, E.A., Whitney, D.C., and Wise, J.M. *MediaMaking: Mass Media in a Popular Culture*, 2nd edn. Thousand Oaks, CA: Sage Publications, 2006.

Hodkinson, P. *Media, Culture and Society: an Introduction*. Los Angeles, CA: Sage Publications, 2011.

Laughey, D. *Key Themes in Media Theory*. London: Open University Press, 2007.

Marris, P. and Thornham, S. *Media Studies: a Reader*, 2nd edn. New York: New York University Press, 2000.

Stevenson, N. *Understanding Media Cultures: Social Theory and Mass Communication*, 2nd edn. Thousand Oaks, CA: Sage Publications, 2002.

Storey, J. *An Introduction to Cultural Theory and Popular Culture*, 2nd edn. Athens, GA: University of Georgia Press, 1998.

Strinati, D. *An Introduction to Theories of Popular Culture*. New York: Routledge, 1994.

Taylor, L. and Williams, A. *Media Studies: Texts, Institutions and Audiences*. Oxford: Blackwell, 1999.

Tebbel, J. *Between Covers: the Rise and Transformation of Book Publishing in America*. New York: Oxford University Press, 1987.

Tebbel, J. and Zuckerman, M.E. *The Magazine in America 1741–1990*. New York: Oxford University Press, 1991.

Williams, K. *Understanding Media Theory*. London: Arnold, 2003.

NOTES

1. S.I. Hayakawa, *Language in Thought and Action* (New York: Harcourt, Brace and Company, 1941), 31–3.
2. J. Cullen, *The Art of Democracy: a Concise History of Popular Culture in the United States* (New York: Monthly Review Press, 1996), 23–4.
3. Cullen, 48.
4. Newspaper Association of America, last updated September 4, 2012, http://www.naa.org/Trends-and-Numbers/Circulation-Volume/Newspaper-Circulation-Volume.aspx (accessed August 18, 2013).
5. M. Driscoll, Print Book Sales Fell in 2012 – But No Faster Than They Did in 2011, Says Nielsen, *The Christian Science Monitor*, January 8, 2013, http://www.csmonitor.com/Books/chapter-and-verse/2013/0108/Print-book-sales-fell-in-2012-but-no-faster-than-they-did-in-2011-says-Nielsen (accessed March 31, 2013).

6. T. Schatz, The Return of the Hollywood Studio System, in *Conglomerates and the Media*, E. Barnouw et al. (eds) (New York: The New Press, 1997), 73–106.

7. B. Stelter, Ownership of TV Sets Falls in U.S., *The New York Times*, May 3, 2011, http://www.nytimes.com/2011/05/03/business/media/03television.html (accessed March 31, 2013). See also Nielsen Estimates Number of U.S. Television Households to be 115.7 Million, *The Nielsen Company*, May 3, 2011, http://www.nielsen.com/us/en/newswire/2011/nielsen-estimates-number-of-u-s-television-homes-to-be-114-7-million.html (accessed October 14, 2013).

8. U.S. Homes Add Even More TV Sets in 2010, *The Nielsen Company*, April 28, 2010, http://www.nielsen.com/us/en/newswire/2010/u-s-homes-add-even-more-tv-sets-in-2010.html (accessed October 14, 2013).

9. Snapshot of U.S. Television Usage, *The Nielsen Company*, September 23, 2010, http://www.nielsen.com/us/en/newswire/2010/snapshot-of-u-s-television-usage-what-we-watch-and-how.html (accessed March 31, 2013).

10. K.M. Mendolera, *State of the Media Report 2012: Emerging and Evolving* (Vocus Media Research Group, 2012), 11.

11. S. Donohue, LRG: 87% of Households Subscribe to Cable or Satellite TV, *FierceCable*, July 5, 2012, http://www.fiercecable.com/story/lrg-87-households-subscribe-cable-or-satellite-tv/2012-07-05 (accessed March 31, 2013).

12. L. Manovich, New Media from Borges to HTML, in *The New Media Reader*, N. Wardrip-Fruin and N. Montfort (eds) (Cambridge, MA: The MIT Press, 2003), 16–17.

13. F. Biocca, New Media Technology and Youth: Trends in the Evolution of New Media. *Journal of Adolescent Health* 27, 2000, 23.

14. K. Zickuhr and A. Smith, *Digital Differences* (Washington, DC: Pew Research Center's Internet & American Life Project, April 13, 2012), 4.

15. V. Vahlberg, *Fitting into Their Lives: a Survey of Three Studies about Youth Media Use* (Arlington, VA: Newspaper Association of America Foundation, 2010), 5.

16. *State of the Media: The Cross-Platform Report, Quarter 1, 2012 – US* (The Nielsen Company, 2012), 4. See also *State of the Media: Consumer Usage Report 2011* (The Nielsen Company, 2012).

17. T. Eagleton, *The Illusions of Postmodernism* (Oxford: Blackwell, 1996), vii.

18. A. Toffler, *Future Shock* (New York: Random House, 1970), 249.

19. J. Naisbitt, *Megatrends: Ten New Directions Transforming Our Lives* (New York: Warner Books, 1982), 99–100. This number includes industry and trade publications, as well as commercial or consumer magazines.

20. M. Waters, *Globalization*, 2nd edn (New York: Routledge, 1995), 1.

21. J. Baudrillard, *Simulacra and Simulation*, trans. S.F. Glaser (Ann Arbor, MI: University of Michigan Press, 1994), 1.

22. Baudrillard, 6.

23. J.W. Chesebro and D.A. Bertelsen, *Analyzing Media: Communication Technologies as Symbolic and Cognitive Systems* (New York: The Guilford Press, 1996), 22.

24. M. Stephens, *The Rise of the Image the Fall of the Word* (New York: Oxford University Press, 1998), 78–9.

25. According to Paul Ricoeur, the hermeneutics of suspicion is "a method of interpretation which assumes that the literal or surface-level meaning of a text is an effort to conceal the political interests which are served by the text. The purpose of interpretation is to strip off the concealment, unmasking those interests." Quoted in *Philosophy: the Classic Readings*, D.E. Cooper and P.S. Fosl (eds) (Oxford: Wiley-Blackwell, 2010), 184. Ricoeur writes, "Hermeneutics seems to me to be animated by this double motivation: willingness to suspect, willingness to listen; vow of rigor, vow of obedience" [P. Ricoeur, *Freud and Philosophy: an Essay on Interpretation* (New Haven, CT: Yale University Press, 1970), 27; see also pp. 32–3)].

26. E.W. Said, *Humanism and Democratic Criticism* (New York: Columbia University Press, 2004).

27. H. Hardt, *Critical Communication Studies: Communication, History and Theory in America* (New York: Routledge, 1992), xi.

28. Said, 12.

29. Hardt, x.

30. K. Burke, *Permanence and Change*, revised edn (Los Altos, CA: Hermes Publications, 1954), 49.

Part I

Media Industries:
Marxist, Organizational,
and Pragmatic Perspectives

2 Marxist Analysis

KEY CONCEPTS

ADVERTISING
BASE
CELEBRITY
CONCENTRATION

CONGLOMERATION
HISTORICAL MATERIALISM
JOINT VENTURES
INTEGRATION
LOGIC OF SAFETY
MARXISM

MULTINATIONALISM
PLANNED OBSOLESCENCE
PROFIT-MOTIVE
SPECTACLE
SUPERSTRUCTURE
SYNERGY

The Secret Circle, a supernatural drama about a coven of teen witches in the fictitious community of Chance Harbor, WA, debuted on the CW television network in September 2011 with many indicators of success. In addition to deriving its source material from a popular series of young adult novels by author L.J. Smith, the new series scored a coveted broadcast slot following the network's most popular program, *The Vampire Diaries* (another show sourced from Smith's literary work). Moreover, the paranormal juggernaut *Supernatural* was entering its seventh season on the CW at the same time, suggesting that its dedicated audiences might also be open to adopting the spellbinding *The Secret Circle* as well. To some degree these strategic overlaps paid off. *The Secret Circle*'s viewership fluctuated throughout its nine-month run, but the program managed to conclude the 2011–12 season as the CW's most watched new series, making it the third most watched series overall for the network (ahead of more proven performers like *One Tree Hill* and *Gossip Girl*).[1]

Fans of the show were understandably puzzled, then, to learn in May 2012 that the CW had decided not to renew *The Secret Circle* for a second season. Why would the network cancel something so popular, especially when it appeared to fit so well with its brand? One likely answer is cost; *The Secret Circle* was tremendously expensive to produce when compared to other new CW series.[2] While fellow fledgling programs like *Hart of Dixie* and *Ringer* could be filmed in hotspots like New York and Los Angeles, *The Secret Circle* required more expensive, on-location shoots in and around the Pacific Northwest and Canada. Furthermore, no other new series on the network required the costly special effects that *The Secret Circle*'s witches necessitated. Despite

Critical Media Studies: An Introduction, Second Edition. Brian L. Ott and Robert L. Mack.
© 2014 John Wiley & Sons, Inc. Published 2014 by John Wiley & Sons, Inc.

these practical concerns, fans of the program launched an online campaign called "Save The Secret Circle," encouraging the CW or other sympathetic networks (ABC Family, MTV, Syfy, etc.) to renew the series.[3] Although fans circulated online petitions, wrote letters to television executives, and inundated the offices of Warner Bros. with 2,500 postcards and ABC Family with 300 lbs of plastic gold coins, no network picked up the series for a second season.

The cancellation of *The Secret Circle* is as an important reminder to media consumers about the powerful role that economic factors play in shaping our media landscape. Though the program had strong ratings and a dedicated audience, its high production costs prevented it from being profitable enough to renew. In many ways, this case study illustrates the critical perspective in media studies commonly referred to as Marxist analysis. Generally speaking, Marxist media scholars are interested in how economic contexts and imperatives impact the production and distribution of media content. Books, films, and television shows do not just spontaneously occur: all are created as *products* to be bought and sold in a greater system of commodity exchange. Marxist scholars are concerned with how the idea of media content as product, in turn, shapes the way it looks and circulates.

We begin this chapter with an overview of Marxist theory before turning our attention to patterns of media ownership, focusing on how concentration, conglomeration, integration, and multinationalism diminish competition, maximize profits, and exploit foreign markets. In the next portion of the chapter, we explore several of the key strategies of profit maximization utilized by multinational media conglomerates to increase their bottom line and maintain their economic dominance. Then, we examine the role that advertising plays in the media industry, looking at its changing dynamics over time. We conclude the chapter by considering how media ownership patterns and strategic practices reduce diversity in media content, limit the breadth of voices and ideas found in media, and fuel cultural imperialism.

Marxist Theory: an Overview

Marxism is both a social theory and a political movement rooted in the idea that "society is the history of class struggles." Its origins lie in the work of Karl Marx and Friedrich Engels, who collaborated on *The German Ideology* in 1845 (though it was not published until long after their deaths) and the *Communist Manifesto* in 1848. Marx, who was born in Prussia in 1818, is the more well known of the two due, in part, to his single-authored works, including *The Poverty of Philosophy* (1847), *Theories of Surplus Value* (1860), *Capital* (1867), *A Contribution to the Critique of Political Economy* (1859), and *Economic and Philosophic Manuscripts of 1844*, which was published posthumously in 1930. The central premise of Marxism is that the mode of production in society (i.e. its underlying economic structure and practices) determines the social relations of production (i.e. its class structure). This theory understands and makes sense of the world through the perspective of **historical materialism**, which regards the character of social life to be a reflection of the material conditions that exist at a particular historical juncture.

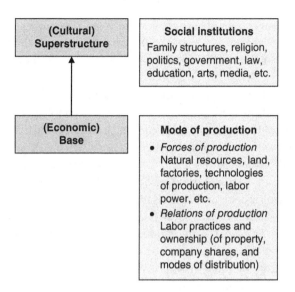

Figure 2.1   Marx's base/superstructure model.

Marx believed that the material world (i.e. natural phenomena and processes) precedes human thought: that the external, concrete, material conditions of social existence determine or ground human consciousness. As such, Marxism is considered a *materialist* philosophy rather than an *idealist* philosophy; idealists maintain that ideas, not material conditions, determine social existence. Marx also believed that the material conditions of societies change over time and must, therefore, be viewed in historical context. As he explains in the Preface to *A Contribution to the Critique of Political Economy*:

> In the social production of their existence, men [*sic*] inevitably enter into definite relations, which are independent of their will, namely relations of production appropriate to a given stage in the development of their material forces of production. The totality of these relations of production constitutes the economic structure of society, the real foundation, on which arises a legal and political superstructure and to which correspond definite forms of social consciousness. The mode of production of material life conditions the general process of social, political and intellectual life. It is not the consciousness of men that determines their existence, but their social existence that determines their consciousness.[4]

Marxism, then, holds that social consciousness, as encoded in institutions such as religion, politics, government, education, law, and art and media, which Marx collectively referred to as the cultural **superstructure**, reflects or mirrors the material conditions of society, which he termed the economic **base**. Figure 2.1 represents Marx's famous base/superstructure model.

For Marx, the cultural superstructure and the social institutions that comprise it operate in the realm of ideas or *ideology*. Thus, to understand the ruling ideas or dominant ideology in society, one needs to attend to the material mode of production in that society. As Marx and Engels explain in *The German Ideology*:

> The ideas of the ruling class are in every epoch the ruling ideas: i.e. the class which is the ruling *material* force of a society is at the same time its ruling *intellectual* force. The class

which has the means of material production at its disposal, consequently also controls the means of mental production.... The ruling ideas are nothing more than the ideal expression of the dominant material relations, the dominant material relations grasped as ideas.[5]

The mode of production within any society is characterized by two elements: its *forces of production* such as the land, natural resources, and technology needed to produce material goods, and its *relations of production* such as labor practices and ownership (of property, company shares, or the ways goods are distributed). According to Marx, a society based on a capitalist mode of production is inherently exploitive because it creates two classes, a working or proletariat class and a ruling or bourgeois class.

Since the bourgeoisie owns and controls the means of production in society, the only commodity that the proletariat has to sell is its labor. For Marx, the ruling class exploits the economic value (i.e. labor) of the working class to increase surplus value or profits. But the capitalist system in many countries has changed dramatically since Marx developed his Labor Theory of Value, and the division of labor that produced such a harsh divide between the haves and the have-nots in the past has been replaced by a system that sustains a large middle class, the petty or petite bourgeoisie, of small business owners and white-collar workers (i.e. lawyers, doctors, professors, etc.). Their ideological domination – and it is domination (e.g. the middle class still behaves in a manner that sustains the ruling elite) – appears to be less grounded in their working conditions. This has led many contemporary Marxist scholars to reject *deterministic* models, which they label "vulgar Marxism," that see the superstructure as having no autonomy from the economic base. While Marxist critics are still interested in who owns and controls the means of production in society, they also recognize that ideology can and does influence modes of production. Thus, for them, the process is much more dialectical than unidirectional, and it is this dialectic which they wish to understand.

Capitalism is driven by the continuous desire to increase capital, an ideology known as the **profit-motive**. Contemporary Marxist critics, many of whom adopt the label *political economists*, investigate both the prevailing patterns of media ownership and how the logic of capital, or profit-motive, influences media business practices. There is good reason to do so, as the media are big business... *very* big business! According to the professional services firm PwC (formerly PricewaterhouseCoopers), in 2011, entertainment and media was a $1.6 trillion a year global business, involving internet access ($317 billion), advertising ($486 billion), and consumer spending ($802 billion).[6] PwC projects that, by 2016, entertainment and media will have grown into a $2.1 trillion business. Of the $802 billion in consumer spending on media globally in 2011, $265 billion was spent in North America alone. Table 2.1 breaks down these numbers by media industry.

Given the staggering size of these numbers, it is useful to consider media consumption on a more personal level. Table 2.2 summarizes how much money the typical US consumer has spent on select media since 2004. These data suggest that in 2012, the average American consumer spent more than $1,000 a year reading, viewing, listening to, and downloading media content.

Table 2.1   Consumer spending by media industry in 2009 and 2011 (in billions of dollars)

	Globally		North America	
	2009	2011	2009	2011
Media industry				
TV subscriptions and fees	191	216	75	80
Music	53	50	18	17
Filmed entertainment	81	83	34	33
Video games	54	57	15	14
Consumer magazines	46	44	10	9
Newspapers	77	77	11	10
Radio	15	15	2	3
Consumer books	114	112	33	32
Business-to-business	146	148	66	67
Total consumer spending	**776**	**802**	**264**	**265**

Source: PwC, *Global Entertainment and Media Outlook 2012–2016*, June 2012. Note: numbers may not add up to total due to rounding.

Table 2.2   US consumer spending on select media per person per year (in dollars)

	2004	2006	2008*	2010*	2012*
Publishing industry					
Newspapers	51.92	49.23	45.78	43.85	44.41
Consumer books	94.60	99.56	105.52	110.75	117.45
Consumer magazines	47.33	44.46	44.42	44.31	43.49
Motion picture and sound recording					
Box office	37.50	36.38	38.16	38.18	39.66
Recorded music	51.97	49.48	43.11	42.63	43.33
Broadcast industry					
Cable and satellite TV	256.30	306.60	354.51	400.78	443.61
Broadcast television	.09	.90	3.16	6.81	11.06
Broadcast and satellite radio	1.19	5.76	9.31	12.25	14.26
New media					
Internet services	60.31	54.06	59.53	67.42	73.48
Home video	125.36	114.12	107.24	105.93	105.22
Video games	33.61	33.91	55.77	75.36	90.59

Source: US Census Bureau, *The 2010 Statistical Abstract*, Table 1094, Media Usage and Consumer Spending: 2004 to 2012. *Projected numbers.

Patterns of Media Ownership

Adopting a historical materialist perspective, Marxist analysis of mass media begins by examining the means and relations of production under contemporary capitalism, or what Marxist critic Fredric Jameson calls *multinational capitalism*. Like all economic systems, capitalism changes over time. The information-based service economy of the twenty-first century is substantially different than the industrial-based manufacturing economy of the nineteenth and twentieth centuries. It is vital, therefore, to consider how the media industry is organized and controlled today. Toward that end, this section investigates four current and deeply intertwined patterns of media ownership: concentration, conglomeration, integration, and multinationalism.

Concentration

The media and entertainment industry in the USA and much of the world is highly **concentrated**, meaning that it is owned and controlled by a small group of powerful companies. The domination of an entire industry by just a few companies is sometimes referred to as an *oligopoly*, as opposed to a *monopoly* in which one company dominates an entire industry. Microsoft's domination of the software industry, for instance, is often considered a monopoly. Oligopolies reduce competition by making it all but impossible for small, independent, or start-up companies to survive in the marketplace. The big companies typically buy up the small companies or drive them out of business. Once an industry becomes highly concentrated, the few remaining companies function more like a cartel or partners than competitors. They each control such a large piece of the industry pie that the other companies do not constitute a real threat to their success.

Concentration occurs both *within* particular media industries such as music, which is dominated by three major companies (Universal Music Group, Sony Music Entertainment, and Warner Music Group), and *across* the media industry as a whole. In the USA, the media industry is dominated by six massive corporations that we have dubbed "The Big Six." Each year, Fortune 500 ranks America's largest and most profitable corporations. In 2012, five of the companies ranked in the top 200 on Fortune's list were in the entertainment industry: The Walt Disney Company (ranked 66), News Corp. (ranked 91), Time Warner (ranked 103), Viacom (ranked 177), and CBS (ranked 188). To these five companies, we would add Comcast – a cable and telecommunications company that became a major player in the media industry in 2011 when it paid General Electric $6.5 billion dollars for the controlling stake (51%) in NBC Universal.

Although there are certainly other large, very profitable US-based media companies, such as Gannett Co., The Hearst Corporation, Tribune Company, The Washington Post Company, Clear Channel, and Liberty Media, they are better classified as second-tier media companies because their profits within the media industry are relatively small compared to the Big Six, at least, at present. As a way of demonstrating the domination of the Big Six, consider the scope and power of Time Warner, the third largest entertainment and media conglomerate in the USA behind The Walt Disney Company and News Corp. In 2011, Time Warner's total revenues were nearly $29 billion, an 8 percent increase over the previous year. But where does all this money come from? To answer that question, we need to look at Time Warner's corporate structure, which is divided into four major units, each of which owns dozens of brands and subsidiary companies: Turner Broadcasting System, Warner Bros. Entertainment, Home Box Office, and Time Inc.

The Turner Broadcasting System consists of news and entertainment networks such as CNN, HLN, TBS, TNT, truTV, Turner Classic Movies, Cartoon Network, Adult Swim, and Boomerang. In 2011, just one of those networks, TBS, reached approximately 99.9 million US television households and was home to basic cable's number one sitcom, *The Big Bang Theory*, as well as other popular syndicated shows such as *The Office* and *Family Guy*.[7] Meanwhile, Home Box Office, which features its original programming like *True Blood*, *Game of Thrones*, and *Boardwalk Empire*, was the number one domestic premium pay television service in 2011. Warner Bros. Entertainment played its part by releasing 22 films in 2011, including *Green Lantern*, *Harry Potter and the Deathly Hallows: Part 2*, *The Hangover Part II*, and *Horrible Bosses*, which grossed a combined $4.7 billion in total box office receipts ($1.83 billion domestically, $2.87 billion internationally). Warner Home Video – the distribution arm of Warner Bros. Entertainment – captured 21.9 percent of all US consumer spending on DVDs and Blu-rays, the most of any studio. Similarly, Time Inc., which distributes 95 magazine titles worldwide, captured 20 percent of all US magazine advertising spending. Time Inc. estimates that more than 50 percent of all American adults read at least one of its magazines every month, and that more than 100 of its magazines are sold in the USA every minute. Figure 2.2 provides a detailed list of Time Warner's corporate holdings as of January 2013 and also highlights the second ownership pattern: conglomeration.

Conglomeration

A second prevailing and closely related pattern of media ownership is **conglomeration**, the corporate practice of accumulating multiple companies and businesses through startups, mergers, buyouts, and takeovers. Whereas concentration describes the media industry as a whole and its increasing consolidation into the hands of fewer and fewer corporations, conglomeration describes a corporate structure in which a parent company owns and controls a host of subsidiary companies. Some scholars reserve the term conglomerate to describe large corporations whose *media holdings* reflect only one dimension of their overall corporate portfolio. General Electric (GE), which manufactures home appliances and light bulbs, is a good example in this regard.

Time Warner (January 2013)

TURNER BROADCASTING SYSTEM

Adult Swim
Amo El Cine
Boomerang
Cartoonito
Cartoon Network
Cartoon Network Too
Chilevisión
CNN
CNN International
Glitz*
HLN
HTV
I.Sat
Infinito
MondoTV
MuchMusic
POGO
Tabi
TBS
TCM
  TCM Asia
  TCM Australia/New Zealand
  TCM France
  TCM Latin America
  TCM Spain
  TCM UK
The Smoking Gun
Tooncast
truTV
TNT
Turner Sports
Joint Ventures
  Boing
  Cartoon Network Korea
  CNNj
  CNN Chile
  CNNMexico.com
  CNN Türk
  CNN-IBN
  Q-TV
  WB

WARNER BROS. ENTERTAINMENT

Warner Bros. Home Entertainment
  Group
Warner Home Video
Warner Bros. Digital Distribution

Warner Bros. Advanced Digital
  Services
Warner Bros. Interactive
  Entertainment
Warner Bros. Technical Operations
Warner Bros. Anti-Piracy Operations
Warner Bros. Pictures Group
  Warner Bros. Pictures
  Warner Bros. Pictures International
Warner Bros. Television Group
  Warner Bros. Television
  Telepictures Production
  Warner Horizon Television
  Warner Bros. Animation
Warner Bros. Domestic Television
  Distribution
Warner Bros. International
  Television Distribution
  Warner Bros. International
  Television Production
Warner Bros. International Branded
  Services
  Studio 2.0
  The CW Television Network
Consumer Products
DC Entertainment
Studio Facilities
International Cinemas
Live Theater

Home Box Office

HBO
HBO on Demand
HBO GO
Cinemax
Cinemax on Demand
MAX GO
HBO2
HBO Signature
HBO Family
HBO Comedy
HBO Zone
HBO Latino
More Max
Action Max
Thriller Max
5 Star Max
W Max
Outer Max
@ Max

**HBO & CINEMAX BRANDED
SERVICES AVAILABLE IN:**

Asia

Bangladesh
Brunei
Cambodia
China
Hong Kong
India
Indonesia
Macau
Malaysia
Maldives
Mongolia
Nepal
Pakistan
Palau
Papua New Guinea
Philippines
Singapore
South Korea
Sri Lanka
Taiwan
Thailand
Vietnam

Europe

Bosnia & Herzegovina
Bulgaria
Croatia
Czech Republic
Denmark
Finland
Hungary
Kosovo
Macedonia
Montenegro
Moldova
Norway
Poland
Romania
Serbia
Slovak Republic
Slovenia
Sweden

Figure 2.2   Time Warner brands and supporting organizations. TIME WARNER, JANUARY 2013. http://www.timewarner.com/our-content/

Latin America

Argentina
Aruba
Bahamas
Barbados
Bolivia
Bonaire
Brazil
British Virgin Islands
Chile
Colombia
Costa Rica
Curaçao
Dominican Republic
Ecuador
El Salvador
Grenada
Guatemala
Honduras
Jamaica
Mexico
Nicaragua
Panama
Paraguay
Peru
St. Lucia
St. Maarten
Suriname
Trinidad
Uruguay
Venezuela

TIME INC.

United States

All You
CNNMoney.com
Coastal Living
Cooking Light
Entertainment Weekly
ESSENCE
FanNation
FORTUNE
GOLF
Health
InStyle
LIFE
Money
My Home Ideas
My Recipes
PEOPLE
People en Español
People StyleWatch
Real Simple
Southern Living
Sports Illustrated

Sports Illustrated for Kids
Sunset
This Old House
TIME
TIME for Kids

International

Grupo Editorial Expansión

balance
Chilango
Chilango.com
CNNExpansión.com
CNN México
Cronos°
Dinero Inteligente
ELLE
Endless Vacation
Expansión
IDC Asesor Juridico y Fiscal
IDC Online
InStyle
Life and Style
Loop
Manufactura
mediotiempo.com
metroscubicos.com
Obras
Quién
Quién.com
Quo
Revolution
Travel & Leisure, Mexico
Vuelo

IPC Media

25 Beautiful Homes
Amateur Gardening
Amateur Photographer
Angler's Mail
Beautiful Kitchens
Chat
Chat – It's Fate
Country Homes & Interiors
Country Life
Cycle Sport
Cycling Active
Cycling Fitness
Cycling Weekly
Decanter
Essentials
European Boatbuilder
Eventing
Feelgood Games
Golf Monthly
Good to Know

Good to Know Recipes
Homes & Gardens
Horse
Horse & Hound
HousetoHome
Ideal Home
InStyle
International Boat Industry (IBI)
Livingetc
Look
Marie Claire
Motor Boat & Yachting
Motor Boats Monthly
Mountain Bike Rider (MBR)
Mousebreaker
NME
Now
Nuts
Pick Me Up
Practical Boat Owner
Rugby World
Shooting Gazette
Shooting Times
ShootingUK
Soaplife
Sporting Gun
Style at Home
SuperYacht Business
SuperYacht World
Teen Now
The Field
Trusted Reviews
TV & Satellite Week
TVeasy
TV Times
Uncut
Volksworld
VW Camper & Bus
Wallpaper*
What Digital Camera
What's on TV
Woman
Woman Special Series
woman&home
woman&home Feel Good Food
woman&home Feel Good You
Woman's Own
Woman's Own Lifestyle Series
Woman's Weekly
Woman's Weekly Fiction Series
Woman's Weekly Home Series
Woman's Weekly Living Series
World Soccer
Yachting Monthly
Yachting World
YBW.com

Figure 2.2 Continued

GE owned the controlling stake in NBC Universal (NBC, MSNBC, Syfy, E! Entertainment Television, USA Network, Golf Channel, Bravo, Oxygen, Telemundo, Universal Pictures, etc.) until January 2011, when Comcast became the majority owner (51%) in the company. Since media companies are among some of the most powerful corporations in the world, we regard each of the Big Six as conglomerates even though the majority of their holdings are restricted to media.

Let us take a closer look at how a media giant like The Walt Disney Company becomes a conglomerate. Like many conglomerates, The Walt Disney Company has rather humble origins, having been started as a small animation studio in 1923 by brothers Walt and Roy Disney. Early success at Walt Disney Studios (originally Disney Brothers Cartoon Studio) led to the formation of three other companies in 1929, Walt Disney Enterprises, Disney Film Recording Company, and Liled Realty and Investment Company. These companies later merged under the name Walt Disney Productions in 1938. In an effort to expand its business, the company began designing its theme parks in 1952 and formed Buena Vista Distribution to distribute Disney's feature films two years later. But Walt Disney Productions did not become The Walt Disney Company until February of 1986, by which time it also included the Disney Channel and a new film label, Touchstone Pictures. Under the leadership of Michael Eisner, the company conducted a series of key acquisitions in the 1990s, including independent film distributor Miramax in 1993, which it sold in 2010 after a 17-year partnership, and perhaps more importantly Capital Cities/ABC, a $19 billion transaction, in 1996.[8] During the 1990s, it also established Hyperion, a book-publishing division. By decade's end, The Walt Disney Company had grown into a global empire with powerful interests in all four of the mass media industries.

In 2004, Disney narrowly escaped a hostile takeover attempt by Comcast, an event that contributed to Michael Eisner's replacement as CEO by Robert Iger the following year. Shortly after Iger assumed the reins, Disney acquired Pixar Animation Studios in a transaction worth $7.4 billion. "Disney's performance during Iger's first year," reports the company's website, "was stellar, with record revenues, record cash flow and record net earnings for fiscal year 2006."[9] Presently, Disney is organized into five major business segments: *Media Networks* (ESPN, Disney Channels Worldwide, ABC Family, SOAPnet, A&E Television Networks, Hyperion Books), *Parks and Resorts* (Walt Disney World Resort, Disneyland Resort, Aulani, a Disney Resort & Spa, Disneyland Paris, Hong Kong Disneyland Resort, Shanghai Disney Resort, Tokyo Disney Resort, Disney Vacation Club, Disney Cruise Line, Adventures by Disney), *Studio Entertainment* (Walt Disney Studios Motion Pictures, Marvel Studios, Touchstone Pictures, Disneynature, Walt Disney Animation Studios, Pixar Animation Studios, Disney Music Group, Disney Theatrical Group), *Consumer Products* (Disney Licensing, Disney Publishing Worldwide, Disney Store), and *Interactive* (Disney Interactive Media and Disney Interactive Games). Table 2.3 charts The Walt Disney Company's revenues in each of these areas over the past decade.

Table 2.3   Annual revenues for The Walt Disney Company (in billions of dollars)

	2002	2004	2006	2008	2010	2012
Media Networks	9.7	11.8	14.6	15.9	17.2	19.4
Parks and Resorts	6.5	7.8	9.9	11.5	10.8	12.9
Studio Entertainment	6.7	8.7	7.5	7.3	6.7	5.8
Consumer Products	2.4	2.5	2.2	2.4	2.7	3.3
Interactive*	—	—	—	.7	.8	.8
Total revenues	**25.3**	**30.8**	**34.3**	**37.8**	**38.1**	**42.3**

Source: The Walt Disney Company, *2006 Annual Report, Fiscal Year 2010 Annual Financial Report and Shareholder Letter*, and *Fiscal Year 2012 Annual Financial Report and Shareholder Letter*. Note: numbers may not add up to total due to rounding. *This revenue category was added after 2006.

Integration

Media conglomerates are by definition integrated. **Integration** is an ownership pattern in which the subsidiary companies or branches within a corporation are strategically interrelated. Corporations can be integrated vertically, horizontally, or both. *Vertical integration* describes a corporation that owns and controls various aspects of production and distribution *within* a single media industry like publishing or broadcasting. Vertical integration can significantly increase the profits associated with a media product by allowing the parent corporation to oversee all stages of its development, everything from its production and marketing to its distribution and exhibition. A media conglomerate that owns record copyrights, record labels, sound recording studios, and record clubs, stores, or other distribution outlets would possess strong vertical integration in the music industry, for instance.

The filmed entertainment division at Viacom offers a concrete example of vertical integration. In 1972, Paramount Pictures produced the Oscar-winning film *The Godfather*, which had grossed $134 million in the USA by 1973. But domestic box office receipts are far from the end of the story. Today, Paramount Home Entertainment markets and distributes the film on DVD, Worldwide Television Distribution negotiates its broadcast on TV, and Famous Music licenses the use of its soundtrack. All of these companies, which continue to generate profit from *The Godfather* franchise, are part of the Paramount Pictures Corporation, a wholly owned subsidiary of Viacom.

The popular, conspiracy-driven TV drama *The X-Files* (1993–2002) provides a second example of the benefits of vertical integration. The Fox Broadcasting Company produced the show, which then aired in first-run production on the FOX network. In addition to the profits generated by its initial airing, Twentieth Television, a division of Fox Television, syndicated three rounds of reruns on local Fox affiliates and other stations, collecting an additional $35 million a year. Meanwhile, FX, one of Fox's numerous cable networks, also aired the show in rerun, generating $69 million more in annual profits. In total, Fox's yearly profits from *The X-Files*, after subtracting production costs of course, exceeded $180 million dollars,[10] a rather impressive figure when one considers it was only one television show produced by Rupert Murdoch's media conglomerate News Corp.

Horizontal integration describes an ownership pattern in which a corporation dominates one stage (or level in the value chain) of the production process. This typically takes one of two forms. Some firms achieve horizontal integration through ownership of multiple media outlets in one market, thereby reducing competition. A company like News Corp, which owns 35 Fox television affiliate stations, several of which are in the same markets, for instance, has strong horizontal integration. If a company controlled all or nearly all the radio stations, TV stations, or newspapers within a market, then it would have a horizontal *monopoly* in that market.[11] As we will see in Chapter 4, the 1996 Telecommunications Act, which eliminated or relaxed ownership restrictions in the USA, has increased this form of integration. A second way for a corporation to achieve horizontal integration is to own and control companies *across* various media industries, but typically at the same level of production, distribution, or exhibition.[12] This corporate structure is sometimes referred to alternatively as *cross-media ownership*. Like vertical integration, horizontal integration can have tremendous financial benefits, namely by enhancing synergy, a concept we will explore shortly. As Table 2.4 demonstrates, all of the Big Six US media conglomerates are horizontally integrated.

Multinationalism

A fourth pattern of contemporary media ownership is **multinationalism**, or a corporate presence in multiple countries, allowing for the production and distribution of media products on a global scale. Multinationalism should not be confused with globalization, however. As we saw in Chapter 1, globalization is a complex set of economic and political processes, and while globalization may be contributing to the rise of multinational corporations, it cannot be reduced to this ownership trend. Multinational media conglomerates, also known as TNCs (short for transnational corporations), do not simply (re)distribute a static, pre-packaged product developed in one locale to various countries around the globe, nor do they completely reinvent the proverbial wheel each time. National differences in regulatory policies as well as cultural values means that TNCs often partner with national media companies to produce and distribute media that will be successful in that country or region. In some cases, the "foreign" companies owned by TNCs are former local or independent media that they have simply bought out. For most media conglomerates, international markets represent potential profits that are just too tempting to resist.

Table 2.4 Horizontal integration of the Big Six US media conglomerates (January 2013)

	Print media	Film and sound	TV and radio	New media
The Walt Disney Company (Robert A. Iger, CEO)	Disney Press, Hyperion Books, Voice, Marvel Publishing, *ESPN The Magazine*	Walt Disney Pictures, Marvel Studios, Pixar Animation, Lucasfilm Ltd., Touchstone Pictures, Walt Disney Records, Hollywood Records (Mammoth and Buena Vista Records), Lyric Street Records	ABC Family, Disney Channel, Disney Junior, SOAPnet, ESPN (80%), A&E (50%), Lifetime (50%), HISTORY (50%), BIO (50%), LMN (50%), H2 (50%)	ABC.com, Disney.com, ESPN3, WatchESPN, Spoonful.com, Babble.com, DisneyBaby.com, BabyZone.com, Go.com, Hulu (32%), Disney Interactive Games
Time Warner (Jeffrey Bewkes, CEO)	Warner Books, DC Comics, *People, Time, Sports Illustrated, Entertainment Weekly, InStyle, Fortune*	Warner Brothers Pictures, New Line Cinema, Castle Rock, DC Entertainment	CNN, TBS, TNT, Cartoon Network, truTV, Turner Classic Movies, Adult Swim, HLN, HBO, Cinemax, The CW (50%)	CNN.com, DCComics.com, TMZ.com, KidsWB.com, NBA.com, NCAA.com, PGA.com
News Corp (Rupert Murdoch, CEO)	HarperCollins, Zondervan, Dow Jones, *Wall Street Journal, Barron's, New York Post*	Twentieth Century Fox, Fox 2000 Pictures, Fox Searchlight Pictures, Fox Music, Blue Sky Studios	FOX, FOX News FX, FUEL TV, SPEED, FSN, MyNetworkTV, Big Ten Network (51%), National Geographic Channel (70%)	FOX.com, Amplify, IGN Entertainment, AskMen, Making Fun, Wireless Generation, Hulu (32%), MySpace (until June 2011)
Viacom (Philippe Dauman, CEO)	(Viacom has not owned any print media since its split with CBS in December 2005)	Paramount Pictures, Paramount Vintage, MTV Films, Insurge Pictures, Nickelodeon Movies	MTV, VH1, CMT, Nickelodeon, Nick Jr., Nick at Nite, Comedy Central, SPIKE, TV Land, Logo, BET, CENTRIC	ParentsConnect, GoCityKids, Atom Entertainment, Shockwave, Nick.com, GameTrailers
CBS Corporation (Leslie Moonves, CEO)	Simon & Schuster, Pocket Books, Scribner, The Free Press	CBS Films	CBS, Showtime, The CW (50%), The Movie Channel, FLIX, CBS Radio	CBS Interactive, CBSSports.com, Last.fm, CNET
Comcast (Brian L. Roberts, CEO)	(Comcast does not currently own any print media)	Focus Features, Universal Pictures, Universal Home Entertainment	NBC, MNBC, E!, USA Network, Bravo, Oxygen, Golf Channel, Syfy, CNBC, Chiller, G4, Telemundo, The Weather Channel Companies	Fandango, DailyCandy, Television Without Pity, iVillage, CNBC Digital, Plaxo, NBC.com, Hulu (32%), Comcast Interactive Media

The German-based media conglomerate Bertelsmann provides an excellent example of a powerful multinational media conglomerate. Consider the expansive reach of Bertelsmann's broadcasting production and distribution company, RTL Group:

> Each day, more than 170 million viewers in Europe watch TV channels operated by RTL Group: RTL Television, Super RTL, Vox or N-TV in Germany; M6 in France; Antena 3 in Spain, RTL 4 in the Netherlands; RTL TVI in Belgium; and RTL Klub in Hungary to name only a few .... RTL Group's content production arm, Fremantle Media produces more than 10,000 hours of programming every year. In 22 countries, Fremantle Media creates and produces a range of award-winning programmes including primetime drama, serial drama, entertainment, factual and comedy. With programming rights in about 150 countries, Fremantle Media is also the largest independent TV distribution company outside the United States.[13]

Like RTL Group, Bertelsmann's book publishing division Random House is a global giant that prides itself on penetrating foreign markets.

> With more than 11,000 new books issued a year and 500 million books sold annually, Random House is the world's largest general-interest book publisher. ... The publisher presents a broad spectrum of editorial voices comprised of nearly 200 editorially independent imprints in 15 countries. These include historic publishing houses such as Doubleday and Alfred A. Knopf (USA); Ebury and Transworld (UK); Plaza & Janés (Spain); Sudamericana (Argentina) and Goldmann (Germany).[14]

Bertelsmann's global domination in the book-publishing industry is mirrored by News Corp.'s massive international newspaper empire, Time Warner's global supremacy in the magazine industry, and Viacom's media networks, which "reach approximately 700 million households in over 160 countries and territories worldwide via more than 200 locally programmed and operated TV channels and hundreds of digital and mobile TV properties."[15]

While all of the Big Six US-based media companies are multinational conglomerates, none has the global reach of The Walt Disney Company. Here is what Disney CEO Robert Iger told shareholders in the Fiscal Year 2012 Annual Financial Report and Shareholder Letter:

> Our high-quality content translates into new businesses and new markets around the world, and we continue to see enormous growth potential in emerging countries. There is a rapidly growing middle class in these markets, with rising disposable income, and a desire for the kind of family entertainment Disney creates. In addition to continuing to expand our presence in both China and Russia, this year we also made our largest investment in India to date, acquiring UTV to become India's leading film studio and TV producer. The deal also added six of the country's most popular entertainment, news, and film channels to our portfolio, so we're now one of India's premier broadcasters as well, reaching more than 100 million viewers every week. The UTV deal also positioned us as a significant player in the digital media space, thanks to Indiagames, the number one mobile gaming company in this market.[16]

In addition to its media assets in India, in the preceding letter, Iger mentions both Russia, where, in 2011, Disney launched a free-to-air channel that reaches 40 million homes or about 75 percent of the country's viewers, and China, where Disney recently opened the Shanghai Disney Resort. Through its media content, worldwide resorts and theme parks, and unparalleled toy merchandizing capability, Disney is truly a global force in entertainment. The Walt Disney Company is not alone of course, as all six of the major US-based media companies are fully integrated, multinational conglomerates.

Strategies of Profit Maximization

As we have just seen, ownership and control of the mass media is driven by a profit-motive. But ownership alone does not guarantee financial success. Thus, the few multinational conglomerates that dominate the media industry utilize a series of strategies to maximize profits. We are using the term *strategy* here in a very specific way consistent with the French sociologist Michel de Certeau. For de Certeau, strategies are the exclusive domain of the "strong" or subjects of will and power. "A strategy," he writes, "assumes a place that can be circumscribed as *proper* (*propre*) and thus serve as the basis for generating relations with an exterior distinct from it (competitors, adversaries, 'clientèles,' 'targets,' or 'objects' of research)."[17] De Certeau contrasts strategies with *tactics*, which he defines as the everyday practices used by the "weak" to resist domination (tactics will be explored in Chapter 12). The distinction between strategies and tactics hinges on ownership; only those who have a "place" to stockpile their winnings can carry out strategies. Five key strategies of profit maximization in the media industry are: synergy, planned obsolescence, the logic of safety, celebrity and spectacle, and joint ventures.

Synergy

The first key strategy of media conglomerates is **synergy,** or the involvement of multiple subsidiary companies in the cross-development, production, and distribution of a media brand for the purpose of "exploiting it for all the profit possible."[18] Synergy is made possible by horizontal integration, and since each of the Big Six is horizontally integrated, the examples are virtually endless. Time Warner, which owns DC Comics and publishes over 900 comic book titles, for instance, frequently has "DC Comics' characters appear in comic book live-action and animated series, direct-to-video releases, collectors' books, online entertainment, licensing and marketing deals, consumer products, graphic novels and feature films."[19] Characters such as Superman and Batman, who started out as comic book heroes, have both repeatedly found their way onto the big screen in feature films produced and distributed by Warner Bros. Entertainment. The television series *Smallville*, which also taps the Superman mythology, was produced by Warner Bros. Television and aired on the Warner Bros. network. Similarly, the Academy Award-winning 1989 film *Batman*, which grossed a record-setting (at the time) $40,489,746 during its opening weekend, was released in conjunction with two albums.[20] The first was Prince's *Batman* soundtrack on Warner Brothers Records, which debuted at number one on the Billboard 200 charts and went multi-platinum, selling 11 million copies worldwide. The second album, also released on Warner Bros. Records, featured the original score composed by Danny Elfman.

Increasingly, the summer blockbuster lies at the heart of cross-promotional efforts. In fact, big-budget films often only get made today if they can demonstrate strong cross-promotional potential. Typically, this means a film that will appeal to a wide audience and can be marketed to children through toy lines and the fast-food industry. While no media conglomerate has perfected this formula better than Disney, MCA/Universal offers one compelling example. We are speaking, of course, about the 1993 mega hit *Jurassic Park*. Created by Steven Spielberg and based on the Michael Crichton book by the same name, *Jurassic Park* cost Universal Studios a whopping $56 million to produce.[21] So, MCA/Universal could not take any chances and undertook a $65 million licensing and promotional campaign, which involved making deals with over 100 companies from Kenner and Kellogg's to SEGA and Ocean Software to market 1,000 products.[22] The marketing hype paid off and *Jurassic Park* cleared a record $50 million its first weekend, eclipsed $100 million in 9 days, and eventually grossed over $350 million in the USA and Canada. But as Thomas Schatz notes, "Its overseas box-office performance was even stronger, and together with its huge success on video cassette [distributed by MCA/Universal Home Video], pay-cable, and other ancillary markets pushed the film's revenues to well over a billion dollars."[23] The film's international success was due in part to screenings of the film's trailer in Japan through Panasonic, a company owned by Matsushita Electric Industrial Co. and the parent corporation of MCA/Universal. Nor did the profits end with the film. In 1996, a year after the Canadian media conglomerate Seagrams purchased MCA/Universal from Matsushita, Jurassic Park – The Ride opened at Universal Studios Hollywood, boosting attendance at the park by 40 percent compared with the previous year.

Planned obsolescence

One of the central challenges faced by the media industry is getting consumers to consume media continuously, especially when the content endlessly being churned out is formulaic rather than creative (see the logic of safety below). One strategy designed to accomplish this is planned obsolescence. According to *The Economist*, **planned obsolescence** "is a business strategy in which the obsolescence (the process of becoming obsolete – that is, unfashionable or no longer usable) of a product is planned and built into it from its conception. This is done so that in [the] future the consumer feels a need to purchase new products and services that the manufacturer

Table 2.5   US consumer spending on home video rental and sales, 2000–10 (in billions of dollars)

	2000	2002	2004	2006	2008	2010
VHS/UMD	11.4	9.6	4.4	0.4	0.1	0.0
DVD	2.4	8.6	16.7	20.2	18.4	14.0
BD/Hi-Def	0.0	0.0	0.0	0.0	0.9	2.3
Digital	0.7	0.7	0.7	1.0	1.6	2.5
Total revenues	**14.5**	**19.0**	**21.8**	**21.6**	**21.0**	**18.8**

Source: DEG Year-End 2010 Home Entertainment Report, 2011.

brings out as replacements for old ones."[24] As Giles Slade explains in his 2006 book, *Made to Break: Technology and Obsolescence in America*, planned obsolescence takes one of two forms: technological obsolescence and psychological obsolescence.[25] *Technological obsolescence* occurs when a development in technology causes the previous generation of that technology to become obsolete, such as how CDs have made cassette tapes obsolete and digital music is now making CDs obsolete. *Psychological obsolescence* arises not when a new technology replaces an older one, but when a new style or product replaces an older style or product such as the way new music is endlessly turned into hits through frequent radio play. Let us look at both of these processes in more detail.

Technological obsolescence is a mainstay of the media industry. The sound recording and film industries are forever releasing their content in new formats, which requires users both to regularly upgrade their playback equipment and to repurchase media content they already own in the new format. Just as the shift in audio from LP record to cassette tape to CD to digital file forced the serious music collector to reinvest in an entirely new music library, the shift in video from VHS tape to DVD to BD/High-Def to digital is causing serious movie collectors to restock their libraries as well. Table 2.5 demonstrates the shift in consumer spending on home video rental and sales across these formats over the decade of the 2000s. And if someone really enjoys listening to music or watching videos, she or he can only resist the "upgrade" for so long, as eventually media producers will stop producing media in the old format, effectively making the technology that plays the old format obsolete.

Though the strategy of technological obsolescence can be found in all sectors of media, it is particularly evident in the video game industry where new game consoles are released every couple of years. Many of these systems are specifically designed to prevent *backwards compatibility*, meaning that the newer systems will not play older games. In 2010, about 41 percent of US households owned a 7th generation game console, which includes Microsoft's Xbox 360, Nintendo's Wii, and Sony's PlayStation 3, and about 23 percent owned a handheld console like the Nintendo DS and Sony PSP.[26] The current generation of consoles/handheld games has hurt the PC game market and made previous generations of game consoles obsolete. When was the last time you heard someone say, "Hey, wanna come over tonight and play Atari?" Forecasters predict it will not be long, however, before online and wireless gaming overtakes the console market, thereby making them obsolete.

Whereas technological obsolescence is tied to innovations in technology, psychological obsolescence is tied to the manipulation of time. "This was the great achievement of the newspaper," explains Nicholas Garnham, "which, by creating rapidly decaying information, created thereby a constant need to re-consume."[27] The production of daily news in newspapers, then morning and afternoon news on broadcast TV, and finally up-to-the minute news on 24-hour cable news networks has created a media product ("the news") that must be continuously updated, making older news obsolete. When was the last time you read a week-old newspaper or digitally recorded the news to watch at a later date? Nor is psychological obsolescence limited to the news media. The ongoing success of the music industry depends upon consumers continuously developing an interest in new artists. Thus, new musical artists must constantly be discovered, packaged, and sold by the music industry as "the next big thing." Horizontal integration has allowed media conglomerates to fulfill the need for the next big thing in music through singing competitions on television. *American Idol*, *The X Factor*, and *The Voice* are designed not so much to find stars as to create them, which in turn creates new "hit" music to purchase.

Logic of safety

A third strategy of profit maximization is the **logic of safety**, which is based on two principles: the belief that "nothing succeeds like success" and the idea that "change" is financially risky. Because of the first principle, when a format or concept meets with financial success, media companies have a strong incentive to replicate it. Since exploiting proven formulas is driven by risk avoidance, media companies are, in most circumstances, reluctant to produce highly original, innovative, or creative content. The reward of trying something new and unproven, which may fail, is simply not worth the financial risk. Hence, the major media conglomerates have perfected the art of imitation, which comes in three basic flavors: sequels, remakes, and spin-offs. Let us begin with movies, which are especially costly to make. In 2007, the average cost to produce and market a Hollywood film was $106.6 million.[28] If a studio is going to invest that kind of money upfront, then they want a guarantee of success, or at least as close to a guarantee as they can get. So, in 2009, when *The Hangover* (distributed by Warner Bros.), which cost a comparatively small $35 million to produce, grossed $277 million domestically and another $190 million at the foreign box-office, making it the highest-grossing R-rated comedy in US history, a sequel was a safe bet. And when the sequel, *The Hangover Part II* (2011), grossed $581 million in box-office receipts worldwide, out-earning the original, it ensured that – despite how badly the sequel sucked – the franchise would be, at least, a trilogy. The virtually unwatchable *The Hangover Part III* was released in 2013.

The Hangover was itself already a rehash of a familiar Hollywood formula, the over-the-top and out-of-control bachelor party film. Sometimes film production houses show even less originality, recycling not just a generic formula, but actual films. Two popular US films that drew their inspiration from foreign cinema are David Fincher's 2011 mystery thriller *The Girl with the Dragon Tattoo*, which is a remake of the 2009 Swedish film, *Män Som Hatar Kvinnor*, and Martin Scorsese's 2006 Oscar-winning *The Departed*, which is a remake of the 2002 Hong Kong crime-thriller *Infernal Affairs*. Hollywood is also quite content to copy itself, as suggested by recent remakes such as *Total Recall* (2012/1990), *Footloose* (2011/1984), *The Karate Kid* (2010/1984), *Clash of the Titans* (2010/1981), *King Kong* (2005/1976), and *The Manchurian Candidate* (2004/1962). In the music industry, remakes or "covers" are almost as numerous as artists. Some notable recent covers include: Cee Lo Green's cover of Band of Horses' "No One's Gonna Love You," Adele's cover of The Cure's "Lovesong," Linkin Park's cover of Adele's "Rolling in the Deep," Three Days Grace's cover of Michael Jackson's "Give In to Me," Lizzie's cover of Lady Gaga's "Bad Romance," the White Stripes' cover of Dolly Parton's "Jolene," Taylor Swift's cover of Rihanna's "Umbrella," and Johnny Cash's cover of Nine Inch Nails' "Hurt."

Although television also produces remakes – it is especially well known for adapting successful British shows like *The Office*, *Pop Idol* (becoming *American Idol*), and *Who Wants to be a Millionaire?* – the more common strategy is what sociologist Todd Gitlin calls "recombinancy." Television is a particularly formulaic medium. Not only can audiences count on popular genres such as the game show, drama, situation comedy, and reality TV, but they can also count on sub-genres with very specific traits. Primetime would simply not be complete without a medical drama, crime drama, legal drama, and police drama, for instance. In many instances, when a show is nearing the end of its run, producers will simply create a spin-off that focuses on a popular or even secondary character from the original. *All in the Family* spun off *The Jeffersons*, *Mary Tyler Moore* spun off *Lou Grant*, *Happy Days* spun off *Laverne & Shirley*, and *Dallas* spun off *Knots Landing* to name just a few. More recently, when a show has been particularly successful, producers have simply spun off additional versions of the same thing, as has happened with NBC's *Law and Order* and CBS's *CSI*, *Criminal Minds*, and *NCIS*.

But regardless of whether it is movie sequels, music remakes, or television spin-offs, they all share the logic of safety. Indeed, when "innovation" does emerge in the media industry, it is typically because a small, independent producer has "broken the rules." When this occurs, the "emergent rules" are quickly co-opted and endlessly reproduced by the large conglomerates, or the smaller company is simply bought out. This is precisely what happened at Miramax. After the unlikely success of controversial films like *sex, lies, and videotape* (1989), *Tie Me Up! Tie Me Down!* (1990), and *The Crying Game* (1992), Disney acquired Miramax in 1993. Releasing future films such as *Pulp Fiction* (1994), *Chasing Amy* (1997), and *Kill Bill* (2003) under the Miramax label allowed Disney to branch into more risqué film making without endangering its wholesome, family image.

Celebrity and spectacle

A fourth strategy of profit maximization involves the deeply interconnected concepts of celebrity and spectacle. Whereas the logic of safety could be said to rule the *form* of media (suggesting what general formats, formulas, and patterns to follow), celebrity and spectacle might be said to govern the *content* of media (suggesting what particular ingredients to include). The concept of **celebrity** refers to "those people who are well known for their well-knownness."[29] This includes high profile public officials, popular entertainers and artists, and others who seize, if only momentarily, the public spotlight. If history has proven anything in the media industry, it is that audiences will pay to consume virtually anything that features celebrity personalities. Celebrity, it should be noted, has nothing to do with talent, only with well-knownness. Consequently, socialite Kim Kardashian gained media fame in 2007 after a sex tape of her and singer Ray J went public. Interest in the tape and the lawsuit that ensued allowed Kardashian to spin her newfound fame into a series of successful reality TV shows, including *Keeping Up with the Kardashians*, *Kourtney and Kim Take New York*, and *Kourtney and Kim Take Miami*. As of 2010, Kim Kardashian was the highest-paid woman in reality TV, making an estimated $18 billion per year according to *Forbes*.[30]

When celebrities are unavailable or too expensive to feature in media, the media industry frequently resorts to its other proven content strategy: spectacle. The concept of **spectacle** describes the media's obsession with the sensational and arresting, scandalous and shocking dimensions of a situation or context. It refers to that which grabs hold of our attention either because it is tantalizing or startling. So prevalent is the role of spectacle that Guy Debord argues in his 1967 book, *The Society of the Spectacle*, our whole society submits to its logic. In its opening pages, Debord explains:

> Understood in its totality, the spectacle is both the outcome and the goal of the dominant mode of production. It is not something *added* to the real world – not a decorative element, so to speak. On the contrary, it is the very heart of society's real unreality. In all its specific manifestations – news or propaganda, advertising or the actual consumption of entertainment – the spectacle epitomizes the prevailing mode of social life. It is the omnipresent celebration of a choice *already made* in the sphere of production, and the consummate result of that choice.[31]

For Debord, our whole society has become little more than *spectacle* – mere exhibition and display. Through the endless reproduction of shocking images, be they of sex or violence, and glitzy promotions, the media collapses news into entertainment and entertainment into life. The production of a hyper-sensational world through spectacle ensures that viewers will attend to media. After all, its depiction of life is more compelling than life itself. Consider gangsta rap's creation of what Debord calls a "real unreality," in which multi-million-dollar artists who drive luxury automobiles, cover themselves in bling, and work for transnational media conglomerates rap about gang violence, growing up in the hood, and stickin' it to "the man." While all of these are very real social phenomena, gangsta rap glamorizes them, pimps them as lifestyles or commodities that can be attained and lived at the level of style and appearance. Life imitates art, which imitates nothing at all.

On some rare occasions celebrity and spectacle collide, creating *hyper-spectacles* or self-perpetuating media frenzies that dominate all forms of media for an extended period of time. The Clarence Thomas–Anita Hill hearings, the Rodney King beating, the O.J. Simpson trial, and the deaths of Princess Diana and Michael Jackson are all examples of such hyper-spectacles. What separates these hyper-spectacles from ordinary spectacles is (1) the intersection of celebrity and tragedy, (2) the scope and intensity of the media coverage (i.e. the story's ability to dominate all media and to disrupt normal programming), and (3) the resistance of the story to information decay. Take the O.J. Simpson case as an example. According to Paul Thaler, "From June 1994 through October 1995, the Simpson story overtook our culture, sweeping away all other news – in fact, virtually all other public discussion – in its path."[32] This hyper-spectacle began on June 17, 1993 with the nationally televised low-speed chase of Simpson's white Bronco five days after the brutal murder of his ex-wife, Nicole Brown Simpson, and her friend, Ronald Goldman. The three major broadcast networks (ABC, NBC, and CBS) and CNN all interrupted their regular programming to cover the police chase live. In the days and weeks following the chase, there was an explosion of newspaper headlines, magazine articles, books, and primetime TV specials. Diane Furno-Lamude offers this summary of the media coverage:

> In the *Los Angeles Times*, the Simpson story appeared on the front page for more than three hundred days after the murders. Additionally, when the criminal trial began, every local Los Angeles station except one carried it live. The major evening news broadcasts devoted more time to the Simpson case than they had given to Bosnia and the Oklahoma City Bombing combined.[33]

Low-cost to produce and able to capture the attention of large audiences for long periods of time, hyper-spectacles are profit-generating machines, which suggests that the media industry has a vested interest not just in covering them, but in creating them.

Joint ventures

Given the high costs of television, sound, and film production, media conglomerates often undertake **joint ventures** to reduce financial risks. By splitting the costs of a new venture, neither corporation has to bear the full financial burden should the venture fail. In 2004, the major media conglomerates had, according to Ben Bagdikian, "a total of 141 joint ventures, which makes them business partners with each other."[34] Today, two US television networks are the result of such partnerships. Prior to the late 1980s, a 24-hour all-comedy cable network had never been tried. So, it was hardly a surprise when Time Warner's The Comedy Channel merged with Viacom's HA! to form Comedy Central in 1991. For 12 years, both companies retained 50 percent ownership in the network. The venture was so successful that Viacom had to pay Time Warner a massive $1.2 billion to acquire its share of the cable network in 2003. A more recent joint venture is the CW Television Network, which is owned in equal parts by the CBS Corporation and Time Warner. The CW was launched in 2008 following the collapse of CBS's UPN and Time Warner's WB networks. While neither company was able to sustain a sixth major network on its own, the partnership has allowed both companies to continue to appeal to a younger audience, whose average viewer (34-year-old), 10 years junior to its nearest competitor, FOX (44-year-old), making it an attractive demographic to advertisers.[35]

Another reason media conglomerates might join forces is to expand their control in a particular industry. In 2004, for instance, Sony Music Entertainment (a Sony Corporation company) merged with Bertelsmann Music Group (a Bertelsmann company) to form Sony BMG Music Entertainment. Sony BMG immediately joined EMI, Universal, and Warner as one of the, at that point, Big Four music companies. The merger also reportedly allowed the two parent companies to cut roughly 2,000 jobs, saving them nearly $350 million a year. Sony Corporation of America, a subsidiary of Japan's Sony Corporation, acquired Bertelsmann's 50 percent stake in Sony BMG in 2008, adopting the Sony Music Entertainment label once again. As of February 2013, Sony Music Entertainment was the second largest record company behind Universal Music Group (UMG), which is owned by the French media conglomerate Vivendi. Partnerships like those described in this section are fairly common due, at least in part, to the fact that major media conglomerates often have *interlocking directorates*. Each of the Big Six conglomerates is overseen by a board of directors whose board members will often sit on multiple boards, making them interlocked. The people deciding what is good for one media conglomerate, then, are likely to be some of the same people deciding what is good for another. One consequence is joint ventures.

Advertising

In the previous section, we examined a few of the strategies that media conglomerates use to maximize consumer profits. But to focus only on the profits generated by the sale of media products would be to overlook a significant source of revenue in the media industry, namely advertising. **Advertising** is a form of communication and marketing designed to persuade audiences to feel and/or behave a certain way toward a product, service, or corporate brand, and it plays a central role in media industry profits. Advertising is a relatively modern invention that emerged in the latter half of the nineteenth century. Indeed, prior to 1851, Anne McClintock explains, "it was generally regarded as a confession of weakness, a rather shabby last resort."[36] But by the late 1800s, with the Victorians consuming 260,000 tons of soap

Table 2.6   Major media advertising spending in the USA, 2009–12 (in billions of dollars)*

	2009	2010	2011	2012
TV	53.8	59.0	60.7	64.5
Internet/Digital	22.7	25.8	32.0	37.3
Newspapers	24.8	22.8	20.7	19.1
Magazines	15.5	14.7	15.2	15.2
Radio	14.3	15.3	15.2	15.5
Directories	10.3	9.3	8.2	7.5
Outdoor	5.9	6.1	6.4	6.8
Total	**$ 147.2**	**$ 153.0**	**$ 158.3**	**$ 166.0**

Source: eMarketer, March 2011, http://www.iab.net/insights_research/industry_data_and_landscape/1675/1707493 and September 2012, https://www.emarketer.com/Coverage/AdvertisingMarketing.aspx. Note: numbers may not add up to total due to rounding. *Major media excludes advertising spending on cinema, which according to ZenithOptimedia averaged about $2.5 billion per year during this period.

a year, "soap manufactures began to pioneer the use of pictorial advertising as a central part of business policy."[37] Chief among its innovators was Thomas J. Barratt, whose public gimmicks, targeted slogans, and image campaigns for Pears Soap have earned him the title as the "father of advertising."[38] Today, advertising – whether in print, broadcast, or digital media – subsidizes much of the media content we consume.

Estimating the precise amount spent on advertising each year is no easy process. Part of the difficulty is in deciding what to include in the calculations. Some estimates of advertising spending include commercial, non-commercial, and political advertising, while others focus exclusively on commercial advertising. Similarly, some estimates include both measured and unmeasured advertising spending and others do not. *Measured advertising spending* typically includes expenditures for network and cable TV, consumer magazines, newspapers, internet, radio, and outdoor (billboards, benches, etc.), while *unmeasured advertising spending* often includes expenditures for direct mail, telemarketing, and catalogues. Despite these difficulties, eMarketer estimates that global spending on measured media advertising in 2012 was roughly $532 billion. Of that, about $166 billion was spent on major media in the USA alone, more than three times that of any other country in the world.[39] Table 2.6 breaks down advertising spending in the USA by major media over a 4-year period.

Table 2.6 highlights a few important trends. While advertising spending on newspapers has steadily been declining for over a decade (down from $48.7 billion in 2000 to $19.1 billion in 2012), advertising spending on the internet and digital media has been growing exponentially during that same period (up from $6 billion in 2000 to $37.3 billion in 2012). Meanwhile, advertising spending on TV continues to dominate spending on other media by a wide margin, generating huge revenues for TV networks.

Table 2.7   Cost of a 30-second advertising spot on the 10 highest-priced programs in 2012 (in dollars)

Network	Program	Cost
NBC	*Sunday Night Football*	545,152
FOX	*American Idol Wednesday*	340.825
ABC	*Modern Family*	330,908
FOX	*New Girl*	320,940
FOX	*American Idol Thursday*	296,062
FOX	*The Simpsons*	286,131
FOX	*Family Guy*	276,690
CBS	*The Big Bang Theory*	275,573
CBS	*2 Broke Girls*	269,235
CBS	*Two and A Half Men*	247,261

Source: *Advertising Age*, October 22, 2012.

Advertising Age estimates that in 2010 the total advertising revenue for the four major broadcast networks was as follows: CBS, $6.48 billion; ABC, $5.12 billion; NBC, $4.82 billion; and FOX, $4.49 billion.[40]

In light of the tremendous revenue generated by television advertising, we would like to look more closely at its historical development. On July 1, 1941, CBS launched the first TV schedule with 15 hours of weekly programming, including two 15-minute news programs Monday through Friday. That same day, WNBT (later NBC) aired the first television commercial for Bulova watches during a Dodgers/Phillies game. By 1949, advertisers were spending $12 million a year on television advertising alone, a number that jumped to $128 million in just two short years.[41] In the mid-1960s, a typical 30-second ad spot during a national primetime TV series cost about $20,000–$25,000.[42] Today, that same spot can cost 10 times as much, depending upon a show's ratings. Table 2.7 shows the cost of an average 30-second spot on the 10 highest-priced primetime programs in 2012. But the cost of these spots pales in comparison to those for special events like the Olympics or Super Bowl. During the 2012 Super Bowl, for instance, advertisers paid $3.5 million on average for a 30-second spot, generating $262.5 million dollars in revenue for NBC.[43]

As the cost of producing network television has risen, the TV industry has constantly had to devise new ways of increasing advertising revenue, and raising the cost of ad spots reflects only one strategy. Another strategy has been to shorten the length of ad spots themselves so that more ad spots can be sold. In 1965, every network television commercial was a full 60 seconds in length, but 10 years later only 6 percent were a minute long. By cutting ad spots in half to 30 seconds, networks were able to double the number of ads they could sell. But the price was not cut in half. So, two 30-second ads cost more than one 60-second spot had. Ad spots have continued to get shorter and many spots today are only 15 seconds in length.[44] In the meantime, the total amount of advertising time has steadily grown, while the length of network programming has been trimmed. In 1999, the typical "1-hour" show had been cut to 44 minutes, and the average "half-hour" show had been shortened to 21 minutes.[45] This means that roughly 30 percent of all TV time is taken up by commercials. With the advent of new technologies such as the VCR and remote control that allowed for commercial "zapping," advertisers complained that they were not getting what they had paid for, namely consumers' attention.

So, television adapted yet again, first, by reducing the length of the commercial break between two programs or sometimes eliminating it altogether as a way of preventing viewers from leaving to take a bathroom break between shows. In addition to creating more, shorter commercial breaks, the networks began to sell *product placements*. Instead of characters in television using or wearing generic products, networks began to charge companies to promote their products by highlighting labels and name brands, or simply having characters mention a brand. Films, which until recently did not have commercials, had pioneered the in-text ad much earlier with famous product placements such as Coca-Cola in *Blade Runner* and Reese's Pieces in *E.T.: The Extra-Terrestrial*. Today, if you can make out a brand in television or film, then chances are it is a paid advertisement.

Disney, however, has taken product placement to a whole new level. Rather than merely promoting brands within its media products, the media itself is the brand being advertised. Children's television programs such as the animated series *My Friends Tigger and Pooh* on the Disney Channel function as one long advertisement for the Winnie the Pooh brand and related merchandise. Recent Disney films such as *Toy Story* and *Cars* (both from Pixar), *The Chronicles of Narnia*, *Pirates of the Caribbean*, and *The Avengers* all work similarly to sell everything from T-shirts and sleeping bags to furniture and baby food. Nor is Disney shy about its use of media to sell Disney-related merchandise:

> As the world's largest licensor, Disney is able to extend our storytelling beyond the screen, taking our beloved characters into the daily lives of millions of people. A wide array of merchandise based on some of the world's most iconic franchises such as Mickey Mouse, Disney Princesses, Cars, and Marvel's The Avengers is available in innovative online and retail environments that continue the Disney experience, and take fans even deeper into the stories they love. Disney is also the world's leading children's publisher, using digital technology to create dynamic new reading experiences. In fiscal 2012, we launched a line of digital learning opportunities, based on our successful Disney English Learning Centers in China, to help parents everywhere use their children's favorite characters to share their love of learning. We also expanded our growing Disney Baby brand across North America and are poised to grow it internationally in the coming year.[46]

Advertising in the media is so pervasive that one media scholar, Dallas Smythe, argues that the chief commodity sold in the media today is the audience.[47] The mass media audience is sold to advertisers and advertisers expect to get what they are paying for. So, the media industry has developed increasingly sophisticated strategies to package and sell audiences to advertisers. One such strategy is niche marketing.

Niche marketing is the targeting of a specific segment of the public that shares particular, but known demographic traits such as age, sex, income, etc. Niche marketing is sometimes referred to as *narrowcasting* as a way of distinguishing it from *broadcasting*, a model that targeted a large, anonymous, and undifferentiated audience. The financial benefit of niche marketing is twofold. First, if a media company can deliver a niche audience that is highly sought after, then it can charge a premium for advertising. Say, for instance, a retail business sells skateboards and the business knows from past experience that the vast majority of its customers are ages 12–22 and skewed slightly toward males. The FOX network, whose primetime viewers are the youngest of the four major networks, could charge this business more for a 30-second advertising spot than, say, CBS, where historically more than 50 percent of its primetime viewers are over 50.[48] Because of the network's age demographics, even highly rated programs like CBS's *60 Minutes* are probably not a good place to advertise skateboards. Meanwhile, NBC, which boasts the largest percentage of viewers who earn over $75,000 a year, would be the most logical place to advertise luxury items. In the past, advertising rates were closely tied to audience share. But in this model, many viewers may not have been part of the target demographic an advertiser wished to reach. As media corporations increasingly target narrower audiences, they can charge advertisers premium rates.

A second advantage of niche marketing is that it allows media corporations to target and reach previously untapped markets. As the tastes of some viewers and listeners run counter to popular tastes, these audiences were largely disinterested in the messages propagated by the old broadcast model. Thanks to digital media technologies and platforms, however, highly specialized content can now be delivered to remote places (so long as there is internet access). Historically, the size of a town dictated how many radio stations it had, and therefore how diversified the choice of formats was. A smaller market might only receive three radio stations such as hits, rock, and country. XM radio, by contrast, features 69 different music channels in addition to its news, talk, sports, and entertainment programming, and is available anywhere. Although the music on XM radio is currently commercial-free, this will likely change. When new media are introduced into the marketplace, they frequently court customers with the promise of little or no advertising. But after building a customer base, media moguls generally let advertisers in. Cable television, which started out largely commercial-free, is now saturated with advertising.

Consequences of Ownership Patterns and Profit Maximization

In any capitalist society, the patterns and strategies discussed in this chapter may not seem surprising or abnormal. We are, of course, socialized from birth to see capitalism not as *one possible* economic system, but as *the only* economic system. In such a context, the desire to accumulate wealth appears to be intrinsic and instinctive rather than constructed and learned. But when culture is transformed into nature (i.e. made to seem natural), we do not stop to question it. We do not ask, why does it matter that the media industry is highly concentrated? Or what difference does it make that the major media conglomerates operate according to a logic of safety? The remainder of this chapter begins with a reminder that late capitalism is only one structural (i.e. economic) possibility and that the patterns of ownership, strategies of profit maximization, and advertising practices that emerge in relation to it have significant social and political consequences that affect our lives. Three implications in particular warrant our attention: the reduction of diversity, the restriction of democratic ideals, and the spread of cultural imperialism.

Reduction of diversity

Concentration, which severely restricts competition, integration, which leads to the development of some projects and not others, and the logic of safety, which drastically limits creativity, collectively result in the homogenization of media. Despite the plethora of media outlets and the apparent array of choices today, media products such as music, television, and film are overwhelmingly similar in form and content. The uniformity of media has long been recognized by media scholars and can be traced back to the Frankfurt School, an institute for social research established in Weimar, Germany in 1923. The Frankfurt tradition found its way to the USA in the 1930s when German scholars immigrated there following the rise of National Socialism in Germany. Influenced by Marxism, scholars such as Herbert Marcuse, Theodor Adorno, and Max Horkheimer saw the mass media and popular culture as rigid, formulaic, highly standardized, and clichéd. They argued that media's unending sameness had a pacifying effect on audiences, eliminating the possibility for critical thought, and thereby producing our very consciousness. Though the Frankfurt School has been critiqued for promoting the idea of *false consciousness*, the belief that the masses are duped into blindly accepting the prevailing ideology, their criticisms of standardization are not entirely without merit.

While examples of standardization can be found in any of the media industries, the music industry and especially pop music provides a compelling example. In 1941, Adorno argued that popular music was successful because it was simultaneously standardized (i.e. it was all the same and therefore required no thought or effort to enjoy) and pseudo-individualized (i.e. it was cloaked in false appearance of uniqueness). Adorno explained:

> The necessary correlate of musical standardization is pseudo-individualization. By pseudo-individualization we mean endowing cultural mass production with the halo of free choice or open market on the basis of standardization itself. Standardization of song hits keeps the customers in line by doing their listening for them, as it were. Pseudo-individualization, for its part, keeps them in line by making them forget that what they listen to is already listened to for them, or "pre-digested."[49]

If Adorno's critique sounds overly harsh, allow us to cite an example. In 1997, three brothers from Tulsa, Oklahoma, known collectively as Hanson, became a pop sensation with their song, "MMMBop," which quickly rocketed to number one. Featuring scintillating lyrics such as "In an mmm bop they're gone. In an mmm bop they're not there/Until you lose your hair. But you don't care," MMMBop appeared with 12 other songs (four more of which were hits) on the album *Middle of Nowhere*, which has sold over 10 million copies worldwide. Hanson, along with the near-endless iteration of boy bands and pop queens like Britney Spears, Christina Aguilera, and Avril Lavigne, would suggest that musical innovation and diversity are not only atypical, but also unnecessary for success.

Restriction of democracy

A second social consequence of ownership patterns and profit-maximization strategies in the media industry is the decline of democratic ideals. Democracy is premised on the notion of egalitarianism, the free and open exchange of ideas, and the participation of diverse publics.

But until the relatively recent development and spread of new media, it was virtually impossible for ordinary citizens to share their ideas and opinions with large, remote audiences. Thus, only those who owned and controlled the means of production truly had a "public" voice. Even as access is gradually becoming more democratic through personal and political blogs, for instance, the major media conglomerates continue to function as powerful *gatekeepers*. Gatekeeping is a filtering practice that determines what makes it into the media and what does not. Media such as radio, television, and film remain almost entirely inaccessible to ordinary citizens. And even more democratic media platforms such as YouTube, MySpace, and Facebook are being bought up by the major conglomerates. Often, what starts out as creative, independent art is later co-opted for corporate profit.

By controlling what is included in (and thus excluded from) both news and entertainment media, the major media conglomerates also exercise an *agenda-setting* function. Agenda-setting refers to the power of the media to influence what people are concerned with or care about. By covering some news stories and not others, or by treating some scenarios, themes, and issues in entertainment media and not others, the media greatly influence what the public regards as important. The idea of agenda-setting asserts that media do not influence *what* audiences think, so much as they influence what audiences think *about*. Typically, agenda-setting is discussed in relation primarily to the news media. But entertainment media also exercise an agenda-setting function. The sheer prevalence of cop shows and crime dramas ensures that violence will be viewed as a serious social concern, while the absence of environmental dramas has the opposite effect. Sex and violence are seen as social concerns, in part, because there is so much sex and violence in the media. Meanwhile, genocide and sex trafficking around the globe are of little concern to many Americans because they receive little to no attention in the media.

In addition to gatekeeping and agenda-setting, the major media conglomerates exercise an important *framing* function. Framing describes the viewpoint or perspective that is employed by the news and entertainment media when covering social and political issues. Just as the lens of a camera frames its subject, media frames create particular windows through which audiences view issues. The news media's repeated framing of political issues around a conservative/liberal or left/right binarism, for instance, greatly limits the scope of public debate by marginalizing non-centrist or alternative perspectives. During political campaigns, third-party candidates are rarely taken seriously by the media. The naming and hence framing of third-party candidates as "on the fringe" works to ensure that they will remain there. In short, the gatekeeping (filtering), agenda-setting (focusing), and framing (structuring) functions of the major media conglomerates consistently undermine democratic principles and ideals.

Spread of cultural imperialism

A third consequence of contemporary ownership patterns and profit-maximization strategies many observers warn is *cultural imperialism*. Cultural imperialism describes the exporting of US values and ideologies around the globe, usually to the detriment of local culture and national sovereignty. While local culture certainly inflects upon and influences the media products such as television, film, and music imported from predominantly US-centered media conglomerates, the cultural imperialism hypothesis is rooted in the idea of unequal flow. This idea holds that, while cultural beliefs and values are flowing in both directions, the inward flow is so much greater than the outward flow that over time it causes cultural erosion in poorer countries with less-developed media industries. In some cases, exposure to outside cultural values can have devastating effects on local cultures. There was a significant rise in infant deaths in a number of countries in Africa, for instance, when mothers switched from breast-feeding to bottle-feeding after seeing it repeatedly featured in European and US television programs and advertising. The mixing of infant formula with unsanitary water in this particular region resulted in an epidemic.[50] Furthermore, given the financial resources behind the Big Six, it is often difficult for independent, local production companies to compete with multinational conglomerates. The increasing concentration of highly integrated media companies along with the drive to make profit is clearly not without significant social consequences.

Conclusion

This chapter has looked at the effects of ownership patterns and profit-motive on the creation and circulation of media texts. Though largely masked by their sheer complexity in contemporary society, the means of production ultimately determine the shape and content of media in a Marxist framework. Formed through multiple mergers and buyouts, the six major US-based media conglomerates look to maximize profit whenever possible, leading to a strange combination of standardization and spectacularization in media content as a result of the hegemonic logic of safety. At the same time, the industry's increasing ability to cross-promote and advertise media content drives this fairly uniform product to almost every corner of the Earth. The widespread cultural influence, in turn, restricts democracy, reduces content diversity, and increases the cultural capital of the countries that produce the majority of media today.

If, while reading this chapter, you felt somewhat overwhelmed or depressed at the utter control of the industry presented in the Marxist perspective, you are not alone. Marxist critique is certainly an important contribution to media studies, and indeed one of the oldest, but it is not complete in its ability to understand how the media industry functions. As we will see in the next two chapters, other factors like conventions and government regulations also help shape media content. Media industries represent a special kind of contemporary business, in that they are often in the service of both profit and art, and a strictly economic analysis will always be partial in its ability to explain the inner workings of these increasingly visible companies.

MEDIA LAB I: DOING MARXIST ANALYSIS

OBJECTIVE

The aim of this lab is to utilize Marxist principles to analyze the media. Specifically, students will investigate how patterns of ownership, strategies of profit-maximization, and advertising practices shape the form and content of select magazines.

ACTIVITY

- Divide the class into small groups of 4–5 students each.
- Supply each group with a Time Warner publication such as *People, InStyle, Sports Illustrated, Entertainment Weekly*, or *Time*.
- Ask students to record their answers to the following questions.
  1 Please define and give an example of the following concepts: concentration, conglomeration, integration (both horizontal and vertical), and multinationalism. Note: Your examples for this question do not need to (and likely will not) come from the magazine you have been given.
  2 Identify and describe four specific examples of how the magazine employs strategies of profit maximization.
  3 How do the style, design, and layout of the magazine also reflect a profit-motive? Identify and describe five specific examples.
  4 What role does advertising play in the magazine? How is it incorporated? Cite three specific examples.

SUGGESTED READING

Bagdikian, B.H. *The New Media Monopoly*. Boston: Beacon Press, 2004.

Barnouw, E. *Conglomerates and the Media*. New York: New Press, 1997.

Gandy, Jr, O.H. The Political Economy Approach: a Critical Challenge. *Journal of Media Economics* 1992, 5, 23–42.

Garnham, N. *Capitalism and Communication: Global Culture and the Economics of Information*. Newbury Park, CA: Sage Publications, 1990.

Golding, P. and Murdock, G. Culture, Communications, and Political Economy. In *Mass Media and Society*, J. Curran and M. Gurevitch (eds), pp. 15–32. New York: Edward Arnold, 1991.

Herman, E. and Chomsky, N. *Manufacturing Consent: The Political Economy of the Mass Media*. New York: Pantheon, 1988.

Horkheimer, M. and Adorno, T.W. *Dialectic of Enlightenment*, trans. J. Cumming. New York: Continuum, 2001.

Jhally, S. The Political Economy of Culture. In *Cultural Politics in Contemporary America*, I. Angus and S. Jhally (eds), pp. 65–81. New York: Routledge, 1989.

Marx, K. (with Engels, F.) *The German Ideology including Theses on Feuerbach and Introduction to the Critique of Political Economy*. Amherst, NY: Prometheus Books, 1998.

McChesney, R.W. *Corporate Media and the Threat to Democracy*. New York: Seven Stories Press, 1997.

McChesney, R.W. *Rich Media, Poor Democracy: Communication Politics in Dubious Times*. New York: The New Press, 1999.

McChesney, R.W. *The Problem of the Media: U.S. Communication Politics in the 21st Century*. New York: Monthly Review Press, 2004.

McChesney, R.W. *Communication Revolution: Critical Junctures and the Future of Media*. New York: The New Press, 2007.

Mosco, V. and Wasko, J. *The Political Economy of Information*. Madison, WI: University of Wisconsin Press, 1988.

Murdoch, G. Large Corporations and the Control of the Communications Industries. In *Culture, Society and the Media*, M. Gurevitch, T. Bennett, J. Curran, and J. Woollacott (eds), pp. 118–50. New York: Routledge, 1982.

Schiller, H.I. Not Yet the Post-imperialist Era. *Critical Studies in Mass Communication* 1991, 8, 13–28.

Smythe, D.W. *Dependency Road: Communications, Capitalism, Consciousness and Canada*. Norwood, NJ: Ablex, 1981.

Wasko, J. *How Hollywood Works*. Thousand Oaks, CA: Sage Publications, 2003.

Williams, R. *Problems in Materialism and Culture: Selected Essays*. London, Verso: 1980.

NOTES

1. *CW 2011–2012 Ratings Report Card*, TV Series Finale, http://tvseriesfinale.com/tv-show/cw-2011-2012-ratings (accessed January 3, 2013).

2. For discussion of the show's budget concerns, see Andrew Miller Addresses Fan Efforts to Save The Circle, *Save The Secret Circle*, http://save.thesecret-circle.com/?p=603 (accessed January 3, 2013); Carina Adly MacKenzie, "Secret Circle" Says Goodbye: Britt Robertson Tells Us Season 2 Just is "Not Happening," *Zap2it*, http://blog.zap2it.com/frominsidethebox/2012/06/secret-circle-says-goodbye-britt-robertson-tells-us-season-2-just-is-not-happening.html (accessed January 3, 2013).

3. For a chronology of this group's activities, see the "News" heading on their webpage, *Save The Secret Circle*, at http://save.thesecret-circle.com/?page_id=7 (accessed January 3, 2013).

4. K. Marx, *Selected Writings*, L.H. Simon (ed.) (Indianapolis, IN: Hackett Publishing Company, 1994), 211.

5. K. Marx (with F. Engels), *The German Ideology Including Theses on Feuerbach and Introduction to the Critique of Political Economy* (Amherst, NY: Prometheus Books, 1998), 67.

6. PwC, *Global Entertainment and Media Outlook 2012–2016*, 13th annual edn (June 2012), 50, 52, 54.

7. Time Warner, *Time Warner Annual Report 2011* (2012), 4.

8. Bloomberg Business News, The Media Business; Disney Clears F.C.C. Review of Its Merger, *The New York Times*, February 9, 1996, http://www.nytimes.com/1996/02/09/business/the-media-business-disney-clears-fcc-review-of-its-merger.html?scp=15&sq=disney+abc+merger&st=nyt (accessed February 3, 2013).

9. The Walt Disney Company, *Company History*, http://corporate.disney.go.com/corporate/complete_history_7.html (accessed December 14, 2008).

10. J.L. Roberts, TV Turns Vertical, *Newsweek*, vol.132, no. 16, *October* 19, 1998, 54–6.

11. R.W. McChesney, *Rich Media, Poor Democracy: Communication Politics in Dubious Times* (New York: The New Press, 1999), 16.

12. D. Croteau and W. Hoynes, *Media/Society: Industries, Images, and Audiences* (Thousand Oaks, CA: Pine Forge Press, 2003), 40, 45.

13. *RTL Group – Quality Entertainment on all Stations*, Bertelsmann – Media Worldwide, www.bertelsmann.com/bertelsmann_corp/wms41/bm/index.php?ci=168&language=2&pagesize=A&pagecolor=normal (accessed January 27, 2013).

14. *Random House – Number One in the World of Book Publishing*, Bertelsmann – Media Worldwide, www.bertelsmann.com/bertelsmann_corp/wms41/bm/index.php?ci=24&language=2&pagesize=A&pagecolor=normal (accessed January 27, 2013).

15. Viacom, *Fiscal Year 2012 Annual Report on Form 10-K* (2013), 1.

16. The Walt Disney Company, *Fiscal Year 2012 Annual Financial Report and Shareholder Letter* (2013), 3.

17. M. de Certeau, *The Practice of Everyday Life*, trans. S. Rendall (Berkeley, CA: University of California Press, 1984), xix.

18. McChesney, 91.

19. Time Warner, *Building Brands for a Digital World, 2007 Profile* (2007), 14.

20. For an extended analysis of the Batman brand and franchise, see E.R. Meehan, "Holy Commodity Fetish, Batman!": the Political Economy of a Commercial Intertext, in *The Many Lives of Batman: Critical Approaches to a Superhero and His Media*, R.E. Pearson and W. Uriccho (eds) (New York: Routledge, 1991), 47–65.

21. Crichton's book was published in 1990 by Alfred A. Knopf, Inc., an imprint owned by the New York-based publishing house Random House. At the time, Random House was still an independent publisher, but it was acquired by media giant Bertelsmann in 1998.

22. P.H. Broeske, The Beastmaster: Steven Spielberg Keeps a Tight Rein on His Dino Epic, "Jurassic Park," *Entertainment Weekly*, issue 161, May 12, 1993, www.ew.com/ew/article/0,,305858,00.html (accessed December 14, 2008).

23. T. Schatz, The Return of the Hollywood Studio System, in *Conglomerates and the Media*, E. Barnouw et al. (eds) (New York: The New Press, 1997), 74.

24. Planned Obsolescence, *The Economist*, March 23, 2009, http://www.economist.com/node/13354332 (accessed February 3, 2013).

25. G. Slade, *Made to Break: Technology and Obsolescence in America* (Cambridge, MA, and London: Harvard University Press, 2006), 4–5.

26. The Nielsen Company, *2010 Media Industry Fact Sheet* (2010), 2.

27. N. Garnham, Contribution to a Political-Economy of Mass-Communication, in *Media and Cultural Studies: Keyworks*, rev. edn, M.G. Durham and D.M. Kellner (eds) (Oxford: Blackwell, 2006), 222.

28. R. Verrier, MPAA Stops Disclosing Average Costs of Making and Marketing Movies, *Los Angeles Times*, April 1, 2009, http://articles.

latimes.com/2009/apr/01/business/fi-cotown-mpaa1 (accessed February 3, 2013).

29. N.M. Alpersetein and B.H. Vann, Star Gazing: A Socio-Cultural Approach to the Study of Dreaming about Media Figures, *Communication Quarterly* 45, 2007, 142.

30. The Kardashians, Real Housewives, Teen Moms, Honey Boo Boo and More: How Much Do Reality TV Stars Earn?, *Celebuzz!*, September 17, 2012, http://www.celebuzz.com/2012-09-17/the-kardashians-real-housewives-teen-moms-honey-boo-boo-and-more-how-much-do-reality-tv-stars-earn-analysis/ (accessed February 4, 2013).

31. G. Debord, *The Society of the Spectacle*, trans. D. Nicholson-Smith (New York: Zone Books, 1995), 13.

32. P. Thaler, *The Spectacle: Media and the Making of the O.J. Simpson Story* (Westport, CT: Praeger, 1997), xiii.

33. D. Furno-Lamude, The Media Spectacle and the O.J. Simpson case, in *The O.J. Simpson Trials: Rhetoric, Media, and Law*, J. Schuetz and L.S. Lilley (eds) (Carbondale, IL: Southern Illinois University Press, 1999), 22.

34. B.H. Bagdikian, *The New Media Monopoly* (Boston, MA: Beacon Press, 2004), 9.

35. S. Sternberg, *The Median Age Report* (A Magna Publication, June 30, 2008), 1.

36. A. McClintock, Soft-Soaping Empire: Commodity Racism and Imperial Advertising, in *The Visual Culture Reader*, 2nd edn, N. Mirzoeff (ed.) (New York: Routledge, 2002), 508.

37. McClintock, 508.

38. McClintock, 510.

39. eMarketer, *The Global Media Intelligence Report* (September 2012), iv.

40. R.K. Miller and Associates, *The 2012 Entertainment, Media and Advertising Market Research Handbook*, 12th edn (Loganville, GA: Richard K. Miller and Associates, 2011), 140.

41. S.J. Baran, *Introduction to Mass Communication: Media Literacy and Culture*, 2nd edn (New York: McGraw Hill, 2001), 346.

42. R. Campbell, *Media & Culture: an Introduction to Mass Communication*, 2nd edn (Boston, MA: Bedford/St Martins, 2000), 415.

43. Kantar Media Reports Super Bowl Spending Reached $1.85 Billion over Past Ten Years, January 14, 2013, http://kantarmediana.com/sites/default/files/kantareditor/Kantar-Media-2013-Super-Bowl-Pre-Game-Release.pdf (accessed August 12, 2013).

44. Baran, 347–8.

45. K. Alexander, TV Networks Trim Shows to Make Time for Ads, *Fort Collins Coloradoan*, September 18, 1999, D11.

46. The Walt Disney Company, *Fiscal Year 2012 Annual Financial Report and Shareholder Letter* (2013), 3.

47. D. Smythe, On the Audience Commodity and Its Work, in *Media and Cultural Studies: Keyworks*, rev. edn, M.G. Durham and D.M. Kellner (eds) (Oxford: Blackwell, 2006), 230–56.

48. R. Grover, Must-See TV for Left-Handed Men Under 30: ABC, CBS, and NBC are Increasingly Watched by Niche Viewers, *Business Week*, December 14, 1998, 104. See also M. Schneider, Median Age Report: the Big 3 Earn Their AARP Cards (and Fox Isn't Too Far Behind), *Variety*, August 10, 2010, http://weblogs.variety.com/on_the_air/2010/08/median-age-report-the-big-3-earn-their-aarp-cards-and-fox-isnt-too-far-behind.html (accessed February 3, 2013), and D. Bauder, Young Demographics Don't Rule Network TV, *Herald Tribune*, August 17, 2010, http://www.heraldtribune.com/article/20100817/ARTICLE/8171043 (accessed February 3, 2013).

49. T.W. Adorno (with the assistance of G. Simpson), On Popular Music: 1941, in *On Record: Rock, Pop, and the Written Word*, S. Frith and A. Goodwin (eds) (London: Routledge, 2000), 308.

50. Baran, 551.

3 Organizational Analysis

The Social Network – a 2010 film about computer genius Mark Zuckerberg's development of Facebook – was, by nearly any standard, a huge success. Not only did the film perform well at the box office, grossing more than $96 million domestically as of February 2011, but it also garnered eight Academy Award nominations, winning three. In addition to these accolades, *The Social Network* won four Golden Globe Awards: Best Motion Picture – Drama, Best Director, Best Screenplay, and Best Original Score. One way to understand the film's commercial and critical success is, as we saw in the previous chapter, through the lens of Marxism. As a big budget motion picture released by a multinational corporation, in this case Columbia Pictures (a subsidiary of the Sony Corporation), the film followed a clear logic of safety. The basic story was, after all, hardly novel. Indeed, what attracted screenwriter Aaron Sorkin to the project "had nothing to do with Facebook. The invention itself is as modern as it gets, but the story is as old as storytelling; the themes of friendship, loyalty, jealousy, class and power."[1] While a profit motive rooted in risk aversion, no doubt, contributed to the film's success, it does not tell the whole story.

We can also understand and evaluate the success of *The Social Network* at the level of its technical and aesthetic artistry. To suggest that the film is "safe" (i.e. not especially original) is not also to concede that the film is poorly made. On the contrary, *The Social Network* is a well-crafted film to which numerous talented

Critical Media Studies: An Introduction, Second Edition. Brian L. Ott and Robert L. Mack.
© 2014 John Wiley & Sons, Inc. Published 2014 by John Wiley & Sons, Inc.

professionals contributed. Let's consider the pedigree of just a few of them. The film's director, David Fincher, was hardly a novice, having previously directed successful features such *Alien 3* (1992), *Se7en* (1995), *The Game* (1997), *Fight Club* (1999), *Panic Room* (2002), and *The Curious Case of Benjamin Button* (2008). Meanwhile, screenwriter Aaron Sorkin had already established his talent for writing with films like *A Few Good Men* (1992) and *The American President* (1995), as well as the TV series *The West Wing* (1999–2006). Nor are the director and screenwriter the only key players. Jeff Cronenweth, the film's cinematographer, holds a degree from USC's School of Cinema-Television and had previously served as the director of photography on *Fight Club*, while Angus Wall and Kirk Baxter, the film's editors, had earned Academy Award nods for their editing of *The Curious Case of Benjamin Button*. Since all of these individuals are well trained in specific aspects of film making, we cannot ignore the importance of organizational and professional cultures in understanding media.

Media scholars employing an Organizational perspective seek to understand "why media organizations, a specific medium, or the mass media institution produces the kinds of content it does."[2] In other words, these scholars understand that an organization is more than merely an assemblage of disparate parts. The manner in which media companies organize and divide labor directly influences the character of content they produce. We begin this chapter by tracing the most important aspects of an Organizational perspective, attending to the concepts of structure, process, and organizational and professional conventions. Each of these concepts helps us to better understand how the various facets of an organization come together to form an integrated whole. The latter half of the chapter undertakes an extended analysis of work in a specific industry, the news media, as a way of demonstrating the key role that work practices play in shaping media products. Contrary to popular belief, we contend that the news is not an objective retelling of the day's events, but rather a selective and structured product governed by organizational norms and demands.

Organizational Theory: an Overview

Work is a central feature of daily life, particularly in the USA, where workers put in the longest work hours of any industrialized nation. According to NBC, the average US American logged 1,797 hours of work in 2011, or about 34.5 hours per week. To put this number in perspective, consider that in France the typical worker averages 26.8 hours per week for 1,392 hours per year, while in Germany the typical worker averages 25.6 hours a week for a total of 1,330 hours a year.[3] Since a worker who works 40 hours a week for 52 weeks would log a total of 2,080 hours, the typical US American is working nearly full-time for a full year. With so much time spent at work, it is important to understand what happens there, and how what happens there influences an organization's products and services.

Our work lives are most centrally defined by whom we work with and for. Collectively, employers and employees comprise **organizations**: a system or network of ordered relationships and coordinated activities directed toward specific goals.[4] At a film studio such as Paramount, for instance, there are writers, producers, directors, actors, editors, sound crews, make-up artists, etc. engaged in scripting, shooting, editing, and marketing a particular film. Paramount, like any other organization, has two basic dimensions: structure and process.[5] *Structure* describes the underlying framework that shapes an organization over time, and includes three key elements: hierarchy, differentiation and specialization, and formalization.

1   *Hierarchy*, the first structural element of organizations, refers to the specific arrangement of job roles and positions based upon authority within an organization. Inevitably, some persons or groups have more decision-making power than others within an organization, and thus are central to both the creation and maintenance of a particular corporate culture.
2   *Differentiation and specialization*, the second structural element, accounts for the division of companies into units, departments, and positions, each of which performs specific tasks. To the extent that these tasks require a unique set of skills and training, the positions within an organization are filled by professionals. **Professionals** are individuals who possess expertise in a particular area or field that allows them to accomplish the distinctive tasks of their position. A book editor, for example, is a professional with specialized training and credentials in proofreading and copyediting.
3   *Formalization*, the third structural element, is the degree to which specific practices must conform to accepted organizational and professional conventions. We will discuss the topic of conventions in greater depth shortly, but first let us consider the second major dimension of organizations: process.

Whereas structure describes the underlying framework of an organization, *process* denotes the actual substance erected upon that framework. Structure and process can be likened to Kenneth Burke's notion of "container and thing contained."[6] Although a container has an identifiable shape and form, its contents can vary greatly. The contents are, of course, always shaped and thus constrained to some extent by the container. So, while every organizational member, as an individual, engages in unique behaviors and actions (i.e. process), such behaviors and actions are always constrained, which is to say limited, by the principles of hierarchy, differentiation and specialization, and formalization (i.e. structure). The media critic who adopts an Organizational approach or perspective is interested in the precise ways that structure and process mutually influence one another within a media organization. One productive way of getting after that relationship is by analyzing the communicative practices that occur within organizations and how those practices create and maintain a particular type of organizational culture.

Assessing communicative practices

Every organization develops a unique **organizational culture**: the set(s) of norms and customs, artifacts and events, and values and assumptions that emerge as a consequence of organizational members' communicative practices. In this section, we outline five ways to study an organization's culture: performance, narrative, textual, management, and technology. Before examining these various lenses, however, we wish to stress that communicative practices are dynamic, contingent, and transactional, meaning that they are not static, universal, or bounded, but complex, improvisational, and continuous. To understand an organizational culture, then, one must look at its communicative practices in local, social, and historical contexts, including why, when, where, and how they occur, as well as whether or not they are ignored, legitimated, and/or challenged by organizational members.

1   *Performance.* Performances are expressive (i.e. productive and purposeful) displays (i.e. both process and product) that carry symbolic significance (i.e. meaning and implication) in a particular context.[7] Four important types of organizational performance are ritual, sociality, politics, and enculturation.[8] *Ritual* performances are those personal or organizational behaviors that members engage in on a regular or routine basis. One of the authors of this book, for instance, drinks coffee every morning as he reads his email. This is a personal ritual because it is not necessitated by his job. Such personal rituals are sometimes known as trademark performances because they are strongly associated with particular members. Organizational rituals by contrast, such as attending weekly faculty meetings, involve routine behaviors that are necessitated by or expected within a specific workplace environment. Given the near "sacred" character of some organizational rituals, they can be particularly revealing of an organization's culture. *Sociality*, a second type of performance, refers to the codes of etiquette that are enacted with regard to friendliness, small talk, joking, and privacy within an organization. *Politics* are performed differently in every organization and influence the type and degree of independence, negotiating, and coalition building that are acceptable. A fourth common type of organizational performance, *enculturation*, emphasizes those "communicative performances wherein the newcomer learns the social knowledge and skills of the culture."[9] Although *narratives* are also a type of organizational performance, we have chosen to treat them separately given their unique complexity and importance.

2   *Narratives.* Stories are a ubiquitous feature of organizations, and the stories members tell about their workplace experiences are another way to evaluate the endless (re)creation of an organization's culture. Since stories are inherently selective, what does and does not get storied speaks to an organization's values and norms, as does the frequency with and manner in which stories are told.[10] Narratives can be classified as personal, collegial, or corporate. Personal stories are those that convey individual subjective experiences; collegial stories are those told about other organizational members; and corporate stories are those

told about the organization itself. Each of these story types can function to affirm or discourage certain attitudes and activities within a culture. Narratives that glorify the success of an action or event invite emulation, while those that recount or accentuate failure sound a cautionary tone.[11]

3   *Textual.* Another means of examining an organization's culture is through the texts – written or electronic documents such as company bylaws, policy manuals, procedure handbooks, training manuals, office memos, newsletters, mission statements, reports, etc. – it produces. The purpose of formal texts like those just mentioned is to explicitly identify what are considered to be acceptable and unacceptable actions and activities within an organization. Given the origin and relative permanence of such documents, they tend to represent and reinforce managerial perspectives. Not all texts created within an organization are formal, however. Graffiti, personal employee notes, and "private" emails are all examples of informal, more spontaneous, texts. Whereas formal texts espouse the managerial or company "line," informal texts communicate the views of those in the "trenches." One way of understanding an organization's culture, then, is by examining the differences and similarities between formal and informal texts, between espoused and enacted views. If, for example, a parody of the company newsletter was circulated widely among employees, it might suggest that the newsletter is seen as little more than managerial propaganda.

4   *Management.* A fourth lens through which to evaluate an organization's culture is a managerial perspective. This approach concerns how "organizational culture is developed and directed by managers for the purpose of improving operating efficiencies, enhancing the bottom line, or creating satisfied customers."[12] Though this perspective, which conceives of organizations principally as businesses, emerged initially as a way to assist managers in achieving success by implementing strategies that enhance productivity, performance, and profits, it can be used by critical organizational scholars to evaluate the political consequences of managerial practices. Drawing upon Marxist principles concerning the influence of economic imperatives on corporate culture, for instance, scholars might examine how specific management structures (i.e. the level and flexibility of hierarchy) and practices (i.e. hiring, assessment, promotion) influence both the character of products produced and the quality of employees' lives (i.e. pay, benefits, respect, voice, support, working conditions, etc.) within a particular organization.

5   *Technology.* In the context of an increasingly post-industrial and global economy, information technology (IT) has come to play a central role in the contemporary workplace. From networked communications to data storage and retrieval, IT is vital to the everyday operation of an ever-expanding array of organizations. Consequently, organizational scholars need to examine the ways in which technology structures work activities, as well as "influences organizational members' work roles and work relationships."[13] The quick and easy access to information on wire services, for instance, has decreased the need for news organizations, especially local affiliates, to produce their own

news, thereby altering journalists' daily routines (i.e. how they gather and package news). Technology is not so much a tool for doing one's job more effectively or efficiently today, as it is the very environment in which one does one's job. In remaking the workplace environment, technology has fundamentally altered the skills required to perform some jobs. Indeed, the decreasing cost and increasing availability of IT is directly related to the rise of citizen journalism.

Studying performances, narratives, texts, management, and technology are all ways for scholars to evaluate and assess how communicative practices mediate the tension between structure and process within an organization. The structure/process dialectic is not exclusively an internal dynamic, however. Organizations must also respond to external pressures such as the professional culture that prepares members to work in a profession. Organizational cultures and professional cultures are not the same thing.[14] Whereas an organizational culture is always unique to a specific organization and its practices, a professional culture may extend across many organizations. A **professional culture**, then, refers to sets of norms and customs, artifacts and events, and values and assumptions that emerge as a consequence of formal training (i.e. education, apprenticeships, internships, etc.), membership and participation (i.e. professional associations, conferences, workshops, licenses, etc.), and recognition (i.e. industry awards and honors) within a profession. While an attorney in the USA may work at a specific law firm (or organizational culture), she or he must also earn a juris doctorate (JD degree) from a law school accredited by the American Bar Association and be licensed by the bar association where she or he practices law (or professional culture). To appreciate why workers carry out their jobs as they do, therefore, requires an understanding of both organizational and professional conventions.

Characteristics of conventions

Conventions describe the norms that govern the technical and creative choices made by workers in the execution of their duties, art, or craft. For media workers, conventions influence everything from how one dresses and whom one eats lunch with to the way a news anchor reads news copy and a cameraperson frames particular shots. As these examples suggest, conventions operate at various levels, including a unit or departmental level, corporate level, and finally occupational or professional level. If it were not for conventions, workers would confront a virtually infinite array of options in how to carry out their job-related tasks. Thus, employees internalize and abide by conventions as a matter of practicality. Given the central role that conventions play in how workers carry out their jobs, it is worth considering the chief characteristics and consequences of conventions in greater detail. Conventions are motivated, shared, naturalized, resilient, and directive.

1   *Motivated.* Though conventions may appear to be arbitrary and capricious, they typically develop out of some pragmatic need even if that need is as simple as efficiency or the desire for a sense of community, belonging, and group cohesion. In the academic department of one of the book's authors, for example, faculty members playfully address one another as "professor," instead of by their first names. This communicative practice heightens the sense of community among faculty by creating identification between those members of the department who have doctorate degrees. Feelings of belonging always depend, in part, upon exclusion. The term "professor" fosters this feeling by distinguishing faculty from students, staff, and administrators. Conventions, then, are motivated rather than random. There is some purpose behind them even if that purpose is not immediately self-evident.

2   *Shared.* Although most of the practices in which people engage are purposeful, not all practices – even routine practices – become conventions. For practices to function as norms, they must be internalized by other employees. Simply put, conventions are shared. Creating and maintaining a curriculum vitae (i.e. detailed academic résumé) is a professional convention that academics share. The fact that an individual professor within an academic department routinely uses Microsoft PowerPoint to lecture does not make that practice a convention, as other professors can present course material however they choose to. The use of PowerPoint is a personal practice, not something one does *because* one is a professor.

3   *Naturalized.* A third characteristic of conventions is that they are naturalized and thus largely invisible. Since conventions are "the norm," workers tend to adopt and abide by them unconsciously and unreflectively. When persons act in accordance with the prevailing norms, their behaviors appear to be "natural" rather than "cultural." A common professional convention among students is raising their hand to ask a question. Despite the fact that this book's authors have never once asked students to raise their hands when they have questions, they have all blindly accepted this behavior as convention(al) and norm(al). We are willing to bet that those same students do not raise their hands when they have questions for their friends at dinner, as the conventions of friendship differ from those of education.

4   *Resilient.* Conventions typically endure over time, often as much out of tradition as anything else. The comment, "That's just the way we've always done it," which utilizes an appeal to tradition for instance, is a fairly common response to the question, "Why do you do it that way?" Though conventions are relatively resilient or stable, they are neither fixed nor static. Indeed, as organizational demands change, so too do conventions. As we will see shortly, the rise of new conventions partially accounts for why today's news media looks very different than the news media of just 40 years ago. One of the factors that should be considered by scholars who employ an Organizational approach, then, is why and under what circumstances conventions change.

5   *Directive*. Finally and perhaps most significantly, conventions are *directive*. They sanction or authorize some practices and behaviors, and discourage or disapprove of others. In other words, conventions function not as mere suggestions for possible courses of action, but as unspoken guidelines or rules for the correct or appropriate action. Because of their motivated, shared, naturalized, resilient, and directive character, conventions – be they organizational or professional – have a significant impact on daily workplace practices and consequently on the services and products offered by media companies. Before illustrating this through a specific case study, we briefly reflect on the process of professionalization.

Professionalization

The existence and operation of professional conventions leads to **professionalization** or the socialization of workers to do their work in certain ways and to produce certain kinds of products. Simply stated, professionalization is the internalization of professional conventions as common sense. Consider the "training" of a professional film director like Martin Scorsese, for instance. Although Scorsese's interest in film goes back to his childhood, his formal training did not begin until he was a student at New York University's prestigious film school. We say "formal training," as the mere act of watching films had already begun to educate and professionalize him. Having graduated with an MFA in film directing in 1966, Scorsese now had the professional credentials to begin making Hollywood films. The combination of his personal style (process) and professional training (structure) has led to a career of critically acclaimed films, including the recent, *Hugo* (2011), which won five Academy Awards. In short, Scorsese was taught a set of film-making conventions, which allowed him to become a professional film maker and hence reproduce those conventions in his own work, for which he was recognized as outstanding in his field. None of this is to suggest that Scorsese is not a talented film maker, only to highlight that what counts as "excellence" in film making depends to a large extent on an adeptness with professional conventions.

This brief account of Scorsese's career highlights several interconnected dimensions of professional socialization. Once professional norms harden into common sense, arising often as a consequence of the profit-motive or as a matter of practicality, they establish the standards by which a profession measures quality and competence. These standards, in turn, serve as guides for making hires, conducting annual evaluations, determining promotions, and dispensing awards and recognition. The more fully one has been professionally socialized through one's education and training, the more likely one is to get a job. After all, one already possesses the skills that have been deemed valuable and necessary. Similarly, once in a position, the more one is able to conform to existing professional conventions, the more likely one is to be rewarded with money, promotions, responsibilities, recognition, and praise. Professionals, then, have many powerful incentives to adopt and follow professional conventions even if they are consciously unaware of them. Most professions also have professional societies to which their members belong. These societies generate literature, conduct studies, and host conventions that all function to further reinforce professional norms and conventions. They, in effect, perform the socializing role performed early in one's career by formal education.

The News Media: an In-Depth Case Study

To better understand the ways that media organizations constrain the practices and hence the products of media workers, the remainder of this chapter undertakes a detailed case study of the news media. This section begins by recounting the historical development of the press in the USA, including its professionalization, before turning to a detailed examination of the causes, character, and consequences of journalistic conventions. The news media or "press" have a long and storied history in the USA, one that extends back to Colonial America. The colonies' first newspapers, which began to appear in the late 1600s, bore little resemblance to the newspapers of today. They were typically large, one-sided, single sheets, which earned them the nickname *broadsides*. Broadsides and the multipage newspapers to follow were often overtly political and more than a little critical of the British crown.

Public Occurrences, Both Foreign and Domestic, the first newspaper published in the USA, for instance, was banned after only a single issue – published on September 25, 1690 – because the government objected to Boston publisher Benjamin Harris's unfavorable depiction of British rule. Such setbacks did not deter upstart publishers, however, and during the 1700s colonial broadsides and newspapers were instrumental in challenging British authority and decree and fostering colonial solidarity. The "No *Stamped Paper* to be had" broadside, for instance, reported on colonial efforts to repeal the greatly despised 1765 Stamp Act, which required all colonial newspapers to carry a stamp tax designed to generate revenue for the British government. The Stamp Act along with British efforts to suppress anti-government views and sentiments, which included shutting newspapers down, partially accounts for why the framers of the US Constitution were committed to guaranteeing a "free press" following the American Revolution. The belief in an independent press, free from governmental regulation and interference, is what earned the news media its reputation as the Fourth Estate. As Thomas Jefferson famously wrote:

> I am persuaded myself that the good sense of the people will always be found to be the best army. They may be led astray for a moment, but will soon correct themselves. The people are the only censors of their governors: and even their errors will tend to keep these to the true principles of their institution. To punish these errors too severely would be to suppress the only safeguard of the public liberty. The way to prevent these irregular interpositions of the people is to give them full information of their affairs thro' the channel of the public papers, and to contrive that those papers should penetrate the whole mass of the people. The basis of our governments being the

opinion of the people, the very first object should be to keep that right; and were it left to me to decide whether we should have a government without newspapers, or newspapers without a government, I should not hesitate a moment to prefer the latter.[15]

Jefferson's statement suggests that he saw newspapers as vital to an informed public and thus to a healthy democracy.

As newspapers spread and flourished following the American Revolution, they remained decidedly political. In fact, many newspapers were openly sympathetic toward or even funded by particular political parties and interests: a journalistic model known as the *partisan press*. This trend continued until about the mid-1800s when newspapers, in an attempt to appeal to broader audiences, slowly began to temper their partisan messages in favor of human-interest stories. It was also during this period that six New York newspapers established the first major news wire, the Associated Press (AP), in an effort to exchange news and information more efficiently. This shift along with the relatively inexpensive cost of papers contributed to an explosion of dailies, and triggered fierce competition. Consequently, journalism (especially following the Civil War) became increasingly fascinated with scandal, corruption, and sensational headlines: a practice that came to be called *muckraking* as a result of its fondness for dredging up "muck." The trend toward salacious, personality-centered, entertainment-oriented, soft news only increased as newspapers aggressively competed for readers and advertisers. One of the most famous and nasty competitions occurred in New York between William Randolph Hearst's *Morning Journal* and Joseph Pulitzer's *New York World*. As these and other local rivals battled for greater shares of the marketplace, quality journalism committed to covering hard news was replaced by **yellow journalism**: a style of news that lacked any sense of social responsibility and privileged sensational and even fabricated stories and photos.

Although yellow journalism was prevalent as well as profitable throughout the late 1800s, by the turn of the century it was slowly being challenged by a more responsible model of journalism: one that eschewed tabloid news, sensational stories, publicity stunts, and excessive commercialism in favor of the impartial reporting of information regarded as vital to the public. This shift was due in large part to the increasing professionalization of journalism: a process that "included the founding of journalism schools and professional organizations as well as the formulation of several codes of ethics, such as the one drawn up by the American Society of Newspaper Editors in 1923."[16] Journalistic practices were also influenced by the publication of Walter Lippmann's *Liberty and the News* in 1920. Lippmann, a well-known essayist and editor, wrote that "the present crisis of western democracy is a crisis in journalism" because "there is no steady supply of trustworthy and relevant news."[17] Writing in a broadly libertarian tradition, Lippmann was an ardent advocate for the journalistic standard of **objectivity**, or the reporting of facts in a fair and impartial manner. Although objectivity existed as a journalistic ideal long before Lippmann, he was vital to its widespread adoption as a professional norm following World War I.

Further professionalization of journalism in the twentieth century was fueled by two interrelated factors: growing concern over the possibility of government regulation and the advocacy of social responsibility theory. Fears among newspaper owners and editors that the government might attempt to regulate the press were far from unfounded. The Federal Radio Commission (FRC), for instance, had been established in 1927 to regulate radio following arguments by Commerce Secretary Herbert Hoover that the airwaves belong to the people and therefore ought to serve the "public interest." Mounting pressure for newspapers to submit to similar regulatory efforts ultimately led to the formation of the Hutchins Commission on Freedom of the Press in 1942.

The Commission, which was funded by Time Inc. CEO Henry Luce and headed by University of Chicago President Robert Maynard Hutchins, sought to address the question, "Is the freedom of the press in danger?"[18] Comprised of academics from Yale University and the University of Chicago, whom Hutchins had appointed, the Commission on Freedom of the Press released its final 133-page report, *A Free and Responsible Press*, in 1947. In its report, the Hutchins Commission advocated a code of social responsibility for the press that included five basic services:

1   a truthful, comprehensive, and intelligent account of the day's events in a context which gives them meaning,
2   a forum for the exchange of comment and criticism,
3   the projection of a representative picture of the constituent groups in society,
4   the presentation and clarification of the goals and values of the society,
5   full access to the day's intelligence.

Response to the report was both swift and harsh, especially from journalists and editors who resented the implication that they were not doing their jobs. Despite the indignant response of the press, however, the report had a significant influence on academic thinking, and a "social responsibility" model soon became the standard in journalism schools around the country. The adoption and teaching of a common journalistic model (and, hence, set of practices) fueled the professionalization of the field, and paved the way for the rise of "accredited" journalism schools. One way to understand the history of journalism in the USA, then, is to see it as a story about the gradual transformation of journalists from independent, civic-minded, "ink-stained wretches to college-educated professionals."[19]

News organizations and journalistic conventions

Having reviewed some of the key developments in the history and evolution of journalism, we can now turn our attention to the modern-day news organization and ask how its organizational structure and processes shape the daily output of the media product we know as "news." Ideally, the **news** ought to provide the public with accurate and reliable information that assists them in better participating in civic life in a responsible and informed manner. But in reality, the news is more often, explains Lance Bennett, "what newsmakers (politicians and other political actors) promote as timely, important, or interesting from which news organizations select, narrate, and package for transmission (via communication technologies) to people who consume it."[20] In other words, the news is produced like any other commodity, not discovered or found. To understand the sizeable gap between the ideal and the actuality of what constitutes the news, we must examine the specific professional conventions that govern how news is gathered and reported. Like all conventions, the conventions of news *gathering* and *reporting* did not emerge arbitrarily. They are responses to specific situational demands.

The two major situational constraints on news gathering are the "news hole" and the "news whole," both of which are influenced heavily by the profit-motive discussed in Chapter 2. The *news hole*, or the necessity to deliver the news every day at the same time (i.e. to "fill the hole"), is one of the most powerful institutional forces in journalism and it has resulted in a series of concrete organizational practices and routines. The need to produce the news every day by a specific deadline is a heavy burden for both local and national news outlets. To meet the daily demand for news created by the news hole, journalists rely upon a series of standardized practices for collecting the news that include journalistic beats, news agencies, and punditry and press releases. **Journalistic beats** are the places and institutions where news is expected to occur on any given day, such as police stations and courthouses. These institutions comprise the criminal/legal beat, for instance, and are reliable sources of news. According to Herbert Gans, national news in the USA is overwhelmingly dominated by five beats: incumbent presidents, presidential candidates, leading federal officials, state and local officials, and alleged and actual violators of laws and mores.[21] The reason the news is dominated by a steady stream of stories about crime and politicians, then, is not because these topics and figures are inherently newsworthy, but because news organizations assign reporters to these beats. Mark Fishman describes how this journalistic practice influences what counts as "news" and what does not:

> Some happenings in the world become public events. Others are condemned to obscurity as the personal experience of a handful of people. The mass media, and in particular news organizations, make all the difference.... [A] crucial part of the newsmaking process – the routine work of beat reporters – [...] determines what becomes a public event and what becomes a nonevent.... [R]eporters' "sense of events," their methods for seeing the newsworthiness of occurrences, are based on schemes of interpretation originating from and used by agency officials within the institutions beat reporters cover. Nonevents are specific happenings that are seen as "out of character" within the institutional settings in which they occur.... To seriously entertain these occurrences as potential news would force journalists to question their own methods for detecting newsworthy events.[22]

The events that are systematically excluded from public view (i.e. the so-called nonevents) as a result of prevailing news-gathering conventions, then, are really nothing more than occurrences that, if reported, would call into question the legitimacy of the beats (people and institutions) that reporters depend on for news.

Figure 3.1   President Bush declaring an end to major combat operations in Iraq. J. Scott Applewhite/ AP/PA Photos.

In addition to news organizations gathering news from the same places day after day, they also obtain news from news agencies or wire services. **News agencies** can be corporations such as Reuters that produce and sell stories to other news providers or non-profit cooperatives like the Associated Press that work with large media companies to generate news centrally and distribute it locally. Since the major news agencies generally prepare features and news packages complete with stock images and footage, the stories they provide can generally be used by news organizations with virtually no modification. This is particularly valuable to news organizations that must meet daily print and broadcast deadlines. The use of news agencies as a central means of gathering news explains, at least partially, why the major news networks inevitably cover the same stories every day. The consistency of the news across networks does not arise because various news organizations independently "discover" the same news every day, but because they all collect news from the same beats and news agencies.

A third way that news organizations gather news is through political pundits and press releases. **Punditry** describes news that is pre-packaged by politicians and their communication consultants (i.e. press advisors and public relations managers) to promote a favorable image of a politician and her or his specific policy initiatives.[23] In the interest of *image management*, consultants constantly seek to control both the news situation and message surrounding political actors. The strategies consultants employ to control the news situation are vast and sophisticated, and range from carefully staged, scripted, and acted *pseudo events* to scheduled press briefings where politicians set the agenda.[24] One of the most infamous pseudo events in recent history was President George W. Bush's May 1, 2003 declaration of an end to major combat operations in Iraq aboard the aircraft carrier USS *Abraham Lincoln* under a red, white, and blue banner boldly proclaiming, "Mission Accomplished" (Figure 3.1).

In addition to staging pseudo events, consultants also attempt to manage the image of a politician by controlling the news message. Consultants and pundits accomplish this by packaging their messages as clear, concise slogans, saturating the news with these slogans, and providing some form of evidence that the message is credible. This practice, which depends upon carefully constructed *sound bites*, is often referred to as *political spin*. Such pre-packaged news, though clearly biased, is attractive to journalists because it is delivered directly to them and presented in a form that is easily reportable. Bennett estimates that nearly three-quarters of all political news comes from government officials in the form of interviews, press conferences, press releases, official proceedings, and sanctioned leaks.[25] **Press releases** are strategically prepared written or recorded statements produced for news organizations to announce something that claims to be newsworthy.

Political consultants are not the only ones who use press releases as a strategy for getting carefully controlled messages picked up as news, however. Many major corporations, non-profit organizations, scientific foundations, and even fanatical cults utilize press releases as a way to promote themselves, their views, and their products. In his 2007 book, *It's Not News, It's Fark: How Mass Media Tries to Pass off Crap as News*, Drew Curtis documents that press releases are frequently picked up, oftentimes with no changes, and run as news. Curtis calls this phenomenon the "unpaid placement masquerading as actual article," and notes that it is surprisingly common.[26] Consider, for instance, annual lists such as *People*'s Sexiest Man Alive or *Time*'s 100 Most Influential People. Each year, these magazines circulate press releases about their picks, which are then reported by mainstream news organizations as news. But is the selection and announcement of Channing Tatum as 2012's sexiest man alive really news or just an advertisement for *People* magazine? In a similar vein, big drug companies often release the results of "scientific studies" announcing landmark medical breakthroughs that are in actuality little more than advertisements for their latest designer drug.

Journalistic beats, news agencies, and political pundits and press releases do more than assist news organizations in filling the daily news hole, however; they also aid them in filling it completely or wholly. The *news whole* is our phrase to describe the specific amount of time or space allotted for reporting the news each day. Has it ever seemed strange to you that regardless of the events of the day, nightly national news broadcasts are always precisely 60 minutes long? This means that journalists must gather enough news every day to fill the entire news program, but not so much news that it won't fit in the program. So, how does the need to make the news "fit" daily programming schedules constrain the practices of news gathering? The chief way it does this is by influencing the selection of stories. When journalists are sent into the field to produce news packages that will later be used locally or shared through news agencies, they know that the typical television news package is only 60–90 seconds long. Before they ever became professionals, young journalists were taught the basic formulas for creating news packages in school. Consequently, events and information that do not readily lend themselves to a short, simple, dramatic, and narrative format are commonly ignored or overlooked. Complex issues, even those vital to the public, are far less likely to see the light of your television screen or the front page of your daily newspaper than matters that can easily be reported by answering the routine who, what, where, and when questions.

The strict conventions that govern news gathering are driven in large part by the profit-motive, or the desire of news organizations to produce the news cheaply and efficiently, while simultaneously appealing to the largest audience possible. Audience share is important because it determines what can be charged for advertising time and thus affects advertising revenues.[27] In short, journalists are under considerable economic pressures to find audience-grabbing stories on short deadlines with minimal resources. Consequently, the selection of news stories often has little to do with their *newsworthiness*: their social and informational value to the public. Rather than asking what really matters to people's everyday lives or what is vital for people to know to be able to effectively carry out their civic duties, journalists simply regard the public figures and institutions that comprise their regular beats as newsworthy. Hence, the news is not something that is uncovered, explored, and reported on each day; rather, it is a product or commodity manufactured by news organizations for maximum palatability and profitability. This claim is further evidenced by news-reporting conventions.

One of the perennial issues raised about the news media is its supposed political bias; we say "supposed" because the precise nature of its bias depends upon whom you ask. In *Bias: a CBS Insider Exposes How the Media Distort the News*, Bernard Goldberg argues the news media have a left-wing bias, while in *What Liberal Bias?: The Truth about Bias and the News*, Eric Alterman contends that the news media have a right-leaning bias. The problem with this debate generally, regardless of the side being argued, is that it is utterly relative. To say that the news media have a left-wing bias presumes there is an objective, apolitical position from which to judge it. The debate also assumes (incorrectly) that all news outlets have the same political bias, as though the *New York Times* and *New York Post* or MSNBC and FOX News were identical. The question of political bias in the news is a nonsensical one, then, especially since – despite their obvious political leanings – news outlets largely cover the same stories every day. The far more insidious bias in the news is an informational, not explicitly political one. **Informational bias** refers to how a story is structured and told, and as Lance Bennett notes, most news stories display four informational biases.

1 *Personalization.* Most news stories focus on individuals rather than institutions, and emphasize human-interest angles and emotional impact over and often at the expense of broader social contexts and political perspectives. Simply put, news stories are people-centered; they rely heavily upon interviews, first-person accounts, eye-witness testimony, and expert opinions. The focus on individual people is designed to make stories feel more personal, direct, and immediate. But by focusing on individual actors, such as the President, in a story about economic recession, for instance, audiences are encouraged to view political issues individually rather than socially. Consequently, they are more likely to blame specific political actors for social ills and less likely to understand the underlying factors and root causes of social problems.

2   *Dramatization.* The news is overwhelmingly biased toward the narrative presentation of information. Regardless of the specific issues journalists are reporting on,
those issues tend to be structured as stories, "as contrasted, for example, to analytical
essays, political polemics, or more scientific-style problem reports."[28] Moreover, to
heighten audience interest, journalists frequently focus on the most sensational,
scandalous, and shocking details of a story. The insistence on narrativizing the
news has at least two significant consequences. First, since some issues are difficult
to pictorialize and require sustained analysis, their dramatization leads to inaccurate or misrepresentative reporting (if they get covered at all). Second, since
narratives have beginnings, middles, and endings, dramatized news has the potential
to impose a clean and tidy sense of closure on complex, enduring issues.

3   *Fragmentation.* A third informational bias in the news is the tendency to treat
stories in isolation, ignoring their connection to other stories and the larger contexts in which they occur. Both newspapers and televised newscasts organize the
news into brief, self-contained capsules. This can foster the misimpression that
the world is just a series of random, unrelated events. The compartmentalization
of news stories can obfuscate not only the interconnections among stories, but
also their historical significance. Fragmented news makes the world appear chaotic
and unpredictable. Indeed, the prevalence of fragmented news helps to explain
why the 9/11 attacks were so utterly incomprehensible to most Americans, who
had no context for understanding the connections between the economic and
foreign policies of the USA, and the religious zealotry of Islamic extremists. To
most Americans, the attacks of September 11, 2001 on the World Trade Center
and Pentagon are isolated events with no prior history or context.

4   *Authority–disorder.* The fourth and final informational bias of the news is closely
related to the first three, and in particular, the way that personalized news becomes
dramatized. Since personalization leads to a focus on individuals and dramatization favors the sensational, it is common to depict the individuals and parties
involved in a story as in conflict or tension. This tension is typically represented as
one between authority (i.e. police, government leaders, public officials) and disorder (i.e. criminals, natural disasters, terrorism). Furthermore, since the news is
comprised of individual capsules that require narrative closure, the authority-
disorder tension is generally resolved either in the direction of authority through
the restoration of normalcy or in the direction of disorder and the cynical view
that public officials are incompetent. Consider the news media framing of
Hurricane Katrina, which struck the Gulf Coast and devastated New Orleans on
August 28, 2005. The story was structured around a natural catastrophe (disorder)
and the government's response, as represented by Michael Brown, then Director of
the Federal Emergency Management Agency (FEMA). When the government was
not able to quickly restore normalcy, Brown was fired for his incompetence.

While virtually any news story could profitably be analyzed using the four information
biases just presented, one of this book's authors witnessed a particularly apt example on
the local Fox 31 affiliate one evening. As he was watching reruns of *The Simpsons*,
Ott repeatedly saw a promo for that evening's newscast, which in a deep announcer's

voice alarmingly said: "Ron has a nuclear bomb buried in his back yard! Missiles are buried all over Colorado. See where tonight on Fox 31 News at 9:00." After soiling himself, Ott began to wonder if Ron tried to plant a tree in his backyard would it cause a nuclear holocaust. Fearing for his life, he decided to stay tuned. Despite the hysteria of the promo, this news story did not begin until a full 30 minutes into the broadcast. In a segment dramatically titled, "Nukes In Your Neighborhood" – complete with images of mushroom clouds – reporter Heidi Hemmat informed viewers of the 49 Minute Man missiles located in Colorado "on farms, near churches and schools, throughout small towns across the eastern plain." The mention of farms, churches, and schools heightens fear, making the story more dramatic. She then interviewed farmer Ron Bornhoff, who has a missile near his farm, to personalize the story. After scaring the audience shitless, Hemmat assured viewers the bombs are carefully guarded 24 hours a day by the US military, thereby re-establishing authority and order to the chaotic frame of the story. The story reflects fragmentation to the extent that it stands completely independent of the other news reports that evening. In retrospect, Ott realized that there was no real news here at all, only fear packaged as news for an unsuspecting audience.

The informational biases of personalization, dramatization, fragmentation, and authority–disorder in the news can be visual as well as linguistic. Like journalism more broadly, press photography operates according to a strict set of professional conventions. In the early 1960s, Roland Barthes published two famous studies, "The Photographic Message" and "Rhetoric of the Image," in which he highlighted the distinctive visual codes of press and advertising photography respectively. Barthes recognized that photojournalists are trained professionals who have been taught to take pictures in a particular way, namely so that they evoke strong emotion, appear to be candid, and situate the viewer in the action. Advertising photography, by contrast, creates desire and pleasure, emphasizes careful staging, and places the viewer at a distance from its subject. The noticeable difference in visual codes between photojournalism and advertising is a powerful reminder that no image is objective, and that editors select the images used in the news precisely because they best conform to the norms of photojournalism. Figure 3.2, which depicts Tarana Akbari, age 12, screaming in fear moments after a suicide bombing, is especially adept at modeling the conventions of photojournalism and, thus, won the 2012 Pulitzer Prize for Breaking News Photography. Contrast this image with Figure 3.3, an advertisement for Hot Wheels, which also features a child, but works in a different way. Unlike the press photograph, the advertising image is not particularly emotional or immediate; it is clever and cute, rather than terrifying and tragic.

Conventions of the news magazine

Up to this point, our discussion of the news media has focused primarily on print media. But television is also an important source of news in the USA. Within the TV news industry, there are numerous news formats, ranging from the morning talk show (e.g. *Good Morning America*, *The Today Show*, *The Early Show*) and news commentary program (e.g. *The O'Reilly Factor*, *Hardball with Chris Matthews*) to

Figure 3.2 Pulitzer Prize for Breaking News Photography 2012 – Tarana Akbari, 12, screaming in fear moments after a suicide bomber detonated a bomb in a crowd at the Abul Fazel Shrine in Kabul on Dec. 6, 2011. MASSOUD HOSSAINI/ AFP/GETTY IMAGES.

Figure 3.3 Hot Wheels advertisement. (with permission from Mattel)

the evening news (e.g. *NBC Nightly News, CBS Evening News, ABC News*) and newsmagazine program (e.g. *20/20, Dateline NBC, 48 Hours, Primetime, 60 Minutes*). Each of these formats employs its own distinct formula for organizing and presenting information. In this section, we highlight the formal conventions of the evening newsmagazine by drawing upon Richard Campbell's landmark study, *60 Minutes and the News: a Mythology for Middle America.*

60 Minutes is one of the most successful television shows in history, having finished in Nielsen's top 10 programs a record 23 consecutive seasons. Created in 1968 by Don Hewitt, who remains the show's executive producer, *60 Minutes* has won more Emmy awards than any other news broadcast. The show combines investigative journalism with celebrity journalism, and typically consists of two or three separately produced segments. As Campbell has demonstrated, those segments generally follow one of four well-worn formulas.

1 *News as mystery*. This type of report is what many people think of when they hear the phrase "investigative reporting" because it often involves journalists with hidden cameras, who uncover wrongdoings by playing detective and surprising or ambushing interviewees. For Campbell, stories told using this formula precede in four stages: (1) the identification of key characters, who are framed as villains or criminals; (2) the search for clues of criminal violation; (3) the stalking and ultimate confrontation of the wrongdoer about his or her misdeeds; and (4) an assurance that the wrongdoers have been brought to justice, and safety has been restored. In August 2004, for instance, *60 Minutes* aired a segment titled "Doing Business with the Enemy" that uncovered major US companies such as Halliburton were conducting millions of dollars' worth of business with countries that sponsor terrorism (e.g. Iran).

2 *News as therapy*. This formula places the reporter in the position of analyst or therapist, rather than detective. In his or her capacity as therapist, the journalist performs four key roles: (1) as a social commentator who endows the narrative with moral meaning by placing the interview in appropriate historical, political, or cultural context; (2) as an intimate confidant to whom the interviewee can reveal private, personal details; (3) as a champion of heroic characters or a foil to villainous characters; and (4) as an inquisitor, who asks tough, confrontational questions that probe deviations from popular values. Correspondent Ed Bradley's interview, titled "Being the First Man on the Moon," of the famously private Neil Armstrong about his family and fame in July 2006 is exemplary of this formula.

3 *News as adventure*. The adventure-story formula features plays like a Western and the reporter as tourist or a well-informed traveler in search of drama and adventure. The reporter-tourist is portrayed in three recurring capacities: (1) as viewers' surrogate for exploring and ultimately understanding a new, unfamiliar, or exotic locale; (2) as nostalgic traveler (in search of a simpler, uncorrupted time: a past still reflected in small-town, Middle American values) or as seeker of the authentic, natural or "real" America behind the fast-paced, high-tech modernist exterior; and (3) as protector from foreign or alien values that somehow threaten traditional, American-heartland values. The story of the Moken people, who miraculously survived the tsunami in Asia, illustrates news as adventure. In this June 2007 story, correspondent Bob Bimon traveled to a remote island off the coast of Thailand to learn the secrets of these native peoples in "Sea Gypsies Saw Signs in the Waves."

4 *News as arbitration*. A final formula used in newsmagazines is news as arbitration, which positions the reporter as referee or arbitrator. Of the four formulas, this one shares the most in common with orthodox journalism by featuring the reporter (1) as a neutral observer, (2) who defers to experts or authorities, (3) emphasizes a dialectical rather than expository structure, (4) abandons the search for a clear, unequivocal villain, and (5) resists proving narrative closure and resolution. "The Oil

Sands of Alberta," which aired in June 2006, illustrates the news-as-arbitration formula. The story described the vast oil reserves in Canada and reported on the dependence on fossil fuels and environmental debates that the reserves raise, but did not take sides or suggest what the outcome of these debates will be.

Consequences of news conventions

The professionalization of the news – and more specifically the journalistic conventions involved in news gathering and reporting – has four serious consequences. First, by deciding who and what gets covered (and conversely who and what does not get covered), the news media exercise a powerful **gatekeeping** function: the ability to control access to the public. Due to the pressures on journalists to meet deadlines, some issues, events, and actors are far more likely to be reported on than others. This system privileges organizations and politicians who possess the financial and structural resources to provide newsmakers (i.e. journalists) with ready-made news, and disadvantages alternative, independent, and less well-funded groups and citizens seeking to promote their message. In the political arena, news conventions greatly benefit the two major political parties and their candidates, while marginalizing and ostracizing third-party or independent candidates. This bias is one of the reasons why it makes little sense to debate whether the news is liberal or conservative; the blind reproduction of the two-party system means that news is overwhelmingly centrist.

An additional side-effect of gatekeeping is **agenda-setting**, or the belief that the news media do not influence *what people think* so much as they influence *what people think about*. The news media, by covering some topics and not others, establish the important topics of the day; they, in effect, set the agenda for public dialog. Because so much of what is reported as news is a product of journalistic beats, news agencies, political punditry, and press releases, the news media significantly restrict the diversity of topics on the public's mind. For the most part, if the media are not talking about it, neither is the public. Moreover, driven by profit, news outlets frequently engage in cross-promotional efforts for their parent corporations. Just before Disney released the summer blockbuster *Armageddon* (1998), for instance, ABC News (a Disney subsidiary) repeatedly ran stories about the dangers of asteroids striking the Earth. In this case, the so-called "news" functioned as little more than a film advertisement. Conversely, news outlets occasionally censor stories that could potentially hurt their corporate image such as when the President of ABC News axed a story ABC journalists were working on regarding Disney theme parks hiring known child molesters.[29]

A second and closely related consequence of news conventions is *homogenization*. Just as news-gathering conventions limit the diversity of *what* is covered, news-reporting conventions limit the diversity of *how* it is covered. According to Taylor and Willis, "Working practices contribute to the production of similar and less innovative programs across news production. ... The routines and working practices within news production therefore act to further the shared understanding of the form of news and hence also work to ensure a reproduction of both visual style and approach to content."[30] Despite the infinite number of ways a newspaper could be structured, for instance, there is a remarkable consistency in newspaper layout. Nor are the similarities among papers purely stylistic. Since journalists have been professionalized by their education, training, and experience, different reporters at different newspapers are likely to cover the same story in the same way. The presence of multiple newspapers in one locale, then, only creates "the appearance of choice," as both what they report on and how they report on it are likely to possess greater similarities than differences.

A dramatic increase in soft news is the third major consequence of news conventions. *Soft news* describes news that is high in entertainment value, but low in educational value; this type of news is sometimes referred to as "infotainment" because it is packaged so as to make it look important and informational despite the fact that it has no intrinsic social significance. In contrast to soft news, hard news is characterized by sustained reporting on issues important to people's lives, and in a manner that equips citizens to make informed decisions on public policy and social issues. Soft news appeals to viewers primarily on an emotional level by evoking fear, concern, or outrage. Common topics of soft news include crime (especially heinous crimes like child molestation), alcohol and drugs, gangs and violence, and fires and accidents. The degree to which the news is dominated by these types of stories is sometimes referred to as the *mayhem index*. Although the mayhem index is difficult to quantify, Bennett notes that between 1993 and 1996 the number of news stories about murder on the national news networks increased by 700 percent, while during that same time period, the actual murder rate declined by 20 percent.[31] No story, however, is *inherently* soft or hard news. Even crime stories can be reported as hard news if they focus on the social causes and consequences of violence, rather than on the sensational details of the crime or the tremendous grief of the victim's family. Thus, the prevalence of soft news is a result of how the news is reported, namely according to the four informational biases identified earlier in this chapter, rather than what is reported as news.

The fourth consequence of news conventions concerns the attribution of responsibility for social ills. The ways stories are framed by journalists influences how citizens understand social problems and ultimately whom they hold responsible for those problems. In his book *Is Anyone Responsible?* media scholar Shanto Iyengar argues that most news stories are framed in one of two general ways, either episodically or thematically. "The episodic news frame," according to Iyengar, "takes the form of a case study or event-oriented report and depicts public issues in terms of concrete instance."[32] The thematic news frame, by contrast, is more likely to situate social issues in a broader, abstract context and involve a "'takeout,' or 'backgrounder,' report directed at general outcomes or conditions."[33] Episodic and thematic news frames strongly influence how citizens assign responsibility for social problems. Whereas the episodic frame leads to the blaming of individuals, typically politicians, for social problems, the thematic frame tends to hold all of us accountable for social ills. Based on what we have learned in this chapter, it probably comes as no surprise that the news is dominated by episodic frames. This is because, as Bennett explains, "the (four) information biases in the news add up to news that is episodic."[34] The danger of episodic news is that it does not serve the public well as a basis for social and political action, since it frames problems as individual rather than institutional.

Conclusion

This chapter has explored the media industry from an Organizational perspective by looking at the interplay of structure and process. We learned that organizations consist of various professionals each with specialized skills and duties they have learned through formal training and actual practice. Routine work practices that are unique to a particular organization or profession are known as conventions. To illustrate how these principles actually operate, the chapter undertook a detailed analysis of the news media. Journalistic beats, news agencies, and political pundits and press releases were shown to dominate news-gathering conventions, while four primary information biases (personalization, dramatization, fragmentation, and authority–disorder) were shown to govern news-reporting conventions. Although these conventions may have developed for both pragmatic and economic reasons, they commonly result in news that is narrow, homogeneous, soft, and episodic. Despite the intensive focus on the news in this chapter, professionalization exists across media industries. Magazines, books, music, television, and film are no less the product of professional conventions than is the news and, thus, no less formulaic.

MEDIA LAB 2: DOING ORGANIZATION ANALYSIS

OBJECTIVE

The purpose of this lab is to learn to analyze the media from an Organizational perspective. Specifically, students will investigate how *news-gathering* and *news-reporting conventions* shape the selection and style of news stories.

ACTIVITY

- Divide the class into small groups of 4–5 students each.
- Supply each group with a copy of the university's newspaper.
- Ask students to record their answers to the following questions.
  1. Looking at the newspaper as a whole, what are the primary journalistic beats covered? Hint: A few of them may be unique to a student paper.
  2. Compare the style and layout of this newspaper to other newspapers you are familiar with. How is it similar? Different?
  3. Select one news story from the paper and identify how, if at all, the story reflects the four information biases described by Lance Bennett. Be specific in your answer. How does the language of the article reinforce particular informational biases?
  4. Is the story you selected primarily episodic or thematic in its framing? How do you know?

SUGGESTED READING

Bennett, W.L. *News: the Politics of Illusion*, 6th edn. New York: Pearson Education, 2005.

Bennett, W.L., Lawrence, R.C., and Livingston, S. *When the Press Fails: Political Power and the News Media from Iraq to Katrina*. Chicago, IL: University of Chicago Press, 2007.

Campbell, R. *60 Minutes and the News: a Mythology for Middle America*. Chicago, IL: University of Illinois, 1991.

Cheney, G., Chistensen, L.T., Zorn, Jr, T.E., and Ganesh, S. *Organizational Communication in an Age of Globalization: Issues, Reflections, Practices*. Prospect Heights, IL: Waveland Press, 2004.

Cohen, E.D. (ed.) *News Incorporated: Corporate Media Ownership and Its Threat to Democracy*. New York: Prometheus Books, 2005.

Cohen, S. and Young, J. (eds) *The Manufacture of News: Social Problems, Deviance and the Mass Media*, revised edn. Beverly Hills, CA: Sage Publications, 1981.

Curtis, D. *It's Not News, It's Fark: How Mass Media Tries to Pass Off Crap as News*. New York: Gotham Books, 2007.

Ettema, J.S. and Whitney, D.C. (eds) *Individuals in Mass Media Organizations: Creativity and Constraint*. Beverly Hills, CA: Sage Publications, 1982.

Fallows, J. *Breaking the News: How the Media Undermine American Democracy*. New York: Vintage Books, 1997.

Fenton, T. *Bad News: the Decline of Reporting, the Business of News, and the Danger to Us All*. New York: HarperCollins Publishers, 2005.

Fischman, W., Solomon, B., Greenspan, D., and Gardner, H. *Making Good: How Young People Cope with Moral Dilemmas at Work*. Boston, MA: Harvard University Press, 2004.

Gans, H.J. *Deciding What's News: a Study of CBS Evening News, NBC Nightly News, Newsweek and Time*. New York: Pantheon Books, 1979.

Gardner, H. Irresponsible Work. In *Responsibility at Work: How Leading Professionals Act (and Don't Act) Responsibly*, H. Gardner (ed.), pp. 262–82. San Francisco, CA: Jossey-Bass, 2007.

Iyengar, S. *Is Anyone Responsible? How Television Frames Political Issues*. Urbana, IL: University of Chicago Press, 1991.

Keyton, J. *Communication and Organizational Culture: a Key to Understanding Work Experiences*. Thousand Oaks, CA: Sage Publications, 2005.

Leigh, R.D. (ed.) *A Free and Responsible Press: a General Report on Mass Communication: Newspapers, Radio, Motion Pictures, Magazines and Books by the Commission on Freedom of the Press*. Chicago, IL: University of Chicago Press, 1947.

Lippmann, W. *Liberty and the News*. Princeton, NJ: Princeton University Press, 2008.

McPhee, R.D. Organizational Communication: a Structural Exemplar. In *Rethinking Communication, Volume 2: Paradigm Exemplars*, B. Dervin, L. Grossberg, B.J. O'Keefe, and E. Wartella (eds), pp. 199–212. Newbury Park, CA: Sage Publications, 1989.

Merritt, D. and Rosen, J. *Imagining Public Journalism: an Editor and Scholar Reflect on the Birth of an Idea*. Indiana University School of Journalism, Roy W. Howard Public Lecture, April 13, 1995.

Schmidt, J. *Disciplined Minds: a Critical Look at Salaried Professionals and the Soul-Battering System that Shapes Their Lives*. New York: Rowman & Littlefield Publishers, 2000.

Schudson, M. *Discovering the News: a Social History of American Newspapers*. New York: Basic Books, 1978.

Siebert, F.S., Peterson, T., and Schramm, W. *Four Theories of the Press: the Authoritarian, Libertarian, Social Responsibility, and Soviet Communist Concepts of What the Press Should Be and Do*. Urbana, IL: University of Illinois Press, 1963.

Tuchman, G. Making News by Doing Work: Routinizing the Unexpected. *Journal of Sociology* 1973, 79, 110–31.

Tuchman, G. *Making News: a Study in the Construction of Reality*. New York: Free Press, 1978.

Whitney, D.C., Sumpter, R.S., and McQuail, D. News Media Production: Individuals, Organizations, and Institutions. In *The Sage Handbook of Media Studies*, J.D.H. Downing, D. McQuail, P. Schlesinger, and E. Wartella (eds), pp. 393–410. Thousand Oaks, CA: Sage Publications, 2004.

NOTES

1. D. Callaghan, Face Value: Aaron Sorkin Finds Tragedy in the Creation of Facebook and Makes *The Social Network* an Era-Defining Film, *Writer's Guild of America, West*, October 1, 2010, http://www.wga.org/content/default.aspx?id=4348 (accessed February 9, 2013).

2. D.C. Whitney, R.S. Sumpter, and D. McQuail, News Media Production: Individuals, Organizations, and Institutions, in *The Sage Handbook of Media Studies*, J.D.H. Downing, D. McQuail, P. Schlesinger, and E. Wartella (eds) (Thousand Oaks, CA: Sage Publications, 2004), 394.

3. M.B. Sauter, A. Hess, and L.A. Nelson, Countries Where People Work Least, *NBC.com*, http://www.nbcnews.com/business/countries-where-people-work-least-915292#/business/countries-where-people-work-least-915292 (accessed February 9, 2013).

4. G. Cheney, L.T. Christensen, T.E. Zorn, Jr, and S. Ganesh, *Organizational Communication in an Age of Globalization: Issues, Reflections, Practices* (Prospect Heights, IL: Waveland Press, 2004), 7–8.

5. Cheney *et al.*, 18.

6. K. Burke, *A Grammar of Motives* (Berkeley, CA: University of California Press, 1969), 3.

7. E. Bell, *Theories of Performance* (Thousand Oaks, CA: Sage Publications, 2008), 16–17.

8. M.E. Pacanowsky and N. O'Donnell-Trujillo, Organizational Communication as Cultural Performance, *Communication Monographs* 50, 1983, 135–44.

9. Pacanowsky and O'Donnell-Trujillo, 144.

10. "When multiple organizational members tell (and retell) similar stories, the specifics of the stories accrue and are taken as findings about artifacts, values, and assumptions of an organization's culture" [J. Keyton, *Communication and Organizational

Culture (Thousand Oaks, CA: Sage Publications, 2005), 90].

11. Pacanowsky and O'Donnell-Trujillo, 139.

12. Keyton, 93.

13. Keyton, 112.

14. Keyton, 70.

15. T. Jefferson, Amendment I (Speech and Press), Document 8, Thomas Jefferson to Edward Carrington, in *The Papers of Thomas Jefferson Vol. 5, 1781*, J.P. Boyd (ed.) (Princeton, NJ: Princeton University Press, 1952). http://press-pubs.uchicago.edu/founders/documents/amendI_speechs8.html (accessed March 31, 2009).

16. W. Fischman, B. Solomon, D. Greenspan, and H. Gardner, *Making Good: How Young People Cope with Moral Dilemmas at Work* (Boston, MA: Harvard University Press, 2004), 25.

17. W. Lippmann, *Liberty and the News* (Princeton, NJ: Princeton University Press, 2008), 2, 6.

18. R.D. Leigh (ed.). *A Free and Responsible Press: a General Report on Mass Communication: Newspapers, Radio, Motion Pictures, Magazines and Books by the Commission on Freedom of the Press* (Chicago, IL: University of Chicago Press, 1947), 1.

19. J. Straubhaar and R. LaRose, *Media Now: Communication in the Information Age*, 3rd edn. (Belmont, CA: Wadsworth Publishing, 2001), 118.

20. W.L. Bennett, *News: the Politics of Illusion* (New York: Pearson Education, 2005), 9.

21. H.J. Gans, *Deciding What's News: a Study of CBS Evening News, NBC Nightly News, Newsweek and Time* (New York: Pantheon Books, 1979), 9–11.

22. M. Fishman, News and Nonevents: Making the Visible Invisible, in *Individual in Mass Media Organizations: Creativity and Constraint*, J.S. Ettema and D.C. Whitney (eds) (Beverly Hills, CA: Sage Publications, 1982), 219.

23. This definition of punditry is specific to the USA. In other countries such as the UK, the term is less pejorative and refers to respected experts who offer valuable opinions on news events.

24. Bennett, 142–3.

25. Bennett, 125.

26. D. Curtis, *It's Not News, It's Fark: How Mass Media Tries to Pass Off Crap as News* (New York: Gotham Books, 2007), 60.

27. Bennett, 92.

28. Bennett, 46.

29. Bennett, 99.

30. L. Taylor and A. Willis, *Media Studies: Texts, Institutions and Audiences* (Oxford: Blackwell, 1999), 128.

31. Bennett, 14.

32. S. Iyengar, *Is Anyone Responsible? How Television Frames Political Issues* (Urbana, IL: University of Chicago Press, 1991), 14.

33. Iyengar, 14.

34. Bennett, 53.

4 Pragmatic Analysis

KEY CONCEPTS

AGGRESSOR EFFECT
BYSTANDER EFFECT
CATHARSIS EFFECT
CODE OF ETHICS
CONSEQUENCES
CONTINGENCIES
COPYRIGHT
DIGITAL RIGHTS
MANAGEMENT
ENCRYPTION

HABIT
HISTORICAL VIOLENCE
HYPER-REAL VIOLENCE
INDECENCY
IRONISM
LIBEL

MELIORISM
OBSCENITY
PRAGMATISM
PROFANITY
RELATIVISM
RITUALISTIC VIOLENCE
SLANDER
VICTIM EFFECT

In late October 2011, Texas Representative Lamar S. Smith introduced the Stop Online Piracy Act (SOPA) to the US House of Representatives, triggering perhaps the most spectacular battle over new media regulation in recent memory. Among other provisions, SOPA would have granted the federal government the power to compel search engines to blacklist foreign websites that illegally hosted copyrighted material, as well as to shut down American websites for similarly offending material uploaded by users. On one side of this battle were the Motion Picture Association of America and other professional associations that represented the creators of often-pirated media content. On the other were companies like Google and Facebook, media activists, librarians, and others concerned about the Act's impact on free speech and online information access.

Protests to the bill and its perceived censorship were swift and harsh. Major web hubs like Wikipedia and Reddit, for example, voluntarily went offline for a day, refusing users access in an attempt to symbolize the damage SOPA would do to the internet's collective architecture. The shadowy "hacktivist" organization known as Anonymous went a step further, taking credit for the simultaneous shutdown of websites for perceived SOPA supporters like the US Justice Department and the Recording Industry Association of America. In the wake of these demonstrations, as

Critical Media Studies: An Introduction, Second Edition. Brian L. Ott and Robert L. Mack.
© 2014 John Wiley & Sons, Inc. Published 2014 by John Wiley & Sons, Inc.

well as numerous members of Congress publicly recanting their support for the bill, the House finally announced in January 2012 that it would postpone discussion of online piracy until it conducted further analysis of the various issues involved.

This chapter asks the question, what should be the government's role in media? This relationship, of course, varies greatly from society to society. In some countries, the media is state-owned, -controlled, and -run: a sort of propagandistic arm of the government. In most democratic societies, the media is "relatively" independent of the government, often performing the function of "the Fourth Estate." But even in democratic societies, government and media are not completely independent, and, indeed, the media industry favors some involvement and regulation by the government. Without the formal licensing of radio stations, for instance, different companies would constantly jam or interfere with each other's broadcasts.

But the example of SOPA suggests that the actual practice of regulation is wrought with difficulties. When and under what circumstances is regulation actually necessary? How much regulation is enough without being too much? In the past, attempts to answer this question have often relied on abstract principles such as free speech and public interest. Although these are certainly important principles, without some guiding theoretical framework to suggest how these concepts should be utilized in practice, it is very difficult to approach the relationship between government and media in a critical way. This is where our chapter differs from most on the subject. Rather than presenting an historical overview of government regulation as a loose theme in media studies, we offer the philosophical perspective of Pragmatism as a guiding heuristic for critically evaluating government regulation of the media. We will begin by outlining some of the major tenets and thinkers of Pragmatism before looking at how Pragmatist ideas help us better understand the process of regulation in the American media industries.

Pragmatism: an Overview

Pragmatism is the branch of philosophy that assesses truth in terms of effect, outcome, and practicality. Unlike earlier, metaphysical philosophers who viewed truth as a transcendental constant waiting to be discovered, Pragmatists claim that truth depends on the degree to which a concept or theory provides us with useful results in the process of solving problems. Metaphysical truths by their nature cannot actually be fully known, and many Pragmatists argue that believing or not believing in them has no real bearing on one's daily life. Instead, the truth of an idea or course of action (and therefore its merit) should be based on tangible results and the possible consequences of supporting or disregarding it. As a result, truth becomes a sort of label, a quality that a thing can possess or lack, and it is always dependent on contextual factors.

Pragmatism is often referred to as the only significant American contribution to world philosophy, and the connections between Pragmatism's emphasis on practicality and the American Protestant work ethic are not difficult to see. In addition, almost all key Pragmatic thinkers have come from American institutions. The philosopher Charles Sanders Peirce is credited with actually coining the term in the late nineteenth century, but other key thinkers have played a more important role in developing the philosophy into its current form. We choose to focus on three in this chapter: William James, John Dewey, and Richard Rorty.

William James (1842–1910)

William James was a psychologist and an important early Pragmatic philosopher. In both *Pragmatism* (1907) and its sequel, *The Meaning of Truth* (1909), James in effect "founded" the American school of Pragmatism by popularizing Peirce's own obscure work on the subject (which might have been forgotten otherwise). The union between James's psychological and Pragmatic interests is best represented by his conception of **habit**, or "a pathway of discharge formed in the brain, by which certain incoming currents ever after tend to escape."[1] For James, predictable or habitual ways of thinking and acting arise when external phenomena register upon the brain. The initial adaptation of the brain in response to something lays a mental pathway for the processing of any future experiences with that thing. This means that habit is essentially practical in nature, for without habits, the brain would have to generate new thoughts and actions each time the individual experienced anything. James compares the formation of habits to a bone fracture: a broken bone may heal, but because of its interaction with something external, it is more vulnerable to future injury than a bone that has never been broken. Habits, then, are not idiosyncratic qualities that an individual happens to possess; they are remnants of interactions with the real world which predispose future actions along somewhat predictable lines.

Habits can be negative or positive. Eating lots of ice cream in response to the stress of studying for a math exam, for example, may lead you to overindulge again during future cram sessions until wolfing down Rocky Road becomes easier than long division. At the same time, finding a quiet spot in the library to study may lead to future productive sessions in the same location until you are your class's resident math whiz. The predictability inherent to habit, however, does not mean that it is completely unchanging. New experiences may give rise to new habits or gradually alter existing ones. A concerned roommate who locks up the Rocky Road whenever he sees you whip out your math book might encourage you to abandon the treat and inaugurate some healthier coping habits. Alternatively, people who flood the library during finals week may interrupt your normal study habits and force you to try something else.

Since habits can either help or hinder and are constantly open to revision, James came to believe that "[t]he whole function of philosophy ought to be to find out what definite difference it will make to you and me, at definite instants of our life, if this world formula or that world formula be the true one."[2] In other words, rather than consider the unchanging truths of the universe, philosophers should explore practically how encounters with the world may give rise to better or worse habits within individuals. James's imperative functions as a touchstone for the very material focus of Pragmatism today, but for much of his career he remained focused on what a Pragmatic orientation could do to better the life of the *individual*. It was not until the work of John Dewey that the budding philosophy began to grapple with larger social concerns.

John Dewey (1859–1952)

John Dewey is more popularly known as a great pillar in American educational theory of the twentieth century, but his theories on the nature of education are intrinsically tied to his own Pragmatic philosophy. His major works in relation to Pragmatism include *Reconstruction in Philosophy* (1919) and *The Quest for Certainty* (1929). Echoing James, Dewey believed that ways of thinking were essentially habits, in the sense that human beings generate thought in order to overcome difficulties they encounter in the world. Unlike James, however, Dewey introduced communication and social interaction as critical nodes upon which human habits and thoughts rest. "Apart from communication," he writes,

> habit-forming wears grooves; behavior is confined to channels established by prior behavior. In so far the tendency is toward monotonous regularity. The very operation of learning sets a limit to itself, and makes subsequent learning more difficult. But this holds only of a habit, a habit in isolation, a non-communicating habit. Communication not only increases the number and variety of habits, but tends to link them subtly together, and eventually to subject habit-forming in a particular case to the habit of recognizing that new modes of association will exact a new use of it. Thus habit is formed in view of possible future changes and does not harden so readily.[3]

In short, the ability to communicate with others is what keeps one's habits and thoughts from calcifying.

Dewey's recognition of sociality as the key to altering habits paved the way for his crucial contribution to Pragmatic thought: **meliorism**, or the recognition of the elements present in a historical moment and the use of applied thought to develop ways of improving them.[4] Social problems may exist as products of engrained habits, but the malleable nature of habit also means that these problems can be fixed, especially through communicative and social intervention. With meliorism as his guiding principle, Dewey attempted to shift the focus in American education away from habits of rote memorization and toward an appreciation for flexible problem solving. As the American population changed its habits of thought, Dewey believed, they could work together to correct the many social problems which plagued the time period.

Thus, Dewey mirrors James in his belief that the purpose of philosophy is to correct real and significant problems in the world, but he also extends James's focus on the site of these problems from individual to social levels. His thoughts regarding an essentially Pragmatic education were instrumental in connecting individual evolution to social improvement, and in many ways his work paved the way for the tenets of Pragmatist thought we have today. The budding American philosophy, however, still faced a number of conceptual problems. These problems became the focus of one of the most important scholars in contemporary Pragmatism, Richard Rorty.

Richard Rorty (1931–2007)

Richard Rorty began his career in the 1960s as a scholar of analytic philosophy, a branch of thought related to Pragmatism that roughly aligns philosophical work with the empiricism of the hard sciences. As represented in works like *Consequences of Pragmatism* (1982) and *Contingency, Irony, and Solidarity* (1989), however, he spent much of his career (eloquently) defending Pragmatism as a distinct philosophy and diffusing some of the perspective's perceived weaknesses. Rorty railed against the uselessness of metaphysical philosophy because he found it impossible and sterile. For Rorty, metaphysical philosophical approaches to life are uninspiring, merely the "search for a way in which one can avoid the need for conversation and deliberation and simply tick off the way things are."[5] Those who engage in Pragmatic approaches may give up the awesome search for some deeper, more complete meaning in life, but in turn they gain a more profound understanding of human systems and an appreciation for human agency.

For Rorty, this Pragmatic appreciation is best cultivated through **ironism**, or a commitment to seeing the world in terms of contingent historical descriptions (and *not* in terms of an unchanging essence). An appreciation of language is key to this view. Taking competing philosophical accounts of the world and of human nature not as records of the truth but as more and less useful ways of describing life, those who embrace irony champion "experimenting with the vocabularies which these people concocted. We redescribe ourselves, our situation, our past, in those terms and compare the results with alternative redescriptions which use the vocabularies of alternative figures. We ironists hope, by this continual redescription, to make the best selves for ourselves that we can."[6] Through the comparison of the various vocabularies that constitute knowledge, then, ironists hope in a truly Pragmatic sense to create identities and societies that "work" for those involved in the moment. These social arrangements never adhere for long, however, because being open to doubt and enacting regular revision is the only way to maintain fidelity with the rhythms of living.

The notion of fidelity is also an important factor in Rorty's attempts to overcome one of the common criticisms leveled against Pragmatism: relativism. **Relativism** is the belief that diverse approaches and theories related to a given subject are all equally correct. Action becomes difficult in a relativistic lens because there is no consistent truth to act upon. Because Pragmatism abandons the search for underlying truths on a topic, critics often see it as a relativist approach that cannot practically address the problems it purports to solve. Rorty, however, drew an important distinction between *relativism* in the metaphysical sense and *possibilities* as they apply to the real world. Pragmatists are relativistic when it comes to metaphysics, in the sense that all searches for essential truth are equally valid because none of them actually makes any real difference. But when it comes to lived experience and situations, Pragmatists entertain options only to the point that they can be discussed, tested, and selected in the process of problem solving. "When such an alternative is proposed," Rorty writes, "we debate it, not in terms of categories or principles but in terms of the various concrete advantages and disadvantages it has."[7] As a result, Pragmatists avoid spinning in relativistic circles by staying true to reality, considering and organizing multiple ideas according to their social use.

The collective ideas of James, Dewey, and Rorty regarding practical application, social utility, and informed discernment provide a foundation for a Pragmatic perspective on the government regulation of media industries. The critical assessment of media regulations is fundamentally melioristic in nature, recognizing that aspects of an historical moment may always be improved, but only through human intervention. Furthermore, Pragmatism allows us to judge the worth of regulation according to the perceived outcomes and effects of the regulation. In a very rough sense, regulatory policy is "true," worthy, or good if it clearly benefits American society or helps to concretely correct social problems. Careful consideration of many factors and deliberation between multiple options are the hallmarks of quality government regulation; engaging in such debates helps ensure that the resulting policy best meets the many needs of society. "Bad" regulation, in turn, does not provide definite social benefits or stems from constant, predetermined or uncontested truths and beliefs about the world. We present a formal paradigm for making these judgments below.

A Pragmatic Approach to the Government Regulation of Media

Two concepts provide the standards for evaluation within a Pragmatic approach to media: consequences and contingencies. **Consequences** refer to the clear effects of a given regulation on society at large. Generally, consequences must be beneficial to society if we are to deem the regulation a good one. Does the policy stop advertisers from misrepresenting products and potentially causing harm to significant portions of the population? Does the regulation increase the likelihood that traditionally underrepresented portions of the population share in the production of media messages? The use of consequences as a standard of judgment reflects the Pragmatic focus on the tangible results of a belief as the measure of its truth. It should also be apparent, however, that the above examples are based on contemporary judgments of what actually constitutes a social benefit. People have only recently recognized the increasing of diversity as an important or worthy social goal of regulation. From this example, we can see that consequences are always linked to the historical moment.

The fact that we can only make judgments about consequences as historical individuals speaks to the second standard, **contingencies**, or the factors a regulation should address as a result of context and situation. The social norms of any given moment, as well as predominant mediums or technologies, all form a group of contingent factors that influence the possible types of regulation. Generally, a quality regulation must adequately take into account and respond to the socio-historical factors in play during its creation. In addition, it must consider these factors within the aforementioned framework of social utility. Prior to the invention of the internet, for example, no one dreamed of debating the regulation of virtual or simulated child pornography. The historical advent of the web prompted the need for this debate, and the unique opportunities presented by an online medium directed it, but the debate was still centered on the consequence of protecting children. The use of contingencies to complement our understanding of consequences mirrors the Pragmatist focus on considering multiple options in the process of solving problems, as well as the spirit of doubt that animates Rorty's ironism. In short, then, the best regulatory solutions are those that have beneficial consequences according to the contingencies of their historical moment.

In addition to the contingencies presented by social or historical contexts, the regulation of American media must also respond to a particular set of regular or ever-present contingencies unique to the American context. It may seem strange to you that a factor can be both regular and contingent. Pragmatism itself hinges on a rejection of constants. However, it is important to understand that these factors are *regular in their presence* but *contingent upon one another at any given time*. In other words, government regulation must always respond to these particular factors, and the best regulations balance them, but the degree to which one is valued over the other varies from moment to historical moment.

The first set of regular contingencies is the tension between free speech and public interest. The freedoms of speech and press granted by the First Amendment of the US Constitution guarantee the open expression of ideas and the existence of media outlets beyond federal ownership and control. A media industry that is able to report freely and comment upon events functions as an informal check in the American political system. Taken together, the twin freedoms often give good reason to hold back government regulation that might impede or censor the free circulation of ideas. At the same time, a completely independent media would quickly fall apart. Prior to the government regulation of the radio industry, different private companies would often use the same airwaves and inadvertently jam one another's signal. Before the advent of government-regulated telephone service, it was often necessary for families to possess multiple telephones, one for each privately maintained phone network to which they subscribed.[8] Thus, at times it is necessary for the government to intervene in the interest of the public in order to make a media industry more efficient. The resulting tension between the regular contingencies of free speech and public interest represents a uniquely American dichotomy that debates about government regulation must always consider. Typically, the dominant social norms or political climate of the age will direct which concept trumps the other in relation to regulation. Quality regulation, however, should always consider both.

The second set of regular contingencies is the interplay between government regulation and media self-regulation. These contingencies are in some ways an extension of the public-interest focus above. They are derived from the social responsibility theory of the press, or the notion that the media are in the service of the public and therefore should be guided by issues of public concern. Early media legislators reasoned that airwaves were a publicly owned, finite national resource. Any industry hoping to lease this resource should have the public's interest in mind, and it became the federal government's responsibility to manage airwave use based on this principle. Through the Federal Communications Commission (FCC; which regulates broadcasting, wire, satellite, and cable services) and the Federal Trade Commission (which regulates advertising and public relations), the government has historically used the notion of public interest to decide which radio stations to license, what times questionable content can be broadcast, and more. At times, however, media industries have made the conscious decision to regulate themselves in an effort to reduce the scope of government intervention. While the FCC still controls industry aspects like broadcast licensing, many media outlets have devised their own rules in relation to best practices or questionable content. Again, like the first set of contingencies, the use of federal and industry-based regulation varies with the social and political climate, but the presence of the dialectic always informs new regulatory policy.

Overall, the central tenets of consequences and contingencies provide a Pragmatic framework from which we can evaluate the regulation of American media. Regulation is directly tied to social and historical factors, but the American context also gives rise to the regular contingencies of free speech versus public interest and government versus media self-regulation. With all of these factors to consider, it should be clear that the process of deciding upon the best form of regulation is a difficult one. Government officials and industry representatives have to balance a number of different (and sometimes competing) issues in attempting to address social problems related to the media. The remainder of this chapter will focus on some of the more prevalent issues within the American media and examples of how different bodies have responded through regulation. As you read, pay special attention to the ways in which regular contingencies find expression in specific media policies.

Issues in the Regulation of American Media

The history of American media regulation is full of many compelling topics. This section focuses on six particular thematic areas within media regulation that have rich and varied histories. We have grouped regulations into thematic areas according to the practical ends or problems that they address. Additionally, each section is followed by a brief discussion where we provide our own interpretation of the regulations in question. In this way, we hope to provide you with some initial ideas about how to critically respond to the regulation of media from a Pragmatic stance.

The first three themes deal primarily with patterns of media ownership, and the last three concentrate on issues dealing with media content. The six themes are: combating monopoly, protecting intellectual property, maintaining national interest, promoting diversity, managing morality, and ensuring accuracy.

Combating monopoly

Regulations designed to prevent media monopolies have focused historically on limiting the amount of a given market that any one company can own. These policies cover broadcasting, programming, and a number of other aspects of the industry. Regulations in this tradition often work toward the practical goal of ensuring that healthy competition remains a vital part of the American media landscape.

One of the clearest historical examples of anti-monopoly regulation is the Financial Interest and Syndication Rules (often abbreviated to Fin-Syn Rules). Various television stations proliferated after the medium was introduced in the first half of the twentieth century, but the major networks of ABC, NBC, and CBS came to dominate the airwaves during the 1950s. By enlisting many local stations throughout the country as broadcast affiliates, the networks had an unparalleled and far-reaching influence on the American public. The FCC feared that the three networks were gaining too much power over their remaining competitors, and they instituted the Fin-Syn Rules in 1970 to correct this trend. The primary purpose of the Fin-Syn Rules was to break up the perceived monopoly of the major networks by limiting the networks' financial control over their programming.

Syndication, generally speaking, refers to the process of producing and selling programming. Networks can purchase programs from independent production companies or commission programs from network-owned companies. Prior to Fin-Syn, ABC, NBC, and CBS were all moving toward a vertically integrated syndication system where they produced and broadcast a great deal of their own programming. However, the newly enacted Fin-Syn Rules limited the amount of broadcasted programming to which the major networks could hold financial rights. In combination with the Prime Time Access Rule, which reduced the amount of network-produced programming the three could broadcast between 7 and 11 p.m., the Fin-Syn Rules forced the major networks to purchase syndicated programming from other, smaller production companies. In addition, the rules prohibited the networks from retaining financial rights to off-network syndicated shows (original network programming rerun on non-network stations).

With the rise of the Fox network and the growing popularity of cable throughout the 1980s, the networks slowly began losing their perceived stranglehold on the American media market. Subscribing to cable services and their diverse array of specialty channels was now a viable option for many Americans. The FCC responded to this shifting social trend by relaxing the Fin-Syn Rules in 1993 to allow networks to hold the financial rights to half of their primetime broadcast line-up. In 1995 the FCC abolished them altogether, which (understandably) resulted in a system where the networks produced or co-produced much of their primetime line-ups.[9] As an historical example of government regulation, the Fin-Syn Rules represented an attempt to halt a network programming monopoly and promote the growth of independent stations and production companies as a source of media competition.

The repealing of the Fin-Syn Rules was one example of a larger trend toward federal deregulation (and increased media self-regulation) that characterized the 1980s and 1990s. The most salient example of this deregulation related to media monopoly is the Telecommunications Act of 1996. The Act shifted the regulations on ownership patterns in broadcast, telephone, and cable industries. Prior to 1996, for example, the FCC capped the amount of stations an individual could own at 7 television channels and 14 radio stations (7 each of AM and FM, and only one per market area at that). The new language in the Act abandoned this strict formula and bases current owner-ship rules on relative audience size. Though there is no specific limit on the number of television and radio stations a single broadcaster may own, ownership is restricted to no more than 35 percent of the national audience for television and varies according to market size for radio. The Act also allowed companies to purchase and control multiple mediums in an unprecedented way. This resulted in increased cross-ownership of television and radio stations in the same market, and it allowed cable companies to expand their offerings to telephone services (and vice versa).

The deregulatory spirit of the Act may seem counter-productive for a government hoping to combat media monopolies. However, legislators believed that decreasing ownership barriers would in fact spur competition, increase content quality, and lower prices for consumers. The Act continued to operate within the historical public-interest paradigm because it "equated the public interest with a competitive economic environment … in which consumer and producer desires and needs can be matched efficiently in the marketplace, not structured by regulators."[10] The logic here is that fewer restrictions on ownership result in more possibilities for more people, thereby increasing the potential for competition across all media markets. The Act safeguards against monopoly by instilling a traditional economic system of supply and demand that encourages the media to monitor itself. As we will see, this "free-market" approach to the media is often used to justify acts of deregulation in the American context.

From a Pragmatic perspective, the Fin-Syn Rules and the Telecommunications Act of 1996 invite a mixed judgment. Most media critics of the 1996 Act agree that its free-market logic failed to inspire competition; contemporary media industries are marked by an increase of corporate mergers and conglomerations that resemble monopolies (see Chapter 2). However, the Act was a genuine attempt to respond to the economic, political, and social climate of the 1990s. The Fin-Syn Rules, on the other hand, did not clearly consider multiple contingencies (benefiting smaller pro-duction companies to the obvious detriment of the networks), but they did result in a diversity of programming options for the American public. These examples reveal that the Pragmatic evaluation of regulation is not often a clear process of sorting regulations into "good" and "bad" categories, but rather a nuanced assessment of the factors that inform the creation and effect of a regulation.

Protecting intellectual property

Regulations concerning intellectual property in the media industry deal with legally protecting the creative work of artists. Policies and technologies in this area establish clear parameters regarding what work can be protected, how it should be protected, and any limits placed on that protection. In addition, these regulations also stipulate the ways in which creative work can be legally disseminated and used in the media.

The most familiar form of intellectual property protection is **copyright**, or the granting of exclusive control of a creative work to that work's creator. Although the practical purpose of copyright is to legally award a creator power over the use of his/ her work, its theoretical purpose is to ensure that individuals will continue to generate innovative products. After all, if there were no way for creators to make money from their work, much less stop others from using their works toward financial interests other than their own, why would anyone choose to become a creator? This aspect of copyright is especially important to media industries because they are in the business of marketing and selling innovation. Without new television shows or broadcast technology, the media industry would cease to exist.

The notion of owning one's own creative work is actually spelled out in Article 1 of the US Constitution, but the various resulting copyright laws could not keep up with increasing changes in technology and the media. Congress passed the Copyright Law of 1978 in order to correct many of the problems with earlier laws. As a result of the 1978 Law (and certain Acts in 1998), we now have a flexible system of copyright that is able to keep up with most forms of technological innovation. Contemporary copyright protection gives a work's author/creator the exclusive control over the reproduction, dissemination, and sale of the work. A work retains this protection for the lifetime of its creator plus 70 years, upon which the holder of the copyright can renew it. Moreover, a work is protected the second an author creates it in a physical medium (such as a computer or film strip). This means that authors enjoy the benefits of copyright protection even if they have not officially registered their work. Most importantly, copyright is limited in certain ways: small portions of a work can be copied under the notion of *fair use* (in scholarly contexts, for example), and copyright can only cover the *material expression* of an idea, not the idea itself. You could not copyright your personal interpretation of the events of September 11, 2001, for example, but you could copyright a particular song or screenplay that expresses those views.

The legal system of copyright also stipulates rules regarding the distribution of creative works, and these systems have given rise to additional regulatory agencies within the media industries. Because it would be virtually impossible for musicians to keep track of all of the film directors and television producers who use their copyrighted songs, licensing companies like Broadcast Music Inc. (BMI) and the Recording Industry Association of America manage the collection and distribution of musicians' royalty fees. BMI is even responsible for licensing music for use in nightclubs, hotels, and restaurants.[11] The Motion Picture Association of America performs a similar function in the film industry, gathering royalty fees from the use of films (for example, in the popular DVD board game *Scene It!*).

These companies implement copyright law and represent one of the various ways copyright is actually enforced in the media industries.

A more recent form of intellectual property protection closely related to copyright is industry-based **digital rights management** (DRM for short). DRM refers to any number of different software programs that media industries employ to control the distribution and use of digital intellectual property. It attempts to duplicate for the online/digital world the types of protection granted by copyright and medium in the real world.[12] Digital versions of intellectual property, such as music or movie computer files, are by nature much easier to copy and pirate than their real-world counterparts (CDs and DVDs), so DRM represents an extra level of security attached to these digital versions. This security takes many forms. One of the most familiar to college students is the DRM embedded in products purchased from Apple's iTunes store. Although Apple made all of its music DRM-free in 2009, other types of content available via iTunes (including movies and television programs) are still subject to such management. iTunes limits users from accessing a non-music product on more than five Apple devices at any one time, and users are unable to burn movies to compact disc. Applications for the iPhone and iPad licensed via the iTunes store are also largely confined to individual usage on authorized devices.[13]

In theory, both copyright and DRM seem to represent attempts by the government and the media industry to protect the intellectual property of individuals. However, critics of these systems claim that they actually protect private corporate interests. Some agree that the American system of copyright provides a good way to ensure people are paid for their creative work, but they point out that contemporary copyright law often goes beyond its original, historical intention to unnecessarily hamper creativity and protect businesses.[14] Others claim that the rise of DRM signals a shift away from legal regulatory standards that historically work in the public interest to industry-based technological guards that privilege the rights of owners over customers.[15] Pragmatically speaking, both copyright and DRM work toward correcting issues related to information piracy, but both fall short of ably balancing issues of free speech and the public interest. While copyright at least attempts to preserve public interest through the doctrine of fair use, DRM is almost entirely economic in nature. Thus, they are both somewhat flawed forms of regulation, with DRM being the more significantly problematic of the two.

Maintaining national interest

Media regulations with the goal of maintaining national interest are concerned primarily with American domestic infrastructure and global image. Often most apparent in times of war, these regulations ensure that media technology and practices do not compromise national security and the government's ability to protect the public. Their association with issues of federal privilege and restricted information often makes them quite controversial.

A notable historical example of this type of regulation is the Escrowed Encryption Standard of 1994. **Encryption** is the process of scrambling important digital messages by software so only those who possess a complementary decoding program can read them. As encryption technology increased in complexity throughout the 1980s and 1990s, government officials worried that such systems would hamper the government's ability to intercept communications that undermined national security. The federal government had restricted the export of powerful encryption software to other countries according to the Export Administration Act, but these restrictions had grown increasingly lax since the end of the Cold War.[16] As a result, the Clinton administration enacted the Escrowed Encryption Standard to provide the federal government with a way of gaining access to encrypted messages sent over telephone wires that they felt posed a national threat.

The Standard outlined a system where the government authorized certain companies to manufacture encryption chips (called Clippers) that would then be installed in communications devices like fax machines and computers. An independent executive agency would collect the decoding keys, split them in half and distribute them between two separate facilities. This was primarily a security measure; any half key would be useless without accessing its complementary half in the other facility. The government could appeal to the agency for the two halves of the necessary decoding key only when it had reasonable cause to suspect that a message endangered national security. In many ways, the Escrowed Encryption Standard worked as a trade-off. It offered the public access to powerful encryption software, but it also provided a back door for government officials to decode and read encrypted messages. It was also a way for them to strike a balance "between a person's right to privacy and the government's ability to monitor hostile foreign governments, terrorists and criminals."[17] However, lukewarm reception by technology industries and public backlash over privacy invasion forced the government to abandon the Standard only a few years after its inception.

The Escrowed Encryption Standard was one way the federal government has tried to regulate media in relation to foreign threats. During times of actual war, the government also invokes a number of other regulations on the media, and we can see many examples of these policies in the media coverage of the Iraq War. Embedded journalists, for instance, are often censored in what information they are allowed to broadcast. Award-winning reporters Peter Arnett and Geraldo Rivera were both removed from Iraq on the same day in 2003 for this reason. While Rivera mistakenly revealed on national television the location of the 101st Airborne Division with whom he was stationed, Arnett consented to an interview on Iraqi TV where he spoke critically of the American war effort.[18] Arnett's dismissal echoes the silent regulatory pressure placed on the media overall to keep dissenting opinions on war quiet.[19] A further restriction placed on the media during the Iraq War was the Bush administration's now famous refusal to publish pictures of coffins containing the bodies of American soldiers. Although the administration officially claimed that they halted publication of the photos to maintain the privacy of the soldiers' families, many speculated that it was really an attempt to block negative images of the war from the public eye. The ensuing debate over the pictures between proponents of national interest and freedom of information reflects the greater problem of how to best manage the particular demands of war without sacrificing peacetime standards.[20]

Evaluating the Escrowed Encryption Standard and various wartime policies from a Pragmatic perspective yields fairly negative judgments. The Encryption Standard was a Pragmatic failure because it simply did not make much of an impact at all. Additionally, it failed to gain public support because it neglected to adequately address the contingency of the American right to privacy. Similarly, while some of the wartime policies are Pragmatically functional (limiting Rivera's free speech regarding troop location to protect American forces), others are rather questionable (limiting Arnett's free speech or the publication of coffin photos because they tarnish the national image of the war). Regulations in the service of national interest by their nature champion the public interest over free speech, but better ones carefully consider ways to manage both.

Promoting diversity

Regulations with the end goal of promoting diversity in media industries have attempted in some way to establish a sense of equality in media content. Because wealthy, privileged social groups usually have the most access to media outlets (and very often own them), these regulations are motivated by the desire to ensure that minority viewpoints and perspectives find a place on television and radio as well.

One of the clearest examples of this type of regulation is the Fairness Doctrine established in 1949. The Fairness Doctrine was an FCC policy that urged broadcasting stations to air programming on controversial issues and fairly represent both sides of the issues to viewers. Its supporters justified the Doctrine by claiming that it was in the public interest to hear both sides of an issue. This might sound like a good way to promote diversity, but most scholars agree that it actually decreased the amount of controversial material on air. Rather than give up precious airtime to both sides of a given issue, many television and radio stations avoided covering such costly issues altogether. Furthermore, stations that did choose to cover issues complained that the Doctrine violated their First Amendment rights by dictating parameters of coverage. The rule tended to result in the impression that all ideas and perspectives on an issue are equally good, something not always true in the real world. The FCC voluntarily rescinded the policy in 1987 as a consequence of "free-market" logic and deregulation, but we still find glimmers of its underlying ideology today. When we see a news program invite both a supporter of evolution and a supporter of intelligent design to comment on the origin of humanity, we are looking at vestiges of the Fairness Doctrine. The demise of the Doctrine, however, has also led to the creation of new television and radio programs that communicate a single point of view, like *Fox News* or *Democracy Now!*.

Another example of regulation intended to promote diversity is the equal time rule, which is still in place today. The rule clearly outlines how stations must handle the broadcast of political advertisements for primary or general elections. Television and radio stations cannot refuse airtime to paying political candidates and must charge candidates the lowest rate they would charge other advertisers. Stations must charge all candidates equally. If the station chooses to give free advertising to a particular candidate, it must offer all other candidates an equal amount of free time with a roughly equal audience size (audience size is determined by a number of factors, including time of broadcast or day of the week). As a whole the equal time rule addresses a very narrow part of the industry, but at times it has led to some interesting situations within broadcast media. For example, after actor Arnold Schwarzenegger officially announced his candidacy during the 2003 race for the California governor's office, broadcast television stations were prohibited from airing any of his films under the equal time rule.[21] If they did air a film, they risked having to give time to the other 134 candidates equivalent to the film's length.

Comparing the Fairness Doctrine and the equal time rule from a Pragmatic perspective yields judgments similar to the public perception of these regulations. The Fairness Doctrine had clear negative consequences in that it reduced the amount of controversial issues on air, and it trampled over the regular contingency of free speech by stipulating content. In this sense, the Doctrine was probably not one of the better examples of diversity regulation. The equal time rule, conversely, promoted diversity in a Pragmatically responsible way. The rule results in equal access to the media for all public candidates, and it is built upon contingencies (current rates for advertising, rules that only apply when a station gives away free advertising, etc.). Rather than enforcing a blanket understanding of diversity like the Fairness Doctrine, the equal time rule presents a flexible system of encouraging equality without specifying or restricting content.

Managing morality

Regulations concentrated on the management of morality in media content and programming are one of the more controversial areas in media industry law. Because one cannot truly "legislate" morality without endangering free speech, the types of regulations in this tradition often (1) offer general guidelines rather than definite understandings of issues related to morality and (2) restrict access and consumption of questionable texts rather than their production. The three key types of regulated media content are obscenity, profanity, and indecency.

Obscenity has been a historically difficult term to define, but most obscene media content is sexually explicit in nature. Obscene material is not protected by the freedom of speech. Although this standard has, on occasion, been applied to non-broadcast material, it is overwhelmingly used in the evaluation of broadcast content. The 1973 court case *Miller vs. California* famously defined obscene content according to a three-pronged test. Content is considered obscene when it meets all of the following standards:

1   the average person, applying contemporary community standards, would find that the work, taken as a whole, appeals to prurient interest;

2   the work depicts or describes, in a patently offensive way, sexual conduct specifically defined by applicable state law; and

3   the work, taken as a whole, lacks serious literary, artistic, political, or scientific value.

The regulation of obscene content is straightforward: it is illegal. However, images or words are not obscene until someone challenges them as such in a court of law. In this way, the legal definition of obscenity acts as an informal regulation by shaping the decisions made about content so that it cannot be declared obscene. Remember, if the content does not meet all three of the *Miller* definitions, then it is not obscene.

Profanity is often equated with comedian George Carlin's act about the seven "filthy" words banned from public broadcast: shit, piss, fuck, cunt, cocksucker, motherfucker, and tits. Although speech outside of these seven words can be considered profane, the seven have become the standard for FCC regulation. Generally, the regulation of profanity falls under the greater regulation of indecency. **Indecency** refers to any material that is morally unfit for general distribution or broadcast, and indecent material most often depicts sexual or excremental activities. Unlike obscenity, indecent content is not illegal, but it is regulated in a number of ways. For example, radio and television stations may broadcast indecent programming only between the "safe harbor" hours of 10 p.m. and 6 a.m. when it is unlikely that any children are watching/ listening. Media outlets that do not observe these kinds of rules are subject to FCC fines, loss of broadcasting license, and more. Radio shock jock Howard Stern set records for FCC indecency fines throughout the early 1990s and eventually racked up fines of $1.7 million for his distributor, Infinity Broadcasting.[22]

The management of indecent content is a historically important area of media self-regulation. One of the earliest forms of industry-based content restriction is the Hollywood production code of the 1930s, which was primarily "written by a Jesuit priest and a Catholic layman."[23] It outlined what could and could not be depicted in Hollywood films, and movies that ignored these restrictions could not earn the approval of the Motion Picture Producers and Distributors Association necessary for widespread distribution. Along with the eradication of images of violence and sex, the production code also prohibited the depiction of homosexuality, interracial relationships, and the benefits of illegal activity in films. While prudish and discriminatory by today's standards, the code was an attempt by Hollywood to halt what they perceived to be invasive federal intervention in the movie industry. If industry officials could prove to the government that they could sufficiently regulate themselves, then the government would have less of a presence in the business overall. This, to many film makers, was an attractive trade-off.

Industry-based standards like the production code are still the primary form of moral regulation in Hollywood today, with a few significant changes. Most notably, the burden of managing indecent or questionable material has transferred from film makers to audiences. Access to indecent or violent content is now based on audience age, a decision that recalls the "safe harbor" rule. Instead of maintaining a production code that severely censors the content of films, the Motion Picture Association of America has developed a ratings system (G, PG, PG-13, R, NC-17) that restricts viewers instead. The ratings system maintains freedom of speech for film makers while simultaneously enforcing content standards. Television, music, and video game industries have all followed suit in the last 20 years by developing their own

Table 4.1   Breakdown of television ratings in the USA

Rating	(V) Violence	(L) Language	(S) Sexual situations	Example
TV-Y	***	***	***	*Sesame Street*
TV-Y7	Mild	Mild	***	*SpongeBob Squarepants*
TV-G	***	***	***	*Jeopardy!*
TV-PG	Moderate	Mild	Mild	*NCIS*
TV-14	Strong	Moderate	Moderate	*Family Guy*
TV-MA	Extreme	Strong	Strong	*South Park*

***means none.

ratings systems in relation to questionable content (see Table 4.1 for a breakdown of television ratings). In theory, young children cannot purchase tickets to R-rated films, CDs stamped with a "Parental Advisory" notice, or video games marked T (for Teen) or M (for Mature). However, according to a Federal Trade Commission study on media violence released in September 2000, media industries regularly market these products to minors and young people routinely have access to them.[24] Additionally, a 2012 study by the Parents Television Council suggests that many programs rated TV-PG feature higher levels of sexual innuendo and violence than one might expect.[25] Studies like these question the effectiveness of industry-based media regulation related to indecent or violent content.

From a Pragmatic perspective, the regulation of morality through obscenity, profanity, and indecency is more contingent on socio-historical factors than almost any other form of regulation. However, we can make some initial judgments based on our discussion thus far. The federal regulations of obscenity and indecency are both largely effective because they yield practical results in relation to questionable content while balancing factors like social norms, free speech, and public interest. The general definition of obscenity importantly hinges on whether or not the particular community in which the content is consumed would find the material objectionable, which often binds particular definitions of obscenity to specific geographical locations in the USA. The regulation reduces obscene content overall without applying a blanket standard. Similarly, the restriction of indecent material to particular hours of broadcast limits access to questionable material in the public interest while maintaining notions of free speech. In the end, these regulations are very much in line with the Pragmatic tenets of consequences and contingencies because they control the access of audiences to questionable material while remaining relatively open to contextual, cultural factors.

We cannot say the same for the systems of media self-regulation discussed here. The production code of the 1930s was clearly a negative form of regulation because it was not sensitive to the varied social and historical factors of the time period. Instead of attempting to balance multiple perspectives, the code imposed a very narrow and somewhat religious conception of morality on film makers. In a Pragmatic sense, the code appealed to a constant and predetermined definition of morality rather than a flexible, contingent one, and this definition in turn supported notions of the public interest while greatly restricting free speech. Current ratings standards, on the other hand, champion free speech but do not actually solve the problem of minors' access to indecent and violent material. In Pragmatic terminology, current media ratings systems are ill-conceived forms of regulation because they do not practically address the social problems they are intended to solve. The aforementioned Federal Trade Commission report clearly outlines how to fix this problem: "Self-regulatory programs can work only if the concerned industry associations actively monitor compliance and ensure that violations have consequences."[26] Only with increased vigilance can ratings systems actually result in effective regulatory consequences.

Ensuring accuracy

Regulations aimed at ensuring accuracy primarily deal with the news broadcast and print industries. Equally balanced between government- and industry-based standards, these regulations attempt to prevent the dissemination of false (and possibly damaging) information and provide systems of legal correction if such information does become public. In short, these regulations concentrate on ensuring that journalists and news reporters use media forums to responsibly report the truth to the American public.

The two most important forms of government regulation aimed at ensuring accuracy are the twin legal concepts of slander and libel. **Slander** refers to publicly spoken, untrue, and defamatory statements, while **libel** refers to false printed statements that similarly damage a person's character. Neither is protected under the freedom of speech. While the line between slander and libel was originally very easily understood, the rise of broadcast media has blurred it significantly. After all, news broadcasting relies primarily on the spoken word, but the preparation of news for broadcast resembles the same procedures as print media. Slander and libel laws together force reporters and broadcasters to double check their stories for accuracy. Legal definitions of slander and libel are like definitions of obscenity in that they regulate primarily by guiding the informal decisions made about news content: industry workers avoid disseminating content that is slanderous or libelous. However, these laws also provide a means of legal recourse for defamed individuals who are the victim of slander and libel. If a media outlet is found guilty of slander or libel in a court of law, they often must pay hefty sums in monetary compensation.

Although slander and libel laws represent a significant factor that journalists and newscasters must consider in reporting, there are defenses against them. The most important of these is truth. If a statement is true, no matter how damaging it is to the character of an individual, then it is not subject to slander or libel laws. Similarly, the media is allowed to comment on public figures and their actions under the doctrine of *fair comment*. Because the press is often responsible for acting as a check to governmental powers, they have the right to report and editorialize on aspects of a public figure that may be defamatory as a result. This notion of fair comment also covers the news media's right to judge and critique the products of public institutions (like restaurants) without committing libel.

Even with fairly clear definitions and defenses against slander and libel, however, those within the media industry still find themselves in other binds related to accuracy. Should a journalist publish crucial material if the source of that material wishes to remain anonymous? How soon after a terrible accident should a reporter attempt to interview a victim's family? There are no clear or definite answers to these kinds of questions, and issues like the ones above have given rise to industry-based codes of ethics. A **code of ethics** is a self-imposed set of rules that outlines the ethical strivings of a particular media outlet (goals which typically revolve around notions of truth and fairness), and they often stipulate the particular ways that those within the organization should handle conflicts of interest, ethical dilemmas, and other problem areas. By adhering to a code of ethics, news media outlets ensure that they consistently address issues accurately and fairly for the parties involved.

Within a Pragmatic lens, regulations directed toward ensuring accuracy in the media are relatively effective ones. Slander and libel laws halt potential abuse of the individual and help contain the power of the media in shaping public perception. The heavy penalties that result from slander and libel legal cases push media outlets to remain ever vigilant about the facts that they report. While there has been some slippage between the terms as a result of technological development, the laws still strike a nice balance between maintaining freedom of the press and protecting the public. Similarly, codes of ethics provide reporters and broadcasters with general guidelines for resolving specific issues particular to the news industry. Because it is ultimately the individual who makes the call after consulting the code, these rules are practical without being rigid. Sometimes these codes fail to provide good answers, just as media outlets occasionally commit libel or slander, but in general these regulations give flexible structure to the ways in which the industry approaches notions of truth and accuracy.

Violence in the Media: a Closer Look at Pragmatic Regulation

Many of the regulations we have discussed thus far do not occupy a significant place in the public consciousness. Issues like syndication rights, political advertisements, and libel laws often fail to attract the attention of the typical American media consumer. But the same cannot be said for violence. In fact, one would be hard pressed to point to a media issue that garners more public concern than violence in film, television, music, and video games. Because the *perceived* effects of media violence (especially on children) are so great, concerned parents, special-interest groups, and politicians often respond with extreme, reactionary proposals that border on outright censorship. Soon-to-be Republican Presidential nominee Bob Dole, for instance, made headlines in 1995 when (on a campaign stop in Los Angeles) he condemned the entertainment industry for cultivating moral depravity, deviancy, and cultural contamination. In this section, we advocate a more measured approach that attempts to balance the complex interplay of contingencies and consequences related to media violence. In doing so, we hope to illustrate that a Pragmatic perspective is uniquely suited for discussing and appraising media regulations, be they government- or industry-based.

Violence in the media is often treated in a unified, monolithic way. But representations of violence vary greatly in both form and function, and thus it is vital that the Pragmatist distinguish among the different forms of media violence. A useful starting point in this regard is Henry A. Giroux's differentiation between reflective, gore, and stylized violence.[27] According to Giroux, reflective or **historical violence** "probes the complex contradictions that shape human agency, the limits of rationality, and the existential issues that tie us to other human beings and the broader social world."[28] This type of violence typically accompanies the portrayal of actual historical events and can be seen in films such as *Platoon* (1986), *Schindler's List* (1993), and *Lincoln* (2012). The visual and narrative framing of historical violence invites audiences to contemplate the horrors of war or the historical atrocities perpetrated against particular social groups; it encourages audiences to think critically about the way violence is connected to hatred and social injustice. Historical violence, then, can be said to heighten social consciousness by imparting larger philosophical messages about humanity and its struggles.

Whereas historical violence engenders thoughtful reflection, gore or **ritualistic violence** generates mostly emotional excitement because, in Giroux's words, it is "pure spectacle in form and superficial in content."[29] Depictions of ritualistic violence are typically fast-paced, adrenaline-pumping, sensationalistic, and hyper-masculine. This form of violence is common to both horror (slasher) and action genres, and is exemplified in films like *Rambo: First Blood* (1982), *True Lies* (1994), and the *Transformers* series (2007, 2009, 2011). Rather than imparting social messages, ritualistic violence serves primarily to stimulate and entertain. Consequently, audiences tend to respond to ritualistic violence on a visceral (rather than rational) level. Anyone who has screamed during a gruesome horror scene or clutched his or her seat while viewing an explosive action sequence can attest to the capacity of ritualistic violence to move us at a bodily level.

Giroux's third category of media violence, stylized or **hyper-real violence,** is the most challenging to define. The difficulty arises, at least in part, because it blurs the boundaries between historical and ritualistic violence. To borrow a phrase from the Police song, "Murder by Numbers," hyper-real violence turns "murder into art."[30] Elaborating on the character of hyper-real violence, Giroux explains that it is "marked by technological over-stimulation, gritty dialogue, dramatic storytelling, parody, and an appeal to gutsy realism."[31] Like historical violence, hyper-real violence is extremely realistic and believable. But like ritualistic violence, it is visceral and entertaining (not to mention graphic and shocking). Put another way, hyper-real violence combines the *look* of historical violence with the *feel* of ritualistic violence.

A few films that typify this form of media violence include *Reservoir Dogs* (1992), *The Boondock Saints* (1999), and *Sin City* (2005). Since hyper-real violence lacks the reflective dimension of historical violence, it is unlikely to induce audiences to think critically.

Though not every instance of violence in the media fits neatly into one of Giroux's three categories, his typology nevertheless offers a helpful way to begin sorting through the diverse effects of media violence. Research on media violence suggests that it has four primary effects: the aggressor, victim, bystander, and catharsis effects. Before discussing each of these effects, however, we wish to stress that the relations between media violence and audience actions are complex and indirect, not simple and causal. Moreover, social-environmental factors such as family and viewing contexts as well as individual characteristics like gender, age, and academic achievement influence and mitigate the effects of media violence.[32]

Perhaps the most studied consequence of media violence is the **aggressor effect**, which suggests that exposure to media violence triggers arousal and promotes aggressive behavior. Accounts of this effect typically involve one of three theories: disinhibition, enculturation, or imitation. The theory of *disinhibition* posits that the consumption of media violence undermines the social norms and sanctions against violence that individuals would otherwise abide by. Conversely, *enculturation* theory speculates that long-term exposure to media violence actually constructs violence as the norm and thereby encourages aggressive behavior (through social scripts). In other words, violence begets violence by suggesting it is an appropriate and acceptable response to certain life situations. Finally, the theory of *imitation* maintains that some audiences (most often young viewers who do not fully understand violent displays) will mimic the aggressive behavior they observe in media. Despite decades of study, however, findings related to the aggressor effect are, at best, inconsistent.[33] Part of the problem may be that much of the research does not distinguish among different forms of media violence, which is an important contingency. Imitation, for instance, seems most probable when children consume ritualistic violence, as it is often enacted by a (super)hero and thus positively coded. Meanwhile, disinhibition and enculturation are more likely to result from hyper-real violence, which is morally ambiguous.

Research also suggests that media violence can produce a **victim effect** in which people develop and experience a heightened fearfulness of violence. The victim effect finds support in George Gerbner's empirical work on television and media cultivation.[34] Gerbner argues that individuals who consume heavy amounts of television undergo a process of *mainstreaming* in which they begin to view mediated images as accurate representations of reality. In this theory, repeated exposure to media violence leads to an exaggerated sense of danger or mistrust about the world. Regular viewers of crime dramas like *Law and Order*, *CSI*, and *Criminal Minds*, for example, may develop an unrealistic perception of crime in the USA and subsequently an irrational fear of being the victim of crime themselves. In short, heavy viewing of media violence leads people to see themselves as likely victims in a cruel and scary world. Unlike the aggressor effect, which appears to be connected to specific forms of media violence, the victim effect is probably a consequence of the sum of all violent images circulating in society.

A third major strain of research into media violence concerns the **bystander effect**, which holds that media violence fosters increased callousness about or insensitivity toward violence directed at others. The bystander effect is rooted in the theory of *desensitization*, or the idea that repeated viewing of media violence leads to a reduction in emotional responses to violence and thus an increased acceptance of violence in real life. The basic premise of the bystander effect is that we consume so much violence in the media that we no longer regard it as shocking or abhorrent when we witness it in real life; we are essentially unfazed by it. The potential danger of desensitization and the bystander effect is that people "are less likely to intervene when they witness aggression [and] less likely to take action to prevent aggression" in their everyday lives.[35] Since historical violence promotes social consciousness and ritualistic violence is perceived by most viewers as unrealistic, the bystander effect is almost certainly associated most closely with hyper-real violence.

Finally, some research indicates that media violence can actually have a **catharsis effect**, meaning that it can reduce and alleviate feelings of aggression. Unlike the three previous effects, the catharsis effect is regarded as a pro-social outcome, for it leads to a reduction in real-world violence. Most of the research on the catharsis effect concerns the way that consuming media violence relieves individuals of their own violent urges by allowing them to live vicariously through the actors on screen. But we would like to suggest that catharsis need not be limited to vicarious release. If catharsis is understood in the more general sense of renewal, then it might help to explain how audiences generally respond to historical violence. In contrast to hyper-real violence, which may result in increased aggression, historical violence is likely to reduce aggressive feelings and tendencies by inviting audiences to reflect on the negative social consequences of violence.

What this brief overview highlights is that any attempt to regulate media violence must carefully balance the consequences (aggressor, victim, bystander, and catharsis effects) with the relevant contingencies (various forms of mediated violence such as historical, ritualistic, and hyper-real). Different forms of mediated violence are likely to lead to different effects, which means that media producers and consumers need to stop treating all instances of media violence as identical when making regulatory decisions. In fact, one need only consider the significant problems with the contemporary television ratings system and v-chip technology to see the effect of glossing over these differences.

Historically, the US government has taken a largely "hands-off" approach when it comes to violence on television. Not wanting to break with that tradition or curtail freedom of speech, but facing mounting pressure from lobbyist groups, Congress signaled its desire for the television industry to develop industry-based ratings standards in 1990,[36] and it later enforced the adoption of these standards with the Telecommunications Act of 1996. The implementation of a television ratings system was designed to help parents identify what programming was appropriate for their children. In connection with v-chip technology, which allows select programs to be blocked on individual television sets based on these industry ratings, the system promised to protect children from inappropriate content. In 1999 the FCC required all manufacturers to begin including v-chip technology in US televisions, but by 2001 only 7 percent of parents in the country were actually using the chip to screen content for their children.[37] The technology made little impact in the following years. A 2007 survey by the Kaiser Family Foundation, for example, found that only 16 percent of parents had used the v-chip, while 57 percent did not even know they had one installed in their home television.[38]

One problem with the newly instituted television ratings system and subsequent v-chip technology was that it could not distinguish between historical violence, which might serve educational purposes, and ritualistic and hyper-real violence, which offered little more than shock and titillation. Television ratings typically index the *amount* of violence in a program more than the *type* of violence featured, which means that v-chip technology screens out many potentially pro-social effects of violent depictions (like learning, reflection, or catharsis) along with detrimental ones. In Pragmatic terms, the regulatory logic behind the v-chip is universal ("All televised violence is bad for children") rather than contingent, inspiring a technology ill-suited to the complexity of media today. This decision, in turn, may have marked effects on the television industry in the coming years. The chip has been so badly received that the FCC has signaled its intention to look into regulating violence in the same way that it regulates indecent content.[39] Had those in the television industry who developed the ratings system adopted a more Pragmatic approach to images of violence, the FCC might not be currently exploring ways to increase the federal government's role in regulating violent content.

Conclusion

In this chapter we have looked at many different regulations from a Pragmatic perspective, and those regulations have taken a number of different forms: laws, policies, standards, technologies, etc. While some of the regulations have been clearly beneficial or disastrous, many more fall somewhere in between. The relatively ambiguous nature of most media regulation is indicative of the many factors that legislators and industry representatives must take into account when trying to craft quality guidelines. On top of social and technological issues related to the historical moment, these individuals must also pay special attention to issues of free speech, the public interest, and the ratio between federal and industry-based regulation. The philosophy of Pragmatism helps us to bring order to these various issues, and it provides a good foundation for making evaluations of resulting regulations. In addition, the special emphasis that Pragmatism places on contingencies helps us deconstruct the various factors that inform some of the most pressing regulatory issues facing us today. The regulation of the media is as old as the media itself, but a Pragmatic approach is a relatively new way of understanding the relationship between the two. In short, it helps us make some sense of the historically varied and sometimes confusing terrain of American media regulation.

MEDIA LAB 3: DOING PRAGMATIC ANALYSIS

OBJECTIVE

The aim of this lab is to use the tenets of Pragmatism to understand the regulation of American media. Specifically, students will be generating Pragmatic, original regulations for contemporary problems within American media.

ACTIVITY

- Divide the class into small groups of 4–5 students each.
- Have each group identify a social problem within contemporary American media that affects them. Potential problems include traditional issues like violence in the media or youth access to indecent material, but students should feel free to choose less common problems as well (volume settings on iPods, for example).
- Have each group generate an original regulation to address the problem in 3–4 paragraphs. Students need not address every detail of the regulation, but basic points should be clear. In crafting their regulation, each group should attend to the following.
  1 What are the perceived consequences of your regulation? How are these beneficial? How might they be detrimental?
  2 What historical contingencies does your regulation take into account? In other words, what contemporary political, social, or cultural issues does your regulation attempt to integrate and satisfy?
  3 How does your regulation balance issues of free speech against the public interest? Does it support one more than the other?
  4 Does your regulation rely on federal enforcement, industry enforcement, or both? How?

SUGGESTED READING

Aufderheide, P. *Communications Policy and the Public Interest: the Telecommunications Act of 1996.* New York: The Guilford Press, 1999.

Bandura, A., Ross, D., and Ross, S.A. Transmission of Aggression through Imitation of Aggressive Models. *Journal of Abnormal and Social Psychology* 1961, 63, 575–82.

Danisch, R. *Pragmatism, Democracy, and the Necessity of Rhetoric.* Columbia, SC: University of South Carolina Press, 2007.

Dewey, J. *The Quest for Certainty: a Study of the Relation of Knowledge and Action.* New York: Minton, Balch & Co., 1929.

Dewey, J. *The Public and its Problems.* Athens, OH: Ohio University Press, 1954.

Diffie, W. and Landau, S. *Privacy on the Line: the Politics of Wiretapping and Encryption.* Cambridge, MA: The MIT Press, 2007.

Dubow, E.F. and Miller, L.S. Television Violence Viewing and Aggressive Behavior. In *Tuning in to Young Viewers: Social Perspectives on Television*, T.M. MacBeth (ed.), pp. 117–47. Thousand Oaks, CA: Sage Publications, 1996.

Freedman, D. Dynamics of Power in Contemporary Media Policy-Making. *Media, Culture & Society* 2006, 28, 907–23.

Gillespie, T. *Wired Shut: Copyright and the Shape of Digital Culture*. Cambridge, MA: The MIT Press, 2007.

Giroux, H.A. Racism and the Aesthetic of Hyper-Real. In *Fugitive Cultures: Race, Violence and Youth*, pp. 55–88. New York: Routledge, 1996.

Helprin, M. *Digital Barbarism: a Writer's Manifesto*. New York: Harper Collins, 2009.

James, W. *Pragmatism: a New Name for Some Old Ways of Thinking*. London: Longmans, Green and Co., 1908.

James, W. *Pragmatism and the Meaning of Truth*. Cambridge, MA: Boston University Press, 1978.

Keith, S., Schwalbe, C.B., and Silcock, W.B. Images in Ethics Codes in an Era of Violence and Tragedy. *Journal of Mass Media Ethics* 2006, 21, 245–64.

Leone, R. and Houle, N. 21st Century Ratings Creep: PG-13 and R. *Communication Research Reports* 2006, 23, 53–61.

Lessig, L. *Free Culture: How Big Media Uses Technology and the Law to Lock Down Culture and Control Creativity*. New York: The Penguin Press, 2004.

Postigo, H. Capturing Fair Use for the YouTube Generation: the Digital Rights Movement, the Electronic Frontier Foundation, and the User-Centered Framing of Fair Use. *Information, Communication & Society* 2008, 11, 1008–27.

Rorty, R. Pragmatism, Relativism, and Irrationalism. In *Consequences of Pragmatism (Essays: 1972–1980)*, pp. 160–75. Minneapolis, MN: University of Minnesota Press, 1982.

Russill, C. Through a Public Darkly: Reconstructing Pragmatist Perspectives in Communication Theory. *Communication Theory* 2008, 18, 478–504.

Samoriski, J.H., Huffman, J.L., and Trauth, D.M. The V-Chip and Cybercops: Technology vs. Regulation. *Communication Law & Policy* 1997, 2, 143–64.

Stroud, S. Mindful Argument, Deweyan Pragmatism, and the Ideal of Democracy. *Controversia* 2011, 7, 15–33.

Timmer, J. The Seven Dirty Words You Can Say on Cable and DBS: Extending Broadcast Indecency Regulation and the First Amendment. *Communication Law & Policy* 2005, 10, 179–215.

West, C. *The American Evasion of Philosophy*. Madison, WI: University of Wisconsin Press, 1989.

NOTES

1. W. James, Habit: Its Importance for Psychology, in *The Writings of William James: A Comprehensive Edition*, J.J. McDermott (ed.) (Chicago: University of Chicago Press, 1977), 9.

2. W. James, *Pragmatism and the Meaning of Truth* (Cambridge, MA: Boston University Press: 1978), 30.

3. J. Dewey, *Experience and Nature* (Mineola, NY: Dover, 1958), 280–1.

4. J. Dewey, Reconstruction in Philosophy, in *The Middle Works of John Dewey, Volume 12, 1899–1924: 1920, Reconstruction in Philosophy and Essays*, J.A. Boydston (ed.) (Carbondale, IL: Southern Illinois University Press, 1988), 181–2.

5. R. Rorty, Pragmatism, Relativism, and Irrationalism, in *Consequences of Pragmatism (Essays: 1972–1980)* (Minneapolis, MN: University of Minnesota Press, 1982), 164.

6. R. Rorty, Private Irony and Liberal Hope, in *Contingency, Irony, Solidarity* (New York: Cambridge University Press, 1989), 80.

7. Rorty, Pragmatism, 168.

8. S.J. Baran and D.K. Davis, *Mass Communication Theory: Foundations, Ferment, and Future*, 2nd edn (Belmont, CA: Wadsworth Publishing, 1999), 97.

9. R.E. Caves, *Switching Channels: Organization and Change in TV Broadcasting* (Cambridge, MA: Harvard University Press, 2005).

10. P. Aufderheide, *Communications Policy and the Public Interest: the Telecommunications Act of 1996* (New York: The Guilford Press, 1999), 61.

11. About BMI, *Broadcast Music Incorporated*, http://www.bmi.com/about/entry/about_bmi (accessed February 2, 2013).

12. B. Rosenblatt, B. Trippe, and S. Mooney, *Digital Rights Management: Business and Technology* (New York: M&T Books, 2002).

13. iTunes Store Terms and Conditions, *Apple*, http://www.apple.com/legal/itunes/us/terms.html#SERVICE (accessed February 2, 2013).

14. L. Lessig, *Free Culture: How Big Media Uses Technology and the Law to Lock Down Culture and Control Creativity* (New York: The Penguin Press, 2004).

15. T. Gillespie, *Wired Shut: Copyright and the Shape of Digital Culture* (Cambridge, MA: The MIT Press, 2007).

16. W. Diffie and S. Landau, *Privacy on the Line: the Politics of Wiretapping and Encryption* (Cambridge, MA: The MIT Press, 2007).

17. D. Abrahms, Lawmakers Seek to Ensure Electronic Privacy, *The Washington Times*, March 5, 1996, final edn, B6.

18. P. Johnson and D. Leinwand, TV Networks Pull Arnett, Rivera, *USA Today*, April 1, 2003, 1st edn, 1A.

19. D. Dadge, *The War in Iraq and Why the Media Failed Us* (Westport, CT: Praeger Publications, 2006).

20. T. Shanker and B. Carter, Photos of Soldiers' Coffins Spark a Debate Over Access, *New York Times*, April 24, 2004, late edn, A14.

21. S. Zeidler, Arnold's Films Sidelined During Governor's Bid: Considered TV Air Time: "It May Beg a Competitor to File a Complaint," *National Post (Canada)*, August 14, 2003, national edn, A15.

22. A. Trebbe, Indecency Fine Ripples Stern's Shock Waves, *USA Today*, October 29, 1992, final edn, 1D; D. Wharton, Infinity Hit with 600G Stern Fine, *Daily Variety*, December 21, 1992, 3; FCC Drops Old Stern Fines, *Daily News*, February 7, 2001, 71.

23. H.M. Benshoff and S. Griffin, *America on Film: Representing Race, Class, Gender and Sexuality at the Movies* (Oxford: Blackwell, 2004), 39.

24. Marketing Violent Entertainment to Children: a Review of Self Regulation and Industry Practices in the Motion Picture, Music Recording & Electronic Game Industries, *Federal Trade Commission*, www.ftc.gov/reports/violence/070412MarketingViolentEChildren.pdf (accessed June 19, 2008).

25. What Kids Can See When It's Rated TV-PG, *Parents Television Council*, http://www.parentstv.org/PTC/publications/reports/TVRatings2012/2012_RatingsStudy.pdf (accessed March 4, 2013).

26. Marketing Violent Entertainment to Children, vi.

27. H.A. Giroux, Racism and the Aesthetic of HyperReal, in *Fugitive Cultures: Race, Violence and Youth* (New York: Routledge, 1996), 55–88.

28. Giroux, 63.

29. Giroux, 61.

30. Sting and A. Summers, "Murder By Numbers," *Synchronicity*, A&M (CD release date October 25, 1990).

31. Giroux, 64.

32. E.F. Dubow and L.S. Miller, Television Violence Viewing and Aggressive Behavior, in *Tuning in to Young Viewers: Social Perspectives on Television*, T.M. MacBeth (ed.) (Thousand Oaks, CA: Sage Publishing, 1996), 117–47.

33. J. Staiger, *Media Reception Studies* (New York: New York University Press, 2005), 167.

34. G. Gerbner, Cultivation Analysis: an Overview, *Mass Communication and Society* 1998, 1 (3/4), 175–94.

35. J.L. Freedman, *Media Violence and its Effect on Aggression: Assessing the Scientific Evidence* (Toronto: University of Toronto Press, 2002), 177.

36. D.E. Newton, *Violence and the Media: a Reference Handbook* (Denver, CO: ABC-CLIO, 1996).

37. J. Rutenburg, Survey Shows Few Parents Use TV V-Chip to Limit Children's Viewing, *New York Times*, July 25, 2001, late edn, E1.

38. V. Rideout, Parents, Children & Media, *Kaiser Family Foundation*, http://www.kff.org/entmedia/upload/7638.pdf (accessed March 4, 2013).

39. S. Labaton, F.C.C. Moves to Restrict TV Violence, *New York Times*, April 26, 2007, late edn, C1.

Part II

Media Messages: Rhetorical, Cultural, Psychoanalytic, Feminist, and Queer Perspectives

5 Rhetorical Analysis

KEY CONCEPTS

AESTHETIC
AFFECT
CLUSTER
CONNOTATION
DENOTATION
FORM
GENRE
ICONIC SIGNS
INDEXICAL SIGNS
NARRATIVE
RHETORIC
SEMIOLOGY
SEMIOTIC
SIGN
SIGNIFIED
SIGNIFIER
SIGNIFYING SYSTEM
STRUCTURALISM
SYMBOLS
TEXTS

James McTeigue's 2005 film *V for Vendetta*, which is based on Alan Moore and David Lloyd's graphic novel of the same name, tells the fictional story of a British totalitarian state in the year 2020. The story concerns a vigilante by the name of V – played masterfully by Hugo Weaving – who, in blowing up the Houses of Parliament, aims to inspire the country's citizens to rise up against their authoritarian government. With bold characters, intense drama, and spectacular visual effects, *V for Vendetta* is an engaging and entertaining film. But it is also an allegory: an extended reflection on the erosion and curtailment of civil liberties in the USA during the George W. Bush presidency. The film strives to shake its viewers, like the citizens in the story, out of their political stupor and to mobilize them to reject the repressive policies of their government. And, in that sense, the film functions as rhetoric, as an attempt to shape and influence its viewers' attitudes and actions.[1]

V for Vendetta stages its critique of the Bush administration on a number of levels. At the level of narrative, for instance, visual and verbal accounts of the British government's actions in the film closely parallel Bush administration policies. With "vivid allusions to Abu Ghraib and references to Iraq, Afghanistan and Syria," the film explicitly rebukes administration practices surrounding "surveillance, torture,

Critical Media Studies: An Introduction, Second Edition. Brian L. Ott and Robert L. Mack.
© 2014 John Wiley & Sons, Inc. Published 2014 by John Wiley & Sons, Inc.

fear-mongering, and media manipulation."[2] The film's repeated references to living in a repressive state are viscerally reinforced by the film's camera work and editing; extreme close-ups of V's co-conspirator Evey Hammond (Natalie Portman) foster feelings of captivity, while rapid editing practices in key scenes evoke fear and anxiety. In short, *V for Vendetta* urges audiences to condemn the Bush administration, its "war on terror," and legislation like the Patriot Act. The attempt to move audiences is by no means unique to this film, however. As this chapter demonstrates, our whole media landscape is rhetorical.

Rhetorical scholars of the media, alternatively referred to as Rhetorical critics, analyze texts for the ways they encourage audiences to inhabit certain moods, adopt certain attitudes, and undertake certain actions. These scholars view texts as complex webs of interrelated parts that work together to influence consumers in particular ways. We begin this chapter with an introduction to the concept of rhetoric, emphasizing its inherently suasory character. Then, we illustrate how signs – the basic building blocks of language and most other forms of rhetoric – create meaning by examining the work of three important philosophers of signs. Next, we consider how signs in complex combination form media texts, whose various structures invite and elicit particular responses from audiences. Finally, we conclude by examining how the aesthetic elements of media such as sound and color move audiences at a bodily level through the generation of affect.

Rhetoric: an Overview

The tendency to view popular media products like the film *The Hunger Games*, or the ABC television series *Modern Family*, or the Gotye song "Somebody That I Used to Know," or the video game *League of Legends* as *mere* (which implies only) entertainment obscures the fact that media messages inevitably persuade as well as entertain us. Media messages cannot help but convey meanings, and meanings are never neutral or objective. Consequently, films, television shows, songs, video games, etc. are constantly inviting us to adopt certain attitudes, values, and beliefs, while simultaneously encouraging us to dismiss and discount others. This is because all media products are rhetorical.[3] Historically, rhetoric referred to the ancient art of oratory, or as Aristotle famously defined it, "an ability, in each particular case, to see the available means of persuasion."[4] The art of rhetoric as practiced by Greek politicians in the fifth century BC may seem distant and unrelated to the art of rhetoric as utilized in the spectacular images of *Avatar* (2009). But both instances of rhetoric rely on symbols to influence what and how audiences think and feel. Indeed, if we were to update Aristotle's definition, we might simply define **rhetoric** as the use of symbols by humans to influence and move other humans.[5]

If what is meant by the idea that media products are rhetorical is still not entirely clear, then consider Michael Moore's controversial 2004 film *Fahrenheit 9/11*. The film takes a highly critical look at the role played by big money, oil, and the Bush administration leading up to and following the tragic events of September 11, 2001. Like Moore's previous artistic endeavors (*Roger and Me* and *Bowling for Columbine*), *Fahrenheit 9/11* is a documentary. But many critics, and especially those on the political right, responded to the film with vitriol and venom because of its biased, one-sided presentation of events, an offense that was only further heightened by the film maker's insistence that it was a documentary. The outrage of critics stemmed, at least in part, from the "perception" that documentaries ought to be objective. But as we have already noted, all symbols are value-laden and thus all messages, as symbolic creations, are necessarily biased.[6] As Kenneth Burke explains, "Even if any given terminology is a *reflection* of reality, by its very nature as a terminology it must be a *selection* of reality; and to this extent it must function also as a *deflection* of reality."[7] Thus, it is naïve to think that communication in any form, be it a documentary film or scientific monograph, can be anything other than biased and suasory.[8]

Theories of the Sign

In 1993, the Sweden-based pop group Ace of Base released their smash hit "The Sign," which spent six weeks atop the Billboard Hot 100 chart in the USA. Although the song owes its success to its infectious dance beat, our interest is in the song's mind-numbing lyrics and popular refrain, "I saw the sign and it opened up my eyes. I saw the sign." As cheesy and cliché as these lines may be, they succinctly describe the basic operation of signs. A **sign** is something that invites someone to think of something other than itself, such as the way an image of a person invites one to think of that person or the way the unique letter combination d/o/g invites one to think of a four-legged canine. Since nearly everything has that potential, virtually anything can function as a sign. When multiple people agree on what a sign refers to, we say that it has shared meaning. Shared meaning is, of course, what makes human communication possible. Without it, no social structures or institutions could exist. Moreover, since no sign (no matter how clear it may seem) can guarantee that everyone will interpret it the same way (i.e. understand it to be referring to the same thing), communication is an extremely fragile thing. Think of all the times in your life you have said something to someone that was intended to be innocent, but that was (mis)interpreted as an offense. Signs are significant, then, because they are the fundamental building blocks of meaning and hence communication. In this section, we consider how three prominent scholars have theorized the sign: Ferdinand de Saussure, Charles Sanders Peirce, and Roland Barthes.

Ferdinand de Saussure (1857–1913)

The Swiss linguist Ferdinand de Saussure is generally regarded as "the founder of modern linguistics,"[9] a title he earned by shifting the study of language away from the historical roots (philology) and changing meaning of specific words (semantics) to the study of language as a structured system. Although Saussure never wrote a book, his lectures on linguistics at the University of Geneva were compiled and published posthumously in 1915 under the title of *Course in General Linguistics*. Saussure called his unique approach to linguistics **semiology**, which he defined as "a science which studies the role of signs as part of social life.... It [semiology] would investigate the nature of signs and the laws governing them."[10] Since Saussure understood language as a system of signs, he began by asking what is a sign and what rules does it obey. All linguistic signs, he argued, were a combination of signifier (*signifiant*) and signified (*signifié*). The **signifier**, or sound-image, refers to the material form of a sign as perceived by the senses, such as the word "dog" as heard by a listener. The **signified**, or mental concept, is the idea evoked by the signifier; in this case, the idea of "dogness." Note that an actual dog is not part of this equation. Together, the signifier and signified constitute a sign, which Saussure designated in the manner shown in the diagram.

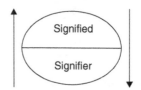

For Saussure, the linguistic sign has two defining traits. First, signs are *arbitrary*,[11] meaning there is no natural correspondence, no necessary relationship, between the signifier and signified. It is precisely because there is no inevitable or inherent link between signifiers and signifieds that the idea of "dogness" can be conveyed by different signifiers: dog (English), *perro* (Spanish), *chien* (French), *cane* (Italian), *Hund* (German), 狗 (Chinese). We could even invent our own word for "dogness," such as *plink*, and if we agreed that *plink* meant "dogness," then we would have a new signifier. It is this principle of arbitrariness that allows Trekkers (fanatical fans of *Star Trek*) to invent and speak in alien languages like Klingon, for instance. The constant creation and addition of new words, like "Truthiness," and the changing meaning of existing words, like "hot" (which went from meaning "extremely warm" to also meaning "cool," "sexy," and "hip" thanks in large part to Paris Hilton), highlight the arbitrariness of signs. "The fact that the relation between signifier and signified is arbitrary means, then," elaborates Culler, "that since there are no fixed universal concepts or fixed universal signifiers, the signified itself is arbitrary."[12] This is to say that while the terms *dog* and *perro* may both evoke the mental idea of "dogness," "dogness" is itself understood differently in different cultures.

The second key trait of the linguistic sign is *linearity*. Since the signifier, being auditory, is unfolded solely in time, it is impossible to utter two distinct linguistic signs simultaneously. Go ahead: try to say two different words at exactly the same time. It is not possible. Saussure recognized that this trait did not hold true for visual signs, which can, in fact, "exploit more than one dimension simultaneously."[13] So, when you look at a photograph, you can process multiple signs simultaneously. Saussure regarded the principle of linearity to be a significant one because it means that signifiers operate in a temporal chain, which if reordered, changes the meaning of what is being said.

Having identified the basic character of signs, let us turn now to Saussure's methods for investigating the rules that govern signs. To understand and appreciate his perspective, we need to introduce three additional ideas: *langue* versus *parole*, synchronic versus diachronic, and difference. For Saussure, it is important to distinguish between *la langue*, the linguistic system, and *parole*, individual speech acts or utterances (i.e. actual manifestations of the sign system). To study *la langue* is to study the rules and conventions that organize the system, while to study *parole* is to study specific uses or performances of language. Saussure was a strong proponent of the former, which he believed to be the proper goal of linguistics. Another distinction of significance to Saussure was that between synchronic and diachronic analysis. *Synchronic analysis*, which was Saussure's principal commitment, concerns the state of language in general: the linguistic system in a static state. It aims to illuminate the conditions for the existence of any language by examining the rules of combination and substitutability within a system. *Diachronic analysis* or evolutionary linguistics, by contrast, concerns the origins of languages and changes in sound or pronunciation over time (phonology). Since such changes are found in *parole*, Saussure did not see diachronic analysis as a suitable method for investigating *la langue*.

The final key concept in Saussure's science of signs is *difference*. Saussure astutely recognized that signs signify by virtue of their difference (i.e. distinctiveness) from other signs. The word "dog" can signify because it sounds and looks different than the words "dig," "frog," and "bag." Though this may seem like an elementary observation, its implications are profound. It suggests that if we cannot distinguish one sign from another, then we cannot communicate. This is what occurs when someone is speaking too softly or mumbling; though we can still hear sounds, we can no longer distinguish among them. Similarly, the difficulty in reading a professor's sloppy handwriting arises from an inability to distinguish those signs from other signs. As long as a sign sounds or looks different from other signs, then it can be used to communicate. The specific character of such differences is unimportant so long as their meaning is socially agreed upon. It does not matter, for instance, what a bishop looks like in the game of chess, only that the bishop, which is bound by certain rules, looks different from the other pieces. Indeed, if one of the bishops in a chess set were lost, the game could still be played using a bottle cap or some other non-chess object so long as both players agreed the bottle cap represented a bishop and was, thus, limited to a bishop's movements. The game could not be played, however, if an extra pawn were made to stand in for the missing bishop since the players would not be able to differentiate that particular pawn (i.e. the one representing the bishop) from the game's other pawns.

Charles Sanders Peirce (1839–1914)

At about the same time Saussure was putting forth his theory of signs in Europe, a Harvard-trained American philosopher by the name of Charles Sanders Peirce was developing his own theory. Peirce called his program **semiotic** (semiotike), which he defined as "the quasi-necessary, or formal, doctrine of signs."[14] Unlike Saussure's theory of signs, which was conveniently compiled into one book, Peirce's work on

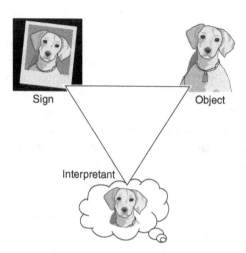

Sign

Object

Interpretant

Figure 5.1
C.S. Peirce's semiotic
theory.

signs spans across his writings and intersects with a diverse array of topics. His notion of semiotic has been distilled from the eight-volume *Collected Papers of Charles Sanders Peirce*, the first two volumes of which appeared in 1932. Peirce's semiotic differs greatly from Saussure's semiology because it both repudiates the principle of arbitrariness and expands the category of signs to include all modes of human communication (not just language). Peirce's semiotic is based upon the triadic relation between sign, object, and interpretant.

"A sign, or *representamen*," as Peirce called it, "is something which stands to somebody for something in some respect or capacity."[15] The "equivalent sign" it creates in a person's mind is the known as the *interpretant*, and the something that the sign stands for is its *object*. In this scheme, the representamen (sign) loosely corresponds to Saussure's idea of the signifier and the interpretant to his notion of the signified. For Peirce, the image or picture of a dog functions as a sign that refers to an object, a real dog, and creates an interpretant, or mental interpretation of the dog (Figure 5.1).

Peirce classified signs into three categories: icons, indices, and symbols. **Iconic signs** operate according to the logic of similarity or likeness; icons are representamens that structurally resemble the objects they stand for. Examples include diagrams, maps, photographs, and other types of images. **Indexical signs** are linked by cause or association to the objects they represent. Since smoke indicates fire, it functions as an indexical sign for fire. Peirce noted that, "anything which focuses the attention is an index," citing the example of a "rap on the door" because it draws our attention to someone's arrival.[16] **Symbols**, the third category of signs, are linked to their corresponding objects purely by social convention or agreement; symbolic signs are learned rather than intuited. As this is how language works, Peirce argued that "All words, sentences, books, and other conventional signs are Symbols."[17] It should be noted that Peirce did not regard these three categories as mutually exclusive, believing instead that certain signs could function in more than one way.

Roland Barthes (1915–1980)

Roland Barthes has been described as "the most important French thinker to emerge from the post-war period."[18] Despite this ringing endorsement, Barthes was famous not so much for proposing intellectually revolutionary ideas, but for refining and expanding upon the ideas of others. As we will see, Barthes's theory of signs, which we term the **signifying system** to distinguish it from semiology and semiotics, draws heavily upon the work of both Saussure and Peirce. The signifying system grew out of Barthes's fascination with how "cultural" practices and beliefs are "naturalized" (i.e. made to appear natural), an idea he first began to explore in his writings on myth (see especially *Mythologies*). Over time, Barthes increasingly began to view myth through the lens of signification, and in particular through Saussure's conception of signs as signifier and signified.

To demonstrate the relation of myth to Saussure's scheme, Barthes famously introduced the distinction between denotation and connotation in *Elements of Semiology* (1964). **Denotation** describes first-order signification or what Barthes called the first "plane of expression."[19] The denotative plane involves the literal or explicit meanings of words and other phenomena. At a purely denotative level, for instance, the word "lion" (signifier) evokes the mental image of a large cat (signified). But Barthes recognized that meaning does not end there, that the signifying system is characterized by process not product.[20] When one hears the word "lion," one may briefly form the mental image of a large cat, but that mental image (as a signifier itself) will evoke still other associations (new signifieds) such as "courage" and "pride." This second plane of expression is what Barthes called connotation. **Connotation** is second-order signification and operates at the level of ideology and myth. While "dog" and "perro" may evoke similar mental images (i.e. denotative meaning), the connotative meaning of dog can vary greatly from culture to culture (everything from "companion" or "family member" to "pest" or "food"). Figure 5.2 visually depicts the relation of denotation to connotation.

The advantage of Barthes's signifying system over Saussure's semiology is not that it illustrates that meaning is always cultural (Saussure was well aware of this fact), but that it emphasizes that meaning is never final or closed.

Like Peirce, Barthes recognized that signs need not be linguistic. Moreover, he agreed that the relationship between the signifier and the signified is not really arbitrary so much as it is *unmotivated*.[21] But even in the case of image-based signifying practices such as photography and cinema or object-based signifying practices such as clothing and food, Barthes found value in the signifier/signified binary. Thus, when

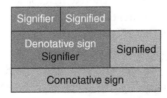

Figure 5.2
The relation of a denotative sign to a connotative sign.

Figure 5.3
Panzani advertisement.
Courtesy of Panzani.

studying images, Barthes would isolate the signifiers and signifieds operating on both the denotative and connotative planes of expression. One of Barthes's most well-known analyses is of an advertisement for Panzani products that appeared in a French magazine (see Figure 5.3).

Barthes argued that the Panzani advertisement comprised three messages (codes): a linguistic message (printed text), a denoted image (non-coded iconic message), and a connoted image (coded iconic message). The linguistic message in advertisements performs the function of anchorage according to Barthes. *Anchorage* limits the (potentially infinite) meanings an image can have by "directing" the reader through the visual signifieds.[22] In other image-based forms such as cinema or comic strips, the linguistic message can also perform a *relay* function, in which the words complement and reinforce the images. For Barthes, the denoted image is analogical in nature, the visual signifier "tomato" referring to the mental idea of "tomato-ness," the visual signifier "net" referring to mental idea of "net-ness," and so forth. Perhaps less obvious is the meaning of the connoted image, which evokes the ideas of freshness or return from market, Italianicity, total culinary service, and "still life." Just as the elements in this image derive their meaning in relation to one another, Barthes believed that each element within a signifying system was dependent upon every other element in that system for its meaning. In other words, not only are the individual signs in a message key to its meaning, but so too are their arrangement in particular texts and rhetorical structures.

Texts and Rhetorical Structures

Signs, of course, rarely exist or function in isolation. Rather, they are combined with other signs to form media products or **texts**. "A text," according to Barry Brummett, "is a set of signs related to each other insofar as their meanings all contribute to the same set of effects or functions."[23] The Panzani advertisement discussed in the previous section, as well as songs, internet sites, video games, television shows, and movies can all be thought of as media texts because the individual signs that comprise them are strategically structured to elicit particular responses from listeners and viewers. Though the organizational pattern of signs that can exist in a text is potentially infinite, there are some general rhetorical structures shared by many, if not all, texts. This section of the chapter focuses on four rhetorical structures in particular: clusters, form, genre, and narrative.

Clusters

Perhaps the most basic rhetorical structure in texts is the **cluster**, or the way individual signs are associated with and dissociated from one another. Expounding on this idea, Kenneth Burke writes, "Now, the work [text] of every writer [or media producer] contains a set of implicit equations. He uses 'associational clusters.' And you [the critic] may, by examining his work [text], find 'what goes with what' in these clusters: what kinds of acts and images and personalities and situations go with his notions of heroism, villainy, consolation, despair, etc."[24] To understand how the clusters in a text are working rhetorically, the critic should begin by identifying the key signs within the text: those signs that are privileged through repetition, intensity, or prominence. In the Candie's Fragrances advertisement (Figure 5.4), for instance, the critic would classify the two perfume bottles as key signs because they are bright, prominently placed in the center of the advertisement, and the focus of the model's attention, a technique designed to focus our attention on them as well. The critic would then ask, what other signs are associated with (i.e. cluster around) these key signs? This would likely lead one to note that the two perfume bottles are swimming in an ocean of condoms. The implicit suggestion, of course, is that wearing Candie's Fragrances will lead to sex … lots and lots of sex! The absence of certain signs or clusters in a text may also be central to its appeal. Notice in the Candie's ad that there is nothing in the medicine cabinet besides condoms and perfume. Other objects (i.e. visual signs) that one might expect to find in a medicine cabinet such as creams, deodorants, and aspirin are all conspicuously missing. These absences are not accidental. Rather they are strategic, as the advertiser does not want to

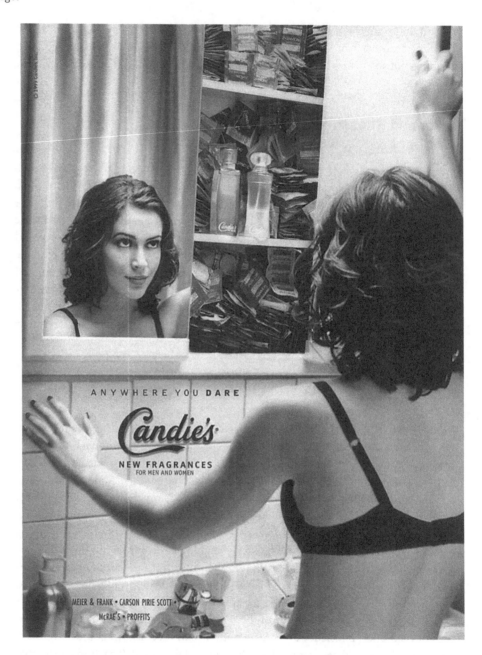

Figure 5.4
Candie's Fragrances
advertisement.
COURTESY OF ICONIX
BRAND/CANDIE'S
FRAGRANCES.

risk consumers associating Candie's Fragrances with rashes, body odor, headaches, and upset stomachs. Finally, the critic explores whether the particular clustering of signs in a text fosters a positive, negative, or ambivalent valence toward the key signs. In the case of the Candie's Fragrances ad, the association of the product with condoms, a half-naked Alyssa Milano, and a pristine, white bathroom all work to make the product more desirable by associating it with a series of positive signifiers.

Form

A second prominent rhetorical structure in texts is form. **Form**, explains Burke, is "an arousing and fulfillment of desires. A work has form in so far as one part of it leads a reader to anticipate another part, [and] to be gratified by the sequence."[25] Simply stated, form is the creation and satisfaction of desire. When a gun is drawn by a character in a film, for instance, it fosters a desire for violence. Although the violence may not occur immediately, which further heightens our desire for it (by withholding or prolonging fulfillment), it must occur eventually; otherwise our desire goes unfulfilled (this is known as "bad form"). If you have ever had a friend break a promise to you, then you know just how frustrating and disappointing bad form can be. Form is at play in virtually all messages. Consider the opening sentence of this paragraph: "A second prominent rhetorical structure in texts is form." This sentence generates a desire to know what "form" is, which the next sentence graciously affords by providing a definition. Similarly, the sentence that immediately precedes the one you are currently reading fulfills the desire to know the significance of the first sentence in this paragraph: a desire created by the phrase, "Consider the opening sentence of this paragraph."

Form comes in a variety of, for lack of a better word, forms. Burke proposes that there are four general varieties of form: progressive form, repetitive form, conventional form, and minor or incidental forms. Progressive form describes the way a story advances step by step, each step following logically from the previous step. "The arrows of our desires," Burke writes, "are turned in a certain direction, and the plot follows the direction of the arrows."[26] Progressive form is particularly evident in television crime dramas such as *CSI*. Each episode begins with a homicide, which (necessarily) leads to the search for a killer. As clues are gathered and analyzed over the episode, suspects are slowly eliminated until the culprit is finally revealed and confronted. Though there may be brief "misdirection" along the way, ultimately the clues will point to the guilt of one individual. The second major type of form, repetitive form, "is the consistent maintaining of a principle under new guises. It is the restatement of the same thing in different ways."[27] Repetitive form can be seen in the actions of most characters on television; they are recognizable to us as "characters" precisely because they repeat the same behaviors over and over again. Though the context changes, Quagmire repeatedly makes sexual advances on *Family Guy*, Phoebe repeatedly behaves eccentrically on *Friends*, and Dr. House repeatedly treats others callously on *House*. Each time we witness these behaviors, it heightens our appetite to see them repeated in a new context. That they are repeated is extremely rewarding because it satiates an appetite created by repetition.

Conventional form, the third major variety of form, is not so much an appeal *within* the text (as progressive and repetitive forms are) as it is an appeal *of* the text. When two friends are trying to decide what movie to go see and one of them says, "I'm in the mood for a romantic comedy," she is articulating a preference based on conventional form. One way of classifying media texts is according to the structural and aesthetic conventions they share. Horror films are scary, action films are thrilling, and romantic comedies are funny, or at least we "expect" them to be. We often select the media texts we do because we desire a particular set of conventions at a particular moment in time. When someone is depressed and chooses to listen to a sad, sappy love song, it is because that *type* of song fulfills the desire to wallow in self-pity. The fourth and final variety, minor or incidental forms, is sort of a catch-all category. It includes the brief, frequently literary devices that may appear within a text such as metaphor, paradox, reversal, contraction, expansion, etc. Minor forms are what allow us to take pleasure in segments, sections, or pieces of larger texts. One may delight, for example, in a particular scene from a film independent from the whole because it creates and fulfills a desire all its own.

Genre

Another way to investigate what media texts mean and how they function rhetorically to move us is through the concept of genre. A **genre** is a class or constellation of messages that share discernible stylistic or formal (syntactic), substantive (semantic), and situational (pragmatic) characteristics.[28] The idea that media messages can be categorized into identifiable genres according to the stylistic and substantive traits they share may seem rather obvious. After all, popular cinematic genres like romantic comedies, psychological thrillers, and horror films each have readily identifiable plot, setting, and character elements. The broad recognizability of these elements allows for the near continuous release of film parodies like *Scary Movie* (2000), *Not Another Teen Movie* (2001), *Date Movie* (2006), *Epic Movie* (2007), *Superhero Movie* (2008), *InAPPropriate Comedy* (2013), etc. What is less obvious, but no less important, is that genres possess stylistic and substantive similarities because they speak to typical or recurrent situations in familiar ways. In other words, genres function as modes of social action; they are patterned responses to situations that audiences perceive as somehow similar or comparable. Romantic comedies are recognizable as romantic comedies, in large part, because they address common relational challenges in formulaic ways – ways that differ noticeably from how Westerns define and frame relational challenges.

The study of genre is typically approached in one of two ways: inductively or deductively. Genres that are arrived at inductively are created by drawing general conclusions based upon the analysis of specific instances. An inductive approach typically corresponds to what are known as *historical genres*. Historical genres, which are rooted in the observation of shared traits across media texts, are well known to most people. Popular television genres such as soap operas, game shows, reality TV, sitcoms, and dramas (crime, medical, and legal) are common examples of historical genres. But let's take a closer look at an example of a historical genre: the daytime talk show. Like other television genres, the talk show has an easily identifiable set of formal and substantive characteristics. For instance, it features a host who interviews guests on a specific topic, incorporates unexpected or surprising elements, involves the interaction of a studio audience, and is seemingly spontaneous and unscripted. But as anyone who

Table 5.1   Comparison of trash and confessional talk shows

Trash talk show	Confessional talk show
Host as (circus) ring leader	Host as (personal) therapist
Everyday people with *outrageous* problems (sensational, salacious, and socially taboo)	*Celebrity* personalities with *ordinary* problems (typical, normal, and common)
Entails conflict and confrontation among guests	Entails friendly, sit-down interviews with guests
Young studio audience that hoots, shouts, and chants	Middle-aged studio audience that asks questions and shares experiences
Contentious, carnivalesque culture	Feel-good, celebrity-friendly gossip culture
Examples: *The Jerry Springer Show, Maury, The Ricki Lake Show, The Jenny Jones Show*	Examples: *The Ellen DeGeneres Show, The View, The Rosie O'Donnell Show, The Oprah Winfrey Show*

regularly watches talk shows will tell you, not all talk shows are equal; there are meaningful differences, for example, between *The Jerry Springer Show* and *The Ellen DeGeneres Show*. Studying these shows and others like them allows us to refine our taxonomy and to distinguish between the "trash" talk show and "confessional" talk show. Though similar in many respects, the trash and confessional talk show are distinct historical (sub)genres typified by the characteristics in Table 5.1.

As we noted at the outset of this section, genres are based not only on the stylistic and substantive traits they share, but also on what they *do* (for audiences) – on the social action they perform in response to recurring situations. Genre operates, then, in much the same manner as does Burke's notion of conventional form. Viewers come to tabloid (trash) and confessional talk shows expecting certain things to happen and to the extent that those things do happen, the shows are formally rewarding. But even more basically, audiences are drawn to those genres in the first place because of the precise manner in which they deal with typical situations and, thus, fulfill particular psychological needs and desires. From this perspective, we might conclude that one reason trash talk shows are appealing is because, in showing us everyday people with outrageous problems, they reassure us that our lives are pretty normal and uncomplicated by contrast. Alternatively, confessional talk shows are appealing because, in showing us celebrities with ordinary problems, they comfort us with the knowledge that all people share in similar struggles. So, while both genres address the difficulties of daily life, they do so in dramatically different ways.

A second way to study genre is deductively, working from a set of general propositions to specific conclusions. In contrast to an inductive approach, as reflected in historical genres, a deductive approach generates and tests *theoretical genres*. Whereas historical genres are based upon generalizations that emerge from the observation of multiple cases (such as our analysis of daytime talk shows), theoretical genres are rooted in the application of general principles to individual instances. To clarify this distinction, consider Diomedes' classification of literary works into three key genres during the fourth century: those in which only the narrator speaks; those in which only the characters speak; and those in which both speak. "This classification," observes Russian literary scholar Tzvetan Todorov, "is not based upon a comparison of works to be found in the history of literature (as in the case of historical genres), but on an abstract hypothesis which postulates that the performer of the speech act is the most important element of the literary work, and that according to the nature of this performer, we can distinguish a logically calculable number of theoretical genres."[29] Film scholar Jane Feuer further clarifies the difference between historical and theoretical genres, noting that the former is "accepted by culture" and the latter is "defined by critics."[30]

Narrative

A fourth rhetorical structure common to media texts is narrative. **Narrative** describes a series of real or fictitious events that occur in (often chronological) succession. For narrative theorist Gérard Genette, narrative can be divided into three levels: story (*histoire*), discourse (*récit*), and narrating (*narration*). To appreciate the rhetorical complexity of narrative, it is worth looking at each of the three levels in greater detail.

1   *Story* refers to what happens to whom in a narrative. It is comprised of events and existents.
    a)   *Events*. The particular events that occur within a story are further divided according to the function they perform: kernels (or nuclei) are the key nodes or hinges that actively contribute to a story's progression and satellites (or catalyzers) are the more minor plot events that fill in the narrative. The distinction between kernels and satellites becomes evident when a story is condensed into its simplest form. Take the following story as an example.

        Villain kills victim. Victim's body is discovered. Hero begins search for villain. Hero discovers clues to villain's crime. Hero captures villain. Villain is punished.

        This is what a story might look like if it were totally stripped of all satellites. Each of these events functions as a kernel because they formally necessitate subsequent cardinal events. The endless array of minor events that connect these kernels will likely be satellites. After dispatching the victim, for instance, the villain may drive home (satellite), attempt to destroy evidence of the crime (satellite), and return to work (satellite). These events are satellites because they can be substituted with other events or even deleted without altering the basic story.
    b)   *Existents*. Stories are also made of existents, which include characters (actants) and indices (informants and setting). Characters are often classified with respect to the actions they perform within a story. In his study of Russian fairy

tales, Vladimir Propp identifies seven typical characters: hero (seeker or victim), villain, donor (provider), helper, princess (sought-after person), dispatcher, and false hero.[31] This list was later streamlined by A.J. Greimas into three pairs (subject/object, sender/receiver, helper/opponent), which he argued accounted not just for the characters in fairy tales, but for those in stories in general.[32] What audiences know about characters – specific details such as their age, hair color, and favorite food – are known as informants, while the location and overall atmosphere in which characters find themselves is called the setting.

2   *Discourse*, according to Genette, describes the actual words, written or spoken, used to tell a story. Since the narratives in contemporary media are increasingly visual, we would add images or pictures along with words to Genette's category of discourse. As is evidenced by the silent film era, words are not a requirement for storytelling. Because signs (i.e. words and images) are never neutral, the specific discourse of a narrative is central to its meaning. The meaning of the event, "boy meets girl," is significantly altered if, in the telling, the narrator says, "a seedy-looking man wearing a dark overcoat confronts Gillian in a dimly lit alley" rather than, "a businessman approaches Gillian at the bar and politely offers to buy her a drink." When analyzing how a narrative functions rhetorically, a critic ought to attend not just to what happens and to whom (i.e. story), but also to the precise language used to tell the story (i.e. discourse).

3   *Narrating*, the third level at which we can approach narrative, refers to the actual act of recounting (the situation *within* which discourse is uttered). It involves questions such as who is speaking, from what perspective or point of view, and in what relation to the listener/audience. To address these questions, Genette proposed analyzing narration along three axes: tense, mood, and voice.

a)   *Tense*. Drawing upon the work of Todorov, Genette understood tense to refer to narrative temporality. Tense, or the temporal relations of the narrative, can further be divided into the categories of order, duration (speed), and frequency. The category of *order* has to do with how time unfolds for the narrator, who may or may not also be a character in the story. Narrators can transport audiences to the past through flashbacks (analepses) or into the future through flash forwards (prolepses), or they can create anticipation for future events through character premonition. The concept of reach refers to how far back or ahead the events the narrator recalls or anticipates lie. The second category of narrative temporality is *duration* or speed, and it involves the relation between the period of time described (story-time) and the period of time required for the telling (discourse-time). According to Sarah Kozloff, there are five possible relations between story-time and discourse-time:[33]

- scene: discourse-time and story-time are roughly equal (such as the technique utilized during the first season of the television series *24*).
- summary: discourse-time is shorter than story-time (such as the way a week can pass in an hour-long program).

- ellipsis: discourse-time is zero (such as the way two or three weeks can pass with a simple cut in film or television).
- stretch: discourse-time is longer than story-time (slow motion).
- pause: discourse-time is longer than story-time, which is zero (freeze-frame).

Frequency, the final category of temporal relations, refers to the number of times a single event or incident is recounted by the narrator. Genette noted four potential expressions of frequency: narrating once what happened once (e.g. "Yesterday, I went to bed early."), narrating *n* times what happened *n* times (e.g. Monday, I went to bed early. Tuesday, I went to bed early. Wednesday, I went to bed early."), narrating *n* times what happened once (e.g. "Yesterday I went to bed early, yesterday I went to bed early, yesterday I went to bed early."), and narrating one time (or rather, at one time) what happened *n* times (e.g. "I went to bed early every day of the week.").

b) *Mood*. Whereas tense (i.e. order, duration, and frequency) describes narrative temporality, Genette employs the term mood to describe the *"regulation of narrative information,"*[34] such as how much or how little is told (distance) and through what channel (perspective). Distance involves the words and thoughts of a character, while perspective or point of view describes who sees in the narrative and his or her capacities of knowledge. Perspective varies greatly, as a story can be told from (focalized through) or about (focalized on) a specific character. In the television series *Sex and the City*, for instance, the story is told from the perspective of Carrie Bradshaw, who frequently shares her personal thoughts. Consequently, viewers are invited to identify with Carrie and to see the world through her eyes.

c) *Voice*. Genette's final category, voice, entails the position, type, and relation of the narrator. Questions of voice include: Is the narrator a character in the story (homodiegetic) or is she or he outside the story-world (heterodiegetic)? What is the narrator's degree of omniscience? Is the narrator reliable? Is the story told in first or third person? Genette regarded the distinction between voice and mood to be an important one because narrative voice frames how audiences understand and relate to narrative mood. While a character in a story may have a particularly optimistic outlook about the future (mood), the audience may know that such optimism is unwarranted because the character is about to experience bad fortune (voice). This is precisely the situation in horror films when the audience is shown (afforded special knowledge by the narrator) that there is a killer hiding under the bed that a character is unwittingly having sex on. Having more knowledge than the character in this case heightens the audience's fear by creating the expectation of violence.

As is likely evident by this point, narratives are complex rhetorical structures involving many variables. Thus, we have included Figure 5.5 to clarify how those variables relate to one another.

Elements of narrative

I. Story (content plane): the totality of narrated events
    A. Events:
        1. kernals (nuclei)
        2. satellites (catalyzers)
    B. Existents:
        1. characters (actants)
        2. indices:
            a. informants
            b. setting (motif)
II. Discourse (expression plane): the actual written or spoken words
III. Narration: the very act (recounting) that produces the discourse
    A. Tense (temporal relations)
        1. order
        2. duration (speed)
        3. frequency
    B. Mood
        1. distance: quantitative modulation
        2. perspective: qualitative modulation
    C. Voice (narrator)

Figure 5.5
The elements of
narrative.

The Material Turn: Affect and Aesthetics

Up to this point, our discussion of a Rhetorical approach to media has focused on how signs or texts – sets of signs working together – create meaning and influence audiences. We have, in keeping with a rather traditional Rhetorical perspective, concentrated on how media appeal to or move us at a purely symbolic, cognitive level. But more recently, Rhetorical scholars have begun to ask how rhetoric moves us at a material, bodily level. Music scholars, for instance, are quick to point out that the melody, harmony, and rhythm of a song do not function in the same manner as the words in a book do, for they do not represent (i.e. stand in for) something else.[35] Yet, these non-symbolic elements of music clearly exert a powerful influence upon us. Our bodies literally feel and experience the rhythm of a song, which may, in turn, prompt us to tap our feet. Similarly, the timbre or grain (the material message) of someone's voice can – independent of what that person is saying (the symbolic message) – sway us depending upon whether it is pleasing or displeasing. Thus, as Rhetorical scholars continue to investigate how messages move audiences, they are increasingly attending to media's materiality as well as its symbolicity.

The historical bias in favor of symbolicity, over and at the expense of materiality, is a consequence of two closely related, but mistaken philosophical assumptions: (1) that the mind and body are separate, independent structures, and (2) that meaning belongs primarily to the purview of the former. Today, most scholars reject the mind/body dualism that originated with the French philosopher René Descartes in the seventeenth century. Critiquing Descartes' view, philosopher Mark Johnson explains:

A person is not a mind *and* a body. There are not two "things" somehow mysteriously yoked together. What we call a "person" is a certain kind of bodily organism that has a brain operating within its body, a body that is continually interacting with aspects of its

> environments (material and social) in an ever-changing process of experience.... In short, "mind" and "body" are merely abstracted aspects of the flow of organism-environment interactions that constitutes what we call experience.[36]

In addition to rejecting the Cartesian mind/body dichotomy, scholars increasingly understand that "*Meaning is grounded in our bodily experiences*,"[37] and that one must study our visceral and corporeal connections to the world to apprehend human meaning-making.

How, then, does one critically assess bodily experiences? As bodies interact with their material surroundings, they experience various energies, intensities, pulsations, and rhythms, which through sensory data (sights, sounds, tastes, smells, and tactility) generate affect. The term affect is often used in a generic sense to refer to emotion. But as Brian Massumi and others have noted, affect and emotion are not precisely the same thing. **Affect** describes an intensity registered directly by the body and, therefore, operates on a non-representational or asignifying register.[38] Emotion, by contrast, is conscious and qualified and, thus, carries a particular valence and meaning. Admittedly, an affect such as a tingling of the skin that one might experience while watching a horror film is often quickly qualified into a recognizable emotion such as fear. To complicate matters further, feelings and moods are states that fall somewhere between affect and emotion, and, indeed, many media scholars use affect, feeling, mood, and emotion interchangeably. So, why bother with these distinctions?

Rhetorical scholars have a well-developed vocabulary and set of critical tools (such as sign, text, cluster, form, genre, and narrative) for analyzing how media operate symbolically, but they lack a detailed vocabulary and sophisticated set of tools for understanding media's fundamental materiality. The distinction between affect and emotion reflects a desire on the part of Rhetorical critics to take seriously the way media move audiences materially. Viewing affect as "primary, non-conscious,... asignifying, unqualified, and intensive"[39] affords critics a tool for studying how matter, which makes up all music, film, television, etc., appeals directly to the human sensorium. Recognizing that matter produces sensation and, hence, affect is an important first step in understanding the materiality of media. But it does not yet explain why specific arrangements of matter such as a film or song may elicit public or shared affect. To address this issue, we must consider the notion of the aesthetic.

Just as the signs that comprise media are organized into signifying or textual structures such as form and narrative, the matter that comprises media possesses sensual or aesthetic properties such as "consonance, dissonance, harmonies of tone, light, colour, sound and rhythm."[40] The **aesthetic**, as we are using it here, refers to those qualities of an artwork that, while asignifying, generate sensual experiences and evoke affective responses from audiences. Unlike textual structures, the aesthetic properties of media do not function to symbolize. As we have already seen, the rhythm of a song does not refer to something outside of itself and, therefore, does not convey a specific meaning. While the aesthetic is not, properly speaking, symbolic, it is, as Debra Hawhee observes, "always and everywhere rhetorical – that

Table 5.2 Comparison of rhetoric's symbolic and material dimensions

	Symbolicity	Materiality
Basis	Symbol or sign	Matter or substance
Mechanism	Signifying structures	Aesthetic properties
Activates	Cognition	Sensation
Type of effect	Meaning	Presence
Induces	Attitudes	Affects

is, productive of effects – and crucially, these effects are produced on and through the live and lively bodies in audiences."[41] We might say, then, that the aesthetic produces *presence effects* – effects that prime our bodies, essentially predisposing us to experience an event and its attendant symbols in a particular way. In a moment, we will consider a few specific ways that the aesthetic induces affective priming, but first we summarize the differences between rhetoric's symbolicity and materiality in Table 5.2.

Although media aesthetics is frequently ignored by Rhetorical scholars because it is seen as involving purely subjective judgments and tastes,[42] it is vital to the way media texts function materially. As Arthur Asa Berger explains with regard to film, "The way a scene is shot – the cutting, the editing, the use of music and sound effects, the lighting, the camera work – conveys a great deal of information and gives a sense of the importance of what we are seeing relative to other images and events in the text."[43] It is useful, therefore, to highlight a few important aspects of media aesthetics. In several of the supporting quotations throughout this section, the word emotional is used in place of the word affective, though the latter term is probably more correct.

1   *Color.* Though color can be symbolic, such as the use of red to mean hot and blue to mean cold, color also has an immediate "emotional quality, which derives partly from personal associations; partly from experience in nature."[44] The ability of color to impact our mood and feelings is well established in both psychological and media scholarship.[45] Indeed, with regard to film, Barbara Kennedy argues that, "Colour functions as the main modulator of sensation."[46] So, for instance, while red stimulates excitement, blue and pink have a calming effect.[47]

2   *Lighting.* Like color, light (or its absence) has a strong symbolic dimension. While light typically signifies good, virtue, and salvation, darkness signifies evil, sin, and doom.[48] But light also operates on a material level and "can have profound effects on emotional states."[49] The intensity, focus, and shape of light can be used to guide or direct attention, to create depth and perspective, and to establish or enhance a particular mood. Since darkness can induce fear, horror films use dimly lit images to reinforce feelings of dread and fright. Meanwhile, films such as *Batman Begins* (2005) and *The Dark Knight* (2008) employ darkness to create a general sense of malaise.

3   *Editing.* Editing describes the sequencing and length of individual shots within film and television, as well as the type (cuts, fades, dissolves, wipes, etc.) and frequency of transitions or shifts between shots. The way moving images are edited can have a profound influence on how an audience feels during a scene. Berger notes, for instance, that "Quick cutting between shots creates a sense of excitement in viewers; they work in a way opposite to that of lingering shots, which slow things down."[50] Identifiable editing practices often emerge in relation to specific media forms, and thus influence the way audiences respond to that form. So, unlike Hollywood's classical narratives, whose editing functions to locate one in time and space, music videos rely on montage, a rapid editing style more likely to generate a sensation of discontinuity.[51]

4   *Movement and framing.* Camera movement (i.e. panning, dollying, and tracking) along with framing techniques, like angle of elevation, can powerfully shape the way audiences feel about a person or event they see on screen. As Ann Marie Seward Barry observes:

> The language of camera angles is...highly manipulative emotionally.... . If the angle is extreme, the attitude becomes emphatic. Low angles (shot from beneath with the camera looking up at a subject) give the subject a sense of importance, power, and respect.... In contrast, when a film is shot from a high place looking down on the figure (that is, high angle), the reverse effect is achieved, and the figure looks small, helpless, and insignificant.[52]

Since camera angles are only one of the many techniques involved in image framing, the critic who wishes to understand the emotional valence created by the camera will need to attend to viewpoint, field of view, and picture composition as well.

5   *Sound.* In media such as television and film, sound is omnipresent; while noises (i.e. sound effects) such as a ringing phone or car engine generate a sense of verisimilitude by actualizing time and space, music plays a central role in establishing mood.[53] In a study of the mode, texture, and tempo of music, for instance, Gregory Webster and Catherine Weir found that major keys, non-harmonized melodies, and faster tempos were more likely to result in happier responses, while minor keys, harmonized melodies, and slower tempos were more likely to evoke sadness.[54] Similarly, Kevin Donnelly has demonstrated how the ephemeral character of film music manipulates audiences' emotions.[55]

The five aspects of media aesthetics discussed here do not constitute a comprehensive list, especially since different media have different aesthetics. When evaluating painting, posters, or photography, for instance, a critic would want to consider balance, shape, and form in place of editing, camera movement, and sound. The study of stationary images and other visual artifacts such as public memorials, buildings, and fashion has become so popular in recent years that it has produced its own rich body of literature known as visual rhetoric.[56] In many ways, the scholarship on specifically visual rhetorics, which typically excludes moving images such as film, video, and television[57] in addition to music, mirrors the basic trajectory of the Rhetorical study of media generally. It began with an almost exclusive focus on the symbolic dimensions of visuality (a bias that is still widely evident), but has slowly begun to recognize the importance of visual imagery's fully embodied, material dimensions. As the Rhetorical approach to the study of media continues to develop, it will need to more fully theorize and appraise the relation between the symbolic and the material.

Conclusion

In this chapter, we have considered what it means to approach media from a Rhetorical perspective by discussing what signs are, how they create meaning, how they combine to form texts, and how texts are structured to appeal to audiences. In the final section, we considered the affective dimensions of aesthetic experience, of how media move us materially and sway us somatically, and contribute to human meaning-making as a fully embodied experience. The Rhetorical approach, as we have described it thus far, reflects a rather structuralist perspective. **Structuralism** is the idea, largely popularized by the anthropologist Claude Lévi-Strauss, that each element in a cultural system derives its meaning in relation to other elements in that system;[58] moreover, it tends to regard such systems (language, food, fashion, kinship, etc.) as relatively closed and independent. This latter assumption has come under some critique from poststructuralists, who tend to view systems as interlocking and structures themselves as more open.

We wish to be careful of drawing too sharp a distinction between structuralism and poststructuralism, however, as most theorists agree that the seeds of post-structuralism are already present in structuralism. Perhaps the most important distinction is in how they conceptualize "texts." In structuralism, the meaning of a text derives from "internal" or immanent structures. The producer and receiver of a text (and to some extent even other texts) are seen as having very little to do with a text's meaning. Poststructuralism, by contrast, sees meaning as a complex interaction among texts (intertextuality) as well as between audiences and texts. The practical consequence of this distinction is that structuralism treats texts as more closed (possessing singular meanings) and poststructuralism treats texts as more open (inviting multiple meanings). The implications of this shift in per-spective are more fully explored in Chapter 10 on Reception theory, which considers the centrality of audiences in meaning-making.

MEDIA LAB 4: DOING RHETORICAL ANALYSIS

OBJECTIVE

The aim of this lab is to critically assess a media text from a Rhetorical perspective. Attending to the rhetoric structures (clusters, forms, genre, and narrative) of a text, students will identify the text's central modes of appeal and influence.

ACTIVITY

*   Divide the class into small groups of 4–5 students each.
*   Show students a recruiting video for one of the armed services (i.e. Army, Navy, Air Force, Marines).
*   Ask students to record their answers to the following questions.
    1   What are the key signs? What other signs cluster around them? What associations and dissociations are invited by the clustering of signs? What is strategically absent from the text?
    2   What formal appetites does the text create? How are they resolved?
    3   Identify three other messages that share at least some structural similarities with the video. What are the similarities? What expectations do they foster?
    4   What is the story being told in the video? What are its main characters and events? What do you notice about the specific discourse being used in the video? What are the characteristics of the narration?

SUGGESTED READING

Barthes, R. *Elements of Semiology*, trans. A. Lavers and C. Smith. New York: Hill and Wang, 1967.

Barthes, R. *Image, Music, Text*, trans. S. Heath. New York: Hill and Wang, 1988.

Bordwell, D. *Making Meaning: Inference and Rhetoric in the Interpretation of Cinema*. Cambridge, MA: Harvard University Press, 1989.

Brummett, B. *Rhetoric in Popular Culture*, 2nd edn. Thousand Oaks, CA: Sage Publications, 2006.

Burke, K. *Counter-Statement*. Los Altos, CA: Hermes Publications, 1931.

Burke, K. *The Philosophy of Literary Form: Studies in Symbolic Action*. Baton Rouge, LA: Louisiana State University Press, 1941.

Campbell, K.K. and Jamieson, K.H. *Form and Genre: Shaping Rhetorical Action*. Falls Church, VA: Speech Communication Association, 1976.

Chandler, D. *Semiotics: the Basics*. New York: Routledge, 2002.

Chatman, S. *Story and Discourse: Narrative Structure in Fiction and Film*. Ithaca, NY: Cornell University Press, 1978.

Culler, J. *Ferdinand de Saussure*, revised edn. Ithaca, NY: Cornell University Press, 1986.

Deming, C. Hill Street Blues as Narrative. In *Critical Perspectives on Media and Society*, R. Avery and D. Eason (eds), pp. 240–64. New York: Guilford, 1991.

de Saussure, F. *Course in General Linguistics*, trans. R. Harris. Chicago, IL: Open Court, 1986.

Feuer, J. Genre Study and Television. In *Channels of Discourse, Reassembled: Television and Contemporary Criticism*, R.C. Allen (ed.), pp. 138–60. Chapel Hill, NC: University of North Carolina Press, 1992.

Fry, N. *Anatomy of Criticism: Four Essays*. Princeton, NJ: Princeton University Press, 1957.

Genette, G. *Narrative Discourse: an Essay in Method*, trans. J.E. Lewin. Ithaca, NY: Cornell University Press, 1980.

Hoopes, J. (ed.) *Peirce on Signs: Writings on Semiotics by Charles Sanders Peirce*. Chapel Hill, NC: University of North Carolina Press, 1991.

Johnson, M. *The Meaning of the Body: Aesthetics and Human Understanding*. Chicago, IL: University of Chicago Press, 2007.

Kennedy, B.M. *Deleuze and Cinema: the Aesthetics of Sensation*. Edinburgh: Edinburgh University Press, 2000.

Kozloff, S. Narrative Theory and Television. In *Channels of Discourse, Reassembled: Television and Contemporary Criticism*, R.C. Allen (ed.), pp. 67–100. Chapel Hill, NC: University of North Carolina Press, 1992.

Massumi, B. *Parables for the Virtual: Movement, Affect, Sensation*. Durham, NC: Duke University Press, 2002.

Metz, C. *Film Language: a Semiotics of Cinema*. Chicago, IL: University of Chicago Press, 1974.

Olson, L.C., Finnegan, C.A., and Hope, D.S. (eds) *Visual Rhetoric: a Reader in Contemporary Communication and American Culture*. Los Angeles, CA: Sage Publications, 2008.

Ott, B.L. The Visceral Politics of V for Vendetta: on Political Affect in Cinema. *Critical Studies in Media Communication* 2010, 27(1), 39–54.

Scholes, R., Phelan, J., and Kellogg, R. *The Nature of Narrative*. 40th anniversary edn. Oxford: Oxford University Press, 2006.

Seiter, E. Semiotics, Structuralism, and Television. In *Channels of Discourse, Reassembled: Television and Contemporary Criticism*, R.C. Allen (ed.), pp. 31–66. Chapel Hill, NC: University of North Carolina Press, 1992.

NOTES

1. See B.L. Ott, The Visceral Politics of V for Vendetta: on Political Affect in Cinema, *Critical Studies in Media Communication* 27, 2010, 39–54.

2. C. Chocano, It's All a Little Murky under the Mask, *Los Angeles Times*, March 17, 2006, E-1, http://articles.latimes.com/2006/mar/17/entertainment/et-vendetta17 (accessed December 11, 2008).

3. The claim that all media are rhetorical should not be taken to mean that media are nothing but rhetorical. On this distinction, see M.J. Medhurst and T.W. Benson, *Rhetorical Dimensions in Media: a Critical Casebook*, 2nd edn (Dubuque, IA: Kendall/Hunt Publishing Company, 1991), xix.

4. Aristotle, *On Rhetoric*, trans. G.A. Kennedy (New York: Oxford University Press, 1991), 14.

5. This is a paraphrase of Burke's definition: "The use of symbols to induce action in beings that normally communicate by symbols" [K. Burke, *A Rhetoric of Motives* (Berkeley, CA: University of California Press, 1950), 162].

6. "[S]peech in its essence is not neutral. Far from suspended judgment, the…speech of people is loaded with judgments. It is intensely moral – its names for objects contain the emotional overtones which give us cues as to how we should act toward these objects. Even a word like 'automobile' will usually contain a concealed choice (it designates not merely an *object*, but a *desirable object*). Spontaneous speech is not a naming at all, but a system of attitudes, of implicit exortations.… speech is profoundly *partisan*" [K. Burke, *Permanence and Change: an Anatomy of Purpose*, revised edn (Los Altos, CA: Hermes Publications, 1954), 176–7].

7. K. Burke, *Language as Symbolic Action* (Berkeley, CA: University of California Press, 1968), 45.

8. The authors of this book reject the idea that invitational rhetoric, which is believed by a small group of scholars to be an alternative to persuasive discourse, is somehow not suasory. Continuing to promote invitational rhetoric as such dangerously obfuscates the ways in which it, like any other form of discourse, necessarily entails and promotes particular biases.

9. J. Culler, *Ferdinand de Saussure* (Ithaca, NY: Cornell University Press, 1986), 15.

10. F. de Saussure, *Course in General Linguistics*, trans. R. Harris (Chicago, IL: Open Court, 1986), 15.

11. Saussure, 67.

12. Culler, 33.

13. Saussure, 70.

14. Quoted in D.S. Clarke, Jr, *Sources of Semiotic: Readings with Commentary from Antiquity to the Present* (Carbondale, IL: Southern Illinois University Press, 1990), 58.

15. Quoted in Clarke, 59.

16. Quoted in Clarke, 71.

17. Quoted in Clarke, 74.

18. M. Ribière, *Barthes: a Beginner's Guide* (London: Hodder & Stoughton, 2002), 1.

19. R. Barthes, *Elements of Semiology*, trans. A. Lavers and C. Smith (New York: Hill and Wang, 1967), 89.

20. One can never, as Barthes would say, arrive at a final signified.

21. Barthes, *Elements*, 50.

22. R. Barthes, *Image, Music, Text*, trans. S. Heath (New York: Hill and Wang, 1988), 40.

23. B. Brummett, *Rhetoric in Popular Culture* (Thousand Oaks, CA: Sage Publications, 2006), 34.

24. K. Burke, *The Philosophy of Literary Form: Studies in Symbolic Action* (Baton Rouge, LA; Louisiana State University Press, 1941), 20.

25. K. Burke, *Counter-Statement* (Los Altos, CA: Hermes Publications, 1931), 124.

26. Burke, *Counter-Statement*, 124.

27. Burke, *Counter-Statement*, 125.

28. C.R. Miller, Genre as Social Action, *Quarterly Journal of Speech* 1984, 70, 152.

29. T. Todorov, *The Fantastic: a Structural Approach to Literary Genre*, trans. R. Howard (Ithaca, NY: Cornell University Press, 1975), 14.

30. J. Feuer, Genre Study and Television, in *Channels of Discourse, Reassembled*, R.C. Allen (ed.), pp. 138–60 (Chapel Hill, NC: University of North Carolina Press, 1992), 140.

31. V. Propp, *Morphology of the Folktale*, 2nd edn (Austin, TX: University of Texas Press, 1968).

32. A.J. Greimas, *Structural Semantics: an Attempt at a Method* (Lincoln, NE: University of Nebraska Press, 1984).

33. S. Kozloff, Narrative Theory and Television, in *Channels of Discourse, Reassembled*, R.C. Allen (ed.), pp. 67–100 (Chapel Hill, NC: University of North Carolina Press, 1992).

34. G. Genette, *Narrative Discourse: an Essay in Method*, trans. J.E. Lewin (Ithaca, NY: Cornell University Press, 1980), 162.

35. M. Johnson, *The Meaning of the Body: Aesthetics and Human Understanding* (Chicago, IL: University of Chicago Press, 2007), 238.

36. Johnson, 11–12.

37. Johnson, 12.

38. B. Massumi, *Parables for the Virtual: Movement, Affect, Sensation* (Durham, NC: Duke University Press, 2002), 25–8.

39. S. Shaviro, *Post-Cinematic Affect* (Washington: 0-Books, 2010), 3.

40. B.M. Kennedy, *Deleuze and Cinema: the Aesthetics of Sensation* (Edinburgh: Edinburgh University Press, 2000), 114.

41. D. Hawhee, *Moving Bodies: Kenneth Burke at the Edges of Language* (Columbia, SC: University of South Carolina Press, 2009), 13.

42. This bias against aesthetic experience is largely inherited from Immanuel Kant. See Johnson, 211–18.

43. A.A. Berger, *Essentials of Mass Communication Theory* (Thousand Oaks, CA: Sage Publications, 1995), 81.

44. A.M.S. Barry, *Visual Intelligence: Perception, Image, and Manipulation in Visual Communication* (Albany, NY: State University of New York Press, 1997), 130.

45. In psychology, see M. Hemphill, A Note on Adult's Color-Emotion Associations, *Journal of Genetic Psychology* 1996, 157, 275–80, and K.W. Jacobs and J.F. Suess, Effects of Four Psychological Primary Colours on Anxiety State, *Perceptual and Motor Skills* 1975, 41, 207–10. In media studies, see B.H. Detenber, R.F. Simons, and J.E. Reiss, The Emotional Significance of Color in Television Presentations, *Media Psychology* 2000, 2, 331–55; M.-C. Lichtlé, The Effect of an Advertisement's Colour on Emotions Evoked by an Ad and Attitude Towards the Ad, *International Journal of Advertising* 2007, 26, 37–62; and P. Valdez and A. Mehrabian, Effects of Color on Emotions, *Journal of Broadcasting & Electronic Media* 1994, 42, 113–27.

46. Kennedy, 115.
47. R. Arnheim, *Art and Visual Perception: a Psychology of the Creative Eye*, The New Version (Berkeley: University of California Press, 1954), 368; see also Barry, 132.
48. Arnheim, 324.
49. Barry, 134.
50. Berger, 83.
51. C. Vernallis, *Experiencing the Music Video: Aesthetics and Cultural Context* (New York: Columbia University Press, 2004), 37.
52. Barry, 135–6.
53. J. Monaco, *How to Read a Film: the Art, Technology, Language, History, and Theory of Film and Media*, revised edn (New York: Oxford University Press, 1981), 179.

54. G.D. Webster and C.G. Weir, Emotional Responses to Music: Interactive Effects of Mode, Texture, and Tempo, *Motivation and Emotion* 2005, 29, 19–39.
55. K. Donnelly, *The Spectre of Sound: Music in Film and Television* (London: British Film Institute, 2005).
56. For an overview of this literature, see B.L. Ott and G. Dickinson, Visual Rhetoric as/and Critical Pedagogy, in *The SAGE Handbook of Rhetorical Studies*, A. Lunsford (ed.), pp. 391–405 (Los Angeles, CA: Sage, 2009).
57. Visual rhetoric scholars are beginning to consider media that include moving images, but historically the focus has been on stationary imagery and artifacts.
58. C. Lévi-Strauss, *Structural Anthropology*, trans. C. Jacobson and B. Grundfest Schopf (New York: Basic Books, 1963), 33.

6 Cultural Analysis

KEY CONCEPTS

AMERICAN DREAM
ASSIMILATION
CONSPICUOUS CONSUMPTION
CULTURAL STUDIES
CULTURE
DIFFERENCE
DOXA

EXCLUSION
EXOTICISM
HEGEMONY
IDEOLOGY
INTERPELLATION
MYTH

OTHERING
STEREOTYPING
STRUCTURE OF FEELING
TOKEN

Despite the mountains of praise heaped upon the film for its groundbreaking forays into 3D technology, James Cameron's *Avatar* quickly became the target of considerable criticism from many different social and political groups after its world premiere in December 2009. Almost everyone appeared to find something offensive about the film's sci-fi narrative, which follows US Marine Jake Sully (Sam Worthington) in his attempts to stop business interests from conquering Pandora, the alien home world of a tribalistic race called the Na'vi.[1] Conservatives blasted the film's rather blunt criticism of economic development and military aggression, as well as its promotion of traditionally liberal concerns like environmental awareness and ethnic diversity. Many liberals, however, bristled at *Avatar*'s depiction of race relations, aligning it with films like *Dances With Wolves* (1990) or *The Last Samurai* (2003) in its portrayal of a white man "saving" an outflanked ethnic group by assimilating into their culture and leading them in battle. A number of feminists criticized the film for its depiction of gender roles, especially when Neytiri, the otherwise independent and strong Na'vi warrior princess, falls in love with Sully and convinces the Na'vi to follow him. Some Christian critics suggested that the film blasphemously promotes the pagan worship of nature over monotheism. One public health group even criticized *Avatar* for endorsing cigarettes.

Critical Media Studies: An Introduction, Second Edition. Brian L. Ott and Robert L. Mack.
© 2014 John Wiley & Sons, Inc. Published 2014 by John Wiley & Sons, Inc.

Behind each of these criticisms lies a basic assumption: *Avatar*'s portrayal of political, social, or religious issues would in turn shape the way that its audiences would perceive these issues in the larger world. In many ways these worries lend credence to the work of scholars who take a cultural or ideological approach to media texts. Scholars in this strand of media studies seek to understand how media texts influence the way we think about the world as political and social beings. Currently described by the scholarly umbrella term Cultural studies, cultural and ideological critics claim that media texts like television shows or newspapers, far from merely reflecting the world around us, always represent a skewed or partial vision of society in relation to class, race, gender, sexuality, age, disability, and a host of other social constructs. In essence, media texts tend to represent particular perspectives on the world and society at the cost of excluding other views, and the worldviews represented in the media are often those of socially powerful or privileged groups.

This chapter begins with a discussion over theories of culture and ideology, concentrating on how the ideologies of any given culture work to normalize and privilege certain perspectives on reality. We then briefly outline the historical development of the British Cultural studies tradition as a way of understanding the political underpinnings of Cultural studies scholarship. Finally, we consider how ideologies influence the construction of media texts in relation to two historically relevant social issues in the Cultural studies tradition: class and race.

Cultural Theory: an Overview

As a way of understanding social organization, **culture** can be a problematic term. Scholars disagree over the best way to conceptualize or understand the issue of culture. In mulling over the idea of culture, sociologist Michael Richardson provides this possible definition: "Culture is simply what human beings produce and the means by which we preserve what we have produced."[2] This definition provides a good foundation for understanding culture: that it is constructed, multifaceted, and uniquely human. However, it is helpful in formulating a specific definition of culture to consider the key ingredients or aspects that make a culture known. The "building blocks" of culture fall into roughly three forms physical, social and attitudinal:

1. The first form of culture is *physical*. Picture a society thousands of years in the future attempting to study and gain knowledge about our current culture. How might they understand us better? The most obvious way would be through the physical objects that we leave behind for them to find, called artifacts. Artifacts are any of the material aspects of daily life that possess widely shared meanings and manifest group (national, social, political) identification to us. Artifacts include clothing, music, television shows, automobiles, computers, comic books, billboards, carnival rides, space shuttles, and more; virtually any manufactured item that you can point to (including this textbook) is an example of an artifact. An artifact is a material, human-made object of a culture.

2. The next form of culture is *social*. After collecting and analyzing our artifacts, the futuristic society studying us will attempt to decipher the social codes and rules that governed the creation of those artifacts. They will attempt to reconstruct the practices or customs of our daily lives, the habitual performances of our particular social conventions. If they found this textbook, for example, they might assume that reading, learning, and critiquing were all social practices of ancient American culture. Similarly, they might formulate some ideas about our hygienic customs if they were to discover any one of the wide assortment of tools related to personal upkeep: toothbrushes, blow dryers, contact lens cases, etc. If artifacts are the products of our shared lives, then customs are our shared, lived experiences: eating, working, dancing, mourning, sex, exercise regimens, driving laws, power hours, etc.

3. The final form of culture is *attitudinal*. Our customs, laws, and traditions reflect particular ways of understanding the world. To continue with our futuristic society example, scholars of the next millennium might piece together enough artifacts to discover that we as Americans tended to support the notion of free speech or the concepts of individualism and personal responsibility. They might find documents with the acronym PLUR, describing the beliefs and attitudes expressed by members of modern rave culture: Peace, Love, Unity, and Respect. In essence, attitudes display the overarching ways a particular culture makes sense of the world and itself, including values, tastes, concepts of right and wrong, religious systems, economic beliefs, or political philosophies.

Now that we have some understanding regarding what constitutes culture, we can begin to pick out some of the common qualities that define culture. First, culture is *collective*. While individuals may be a part of a particular culture, they can never inhabit a culture on their own. Culture must be shared among a group of people. However, it is important to remember that a cultural group in itself may be as large as a nation or as small as a fandom of a syndicated television show. Computer hackers constitute a distinct cultural group; only individuals who participate in hacking know about the artifacts, practices, and attitudes that make up the distinct culture of hackers. Therefore, while culture must be shared among a group of people, it also by definition does not include everyone. Society is always a collection of cultures and co- or subcultures (cultural groups that exist within larger cultural groups), and all individuals will be members of multiple cultural groups at one time.

Second, culture is *rhetorical*. Culture functions symbolically (see Chapter 4). Possessing culture is not natural or inherent to our biology as human beings, but rather a result of our shared symbol systems that allow us to communicate meaning to one another. This means that a culture is sustained and transmitted exclusively through the words and images that carry significance for members of the culture. The artifacts of a particular culture only have significance because members of the culture can *name* them, and the customs or attitudes of a cultural group can only be meaningful because that can be *described* as such. For instance, the report card is a powerful artifact in the culture of American education, but its power only comes from the rhetorical, symbolic aspect of our national culture. There is nothing intrinsically powerful or threatening about a piece of paper with markings on it, and there is nothing that requires an A to mean "outstanding" and an F to mean "failure." Instead, we as a culture have symbolically and rhetorically agreed upon the meaning of the report card.

Third, culture is *historical*. It changes, evolves, mutates, fades, and even disappears over time. Like everything else, culture is subject to the whims and shifts of history. Some cultures have existed for millennia in different forms (Greco–Roman culture, Jewish culture, etc.), and some appear and vanish in a matter of years. A good example of this type of sudden cultural ascent and decline is the Club Kids phenomenon of the 1980s and 1990s. The Club Kids were a subculture within the New York party and nightlife scene of the time. The group dressed in wildly outrageous and androgynous costumes, experimented with a number of drugs, and promoted hedonistic philosophies of life. Although at times club owners paid the group to show up and promote specific venues, they were really a culture unto themselves, oftentimes throwing spontaneous parties in public places throughout New York. The Club Kids culture began to decline in the 1990s, and they are all but non-existent today. They stand as a stark example of how cultures can suddenly form and dissipate depending on the historical moment.

Finally, and perhaps most important to our present discussion, culture is *ideological*. The cultures we inhabit teach us to see the world in some ways and not in others. The attitudes, practices, and artifacts of our everyday lives encourage us as individuals to interpret the world according to certain frameworks of culturally based knowledge. French discourse scholar Michel Foucault provides a stark example of how culture functions to direct our attention in his work on madness.[3] The majority of cultures in Renaissance Europe did not perceive madness as problematic. It existed as a constant in daily life, a factor as unpreventable and prevalent as death. Foucault cites various historical examples and texts, including celebratory "Feasts of Fools" and the works of Shakespeare, to show how madness was intrinsically tied into the cultural fabric of the time. However, the seventeenth century saw the rise of sanitariums and other confinement houses in Europe, and these institutions were responsible for removing undesirable individuals from everyday life: the poor, the indecent, and the mad. The common denominator among all of these groups was their inability to contribute to the newly emerging process of economic production and consumption that marked Europe during the time. Thus, the widespread "lock up" of these individuals "concerns not the relations between madness and illness, but the relations between society and itself, between society and what it recognized and did not recognize in the behavior of individuals."[4] We can see from Foucault's example that the structure of a culture directs its inhabitants to perceive the world in a given way. Although there is always room for individual interpretation, ideology is a powerful and distinct force of interpretation in every culture.

Overall, culture can be described as the collection of artifacts, practices, and beliefs of a particular group of people at a particular historical moment, supported by symbolic systems and directed by ideology. This understanding of culture in general, and ideology in particular, is important for media scholars who see mass media texts like magazines or news programs as a central component in the dissemination of a given culture's ideologies. These scholars analyze media texts to better understand the ideologies that inform their creation, and they hope to better conceptualize how the attitudes and beliefs of a culture find their way into the media we consume every day. Before turning our attention to the specific work of ideological media analysis, however, it is important that we have a better understanding about the role and scope of ideology in contemporary society.

The Functions of Ideology

We already know that cultures give rise to ideologies and that ideologies influence how individual members of the culture see the world, but we still need to understand the subtle ways that ideology accomplishes this directed attention. Remember, an **ideology** is a system of ideas that unconsciously shapes and constrains both our beliefs and behaviors. The way that we unconsciously define the world around us, the explanations about the world that we take for granted, and the unquestioned beliefs that we hold are all the result in some way of our cultural ideologies. The four ways that ideology structures our social world are through limitation, normalization, privileging, and interpellation.

First, a given ideology *limits* the range of acceptable ideas that a person may consider within a particular cultural context. It promotes and legitimates certain perspectives and values while obscuring or devaluing others. This "blinding" function is easy to spot in certain ideologies when the interpretations they promote are regularly identified as biased or one-sided. Republicans and Democrats, for example, both possess ideologies that are made highly visible by the existence of the other party. Each party nevertheless functions as a culture with particular artifacts, customs, and attitudes, providing its members with an ideology that limits interpretation and helps those individuals distinguish between right and wrong, true and false, good and bad.

Some ideologies, however, limit our interpretation of the world in a more unconscious fashion, and we enact or support them often without realizing it. These are ideologies that have become so ingrained in our minds and everyday lived experiences that we fail to notice their influence as ideological. A good example of this kind of unconscious ideology concerns biological sex in contemporary American society. In America we tend to understand the concept of sex according to one of two groups: male or female. The reality, of course, is that the human form can often display physical characteristics of both sexes, leading to a condition known as *intersexuality* (a term that has replaced the more archaic *hermaphrodite*). Intersexuality is more common than most people realize. Approximately one in every 2,000 children is born with sexually ambiguous genitalia,[5] compared to only one in 17,000 born with albinism.[6] Despite the relatively common occurrence of this condition, sexual ideologies in our culture and media erase the presence of intersexuality from everyday thought in many ways. Public restrooms are assigned according to male and female sexes, as are clothing departments in retail stores. The categories for Oscars, Emmys, and other sanctioned media awards are typically divided on the basis of sex. It would be difficult to pick out even one major intersexed character in the history of American television. The two-sex system becomes even more visibly constructed when compared to the complex fabric of Indian society, where the culture recognizes a valid third sex called the Hijra. The Hijra are an assembly of eunuchs, intersexuals, transsexuals, and others that the society understands as neither male nor female. With this knowledge, then, we can see how ideology subtly directs our attention toward perceiving sexuality and biology in America from a certain perspective. We only think about intersexuality and sexual ideologies when we are consciously confronted with the ideas. It is this unconscious form of ideology and the ways it structures our perception that will be the primary focus of the rest of this chapter.

By limiting the possible perceptions or interpretations of the world, ideology also *normalizes* certain aspects of it. This process of defining normalcy is especially important in the realm of social relations. Ideology often makes social relations and arrangements between individuals seem normal, and it makes established relationships of power appear to be the natural order of things. For example, you are probably reading this chapter right now because your instructor assigned it as homework. Your resulting responsibility as a student is to read the chapter and absorb the information for class discussion or tests. Have you ever stopped to question where this student/teacher relationship comes from? Why does the teacher have more authority than you do in your own education? The social roles that we occupy throughout our lifetime, like *child*, *student*, or *employee*, place us into relationships of unequal power as a result of ideological value hierarchies. All social relations are inherently relations of power because all social relations exist in a web of ideologies which award power to certain roles. Your instructor has power, or "the ability to control events and meanings,"[7] only because American cultural ideology often awards authority to highly educated experts in a given field.

The distribution of power in accordance with ideology extends well beyond the college classroom. The ideology of American capitalism, for example, ensures that employers have power over their employees, and this relationship between owner and worker seems to be a natural part of everyday life instead of a culturally constructed system. In some cultures older individuals wield a great deal of power as revered elders, but in American society elderly individuals are often thought of (and therefore treated) as helpless, feeble, or "a drain on the system." Power is, then, inextricably tied up with the ideological constructs of a particular culture. At times relationships of power can be beneficial (after all, you *are* receiving an education even if your instructor has the power), but they are never *natural*. Ideology normalizes these relationships of power and their control over individuals.

This unequal distribution of power between social actors explains one of the most important aspects of ideology: ideology *privileges* some interests over others. In the process of normalizing relations of power, it also informally confirms that the perspectives, qualities, or needs of socially powerful groups are more important or valid than those of socially dominated groups. The capitalist economic and ideological structure of American business culture is full of examples of this distinction. Although employees tend to do much of the actual work in a capitalist business, it is the more socially powerful management and owners that reap the most profits generated from the work. Likewise, most businesses in America favor managerial styles that emphasize masculine qualities like assertiveness, independence, or competitiveness, a fact that helps men move up through a company and often creates difficult situations for women seeking promotion. Outside of business culture, a hotly debated example of power and privilege now is the issue of marriage. As a result of American religious and political ideologies, the institution of marriage as of this writing generally reflects the needs and interests of (socially powerful) heterosexual couples to the detriment of (socially powerless) homosexual couples.

It may seem at this point that ideology permeates every aspect of a culture, fashioning the limits of knowledge and influencing power structures at every level of social organization. This seemingly overarching quality of ideology is central to Louis Althusser's concept of **interpellation**, the fourth function of ideology. Althusser was an Algerian Marxist interested in the ways that ideology controls individuals. He claims that ideology is so infused into the social structure that it actually serves as the force to interpellate us, or the force that calls us into existence as social subjects.[8] Individuals, far from being unique or original, are actually a collection of different ideological systems fused into one identity through the process of "hailing." Hailing occurs when individuals recognize and respond to an encountered ideology and allow it to represent them. Althusser also posits that because culture and ideology necessarily predate the individual, individuals are "always already interpellated."

In order to make the process of interpellation clearer, consider the following questions: At what age do you remember recognizing your particular gender identity? Chances are that before you even consciously took up that identity, your parents had already given you toys, surrounded you with colors, or played with you in ways that communicated the norms or limits of that identity to you. Each of these moments constituted a hailing, or a moment of exchange where you recognized the existence of a way of understanding yourself and responded to it, allowing it to define or constitute you in the process. The process of forming identity is a process of ideological recognition. For Althusser, ideologies exhibit the range of possible identity expressions, and individuals are a collection of the ideologies to which they consciously or unconsciously ascribe. Ideological discourse not only speaks to us, it creates the *us*.

Althusser's assertion that individuals are caught in a web of ideologies from which they draw their individual identities is an interesting perspective on the role of ideology in society, but it also importantly confirms the existence of multiple ideologies circulating throughout a culture. Remember, ideology is an aspect of every culture, and even relatively small subcultures can have powerful ideologies (one only needs to look at historical cults like Heaven's Gate or Jonestown to confirm this point). It should also be clear, however, that not all ideologies carry the same weight on a widespread scale, and we can see that some are more present than others in the minds of most people. The aforementioned concepts of social power and privilege hint at the reason for this imbalance, but something else explains the supremacy of certain ideologies in American culture. It is to these ideas that we turn our attention now.

Ideological Processes: Myth, Doxa, and Hegemony

A number of theories explain how certain ideologies within a culture become widespread, common, or dominant. This section will focus on three interrelated concepts: Roland Barthes's *myth*, Pierre Bourdieu's *doxa*, and Antonio Gramsci's *hegemony*. Although myth and doxa both shed light on how ideology works, hegemony has gained a certain theoretical dominance within the field of ideological analysis. As a result, the majority of this section will focus on ideas surrounding hegemony, and hegemony will be a central theme throughout the rest of the chapter.

In his book *Mythologies*, Barthes outlines a theory of ideological dominance based on the notion of myth.[9] A **myth** is a sacred story or "type of speech" that reaffirms and reproduces ideology in relation to an object. *Mythologies* itself is a collection of essays in which Barthes identifies a variety of cultural objects (toys, soap advertisements, etc.) and investigates them for their mythological components, or "higher" levels of meaning that augment the objects' basic meanings. At some basic level, for example, the video game *Super Mario Bros.* literally means "a video game named *Super Mario Bros.*," but a mythic analysis would investigate the game's larger, culturally connoted meanings. In addition to signifying "video game," *Super Mario Bros.* also relates a classic story of a hero undertaking a voyage to rescue a princess from an evil captor. In this way, the mythological or "higher-level" meaning of the game connotes ideas of bravery, heroism, and masculinity that are central to American ideological formations. The game reinforces certain ideologies above others by making their mythological content seem innocent, everyday, or "natural." Barthes claims that cultural myths normalize the ideologies of the ruling or socially privileged groups and reinforce power differentials between classes.

Another useful concept for exploring the workings of ideology is doxa. According to Bourdieu, **doxa** represents knowledge "which is beyond question and which each agent tacitly accords by the mere fact of acting in accord with social convention."[10] In other words, doxa refers to any constructed aspects of a culture that its members do not really challenge or critically reflect upon. A good synonym for doxa is "common sense." Like myth, doxa supports certain ideologies over others by making them seem natural or simply as "the way things are." Bourdieu, like Barthes, views doxa as intrinsically tied to the ideologies of socially dominant groups. Those with social power wish to preserve the cultural doxa, while those without power seek to resist or alter it.

It is important to realize that expressing a minority opinion is not the same as resisting the "common-sense" ideologies present in doxa, for in many ways doxa is outside the realm of opinion altogether (see Figure 6.1). Consider the process of watching a popular movie at a theater with your friends. The members of your group may disagree over the relative merit of the film, but none of you would be likely to

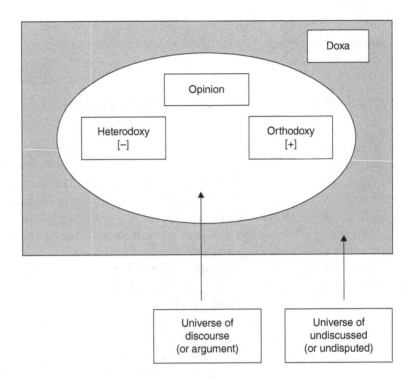

Figure 6.1 Bourdieu's doxa, orthodoxy, heterodoxy.

question why you had to pay to see the film in the first place. The discussion between your friends over their opinion of the film is a part of what Bourdieu calls "the universe of discourse," made up of all of the issues that may be formally agreed upon (othrodoxy) or debated (heterodoxy) in a given society. The process of handing your money over to the theater to gain admittance, however, is a part of the doxa, or "the universe of undiscussed," made up of social rules and processes that go unnoticed and unquestioned. Paying to see the film supports capitalist ideology and reaffirms its "common sense" validity in our cultural context.

Although myth and doxa both lend valuable insight into why certain ideologies are more widespread than others, the concept of hegemony is especially important because it accounts for the *evolution* of dominant ideologies. First proposed by Italian Marxist Antonio Gramsci in the 1920s and 1930s, the concept of hegemony is key in understanding the ascension and persistence of dominant ideologies. **Hegemony** is the process by which one ideology subverts other, competing ideologies and gains cultural dominance through the won consent of the governed (or dominated). Gramsci developed his theory of hegemony to address some of the shortcomings of Marxism. Recall the basic structure of Marxist theory from Chapter 2. Marx believed that ideology was a byproduct of the economic system in any culture, at most a reflection of bourgeois interests used to trick the working class into a false consciousness. He asserted that over time the large working class would recognize this ideological trick and overthrow the relatively small owning class. When this revolution did not occur, Gramsci proposed his theory of hegemony as an explanation for its absence.

An essential function of hegemony involves convincing people to support the existence of a social system that does not support them in return. Marginalized groups do not often protest or revolt against ideologies that overwhelmingly support privileged groups because, on some level, they consent to being dominated. This statement prompts an immediate question: Why would anyone consent to such an arrangement? While dominant ideologies may reflect the desires and interests of socially powerful groups, for these ideologies to *remain* dominant (or hegemonic), they must also feature an additional promise: It is in the best interest of marginalized groups to accept these beliefs as well. Put another way, members of socially powerful groups act to have their worldview accepted as the universal way of thinking, and members outside of these groups come to accept some of these ideologies because they appear beneficial in some way. Gramsci refers to this process as one of "'spontaneous' consent" because it is typically informal or unnoticed.[11]

The best way to understand the spontaneous consent of hegemony is through an example. A number of ideological components within American higher education are not in the best interests of students. One dominant belief, for instance, suggests that college students should pay for their own education, a norm that certainly does not benefit them financially as individuals. Another widespread belief suggests that instructors have the right to influence public perception of students' intellectual ability in the form of assigned grades, a norm that certainly does not benefit most of them socially as individuals. Despite these factors, students still dutifully fork over thousands of dollars in tuition each semester and show up to class with the hopes of getting an A. Why? They consent to these beliefs because other aspects of this belief system promise that it is ultimately in their best interest to do so. Securing a college degree in many ways promises a higher professional pay grade. A system of letter grades promises social prestige to those who achieve high marks. Although presidents, deans, and professors will probably gain more financial and social rewards from the norms of this system than any individual undergraduate, the "spontaneous" consent of the student body ensures that the ideology survives as the norm.

When such consent fails, however, the concept of hegemony also explains how dominant ideologies evolve to contain this failure through a process of flexible appropriation. In such a situation, it is likely that dominant cultural institutions will absorb any challenging beliefs, integrate them into the hegemonic matrix, and re-establish the previous norm. A number of classic studies in the field provide examples of this process. In *Subculture: the Meaning of Style*, for instance, Dick Hebdige looks at the subculture of British punks in the 1980s.[12] The punk movement's emphasis on anarchy and gratification represented a challenge to the hegemonic British ideologies of governance and order. As the punk movement increased in popularity and visibility, they became more of a threat to the traditional, ideological British "way of life." In order to circumvent this threat, dominant institutions in Britain began to absorb punk life into the existing system of hegemonic beliefs. Retail shops began to sell punk clothing, and newspapers began running stories on punks and their families. By integrating the punk movement into dominant economic and cultural systems, the British hegemonic structures sanitized the punk movement and greatly diminished its challenge. "Punk" was, in a sense, absorbed and put in the service of hegemonic ideologies of capitalism and family.

As a result of this function, hegemonic systems never go away. They simply change form through a process of constant give and take between social groups. John Fiske's discussion of jeans is a good example of the regular back and forth struggle that characterizes hegemony.[13] Wearing blue jeans in the 1960s was a sign of opposition to the dominant American culture. As the popularity of such resistance began to take hold, however, retailers responded by creating an elaborate system of different mass-produced styles and designer labels for jeans. Jeans became mainstream and normal. In response, many individuals began to intentionally rip and disfigure their jeans in an attempt to distinguish themselves from the newly established normalcy. Retailers in turn began to fade and destroy their jeans on a large scale. In this way, hegemonic ideological structures maintain control in part through the never-ending process of integration and appropriation of marginalized ideologies.

Overall, the concepts of myth, doxa, and hegemony explain a great deal about the ideologies and power structures of a given culture. Myth is the preservation of ideology through the active retelling of dominant cultural stories. Doxa is the preservation of ideology through silence and maintaining the distinction between what can and cannot be debated. Hegemony is the preservation of ideology through won consent and flexible adaptation toward resistance. For media scholars interested in issues of culture, the concept of ideology helps to explain the structures and themes of a culture's media texts, and the concept of hegemony helps to explain the presence of certain ideologies over others. Scholars do this type of media analysis under the academic banner of **Cultural studies**, an umbrella term for a wide variety of scholarship concerned with culture, ideology, privilege, and oppression. The Cultural studies tradition is relatively new in comparison to other media studies approaches, and it represents an important area in the contemporary discipline of media studies.

Cultural Studies: History, Theory, and Methodology

In a sense, the academic discipline of Cultural studies has two histories. The actual or literal discipline can be traced to 1964 with the founding of the Centre for Contemporary Cultural Studies at the University of Birmingham in the UK. However, the theoretical or conceptual history of Cultural studies actually begins in the early twentieth century. The formation of Cultural studies as a scholarly perspective was in many ways a response to previous conceptions of "culture" as the exclusive realm of the upper class. Based on the works of literary/cultural critics like Matthew Arnold and F.R. Leavis, many academics in Britain at this time limited the definition of "culture" to the best aesthetic products and traditions of contemporary society. In essence, artistic products like operas, high art, and literary classics could be considered culture within this framework. Horse races, quilted blankets, and cartoons could not.

Leavis endorsed literature as an especially important aspect of culture because he believed that great literary works preserved essential moral qualities of a bygone era in British history. Popular fiction, as his wife and fellow scholar Q.D. Leavis characterized it, was "not only formed to convey merely crude states of mind but it [was] destructive of any fineness."[14] From the Leavises' perspective, it was the duty of intellectuals and academics to uphold the legacy of "cultured" literature in order to maintain moral standards in an increasingly industrialized, mediated society like Britain in the 1920s and 1930s. Thus, we can see that defining culture was more than just an arbitrary distinction of aesthetics for these thinkers. Limiting the academic definition of culture was also a political attempt to combat the perceived ills of increased exposure to a popular mediated system that engaged "the unruly desires and immorality of the masses."[15]

Reflecting on this academic movement (widely referred to as Leavisism), we can see that it clearly drew elitist distinctions between culture and mass society along class lines. "Culture" here referred exclusively to the aesthetic forms most accessible to educated or wealthy individuals in society, and "mass society" referred to the activities and products of the lower or working classes. This division held academic sway until the publication of Richard Hoggart's *The Uses of Literacy* in 1958, which disrupted the link between the notion of "culture" and upper-class pursuits.[16] Drawing on his personal experiences as a youth in the British working class, Hoggart outlines a detailed account of working-class culture and its norms in relation to family relationships, neighborhood structures, religious belief, and more. In this way, *Uses* departs from Leavisism by making a claim for the importance of working-class cultural norms, pointing out that issues of morality are not exclusive to the upper class. However, the second half of the book engages in a decidedly Leavisist criticism of mass culture like popular music and "sex-and-violence novels," which Hoggart sees as a threat to the working-class way of life. In retrospect, although Hoggart's work importantly expanded ideas of morality to working-class culture, it also continued the Leavisist tradition by affirming the perceived dangers of popular culture.

Though Hoggart began to break the notion of culture free from its Leavisist roots, the most important scholar in laying the theoretical groundwork for the distinct discipline of Cultural studies is Raymond Williams. The publication of his book *The Long Revolution* in 1961 marked an important turn in the understanding of culture. In it, Williams recognizes the importance of viewing culture from ideal (Leavisist) and documentary (anthropological) standpoints, but he also proposes a third, social definition: "Culture is a description of a particular way of life, which expresses certain meanings and values not only in art and learning but also in institutions and ordinary behavior."[17] For Williams, no analysis of culture is complete without looking at all three of these dimensions. Moreover, this newly proposed social definition extends the idea of culture to include virtually all aspects of contemporary society, considering both high art *and* pop art, literature *and* comics to be important expressions of a particular culture at a particular moment in history. Williams also claims that every culture is governed by a structure of feeling. A **structure of feeling** is the sum of the subtle and nuanced aspects of a historical culture, those aspects not obviously or completely captured in the artifacts of a society. Williams claims that the contours of this structure become most apparent in intergenerational social exchanges or discussions about one's own culture with members of another culture. In many ways, the structure of feeling is intimately related to the aforementioned concepts of myth, doxa, and hegemony.

In expanding the notion of culture to include aspects of everyday pursuits, Williams opened the door for the academic study of mass culture products and institutions. A few years after the publication of *The Long Revolution*, a collective of British academics established the Centre for Contemporary Cultural Studies to study popular culture with special focus on ideological components of the mass media. Stuart Hall, who served as the head of the Centre from 1969 to 1979, wrote an essay entitled "Cultural Studies: Two Paradigms" in 1980 that many consider to be a crucial outlining of the institutionalized Cultural studies approach.[18] The two paradigms indicated in his title are culturalism (work in the tradition of Hoggart and Williams which scrutinizes particular beliefs and activities of individuals in a given culture) and structuralism (work derived from Marx and anthropologist Claude Lévi-Strauss which looks at how social systems limit the activities of individuals through ideology). Hall claims that contemporary Cultural studies brings together the best aspects of each tradition, and that the traditions "pose, together, the problems consequent on trying to think *both* the specificity of different practices and the forms of the articulated unity they constitute."[19]

While Hall appears to give a balanced approach to both paradigms on the surface of the essay, however, some scholars point out that his true scholarly commitments lie more closely with the structuralist focus on ideology.[20] Thus, although the culturalist focus on the meanings made by particular individuals within a culture importantly paved the way for Cultural studies' attention to popular texts, the structuralist concepts of ideology, power, privilege, and oppression have become the primary theoretical hallmarks of the contemporary Cultural studies approach. The culturalist focus has been largely absorbed into an approach based on the ethnographic study of audiences, addressed in Chapter 10 of this book.

This structuralist lens has shaped the Cultural studies discipline across five methodological motifs. First, Cultural studies is *interdisciplinary*. As a method of textual criticism, Cultural studies appropriates and combines theoretical tools from many different fields to assemble a new approach specifically designed to address the text in question. Second, Cultural studies is *pragmatic*. The ideal criticism of texts from a Cultural studies perspective should be practical in nature, toward a specific end, and understandable to a wide variety of people. This practicality is closely related to the third aspect of Cultural studies: it is *political*. Cultural studies scholarship seeks not only to identify particular ideologies, but also to challenge and alter their effects on systems of social (in)equality. Fourth, Cultural studies is *self-reflexive*. Cultural studies scholars adopt a critical awareness of their own social locations and the implications of that positioning. In other words, work within Cultural studies is often hyper-aware of its own socio-political biases, and scholars often acknowledge these limitations within their writing. Finally, Cultural studies is culturally and historically *contingent*. Textual criticism from this perspective is always tied to particular social systems at particular moments in time. Jenkins, McPherson, and Shattuc refer to this dual quality as Cultural studies' commitment to "contextualism" and "situationalism," respectively.[21]

With these five themes as a guiding framework, the remainder of this chapter will look at ideologies of class and race in American media to provide an in-depth understanding of the type of work that constitutes a Cultural studies approach. This decision is purposeful. Issues of class were intimately involved in the historical evolution of British Cultural studies (both in the gradual displacement of "culture" from the upper class and in the Marxist underpinnings of structuralism), and notions of race provided an early and important historical focus to the budding discipline. However, it is important to keep in mind that issues of ideology and power are applicable to the investigation of any social construct in a text: class, race, gender, age, sexuality, disability, etc. To extend the same amount of attention to each of these is beyond the scope of an introductory chapter to Cultural studies, but we address the relationships of some of these constructs to power in Chapters 8 and 9.

Ideology and Media Representations of Class

Cultural studies scholars interested in ideological issues of class look at the ways in which popular media texts communicate, justify, and maintain disproportionate socio-economic status divisions. They also do the reverse, utilizing notions of class to understand the particular structures and effects of media texts. Overall, these scholars analyze the interplay between popular media texts and hegemonic ideologies of class that convince individuals that capitalism and class standing are "natural" forms of social existence.

Social class basically refers to the division of society into the "haves" and the "have-nots." You may already be familiar with many of the more specific ways to discuss class, including the divisions of upper, middle, and lower class, hybrids like upper middle class, and even phrases like "working class" or "working poor." Marx, the pre-eminent theorist of social class, originally divided capitalist society into three major classes: the *bourgeoisie*, or large-business owners who control the means of production; the *proletariat*, or blue-collar workers who sell their labor to the owners; and the *petite bourgeoisie*, or small-business owners and white-collar professionals (doctors, lawyers, etc.) who represent a minority middle class. However, he also envisioned that capitalist societies evolve according to changing social relations. As such, what we now have in American society is a class system reminiscent of Marx's original divisions with two important differences.

The first difference is in the size of the petite bourgeoisie. Unlike in Marx's time, when the petite bourgeoisie or middle class encompassed a relatively small number of professionals, the middle class now represents the largest class division in American society. This growth of the middle class (and relative shrinking of the upper bourgeoisie and lower proletariat classes) is intrinsically tied to the second important deviation from Marx: the rise of information- and media-based occupations in the twentieth century. As computers and technology industries have increased in scope and popularity in the last 50 years, the demand for knowledge-based positions like technicians and programmers has increased as well. This signifies a shift away from a Marxist economy focused on material production toward one focused on mediated information dissemination. Such a shift influenced class distinctions in a number of ways. Newly created white-collar jobs increased the size of the middle class, and ownership became increasingly focused on the *cultural* production of lifestyles and leisure. As you might guess from the ideas discussed thus far in this chapter, the production of culture in these media industries also means the production and reification of ideologies.

Media outlets like television, film, and newspapers consistently impart two important understandings of class in America. On one hand, the American public is bombarded with images that communicate clear class distinctions. Many programs on the Bravo television network, for example, including *The Rachel Zoe Project*, *The Millionaire Matchmaker*, *Million Dollar Listing*, and the various *Real Housewives* incarnations, introduce viewers to the worlds of wealthy and famous Americans. These shows reveal a sharp disparity between the lifestyles of their economically advantaged subjects and the experiences of their largely middle- to lower-class audiences. On the other hand, the media also regularly suggest that all these class distinctions are permeable. Some of the appeal of the above programs may be attributed to the fact that their central personalities, including stylist Rachel Zoe and matchmaker Patti Stanger, appear to have overcome their middle-class childhoods to join the ranks of the economically elite. Films like *Pretty Woman* (1990) and *The Pursuit of Happyness* (2006) also champion the idea that one can transcend class distinctions under the right circumstances.

Two ideologies of class, in turn, help to explain the presence of these messages in American media. The first is the **American Dream**, or the idea that a person's level of success is directly related to the amount of effort or drive they put forth in attaining that goal. The American Dream is one of the most prevalent hegemonic ideologies in American media texts. There is large-scale consent to the American Dream because it promises people a definite avenue toward success and happiness. It boils down all of the complications of modern life into a simple equation (hard work = success), and it symbolically erases real issues of social inequality, class struggle, profit-motive, and others that may provide barriers toward success. In reality, adhering to the American Dream probably does more to transform individuals into compliant workers for capitalist owners than it does to actually elevate their personal socio-economic statuses, but this fact is difficult to see because of hegemonic qualities which veil the interests of the upper class inherent to the ideology. In addition, the repetition of the American Dream over and over in media images like *Pretty Woman* and *The Pursuit of Happyness* helps to solidify the Dream as truth in the popular consciousness.

One of the more celebrated media images in the ideological web of the American Dream is the token. A **token** is an exception to a social rule that affirms the correctness of an ideology. In this case, a token is an individual who has actually fulfilled the promise of the Dream and broken into the upper class based on personal initiative. Although they are exceptions rather than the norm, tokens often gain high visibility within the media because they lend a sense of legitimacy to the American Dream ideology. "If I can succeed," the token says, "then anyone can." Oprah Winfrey and Bill Gates are good examples of tokens regularly discussed in the media; both built vast empires of wealth from fairly meager economic beginnings. Of course, media outlets do not also address the millions of other individuals who do not ever transcend their class despite their personal effort and hard work. In this way, highly visible media tokens symbolically erase the presence of systemic realities that arise from class ideologies.

It should be obvious, however, that the American Dream is not beyond reproach. Even within the media we have films like *Born on the Fourth of July* (1989) that scathingly critique the ideology. Therefore, there must be other ideologies of class that function to hegemonically maintain the status quo. The second important ideology to understand in relation to the media is Thorstein Veblen's idea of conspicuous consumption.[22] **Conspicuous consumption** is the belief that one can attain membership in the "upper class" through the purchase of material goods and services. When people refer to houses as status symbols or express a need to "keep up with the Joneses," they are hinting at this belief. People often consent to the doctrine of conspicuous consumption because it allows them to feel as if they have succeeded in life as a result of owning nice objects. In truth, individuals who believe they have "made it" because of their consumption practices often move only slightly up the scale of the large American middle class. While their lifestyles may appear luxurious compared to viewers' own, for example, most of the individuals featured in *The Real Housewives* series are really members of the upper middle class. As such, the ideology of conspicuous consumption works hegemonically to blind the majority of Americans from realizing what *real* upper-class wealth actually looks like. This concealment in turn works to solidify class distinctions.

Media advertising thrives on the notion of conspicuous consumption and is a primary support system for this ideology. In her book *Born to Buy*, Juliet B. Schor claims that Americans are becoming the target of advertising at increasingly younger ages. "Children," she writes, "have become conduits from the consumer marketplace into the household, the link between advertisers and the family purse."[23] Advertising literally does the work of conspicuous consumption. Its duty is to manufacture desires for products and services within the general public under the guise of consumer choice. As a result of multi-billion-dollar advertising companies, then, ideas of conspicuous consumption are deeply ingrained into the American public from birth and register as the natural or normal consequence of competition and taste.

In sum, the dual ideologies of the American Dream and conspicuous consumption work via media texts to solidify current class divisions in America even while such boundaries appear to be outdated or permeable. In 2010, the top 10 percent of the wealthiest households in America collectively held 76.7 percent of the national wealth (or net worth), while the remaining 90 percent of households commanded only 23.3 percent (see Figure 6.2). In addition, between 1983 and 2010 the share of national

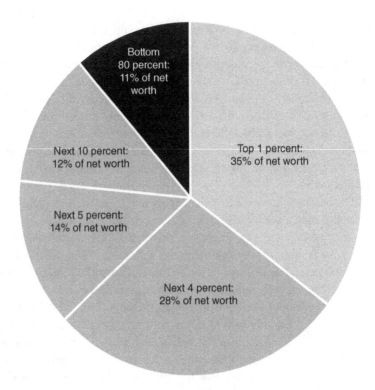

Figure 6.2
US wealth distribution
(in terms of net
worth), 2010.

wealth held by the top 20 percent of households increased by 7.6 percent, which means that the share held by the bottom 80 percent of households decreased by the same amount over the same time period. Of this 7.6 percent share increase, the overwhelming majority (7 percent) actually occurred among only the top 5 percent of households.[24] Such economic disparity points to the fact that class is still a significant structuring factor in many people's lives despite ideological confirmations of the contrary. Of course, class is not the only issue of privilege that continues to operate in this way. Another hotly contested area that often appears to be a non-issue as a result of ideological intervention is race.

Media, Ideology, and Representations of Race and Ethnicity

Cultural studies scholars interested in media representations of race investigate how a culture's racial ideologies help determine the structures of popular media texts like television shows, films, music, and periodicals. They analyze these texts to understand how the media reinforce cultural and ideological power hierarchies, systems that usually award privilege and power to white individuals at the expense of nonwhite individuals. These scholars are especially interested in how media texts reflect hegemonic racial ideologies, concentrating on the ways these texts invite consumers to accept whiteness as the norm in relation to issues of race.

Thomas K. Nakayama and Robert L. Krizek refer to discourses of whiteness in America as "strategic rhetoric."[25] In essence, the images and words most commonly used to discuss whiteness reinforce its privileged place at the center of our understanding of race. Through media representations, social organizations, and even everyday objects, "white" becomes an overarching norm, a privileged non-race against which all other races are measured and compared. Peggy McIntosh outlines a variety of ways this privilege manifests in her own life as a white individual in America: "I can turn on the television or open to the front page of the paper and see people of my race widely represented. … When I am told about our national heritage or about 'civilization,' I am shown that people of my color made it what it is. … I can choose blemish cover or bandages in 'flesh' color and have them more or less match my skin."[26]

Scholarship regarding the media representation of race is vast, but work within this area can be summarized into a group of key concepts that explain how media texts operate across ideological lines within the context of American culture. These concepts are exclusion, stereotyping, assimilation, and othering.

Exclusion

Ironically, a prevalent representation of race in American media is actually better characterized as an *absence* of representation. **Exclusion** is the process by which various cultural groups are symbolically annihilated, or "written out of history," through under-representation in the media. If the media were an actual reflection of race in American culture, then one would expect to see a clear ratio between the size of a racial population in real life and its visible population in television or films. However, research in this area points out that the relationship between population and mainstream media visibility is highly skewed. In other words, racial minorities simply do not "exist" in much of the media that we consume every day, and this absence reinforces ideological power structures by over-representing the dominant white group in media texts.

We can see the process of racial exclusion if we compare the Latino population in America to its representation in mainstream American media. Latinos are the fastest-growing minority population in the USA, numbering about 50.5 million in 2010, or 16 percent of the total US population.[27] To get an idea about how large this number really is, consider the fact that there are more Latinos in the USA than there are Canadians in Canada. If you were to take the entire US Latino population and transform it into a Latin American country, it would have the third largest population by comparison. And yet, despite the obviously large numbers of Latino individuals living in America, images of the lives and issues of Latin American people are largely absent from mainstream American media. The next time you turn on your television, try and find a sitcom that centers on a Latin American family or social group. You might stumble across syndicated episodes of *The George Lopez Show*, *Ugly Betty*, or *Devious Minds* but there is a stronger possibility that you will discover a litany of shows depicting white American social groups like *Friends*, *Seinfeld*, *Roseanne*, or *Everybody Loves Raymond*. Beyond *Teen Wolf* and *Modern Family*, few contemporary programs even feature a Latino character in a lead role. Likewise, many of the more popular or critically recognized films about Latinos since 2000, such as *Y Tu Mamá También* (2001), *Frida* (2002), *The Motorcycle Diaries* (2004), *Volver* (2006), *The Orphanage* (2007), and *The Skin I Live In* (2011), are either produced by foreign film companies or largely focused on the lives of Latino individuals *outside* of the USA.

Overall, systems of symbolic exclusion do not completely remove a Latino presence from American media (as many television shows and films feature Latinos as friends, neighbors, co-workers, or other minor characters), but they do manage to partially erase the perspectives, interests, and needs of the significant US Latino population from the everyday American conscious. As times this lack of symbolic presence justifies more tangible forms of exclusion as well. Rather than hire a Latino actor to play CIA agent Tony Mendez in the 2012 film *Argo*, for example, white director Ben Affleck decided to cast himself in the role instead. Although Affleck attracted significant criticism for doing so, *Argo* also won the 2012 Academy Award for Best Picture, suggesting that Hollywood had little problem with the racial switch.[28] Examples like *Argo* reveal how the exclusion of Latinos and other minority groups from the media reinforces ideological systems of white privilege that construct whiteness as prevalent, multifaceted, normal, and desirable.

Stereotyping

When people of color *do* appear in the media, they often fall victim to the second major form of racial representation. **Stereotyping** is the process of constructing misleading and reductionist representations of a minority racial group, often wholly defining members of the group by a small number of characteristics (see also Chapter 8 for an extensive discussion of stereotyping). Media stereotypes by definition make value judgments about the worth, taste, and morality of another culture, and in doing so they can influence our attitudes, behaviors, and actions toward members of that culture. Racial stereotypes are not always a negative reflection of a culture (the stereotype of the "smart Asian" is a good example of a positive stereotype), but all stereotypes overlook the inherent complexity of a racial group and present media consumers with simplified and flawed representations. These simplified racial caricatures enable systems of white privilege by presenting consumers with a world where the majority of complex, interesting, and realistic characters are white.

One example of a long-standing racial stereotype in US media is that of people of Middle Eastern descent as violent or barbaric terrorists. Even before September 11, 2001, the image of the "Arab terrorist" was prevalent in American films like *Back to the Future* (1985), *True Lies* (1994), *The Siege* (1998), and *Rules of Engagement* (2000). Films that reference the World Trade Center bombing like *United 93* (2006) or *Zero Dark Thirty* (2012) naturally resonate with this stereotype, but it endures elsewhere in films like *American Dreamz* (2006) and *Vantage Point* (2008). When the media are not depicting Middle Easterners as terrorists, other common stereotypes include shady, big-nosed, and often irate individuals who wear turbans and ride camels (*Aladdin*, 1992), drive taxis (*You Don't Mess With the Zohan*, 2008), or own convenience stores (*Four Brothers*, 2005). The repetition and combination of these stereotypical images over time reduces the complex variability of Middle Eastern peoples to a few exaggerated, stock representations. Like the process of exclusion, stereotyping establishes the hegemonic norm of whiteness by largely reducing realistic or affirming images of racial minorities, thereby erasing an accurate presence of them from the minds of many consumers.

The matter of racial stereotyping in the media is a sensitive and delicate one because it raises questions of both perception and intent. Consider, for example, the April 2008 cover of *Vogue* magazine, which features an image of NBA sensation LeBron James clutching Brazilian supermodel Gisele Bündchen. The cover – the first to feature an African American man in the magazine's history – quickly ignited a critical firestorm in the blogosphere.[29] For many, the *Vogue* cover, which was shot by renowned photographer Annie Leibovitz, resembled images of "King Kong," casting James as the dangerous (black) gorilla and Bündchen as the helpless (white) damsel.[30] This interpretation was dismissed by *Vogue* spokesperson Patrick O'Connell, who claimed the image simply "sought to celebrate two superstars at the top of their game[s]."[31] Though the magazine's editors almost certainly did not perceive (let alone intend) the image to be racially insensitive, it nevertheless elicited strong condemnation from those who believed it tapped (even if only unconsciously) into decades-old, racial stereotypes of the "black brute" and "white damsel." In support of this claim, the image is frequently juxtaposed with the World War I recruiting poster shown in Figure 6.3. What we hope this example illustrates is that media executives and editors, even those who have the best of intentions, must be vigilantly on guard against the reproduction of racial stereotypes.

Assimilation

The comparatively small number of media texts that do focus on the lives or experiences of people of color often display the third type of racial representation. **Assimilation** is the process by which media texts represent minority racial groups in a positive light while simultaneously dehistoricizing or stripping them of their cultural identities. These groups are often shown to possess equal or better socio-economic standings than their white counterparts, but issues of past or continued political struggle for that equality are virtually absent. Instead, racial minorities become assimilated into a middle or upper class that largely reflects the perspectives of white individuals. Except for the possibility of a "very special episode" about racism here or there, most of the problems that concern assimilated individuals involve family problems, occupational issues, or romantic pursuits, not issues of social power and oppression that often inform the lives of racial minorities in the real world. In this way, structures of inequality are hidden behind an apparent "face" of diversity in these texts.

Figure 6.3   World War I US Army recruiting poster. ANN RONAN PICTURE LIBRARY/HIP/TOPFOTO.

The quintessential example of a racially assimilating media text is *The Cosby Show*. The Emmy-Award-winning show follows the antics and trials of the Huxtables, an African American, upper-middle-class family led by parents Cliff (Bill Cosby) and Clair (Phylicia Rashad). Cliff is an obstetrician and Clair is a successful attorney, and the family overall represents middle-class achievement and the possibilities of social mobility for racial minorities. In line with the American Dream, *The Cosby Show* suggests that success is open to all those who are talented and hard-working if only they educate and apply themselves. Consequently, the show's viewers may come to think that widespread African American poverty is a result of individual weakness or cultural deficiency instead of systemic and ideological oppression. Shows like *Cosby* and *The Jeffersons* paved the way for other successful African American television shows that displayed tendencies toward assimilation, including *Family Matters* and *The Fresh Prince of Bel-Air*. Compared to the popular 1970s show *Good Times*, which chronicled the life of an African American family in the face of poverty, unemployment, and other social troubles often tied to racial power, these later shows virtually ignored issues of political struggle and "whitewashed" their African American characters.

Like the American Dream, issues of racial assimilation are closely tied to issues of tokenism. A token here is a character or personality of color whose presence in the media supposedly proves that systemic racism and white privilege no longer exist. The logic is that consciously injecting a single racial minority into an otherwise dominant or "white" program means that the program is fairly and realistically representing that minority perspective. In reality, tokens are a surface-level conceit to diversity because the token often displays qualities of hegemonic assimilation. Dixon Wilson, one of the major characters in the 2008 television reboot of *90210*, is a good example of a media token. As the only major African American character on the program (and, indeed, within his adoptive family), Dixon struggles at times with his place in the overwhelmingly white city of Beverly Hills, CA. These racial concerns, however, are effectively obscured by a host of interpersonal conflicts and romantic issues that largely resemble those of his white classmates. Media tokenism is present outside of fictional programs as well, especially in local news teams often made up of one reporter from each major ethnic group that predominates in the area. In a satirical jab at this system, *South Park* creators Matt Stone and Trey Parker have named the only African American child in their titular Colorado town "Token Black."

Assimilation and tokenism support ideological systems of white privilege by constructing middle-class life and norms as implicitly white. Characters and personalities of color assimilated into the white, middle-class media landscape seem to testify to the non-existence of racial ideological power, obscuring real issues of racial dominance and privilege by presenting consumers with images of false diversity. This functions as a tool of hegemony, convincing people to support mainstream media representations because they seem to present a racially equitable world even as the images reinforce current racial power relations.

Othering

The final type of media representation builds from this relationship between "normal" and "white." **Othering** is the process of marginalizing minorities by defining them in relationship to the (white) majority, which functions as the norm or the natural order. The understanding of "white" as a non-race addressed at the beginning of this section is both cause and consequence of othering practices. Examples of othering within the media are often difficult to identify because they rely on the unquestioned ideological assumptions about race and culture that we use to make sense of the world. Harry M. Benshoff and Sean Griffin point out that othering was evident in the predominant practice in early Hollywood to have actors of color play a variety of ethnic characters: "African Americans and Latinos were often hired to play Native American characters, and Hispanic, Italian and Jewish actors played everything from Eskimos to Swedes."[32] This process drew clear distinctions between white and non-white actors, privileging the unique qualities of the former and erasing the individuality of the latter. Though this may seem like an outdated practice, instances of othering still exist today in the entertainment industry. It is common, for example, to run across descriptions of Eddie Murphy, Chris Rock, or Tracy Morgan that characterize them as "black comedians," but it is unlikely that one would ever encounter material describing Daniel Tosh or Jeff Dunham as a "white comedians." A generic "comedian" is assumed to be white unless he/she is specified otherwise.

The notion of othering greatly illuminates the ways many media texts function in America. One of the most prevalent forms of othering involves the ideology of **difference**, or the depiction of subordinate and racialized "others" as a source of pleasure for US American tourists and consumers. Activist bell hooks characterizes this pleasure as a process of "eating the other," where white individuals literally "consume" images and representations of racialized others in order to experience positive feelings. She suggests that within such an ideological structure, privileged white individuals act "on the assumption that the exploration into the world of difference, into the body of the Other, will provide a greater, more intense pleasure than any that exists in the ordinary world of one's familiar racial group."[33] For a better understanding of how this consumption manifests in the media, consider Figure 6.4. From one vantage, the Motorola advertisement is certainly problematic in its reliance on a generic "Asian ninja" stereotype. Further inspection, however, leads to questions about the race of the actual model. It is unclear if she is Asian, Latino, white, or some other race (or combination of races). More problematic than stereotyping, then, is Motorola's use of a generically consumable "Asian-ness" in the image, something depthless that can literally be put on and taken off (or "tried out") for pleasure and excitement.

Another common example of difference in contemporary media involves the hip-hop music industry. Although popular hip-hop musicians are overwhelmingly African American, and the genre is often characterized in the public consciousness as "African American" in style, many hip-hop consumers are

Figure 6.4   Motorola RAZR advertisement. COURTESY OF THE ADVERTISING ARCHIVES.

young, white, middle-class individuals. Ideologies of difference help explain the draw of white suburbanites to this quintessentially African American form: to consume hip-hop is to dabble in the other, to transgress racial norms in a self-gratifying manner. Remember that the notion of gratification is crucial to understanding difference. While it may seem that actions based in difference reject racial norms in a progressively political light, in reality these moves reduce aspects of minority culture to mere products for privileged white individuals to consume toward their own ends.

The other way that othering often manifests in media is through a process of exoticism. **Exoticism** refers to the ideologically-driven circulation and consumption of images of foreign lands that romanticize or mystify other cultures. Exoticizing a racial group often strips them of contemporary political agency by constructing them as primitive, unintelligent, or animalistic. Virtually any issue of *National Geographic* magazine, for example, commits this act. One usually encounters images of scantily clad "tribal groups" while flipping through its pages, and these societies appear largely exotic and bestial in the context of the magazine's stories on foreign lands and unusual animals. While the magazine covers a variety of racial groups in this way, none of them are ever white. In examples like these, then, exoticism positions non-white groups as socially and cognitively inferior to white, "civilized" society.

Thus, while difference represents actively seeking out aspects of non-white cultures as a source of pleasure, exoticism represents a mental distancing and superiority of white culture over others. Together they represent the most prevalent forms of othering in American media. Othering, difference, and exoticism all ideologically reinforce white privilege by making whiteness the invisible and central concept in American race relations. These ideologies equate whiteness with normalcy, and white stands as the unspoken norm around which all other races revolve.

Conclusion

This chapter has looked at how television shows, films, songs, news outlets, and other popular media forms support certain perspectives on social reality over others as a function of ideology. Operating under the ambiguous and flexible label of Cultural studies, scholars in this research vein seek to understand the ways in which the worldviews of socially privileged groups (men, whites, the wealthy, heterosexuals, adults, middle-aged individuals, etc.) are over-represented in the media to the detriment of socially marginalized groups (women, non-whites, the poor, homosexuals, children, the elderly, etc.). They regularly critique media texts for their role in structuring hegemonic and ideological systems of power. Cultural studies is unabashedly political in relation to this goal, and the approach has produced some of the more radical and interesting research in contemporary media studies. The real strength of Cultural studies is its concentration on the ever-changing dynamic between media texts and the social systems that create them. As US society continues to evolve in relation to media images and technology, the Cultural studies approach will continue to provide perspective on how ideology informs these changes.

MEDIA LAB 5: DOING CULTURAL ANALYSIS

OBJECTIVE

The aim of this lab is to utilize concepts of representation to analyze media texts. Specifically, students will investigate how issues of social power and ideology help structure the representation of particular social groups in the contemporary media landscape.

ACTIVITY

- Divide the class into small groups of 4–5 students each.
- Have each group select a cultural group. Students may choose their own groups or they may select a group from the following list: children, elderly, rich, poor, women, men, blacks, whites, Asians, Hispanics, gays, heterosexuals, persons with disabilities.
- Ask students to record their answers to the following questions.
  1 Based on your experiences with the media, with what frequency is your group represented? Do you think this group is over- or under-represented? Why?
  2 What associations (stereotypes) are frequently made with this group? List at least 10. Are these associations generally positive, negative, or both?
  3 Provide examples of specific media texts that either reinforce or challenge the associations you listed in question 2. Which column is longer? Why?

SUGGESTED READING

Althusser, L. Ideology and Ideological State Apparatuses (Notes Toward an Investigation). In *Lenin and Philosophy and Other Essays*, trans. B. Brewster, pp. 85–126. New York: Monthly Review Press, 2001.

Aronowitz, S. *How Class Works: Power and Social Movement*. New Haven, CT: Yale University Press, 2003.

Bell-Jordan, K.E. *Black. White.* and a *Survivor* of *The Real World*: Constructions of Race on Reality TV. *Critical Studies in Media Communication* 2008, 25, 353–72.

Brantlinger, P. *Crusoe's Footprints: Cultural Studies in Britain and America*. New York: Routledge, 1990.

Cloud, D. L. Hegemony or Concordance? The Rhetoric of "Tokenism" in Oprah Winfrey's Rags-to-Riches Biography. *Critical Studies in Media Communication* 1996, 13, 115–37.

Davies, I. *Cultural Studies and Beyond: Fragments of Empire*. New York: Routledge, 1995.

Dyer, R. *White*. New York: Routledge, 1997.

Eagleton, T. *Ideology: an Introduction*. London: Verso, 1991.

Ewen, S. and Ewen, E. *Typecasting: on the Arts and Sciences of Human Inequity*, revised edn. New York: Seven Stories, 2008.

Grossberg, L. *We Gotta Get Out of this Place: Popular Conservatism and Postmodern Culture*. New York: Routledge, 1992.

Hall, S. *Representation: Cultural Representations and Signifying Practices*. Thousand Oaks, CA: Sage Publications, 1997.

Hebdige, D. *Subculture: the Meaning of Style*. New York: Routledge, 1979.

hooks, b. *Black Looks: Race and Representation*. Boston, MA: South End Press, 1992.

hooks, b. *Where We Stand: Class Matters*. New York: Routledge, 2000.

Johnson, A.G. *Privilege, Power and Difference*. New York: McGraw-Hill, 2001.

Kendell, D. *Framing Class: Media Representations of Wealth and Poverty in America*. New York: Rowman & Littlefield, 2005.

Larson, S.G. *Media & Minorities: the Politics of Race in News and Entertainment*. Lanham, MD: Rowman & Littlefield, 2005.

McIntosh, P. White Privilege: Unpacking the Invisible Knapsack. *Peace and Freedom* 1989, July/August, 10–12.

Peterson, R.T. Consumer Magazine Advertisement Portrayal of Models by Race in the U.S.: an Assessment. *Journal of Marketing Communications* 2007, 13, 199–211.

Roediger, D.R. *The Wages of Whiteness: Race and the Making of the American Working Class*, revised edn. New York: Verso, 1999.

Rogers, R.A. Pleasure, Power and Consent: the Interplay of Race and Gender in *New Jack City*. *Women's Studies and Communication* 1993, 16, 62–85.

Shugart, H.A. Sumptuous Texts: Consuming "Otherness" in the Food Film Genre. *Critical Studies in Media Communication* 2008, 25, 68–90.

Torck, D. Voices of Homeless People in Street Newspapers: a Cross-Cultural Exploration. *Discourse & Society* 2001, 12, 371–92.

Torgovnik, M. *Gone Primitive: Savage Intellects, Modern Lives*. Chicago, IL: University of Chicago Press, 1991.

Veblen, T. *The Theory of the Leisure Class*. New York: The Macmillan Company, 1899.

NOTES

1. For some of these different reactions to the film, see D. Itzkoff, You Saw What in "Avatar"? Pass Those Glasses!, *The New York Times*, January 20, 2010, http://www.nytimes.com/2010/01/20/movies/20avatar.html?_r=1& (accessed March 18, 2013).

2. M. Richardson, *The Experience of Culture* (Thousand Oaks, CA: Sage Publications, 2001), 2.

3. M. Foucault, *Mental Illness and Psychology*, trans. unknown (New York: Harper & Row Publishers, 1976).

4. Foucault, 68.

5. How Common is Intersex?, *Intersex Society of North America*, www.isna.org/faq/frequency (accessed February 3, 2013).

6. What is Albinism?, *The National Organization for Albinism and Hypopigmentation*, www.albinism.org/publications/what_is_albinism.html (accessed January 5, 2007).

7. B. Brummett, *Rhetoric in Popular Culture*, 2nd edn (Thousand Oaks, CA: Sage Publications, 2006), 5.

8. L. Althusser, Ideology and Ideological State Apparatuses (Notes Toward an Investigation), in *Lenin and Philosophy and Other Essays*, trans. B. Brewster (New York: Monthly Review Press, 2001), 85–126.

9. Roland Barthes, *Mythologies*, trans. A. Lavers (New York: Hill and Wang, 1972).

10. P. Bourdieu, *Outline of a Theory of Practice*, trans. R. Nice (Cambridge: Cambridge University Press, 1977), 169.

11. A. Gramsci, *Selections from the Prison Notebooks*, ed. and trans. Q. Hoare and G.N. Smith (New York: International Publishers, 2003), 12.

12. D. Hebdige, *Subculture: the Meaning of Style* (New York: Routledge, 1979).

13. J. Fiske, The Jeaning of America, in *Understanding Popular Culture* (Boston, MA: Unwin Hyman, 1989), 1–21.

14. Q.D. Leavis, *Fiction and the Reading Public* (New York: Russell & Russell, 1965), 211.

15. J.P. Surber, *Culture and Critique: an Introduction to the Critical Discourses of Cultural Studies* (Boulder, CO: Westview Press, 1998), 236.

16. R. Hoggart, *The Uses of Literacy: Changing Patterns in English Mass Culture* (Fair Lawn, NJ: Essential Books, 1957).

17. R. Williams, *The Long Revolution* (New York: Columbia University Press, 1961), 41.

18. Surber, *Culture and Critique*.

19. S. Hall, Cultural Studies: Two Paradigms, in *Media Culture & Society: a Critical Reader*, R. Collins, J. Curran, N. Garnham, P. Scannell, P. Schlesinger, and C. Sparks (eds) (Beverly Hills, CA: Sage Publications, 1986), 33–48.

20. A. Milner and J. Browitt, *Contemporary Cultural Theory: an Introduction*, 3rd edn (New York: Routledge, 2002).

21. H. Jenkins, T. McPherson, and J. Shattuc, The Culture That Sticks to Your Skin: a Manifesto for a New Cultural Studies, in *Hop on Pop: the Politics and Pleasures of Popular Culture*, H. Jenkins, T. McPherson, and J. Shattuc (eds) (Durham, NC: Duke University Press, 2002), 3–42.

22. T. Veblen, *The Theory of the Leisure Class* (New York: The Macmillan Company, 1899).

23. J.B. Schor, *Born to Buy: the Commercialized Child and the New Consumer Culture* (New York: Scribner, 2004), 11.

24. L. Mishel, J. Bivens, E. Gould, and H. Shierholz, *The State of Working America*, 12th edn (Washington, DC: Economic Policy Institute, 2012), 379–80.

25. T.K. Nakayama and R.L. Krizek, Whiteness: a Critical Rhetoric, *Quarterly Journal of Speech* 1995, 81, 291–309.

26. P. McIntosh, White Privilege: Unpacking the Invisible Knapsack, *Peace and Freedom* 1989, July/August, 10, 11.

27. K.R. Humes, N.A. Jones, and R.R. Ramirez, *Overview of Race and Hispanic Origin, 2010 Census Briefs* (Washington, DC: US Census Bureau, 2011), 3, http://www.census.gov/prod/cen2010/briefs/c2010br-02.pdf (accessed February 3, 2013).

28. See, for example, M. Lee, Ben Affleck Casts Himself as Tony Mendez in *Argo*, *Racebending*, July 5, 2011, http://www.racebending.com/v4/history/ben-affleck-casts-himself-as-tony-mendez-in-argo/ (accessed February 3, 2013); M. Esparza, Ben Affleck's *Argo* and the Whitewashing of the Mexican-American, *BeyondChron: the Voice of the Rest*, December 4, 2012, http://www.beyondchron.org/articles/Ben_Affleck_s_Argo_and_the_White_Washing_of_the_Mexican_American_10760.html (accessed October 12, 2013).

29. W. Morris, Monkey Business: So is That *Vogue* Cover Racist Or Not?, *Slate*, posted March 31, 2008, www.slate.com/id/2187797/ (accessed April 23, 2009).

30. J. Hill, LeBron Should Be More Careful with his Image, *ESPN.com*, p. 2, updated March 21, 2008, http://sports.espn.go.com/espn/page2/story?page=hill/080320 (accessed April 23, 2009).

31. Vogue Cover with Lebron stirs up Controversy, *TODAY.com*, http://www.today.com/id/23797883/ns/today-today_style/t/vogue-cover-lebromn-stirs-controversy/

32. H.M. Benshoff and S. Griffin, *America on Film: Representing Race, Class, Gender and Sexuality at the Movies* (Oxford: Blackwell, 2004), 56.

33. b. hooks, Eating the Other: Desire and Resistance, in *Black Looks: Race and Representation* (Boston, MA: South End Press, 1992), 24.

7 Psychoanalytic Analysis

KEY CONCEPTS

APPARATUS THEORY
DESIRE
DRIVE
FANTASY
FETISHISM

IMAGINARY
LACK
MALE GAZE
OEDIPUS COMPLEX
PHALLOCENTRISM
PLEASURE PRINCIPLE

REALITY PRINCIPLE
REPRESSION
SCOPOPHILIA
SYMBOLIC
UNCONSCIOUS
VOYEURISM

The 2011 film *Drive* revolves around the mysterious Driver (Ryan Gosling), a movie stuntman in modern Los Angeles whose choice to moonlight as a get-away car driver for local crooks quickly invokes the ire of more dangerous criminals. Although the Driver dreams of leaving his questionable occupations for the glories of the Formula 1 racetrack, real inspiration for change does not come until he meets a single mother named Irene (Carey Mulligan), a neighbor who provides him with a vision of family life for the first time. When a powerful crime lord threatens to kill Irene and her son over her ex-husband's debts, the Driver responds first by trying to raise funds through a heist, and then later by systematically killing everyone involved in the crime lord's local syndicate. The film ends with the mortally wounded Driver cruising out of Los Angeles after making his final kill. While his fate is certainly sealed and he will never see Irene again, he takes some solace in the knowledge that she and her son are at least safe from harm.

The film's title is a double entendre. On the one hand, it clearly refers to the Driver's legal and extra-legal occupational talents, as well as his original means of escaping an unfulfilling life. On the other hand, *drive* is also a fitting synonym for the compulsion the Driver demonstrates in relation to Irene, a woman he hardly knows but to whom he feels a profound and ineffable connection. As the narrative of the film unfolds, it becomes clear that the Driver is, in fact, the one being driven, compelled by some

Critical Media Studies: An Introduction, Second Edition. Brian L. Ott and Robert L. Mack.
© 2014 John Wiley & Sons, Inc. Published 2014 by John Wiley & Sons, Inc.

unknown force to compromise his well-being in order to preserve Irene's own. As spectators watch the Driver transform from a criminal accessory to a single-minded, animalistic killer by the film's end, it seems pertinent to question if he ever had as much control over his decisions as his enigmatic name suggests.

Of course, the title's double meaning would be no surprise to scholars who utilize a Psychoanalytic approach to study the media, for the idea of an unsettling drive that seeks satisfaction without regard to safety or reality forms the theoretical core of psychoanalytic theory. The Austrian psychiatrist Sigmund Freud originally proposed his theory of the drives in order to explain human psychological motivation, and psychoanalytic media scholars subsequently explore how media texts reflect these powerful forces. Although the body of knowledge in this tradition has changed considerably over time, one could say that the approach is generally grounded in the genesis of individual psychology, the psychology of the media text, and the ways in which the two interact in the process of media consumption.

The first half of this chapter outlines the major tenets of Psychoanalytic theory as well as the two major models of human mental development that have heavily influenced media studies (Freudian and Lacanian). The latter half of this chapter traces the historical inception and evolution of Psychoanalytic theory largely in the realm of film studies. For reasons that will become apparent, the vast majority of Psychoanalytic work in media studies has concentrated on film. However, we conclude this chapter by considering recent Psychoanalytic work that also extends this branch of theory beyond the cinema.

Psychoanalytic Theory: an Overview

Psychoanalytic theory may be distinguished from other theories of psychology on the existence and centrality of the **drives**, or "somatic demands upon the mind."[1] In other words, while other branches of psychology are primarily concerned with the influence of external phenomena on mental structure (i.e. behaviorism, social psychology, etc.), psychoanalysis begins with a consideration of how the mind registers the body's internal, biological needs (for nutrition, comfort, sex, etc.) and transforms them into motivating forces, or drives. Different drives arise from different sources and seek out different objects in the world, but all of them ultimately seek satisfaction through the achievement of these objects, a maxim that Freud refers to at times as the **pleasure principle**.[2] The motivating force of hunger, for example, arises from biological needs for nutrition and can be satisfied through the ingestion of edible objects; the sexual drive arises from biological needs for sex and can be satisfied through contact with stimulating objects. Importantly, these examples suggest that the object(s) of a drive and the kind of satisfaction it seeks are highly variable, differing from person to person. One person may find a given object intensely satisfying (chocolate, for example, either in relation to nutrition or to sex), while another person may find that the same object provides no satisfaction whatsoever. One person may seek out an object that others find decidedly non-sexual in order to satisfy an explicitly sexual drive (i.e. feet, uniforms, etc.). Here we do not mean to imply that people choose these objects or know why they provide satisfaction. Very often people cannot explain these types of attractions, and we will address the source of this inexplicable variability in a moment. For now it is most important to realize that it is the variability of objects and aims that distinguishes drive from hard-wired instinct. Freud's theory of the drives attempts to account for the wide variety of motivating tastes and practices that we see uniquely manifest among human beings.

The complicated variability of objects and aims also means there is more opportunity for the drives to be halted in their attempts to find satisfaction. What if people cannot financially afford the specific objects that would seem to satisfy their drives? What if the given object of a drive is socially unacceptable, or possession of the object is punishable by law? Unfortunately, the motivating force of the drives does not diminish or disappear in these instances. Instead, the drives become frustrated, repressed, or sublimated (redirected into easier or more socially acceptable channels). Freud refers to this constant curbing of the drives according to possibility, law, or social convention as the **reality principle**, and in the interplay between pleasure-seeking and the realistic limits placed on that activity, human mental structure is born.

In order to explain this interplay between drive and reality, Freud proposes two different topographies, or maps of mental life, in his work. Neither topography is more "correct" than the other; each simply sheds light on different aspects of the interplay. Freud proposes the primary topography in his first major book, *The Interpretation of Dreams*: the unconscious, pre-conscious, and consciousness.[3] When a drive becomes blocked in the achievement of its object for any of the various reasons outlined above, Freud suggests that the mind copes with this frustration by repressing or submerging the wish for the object into the **unconscious**, a mental screen behind which the individual cannot clearly or consciously recognize. The relationship between drives/wishes and the unconscious is less like a penny in a piggy bank and more, to borrow a metaphor from Freud, like an iceberg in the ocean. The ocean does not neatly "contain" the iceberg, but it does mask the majority of it from being seen. **Repression**, or the immersion of a drive beneath the unconscious, temporarily relieves the sense of frustration, but the drive always waits for an opportunity to make itself known again in either the pre-conscious or to consciousness. The pre-conscious is the link between the unconscious and consciousness, and through it repressed drives most commonly bubble up to consciousness in the form of dreams. In fact, Freud would suggest that we often "get what we want" in our dreams because they often originate from repressed drives. Should the dream be so intense that the dreamer remembers it upon waking, the drive becomes somewhat known to consciousness, though often obscured beneath layers of dream symbolism. The drive may also come to manifest in conscious life as so-called "Freudian" slips of the tongue or as otherwise unexplainable medical symptoms that symbolize fixations on wished-for objects.

At this point you may be asking: But where do the drives originate in this schema, and what manages their repression? Freud's second topography, involving the id, ego, and superego, helps to clarify these questions.[4] The id is the part of the mind present from birth, the source of the drives regulated by the pleasure principle. The ego is an outcropping of the id, the part of the id closest to consciousness that develops as the individual becomes aware of reality. As such, the ego is responsible for curbing the drives according to the reality principle. As Freud explains,

> [I]n its relation to the id [the ego] is like a man on horseback, who has to hold in check the superior strength of the horse; with this difference, that the rider tries to do so with his own strength while the ego uses borrowed forces. The analogy may be carried a little further. Often a rider, if he is not to be parted from his horse, is obliged to guide it where it wants to go; so in the same way the ego is in the habit of transforming the id's will into action as if it were its own.[5]

We can see in this analogy that the drives of the id remain powerful motivating forces despite the limitations brought upon them by the ego. At its strongest the ego is able to repress a drive temporarily, but more often the ego must settle for sublimating or channeling the drive into other, more acceptable objects and aims. Thus, a person who yearns for a socially-unacceptable object of the sexual drive (an animal, for example) may settle for a more acceptable, approximate object instead (like a sex toy). Just because we cannot eat delicious food at all hours of the day does not mean that we give up food altogether; instead, we satiate our hunger by dividing our eating habits into socially recognizable meals. The "borrowed forces" to which Freud refers that allow the ego to accomplish these regulations are the superego, the part of the ego that functions as the representative of reality. The superego houses the individual's understandings of morality and cultural propriety, first gleaned from primary caregivers and then the world at large. It is the part of the mind that equips the ego with common sense, shame, and a host of other tools that encourage the repression and/or redirection of the drives.

It is important to note that the two topographies are not interchangeable. The id is not synonymous with the unconscious, although a great deal of the id is often unconscious. The ego is not reducible to consciousness, although we are more consciously aware of the ego than we are of the id. If we return to the iceberg metaphor, however, we might be able to equate the first topography with the oceanic landscape and the second with the iceberg itself. The ocean here would represent the unconscious and the sky, consciousness. The lower strata of the iceberg, the vast majority of which is submerged, would represent the id, while the smaller outcropping of ice that floats above water would be the ego/superego complex. The indistinct watermark and the bobbing of the iceberg itself would represent the activity of the drives seeking to be known, as well as the weight of the ego and superego pushing them back.

Psychoanalytic media theorists are primarily interested in the ways that technology and media texts function as objects of these drives, or at least mimic the interplay between the drives and reality that we have discussed thus far. The means by which the components of the interplay form within the individual, however, is still a source of considerable debate among psychoanalysts, one that must be addressed before we can turn our attention to the media. As a result, the next two sections address two theories of human mental development that have most influenced psychoanalytic media studies.

Freudian Development

When most people are asked to identify the animating force of Sigmund Freud's work, they consistently provide the same answer: Sex. This conclusion is, however, only partially true. Although Freud posited the existence of numerous motivating drives early in his career, he eventually came to believe that human motivation results from *two* basic drives: the sexual drive and the death drive.[6] The sexual drive, also called Eros, compels the individual to connect with others and the world, fueling sexual/reproductive acts as well as lesser drives associated with other physical comforts and the continuation of life. The death drive, also called Thanatos, compels the individual toward division from others and a rejection of the living world, often manifesting as aggression or other destructive impulses. The twin drives are distinct but often inseparable, as even basic acts like eating involve both the destruction and continuation of life.[7] Freud believed, however, that the sexual drive is more accessible to speculation than its destructive counterpart; we often only catch glimpses of the death drive as it operates within or alongside the sexual.[8] As a result, sex plays a more prominent role than death in his theories of human development.

Freud's theory of human mental development begins with the notion that humans are born "polymorphously perverse," or with the ability to experience sexual pleasure in many different ways. The restriction of sexual pleasure to more common under-standings (genital contact, orgasm, etc.) is something that the individual only comes to learn later on. Early evidence of this diversity can be witnessed in the first of three developmental stages, the oral stage, where the mouth and the act of sucking take on primary significance. Although the ostensible purpose of sucking is nourishment, "the baby's obstinate persistence in sucking gives evidence at an early age of a need for satisfaction which … strives to obtain pleasure independently of nourishment and for that reason may and should be termed *sexual*."[9] In other words, while the sucking mechanism allows the infant to eat, it also lends itself to other pleasures as well. It may be helpful here to think again on the nature of the drive. While nutrition is certainly a biological need and the act of sucking is instinctual, a variety of objects can come to satisfy this mechanism (including non-nutritional objects like a pacifier or a thumb), suggesting that there is more to the impulse than purely biological satisfaction.

Progression through the next two developmental stages (anal and phallic) in the first few years of life involves similar experience of sexual pleasures that result from parts of the body coming into contact with a diversity of objects. In fact, Freud would suggest that the particular objects that any given individual encounters in these stages (as well as his/her interaction with these objects) would be a great predictor of the objects that come to satisfy the individual's adult drives. One reason that people can-not often explain *why* they find a particular object gratifying is because it references or mimics an object they encountered during this time period, before they were fully aware of themselves and the world. Freud even believed that it was possible for adults to become arrested in these stages, fixated on objects, areas of the body, or activities heightened during this time (such as consumption, retention, expulsion, etc., as well as with objects that lend themselves to these acts).[10]

A particularly important "object" for the developing child during the stages is the mother. Because the mother is often the provider of many other satisfying objects, Freud suggests that she also becomes an object of sexual satisfaction for the child, an attraction which would lead to incestuous situations later on if not curtailed. Such denial occurs through the resolution of the **Oedipus complex**, where the father intervenes and forbids the child from taking the mother as an object of the sexual drive under the threat of "castration."[11] Freud suggests that this threat is embodied in the father's phallus, which simultaneously signals the father's own sexual power and the child's powerlessness. The Oedipal prohibition is critical because it serves as a template for all future repression and makes way for the development of the moralizing superego. Successful navigation of the complex, then, sets the child on a path where socially sanctioned forms of sexuality and object choice emerge after puberty, while failure to give up the mother as object at this stage results in a host of consequently troubled or even psychotic mental states. This is why the murderous actions of Norman Bates, the titular character of Alfred Hitchcock's 1960 film *Psycho*, may be explained above all as a result of his unnatural attachment to his mother.

Freud's commitment to the sexual nature of human motivation and his framing of gender/family norms from the time period as ahistorical truths have invoked considerable criticism from many academics. Without these questionable decisions, however, his work may have never seen the light of day, and we would not have access to his essential insights regarding the existence of the drives and their role in creating the human subject. One line of thinking that has attempted to shore up some of Freud's perceived weaknesses belongs to the French psychoanalyst Jacques Lacan, and so it is to his work that we now turn.

Lacanian Development

The first critical difference between Freud's theories of mental development and those of Jacques Lacan returns us, as always, to the drives. Whereas Freud concentrates on the sexual drive toward union and suggests that we can only understand the death drive in relation to it, Lacan posits the opposite: All drives, including the sexual, are essentially death drive, in the sense that there is something about all drives that compel the individual beyond permanent connections to any real objects.[12] Once a drive achieves its object, in other words, it is not satisfied forever; there is always more to eat and the potential for more sexual partners. The various connections with the world that Freud asserts as the basis of the sexual drive are illusory, for that very same drive always compels the individual away from permanent connections with any particular objects.

What is this "something" about the (death) drives that encourages individuals to always move on to new objects? Lacan proposes the conceptual triad of need, demand, and desire to account for this question, and this trio is central to his developmental theory.[13] Need is, as it is in Freud, purely biological; human beings are born with needs for nutrition and comfort that must be met. Demand is a need made symbolic, first put to language by another person (since a newborn cannot speak). Marie-Hélène Brousse explains it this way:

> A baby has a need that is biologically defined and that has an object biologically related to that need. Milk is related to hunger. What happens? As a little human being, it is situated in a linguistic environment. Its mother talks, before it is born and from the moment it is born too. She talks all the time, even when giving the baby the objects its need requires. Her use of the signifier or language has consequences on the feeding of the need. For example, she gives the baby milk at times in a specific way. For need to be satisfied, a little human being has to deal with the Other's demand. To be satisfied it has to take the Other's demand into account.[14]

In opposition to Freud, then, who suggests that the drives are motivators merely present in the id from birth, Lacan interprets the drives as the result of one's biological needs meeting the symbolic demands that one's caregiver places on the satisfaction of those needs. Put another way, one cannot experience motivation until one understands the parameters in which the motivation can occur. It is this emphasis on the power of language and communication in the formation of mental motivations that makes Lacan very popular among media scholars interested in the ways that media symbols and images engage our minds.

Importantly, exposure to the caregiver's demands also encourages the child to begin making primitive demands of its own, or using symbols to communicate its otherwise non-symbolic needs. Crying for food is perhaps the best example of this kind of demand. Whereas a biological need is either filled or unfilled, however, the social nature of the demand adds a critical layer of complication: The request to fill the need can now be *denied* by the caregiver. Before language, the child merely *required* milk, whereas the child who *asks* for milk can be refused. This means that every demand really has two requests: A request for a specific object *and a request not to be denied*, to be recognized (or loved) by the caregiver. The first request is easy to meet as long as the specific object is readily available, but the second request is quite difficult to fill. How, Lacan asks, can we ever be sure that the caretaker really loves us? What must the caretaker do to prove this love and fulfill this request? Because these questions can never be answered with absolute certainty, the question of love and recognition remains open. This openness is the genesis of **desire**, the unquenchable yearning for love or recognition that no one else can ever perfectly or absolutely fill. Desire is the "something" in the drives that keeps them from ever settling on a particular object. Achieving an object is never wholly satisfying because it may satisfy our needs, but it cannot satisfy our desires.

Lacan poses three "orders" of human experience that help to trace the transformation of the individual's need into desire: The Real, the Imaginary, and the Symbolic. Lacan altered his definition of the Real many times throughout his career, but it is best understood as that part of life which cannot be put into language, or what cannot be articulated as a demand. The **Imaginary** is a primary developmental space in which the child learns to make demands; it is the realm of chaotic images and sensory impressions into which the child is born. The child has no sense of self or ego in the Imaginary, but a crucial developmental moment here known as "the mirror stage" begins to organize "the agency known as the ego, prior to its social determination, in a fictional direction."[15] At this point the child learns to recognize and identify with its own image (most often reflected in a mirror), an immensely pleasurable impression of perfection and wholeness that the child incorporates as the basis of its later ego.

The ego fully materializes as the child acquires the ability to use language and make more coherent demands on others, an acquisition that marks its movement from the Imaginary to the **Symbolic**, or the cultural order of meaning maintained through words and symbols. Lacan suggests that this transition is the culmination of the Oedipus complex, a process that has much more to do with language than Freud initially thought. The complex unfolds as follows: The primary caregiver, often but not necessarily the mother, stands as a critical figure within the ego-less perfection of the Imaginary. The "phallus" is the Lacanian term for any object that the child believes the primary caregiver desires within this order.[16] Because the child comes to desire recognition from the primary caregiver above all else here through the exchange of demands, he/she reasons that the best way to attract such recognition is to try to become the phallus, or the object of the caregiver's desire. At this point a secondary caregiver, often but not necessarily the father, intervenes and denies the child the possibility of this transformation, breaking him/her free of the lure of the primary caregiver's desire through the introduction of language, law, and social convention (in other words, through the introduction of social reality). Since the "father" denies the child's ability to become the phallus, Lacan suggests that the child is effectively "castrated."

Both developmental possibilities at this point come with drawbacks. Children who refuse to give up the quest to become the phallus and forsake the Symbolic order come to possess an identity marked by some degree of psychoses, for the child can never formulate an articulable ego or accept fully the limitations of cultural convention transmitted through language. Giving up the quest and accepting language allows for a coherent ego that the child can present to others through symbols, but it also dooms him/her to living with the insatiable motivation of desire. Lacan refers to the experience of the gap between the Imaginary and the Symbolic which allows for the possibility of desire as **lack**, and the part of the self lost in the transition between orders (the part that cannot be articulated or spoken about) becomes the unconscious.

For Lacan, then, the idea of identity or consciousness is entirely a fiction, one born out of misrecognition of individual wholeness in the mirror stage and solidified in a system of language where subjects can only ever *attempt* to represent themselves. His psychoanalysis is clearly very different from its Freudian counterpart in the way it uses language instead of sex to explain the infant's development and the subsequent mental structures of individuals. Although they conceive of the conscious/unconscious divide quite differently (see Table 7.1), both strands of Psychoanalytic theory offer important insights into the ways that unconscious motivations influence human behavior.

Table 7.1   Comparison of Freud and Lacan

	Freud	Lacan
Pre-Oedipal stage	Polymorphous perversity regulated by the pleasure principle. Sexual pleasure experienced in *oral*, *anal*, and *phallic* stages.	*The Imaginary*: pre-linguistic order dominated by images and sensory impressions. *Mirror stage*: child misrecognizes self as complete and in control; lays basis for eventual ego formation.
Post-Oedipal stage	Identity based on constant curbing of pleasure principle according to reality principle.	*The Symbolic*: linguistic and cultural order where identity arises from attempts to represent self in language.
Drives brought into accordance with reality and its objects via…	*Repression*: socially unacceptable desires for objects suppressed from consciousness but retain influence.	*Desire*: drives possess an extra, insatiable quality that results when biological needs become articulated demands.
Definition of the unconscious	Personal psychical screen that masks repressed desires and attempts to make them known/felt.	Aspects of the self that cannot be articulated in language, formed in the transition to the Symbolic.
The phallus	Actual: the father's penis that represents sexual power and masculine presence to the child.	Metaphoric: imagined object of the "mother's" desire in the Imaginary, denied to the child by the "father."

Now that we have a basic understanding of psychoanalysis, you may be wondering what concepts like *drive*, *repression*, or the *mirror stage* have to do with the media that we consume every day. To better understand the connection, consider the following questions: Why do people continue to attend movie theaters when they can just rent films or watch them via a subscription service at a fraction of the cost? Why do some people watch the same movie over and over again, year after year? Why do we see new movies when we recognize that the vast majority of them rely on the same conventions or plotlines as those we have seen before? Potential answers to these questions can be found in psychoanalysis. Generally speaking, film scholars have historically used psychoanalytic concepts to explain the structure and appeal of films according to the motivations discussed in the works of Freud and Lacan. They claim that there is something unique about the movie theater venue, the edited shot sequence of film, and the bond between the spectator and filmic narrative that is wholly psychological. They believe that the relationship between drive and reality inherent in each of our lives plays out on American movie screens every day, and we watch movies to negotiate this tension in our daily lives. In order to understand how this process takes place, we will now turn our attention to some general assertions of Psychoanalytic media studies and the ways that these translate into specific theories.

Psychoanalytic Studies of Media

Scholars in this tradition draw on a number of different theoretical foundations when attempting to understand films and other forms of media, but most agree on a few overriding principles. First, films are structured in such a way that they activate the desires of the unconscious. When we watch a movie or gaze at an advertisement, we do so because it allows us to experience the parts of ourselves that are there but not consciously known. In Freudian terms, this means that some media are constructed in such a way to allow us to indulge in unconscious, repressed, or socially prohibited pleasures. From a Lacanian perspective, this means that the structure of some media allows us to overcome lack and access the Imaginary pleasures which language divides from our conscious mind. Perhaps it is helpful overall to consider film as a tool for temporarily undermining the hold of the reality principle and allowing the pleasure principle a bit more free reign over our psyche.

Second, given its basis in sex, many scholars also agree that psychoanalytic theory is uniquely equipped to explain depictions of gender in American media, especially as they pertain to cultural phallocentrism. **Phallocentrism** is a social condition where images or representations of the penis carry connotations of power and dominance. Both Freud and Lacan point to the male phallus as an influential symbol in the creation of the human psyche (although Lacan claims it has more of a metaphoric power than does Freud). In both strands of psychoanalysis, the powerful father figure is defined by having command of the phallus, while the rejected mother is defined by her lack of one. For Lacan especially, navigating the Oedipus complex and entering the Symbolic realm of language becomes intertwined with the notion that men are powerful and women are powerless in society, an erroneous understanding prompted by social patriarchy (see Chapter 8). To witness the desirability of the penis in contemporary culture, one need only consider how many tools and structures made to signal awe and power are phallic in shape: rifles, rockets, skyscrapers, the Washington Monument, and more. This logic of desire also occasionally forms the basis of media texts like the Diesel advertisement in Figure 7.1. In essence, within a phallocentric culture, the penis tacitly functions as the object of everyone's desire. One can see, then, why some feminists like Juliet Mitchell have turned to psychoanalytic theory in order to address how the social systems we encounter at an early age infuse our developing minds with constructed notions of gendered power and inequality.[17]

The three major areas of Psychoanalytic film studies discussed here are apparatus theory, the male gaze, and fantasy. There are many divergent strands of psychoanalytic theory and equally divergent forms of textual criticism that accompany them,

Figure 7.1 Diesel
advertisement.
Courtesy of The
Advertising Archives.

but these three represent a somewhat clear trajectory of theoretical development
appropriate to an introductory chapter on psychoanalysis. After establishing this
baseline, the chapter will conclude with a brief discussion regarding other significant
developments within Psychoanalytic media studies.

Apparatus theory

First proposed by scholar Jean-Louis Baudry, **apparatus theory** is the earliest
psychoanalytic approach to film. This approach claims that the actual environment
and machinery of the cinema activates a number of psychoanalytic motivations
within spectators. In his analysis of Plato's famous cave allegory, Baudry points out
that "the text of the cave may well express a desire inherent to a participatory effect
deliberately produced, sought for, and expressed by cinema."[18] In other words, the
same unconscious drives which fueled Plato's writings may have also inspired the
creation of the modern movie theater and the genesis of film itself. Here Baudry is
suggesting that all human beings throughout time have experienced the repression of

drives or their transformation into desire as a result of psychical development, and film is simply the contemporary means by which we negotiate these mechanisms.

The mechanics of cinema allow for this negotiation in a number of ways. According to Baudry the actual context of viewing a movie in a theater "reconstructs the situation necessary to the release of the 'mirror stage' discovered by Lacan."[19] The theatrical environment, in other words, plays upon the process of image identification first enacted in the Lacanian mirror stage. Lacan points out that the child approaching its mirror image lacks significant motor control and relies mostly on vision to understand the world. The mirror stage is pleasant and confirming for the child precisely because it displays a false sense of wholeness and control to make up for this lack. Baudry explains that the conventions of the theater (giant images on the screen, a passive, seated audience) also create a sense of visual dominance and restricted movement, causing viewers to again unconsciously rejoice in mirror stage feelings of wholeness, mastery, and control while watching the film.

For Baudry, then, the narrative or content of the film is not as appealing as the actual process of viewing because "the spectator identifies less with what it represented, the spectacle itself, than what stages the spectacle, makes it seen, obliging him [sic] to see what it sees."[20] He also draws connections between the movie theater and the womb, claiming that the context of watching a movie in a theater causes viewers to unconsciously regress back to the Imaginary and pleasurable experience of a connection to the primary caregiver. This assertion may seem odd until we consider the manner in which theater audiences actually watch films. The darkness of the theater and the relative immobility of spectators both suggest aspects that break us from our daily routine and recall womb-like qualities.

Christian Metz, another scholar interested in the psychoanalytic aspects of film, agrees with Baudry's basic understanding of the cinematic apparatus and extends it in important ways. Metz recognizes that identification is an important component of the apparatus, but he claims that it also taps into the Freudian drives of voyeurism and fetishism. The conceptual trio of identification, voyeurism, and fetishism provide a foundation for a great deal of Psychoanalytic work to follow Metz, and it is important to understand how each of these notions informs the spectator/film relationship.

Like Baudry, Metz asserts that identification with the screen occurs by re-enacting the confirming mirror stage for viewers, but he points out that it can never actually function as a mirror. Because the film can never reflect back the actual image of the viewer, the relationship between the viewer and the screen/mirror is primarily one of identification with *the actual ability to perceive* first encountered in the mirror stage. In his book *The Imaginary Signifier: Psychoanalysis and the Cinema*, Metz characterizes the viewer's mental process thus:

> I know that I am perceiving something imaginary...and I know that it is I who am perceiving it. This second knowledge divides in turn: I know that I am really perceiving, that my sense organs are physically affected, that I am not phantasizing, that the fourth wall of the auditorium (the screen) is really different from the other three....In other words, the spectator *identifies with himself* [sic], with himself as a pure act of perception (as wakefulness, as alertness).[21]

In this way, instead of merely regressing back to the context of the mirror stage as Baudry claims, spectators experience the mirror stage's process of perception by establishing a primary identification with the camera's field of vision as it captures the events in the film. This in turn leads to a secondary identification with the looks of characters in the film whose points of view are captured in film shot and editing techniques. In essence, Metz claims that viewers know that they are not seeing themselves in the screen/mirror, but they do resonate with the actual mirror-stage processes of perceiving and identifying with images outside of themselves by aligning themselves with the scope of the camera and the looks of the characters.

After establishing these primary and secondary identifications with the apparatus, Metz claims that viewers participate in what he calls "the passion for perceiving," or scopohilia. **Scopophilia** refers to pleasure that comes from the process of looking, and Freud identifies it as one manifestation of the sexual drive. Should the aim of the drive deviate from actually acquiring its object, "visual impressions remain the most frequent pathway along which libidinal excitation is aroused."[22] For Metz, derivatives of scopophilia like voyeurism and fetishism help explain the draw of the movie theater and the fascination with film.

Voyeurism, or the process of experiencing pleasure by watching a desired object or person from a distance, is a powerful concept at work in the movie theater. Maintaining a distance between looker and object is key to the pleasure of voyeurism, and Metz sees this distinction as a result of the very nature of desire and lack. Remember that, according to Lacan, one's desires can never be fully satisfied, for they are based on a fundamental uncertainty. Achieving an object of the drive never quite satisfies us because we soon discover that the object cannot fulfill every yearning. Put another way, our desire for an object is stronger when we are at a distance, *before* we achieve the object and discover its imperfections. Metz recognizes that many arts rely upon activating the voyeuristic tendencies inherent in viewers, but film is an especially potent realm of this type of scopophilic pleasure. Like the theatrical performance of plays, cinema screenings place viewers at a distance from the object watched. However, unlike live drama, the objects are not actually present in the movie theater. There is no true exhibitionist complement to the cinematic voyeur, no actual object or person to be watched beyond the flat, projected image. This absence increases the perception of distance and lack between voyeur and object, in turn increasing the possibility of scopophilic pleasure.

Fetishism, or the psychic structuring of an object or person as a source of sexual pleasure, is another Freudian concept bound to the notion of looking that helps explain the draw of the cinematic apparatus. For Freud, fetishizing is an important part of navigating the Oedipus complex which helps to explain the otherwise inexplicable attraction in later life to objects that many would deem "non-sexual." In the complex the child comes to understand for the first time that a power differential exists between the mother and father on the basis of who possesses the phallus. The child thus has two contradictory thoughts: (1) all caretakers are powerful, and (2) some caretakers are more powerful than others. In paraphrasing Freud, Metz claims that the child will "retain its former belief *beneath* the new one, but it will also hold to its new perceptual observation while disavowing it on another level."[23] The knowledge that some can lack the powerful phallus terrifies the child and forces him/her to imagine the implications of his/her own loss or lack. This "castration" anxiety is so great that the child will sometimes fixate on a nearby object in the physical environment, transforming it into a fetish that denies the potential absence of the phallus and becomes a source of pleasure in itself. The fetish effectively "puts a 'fullness' in place of a lack, but in doing so it also affirms that lack. It resumes within itself the structure of disavowal and multiple belief."[24]

Metz sees fetishism operating in the cinematic apparatus through a disavowal inherent to the watching process. On one hand, viewers understand that the objects, characters, and events unfolding in the film before them are not real. On the other hand, quality films will attempt to mimic real life as much as possible and instill within viewers a sense of realism. Viewers, wrestling with the tension between consciously disavowing the film's truth and unconsciously believing the story as true, turn their attention to a fetish to relieve this discomfort. For Metz, the diversionary cinematic fetish is the machinery of the film itself, the director's techniques that help frame and progress the film. "The cinema fetishist," Metz writes, "is the person who is enchanted at what the machine is capable of."[25] Thus, the apparatus is the site where viewers relive Oedipal conflict and anxiety, and they negotiate these negative feelings again through the process of fetishism.

Apparatus theory (and especially the work of Metz) provides an important foundation for the field of Psychoanalytic media studies, but one would be hard pressed to find a scholar today who wholly supports this viewpoint. In many ways apparatus theory is considered a historical moment rather than a vibrant area of contemporary research. Critics of apparatus theory claim that it is a naïve approach to film that ignores a number of cinematic qualities (sound, historical context, etc.), and Feminists critique the approach for its relative silence toward issues of gender inequality and representation in film. In fact, this critique represents the next significant application of psychoanalytic theory in film scholarship, a body of work centered on how psychoanalysis influences the depiction and reception of gender in film.

The male gaze

With the publication of Laura Mulvey's landmark piece "Visual Pleasure and Narrative Cinema" in 1975, some Psychoanalytic media scholars began shifting their attention away from the context of the cinema and focused more on the actual form and narrative of the films involved. This shift opened up a field of study on what has become known as the **male gaze**. In her article, Mulvey contends that the film viewer is not merely called upon to participate in unconscious desire via the apparatus theories of Baudry and Metz, but that the cinema itself uses psychoanalytical concepts of desire, identification, voyeurism, and fetishism to frame the narrative across gendered, ideological lines.[26] It is no accident that the protagonists of many film narratives are male, and Mulvey asserts that Metz's matrix of identification and scopophilia actually operates within a powerful phallocentric frame of reference.

Remember that within a phallocentric frame, men are defined by the presence of the powerful phallus, and masculinity and male sexuality are defined by favorable concepts of action and primacy. Women are defined by an absence of the phallus, and therefore femininity and female sexuality are associated with passiveness and powerlessness. In considering this perspective, Mulvey writes:

> There is an obvious interest in this analysis for feminists.... It gets us nearer to the roots of our oppression, it brings an articulation of the problem closer, it faces us with the ultimate challenge: how to fight the unconscious structured like a language (formed critically at the moment of arrival of language) while still caught within the language of the patriarchy. There is no way in which we can produce an alternative out of the blue, but we can begin to make a break by examining patriarchy with the tools it provides, of which psychoanalysis is not the only but an important one.[27]

Accordingly, Mulvey turns to psychoanalysis to propose a theory of the cinema that associates desire and looking with gendered power. She melds concepts of identification and scopophilia with the male-presence and female-absence thesis of phallocentrism to arrive at a structure for filmic narrative: male/subject/looker and female/object/looked at. Within classic film narrative, Mulvey claims that male characters are active subjects who look upon female characters as passive objects. Likewise, the look of the camera, the way that the shot decisions of the director frame the narrative, is also inherently male and places the female body on display for audiences. Taken together, these two concepts form Mulvey's notion of the male gaze. In accessing a film through this male gaze, film spectators experience unconscious, scopophilic pleasure in two ways: (1) by identifying with the male gaze of the camera as it concentrates on female characters, and (2) by identifying with the male characters who gaze at female characters within the film itself.

In order to understand how Mulvey's thesis builds upon Metz's insights, as well as how her ideas may find continued application in media beyond film today, consider the Nikon advertisement in Figure 7.2. We would suggest that part of the appeal of this ad arises from Metz's understanding of voyeurism. Though the ad directly references the popular image of the "Peeping Tom," the extremely large camera screen framing the models on the bed effectively creates one more voyeur here: the consumer of the ad itself. In the same way that a film screen mediates between the viewer and the projected object in Metz's work, the Nikon camera screen establishes an illusory barrier between the models in the ad and anyone who encounters it. In both cases, the screens draw attention to the impossible distance between the viewer and the mediated object, which in turn mirrors the experience of lack at the core of Psychoanalytic desire. At the same time, Mulvey would consider it no accident that the gazed upon objects in the ad are *women*, while the implied voyeurs here are *men* (or Peeping *Toms*). Like many deployments of gazing in mainstream media, the ad frames the ability to look as masculine and the ability to draw the look as feminine, which intensifies its scopophilic potential. In the process of gazing at the image, consumers are encouraged to identify with the look of the camera or the look of the

The Nikon S60. Detects up to 12 faces.

Nikon

Figure 7.2   Nikon S60 advertisement. COURTESY OF THE ADVERTISING ARCHIVES.

implied voyeurs within the scene itself. All of these positions, however, are masculine in nature.

Although Mulvey was primarily concerned with the narratives of classical Hollywood cinema, one can still find the male gaze operating in contemporary films as well. The 1997 science fiction blockbuster *The Fifth Element* provides an excellent example.[28] The film follows rugged anti-hero Korben Dallas (Bruce Willis) as he teams up with a ragtag group of individuals to assemble an elemental weapon that will save the world from destruction at the hands of an evil industrialist named Zorg (Gary Oldman). Besides the blatant objectification throughout the film of the young and sexy "fifth element" Leeloo (Milla Jovovich), a futuristic opera scene about halfway through the narrative provides a striking example of how the male gaze maintains an enduring presence in cinema today.

Dallas receives an invitation to the opera in order to collect parts of the weapon from the alien diva Plavalaguna. Although on a strict military mission to save the world, Dallas finds himself utterly enraptured during her performance. Plavalaguna is not a human female, but the character exudes femininity through her voice, actions, and physical appearance (including the features of her chest which suggest human breasts). The camera sweeps around her throughout the scene and positions her as an object to be consumed visually by audiences both inside and outside of the actual film. As a result, the actual audience can experience scopophilic pleasure by looking at the diva on screen *and* by identifying with the audience watching her within the film. This double identification is intensified by camera work that establishes a visual (but uneven) connection between the diva and Dallas during the show. At times the camera focuses solely on the diva from a low angle, and the audience understands that they are looking up to the stage from Dallas's front-row perspective. However, in the return shot where one would expect to see Dallas in a similar way through the diva's eyes, instead the camera hovers just to the side of her head (which viewers can see on the screen). In this way, the film invites viewers to identify with Dallas looking at the diva but not with the diva looking at Dallas. Here again, the man is the subject looking and the woman is the object looked at.

The interpretive power of the male gaze does not end here. Mulvey asserts that all female objects will eventually create anxiety for viewers/subjects because their very existence as woman references the absent phallus, Oedipal "castration," and social shortcoming. In order to contain the threat of castration they represent, Mulvey claims that female characters in film are neutralized through various narrative developments of voyeurism and fetishism. Voyeuristic mechanisms in the film, for example, often invite viewers to experience a "preoccupation with the re-enactment of the original trauma (investigating the woman, demystifying her mystery)" even as the film's narrative typically features a "devaluation, punishment or saving of the guilty object."[29] In other words, many films associate acts of looking with depictions of sadism or feminine frailty because the link creates the illusion of control over (and punishment of) the offending female object. Narrative developments based in fetishism, conversely, disavow castration anxiety by transforming the female object into a source of sexual beauty and pleasure. This is most often achieved by diverting attention away from the complexity of the female character and toward specific parts of her body.

Sometimes the female object within the narrative experiences both voyeuristic punishment and fetishism, as is the case with Plavalaguna in *The Fifth Element*. Moments after she finishes her hypnotic performance, a group of alien bounty hunters break into the opera house and brutally gun down the diva in front of the entire audience. Dallas, rushing to her aid, finds her in her last breaths explaining that the weapon pieces he is looking for are actually inside of her body. After a moment's hesitation, he slowly reaches into her gunshot wounds and removes the pieces as she dies in his arms. In this way, the female diva as threatening object is punished with a violent death and fetishized when the film reduces her to nothing more than a supple chest cavity containing the weapon.

Because practices of looking and voyeurism are not confined to the cinema, however, it is possible to discover the sadistic punishment and fetishistic reduction of women in other forms of media as well. The advertisements in Figures 7.3 and 7.4 illustrate this tendency. While heaving a woman's incapacitated body into an automobile trunk may seem like a convoluted way to display and advertise Jimmy Choo shoes, the depiction of this act makes a bit more sense within the Psychoanalytic register of the male gaze. The ad invokes scopophilic pleasures organized around a female object while simultaneously punishing her weakness and relieving any unconscious anxieties that she may summon in the audience. Compared to this dire desert, the posh bedroom in the Dolce & Gabbana ad may seem like a far less dangerous location to advertise designer clothing, but we would suggest that this image quashes viewer anxieties by performing a different sort of violence on the female object, namely a "decapitation" that reduces her fetishistically to a pair of legs.

Figure 7.3 Jimmy Choo advertisement. COURTESY OF THE ADVERTISING ARCHIVES.

Before moving any further, it is important to pause and note an important distinction. The fact that the gaze of the camera in contemporary society is inherently male (and heterosexual, for that matter) does not preclude other social groups from gaining scopophilic pleasure from gazing. It would be ridiculous to say that only men gain pleasure from watching movies or looking at advertisements; the sheer popularity of these institutions in America speaks against the fact. Instead, research on the gaze points to the ways that film and other forms of media can tap into mental structures and orient us to receiving unconscious pleasure across gendered, ideological lines. All spectators can experience the pleasure of looking in the media, but texts often ask them to do so by identifying with a masculine perspective (as Mulvey later asserted in a 1981 article[30]). For Mulvey, that process of identification supports systems of social inequity and decreases the possibility of viewing positions based in the experiences of subjugated groups finding a place in mainstream media.

Figure 7.4
Dolce & Gabbana
advertisement.
COURTESY OF THE
ADVERTISING ARCHIVES.

Despite the interpretive utility and political importance of the male gaze, a nagging question remains: Is it outdated? Mainstream media representations of gender have certainly become more complex since the publication of Mulvey's thesis in 1975. How, for example, might Mulvey account for the existence of something like Steven Soderbergh's 2012 film *Magic Mike*, which follows the lives of a group of male strippers living in Florida? In this mainstream film and in others, the male body is framed as a sexual object with the same visual codes that she reserves for the female body, suggesting that her thesis may no longer apply. Many scholars note, however, that films and other forms of media which appear to objectify the male body also regularly feature codes that simultaneously negate such objectification. In his analysis of the male pin-up in popular magazines, for example, Richard Dyer claims that erotic images of men always contain "instabilities."[31] Though objectified, the male model often denies the look of the spectator by looking away from the camera or positioning his body in ways to connote ideas of power and independence. Male objects tend to be portrayed as more active than their female counterparts, and the "natural" link between muscles and the male object also works to break the image free of passive connotations. While instances of male objectification do occur, then, they carry connotations of power and activity that are typically absent in representations of female objects.

This disavowal of the male as object manifests in other ways as well. Steve Neale notes that though the male body does work as a spectacle in older films like *Spartacus* and *Ben Hur*, those images come to audiences primarily through the looks of other characters who fear or hate the objectified characters (thereby dampening the possibility of erotic desire).[32] Male bodies that *do* carry an air of erotic appeal are also often feminized, such as the body of Rock Hudson in the melodramas of Douglas Sirk. Kenneth MacKinnon suggests that these codes are so instantiated that audiences regularly assume a male object to be a source of pleasure for some other social group than themselves.[33] To illustrate this point, MacKinnon notes the reaction of his students in a film seminar to music videos that prominently objectify and sexualize the male body:

> An older woman thought that it was surely meant for teenaged girls; a younger woman was sure that it was meant for gay males; and a remarkably "out" male who should, by the latter's logic, have recognized his centrality in the audience for those videos claimed with certainty that they were not for "the likes of" him.[34]

From this example MacKinnon concludes that the male object often only ever has fictitious or assumed spectators, which certainly diminishes its status as an object.

Rather than contradict Mulvey's theory of the male gaze, then, many scholarly discussions of the male object tend to reinforce her thesis that "the male figure cannot bear the burden of sexual objectification."[35] The treatments of many images of the male body tacitly fortify the widespread logic of the male gaze by denying men any significant object status. At the same time, there is more to media than just the framing of its objects, and some scholars have theorized the existence of female and queer gazes on the basis of narrative, aesthetic, and other media conventions.[36] These theorists assert that Mulvey's distinction between male subject and female object is not nearly as clear or explanatory as it may originally appear, and the process of identification with the media is actually far more complicated than she claims. One of the most prominent areas of study that reflects this destabilization of the subject/object relationship is fantasy theory.

Fantasy

In her 1984 article "Fantasia," Elizabeth Cowie draws upon the work of Freudian scholars Jean Laplanche and Jean-Bertrand Pontalis to explain how psychoanalytic theory may allow for more fluid or mobile processes of identification in films than Mulvey proposes.[37] A **fantasy** is a mental representation of conscious or unconscious wish fulfillment, and (following Freud) Laplanche and Pontalis see it as a primary aspect of mental development. Fantasy is born in the moment that the suckling child begins to gain sexual satisfaction from feeding; the child wishes for and fantasizes about being with the object (typically the mother's breast, or a bottle) when the object is absent. From this understanding we can assume two qualities of fantasy. First, *wishing creates fantasy*, and we fantasize only because we wish for objects of the drive. Second, fantasy is a *scene* of the drive. It is not the drive in itself, but rather a mental structure that contains the drive and stages the achievement of its object.

Fantasy also importantly allows us to assume multiple perspectives. For Freud and Laplanche, this ability to identify with multiple perspectives in fantasy comes from the primal or first fantasy: A fantasy about the sexual union of the mother and father that created us.[38] Conscious or unconscious fantasies about this moment involve multiple parties, and in considering the perspectives of those parties we establish a template for all future fantasies. Put another way, a child might fantasize about watching the father and mother engaging in the sexual union that created the child, and within the fantasy that child might identify with the father, the mother, its own watching self, another person watching, etc. In this light, we can see that fantasy is just as fundamental as the pleasure principle and other mechanisms of early mental development. However, just as many of our drives remain beyond our conscious recognition, much of the fantasy we experience as individuals also manifests unconsciously.

It is this type of unconscious fantasy that primarily informs the work of media scholars in this tradition. They claim that films engage us like a fantasy that happens to be outside of our heads, inviting us to unconsciously identify with multiple parties in the narrative in order to work through and satisfy our drives. Because we can identify with multiple perspectives in the filmic/fantasy scene, these scholars question Mulvey's notion that audiences gain pleasure from only identifying with the watching male subject on screen. Instead, the film operates as a phantasmic space where spectators can identify with the camera's gaze, same-sex characters, opposite-sex characters, objects, and virtually any other aspect of the narrative. Pleasure comes not from visually consuming the female objects in the film through the male gaze as Mulvey claims, but rather in identifying with characters involved in achieving the objects of their drive/desire on screen. Instead of identifying solely with the male protagonist as he searches to fill his lack in the narrative, audiences in fantasy are free to identify with any aspect of the quest (or with multiple aspects at different times during the film).

Much like Metz's earlier claims about voyeurism in film, Cowie asserts that pleasure in the filmic fantasy comes from the endless deferment of Lacanian desire within the narrative. Recall that desire is predicated on the person being removed from the desired object, and desire is motivating until the person achieves the object. As such, spectators identifying with characters in the film-as-fantasy gain pleasure in the narrative moments that defer and prolong desire, not in the moments where characters actually achieve the objects of their desires. As Cowie puts it, although narratives almost always come to closure by the end,

> inevitably the story will fall prey to diverse diversions, delays, obstacles and other means of postponing the ending. For though we all want the couple to be united, and the obstacles heroically overcome, we don't want the story to end. ... The pleasure is in how to *bring about* the consummation, is in the happening and continuing to happen; is how it will come about, and not in the moment of *having happened*.[39]

In this tradition, then, we engage films because they represent public fantasies that allow us to work through unconscious drives and wishes. We identify with a range of subject positions within the overarching narrative of the film, a narrative that often represents the quest for a desired object. Pleasure in watching, however, comes from the moments in the film when the quest is prolonged or stunted, such as the introduction of the antagonist or other obstacles that keep the protagonist from reaching his/her goal.

The 2003 film *Girl with a Pearl Earring* provides an excellent example of the fantasy approach discussed thus far. The film is a fictional account of how the famous Johannes Vermeer painting of the same name came to exist. It follows the painfully slow seduction of house servant Griet (Scarlett Johansson) by the tortured artist (Colin Firth) and his decision to secretly paint her as his masterpiece. The minimal dialog in the film, coupled with its dreamlike reliance on color and ambient sound, makes it an especially ample fantasy environment for spectators.

A forbidden mutual attraction is present from the first contact between Griet and Vermeer: she for his artistic brilliance and he for her inspiring beauty. Their "courtship" is achingly drawn out and deferred countless times, embodying the fantasy construct of unattainable desire. Spectators who engage the film as fantasy can identify with either or both characters as they yearn for each other throughout the film, and the postponed consummation of their relationship provides the environment where desire continues to thrive. The film is peppered with moments where the two are just barely kept apart. At one point, while teaching Griet to mix and produce paint, Vermeer allows his hand to casually fall near her own at the work table. He pauses before barely inching his hand toward hers. Startled, she looks at it, but the two are interrupted before she can accept his tender offering. In these moments, where outside influences continually divide the characters, viewers can experience the motivation of their own unfulfilled, unconscious desires for objects.

The ending of the film is equally (un)satisfying. Shortly after Vermeer paints her into his masterpiece, Griet is banished from the home by his envious wife Catherina. The final scene of the film, however, shows another servant arriving at Griet's new residence with a package from Vermeer. Inside the package are Catherina's pearl earrings that the artist had Griet wear while posing for the painting. Again, their desire for one another is endlessly deferred in this open-ended conclusion, which stands in stark contrast to the more typical Hollywood ending of a couple's union or marriage. Spectators are left pondering the future of Griet and Vermeer, contemplating the unfulfilled desire between the two while unconsciously activating personal desires as well.

Fantasy theory's basis in narrative and the fluid process of identification represents an attempt to compensate for the perceived limitations of apparatus theory and ideas regarding the male gaze. Still, Teresa de Lauretis fairly criticizes this approach for overlooking some key discrepancies about psychoanalytic fantasy:

> [F]irst, a particular fantasy scenario, regardless of its artistic, formal, or aesthetic excellence as filmic representation, is not automatically accessible to every spectator; a film may work as fantasy for some spectators, but not for others. Second, and conversely, the spectator's own sociopolitical location and psycho-sexual configuration have much to do with whether

or not the film can work for her as a scenario of desire, and as what Freud would call a "visualization" of the subject herself as subject of the fantasy: that is to say, whether the film can engage her spectatorial desire or, literally, whether she can see herself in it.[40]

De Lauretis acknowledges, in other words, that we all fantasize, but she reminds us that the contents of those fantasies are unique to each person. Consequently, there is no reason to believe that the specific narrative content of a particular film appeals uniformly to everyone.

Fantasy theory is one of the last concerted gestures within psychoanalytic film studies, which has somewhat fallen out of vogue since the 1980s. Contrary to those who suggest that other approaches to the media have completely eclipsed Psychoanalysis, however, some media scholars continue to use Psychoanalytic concepts in order to investigate particular texts and technologies for the ways they might resonate with mental forces. These developments represent the best chance for another movement within Psychoanalytic media studies like those we have outlined in this chapter, so we conclude our exploration with them.

Contemporary Scholarship in Psychoanalytic Analysis

While Psychoanalysis remains a viable means for explaining the appeal of media texts today, scholars have largely moved away from the comprehensive perspectives of apparatus theory, the male gaze, and fantasy in favor of more localized or case-specific approaches.

In essence, these scholars acknowledge that Psychoanalytic theories may no longer have widespread conceptual purchase, but they also argue that Freudian and Lacanian insights are sometimes the most useful tools for understanding the narrative or structural elements of a given text.

David Rudd's analysis of Neil Gaiman's *Coraline* is a good example of this trend.[41] The novel revolves around the fantastic adventures of Coraline, a young girl who attempts to leave her inattentive parents by escaping into a mirror universe where everything is the opposite of her own. Although initially charmed by the extreme attention and praise she receives from her new, doting parents, Coraline comes to realize that her "other mother" also plans to trap her in the bizarre universe forever. The woman is, in effect, (s)mothering Coraline to death. Rudd reads *Coraline* in part as an allegory for the Lacanian developmental trajectory of need, demand, and desire. Desire, as a product of language, fuels our constant yearning for love and recognition from the (m)other, but fulfillment of this yearning is constitutively impossible unless we somehow forsake the social/Symbolic realm of language for the specular confusions of the Imaginary (in short, psychosis). The mirror world and the fulfilling "other mother" in *Coraline* are dangerous precisely because they embody:

> all that we need to set aside in order to live, but which will continue to shadow us, and which, indeed, can at times seem appealing. In pursuing her wish to be special, then,

Coraline comes too close to realizing her desires. After this realization, Coraline spends the rest of the book trying to re-establish a distance, to rebuild the fantasmatic screen that allows her to function in the world.[42]

Coraline and its filmic adaptation may be intended for young adults, but Rudd suggests that its underlying Psychoanalytic structure should resonate with all audiences who experience the temptations and dangers of desire.

Some scholars take this interpretive logic a step further when they suggest that media texts which appear to be particularly open to Psychoanalytic readings might also be viewed as reflections or "symptoms" of deeper cultural developments and anxieties. Much like Freud and his contemporaries used knowledge of the drives and the Oedipus complex to probe the depths of patients' psyches and discover the roots of their neuroses, some media scholars utilize Psychoanalytic concepts to "diagnose" cultural and historical moments through the mental structures or processes presented in media of the time. Psychoanalytic understandings of paternal influence, for example, allow Joshua Gunn to link the "father trouble" at the heart of the films *Fight Club* (1999) and *War of the Worlds* (2005) to larger cultural issues of personal identity and power at the beginning of the twenty-first century.[43] In the first instance, Gunn and Thomas Frentz argue that relations between the three primary characters in *Fight Club* are fundamentally Oedipal. The film's extreme violence may be read as representation of the psychoses that results when the paternal figure fails to intervene on the mother–child dyad. Interestingly, this cinematic violence strongly mirrored (and at times inspired) increasing amounts of actual violence at the time of the film's release, leading the authors to conclude that *Fight Club* may in fact index a modern yearning for order that can combat a diffuse cultural "psychosis," or a pervasive inability to reconcile personal identity with social reality. Gunn makes a somewhat resonant argument in his essay on *War of the Worlds*. Here the actions of main character Ray Ferrier (Tom Cruise), a father trying to protect his family during an alien invasion, are akin to the prohibitionary and structuring responsibilities of the paternal figure within the Lacanian Oedipal moment. While *Worlds* activates viewers' need for security in the same way that *Fight Club* dramatizes yearnings for accountability, Gunn is troubled by the way that director Steven Spielberg yolks the unconscious paternal function to very specific political events the time of its release, most notably the terrorist attacks of 9/11 and the Bush Administration's bid for global power. Ultimately, *Worlds* stages a disaster so that its viewers come to wish for a "father" who can protect them outside of the theater as well. As Gunn summarizes it, "*War of the Worlds* unwittingly teaches spectators how to love a dictator" in part by tapping into the deepest layers of the unconscious.[44]

Such symptomatic readings of culture are, of course, possible beyond the medium of film as well. In *Television and Youth Culture: Televised Paranoia*, Jan Jagodzinski argues that the sudden appearance of paranoid and/or "parentless" teenagers on television programs like *Roswell*, *Dawson's Creek*, and others since the late 1990s indicates a much more fundamental, "post-Oedipal" shift within American life.[45] Eternal youth, he notes, is currently an ideal to which many people aspire. Infants are encouraged to grow into their youth more quickly, and adults are pressured to hold onto it longer. If *everyone* is a youth, however, then there is no Oedipal authority to hold people accountable to social reality, resulting in what Jagodzinski calls a widespread "orphan" subjectivity rife with paranoia. Thus, the now common image of the televised teenager who does not attend classes regularly, who secretly battles a variety of supernatural forces, or who only occasionally checks in with largely absent/clueless parents is not an entirely random trend. Instead, Jagodzinski suggests, these paranoid and defensive teens reflect deeper Psychoanalytic issues that accompany a contemporary cult(ure) of youth.

Although the interpretive and symptomatic approaches to texts are both well represented in contemporary Psychoanalytic media studies, a smaller group of scholars utilize Freudian and Lacanian ideas to understand the appeal of certain technologies independent of specific content. Perhaps the best application of psychoanalysis in this approach is in relation to the internet. In a sustained project across a number of different publications, for example, Jodi Dean argues that part of the popularity of web technology stems from its ability to host the compulsive nature of the drive.[46] Lacan suggests that the drive would prefer to endlessly circulate around its object rather than ever actually reach it, a logic that Dean sees replicated in hyperlinking, Facebook "liking," blog posting, and other activities that come to construct a circuit of constant and interminable activity on the web. This resonance between mind and machine is not accidental. Dean suggests that these new technologies and platforms signal the historical rise of "communicative capitalism," where a small cadre of tech wizards and corporations benefit financially from the unconscious capture of a population lulled into political complacency. In short, what seems like genuine participation in the public sphere of the internet is nothing more than the chaos of endless chatter, inspiring little to no action. Dean ultimately suggests that people (and specifically the political Left) need to overcome the seductive pull of new media technologies if genuine political change will ever be possible.

However, Slavoj Žižek, arguably the most popular Psychoanalytic media scholar of our age, disagrees with Dean's thesis to some degree.[47] Žižek also sees a strong resonance between Psychoanalytic mechanisms and the web, but he is less ready to assume that the technology automatically and unconsciously captures its users. Instead, after outlining four popular theses regarding the Psychoanalytic implications of the internet (which are somewhat beyond the scope of our introductory chapter), Žižek concludes by recognizing that there is more to the relation than just the technology–user interface:

> What if it is wrong and misleading to ask which of the four versions of the libidinal or symbolic economy of cyberspace that we outlined (the psychotic suspension of Oedipus, the continuation of Oedipus with other means, the perverse staging of the law, and traversing the fantasy) is the "correct" one? What if these four versions are the four possibilities opened up by the cyberspace technology, so that, ultimately, the choice is ours? How will cyberspace affect us is not directly inscribed into its technological properties; it rather hinges on the network of sociosymbolic relations (e.g. of power and domination) which always and already overdetermine the way cyberspace affects us.[48]

Žižek thus underscores Dean's careful attention to the economic relations of the current era while also reminding us that internet technology should not be automatically forsaken for its Psychoanalytic properties.

Conclusion

This chapter has looked at how the Psychoanalytic concept of drive helps explain the structure of media technologies and texts, with film as the historically predominant area of analysis. Psychoanalytic theorists Sigmund Freud and Jacques Lacan provide a somewhat overlapping understanding of the formative process that results in an individual's psychical structure, and their respective theories of repression and desire each help shed light on why films and other forms of media appeal to audiences based on this mental formation. The three approaches to film outlined in this chapter (apparatus theory, theories of the male gaze, and fantasy theory) all attempt to explain how the early structuring of the human mind results in the particular management of film in society: filmic evolution, screenings, shot sequences, characterization, narratives, etc. Contemporary scholars have extended these approaches by questioning their assumptions about the nature of gender, sexuality, and desire, resulting in a vibrant field of Psychoanalytic research today. Although Psychoanalytic approaches to media texts are not as popular as they were in the 1970s and 1980s, Psychoanalytic scholars continue to present the field of media studies with a fascinating synthesis of psychology with books, film, television, and the internet. If nothing else, psychoanalysis provides us with a multifaceted interpretation of the psyche, an important perspective on contemporary media, and a language to articulate the at times inexplicable attraction we feel toward popular texts.

MEDIA LAB 6: DOING PSYCHOANALYTIC ANALYSIS

OBJECTIVE

The aim of this lab is to utilize Psychoanalytic concepts to analyze media texts. Specifically, students will investigate how notions of the male gaze work to structure the "look of" and "look within" magazine advertisements.

ACTIVITY

- Divide the class into small groups of 4–5 students each.
- Display the advertisements for Candie's Fragrances and Shockwaves shown in Figures 7.5 and 7.6.
- Ask students to record their answers to the following questions.
  1 How do the concepts of scopophilia, voyeurism, and fetishism help to account for the appeal of these advertisements?
  2 How, if at all, is the male gaze activated in these advertisements? In answering this question, please attend carefully to the matters of identification (who are viewers invited to identify with?) and the object/subject dichotomy.
  3 What role, if any, does phallocentrism play in these advertisements?

Figure 7.5
Candie's Fragrances
advertisement.
Courtesy of Iconix
Brand/Candie's
Fragrances.

Figure 7.6
Shockwaves
advertisement.
COURTESY OF THE
ADVERTISING ARCHIVES.

SUGGESTED READING

Bateman, A. and Holmes, J. *Introduction to Psychoanalysis: Contemporary Theory and Practice.* New York/London: Routledge, 1995.

Baudry, J.-L. Ideological Effects of the Basic Cinematographic Apparatus. In *Film Theory and Criticism: Introductory Readings*, 5th edn, L. Braudry and M. Cohen (eds), pp. 345–55. New York: Oxford University Press, 1999.

Biesecker, B. No Time for Mourning: the Rhetorical Production of the Melancholic Citizen-Subject in the War on Terror. *Philosophy & Rhetoric* 2007, 40, 147–69.

Chaudhuri, S. *Feminist Film Theorists: Laura Mulvey, Kaja Silverman, Teresa De Lauretis, Barbara Creed.* New York/London: Routledge, 2006.

Cooper, B. "Chick Flicks" as Feminist Texts: the Appropriation of the Male Gaze in Thelma & Louise. *Women's Studies in Communication* 2000, 23, 277–306.

Cowie, E. *Representing the Woman: Cinema and Psychoanalysis.* Minneapolis, MN: University of Minnesota Press, 1997.

de Lauretis, T. *Alice Doesn't.* Bloomington, IN: Indiana University Press, 1984.

Elliot, A. *Psychoanalytic Theory: an Introduction*, 2nd edn. Durham, NC: Duke University Press, 2002.

Evans, D. *An Introductory Dictionary of Lacanian Psychoanalysis.* New York/London: Routledge, 1996.

Fink, B. *The Lacanian Subject: Between Language and Jouissance.* Princeton, NJ: Princeton University Press, 1995.

Freud, S. *Introductory Lectures on Psycho-Analysis*, trans. J. Strachey. New York: W.W. Norton & Company, 1966.

Freud, S. *An Outline of Psycho-Analysis,* trans. J. Strachey. New York: W.W. Norton & Company, 1970.

Gunn, J. Refitting Fantasy: Psychoanalysis, Subjectivity, and Talking to the Dead. *Quarterly Journal of Speech* 2004, 90, 1–23.

Gunn, J. and Hall, M.M. Stick it in Your Ear: The Psychodynamics of iPod Enjoyment. *Communication and Critical/Cultural Studies* 2008, 5(2), 135–57.

Lacan, J. *Écrits*, trans. B. Fink. New York: W.W. Norton & Company, 2006.

Manlove, C.T. Visual "Drive" and Cinematic Narrative: Reading Gaze Theory in Lacan, Hitchcock and Mulvey. *Cinema Journal* 2007, 46, 83–104.

Metz, C. *The Imaginary Signifier: Psychoanalysis and the Cinema*, trans. C. Britton, A. Williams, B. Brewster, and A. Guzzetti. Bloomington, IN: Indiana University Press, 1982.

Mitchell, J. *Psychoanalysis and Feminism.* London: Penguin, 1974.

Narine, N. Global Trauma and Narrative Cinema. *Theory, Culture & Society* 2010, 27, 119–45.

Penley, C. *The Future of an Illusion: Film, Feminism, and Psychoanalysis.* Minneapolis, MN: University of Minnesota Press, 1989.

Rushing, J.H. and Frentz, T.S. *Projecting the Shadow: the Cyborg Hero in American Film.* Chicago, IL: University of Chicago Press, 1995.

Van Haute, P. *Against Adaptation: Lacan's "Subversion" of the Subject.* New York: Other Press, 2002.

Žižek, S. *Enjoy Your Symptom! Jacques Lacan in Hollywood and Out.* New York/London: Routledge, 1992.

NOTES

1. S. Freud, *An Outline of Psycho-Analysis*, trans. J. Strachey (New York: W.W. Norton & Company, 1970), 17. See also S. Freud, Instincts and Their Vicissitudes, in *The Freud Reader*, P. Gay (ed.), trans. J. Strachey (New York: W.W. Norton & Company, 1989), 562–8.

2. For a succinct description of the pleasure and reality principles as they relate to the drives, see S. Freud, *Introductory Lectures on Psycho-Analysis*, trans. J. Strachey (New York: W.W. Norton & Company, 1966), 443–4.

3. S. Freud, *The Interpretation of Dreams*, trans. J. Crick (New York: Oxford University Press, 1999), 346–74.

4. S. Freud, *The Ego and the Id*, trans. J. Riviere and J. Strachey (New York: W.W. Norton & Company, 1960).

5. Freud, *The Ego and the Id*, 19.

6. S. Freud, *Beyond the Pleasure Principle*, trans. J. Strachey (New York: W.W. Norton & Company, 1961).

7. Freud, *An Outline*, 18.

8. Freud, *The Ego and the Id*, 37–40.

9. Freud, *An Outline*, 24.

10. See S. Freud, The Sexual Aberrations, in *Three Essays on the Theory of Sexuality*, trans. J. Strachey (New York: Basic Books, 1962), 1–38.

11. Freud, *The Ego and the Id*, 26–32; Freud, *Introductory Lectures*, 408–16; Freud, *An Outline*, 69–78.

12. Of course, Lacan arrives at this conclusion through much more complicated means than we can explore in an introduction to his work, but curious readers may consult the following essays for the basis of these ideas: Position of the Unconscious, in *Écrits*, trans. B. Fink (New York: W.W. Norton & Company, 2006), 703–21; The Deconstruction of the Drive, in *The Four Fundamental Concepts of Psychoanalysis*, J.-A. Miller (ed.), trans. A. Sheridan (London: Vintage, 1977), 161–73.

13. See J. Lacan, The Subversion of the Subject and the Dialectic of Desire in the Freudian Unconscious, in *Écrits*, trans. B. Fink (New York: W.W. Norton & Company, 2006), 672–702.

14. M.-H. Brousse, The Drive (I), in *Reading Seminar XI: Lacan's Four Fundamental Concepts of Psychoanalysis*,

R. Feldstein, B. Fink, and M. Jaanus (eds) (Albany, NY: State University of New York Press, 1995), 106.

15. J. Lacan, The Mirror Stage as Formative of the I Function, in *Écrits*, trans. B. Fink (New York: W.W. Norton & Company, 2006), 76.

16. See the discussion of the "imaginary phallus" in D. Evans, *An Introductory Dictionary of Lacanian Psychoanalysis* (New York/London: Routledge, 1996), 142.

17. J. Mitchell, *Psychoanalysis and Feminism* (London: Penguin, 1974).

18. J.-L. Baudry, The Apparatus: Metaphysical Approaches to the Impression of Reality in Cinema, in *Film Theory and Criticism: Introductory Readings*, L. Braudy and M. Cohen (eds), 5th edn (New York: Oxford University Press, 1999), 767.

19. J.-L. Baudry, Ideological Effects of the Basic Cinematic Apparatus, in *Film Theory and Criticism: Introductory Readings*, L. Braudy and M. Cohen (eds), 5th edn (New York: Oxford University Press, 1999), 353.

20. Baudry, Ideological Effects, 354.

21. C. Metz, *The Imaginary Signifier: Psychoanalysis and the Cinema*, trans. C. Britton, A. Williams, B. Brewster, and A. Guzzetti (Bloomington, IN: Indiana University Press, 1982), 48–9.

22. Freud, *Three Essays*, 22.

23. Metz, 70.

24. Metz, 71.

25. Metz, 74.

26. L. Mulvey, Visual Pleasure and Narrative Cinema, in *Media and Cultural Studies: Keywords*, M.G. Durham and D.M. Kellner (eds) (Oxford: Blackwell, 2006), 342–52.

27. Mulvey, Visual Pleasure, 343.

28. B. Ott and E. Aoki, Counter-Imagination as Interpretive Practice: Futuristic Fantasy and *The Fifth Element*, *Women's Studies and Communication* 2004, 27(2), 149–76.

29. Mulvey, Visual Pleasure, 348.

30. L. Mulvey, Afterthoughts on "Visual Pleasure and Narrative Cinema" Inspired by King Vidor's *Duel in the Sun*, in *Feminist Film Theory: A Reader*, S. Thornham (ed.) (New York: New York University Press, 1999), 122–30.

31. R. Dyer, *Only Entertainment* (New York: Routledge, 1992).

32. S. Neale, Masculinity as Spectacle: Reflections on Men in Mainstream Cinema, in *Feminism and Film*, E.A. Kaplan (ed.) (New York: Oxford University Press, 2000), 253–64.

33. K. MacKinnon, After Mulvey: Male Erotic Objectification, in *The Body's Perilous Pleasures: Dangerous Desires and Contemporary Culture*, M. Aaron (ed.) (Edinburgh: Edinburgh University Press, 1999), 13–29.

34. MacKinnon, 18.

35. Mulvey, Visual Pleasure, 347.

36. See, for example, M.A. Doane, Film and the Masquerade: Theorizing the Female Spectator, in *Feminist Film Theory: a Reader*, S. Thornham (ed.) (New York: New York University Press, 1999), 131–45; T. De Lauretis, *Alice Doesn't* (Bloomington, IN: Indiana University Press, 1984); M. Hansen, Pleasure, Ambivalence, Identification: Valentino and Female Spectatorship, in *Feminism and Film*, E.A. Kaplan (ed.) (New York: Oxford University Press, 2000), 226–52; S. Drukman, The Gay Gaze, or Why I Want My MTV, in *A Queer Romance: Lesbians, Gay Men and Popular Culture*, P. Burston and C. Richardson (eds) (New York: Routledge, 1995), 81–95.

37. E. Cowie, Fantasia, in *Representing the Woman: Cinema and Psychoanalysis* (Minneapolis, MN: University of Minnesota Press, 1997), 123–65.

38. Freud references his theory of the primal fantasy or scene, as well as some general comments on the existence and role of fantasy, in *Introductory Lectures*, 458–68.

39. Cowie, 133.

40. T. de Lauretis, The Subject of Fantasy, in *Feminisms in the Cinema*, L. Pietropaolo and A. Testaferri (eds) (Bloomington, IN: Indiana University Press, 1995), 64.

41. D. Rudd, An Eye for an I: Neil Gaiman's *Coraline* and Questions of Identity, *Children's Literature in Education* 2008, 39, 159–68.

42. Rudd, 166–7.

43. J. Gunn, Father Trouble: Staging Sovereignty in Spielberg's *War of the Worlds*, *Critical Studies in Media Communication* 2008, 25(1), 1–27; J. Gunn and T. Frentz, Fighting for Father: *Fight Club* as Cinematic Psychosis, *Western Journal of Communication* 2010, 74(3), 269–91.

44. Gunn, Father Trouble, 3.

45. J. Jagodzinski, *Television and Youth Culture: Televised Paranoia* (New York: Palgrave Macmillan, 2008).

46. J. Dean, *Blog Theory: Feedback and Capture in the Circuits of Drive* (Malden, MA: Polity, 2010). See also J. Dean, *Publicity's Secret: How Technoculture Capitalizes on Democracy* (Ithaca, NY: Cornell University Press, 2002); J. Dean, *Democracy and Other Neoliberal Fantasies: Communicative Capitalism and Left Politics* (Durham, NC: Duke University Press, 2009).

47. S. Žižek, Cyberspace, or, How to Traverse the Fantasy in the Age of Retreat of the Big Other, *Public Culture* 1998, 10(3), 483–513.

48. Žižek, 511.

8 Feminist Analysis

KEY CONCEPTS

ESSENTIALISM
FEMINISM
GENDER
GLASS CEILING
PATRIARCHY
POSTFEMINISM

SEX
SEXISM
STEREOTYPE

When R&B singer India.Arie proclaimed "I Am Not My Hair" on her 2006 album *Testimony: Vol. One, Life & Relationship,* she drew attention to an interesting aspect of contemporary American culture. Hair is an important way we express who we are in our society. In particular, it is a key way we mark gender norms. Scores of products and procedures exist for women to remove "unsightly" hair from their legs, face, underarms, and bikini area. *Newsweek* magazine even caught flak in October 2008 when it featured Republican Vice Presidential candidate Sarah Palin on a cover but failed to airbrush out the hair on her upper lip. At the same time, hair-coloring kits marketed toward men emphasize masking gray hair in order to shake off the image of old age. Baldness is an even more "unmanly" condition, and a variety of shampoos, medications, and procedures exist to help men continue to look virile with a full mane of hair. In each of these examples, the biological quality of hair becomes a way that we understand the cultural rules surrounding what it means to be masculine or feminine.

The associations and meanings made between biology and culture exemplified by hair are at the heart of Feminist analysis. Feminist scholars concentrate on how biological categories like male and female become conflated with cultural expectations of gender, resulting in discriminatory social systems that privilege men over women. Feminist media scholars, in particular, concentrate on revealing the limiting nature of mass media texts that reinforce dominant social understandings of sex and gender. As a result, feminism, like Cultural studies (see Chapter 6), is also

Critical Media Studies: An Introduction, Second Edition. Brian L. Ott and Robert L. Mack.

marked by a political commitment to deconstruct these oppressive systems in order to transform society into a more equitable place for diverse peoples.

This chapter focuses on the place of feminism in understanding media texts. We begin with an introduction to feminism, paying particular attention to the ways in which it concentrates on issues of gender as a whole (and not, as is often portrayed in the mass media, the needs of women alone). After briefly considering the roles and functions of stereotypes, we spend the bulk of this chapter deconstructing common stereotypes of masculinity and femininity in the media and considering the impact of the "postfeminist" sensibility on the project of Feminist media studies.

Before we continue, though, we feel it is necessary to first address a pressing issue. "Feminism" represents a fairly broad theoretical approach to media texts. There are many different kinds of feminism that each stress particular aspects of social power and difference over others. In order to present an introduction to feminism without sacrificing its essential spirit, this chapter will concentrate on the main theoretical impulse(s) behind the tradition before considering representations of gender and sex in the media. If you find this theoretical introduction compelling, we encourage you to explore the diverse body of feminist scholarship at your leisure. See the Suggested Reading section at the end of this chapter for suggestions.

Feminism: an Overview

Feminism, broadly, is a political project that explores the diverse ways men and women are socially empowered or disempowered. It is often a highly charged word that requires some explanation to fully understand. Contrary to popular belief, contemporary feminism is not anti-male. As cultural critic bell hooks defines it in *Feminism is for Everybody*, "feminism is a movement to end sexism, sexist exploitation, and oppression."[1] **Sexism** is discrimination based upon a person's sex. Instead of targeting individual men or even men as a social group, feminism seeks to reveal and eradicate socially ingrained *systems* of sexism that harm *all* individuals in some way. In short, feminism is a political project focused on deconstructing sexist oppression present in our everyday norms and experiences.

A number of interlocking factors contribute to the creation of a sexist social system. The first is the confusion between sex and gender.[2] **Sex** refers to the innate, biological differentiation between men and women: anatomy, reproduction, hormone production, and the like. **Gender**, on the other hand, refers to the culturally constructed differences between men and women: tastes, roles, activities, and more. It is a biological fact that only women can give birth to children, but the tendency to view women as nurturing and mothering is a gendered quality. A good way to distinguish between sex and gender is to look at the respective categories they govern. Sex refers to the categories male and female, while gender refers to the categories masculine and feminine. A Y chromosome is a male trait, whereas aggressiveness is a masculine one. Trouble arises when societies such as ours confuse gendered qualities with sexual ones, understanding culturally constructed norms as innate biological traits. The common belief in American society, for example, that women are naturally more emotional than men is a result of this confusion. The belief that gender distinctions are innate and natural is called **essentialism**.

Another factor intrinsic to our sexist social system is patriarchy. **Patriarchy** is a system of power relations in which women's interests are subordinated to those of men. Essentializing a group is one way of defining them and marking their worth, and patriarchy essentializes women in a way that devalues them while predominantly serving the interests of men. We can see patriarchal logic especially in relation to economics in America. If we believe that women are innately more nurturing than men, then it "makes sense" for women to stay home with newborn children while men continue to work, earn money, and contribute to their skills sets or résumés. If we believe that women are biologically predetermined to fail at math and science, then it "makes sense" that the majority of workers in high-paying engineering and medical occupations are men. Patriarchal systems empower men and disempower women by making constructed, gendered power imbalances seem natural and innate. The often tangible benefits that men reap from this system make them less likely to challenge patriarchy than women.

Does the fact that men benefit from patriarchy mean that all men are sexist? Yes and no. To understand the difference between individuals and social systems, we turn to an analogy adapted from Allan G. Johnson's *Privilege, Power and Difference*.[3] Do you consider yourself an excessively greedy person in your everyday life? Probably not. Most of us think of greed as a negative character trait. However, would you say that you have expressed greedy traits while playing the game *Monopoly* at some point in your life? Probably so. Most of us have spent a rainy afternoon buying up properties on the *Monopoly* board and showing little financial mercy when our siblings, parents, or friends land on them. We may not consider ourselves greedy individuals, but we exhibit extremely greedy traits when playing *Monopoly*. The same can be said about how we act in sexist social systems. We may not consider ourselves sexist in the sense that we do not consciously discriminate against people in our everyday life, but when we play the "game" of sexism – when we go out into the world and take part in social systems that are inherently sexist – we, in a sense, are sexist as well. Social systems cannot happen without people, just as *Monopoly* cannot play itself, but we enact social systems and board games according to rules determined before we as individuals joined. So, to answer the question posed at the beginning of the paragraph, yes, all men are sexist. But so are all women, because we are all playing by the rules of the game when we unconsciously enact sexist social conventions. At the same time, many women and some men have attempted to reject the rules as much as possible in their individual lives. These individuals are feminists.

Understanding that we are all subject to sexist social rules opens up additional understanding about feminism. Feminism attempts to recognize and disable patriarchal social systems that disempower individual women, but recent feminist scholarship has also begun looking at the ways in which patriarchy harms individual men. The gendered expectations that patriarchy places on women also exert pressure on men, often demanding that men show little emotion, avoid certain occupations, or act as the breadwinner for their families. This fact underscores the wide scope of the contemporary feminist project. Everyone is harmed by sexist social systems, although patriarchal power relations increase the harm they do to women. Both men and women enact these systems, and both women and men can be feminists in their attempts to resist them.

Feminist media scholars understand media texts as products of sexist social systems, and they look especially at the ways in which patriarchal systems of power inform the creation of media texts. Scholars in this tradition analyze television programs, films, magazines, radio programs, and internet sites to understand how these texts reflect, support, and create systems of unequal gendered power. Although contemporary feminist scholarship is complex in its analysis of the media, the issue of gendered representation and stereotypes is a historically primary focus that still has relevance for today. The remainder of our discussion on feminism will concentrate on media representations of gender and how particular media texts express stereotypes. First, however, it is important to fully understand the social role of stereotyping.

Stereotyping in American Media

A **stereotype** is a misleading and simplified representation of a particular social group. You are probably familiar with many stereotypes already: The elderly drive badly, fraternity members enrolled in college to party, and people from the Southern US are not very smart. Stereotypes are damaging because they gloss over the complex characteristics that actually define a social group and reduce its members to a few (usually unfavorable) traits. When these stereotypical representations become commonly accepted in the media, the result is often the social oppression and disempowerment of individuals within the stereotyped group. Many people have had experiences with stereotypes. And yet, if the vast majority of people know that stereotypes are false and socially damaging, why do they persist in life and the media? There are a few different answers to this question.

A conventional (and nonetheless accurate) critical explanation for the presence of stereotypes in the media is something akin to the following: socially powerful groups like men have greater access to media outlets as a function of privilege, and this access grants them the ability to represent their particular impressions of other social groups to the widest audiences. These perspectives are often stereotypically reductionist, but they become the most widely known and accepted representations of these social groups. While the repetition of stereotypes is certainly a powerful force in securing their place in the American context, however, it is important to consider how other qualities of stereotypes contribute to their presence in the media as well.

First, everyone stereotypes. Stereotyping helps individuals make sense of an increasingly complex contemporary society. As social creatures we absorb and reflect upon the experiences we have with others, and we use past experiences to make sense of present and future interactions. Stereotypes, or mental categories of people we carry with us, allow us to quickly process incoming information about strangers by greatly reducing the amount of information we have to absorb. If we actually took the time to notice the subtle nuances of every individual we encounter on a daily basis, then we would spend much more time in our lives discussing social issues with every street petitioner and the pros and cons of long-distance service with every telemarketer. Stereotypes, however inaccurate, form mental shortcuts that allow us to quickly make snap judgments about individuals and move on.

Moreover, for such simplistic reductions of character, widespread social stereo-types are actually rather intricate in their construction. You may have heard the say-ing that there is a "kernel of truth" to every stereotype. This is true to the extent that stereotypes often blend realistic aspects of life, material conditions, and social roles into inaccurate assumptions and false traits. The continuing power and "strength of stereotypes lies in this combination of validity and distortion."[4] Stereotypes persist in the media because they have enough truth to *sound* plausible without much critical thought. To complicate the matter even more, sometimes members of socially oppressed groups will believe the stereotypes they see in the media to be true and emulate them.[5] Here stereotypes mimic reality by actually creating it. Stereotypes often persist, then, because it is difficult to distinguish their truth from falsity.

The fact that everyone stereotypes to some degree, and that aspects of stereo-types often ring true, helps explain a rather unique function of stereotypes in the media. The stereotypes we see in the media often lend texts a certain sense of credibility with audiences.[6] When we see a sitcom with a foreign exchange student speaking in broken English, or watch a movie that features a group of black gang members, these representations unfortunately "ring true" with the stereotypical knowledge we already have as members of society. In other words, media images that feature stereotypes gain an informal credibility because they match some of the common stereotypes people use every day to reduce information processing. Media producers who present textual representations that challenge social stereotypes risk losing this informal credibility. While the media create and reinforce stereotypes just as much as they use them to attract audiences, the issues of stereotyping and credibility remain a powerful influence.

In discussing these issues, we do not wish to give the impression that the media use of stereotypes is permissible because stereotyping is a human tendency, a quasi-reflection of reality, or an effective way to appeal to audiences. We also do not excuse individuals who ignorantly hold racial, gendered, sexual, or other stereotypes. Stereotypes are harmful by nature, and we should work to eradicate them as much as possible. In this section we simply hope to situate our discussion of gendered stereotypes within a larger framework of the complex ways that stereotyping operates in the media and society. It deepens our understanding of the power and place of the various mediated stereotypes we will look at. As we address these in detail in the next section, keep these various aspects of stereotypes in mind. Consider how issues like human tendency, reflections of reality, or audience adaptation methods inform the creation of these stereotypes.

Gendered Stereotypes in American Media

Exceptions exist for every rule. Recognizing exceptions is the mark of quality scholarship and true understanding. With that in mind, the stereotypical images of gender we discuss in this section signify some of the general, overarching, historical trends within media representation most apparent in Feminist criticism. They are by no means absolute truths: the contemporary American media landscape is far too diverse to fit only within the narrow range of these stereotypes. However, as archaic as they may sound, these classic stereotypes continue to thrive in media today, and concentrating on these particular stereotypes will provide a useful initial glimpse into the process of Feminist analysis.

The constructed opposition of masculinity and femininity provides a binary understanding of gender in American society, so it is understandable that many gendered stereotypes in the media also function as complementary inverses of each other. In general, stereotypes of masculinity are defined by power, significance, agency, and social influence. Stereotypes of femininity are defined by powerlessness, insignificance, passiveness, and limited control. Although these trends construct narrow gender norms for individual members of both sexes, they reinforce patriarchal systems of power by supporting the domination of men over women. The four interrelated, stereotypical binaries we focus on in this section are active/passive, public/private, logical/emotional, and sexual subject/sexual object.

Active/passive

Mainstream media representations of men and masculinity are often marked by strength and activity. Advertisements tend to depict men engaging in sports, working with tools, or driving powerful vehicles, and the models in these advertisements are often full of vitality or in good physical shape. Images of women, on the other hand, tend to emphasize passiveness and weakness. Female models often simply sit or stand beautifully to advertise their product, and many of them possess dangerously underweight figures.[7] This general contrast between men and women in advertising is striking, and the repetition of this motif across many different kinds of ads makes the distinction seem normal. Notions of power and physical prowess begin to define masculinity and "being a man" in American society, while femininity and "being a woman" are tied to passive acceptance and helplessness.

Consider the difference in gendered representation between the two "Got Milk?" advertisements in Figures 8.1 and 8.2. The advertisement with Jackie Chan exudes masculinity. The daring aerial escape from a burning car constructs Chan as physically strong and in control of his situation, so much so that he can kick a milk bottle with precision despite a rather threatening environment. While there is a great deal of activity in the scene itself (an ascending helicopter and raging flames, for example), the focus here is on Chan's agency. In fact, Chan is so sure of his abilities in this situation that we see him literally laughing in the face of danger and taking time to educate readers on the

Figure 8.1 Milk advertisement with Jackie Chan. Courtesy of The Advertising Archives.

Figure 8.2 Milk advertisement with Kate Moss. Courtesy of The Advertising Archives.

importance of drinking milk. The cityscape that fills the background of the advertisement reminds us that action always requires a context; a subject's actions make no sense unless we understand what prompts them. Additionally, this advertisement conjures many images of Chan's film career, where the actor often portrays a powerful martial artist. Even if one has never seen a Jackie Chan film before encountering this advertisement, the image reflects the "action hero" trope popular in mainstream Hollywood films.[8] Overall, the Chan advertisement taps into many different American cultural codes in order to present an image of masculinity marked by power and strength. In some ways it is easy to forget that this is an advertisement for milk.

The advertisement with model Kate Moss provides a marked contrast to that of Chan. Glancing back over her shoulder, her arm shielding her breasts from the curious eye of the camera/viewer, Moss's pose is innocent and inviting. She is naked and therefore completely vulnerable, and her body is certainly on display for the viewer in a way that Chan's is not. The text, which references Moss's famous facial bone structure, draws additional attention to her physical beauty rather than her abilities or talents. A recognizable background would at least allow readers to imagine Moss reacting to her environment, but the lack of any context here signals that Moss is merely to be visually consumed like a piece of art. The image of Moss also invokes the cultural notion of the pretty, demure model, an individual whose entire career involves constantly being directed by others. Through these various visual cues and references, the advertisement presents an image of femininity defined by passivity and vulnerability. Whereas the Chan ad implies that drinking milk will make readers active and strong, the Moss ad suggests that drinking milk will leave one passive and exposed.

Public/private

The binary of active man/passive woman helps shed light on other, related gendered stereotypes. Popular American television shows often draw sharp distinctions between men and women in relation to public and private spheres. Because men are represented as active and strong, they also tend to fulfill the role of "family provider" in media texts. Audiences often encounter scenes in which men are working on the job as the breadwinner for their families. Women, in contrast, are coded as passive and weak, and media texts tend to represent women as the "family nurturer" as a result. The common media sitcom image of the housewife is the most obvious expression of this domestic stereotype. Here the woman's responsibility is to nurture the family by cleaning the house, taking care of children, and fixing meals. Older television couples, such as Fred and Wilma Flintstone or Ward and June Cleaver (of *Leave it to Beaver*), perfectly embody these binary stereotypes.

Contemporary audiences may consider the provider/nurturer stereotype to be a gross oversimplification, and it is true that some media texts portray heterosexual couples with a much more fluid understanding of family roles. However, despite examples of progressive programs, these gender stereotypes continue to endure in popular American television programming. *The Simpsons* is an excellent example of this type of representation. Homer Simpson may be inept in his job at the Springfield Nuclear Power Plant, but he is still the sole source of income for the cartoon family. Throughout the run of the show, audiences have laughed at Homer's various misguided but heartfelt attempts to provide for his family. In the first full-length episode of the series, for example, Homer fails to get a Christmas raise and takes a job as a mall Santa to earn the money necessary for Christmas presents. Although he loses the Santa job and gambles away his meager paycheck at the Springfield dog track as a last option, he ends up securing a "Christmas" puppy for the family in the process. At various points throughout the series, Homer also works as a monorail conductor, a snowplow operator, and a manager for a country singer in order to be an effective breadwinner for his family.

In contrast, Homer's wife Marge spends most of her days as the doting housewife taking care of the Simpson family. Multiple episodes reinforce Marge's centrality to the Simpson home. In one episode Marge cracks under the pressure of her domestic responsibilities and leaves the family for a relaxing vacation, upon which the household promptly falls apart. Homer is at a loss without Marge's nurturing skills and ends up "misplacing" their youngest daughter Maggie. When Marge eventually returns, the family begs her to never leave them again. We see this theme again in a later episode where Marge is injured at a ski resort and leaves her domestic responsibilities to her daughter Lisa. The home devolves into a complete mess in only a few days. Apparently, the Simpson home cannot survive without Marge as its domestic nucleus. Additionally, even though Marge takes on various jobs throughout the series (including as an actress, an artist, and a pretzel-maker), these never last longer than an episode. When Homer fails at his second jobs, he can always return to the power plant. Marge simply returns home.

Logical/emotional

The association of the public, working sphere with men and the private, domestic sphere with women feeds into a third related gender binary: logic/emotion. Traditionally, media texts construct logic as a masculine trait and emotion as a feminine one. The masculine public sphere is related to politics and decision-making, so masculinity is marked in turn by the kinds of rational thinking associated with these processes. The private sphere is concerned with family and nurturance, and femininity is defined by irrational or emotional impulses as a result. A classic form of this stereotypical dualism is the association of men with mental processes and women with bodily ones, and the effect on our perceptions of gender is very much the same.

A striking example of the logical/emotional binary can be found on the popular syndicated television series *Star Trek: The Next Generation*. The characters of Data and Deanna Troi are clear manifestations of these gender stereotypes. Data (Brent Spiner), the starship Enterprise's lieutenant commander, is an android: a "mechanical man" made completely of circuitry and wires. His technology is sophisticated enough that the crew considers him an individual, but Data lacks the ability to feel emotion. He approaches problems throughout the series with a cool logic and clear predilection for reasoned decision-making. Although Data experiments with humor and special devices that give him the ability to emote throughout the series, these choices often diminish his problem-solving skills (and at times even put his crew in danger). Data, then, never really achieves his desire to be a "fully-feeling" human.

Deanna Troi (Marina Sirtis) is the exact opposite of Data. As the ship's psychological counselor, she is responsible for listening to crewmembers' problems and helping them through their emotional issues. Deanna is also part Betazoid, an alien race in the *Trek* universe who can empathically sense what others are feeling. This factor heightens her counseling abilities and often positions her as the ship's moral conscience and emotional expert. Deanna's empathic abilities, however, backfire at certain times when she cannot stop the flood of others' emotions from overtaking her, actually becoming an emotional "dumping ground" for an evil alien in one episode.

Data and Deanna are nearly perfect examples of the logical/emotional gender binary. Despite their best efforts to resist, each character is dominated by a stereotypically gendered way of understanding the world around them. While (masculine) Data cannot experience emotion, (feminine) Deanna sometimes cannot *stop* experiencing emotion. This duality is especially interesting in light of the original character sketches producers used while casting actors for the series. While Data should be "in perfect physical condition and…appear very intelligent," Deanna need only be "tall (5′8–6′) and slender, about 30 years old and quite beautiful."[9] Such a distinction begins to illustrate the subtle connections between stereotypes. Beauty, emotion, and femininity are stereotypically bound together in a single character in this text.

Sexual subject/sexual object

The final gendered binary is related very strongly to the first three. Masculine stereotypes of strength, ability, and intelligence often translate into media images of sexual subjectivity. In other words, media texts tend to identify men as sexually powerful and pursuant. To be masculine is to be "in charge" of the sexual encounter, to direct its progress and "make it happen." Feminine stereotypes of weakness and emotion in turn give rise to the sexual objectification of women. Media representations of women construct them as sexual conquests to be pursued and lusted after. To be feminine is to be available, responsive, and open to male sexual advances. The famous French feminist Simone de Beauvoir captures the sexual subject/object binary poetically in her treatise on the oppression of women, *The Second Sex*:

For him she is sex – absolute sex, no less. She is defined and differentiated with reference to man and not he with reference to her; she is the incidental, the inessential as opposed to the essential. He is the Subject, he is the Absolute – she is the Other.[10]

Journalist Naomi Wolf echoes de Beauvoir in her proposal of the *beauty myth*, or the cultural beauty standards that continue to control women in an apparently progressive society. For Wolf, "the beauty myth tells a story: The quality called 'beauty' objectively and universally exists. Women must want to embody it and men must want to possess women who embody it."[11]

Examples of the sexual subject/object binary cut across media texts, ranging from relatively innocent representations to more obviously hedonistic ones. The Disney film *Sleeping Beauty* (1959) is a good example of a relatively chaste children's media text that nevertheless hinges on this binary. Princess Aurora falls into a deep slumber after pricking her finger on a spinning wheel spindle cursed by the evil fairy Maleficent. The only act that can break the curse and wake the Princess is a kiss from her true love, Prince Philip, who spends the second half of the film attempting to break free of Maleficent's clutches in order to reach Aurora. The entire narrative resolution rests on Philip's pursuit of Aurora, who passively awaits her prince while sleeping atop a high castle tower (very much on sexual display in a beautiful bed). In this text, Philip is clearly the active, pursuant sexual subject, and Aurora is the passive, waiting sexual object he seeks. The film itself is not highly or explicitly sexual, but it certainly promotes this stereotypical binary.

Of course, this binary is even more present when the sexual content of the text is more explicit. The number of mainstream "sex comedies" that portray horny young men pursuing women as conquests is almost too large to count: the *American Pie* series (1999–2012), the *Porky's* series (1982–5), *Animal House* (1978), *Old School* (2003), *Superbad* (2007), etc. The advertisement for Wild Turkey in Figure 8.3 provides another example that frankly links masculinity to sexual power. The strip club here is empty except for the erotic dancer and her male customer, who appears to have enough influence or money to command a private dance. Importantly, he stares at her body instead of her face, which is not accidentally cropped out of the image. We are to understand her as a sexual object and *not* a person here. Any notion that this man is possibly transfixed or otherwise powerless in the presence of the dancer is obliterated by the caption, which reminds the viewer that this man is fully in control of this sexual situation. Indeed, the thinly veiled substitute of the Wild Turkey bottle for his own anatomy suggests that he is primed to move the sexual encounter forward.

In some ways the subject/object distinction differs from the others we have discussed thus far because it can function as the basis for a relationship between media text and media consumer. In other words, rather than confine the notion of sexual pursuit to the "world" of the text, many media texts feature women as sexual objects with the (assumably male) consumer of the text as a complementary sexual subject (see Chapter 7 on Psychoanalytic analysis for an in-depth discussion of this

Figure 8.3   Wild
Turkey advertisement.
Courtesy of The
Advertising Archives.

relationship). Advertising is especially notorious for establishing and trading upon this type of relationship, with representations of female objects that range from merely suggestive (Figure 8.4) to outright pornographic (Figure 8.5). The popular men's magazine *Stuff* provides another example. The magazine presents a variety of "stuff" supposedly pertinent to the contemporary man's life: technology, movies, music, and women. In fact, virtually every cover of the magazine features a young, scantily clad woman in a sexually provocative pose. By constructing women as mere "stuff" for men's enjoyment, on the same level as golf clubs or video games, the magazine reinforces the traditional sexual subject/object distinction.

Overall, gendered stereotypes of masculinity and femininity influence the possible roles that men and women can fulfill in society. Although by no means do these images dictate or control how men and women should act, they are powerfully persuasive in constructing the social rules we tend to live by unconsciously. When we belittle sexual harassment policies or dissuade young girls from playing football, or when we raise our eyebrows at the mention of a "stay-at-home" dad or encourage young boys to look tough and hold back tears, we are enacting the social rules regarding gender disseminated by the media. It is in these moments that supposedly "outdated" gender stereotypes continue to manifest as very real influences on our lived experience. Although patriarchal systems of power ensure that media stereotypes tend to affect women more than men, in truth all individuals are harmed by these limiting images.

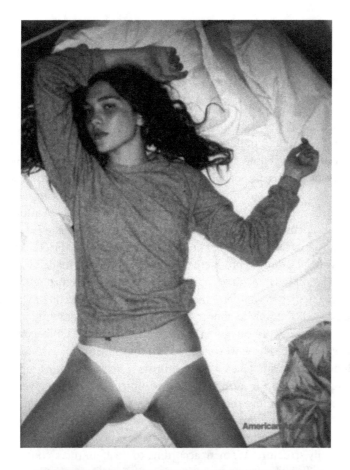

Figure 8.4 American Apparel advert. COURTESY OF THE ADVERTISING ARCHIVES.

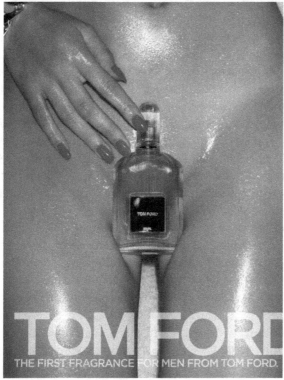

Figure 8.5 Tom Ford advertisement. COURTESY OF THE ADVERTISING ARCHIVES.

Postfeminism and Media Representation

Although difficult to clearly define, **postfeminism** broadly refers to a conceptual shift within the popular understanding of feminism: an evolution in feminist emphasis from the systemic oppression of all women to the empowerment of individual women. It is important to look at the history of feminism to fully understand the role of postfeminism. The term *first-wave feminism* refers to nineteenth- and early twentieth-century activists like Elizabeth Cady Stanton and Susan B. Anthony who primarily fought for women's right to vote. *Second-wave feminism* refers to activists in the 1970s like Gloria Steinem and Betty Friedan who fought for women's workplace and reproductive rights. The progress made by second-wave feminists in relation to women's occupational and sexual roles throughout the 1970s prompted some people to wonder if the feminist goal of sexual equality and freedom had been achieved. Those who continued to interrogate the systemic role of gender in relation to other identity categories (race, class, disability, etc.) became members of *third-wave feminism*. Those who claimed that the systemic focus of feminism had, indeed, "done its job" were labeled postfeminists. The postfeminist logic was fairly straightforward. Since prior incarnations of feminism had finally given women an "equal" place in society, any remaining feminist project should turn attention to women's "individualism, sophistication and choice."[12] Additionally, postfeminists critiqued second-wave feminists for what they saw as an overly negative view of the traditional family structure. Women, according to postfeminists, could have both a career and a family, be both empowered and nurturing. Quite simply, women could be whatever they wanted to be.

Beyond this historical positioning, however, it is difficult to pin down a clear definition of what it means to be a postfeminist today. Rosalind Gill, responding to this relative lack of understanding, frames postfeminism as an emerging "sensibility" made up of a number of interrelated aspects: (1) a melding of femininity, female sexuality, and the body as a response to an increasingly sexualized culture, (2) the dominance of philosophies of individual choice and responsibility, with a concurrent focus on self-discipline and surveillance, (3) the support of theories of irrevocable sexual difference between men and women, and (4) a reliance on irony and "knowingness" as a means of navigating cultural messages.[13] Gill points to a number of media texts as evidence of these qualities, including women's magazines and popular "make-over" television shows, in order to show how qualities like sex differentiation and self-surveillance manifest in diverse media outlets. Her identification of these qualities does not indicate her embrace of them. In fact, she remains rather suspicious of the supposed empowerment that postfeminist doctrines of individualism, sexuality, and choice offer to women. In reflecting on postfeminism's philosophy of choice and women's claim to acting sexy "for themselves," she points out that:

> it presents women as entirely free agents and cannot explain why – if women are just pleasing themselves and following their own autonomously generated desires – the resulting valued

"look" is so similar – hairless body, slim waist, firm buttocks, etc.... It simply avoids all the interesting and important questions about the relationship between representations and subjectivity, the difficult but crucial questions about how socially-constructed, mass-mediated ideals of beauty are internalized and made our own.[14]

Gill's suspicion is indicative of many Feminist media scholars' perspective on the postfeminist sensibility, and it gets at the heart of a current debate over postfeminism, especially in relation to media studies. On one hand, the rise of postfeminist discourses helps explain the presence of some media representations of gender that apparently challenge classic stereotypes. Scholars disagree over when postfeminist ideals of women's empowerment and agency really took hold in the media,[15] but since the 1980s media representations of women have increasingly depicted them as able, intelligent individuals. Media texts like *Bridget Jones's Diary* (2001), *Private Practice*, *Sex and the City* and *Scandal* feature strong, independent heroines who mostly have the ability to satisfy their own economic, sexual, and emotional needs. These images are a far cry from the images of the doting housewife, the emotional wreck, or the passive sexual object that dominated earlier media representations of women. On the other hand, as we have pointed out in this chapter, many traditional gender stereotypes continue to pervade the media. Echoing Gill's sentiments, Angela McRobbie suggests that postfeminist claims regarding the inapplicability of earlier feminist politics are ill-founded and ignore the fact that real, systemic, gendered inequity continues to inform the lives of many women.[16] Patriarchal power structures may have loosened their hold on women, but they are far from gone.

An excellent example of media textual analysis that looks at the interplay between the postfeminist sensibility and continuing issues of women's oppression is Karen C. Pitcher's analysis of the popular *Girls Gone Wild* video/DVD series.[17] The series, which captures young, often inebriated women stripping at hedonistic gatherings like spring break celebrations or Mardi Gras, in some ways exemplifies the doctrines of choice and personal sexual agency that postfeminists espouse. Pitcher even quotes some women who star in the videos as saying that they consciously participate in the taping as a display of sexual freedom. The larger context of the series production, however, effectively strips the interaction of any significant, widespread emancipatory potential. Women's ability to choose, Pitcher contends, is largely constructed or staged within the filming context, resulting in a system of economic exploitation. The company that produces the series always includes footage of women giving their consent to be filmed, a move curiously absent in the series' mirror project, *Guys Gone Wild* (where men of similar age and state of drunkenness strip). Pitcher sees this absence as crucial to the ways the videos function in a patriarchal system:

For these men, consent and agency is an unproblematic given, so much so it need not be included in the footage. Thus, even in a complete gender-role reversal format, *Guys Gone Wild* reinforces the ways in which voluntarily disrobing on camera entails little from men but requires an elaborate staging of agency for women. While *Guys Gone Wild* may be framed as the "mirror image" of *GGW*, its erasure of the consent and reward scenes ultimately highlights the distorted representation of agency that *GGW* fosters.[18]

In the end, postfeminist themes of choice become a means toward economic domination as *Girls Gone Wild* producers commandeer agency as a way of popularizing the series. Clearly, merely asserting that patriarchy is gone does not make it so.

The tension between feminism and postfeminism exists even in far more "innocuous" texts than the *Girls Gone Wild* series. In the popular American book and film series *The Hunger Games*, for example, the main character Katniss Everdeen appears to challenge traditional representations of femininity. Raised in the harsh world of Panem, a futuristic society erected upon the ruins of a fallen United States, 16-year-old Katniss is independent, intelligent, and brave. Though initially terrified of representing her home district in the annual Hunger Games (a lethal, state-sponsored Olympics), she also realizes that she possesses many skills which other women in her district lack. These skills are instrumental to her survival and eventual victory in the Games. Her open defiance of state tradition on national television at the end of the first book, however, makes her a popular folk hero and a wanted citizen by the government. As the state attempts to destroy their new victor and stamp out a series of social rebellions inspired by her action, Katniss joins forces with an underground revolutionary movement and assumes the mantle of the Mockingjay, or the symbol of freedom for the oppressed peoples of Panem.

Despite these images of empowerment and choice, Katniss is not completely free of more traditional stereotypes of women. Although at first indifferent to her fellow Games participant Peeta Mellark, for instance, Katniss quickly finds herself embroiled in a love triangle with him and fellow survivalist Gale Hawthorne. As the series progresses, Katniss appears to spend less time worrying about the unprecedented social revolution she sparked and more time agonizing over her conflicted romantic feelings. Additionally, for all of her trademark self-reliance, Katniss's actions are largely guided throughout the series by two male authorities: Haymitch Abernathy, a past Games winner from her home district who functions as her mentor, and Cinna, a personal stylist who functions as her friend and confidant. Many of Katniss's best strategies in and out of the Games come from these two men. It is Cinna, for example, who engineers Katniss's signature "girl on fire" and Mockingjay looks that become the crucial symbols of rebellion in the series. These narrative points, then, coupled with the fact that Katniss must essentially mother her young sister Primrose (as well as Rue, a participant in the Games), suggest that even a revolutionary cannot completely escape mainstream codes that represent women as emotional, deferential, or domestic.

It is probably safe to say that the *Hunger Games* series is representative of a more general impulse within contemporary American media in relation to issues of gender. The series is certainly progressive when compared to older media texts with defined gender stereotypes, but it is also problematic in its maintenance of certain stereotypical themes (and perhaps does even more damage by concealing them within overarching messages of female empowerment). In analyzing *The Hunger Games*, we can see that neither the extreme postfeminist nor traditional second-wave assessments of media representation of gender are wholly correct. In truth, many media texts today are complex presentations that require careful deconstruction across many layers of meaning, and Feminist media scholarship is constantly examining and assessing the complexity of these texts.

Consequences of Sexist Media Representation

Media texts influence people. The television shows we watch, the albums we listen to, and the websites we visit give us an impression about the world and how we should live in it. We have probably all been moved to tears by a particular film or convinced to purchase a product by a clever advertisement. So when media texts present us with skewed images of gender and sexuality, it is understandable some people will take those stereotypes as "the truth" and act upon them. In this section we wish to outline some of the major, real-world consequences of sexist stereotypes in the media. Far from existing as mere entertainment, these images are crucial in constructing the social world of American culture.

One of the most prevalent material effects of mediated gender stereotypes is a modern proliferation of eating disorders. Stereotypes that construct women as passive or sexually attractive also tend to emphasize the absolute necessity of a slender figure. American daytime and prime-time television shows routinely portray female characters as skinnier than their male counterparts, while the remaining "overweight" characters are less likely to be portrayed in a romantic light.[19] Dieting advertisements which once focused on overall weight now regularly talk about zapping problem areas that are "soft, loose or 'wiggly'" in an effort to rid the body of any sign of fat.[20] Ironically, advertisements for food continually encourage Americans to indulge in excess even as we learn that "fat is bad." Advertising analyst Jean Kilbourne views eating disorders as one of the primary ways that "women cope with the difficulties in their lives and with the cultural contradictions involving food and eating."[21] Stereotypical images of "passive femininity" present women with an unhealthy, underweight, and virtually impossible body image that many internalize and destructively pursue.

Although eating disorders are certainly a significant problem for many women, recent research suggests that many men also suffer from body dysmorphia as a result of mediated, sexist stereotypes. In 2000, Pope, Phillips, and Olivardia published *The Adonis Complex: the Secret Crisis of Male Body Obsession*, bringing popular attention to male eating disorders for the first time.[22] Though not an officially accepted medical term, the so-called Adonis Complex is a catch-all condition that refers to "an array of usually secret, but surprisingly common, body image concerns of boys and men."[23] These concerns include dissatisfaction with one's musculature, body-fat ratio, and size, issues that often result in steroid use, unhealthy weightlifting practices, and eating disorders like anorexia and bulimia. The authors cite the increasing images of "perfect" men in the media as a significant cause of the Complex demonstrating for example, how sexually risqué images of men have steadily risen to be just as common as images of women in popular women's magazines. These representations of men, usually shown with slender waists, rock-hard abs, and/or huge biceps, place pressure on individual men to live up to nearly impossible standards of masculinity. *The Adonis Complex* revealed that eating disorders resulting from media representations of gender are not just a woman's problem. The active/passive gender binary gives rise to a culture of the figure where being "too big" is as deadly as being "too thin."

The role of media texts in exposing consumers to impossible or unhealthy body types is certainly an important one to examine, especially when those images result in harmful personal choices. It is also necessary, however, to understand how these texts influence the make-up of social institutions. Media representations are the result of cultural attitudes toward sex and sexuality, but stereotypes also reinforce those attitudes and help shape them through workplace and government policies. One of the most apparent areas of the institutionalized discrepancy between the sexes is the issue of pay. In 2009 the US Department of Education released statistics that suggest that college-educated women earn 82 cents for every dollar earned by their male counterparts. Although some of this discrepancy can be explained by the fact that women tend to enter lower paying fields that resonate with stereotypically feminine traits (including education and social work), even industry-specific comparisons between the sexes reveal that women tend to earn 7 percent less pay then men.[24] Furthermore, women who *do* attempt to enter the upper echelons of the working world by pursuing management positions often come up against the **glass ceiling**, or informal, gendered workplace policies that allow women to progress only so far in promotion. The logic is that women often lack the (traditionally masculine) qualities of assertiveness and rational thinking that management positions require. Thus, media representations of femininity that position women as meek, subservient, or overly emotional contribute to a culture where it is permissible for women to earn less and have fewer occupational opportunities.

Conclusion

Throughout this chapter we have looked at how media representations of sex and sexuality contribute to social systems of unequal power distribution. Although contemporary feminist analysis is a highly complex and varied critical tradition, we have addressed some of the major issues regarding representation that this approach contributes to the field of media studies. Media representations of men tend to define masculinity according to power, agency, rationality, and sexual prowess, while images of women mark femininity according to passiveness, domesticity, emotion, and beauty. It is the goal of Feminist analysis to deconstruct popular media texts to reveal these false binaries and the systems of inequity that they support. At the same time, feminists remain wary of postfeminist sensibilities that too quickly proclaim the end of patriarchy and the primacy of female individualism and choice. These competing interpretations of gender in contemporary society give rise to confusing, often contradictory messages about the various roles of men and women. Feminist analysis, then, is also a way of beginning to untangle these texts and tease out their social, cultural, and political implications.

Because feminism has often unfairly garnered the reputation of being anti-male, we wish to conclude this chapter by again reiterating that stereotypes of femininity and masculinity are both damaging to individual media consumers in everyday life. Everyone suffers when skewed media stereotypes become the basis for social interaction. Although patriarchal systems of power ensure that representations of women are more restricted and harmful, even representations of men encourage limited modes of action and identification for those individuals. Thus, it is in everyone's interest to participate in the types of analyses outlined by Feminist scholars. It is only by interrogating *all* constructed representations of gender and sexuality that we can move beyond the harmful social structures that characterize contemporary life.

MEDIA LAB 7: DOING FEMINIST ANALYSIS

OBJECTIVE

The aim of this lab is to utilize concepts of Feminist theory to analyze media texts. Specifically, students will investigate how stereotypes of gender and sexuality function as a convention of American television.

ACTIVITY

- Divide the class into small groups of 4–5 students each.
- Show a short clip (5–6 minutes) of a contemporary, mainstream American situation comedy. We suggest programs like *New Girl*, *Mike & Molly*, or *Family Guy*. Older sitcoms, such as *Home Improvement*, as well as reality programs like *The Bachelor* or *The Bachelorette*, may also be used as points of comparison if time permits.
- Ask students to record their answers to the following questions.
  1   What gender stereotypes discussed in this chapter (active/passive, public/private, logical/emotional, sexual subject/sexual object) do you see present in the text?
  2   What additional gender stereotypes not addressed in this chapter can you identify? How might they be related to the four listed above?
  3   Are there any examples of gender reversals in the text? (For example, men acting emotionally, or women in the workplace.)

SUGGESTED READING

Banet-Weiser, S. Girls Rule!: Gender, Feminism, and Nickelodeon. *Critical Studies in Media Communication* 2004, 21, 119–39.

Bell, E., Haas, L., and Sells, L. (eds) *From Mouse to Mermaid: the Politics of Film, Gender, and Culture*. Bloomington, IN: Indiana University Press, 1995.

Bordo, S. *Unbearable Weight: Feminism, Western Culture, and the Body*. Berkeley, CA: University of California Press, 1993.

Bordo, S. *The Male Body: a New Look at Men in Public and Private*. New York: Farrar, Straus and Giroux, 1999.

Brooks, A. *Postfeminisms: Feminism, Cultural Theory and Cultural Forms.* New York: Routledge, 1997.

Butler, J. *Gender Trouble: Feminism and the Subversion of Identity*, 10th anniversary edn. New York: Routledge, 1999.

Connell, R.W. *Masculinities.* Berkeley, CA: University of California Press, 1995.

de Beauvoir, S. *The Second Sex*, trans. H.M. Parshley. New York: Alfred A. Knopf, 1952.

Dow, B. *Prime-Time Feminism: Television, Media Culture, and the Women's Movement Since the 1970's.* Philadelphia, PA: University of Pennsylvania Press, 1996.

Dow, B. and Condit, C. The State of the Art in Feminist Scholarship in Communication. *Journal of Communication* 2005, 55, 448–78.

Haraway, D.J. *Simians, Cyborgs, and Women: the Reinvention of Nature.* New York: Routledge, 1991.

Hernandez, D. and Rehman, B. (eds) *Colonize This! Young Women of Color on Today's Feminism.* New York: Seal Press, 2002.

Holland, S.L. The Dangers of Playing Dress-Up: Popular Representations of Jessica Lynch and the Controversy Regarding Women in Combat. *Quarterly Journal of Speech* 2006, 92, 27–50.

hooks, b. *Feminism is for Everybody: Passionate Politics.* Cambridge, MA: South End Press, 2000.

Hylmo, A. Girls on Film: an Examination of Gendered Vocational Socialization Messages Found in Motion Pictures Targeting Teenage Girls. *Western Journal of Communication* 2006, 70, 167–85.

Johnson, A.G. *Privilege, Power and Difference.* New York: McGraw Hill, 2001.

Johnson, D. and Swanson, D.H. Undermining Mothers: a Content Analysis of the Representation of Mothers in Magazines. *Mass Communication & Society* 2003, 6, 243–65.

Kaplan, E.A. Feminist Criticism and Television. In *Channels of Discourse, Reassembled: Television and Contemporary Criticism*, R.C. Allen (ed.), pp. 247–83. Chapel Hill, NC: University of North Carolina Press, 1992.

Katz, J. *The Macho Paradox: Why Some Men Hurt Women and How All Men Can Help.* Naperville, IL: Sourcebooks, 2006.

Lind, R.A. and Salo, C. The Framing of Feminists and Feminism in News and Public Affairs Programs in US Electronic Media. *Journal of Communication* 2002, 52, 211–28.

Moraga, C. and Anzaldua, G. (eds) *This Bridge Called My Back: Writings by Radical Women of Color.* New York: Kitchen Table: Women of Color Press, 1984.

Rodgers, S., Kenix, L.J., and Thorson, E. Stereotypical Portrayals of Emotionality in News Photos. *Mass Communication & Society* 2007, 10, 119–38.

Shugart, H.A., Wagoner, C.E., and O'Brien Hallstein, D.L. Mediating Third-Wave Feminism: Appropriation as Postmodern Media Practice. *Critical Studies in Media Communication* 2001, 18, 194–210.

Tasker, Y. and Negra, D. *Interrogating Postfeminism: Gender and the Politics of Popular Culture.* Durham, NC: Duke University Press, 2007.

Vavrus, M.D. Domesticating Patriarchy: Hegemonic Masculinity and Television's "Mr. Mom." *Critical Studies in Media Communication* 2002, 19, 352–75.

Wolf, N. *The Beauty Myth: How Images of Beauty are Used Against Women.* New York: William Morrow and Company, 1991.

NOTES

1. b. hooks, *Feminism is for Everybody: Passionate Politics* (Cambridge, MA: South End Press, 2000).

2. Understanding socially constructed qualities of gender as biological constants does contribute to systems of patriarchal power. However, contemporary queer feminist scholarship has also productively challenged this classic distinction between gender and sex. See J. Butler, *Gender Trouble, Feminism and the Subversion of Identity*, 10th anniversary edn (New York, Routledge, 1999). This is also heavily discussed in Chapter 9.

3. A.G. Johnson, *Privilege, Power and Difference* (New York: McGraw Hill, 2001).

4. T.E. Perkins, Rethinking Stereotypes, in *Turning it On: a Reader in Women & Media*, H. Baehr and A. Gray (eds) (New York: Arnold, 1996), 21.

5. R. Dyer, Stereotyping, in *Media and Cultural Studies: Keyworks*, revised edn, M.G. Durham and D.M. Kellner (eds) (Oxford: Blackwell, 2006).

6. T. Linn, Media Methods that Lead to Stereotypes, in *Images that Injure: Pictorial Stereotypes in the Media*, 2nd edn, P.M. Lester and S.D. Ross (eds) (Westport, CT: Praeger, 2003), 23–7.

7. K. Walsh-Childers, Women as Sex Partners, in *Images that Injure: Pictorial Stereotypes in the Media*, 2nd edn, P.M. Lester and S.D. Ross (eds) (Westport, CT: Praeger, 2003), 141–8.

8. S. Bordo, *The Male Body: a New Look at Men in Public and Private* (New York: Farrar, Straus, and Giroux, 1999).

9. L. Nemecek, *The* Star Trek: The Next Generation *Companion* (New York: Pocket Books, 1992), 13.

10. S. de Beauvoir, *The Second Sex*, trans. H.M. Parshley (New York: Alfred A. Knopf, 1952), xix.

11. N. Wolf, *The Beauty Myth* (New York: William Morrow and Company, 1991), 12.

12. S. Thornham, *Women, Feminism and Media* (Edinburgh: Edinburgh University Press, 2007), 16.

13. R. Gill, Postfeminist Media Culture: Elements of a Sensibility, *European Journal of Cultural Studies* 2007, 10(2), 147–66.

14. Gill, 154.

15. See B. Dow, *Prime-Time Feminism: Television, Media Culture, and the Women's Movement Since the 1970's* (Philadelphia, PA: University of Pennsylvania Press, 1996); A. McRobbie, Post-Feminism and Popular Culture, *Feminist Media Studies* 2004, 4(3), 255–64.

16. McRobbie, Post-Feminism.

17. K.C. Pitcher, The Staging of Agency in *Girls Gone Wild*, *Critical Studies in Media Communication* 2006, 23(3), 200–18.

18. Pitcher, 215.

19. S.E. White, N.J. Brown, and S.L. Ginsberg, Diversity of Body Types in Network Television Programming: a Content Analysis, *Communication Research Reports* 1999, 16(4), 386–92.

20. S. Bordo, *Unbearable Weight: Feminism, Western Culture, and the Body* (Berkeley, CA: University of California Press, 1993), 190.

21. J. Kilbourne, *Deadly Persuasion: Why Women and Girls Must Fight the Addictive Power of Advertising* (New York: The Free Press, 1999), 116.

22. H.G. Pope, Jr, K.A. Phillips, and R. Olivardia, *The Adonis Complex: the Secret Crisis of Male Body Obsession* (New York: The Free Press, 2000).

23. Pope *et al.*, 6–7.

24. Despite Progress, Study Finds Gender Pay Gap Persists, *USA Today*, October 24, 2012, final edn, 2B.

9 Queer Analysis

KEY CONCEPTS

CAMP
DISCURSIVE CONSTRUCTION
FOURTH PERSONA
GENDER PERFORMATIVITY
HETERONORMATIVITY
QUEER THEORY

REPRESENTATION
SEXUAL OTHERING
SEXUALITY
TEXTUAL WINK
VISIBILITY

To the casual viewer of *Glee*, Fox's wildly popular television program about a group of musically gifted high school students in Lima, Ohio, a fourth season conversation between Sam Evans (Chord Overstreet) and Brittany Pierce (Heather Morris) may not have seemed very remarkable. It occurs after Brittany turns away from Sam's first romantic advance:

BRITTANY: "I can't."

SAM: "Is it my lips?"

BRITTANY: "No. Your lips are so soft and horizontal. I just like you too much to put you in danger."

SAM: "Santana broke up with you."

BRITTANY: "No, it's not just Santana. It's, like, all the lesbians of the nation. And I don't know how they found out about Santana and I dating, but once they did, they started sending me, like, tweets and Facebook messages on Lord Tubbytin's wall. I think it means a lot to them to see two hot, popular girls in love, and I worry that if they find out about you and I dating that they'll turn on you and get really violent and hurt your beautiful face and mouth."

SAM: "I'm not scared of them."[1]

To a specific subsection of the show's dedicated fan base, however, the conversation added insult to injury. Many of those who appreciated *Glee*'s depiction of a loving, long-standing lesbian relationship between Brittany and fellow cheerleader Santana

Critical Media Studies: An Introduction, Second Edition. Brian L. Ott and Robert L. Mack.
© 2014 John Wiley & Sons, Inc. Published 2014 by John Wiley & Sons, Inc.

Lopez (Naya Rivera) felt betrayed when fourth season spoilers suggested that Brittany would find solace after her sapphic break-up in the arms of a man.[2] Although a number of these fans *did* take to social media outlets in order to voice their displeasure with this narrative turn, the writers' decision to frame them in actual dialog on the program as obsessed, violent internet users seemed like a mean-spirited swipe. After all, surely intense fan commitment to characters and story is the very thing that gets a program like *Glee* to a fourth season?

Such anger and backlash may make more sense if placed in the context of those passions generally stirred up by ambiguous sexual representation on television. As *AfterEllen* blogger Elaine Atwell noted in her own reaction to the *Glee* scene, "[w]e all like to talk a big game about accepting bisexuals, but actually doing it, both in the real world and television, can be a challenge."[3] A charitable reading following this logic, then, may have interpreted Brittany's bisexuality as only the most recent example of diversity on a program that had already won multiple GLAAD (formerly the Gay & Lesbian Alliance Against Defamation) Media Awards for its recognition of non-heterosexual people. Fans who found fault with the writers' decision had simply failed to interrogate their own sexual hang-ups. Still, even with this explanation, it is difficult to ignore the nagging issue that fueled fan outcry in the first place: Absent the debated scene, Brittany and Sam's interaction during the fourth season looked like any other budding heterosexual romance on television at the time.

The questions that *Glee* poses about human sexuality and its depiction in mainstream media are precisely those that interest scholars approaching media texts from a Queer vantage. The perspective of Queer theory, discussed at length below, does not lend itself to easy definition as an analytical perspective, which is part of the reason we reserve it for the final chapter in our section on media texts. Rather than a perceived weakness, however, this lack of coherence is Queer theory's contribution to critical media studies. Generally speaking, Queer media scholars attempt to understand how media texts, as significant outlets of cultural discussion, contribute to the ordering of human understanding surrounding gender, sex, and sexuality. The specific notion of queerness in this perspective – of ambiguity, performance, and play – becomes a powerful way to refuse this structured understanding, a refusal that in turn challenges prevailing cultural norms and the power relations that they reinforce.

This chapter is roughly divided into three major thematic sections, which we label "visibility I," "visibility II," and "invisibility." The first two sections take up the project begun in Chapter 8 (Feminist Analysis) by looking at traditional sexual stereotypes in the media and supposedly "positive" depictions of non-heterosexuals. Here we consider how images of heterosexuality and homosexuality, replicated across media and time, create a binary understanding of sexuality that privileges heterosexuality and marginalizes homosexuality (even in many instances which appear to be progressive). The final section, invisibility, is our term for scholarship which attempts to identify a Queer presence in media texts despite a lack of any explicit reference to queerness within them. Here our discussion of *camp* and the *fourth persona* (or "textual winking") complicates the stereotypes addressed in the first two sections and, in some ways, provides avenues for their remedy. Before we consider the Queer analysis of the media, however, it is important to have a general understanding of Queer theory. We lay out the major tenets of this perspective below.

Queer Theory: an Overview

Queer theory is an interdisciplinary perspective that seeks to disrupt socially constructed systems of meaning surrounding human sexuality. **Sexuality** is an enduring emotional, romantic, or sexual attraction toward others based upon their gender or sex. Americans traditionally interpret sexuality in terms of identity according to the binary of heterosexuality and homosexuality; the fact that even "alternate" forms of sexual identity like bisexuality are understood in reference to this binary speaks to its primacy. Generally speaking, Queer theorists assert that such an understanding misrepresents the full spectrum of human sexuality. Sexuality is fluid and difficult to categorize, and as a result the rather simple identity categories we use to name sexuality can never fully represent any individual's actual, varied sexual drives. Queer theorists work to expose the shortcomings of these labels and show how they function to support systems of social power and privilege.

Let us pause here and consider the full meaning of the above paragraph. A woman who prefers to have sex with men is not inherently heterosexual; she is simply a woman who has sex with men. Growing up in American society, this woman likely took part in the institutions and stories circulating throughout the culture that taught her such attractions and behaviors are properly called "heterosexual." Unconsciously, she probably adopted that word, "heterosexual," in order to identify herself. *But there is no actual connection between that word and her individual sexual drives and practices.* Instead, heterosexuality (like homosexuality) is a cultural construction that functions as a heuristic, a mental shortcut, which people draw upon to describe their sexual practices. While the experience of this thing we call *sexuality* may be particular to each individual, the social constructions of *heterosexuality* and *homosexuality* are cultural categories humans use to make sense of their personal sexual practices. Key to our discussion of the media, then, is how these categories function in society: just as mistaking gender expectations for inherent biology gives rise to sexist social systems (as we discussed in Chapter 8), assuming that the heterosexuality/homosexuality binary represents human sexuality results in the unequal distribution of social power. Put another way, *heterosexuality* and *homosexuality* are cultural constructions like *masculine* and *feminine*. They allow for the social classification, essentializing, and (dis)empowerment of the groups that identify with them.

The system of inequity derived from the heterosexual/homosexual binary is called **heteronormativity** (or heterosexism). It refers to a diverse set of social practices that function (1) to perpetuate the heterosexual/homosexual binary and (2) to privilege heterosexuality. Heteronormative social practices maintain the distinction between heterosexuality and homosexuality out of necessity. Remember that sexism rests upon the visible differences between men and women, and systems of sexist power seem to have some biological or physical component to support them. When talking about the social roles or powers of men and women, we can (for the most part) easily point to individuals that fill the categories of *men* and *women*. However, we think of an individual's sexuality as largely a psychic or internal component, and many actions that we would attribute to this component tend to occur behind closed doors. As a result, heteronormative social practices must convince people that the distinct categories of heterosexuality and homosexuality do exist even if they are not as easily demarcated as biological sex.

This binary must exist if heterosexuality is to be considered normal or desirable, the second function of heteronormative social practices. Homosexuality provides a point of contrast to heterosexuality, or, as Queer theorist Eve Kosofsky Sedgwick puts it, "[t]he gay closet is not a feature only of the lives of gay people."[4] In the same way that our understanding of "night" could not exist without "day," the norm of heterosexuality could not exist as a coherent category without homosexuality as its "abnormal" opposite. The process of stigmatizing homosexuality (or really any non-heterosexual practice) in order to privilege heterosexuality is called **sexual othering**. We can see examples of heteronormativity and sexual othering widely in American culture. When people are asked to consider what the ideal nuclear American family looks like, for instance, they will often default to a picture of a husband and wife with two or three children. There are variations on this theme (the addition of a grandparent or pet, or increasingly a single parent), but the core image is almost always exclusively heterosexual. Here homosexual couples represent the abnormal, the other, and the non-ideal. Moreover, identifying as heterosexual in American society grants individuals easy access to a variety of social practices denied to others, including marriage in many states, insurance benefits, medical visitation rights, and more. Even the American-English language reveals the inequity. There are countless derogatory terms one can use to degrade a non-heterosexual person, and many of these words (like *faggot* or *dyke*) have become epithets that can broadly refer to anyone in a negative fashion. However, outside of select terms used at times by members of the Lesbian, Gay, Bisexual, and Transgendered (LGBT) community (like *breeder*), there are no widely accepted words to ridicule heterosexuals on the basis of their sexuality. Feminist scholar Adrienne Rich suggests that these privileges are so engrained in American society that heterosexuality is best understood as "compulsive," in the sense that people (and women in particular) are coerced into identifying with the social definitions and norms of heterosexuality from birth.[5] Heteronormative practices, then, encourage individuals to identify with heterosexuality from an early age and regularly re-convince people that it is mutually exclusive of homosexuality.

Two important Queer theorists, Michel Foucault and Judith Butler, provide overlapping understandings of the historical origin of the powerful sexual binary we have discussed thus far. In *The History of Sexuality, Volume 1: An Introduction*, Foucault outlines his theory of sexuality as a **discursive construction**, or a product of social forces and ways of talking about the world at a given historical moment.

For Foucault, one of the crucial moments that contributes to our contemporary understanding of sexuality occurred near the beginning of the nineteenth century, which witnessed an explosion of talk around "peripheral" sexual identities. Prior to this time period, the majority of people in the Western world largely viewed sexual acts which violated the marital pact (sodomy, bestiality, etc.) as acts alone, or as isolated aberrations and passing indiscretions. A man, in other words, could certainly have a sexual encounter with another man prior to this time, but any public discussion of the matter largely concentrated on how the encounter related to the institution of marriage (and especially his own, if he happened to be married). Then something changed. Medical and legal documents in the nineteenth century began to discuss and frame these acts not as passing transgressions, but as indicators of more enduring, often "perverse" sexual identities. Suddenly, one could talk about sexuality in ways that did not exclusively relate to what married couples did behind closed doors. As Foucault puts it pointedly: "The sodomite had been a temporary aberration; the homosexual was now a species."[6]

What happened to bring about this change? Working backward through time from this example and from others, Foucault finally suggests that sexuality, understood as a quality of one's personal identity, is a product of class warfare in the eighteenth century. He contends that the previous legitimacy of bloodlines and aristocratic titles began to crumble during this time, and as a result the bourgeoisie or ruling classes throughout the Western world needed something new which could distinguish its members from the working classes they exploited. This new thing was sexual identity. "With the investment of its own sex by a technology of power and knowledge which it had itself invented," Foucault writes, "the bourgeoisie underscored the high political price of its body, sensations, and pleasures, its well-being and survival."[7] For the first time ever, then, powerful people began talking about themselves as if they possessed a thing called a *sexuality*, a part of themselves which demanded special attention and protections from medical and legal establishments. Only after being firmly instilled as a quality of the upper class did the concept of individual sexuality historically spread to the lower working classes, extending consequent medical and legal protections as a way of maintaining a healthy, reproducing workforce in a rapidly industrializing world. Once everyone had a sexuality, however, the heterosexual/homosexual binary (as well as a variety of other ways of classifying sexuality) appeared in the following century as a means of further dividing the world into privileged and oppressed groups.

Does Foucault's theory of sexuality as a discursive construction mean that our own sexual attractions and orientations have no basis in ourselves? Is sexuality a lie? In short, yes and no. These are difficult questions to answer. Much of Foucault's work supports the notion that the ways people talk about a topic create the truth of the topic, especially when it comes to the topic of ourselves. At the same time, talk cannot exist without people to do the talking. Rather than solving this chicken-and-egg issue, then, we believe that more productive questions regarding Foucault's history for Queer theory are: How does this understanding of sexuality break the concept free of the binaries that inscribe people into unequal relations of power?

How does Foucault's conception of sexuality as a negotiable historical construct, rather than internal, constant component, allow for more playful, disruptive understandings of sexuality?

One of the most significant developments of Foucault's theory of sexuality in line with these questions is Judith Butler's work on gender performativity in her book *Gender Trouble: Feminism and the Subversion of Identity*. Performativity is a difficult concept to define, but it generally refers to a school of thought that traces the source of internal identity structures to external actions. A theory of **gender performativity**, then, would claim that actions which appear to be the manifestation of an inner quality called "gender" are in fact the only force that constitutes the concept of personal gender in the first place. To understand this relationship more clearly, consider Butler's own comparison of gender performativity to Foucault's discussion of the human soul in his book *Discipline and Punish*:

> The figure of the interior soul understood as "within" the body is signified through its inscription *on* the body, even though its primary mode of signification is through its very absence, its potent invisibility. The effect of a structuring inner space is produced through the signification of a body as a vital and sacred enclosure. … In this sense, then, the soul is a surface signification that contests and displaces the inner/outer distinction itself, a figure of interior psychic space inscribed *on* the body as a social signification that perpetually renounces itself as such.[8]

In other words, we cannot understand the soul as something sacred unless we first characterize the body as that *which can hold* something sacred. For Foucault, our knowledge of the soul does not in turn influence our knowledge of the body or what makes us human. Instead, the ways we "produce" knowledge of the body through talk in effect "produces" the soul inside it.

Butler suggests that the same principle operates in relation to gender: people act according to the gender conventions of a given society, and acting in accordance with these conventions over a period of time produces a sense of gender identity as a personal or internal quality. A little boy, for example, long before he understands himself as "masculine," may find that his parents praise him for being "a man" when he happens to knock over a tower of blocks. The more often he receives this praise for knocking over blocks, or enacting fights between action figures, or wrestling with his cousins, the more likely he is to continue these actions in order to be "the man" that his parents and society appear to want out of him. Looking back on his childhood many years later, he may incorrectly identify such behaviors as a manifestation of an inherent gender identity, when in fact Butler would suggest that these actions and the social system in which he lived produced an internal sense of masculinity.

At this point you may be asking: What does a discussion of gender performativity have to do with sexuality? Butler suggests that the only "intelligible" genders in modern society "are those which in some sense institute and maintain relations of coherence and continuity among sex, gender, sexual practice, and desire."[9] Even though an internal sense of gender arises from our actions, once it is instantiated as an identity, these internalized conventions may in turn influence the way we exist as sexual beings. One need only consider the existence of gender reassignment surgery or the proliferation of sexual augmentation procedures to see that gender norms can influence what it means to "be" a man or woman, literally. Furthermore, the gendered conventions to which individuals adhere and from which they draw a sense of gender identity may be complicated constellations of different actions, but sexual actions are almost always primary within these formations. It is unlikely that the parents of the little boy in our previous example would deem him "a man" for simply breathing; that action has nothing to do with masculinity in contemporary American society. Playfully chasing a little girl on the playground, however, might inspire some encouragement because heterosexual activity is deeply entwined with notions of masculinity in the same cultural context (and, we would venture, in many others). In fact, Butler claims that "the internal coherence or unity of either gender, man or woman, ... requires both a stable and oppositional heterosexuality."[10] Part of the value of Butler's theory, then, is in how she reveals the largely unquestioned and unconscious origin of masculine and feminine gender identities, as well as the deep investment of those identities in heteronormative social systems.

Another value of Butler's theory is its concentration on *acts* as the seat of gender, or the link between society and the individual. Understanding gender as a series of acts means that people do have the potential to act differently, which is also to say that they have the potential to construct gendered and sexual identities which differ from the mainstream. People certainly do not have *complete* freedom to do so, in the sense that any social system invested in maintaining convention will often find a way to censor or punish those who do not conform, but some limited acts that can disrupt the traditional formations of male/masculine/woman-desiring and female/feminine/man-desiring are possible. At the end of *Gender Trouble*, Butler offers the notion of drag as one example of this kind of disruption. Drag performances call attention to the lack of clear association between gender, sex, sexual practice, and desire; they exist despite the fact that they challenge conventional associations between the different nodes of identity. Butler points out that drag also draws attention to the notion of performance itself, revealing the vast continuum of combinations available when gender is performative rather than a constant conception of one's identity. Though drag is not itself resistive, in the sense that it still relies upon coherent categories of gender even in its recombinations, it is a site of conflation and ambiguity from which resistance can be thought.

We will take up the notion of queer resistance in our section on media invisibility. For now it is most important to consider how Foucault and Butler's analyses of heteronormative social systems also lay ground for their undoing. The fact, however, that Queer theorists attempt to destabilize the sexual binary and reveal heterosexual privilege does not mean that Queer theory as an approach is opposed to individual sexual practices or feelings that might be labeled heterosexual. Instead, as Michael Warner puts it in his introduction to *Fear of a Queer Planet*, the word "'queer' gets a critical edge by defining itself against the normal instead of the heterosexual."[11] In the same way that feminists work against sexist *systems* and not individual men (as we discussed in Chapter 8), Queer theorists work against the systemic normalization of heterosexuality and not individual heterosexuals. Originally a derogatory word, "queer" is often used now as an umbrella term to refer to any and all people whose individual sexualities do not fit into the traditional understanding of heterosexuality. "Queer" has also come to symbolize a rejection of clear sexual definitions in one's scholarship, interaction, and daily life.

In the research tradition that forms the basis of the following section on queer visibility and media representation, Queer theorists look at the ways in which popular media texts promote heterosexuality as normal and other forms of sexuality as deviant, abnormal, or "other." They are interested in understanding and critiquing the ways that media texts paint a picture of the world where sexuality fits conveniently into particular categories according to conventional meanings. Like feminists, they are politically committed to educating individuals about the falsity of sexual binaries and reforming the American media system. Although the focus on upsetting constants makes the perspective a difficult one to pin down, the section on visibility will look at some of the important issues Queer theory has brought to light in relation to media representations of sexuality.

Queerness and Visibility I: Sexual Stereotypes in American Media

In maintaining a clear binary conception of sexuality, heteronormative systems persuade us to sort sexual practices and messages into one of two categories. This establishes a cultural understanding of sexuality where being "heterosexual" means displaying characteristics differently from those who are "homosexual." This binary understanding, in turn, leads to media stereotypes that exist in opposition to one another. We outline a number of these stereotypes below. It may seem strange to you that images of heterosexuality can also be stereotypes, since the word is commonly used to refer to images of marginalized social groups. However, this is exactly the point of Queer theory: any conception of sexuality is culturally constructed and distorting. That fact that heterosexual stereotypes do not appear to be constructions speaks to the power of heteronormative systems.

Natural/deviant

We have already discussed the normalization of heterosexuality and the stigmatization of homosexuality in this chapter, but it is important to understand how these meanings influence the content of popular media texts. The actual number of heterosexual and homosexual characters and personalities in American media is wildly disproportionate. Heterosexuality becomes natural simply by functioning as the overwhelmingly present type of sexual identity in popular media texts. In order to mark its 1,000th publication,

Figure 9.1 JBS
advertisement.
COURTESY OF THE
ADVERTISING ARCHIVES.

the pop culture magazine *Entertainment Weekly* dedicated an entire issue in 2008 to the "new classics" in American media, a collection of the best films, television shows, albums, and books of the previous 25 years.[12] Out of the top 50 best television shows produced during this time period, a surprising number (20) contain non-heterosexual characters or personalities. However, many of these programs feature these individuals in secondary roles (*The Simpsons*, *Roseanne*, *Friends*), only in select seasons (*Survivor*, *The Real World*), or only occasionally (*Seinfeld*, *thirtysomething*, *NYPD Blue*). Other programs portray gay or lesbian characters in a negative or stereotypical fashion (*South Park*), and many programs had limited reach on the cable network HBO (*Sex and the City*, *The Sopranos*, *The Wire*). Of the top 50 television shows produced during this time period, only a handful could legitimately claim to regularly feature non-heterosexual characters in primary roles (*Buffy the Vampire Slayer*, *ER*), and only two focus extensively on the lives of homosexual characters (*Six Feet Under*, *My So-Called Life*). NBC's *Will and Grace*, perhaps one of the most popular television shows to feature queer characters during this time, came in at number 53. With so few representations of non-heterosexual characters, it is clear that heterosexuality functions as the overwhelming norm in US television programming.

Frequency of representation is not the only way to gauge the normalcy of heterosexuality in media. Consider the JBS advertisement for men's underwear in Figure 9.1. Though easy to overlook in relation to the nearly naked female model, the caption in the bottom left corner reads: "Men don't want to look at naked men."

The joke, of course, is that – while ads for men's underwear typically feature male models – JBS's male consumers would rather look at scantily clad women. So, the advertisement places a hyper-sexualized woman wearing men's briefs in a hyper-masculinized role (pouring beer on morning cereal). But the humor only works (makes sense) if the viewer implicitly agrees with the heteronormativity of the ad, which suggests *all* men prefer looking at nearly naked women. That many men would prefer to look at a scantily clad male model points to the ad's ideological bias, which constructs the notion of ideal masculinity as exclusively heterosexual.

Given its historical lack of representation, it makes sense that early Hollywood often used homosexuality as a marker for deviance or criminality. Many older films link homosexuality to abnormal or antisocial behavior, affirming heterosexuality as normal in the process. For example, while the shifty Joel Cairo (Peter Lorre) in the noir thriller *The Maltese Falcon* (1941) never declares his sexuality, he is coded as homosexual through an effeminate voice, mannerisms, and impeccable dress (remember that this coding "works" because of the cultural links between gender norms and sexuality that Butler identifies). These dimensions of the character are unimportant to the plotline except to signal to audiences that the character is homo-sexual, abnormal, and therefore untrustworthy or dangerous (which, over the course of the film, turns out to be true). Similarly, Alfred Hitchcock's *Rope* (1948) tells the story of two young men (played by John Dall and Farley Granger) who strangle a former classmate in an attempt to prove that they can get away with murder. They go so far as to lock the victim's body in a chest, transform it into a table, and invite unwitting guests (including the victim's mother and a beloved former teacher) over for a macabre dinner. Although the murderers' homosexuality is never explicitly recognized in the film, the dialog between the two was enough to signal as much to audiences at the time.[13] The connection between "deviant" homosexuality and murder appears in other Hitchcock films as well, including his much-lauded *Strangers on a Train* (1951).

Although the tendency to associate homosexuality with deviance and criminality is largely a thing of the past, we still see vestiges of this formula in contemporary films. The villain Scar in *The Lion King* (1994) is a good example of this coding. Compared to the masculine and brave king of the pride, Mufasa, Scar is skinny and rather effeminate with his sculpted mane, limp paws, and "a feminine swish in his walk."[14] His eyelashes are long and sit atop rather colorful eyes, which are reminis-cent of cooing Hollywood starlets of the 1930s. In the film Scar ruthlessly murders Mufasa and drives young prince Simba away from the pride in order to secure his place as ruler of the African savannah. It would be a stretch to say that Scar the lion is homosexual, but his character certainly echoes some of the earlier Hollywood visual cues that link homosexuality to evil, and the threat he poses to the image of the nuclear, heterosexual family we discussed earlier is clear. Other contemporary films that link queerness to deviance, abnormal behavior, and especially murder include *The Silence of the Lambs* (1991), *Basic Instinct* (1992), *The Shawshank Redemption* (1994), *Braveheart* (1995), *The Talented Mr. Ripley* (1999), *300* (2006), and *Jennifer's Body* (2009).

Monogamous/promiscuous

On top of drawing clear distinctions between heterosexuality and homosexuality, American media also tend to characterize the very nature of these categories by linking heterosexuality to monogamy and homosexuality to promiscuity. Think quickly: how many popular romantic comedies in the last decade can you name? Now, how many of those movies ended with two heterosexual main characters entering a monogamous relationship by the end of the film? Can you think of any where the relationship was monogamous *but not* one of marriage? In truth, the entire genre of the mainstream American romantic comedy relies on the eventual, monogamous coupling of heterosexual characters, and the genre supports the long-standing stereotype that associates heterosexuality with monogamy.

This is not to say that heterosexuals in the media are always monogamous. MTV's *The Real World* would be far less interesting if that were the case. It is important, however, to take frequency into account when looking at this stereotypical binary. Media images of promiscuous heterosexuals certainly exist, but they represent one of the many varied ways of "being" heterosexual in the American media. Homosexual characters show up less often in American films and television shows, and when they do they often exhibit a "hyper-sexual" drive that encourages coupling with multiple partners. The lower frequency of homosexual characters in the media coupled with their often inflated sexual appetites results in particularly damaging, stereotypical images.

An example of this hyper-sexuality is the short-cartoon series *The Ambiguously Gay Duo*, which ran intermittently on *The Dana Carvey Show* and *Saturday Night Live* between 1996 and 2007. Although clearly poking fun at other male/male superhero duos like Batman and Robin, *The Ambiguously Gay Duo* nevertheless taps into cultural stereotypes that link queerness to an insatiable, almost perverted sex drive. The cartoon bristles with homosexual innuendo as it follows the adventures of superheroes Ace and Gary. The duo's super-vehicle, for instance, is shaped like a giant phallus, complete with laser beam that fires from the faux urethra. When not using the phallus-mobile, the two heroes travel by flying through the air in a pose reminiscent of anal intercourse. In different episodes viewers watch as the duo disables a threatening pterodactyl by "deep-throating" its beak, breaks into an evil robot by pushing through its rear end, and celebrates their regular victories with a congratulatory pat on the rump. While the duo may be ambiguously gay, they are clearly hyper-sexual.

The Dolce & Gabbana advertisement in Figure 9.2 provides another example of how this stereotype can manifest in the media. The nature of the image may be unclear at first glance, which in fact draws the viewer in even more deeply. After extended contemplation we would suggest that the ad depicts an "audition" for those hoping to model for the famed fashion house. As the two seated figures in the background inspect the nude candidate before them, the standing model unzips his pants and prepares to assume a similar reclining position. The model seated all the way to the left undoing his tie can only be a third candidate. The overall impression of the

Figure 9.2   Dolce & Gabbana advertisement.
COURTESY OF THE ADVERTISING ARCHIVES.

ad, then, is that the men seated together will not be satisfied until they have looked at multiple naked men, perhaps more than even those displayed in the image. Nothing in the ad says that any of these men identify as queer or homosexual, but its resonance with the stereotype of queer promiscuity is difficult to deny.

Most often, however, promiscuous queer characters appear alongside their monogamous, heterosexual counterparts, reinforcing the difference between the two and typically affirming the latter as desirable. A good example of this pairing is at the center of the 2010 film *Scott Pilgrim vs. The World*, based on a popular graphic novel series of the same name. In the film, guitar player Scott Pilgrim (Michael Cera) falls in love with the beautiful Ramona Flowers (Mary Elizabeth Winstead), but in order to secure their relationship, he must first defeat seven of her ex-boyfriends in a series of fantastic battles modeled after the world of video games. Scott's best friend and mentor through these trials is his gay roommate, Wallace Wells (Kieran Culkin), who, in contrast to Scott's almost chivalrous devotion to Ramona, flirts with and beds a string of interchangeable male partners throughout the course of the film. Although Scott begins to pursue Ramona while still technically dating his girlfriend Knives Chau (Ellen Wong), a brief exchange between Scott and Wallace suggests that he is violating fundamental rules of heterosexual partnership, rules which Wallace is free to ignore:

WALLACE: "You have to break up with Knives, that poor angel, today."
SCOTT: "But it's hard. ..."
WALLACE: "If you don't, I'm going to tell Ramona about Knives. I swear to God, Scott."

SCOTT: "What?" (Wallace's most recent fling walks through the room to the kitchen.)
WALLACE: "Hey, Jimmy."
SCOTT: (Pointing) "Double standard!"
WALLACE: "I didn't make up the gay rule book. Look, you got a problem with it, take it up with Liberace's ghost."
SCOTT: "You're a monster."[15]

The film ends when Scott successfully defeats the seventh boyfriend, leaves Knives for good, and overcomes his previous romantic shortcomings in order to join Ramona in a presumably monogamous relationship. Wallace, on the other hand, seems content with his most recent sexual acquisition by the end credits, but the film does not frame him in nearly the same redemptive (read: positive) terms.

Gender clarity/gender ambiguity

Perhaps one of the most glaring stereotypes surrounding sexuality in the media returns us to Butler's point about the link between gender and sexual norms. Although there is no absolute association between a person's gender (masculinity/ femininity) and his or her sexuality, media texts often portray heterosexuals as having stable gender roles and homosexuals as having unstable ones. To put a slight spin on Butler, one of the things which makes a character "intelligibly" heterosexual is a definite adherence to masculinity in men and femininity in women. Homosexual characters, on the other hand, tend to shift unpredictably between classic and opposite gender roles, or they blend aspects of masculinity and femininity in original ways. While Queer theorists celebrate this sort of gender fluidity as a way to eradicate sexual classification, the ambiguity in mainstream media texts more often works to create discomfort in mass audiences toward gay and lesbian personalities. In other words, gender androgyny tends to result in a threatening, unsettling sense that "things are not quite right" with queer characters and personalities.

There are countless historical instances where mediated gender ambiguity has caused discomfort among American audiences: David Bowie's original stage performances, reaction to Neil Jordan's 1992 film *The Crying Game*, news commentary surrounding Rosie O'Donnell's coming out, etc. However, *Queer Eye for the Straight Guy*, which ran on the Bravo television network from 2003 to 2007, is a particularly salient example because it relies on the interaction between clear heterosexual gender roles and ambiguous homosexual ones. Each episode of *Queer Eye* follows the Fab Five (a group of gay men who specialize in refined living) in their attempts to make over a hapless, heterosexual male so that he may in turn impress a doting wife or girlfriend. The show implies that the male subjects of these makeovers are often too masculine to care (or indeed even know) about how to groom themselves, choose fashionable clothing, or comprehend the details of interior design. Their heterosexual female counterparts, the wives and girlfriends on the show, enact complementary feminine gender norms by coaxing their partners into getting a makeover and showering them with praise by the episode's conclusion. In short, "men are men" and "women are women" on *Queer Eye*.

That is, except for the Fab Five. In contrast to the heterosexual couples they transform, the Fab Five form a continuum of gender norms on the show that resists easy classification of masculinity. Media critic David Weiss claims that in the Five we see a multiplicity of gender performances that confound and blend traditional understandings of masculinity and femininity.[16] The flamboyant fashion expert Carson, for example, will sometimes refer to himself in feminine terms (comparing himself to famous female stars like Annette Funicello or Ellen DeGeneres). The grooming expert Kyan, conversely, regularly attempts "manly" bonding with the heterosexual subject through a proliferation of high fives and the use of the word "dude." The various gender performances of the Fab Five give the impression that homosexuals are less clear in their gender orientation than the heterosexual couples, and the degrees of bewilderment that the couples visually demonstrate toward the Five (varying from delight to discomfort) further serve to underscore these differences. While some scholars have claimed that the show escapes stereotyping by presenting viewers with multiple masculinities, it still clearly participates in distinguishing between heterosexual and homosexual individuals on the basis of gender clarity and ambiguity, respectively.

Queerness and Visibility II: the Problems with "Positive" Representation

Thus far we have discussed some of the many sexual stereotypes that characterize heterosexuality and homosexuality in the American media. Deconstructing these stereotypes is an important first step in understanding the representation of sexuality in media. Another important area of research within queer visibility, however, looks at how increasing numbers of apparently non-stereotypical representations in the contemporary era continue to bolster heteronormative systems of power. Although there are certainly more media images of queer individuals today than ever before, it is important to understand that **visibility** (the number of queer characters or personalities present in the media) and **representation** (the way that those queers act, feel, and engage with the world) are two different concepts. The increase in queer personalities – and perhaps an attendant reduction of queer stereotypes – in the media does not necessarily result in an increase in *politically potent* images. Instead, these images often enact heteronormativity in other, less visible ways.

Kevin G. Barnhurst represents queer visibility in the media as a paradox.[17] Increasing the visibility of certain non-heterosexual characters, personalities, or themes necessarily overlooks others. As certain aspects of queer life become more prominent in the media, others become ignored. Visibility results in invisibility. The drama of the coming-out tale, for example, often dominates many media texts that feature homosexual characters, but the resulting centrality of "coming out" to homosexual life in the popular consciousness obscures the very simple problems that homosexuals and heterosexuals share every day as humans. Framing the disclosure of one's sexuality in terms of *drama*, then, becomes a new way to "other" homosexuals. The same could be said for what Barnhurst calls "professional queers:" official media liaisons and heads of LGBT organizations, queer journalists, etc. As the American population becomes more accustomed to seeing these "types" of gays and lesbians in the media, it becomes easier to overlook the activities of non-famous queer people in their everyday lives. Those who take their cues about gay life solely from journalists Rachel Maddow and Anderson Cooper, for instance, are likely to have a fairly skewed conception of what it means to be queer in the twenty-first century. Barnhurst's framework is important to consider because it reminds us that increased visibility is not always diverse visibility. Some aspects are always obscured.

Other scholars have pointed out that particular examples of queer visibility are not always as progressive as they might initially seem. One of the most prominent examples of media visibility in recent memory is the simultaneous coming out of comedian Ellen DeGeneres and her character, Ellen Morgan, on the popular television show *Ellen* in 1997. DeGeneres's decision caused a firestorm of controversy, but media critics also hailed it as a milestone in the representation of sexual minorities in American television. After all, Ellen Morgan was not criminal, oversexed, or terribly masculine: she was simply a funny woman who happened to be attracted to other women. And yet, as Bonnie J. Dow has pointed out, the representation of lesbianism on *Ellen* was still problematic.[18] The show positioned Ellen's newfound sexuality as an issue which heterosexual family members, friends, and co-workers learned to accept (or did not). In short, it constructed homosexuality as a problem and source of conflict. The show went on to poke fun at Queer politics for being too "radical" and instead focused on homosexuality as an exclusively personal issue (which, in reality, it is not). In portraying lesbianism predominantly through the reactions of straight characters on the show and ignoring the potentially threatening dimension of Queer politics, "*Ellen* was a sitcom about a lesbian that was largely geared toward the comfort of heterosexuals."[19]

Ellen is no longer on the air, but we continue to see a very similar logic at work in more contemporary television programs like ABC's *Modern Family*. As its title suggests, the program overwhelmingly portrays its central homosexual couple according to classic, heteronormative standards. Cam (Eric Stonestreet) and Mitch (Jesse Tyler Ferguson) have been committed partners for years and organize much of their time around their adopted daughter, a decision that largely replicates the heterosexual "good life" and obscures the desirability of any alternative queer life choices. Moreover, while the extremely flamboyant Cam spends his days at home caring for their daughter, the uptight Mitch financially supports the family as an attorney. Far from embracing the social and economic potentials of their unique relationship, then, the two men simply resemble many other heterosexual husband and wife duos on television. *Modern Family* may be praised for its attempts to complicate the notion of "family" in the current era (and perhaps as well for addressing social and political difficulties queers face to a greater degree than *Ellen*), but it still largely ends up reinforcing traits and values that mainstream, presumably hetero-sexual viewers would recognize and enjoy.

Thus, we can see that the mere presence of positive queer characters or themes does not guarantee the unproblematic representation of sexual minorities in American media. Visibility and representation are not synonymous, and a promi-nence of queerness does not always guarantee an absence of heteronormativity. Media texts that feature queer characters have grown increasingly complex in the ways they represent human sexuality, but many of these contemporary texts are simultaneously affirming and damaging. We conclude our analysis of Queer visibility, then, with a brief discussion of the effects this representation has on media audiences.

Consequences of Heteronormative Media Representations

In Chapter 8 we outlined some of the consequences of sexist media representations on actual women and men in their everyday lives. In this section we continue that project by considering the potential effects of heteronormative media representa-tions on queer and non-queer individuals. At this point, the last chapter in the media texts section of this textbook, you should have a fairly clear idea that media repre-sentations have both positive and negative effects on individuals in the real world. People often turn to the media, consciously or unconsciously, in order to form values about the world we live in today, and those values influence the impressions we have of ourselves and society. When we form values and impressions on the basis of heteronormative media representations, we run the risk of continuing current and unequal power relations.

Like images of gender, the various sexual stereotypes we see in the American media contribute to a social system defined by fairly restricted sexual expectations. The oppositional images of natural, monogamous, secure heterosexuals and deviant, oversexed, androgynous homosexuals supports the notion that there are only two ways of being sexual (and that those two ways are nothing alike). These images are detrimental to queer individuals by making them seem bizarre and threatening. However, they also do some harm to heterosexuals by laying out a fairly limited life script, a fact underscored by the supposedly positive but starkly uniform images of "heterosexualized" queer characters in the media today. It is absolutely true that heteronormative practices lead to a system where non-heterosexuals bear the overwhelming brunt of discrimination and hatred, but these practices also make it difficult for heterosexuals who may wish to resist the doc-trines of marriage or having a family to do so. In this way, stereotypes of sexuality permeate and structure the lives of every individual.

Moreover, the relative absence of queer individuals in the media results in limited models of identification for actual queer populations in the real world. In his account of contemporary gay life, *The Culture of Desire*, journalist Frank Browning recalls the importance of such identification in exploring his own sexuality while attending high school:

> What all of us were doing was sorting through the rush of sensual responses our bodies were offering up, calling on all the available plots of family, church, television, and paperback novels to enable us to savor some and discard others. ... By what we said, and by what we contrived to be overheard saying, we learned (or didn't) whether we were exploring the same mysteries, whether we were inhabiting common plots.[20]

Early on Browning discovered that his "story's plot showed no sign of connection to any of the other plots other young men were following."[21] People draw upon the stories in the media to learn more about themselves, and heteronormative systems of power limit the amount of images with which members of disempowered groups can identify. Whereas young heterosexuals have a variety of (presumably) heterosexual characters and personalities in the media to emulate, queers have fewer unproblematic images to consider. This requires young queer individuals to be more media literate and vigilant in order to separate useful, positive images from stereotypical, negative ones.

The lack of symbolic resources is an important effect to consider, especially in an increasingly media-saturated world like our own, but heteronormative representations extend beyond the individual to reinforce public prejudices and help shape social policies that affect entire queer populations as well. The fact that the overwhelming majority of characters and personalities in the American media are heterosexual contributes to a social system that often marginalizes the interests and needs of queer people. The Human Rights Campaign website lists a number of legal statutes that solidify heteronormative practices into law. Until 2013, for example, the Defense of Marriage Act defined a marriage in the USA as a legal union between one man and one woman, which meant that any federal protections or benefits contingent on marriage would not be extended to same-sex couples. These included benefits that many would consider basic aspects of contemporary life, including social security, certain forms of tax relief, workplace medical leave, and more.[22] Although some states and certain companies took the initiative to extend some of these benefits to same-sex couples in limited fashions, there was no federal mandate that guaranteed this protection (and companies often did so at a cost to themselves). The Act guided and reinforced by the kinds of social prejudices embodied in the media, was clearly in support of heteronormative systems of power. Although the Supreme Court deemed the definitional parts of the Act unconstitutional in 2013 (echoing the 2011 repeal of the US military's "don't ask, don't tell" policy), as of this writing the majority of states in the USA still explicitly prohibit same sex marriage and do not have to recognize same sex marriages granted by other states. Policy programs which codify heteronormativity are open to revision, then, but without better representation in the media as a tool of public opinion, such change is likely to come slowly.

Given the many problems of Queer visibility, as well as the social issues influenced by these problems, the possibility for genuinely positive, powerful, or resistive representations of queerness in mainstream media may seem unlikely. In the next and final section on Queer "invisibility," however, we suggest that returning to the ambiguity at the center of Queer theory and resisting the notion of definite representation may be the best hope for such a project in the media today.

Queerness and Invisibility: Camp and the Fourth Persona

Why, asks Richard Dyer in a famously circulated essay, do so many gay men seem to love film star Judy Garland?[23] After all, there is nothing explicitly "gay" about her. She did not publicly identify as a lesbian during her lifetime, and she never played an openly lesbian character in a film. And yet, somehow, Garland functioned as an integral part of a developing gay subculture during the second half of the twentieth century. As Dyer notes, underground gay magazines and newsletters often featured stories about Garland's life and provided in-depth coverage of her live musical performances. For many years gay men even used the phrase "Friend of Dorothy" as a code word for their sexual preference in public spaces, referencing Garland's most famous role in *The Wizard of Oz* (1939).

How can an aspect of the media like a celebrity image or feature film that never explicitly mentions queerness come to signify a Queer understanding of the world and/or attract queer audiences? "Invisibility" is our catch-all term for two mechanisms that make this relationship possible: camp and the fourth persona. Both concepts explain how queerness may exist "between the lines" of an otherwise mainstream or heteronormative media text, providing hidden material which queer audiences and those sympathetic to queer experiences might discover and activate. Both mechanisms may be wielded consciously or unconsciously by media authors, and it is not always possible to say that either are clearly "there" in a given media text. As one might imagine, such ambiguity often allows for the effective evasion and undermining of heteronormative social standards, as well as a unique set of new problems.

Camp

Like many other concepts we have addressed thus far in this chapter, camp is a difficult term to define. The literary critic Susan Sontag defined camp as a way of seeing the world "not in terms of beauty, but in terms of the degree of artifice, of stylization."[24] Style is certainly important to camp, but the two are not quite synonymous; there is often an element of seriousness in camp which is not required of style. As the twentieth-century novelist Christopher Isherwood notes, "you can't camp about something you don't take seriously. You're not making fun of it; you're making fun out of it."[25] Perhaps Jack Babuscio provides the best understanding of camp when he defines it as "those elements in a person, situation, or activity which express, or are created by, a gay sensibility. Camp is never a thing or person *per se*, but, rather, a relationship between activities, individuals, situations, *and* gayness."[26] A gay sensibility, in turn, is "a creative energy reflecting a consciousness that is different from the mainstream; a heightened awareness of certain human complications of feeling that spring from the fact of social oppression; in short, a perception of the world which is colored, shaped, directed, and defined by the fact of one's gayness."[27] Pulling these various understandings together, then, we may define **camp** as a collection of stylistic elements that, as they happen to converge around and/or within a specific media text, resonate with the experiences of queer individuals living within a heteronormative social system.

Allow us to draw some distinctions. The fact that camp is tethered to queer experiences under heteronormativity does not mean that a text must be explicitly queer in content, or even created by queer individuals, to qualify as camp. Camp refers to an association of stylistic elements, so while some texts are structured with these elements in mind in order to reflect such experiences purposefully, many others become camp quite accidentally. Furthermore, the notion of camp is not wholly exhausted by the idea of textual composition. To some degree camp relies on an audience that can truly witness it, or recognize the association of elements for what they are (as reflections, in other words, of queer life experiences). This is another reason why media texts which may not be camp at the time of their creation become camp at a later date; the text's early audiences could not "read" the text for its camp qualities in the same ways that later audiences can.

Babuscio suggests four elements that may mark a text as camp: irony, theatricality, humor, and aestheticism. These elements need not all be present in every camp media text, but the more of them that appear within a given text, the more likely that the text is an example of camp. We address each one of these elements in turn below. Additionally, in order to clarify the notion that a text may qualify as camp without ever explicitly referencing homosexuality or queerness, we have decided to illustrate each element in relation to Drew Goddard and Joss Whedon's critically acclaimed 2011 horror film *The Cabin in the Woods*. Primarily through the use of camp elements, we believe, the film provides fresh perspective on the cliché horror narrative of teenagers traveling to a remote, wooded area for a weekend of debauchery, only to find themselves terrorized and slaughtered by unimaginable evil.

1   *Irony*, according to Babuscio, is "the subject matter of camp, and refers here to any highly incongruous contrast between an individual or thing and its context or association."[28] Common contrasts he notes in mainstream media include masculine and feminine, youth and age, the sacred and the profane, and high and low social status. Ironic contrasts in camp media index the queer experience within heteronormative social systems by replicating the sexual binary at its core; homosexuality often appears "out of place" when compared to heterosexuality in the modern era.

Irony is key to the pleasure of watching *The Cabin in the Woods*. Very early on the film frames the well-worn "deadly, isolated cabin" theme as the product of a bureaucratic agency charged with arranging an annual sacrifice of five teenagers, a ritual which, if carried out successfully, will prevent monstrous gods slumbering beneath the earth from awakening. Cliché plot points within this sub-genre (including the attempts of a grizzled stranger to turn the teenagers back from certain doom, acts of debauchery within the cabin, and the survival of a "final girl") are all presented as key aspects of the ritual which must be followed closely if the gods are to be appeased. In fact, the shadowy agency is revealed to have a similar department stationed in each country, and each department's sacrificial scenario closely resembles the horror conventions and clichés of that country (Japan's scenario, for example, involves a ghost tormenting children trapped in a school room, recalling films like *Ringu* [1998], *Battle Royale* [2000], and *Ju-on: The Grudge* [2002]). The irony of *The Cabin in the Woods*, then, manifests in different juxtapositions of fantasy and reality. The film contrasts the fantastic horrors of the synthesized cabin against the humdrum realities of the bureaucratic agency, and viewers contrast their actual previous experiences with the sub-genre (in films ranging from *The Evil Dead* [1981] to the *Friday the 13th* franchise) against the fictional story unfolding before them.

2   *Theatricality* refers to an interpretation of life as theater and as performance (see also the discussion of dramaturgy in Chapter 11). Babuscio suggests that this trait manifests in camp media most often through heightened narrative attention to roles and other issues of appearance. The notion of playing a role or emphasizing the style of a thing over its substance mimics the queer experience of "passing" or "playing" heterosexual, a common survival tactic for queer individuals under heteronormativity.

     Theatricality is certainly an important component of *The Cabin in the Woods*. Not only does the agency produce its cabin scenario as something of a reality television show (complete with hidden cameras and a cloistered cast), but the notion of role-playing takes on a special significance within the fantastic narrative. For the ritual to work each year, the sacrificial victims must embody five ancient archetypes: Warrior, Scholar, Fool, Whore, and Virgin. This is why so many hapless groups who descend upon a menacing cabin in American film feature an athlete, a nerd, a stoner, a vixen, and, well, a virgin. Additionally, the Whore must be sacrificed first, and after the other three die in any order, the Virgin may either live or die. Thus, the subject of *The Cabin in the Woods* is a highly orchestrated performance, with the characters caught up in the difference between their "real" selves and the roles they were seemingly born to play.

3   *Humor* is a common element of many media texts, but Babuscio suggests that it takes on a special form and significance within camp media. Although it elicits laughter, camp humor is also often "painful" in the sense that it arouses sympathy "for the person, thing, or idea that constitutes the target of an incongruous contrast."[29] This means that the humor found in camp texts is often bitter, biting, or dark; audiences laugh at the targets of jokes as much as they feel badly for them. For Babuscio, this unique form of humor embodies a common strategy of many queer individuals, who utilize it as a coping mechanism and as an outlet for expressing anger at the everyday slights and incongruities that mark their experiences under heteronormativity.

Almost all of the humorous notes in *The Cabin in the Woods* are biting and dark. This is perhaps clearest in an early scene when the agency lures the teenagers down into the cabin's basement, which houses a variety of beautiful and uncommon objects. Part of the ritual demands that the victims select their own mode of sacrifice, so each object in the basement is linked to a different stock movie monster that will be unleashed when the victims engage it. As the teenagers explore the basement, the film depicts the members of the agency placing frenzied monetary bets on which monster will be unleashed. The scene is extremely funny and excruciatingly painful for audience members, who know that the teenagers are selecting certain death even as the bureaucracy playfully mocks them, and its logic continues throughout the film. Once the teenagers end up releasing the "zombie redneck torture family," for example, the agency fills releases pheromones into the woods so that the vixen and athlete are induced to have sex. The audience here may marvel at the clever management of sub-genre clichés even as they know what such playfulness means for the teenagers (in this case, the vixen's exceptionally gory and painful death).

4   *Aestheticism* is perhaps the most difficult camp trait to define. It generally refers to a spirited rejection of historical conventions and moralities through personal taste or style, as well as an elevation of individuality over group concerns or needs. In essence, aesthetics in camp media are often presented as tools for asserting control over one's life and environment. As such, it mimics another strategy by which queer individuals cope with heteronormativite society; artful self-presentation and the creation of spaces marked as uniquely "queer" are both important ways by which people might reclaim power and influence which has otherwise been denied to them.

The Cabin in the Woods is aesthetically slick in the sense that its visual references to scores of other horror films (via its setting, characters, and objects) simultaneously constitute an homage and a criticism of its cinematic predecessors. Its playful take on the decidedly serious conventions of the sub-genre is what makes the film so unique; even the narrative ultimately supports notions of irreverence and individuality. Things for the agency go horribly awry when the bumbling stoner character manages to survive his encounter with a zombie, thereby endangering the carefully mechanized ritual and, by extension, the world. Even when the stoner realizes the purpose of the cabin, he refuses to sacrifice himself, and the film ends with a massive, god-like hand reaching out of the ground and smashing the cabin to bits. While audiences may find themselves cheering on the stoner's decision to defeat the agency, it is also difficult to imagine a scene that better opposes the many acts of heroism which mark mainstream fantasy/horror/sci-fi cinema.

Through the elements of irony, theatricality, humor, and aestheticism, camp embodies some of the lived experiences of queer individuals and provides a means for their hidden expression in mainstream media. Even media texts that never explicitly reference queerness may come to express a queer perspective of the world, as we can see from

The Cabin in the Woods. The "invisibility" of camp, or the ways it manages to find expression without announcing itself as such, is both a strength and a weakness. On the one hand, camp represents queer experiences in a way that is often less suscep- tible to the stereotypes and heteronormative appropriations that plague more overt representations (as we discussed in our sections on visibility). Its lack of clarity as a presentational mode nicely resonates with Queer theory's own commitment to subversion. Like Butler's comments about drag, camp celebrates the indeterminacy and artifice which haunt all discursive constructions and indicates points of their undoing. On the other hand, the fact that audiences can willfully ignore or overlook the subtleties of camp means that its full expression (and, by extension, any important social conversations it might bring about) is rare.

The Fourth Persona and the "Textual Wink"

Another means by which queer experiences and perspectives might find subtle expression in mainstream media is through the use of the fourth persona. Within rhetorical studies, *persona* refers to a subject position within a given text, and the rhetorician Edwin Black is credited with defining the first and second personas.[30] The *first persona* in a media text is the sense of the author(s) that the text projects. Listening to a song or watching a music video by the musical group One Direction, for example, imparts a certain impression about the boy band members to listeners: here are five young men from the UK who enjoy good times and the company of women their age. Regardless of whether or not audiences approve or disapprove of this image, they will nevertheless recognize it as the "preferred" persona being projected.

By extension, the *second persona* is the image of a text's target or preferred audience, again indicated through particular textual features. Listening to songs or watching music videos by One Direction imparts the distinct impression that their music is designed for pre-teen and teenage girls. We can point to specific features of the texts that give rise to this impression: the frequent use of high school social events as a backdrop in music videos indicates the age of the preferred audience, and, of course, the frequent invocation of the word "girl" in lyrics indi- cates its gender. Middle-aged men are free to enjoy One Direction songs, but doing so will likely result in feelings of guilt, as though they are poaching on someone else's territory. In this instance, middle-aged men (and middle-aged women, and teenage boys) would constitute the *third persona* of the text, or the audience that the text purposefully ignores but which nevertheless haunts it through the absence.[31]

The **fourth persona**, then, is another projection or impression of the author(s) indicated though textual features, but it is a projection that only some audiences will ever notice.[32] Its innovator, Charles E. Morris III, suggests that the persona maintains this quasi-hidden quality by dividing the audience of the text into "clairvoyants" (a subsection of the audience who can sense the persona) and "dupes" (a much larger section of the audience who fails to detect it and concentrates instead on the image of the *first persona*). The use of a fourth persona, then, allows the author of a text to "pass" strategically, appearing to the dupes as one thing and to the clairvoyants as quite another. Importantly, a fairly strict division between these groups is what distinguishes the fourth persona from something like an inside joke or an intertextual reference. In these latter two instances, someone may not understand a certain reference, but that person still typically recognizes that it is meaningful for *someone*. He or she is simply not the intended audience. In the operation of the fourth persona, the dupes do not even realize that a reference has been dropped. They continue to believe that they received the real or correct impression of the author, unaware of what the clairvoyants detect.

How do clairvoyants come to recognize the existence of the fourth persona when so many dupes miss it? Morris suggests that part of the reason they are "clairvoyant" is because they share something intrinsic with the author, a link which also forms the basis of the persona. Furthermore, the persona takes concrete form as a **textual wink**, or a feature of the text which only the clairvoyants will find meaningful based upon their similarity to the author. The wink is a signal for clairvoyants to look more critically at a text than the dupes do, scrutinizing it for additional understandings it may reveal about the author and the text.

In order to understand how the fourth persona might function within mainstream media, consider the discussion surrounding a seventh season performance on Fox's reality television series *So You Think You Can Dance*. The competition typically pairs male and female contestants together for weekly choreographed dance routines, and only a handful of male–male pairings occurred during first through sixth seasons. Furthermore, in these few instances, the choreography positioned the male duos as warring princes, baseball players, and in other stereotypically masculine (and ostensibly heterosexual) roles.[33] As a result, a seventh season male–male duet about emotional vulnerability and betrayal was something noticeably different for the program. Dancers Neil Haskell and Kent Boyd, along with choreographer Travis Wall, explained the message of the piece in a package broadcast before the number:

TRAVIS: "The story is about two guys who are best friends."

NEIL: "We've grown together; we've really built this great friendship together …"

KENT: "I learn that Neil wasn't the friend that I thought he was."

NEIL: "We're at the point in our friendship now where I need to move on, and even if it does hurt Kent, I just really need to move forward."

KENT: "He's never there for me. He did something really mean to me and just stabbed me in the back."

TRAVIS: "When Kent gets stabbed in the back, it's a pain in your heart, your stomach. You want to throw up. And then he turns around and looks at him, and he's like 'You're not going to get away with this.'"

KENT: "I decide that I'm not going to put up with this, and I actually do fight back. [But] I come to the realization that I just need to walk away, and that it's not worth all the trouble. Me and Neil just got to go on our separate paths."[34]

Thus, the uncharacteristic performance was nevertheless a powerful exploration of friendship between men, as well as the sheer aggressions unleashed when such a friendship turns sour.

At least, this was the interpretation of the routine tacitly forwarded by many of the mainstream media bloggers who recapped the episode in the following days.[35] A smaller subsection of bloggers from the queer online community, however, suggested that the piece was not so much about friends as it was about *boyfriends*. Under the cheeky headline "The Completely Not Gay *Dance* Between These 2 Twinks," Queerty blogger Sarah Nigel quipped,

> [Judge] Adam Shankman's on-air mock proposal to [judge] Nigel Lythgoe wasn't the only thing gay about last night's *So You Think You Can Dance*. Alum Neil Haskell, who is straight but has no problem with you thinking otherwise, appeared on stage to dance with current contestant Kent Boyd, whose [*sic*] might also play for our team. It was not romantic at all! Kidding.[36]

AfterElton's Dennis Ayers was a bit more forthright: "'[B]est friends' my ass! The dance was gorgeous and passionate and was clearly about something more than a platonic male friendship."[37] History seems to support this second interpretation to some degree. Within a year of the original broadcast, the same two dancers would go on to perform the routine during the opening ceremonies for LGBT Heritage Month in Los Angeles.

The notion of the fourth persona and the textual wink explains how different audiences could respond differently to exactly the same broadcast. The packaging before the number, as well as judges' comments after the dance, duped many viewers into believing that the routine concerned nothing more than platonic betrayal. Only a handful of "clairvoyants" here saw through the veil to the "real" meaning of the dance as an extension of choreographer Travis Wall. Wall's (non-hetero)sexuality has been an open secret on the show since he joined it as a competitor in the second season,[38] and it was this commonality with the queer blogging community that allowed them to catch the wink within his dance. Like any other use of the fourth persona, this choice served a strategic function. More than two years after the initial broadcast, while discussing the possibility of queer romantic choreography on the show, Wall acknowledged to *The Huffington Post* the necessity of strategically "passing" Neil and Kent as straight in order to inspire the viewing audience to vote:

> I think [same sex choreography] could tell the story of a relationship, but it doesn't have to be romantic because, half the time on "So You Think You Can Dance," it's about the voting. If that was a romantic duet, no one would have ever voted for Kent. He would have missed out on the finale spot because of my trying to change the world and trying to make a statement. It wouldn't have been fair to the contestant. My job as a choreographer is not to make a statement; it's to make the contestant safe for next week.[39]

We would say, however, that Wall's use of a fourth persona in the dance *did* allow him to make a statement despite his first persona duties as a choreographer. It was simply a statement that only part of his audience would ever understand.

The fourth persona, then, as another "invisible" means by which queer perspectives find a voice within a heteronormative media landscape, has many of the same strengths and weaknesses as camp. While its hidden quality gives it a certain subversive edge, allowing clairvoyants to playfully undermine the heteronormative readings carried out by the dupes, its tendency to evade detection by large sections of the audience means that many will never realize that something novel is occurring. Perhaps the fourth persona is most important, then, as a way for queer authors and audiences (and really any members of the same "hidden" social population) to communicate with one another secretly through popular media texts. In a world where queer presence in the media is rare and representations are often problematic, the fourth persona may play a key role in providing queer individuals with some sense of community.

Conclusion

In this chapter we have considered how media representations of heterosexuality and homosexuality contribute to a system of unequal power relations between individuals in society. By drawing on the work of Michel Foucault and Judith Butler, Queer theorists seek to critique these representations and deconstruct heteronormative social systems. Part of this project involves the analysis of how the mass media portray heterosexuals and homosexuals differently in popular texts. Another part discerns the difference between visibility and representation, understanding that the mere presence of queer characters is not enough to make a text progressive. A final part looks for "invisible" aspects of queerness that somehow find a way between the lines of otherwise heteronormative texts. We can see, then, that Queer analysis is a diverse project with many different goals. In a sense, this applicability across many fronts is fitting for a perspective that refuses to be clearly pinned down.

Again, like in Chapter 8 on Feminist analysis, we stress here that Queer analysis as a theoretical perspective on the media is not only appropriate for scholars who may also identify as queer. Stereotypes and unquestioned understandings of sexuality work to place limits on all people in relation to issues of personal identity, practice, and desire, regardless of how we conceive of ourselves in the bedroom. While heteronormative social systems place greater limits on individuals who identify as homosexual, resulting in both symbolic and material disadvantages, those who identify as heterosexual are also inscribed into relations of power. Only the vigilant and careful consideration of media representations of sexuality can begin to overcome these systems of unequal relation. From this perspective, only by "queering" everyone can we begin to make the world a more equitable place to live.

MEDIA LAB 8: DOING QUEER ANALYSIS

OBJECTIVE

The aim of this lab is to utilize concepts of Queer theory to analyze media texts. Specifically, students will investigate popular and supposedly "queer" movies for the ways in which they challenge and reinforce understandings of visible and invisible sexuality.

ACTIVITY

- Divide the class into small groups of 4–5 students each.
- Play a short clip (5–6 minutes) of a popular movie widely recognized for its inclusion of queer characters. Potential films include *The Rocky Horror Picture Show, The Crying Game,* or *To Wong Foo, Thanks for Everything! Julie Newmar.*
- Ask students to record their answers to the following questions.
  1 How, if at all, does the representation in the clip reinforce systems of heteronormativity? How do you know?
  2 What stereotypes of heterosexuality and homosexuality are present in the clip?
  3 How does the clip link sexuality and gender? In your opinion, do these associations reinforce or challenge heteronormativity?
  4 How, if at all, does the clip feature the four qualities of camp? Do these features help to undermine other, potentially heteronormative aspects of the presentation?

SUGGESTED READING

Benshoff, H.M. *Monsters in the Closet: Homosexuality and the Horror Film.* New York: Manchester University Press, 1997.

Berlant, L. *The Queen of America Goes to Washington City: Essays on Sex and Citizenship.* Durham, NC: Duke University Press, 1997.

Bersani, L. *Homos.* Cambridge, MA: Harvard University Press, 1995.

Brookey, R.A. and Weterfelhaus, R. Hiding Homoeroticism in Plain View: the *Fight Club* DVD as Digital Closet. *Critical Studies in Media Communication* 2002, 19, 21–43.

Burston, P. and Richardson, C. (eds) *A Queer Romance: Lesbians, Gay Men, and Popular Culture.* New York: Routledge, 1995.

Butler, J. *Bodies That Matter: On the Discursive Limits of "Sex."* New York: Routledge, 1993.

Butler, J. *Gender Trouble: Feminism and the Subversion of Identity*, 10th anniversary edn. New York: Routledge, 1999.

Cramer, J.M. Discourses of Sexual Morality in *Sex and the City* and *Queer as Folk. Journal of Popular Culture* 2007, 40, 409–32.

Dow, B. *Ellen*, Television, and the Politics of Gay and Lesbian Visibility. *Critical Studies in Media Communication* 2001, 18, 123–40.

Foucault, M. *The History of Sexuality, Volume 1: an Introduction*, trans. R. Hurley. New York: Vintage Books, 1990.

Gamson, J. *Freaks Talk Back: Tabloid Talk Shows and Sexual Nonconformity.* Chicago, IL: University of Chicago Press, 1999.

Goltz, D.B. Laughing at Absence: *Instinct* Magazine and the Hyper-Masculine Gay Future? *Western Journal of Communication* 2007, 71, 93–113.

Gross, L. *Up From Invisibility: Lesbians, Gay Men, and the Media in America*. New York: Columbia University Press, 2001.

Halberstam, J. *Female Masculinity*. Durham, NC: Duke University Press, 1998.

Johnson, A.G. *Privilege, Power and Difference*. New York: McGraw Hill, 2001.

Katz, J.N. *The Invention of Heterosexuality*. New York: Dutton, 1995.

Rich, A. Compulsory Heterosexuality and Lesbian Existence. In *Blood, Bread and Poetry: Selected Prose 1979–1985*, 23–75. New York: W.W. Norton & Company, 1986.

Russell, V. *The Celluloid Closet*, 2nd edn. New York: Harper & Row, 1987.

Sedgwick, E.K. *Epistemology of the Closet*. Berkeley, CA: University of California Press, 1990.

Shugart, H.A. and Waggoner, C.E. *Making Camp: Rhetorics of Transgression in US Popular Culture*. Tuscaloosa, AL: Alabama University Press, 2008.

Sloop, J.M. *Disciplining Gender: Rhetorics of Sex Identity in Contemporary US Culture*. Amherst, MA: University of Massachusetts Press, 2004.

Warner, M. (ed.) *Fear of a Queer Planet: Queer Politics and Social Theory*. Minneapolis, MN: University of Minnesota Press, 1993.

Warner, M. *Publics and Counterpublics*. New York: Zone Books, 2002.

Weiss, A. *Vampires and Violets: Lesbians in Film*. New York: Penguin, 1992.

NOTES

1. B. Falchuk (dir.), Swan Song, *Glee* [television broadcast] (Century City, CA: 20th Century Fox). Original air date December 6, 2012.

2. See H. Hogan, "Glee" Graphed: the Brampocalypse Cometh, *AfterEllen*, December 4, 2012, http://www.afterellen.com/content/2012/12/glee-graphed-brampocalypse-cometh (accessed January 20, 2013).

3. As quoted in H. Hogan, The Lesbian Blogging Community Responds to "Glee"'s Commentary on the Lesbian Blogging Community, *AfterEllen*, December 7, 2012, http://www.afterellen.com/the-lesbian-blogging-community-responds-to-glees-commentary-on-the-lesbian-blogging-community/12/2012/ (accessed August 23, 2013).

4. E. Sedgwick, *The Epistemology of the Closet* (Berkeley, CA: University of California Press, 1990), 68.

5. A. Rich, Compulsory Heterosexuality and Lesbian Existence, in *Blood, Bread and Poetry: Selected Prose 1979–1985*, 23–75 (New York: W.W. Norton & Company, 1986).

6. M. Foucault, *The History of Sexuality, Volume 1: an Introduction*, trans. R. Hurley (New York: Vintage Books, 1990), 43.

7. Foucault, 123.

8. J. Butler, *Gender Trouble: Feminism and the Subversion of Identity*, 10th anniversary edn (New York: Routledge, 1999), 172.

9. Butler, *Gender Trouble*, 23.

10. Butler, *Gender Trouble*, 30.

11. M. Warner, Introduction, in *Fear of a Queer Planet: Queer Politics and Social Theory*, M. Warner (ed.) (Minneapolis, MN: University of Minnesota Press, 1993), xxvi.

12. The New Classics, *Entertainment Weekly*, June 27 and July 4 (double issue), 2008.

13. V. Russell, *The Celluloid Closet*, 2nd edn (New York: Harper & Row, 1987).

14. H.M. Benshoff and S. Griffin, *America on Film: Representing Race, Class, Gender and Sexuality at the Movies* (Oxford: Blackwell, 2004), 19.

15. E. Wright (dir.), *Scott Pilgrim vs. The World* [film] (Universal City, CA: Universal Pictures, 2010).

16. D. Weiss, Constructing the Queer "I": Performativity, Citationality, and Desire in *Queer Eye for the Straight Guy*, *Popular Communication* 2005, 3(2), 73–95.

17. K.G. Barnhurst, Visibility as Paradox: Representation and Simultaneous Contrast, in *Media/Queered:*

Visibility and Its Discontents, K.G. Barnhurst (ed.) (New York: Peter Lang, 2007), 1–22.

18. B.J. Dow, *Ellen*, Television, and the Politics of Gay and Lesbian Visibility, *Critical Studies in Media Communication* 2001, 18(2), 123–40.

19. Dow, 129.

20. F. Browning, *The Culture of Desire: Paradox and Perversity in Gay Lives Today* (New York: Vintage Books, 1994), 17.

21. Browning, 16.

22. An Overview of Federal Rights and Protections Granted to Married Couples, *Human Rights Campaign*, http://www.hrc.org/resources/entry/an-overview-of-federal-rights-and-protections-granted-to-married-couples (accessed January 31, 2013).

23. R. Dyer, Judy Garland and Gay Men, in *Heavenly Bodies: Film Stars and Society*, 2nd edn (New York: Routledge 2004).

24. S. Sontag, Notes on Camp, in *Against Interpretation* (New York: Picador, 1966), 277.

25. C. Isherwood, From *The World in the Evening*, in *Camp: Queer Aesthetics and the Performing Subject*, F. Cleto (ed.), 49–52 (Edinburgh: Edinburgh University Press, 1999), 51.

26. J. Babuscio, Camp and the Gay Sensibility, in *Queer Cinema: the Film Reader*, H. Benshoff and S. Griffin (eds), 121–36 (New York/London: Routledge, 2004), 122.

27. Babuscio, 121.

28. Babuscio, 122.

29. Babuscio, 127.

30. E. Black, The Second Persona, *Quarterly Journal of Speech* 1970, 56(2), 109–19.

31. P.C. Wander, The Third Persona: an Ideological Turn in Rhetorical Theory, *Central States Speech Journal* 1984, 35, 197–216. C.E. Morris III, Contextual Twilight/Critical Liminality: J.M. Barrie's *Courage* at St. Andrews, 1922, *Quarterly Journal of Speech* 1996, 82(3), 207–27; C.E. Morris

III, Pink Herring & The Fourth Persona: J. Edgar Hoover's Sex Crime Panic, *Quarterly Journal of Speech* 2002, 88(2), 228–44.

32. D. Ayers, Who Stabbed Travis Wall in the Back?, *AfterElton*, August 5, 2010, http://www.afterelton.com/tv/2010/08/sytycd-travis-wall-stabbed (accessed January 23, 2013).

33. A. Cooper (pro.), Top Four Perform, *So You Think You Can Dance* [television series] (New York/Century City, CA: Core Media & 20th Century Fox). Original air date August 4, 2010.

34. See, for example, K. Ward, "So You Think You Can Dance" Recap: Four Score! It's Down to the Wire for the Remaining Finalists, *Entertainment Weekly*, August 5, 2010, http://tvrecaps.ew.com/recap/so-you-think-you-can-dance-recap-season-7-episode-20/ (accessed January 23, 2013); R. Crouch, *So You Think You Can Dance* Episode Recap: "The Top Four Perform," *TV Guide*, August 5, 2010, http://www.tvguide.com/tvshows/so-you-think-you-can-dance/episode-20-season-7/191775 (accessed January 23, 2013).

35. S. Nigel, The Completely Not Gay *Dance* Between These 2 Twinks, *Queerty*, August 5, 2010, http://www.queerty.com/the-completely-not-gay-dance-between-these-2-twinks-20100805/ (accessed January 23, 2013).

36. Ayers, Who Stabbed?

37. D. Ayers, So You Think You Can Interview Travis Wall, *AfterElton*, July 5, 2011, http://www.thebacklot.com/so-you-think-you-can-interview-travis-wall/07/2011/ (accessed August 23, 2013).

38. J. Etkin, Travis Wall Talks "All The Right Moves," "So You Think You Can Dance," Emmys and More, *The Huffington Post*, August 22, 2012, http://www.huffingtonpost.com/2012/08/21/travis-wall-all-the-right-moves_n_1820120.html (accessed January 23, 2013).

Part III

Media Audiences: Reception, Sociological, Erotic, and Ecological Perspectives

10 Reception Analysis

KEY CONCEPTS

CODE
DECODING
ENCODING
ETHNOGRAPHY
HERMENEUTIC DEPTH

INTERPRETIVE COMMUNITIES
MEMORY
POLYSEMY
POLYVALENCE
RECEPTION THEORY
RESISTIVE READING
STRATEGIC AMBIGUITY

There is a feeling that I had Friday night after the homecoming game that I don't know if I will ever be able to describe except to say that it is warm. Sam and Patrick drove me to the party that night, and I sat in the middle of Sam's pickup truck. Sam loves her pickup truck because I think it reminds her of her dad. The feeling I had happened when Sam told Patrick to find a station on the radio. And he kept getting commercials. And commercials. And a really bad song about love that had the word "baby" in it. And then more commercials. And finally he found this really amazing song about this boy, and we all got quiet.

Sam tapped her hand on the steering wheel. Patrick held his hand outside the car and made air waves. And I just sat between them. After the song finished, I said something.

"I feel infinite."

And Sam and Patrick looked at me like I said the greatest thing they ever heard. Because the song was that great and because we all really paid attention to it. Five minutes of a lifetime were truly spent, and we felt young in a good way. I have since bought the record, and I would tell you what it was, but truthfully, it's not the same unless you're driving to your first real party, and you're sitting in the middle seat of a pickup with two nice people when it starts to rain.[1]

If you are anything like Charlie, the narrator in Stephen Chbosky's *The Perks of Being a Wallflower* excerpted above, you can probably think of at least one song that holds a unique significance for you. Perhaps the narrative of the song is related to your life,

Critical Media Studies: An Introduction, Second Edition. Brian L. Ott and Robert L. Mack.
© 2014 John Wiley & Sons, Inc. Published 2014 by John Wiley & Sons, Inc.

and maybe even the artist who sings it is important to you, but neither of those aspects fully captures what the song *means*. Perhaps this song is the one that played during the slow dance at your senior prom, the last time you saw a grandparent, or even (like Charlie) on the way to your first real high school party. No matter how many other people you encounter who claim to know and love this song, none of them will have the same meaning for it as you do because none of them were dancing, dealing with loss, or growing up with you.

This chapter asks the question: What is the role of the actual audience in the process of meaning-making in the media? Reception scholars primarily seek to understand the personal meanings that individuals make of mass media texts in relation to their lived social systems and experiences. Often by interviewing audience members or observing the environments where they read, watch, and listen, Reception scholars provide the field of media studies with a unique perspective on the power of audiences in shaping the media landscape. Instead of looking at how media content or production practices influence helpless media consumers, Reception analysis supports the notion of an "active" audience constantly reformulating the meanings of a media text across lines of race, class, gender, sexuality, and more.

This chapter will begin with a brief overview of Reception theory, especially as a response to more traditional audience studies, before looking at three contemporary Reception theories that shed light on how audiences make original meaning out of media texts. These theories are conceptually distinct but broadly convergent, and it is important to understand how they build upon one another to create an overarching understanding of the active audience. The chapter ends with a discussion of the primary research method for Reception scholars, ethnography, and considers two of the most famous examples of this approach in media research: David Morley's *Nationwide* study and Jackie Stacey's work on memory and stardom.

Reception Theory: an Overview

Reception theory refers to a diverse body of work that nevertheless commonly stresses audience interpretation as a primary source of meaning in the media. Proponents in this vein argue that the meaning of a text is never inherent; meaning only arises in the interaction between text and audience member. In relation to literature, for example, Wolfgang Iser notes that "as the reader uses the various perspectives offered [to] him by the text in order to relate the patterns and the 'schematized views' to one another, he [sic] sets the work in motion, and this very process results ultimately in the awakening of responses within himself."[2] Iser suggests that there are always some aspects of fictional narratives that are "unwritten" or left unaddressed by an author. Reading involves imagining or filling in these details, and by doing so the reader influences the meaning he/she makes of the text. Of course, the same process could be said to operate in relation to many other forms of media as well. No newspaper story or Wikipedia entry can relate every detail on a subject. Few films explicitly address what happens to the main characters after the credits roll. As a result, audiences always have some ability to add their own perspectives to a media text. Reception scholars admit that media owners might have the economic power to craft media texts with particular messages, but it is audiences who determine what a text ultimately signifies to them and how it actually functions in their own lives.

The historical advent of Reception theory in media studies was in many ways a response to more traditional, social scientific approaches to the audience that concentrated on measuring the effects of messages on mass consumers. As such, we believe it is important to summarize these approaches briefly in order to provide perspective on the more critical (and, we believe, more important) tradition of Reception analysis. The earliest model of media effects research conceived of the audience as mindless vessels ready to receive media messages. Sometimes dubbed the "hypodermic needle" approach, this research tradition predominantly sought to discover how the mass media "injected" particular meanings into consumers. Researchers assumed here that media messages meant only exactly what producers intended them to mean, and audiences were unable to ignore or negotiate these meanings. The weaknesses of this approach should be obvious: messages do not mean the same thing to every person, and the audience does not just passively absorb any and all media messages. As a result, media scholar Paul Lazarsfeld and his colleagues proposed the "two-step flow" model as a more nuanced version of the hypodermic needle approach.[3] This model posited the existence of opinion leaders, or certain individuals in the audience that attended more carefully to media than others. Mass media messages would influence these individuals, who would in turn disseminate the information to secondary audiences. Although the two-step model recognized a bit more activity on the part of the audience, it was still problematic because it supported the notion that the meanings of media messages were clear and definite.

Other empirical media effects research looks at the ways in which media messages could have broad, collective effects on the larger population. One of the most significant that still continues today is cultivation analysis, first proposed by George Gerbner.[4] Gerbner argues that individuals who watch heavy amounts of television are hyperconscious to issues of danger and violence in their everyday lives. His theory suggests that heavy-viewing audiences develop a distorted view of reality and believe that violence is more prevalent in society than actual statistics support. This kind of widespread effect is mirrored in the work of Donald Shaw and Maxwell McCombs and their theory of media agenda-setting.[5] Shaw and McCombs claim that popular media outlets like news stations tell the American public what to think about and how to think about it: they set the national agenda and fuel public concern. Cultivation analysis and agenda-setting are both more complex and developed approaches than the hypodermic needle or two-step models, but they continue the tradition of positioning the audience as mindless consumers who believe and follow most of what they see in the media.

One early approach to studying the audience that significantly departs from the others mentioned here is uses and gratifications theory.[6] This perspective was the first to begin "thinking of audiences as empowered to select their access to specific media and to use that media within the ranges of possibility."[7] Uses and gratifications theory assumes that individuals consciously consume media texts for their own ends, purposefully reworking textual meaning in order to integrate the text into their daily life. Instead of passively absorbing given meanings, audiences are selective in which media they consume and how they choose to use it. Audiences may engage media as a means of escapism, as a source of information, or even as a form of interpersonal relationship. In short, this perspective reverses the classic understanding of audiences by revealing how they use the media (instead of how the media may use them).

Although uses and gratifications theory is often critiqued for being overly optimistic about the audience, it is important to recognize it as an historical development in Reception analysis. Some of the analytical methods utilized by these researchers helped pave the way for contemporary ethnographic research on audiences. Moreover, the theoretical underpinnings of Reception theory were borne out of the criticisms leveled against uses and gratifications theory for assuming *conscious* activity on the part of the audience. Much Reception theory claims that while consciousness may be a factor for some individual consumers, audience members as a whole can refashion dominant media meanings without being completely cognizant of the process. A fully formulated understanding of this reasoning first crystallized in the encoding/decoding model.

Encoding/Decoding: Stuart Hall

Perhaps the most significant, early conceptual paradigm within Reception theory is Stuart Hall's encoding/decoding model (see Figure 10.1), originally published as a polemic against the classic models of audience effects research. Hall is best known for his ideological critiques within the field of British Cultural studies, and the model's emphasis on the production, negotiation, and reception of ideological messages between classes reflects this background. The model recognizes the role of media institutions and owners in engineering media texts with particular messages, but it also accounts for the various ways in which active audiences of different classes can consume and rework these hegemonic or dominant meanings. In a general sense, it outlines all of the possible ways in which the intended meaning of a text can be potentially reworked in the hands of an active audience.

Hall begins with the basic premise that "there is no intelligible discourse without the operation of a code."[8] A **code** is a set of rules that govern the use of visual and linguistic signs within a culture. Popular codes, like Morse code or so-called Pig Latin, are systems where users can disguise a message by translating it according to particular rules. Hall's notion of code is much broader but relies on the same principle. When you want to communicate something meaningful to a friend, you have to "translate" the thought in your head into a verbal sentence. The English language is the code you use in this instance. You could also use sign language or even

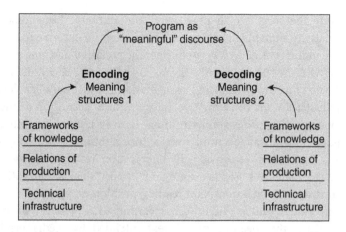

Figure 10.1 Hall's encoding/decoding model.

paint a picture that expresses this same thought; both of these are alternative codes to the English language. Any image or word we can comprehend, for Hall, is the result of a code.

Codes are never neutral in the sense that that they are always *representations* of meaning, not meaning itself, and they reflect the partiality inherent to any representation. Feminist theory is a code that encourages its users to generate and interpret ideas according to issues of gender and power. Christian theology is a code that prompts followers to disseminate and understand messages according to ideas of love and redemption. The codes we use lead to certain ways of seeing the world, and they compel us to interpret the world according to the rules of the code. This interpretation occurs in two related moments. **Encoding** is the process of creating a meaningful message according to a particular code, while **decoding** is the process of using a code to decipher a message and formulate meaning. The key insight of Hall's model is the recognition that "the codes of encoding and decoding may not be perfectly symmetrical."[9]

The left-hand "encoding side" of the model is primarily concerned with how dominant ideologies come to exist in mass-mediated texts. The codes that media industries use to create media texts are typically marked by dominant ideologies. Some industry codes, for example, reflect stereotypical understandings of race and gender (addressed in Chapters 6 and 8). When media producers use these codes to generate media texts (encoding), the ideologies implicit in the code also shape the representations of race and gender in a hegemonic way. The resulting meaning is called the "preferred reading" or desired interpretation of the text: "preferred" in the sense that *this* understanding of race and gender reinforces systems of unequal social power which in turn support media industries. The encoding of preferred meaning in Taylor Swift's break-up anthem "We Are Never Getting Back Together," for instance, would be the encoding of meanings about the lessons learned from the end of a heterosexual relationship. Other implicit preferred meanings might be that "true" love is worthy of pursuit, and that being tough after a break-up is an admirable quality. These are all preferred meanings because they are the result of the dominant codes that constitute the song, which draw from and reinforce hegemonic ideologies (heteronormativity, individualism, etc.), whose popularity in turn benefits the mainstream music industry. A good way to consider the preferred meaning of a media text is to think of what the text apparently "means" on a thematic or cultural level. It is the aspect of the text that draws from and validates dominant cultural ideologies.

Media industries want consumers to interpret texts according to the preferred meaning by employing codes similar to those used in production, but Hall points out that this does not always occur in practice. The right-hand "decoding side" of the model shows how audiences can actually interpret or "read" media texts according to three possible codes or positions: dominant, oppositional, and negotiated. Media audiences operating from a dominant reading position employ a code identical to the industry code and understand the text according to its preferred meaning. These audiences decode the meaning of the text intended by media producers and consciously or unconsciously accept it as true. Communication is "perfectly transparent" here because both parties are using the same code. If the first time you heard "We Are Never Getting Back Together," you thought, "What a catchy break-up song!" and jammed out to it in your car, you probably performed a dominant reading of the song. In other words, you probably accepted the song as meaningful to the extent that it features messages about the necessary trials of heterosexual love and the importance of self-reliance.

If upon hearing the song, however, you quickly switched radio stations and cursed the rise of the pop music love ballad, you probably performed an oppositional reading instead. Oppositional reading is not the same as misunderstanding. For Hall, a media consumer who decodes meaning from the oppositional position "detotalizes the message in the preferred code in order to retotalize the message within some alternative framework of reference."[10] These audiences recognize the preferred reading and dominant code in a text but reject them in favor of a completely different code (and, therefore, a different meaning). For instance, listeners who view the pop music industry as a vapid profit machine might employ a (Marxist) perceptual code that rejects Swift's messages of self-sufficiency and empowerment. Instead, the meaning that they decode from the song might recognize "We Are Never Getting Back Together" as the latest in a long line of moneymaking schemes by the music industry.

Dominant and oppositional reading strategies represent two of the three possible decoding positions, but in reality they are relatively rare. In truth, it is better to view them as ends on a complex continuum that predominantly features the diverse practices of the third category: negotiated reading. The majority of media consumers interpret media texts from a negotiated position, meaning that they decode part of the text in accordance with the industry code and part of it with an alternative code. These audiences mesh the preferred reading of the text with their personal perspectives and interpretations and produce meaning that is only partially reminiscent of the preferred. Typically, a negotiated reading "acknowledges the legitimacy of the hegemonic definitions to make the grand significations (abstract), while, at a more restricted, situational (situated) level, it makes its own ground rules."[11] It accepts the large-scale meanings while simultaneously assigning personal meanings.

This "hybrid meaning" of negotiated reading can take many forms. For example, some consumers who listen to "We Are Never Getting Back Together" might accept its ideologies of heteronormativity and self-reliance, but they might also read the song as an example of female empowerment. Queer individuals who listen to "We Are Never Getting Back Together" might reject the implied heterosexual love in the song, but they might accept the messages of self-reliance in times of emotional crisis. The notion of negotiated readings also helps us understand the various ways that people "use" media texts in their daily lives. When we watch individuals performing "We Are Never Getting Back Together" in talent shows, or in their living rooms via YouTube, we are watching a negotiated reading. There is a dimension of meaning for the performer we cannot access by simply looking at the ideologies of the song's lyrics.

Hall views the encoding/decoding process as cyclical. Each exchange of messages between media producers and consumers (every encoding and subsequent decoding) alters the codes and frameworks of knowledge from which both sides operate. The public reception of "We Are Never Getting Back Together" necessarily influenced which song would become Swift's follow-up hit. Although the encoding/decoding model was the first of its kind to recognize the roles of media producers and audiences in determining the meaning and influence of media texts, it also has a number of conceptual problems: If the encoding and decoding sides always affect one another, where does a text really "begin" in the model? How is it possible to determine the preferred encoded meaning without engaging in a process of decoding first? These questions and others have led other scholars to look at textual negotiation in a less-structured way through the notion of polysemy.

Polysemy: John Fiske, Celeste Condit, Leah Ceccarelli

The word *polysemy* literally translates to "many meanings." As proposed by television scholar John Fiske, **polysemy** refers to the relative openness of media texts to multiple interpretations. A polysemic text is one that can signify a number of different meanings to many different members of the audience. NBC's *Community* is a fairly polysemic text because it blends together the generic conventions of a sit-com, parodies of popular narratives, and diverse intertextual references into a complex piece of television programming. Different audiences will make different meanings of *Community* based on their background and knowledge of American popular culture. Emergency broadcast announcements, on the other hand, have limited polysemic potential. There is only so much a color bar and a loud screeching sound can mean to American audiences. These examples suggest that a text must be polysemic in order to be popular, and the most popular texts are often those most open to audience interpretation (just think of the moral ambiguity at the heart of popular television shows like *Mad Men* and *Revenge*).

The notion of popularity becomes an overriding construct that Fiske uses to understand the role of power and the negotiation of meanings in a text. He concedes that all popular texts must have a foundation of dominant social conventions shared by audiences. Quite simply, "a text can appeal to this variety of audiences only if there is a common ideological frame that all recognize and can use, even if many are opposed to it."[12] This foundation of dominant understandings, however, cannot fully contain all of the meaning in a media text, a fact that always results in the recognition of what Fiske labels "semiotic excess." This excess is the surplus of signifiers in the text that do not reference clear signifieds, and the degree of polysemy in a text is relative to the text's level of semiotic excess. Polysemy is, therefore, not a quality a text either possesses or lacks, but an ever-present aspect of the text that can be measured in terms of *more* or *less*. The greater the semiotic excess and polysemy of a text, the more audiences can negotiate and manage personal meanings. This understanding of texts leads Fiske to view most television programs as "producerly," a term he uses to denote an open, writerly text (see Chapter 11) that is also popular. A producerly text "relies on discursive competencies that the viewer already possesses, but requires that they are used in a self-interested, productive way."[13]

A clear example of a producerly text that exemplifies the tenets of polysemy is the CW network's *Supernatural*. The long-running program is a complex narrative that follows the Winchester brothers (Jensen Ackles and Jared Padalecki) in their attempts to rid the world of demons, ghosts, and other mythical creatures. On the one hand, *Supernatural* relies on a number of American ideological assumptions (the struggle between good and evil, the importance of family, the re-invention of the self) and televisual conventions (seasonal story arcs, cliffhangers, flashbacks). These are the aspects of the show that make it popular among American audiences because they are culturally familiar. On the other hand, *Supernatural* is also predicated on the gradual unwinding of secrets that represent free-floating signifiers and semiotic excess. Viewers encounter narrative moments (hints regarding the brothers' destinies, allusions to plots hatched in heaven and hell, roguish characters with dubious intentions, etc.) that do not possess immediate or clear meanings within the context of the story. The joy of *Supernatural* for many of its fans is the speculation that it generates around these elements, and scores of online forums exist where people can share their thoughts and interpretations. In this way, *Supernatural*'s polysemic ambiguity makes it ripe for multiple readings from different individuals.

Fiske's theory of polysemy re-imagines Hall's encoding/decoding model by aligning Hall's notion of preferred meaning with communal audience decoding practices and his concepts of negotiated or oppositional reading with semiotic excess. Thus, the management of meaning from a polysemic perspective is neither linear nor cyclical, and it is best viewed as a ratio between convention and excess on the part of the reading audience. Polysemy is an important contribution to Reception analysis because it recognizes two levels of potential meaning in any given media text, and it allows scholars to understand the "place" in the text where audiences engage their personal experiences and attitudes. Fiske is one of the strongest proponents of audience power in contemporary media studies, and his theory of polysemy (where meaning can never be fully controlled by producers) reflects that scholarly commitment.

Naturally, such a singular perspective on the audience has its critics. In her essay "The Rhetorical Limits of Polysemy," Celeste Condit outlines a number of issues that Fiske overlooks.[14] The first is a lack of oppositional codes on the part of most audience members. Oppositional codes, such as Marxism or Feminism, are ways of understanding the world that contradict dominant American ideologies. Because most audience members simply do not have access to these codes, it would be difficult to interpret a media text in the truly novel way that the theory of polysemy implies. Condit also critiques Fiske for ignoring the disproportionate amount of internal work required in generating personal meaning against the dominant meanings in the text. Socially privileged groups whose views resonate most with the conventional level of textual meaning experience pleasure more easily than marginalized groups who must work to pull meaning from the semiotic excess. This leads Condit to question Fiske's assumption that television is a democratic medium, instead asserting that media texts are "compromises that give the relatively well-to-do more of what they want, bringing along as many economically marginal viewers as they comfortably can."[15]

Condit goes on to point out that even the diversity of programming on television tends to reinforce particular messages about cultural issues, and the historical moment that contextualizes a media program also importantly influences its reception. Both of these factors position television as a more determined medium than Fiske's notion of polysemy allows. In light of the shortcomings of polysemy, Condit proposes the notion of polyvalence as a more applicable term. **Polyvalence** "occurs when audience members share understandings of the denotations of a text but disagree about the valuation of those denotations to such a degree that they produce notably different interpretations."[16] In other words, audiences understand the actual content of media texts in a similar way, but they disagree on the merit or value of that information. One needs to look no further than film critics to see this point. Although most reviewers share common perceptions about how a film's plot develops or the role of characters, their overall assessments of the work can be strikingly diverse. Polyvalence differs from polysemy in that the difference between audience members is one of *connotation*, not of *meaning* as a whole.

Whether viewed as polysemy or polyvalence, the recognition of multiple dimensions of meaning in a text opens up new understanding in media studies and Reception analysis. These approaches shake off the problematic structuring of the encoding/decoding model while still retaining a focus on the interplay between media producers and audiences. Both Fiske and Condit, however, somewhat ironically operate within a textual paradigm even as they concern themselves with methods of reception. They both (unreflectively) consider how polysemic *texts* enable audiences to negotiate meaning. This is understandable if one remembers that prior to the notion of an "active audience," many media scholars focused on the industry and textual issues outlined in the first two sections of this textbook. The work of many early Reception theorists (like Fiske and Condit) reflects this tendency to consider the text as central, and it was not until Reception theory developed into a more distinct body of work that scholars began interrogating its internal assumptions.

One of the most significant contributions to the refinement of Reception theory and polysemy is Leah Ceccarelli's 1998 article "Polysemy: Multiple Meanings in Rhetorical Criticism."[17] Until this point, many Reception theorists had used the concept of polysemy to explain audience interpretive practices without clearly identifying whether it exists as a quality of the audience, the text, both, or neither. In essence, "the term 'polysemy' is itself polysemous."[18] Ceccarelli is not concerned with pinning down an essential meaning for the term, but she does attempt to understand how it can function through different bodies in different ways toward different ends. Although she is primarily interested in how polysemy functions rhetorically across disciplines, her outline of the three primary "types" of polysemy helps us better understand the process of audience reception in media studies. These three types are resistive reading, strategic ambiguity, and hermeneutic depth.

When scholars view polysemy as a quality of the audience, they are conceptualizing it as a tool of resistive reading. **Resistive reading** is the active, audience-based creation of textual meaning that is contrary to the meaning intended by the text's author, creator, or producer. Here marginalized audiences use the concept of polysemy to distort or transform the messages that reflect the needs and interests of dominant groups. Resistive reading is very close to Hall's notion of oppositional reading in the sense that both rely on audience access to oppositional codes to interpret the message. A Feminist reading of magazine advertisements, for example, is an act of resistive reading. Rather than interpreting the message as an advertisement for a useful product at a good price (which one needs to purchase *right now*), a Feminist resistive reading would understand the advertisement as a text that primarily reinforces the subjugated role of women in society. Polysemy is crucial here because it explains how feminist audiences open up oppositional fields of meaning in a given text.

When scholars view polysemy as a quality of the text and its creator, conversely, they are conceptualizing it as an instance of strategic ambiguity. **Strategic ambiguity** is the intentional decision to craft a vague, semantically rich text that is purposefully open to multiple interpretations. When textual producers are faced with conflicting demands from different audiences, they may navigate through these expectations by attempting to satisfy all of them with the same text. The use of strategic ambiguity is rhetorical in the sense that it is often tied to a specific situation: particular conflicting audiences at a particular historical moment. The annual State of the Union address is often a good example of a strategically ambiguous text. In the address the president must attempt to satisfy a number of different conflicting audiences across areas like political affiliation, income level, or geographic location. Clear plans are less common than general commitments in the address, which allows these different audiences to interpret plans for the coming year as they see fit. Polysemy allows for ambiguity in this instance.

Finally, when scholars view polysemy as a quality of the critic or analyst, they are conceptualizing it as a dedication to hermeneutic depth. **Hermeneutic depth** refers to the critical recognition of multiple meanings in a text as the source of its overall meaning. When scholars imbue a text with hermeneutic depth, they engage it as a site of academic play and problematize any apparently singular meaning. This process reveals the multiple meanings of the text and encourages the understanding of many, sometimes conflicting interpretations. The textbook you are currently reading is in many ways an extended project in service of hermeneutic depth. We began with the text of "American media" (understandably large and complex) and have run it through eight different perspectives by now. None of these perspectives is wholly correct or incorrect, and true understanding only comes in recognizing the (in)applicability of each one at different times. This lack of clear meaning *is* the meaning. Here polysemy becomes a way of achieving hermeneutic depth, a bridge toward deeper, more complex understandings of texts.

Ceccarelli's landmark essay shed critical light on how different types of polysemy function in different ways toward different ends. Her categorization also better distinguishes between text and audience in the process of audience meaning-making, which is its major strength and weakness for Reception theory. On one hand, by clearly distinguishing between resistive reading, strategic ambiguity, and hermeneutic depth, she reminds Reception theorists to be more conscious in their use of the term and their scholarly worldview. On the other, she implicitly recognizes audience-based and text-based polysemy as equally prevalent and valid. While this may be true, it is not helpful for Reception theorists attempting to understand all of meaning from the audience perspective. Instead, this type of holistic viewpoint forms the central component in the final theoretical section we will consider.

Interpretive Communities: Stanley Fish

Stanley Fish is an important literary critic in the tradition known as reader-centered or reader-response criticism, but his work on textual interpretation is just as applicable to media studies as it is to the analysis of literature. Unlike Hall and Fiske, who recognize some degree of ideological or authorial power in texts as a result of their production, Fish claims that all meaning resides in the readers and audiences of texts. Meaning simply cannot exist outside of audience interpretation. The interpretive strategies we already possess as audience members, he writes,

> are not put into execution after reading (the pure act of perception in which I do not believe); they are the shape of reading, and because they are the shape of reading, they give texts their shape, *making* them rather than, as it is usually assumed, *arising* from them.[19] (emphasis added)

In other words, until audience members engage a media text and begin to read or interpret it, that text literally means nothing. The strategies we use to interpret the text direct us to understand the words and images in a particular way. Only then does the text actually *mean* anything. Although we tend to think that our varied perspectives allow us to access the different kinds of meaning implicit in a text, it is actually the other way around: our ways of understanding create meaning in the text, the only meaning a text can have. Any meaning we generate, anything we notice, "has been *made* noticeable ... by an interpretive strategy."[20]

This thinking quickly leads to problems. After all, if every individual makes unique and personal meaning out of a text through the process of reading it, then how is it possible that some people tend to read some texts in roughly the same way? If an individual interprets texts according to particular strategies, how can that individual read two similar texts in very different ways? And where do these strategies come from in the first place? Fish's answers to these questions can be found in his notion of **interpretive communities**, or groups who interpret texts similarly because they share similar social positions and experiences. New Yorkers might interpret a film about New York society differently from Arizonans who watch the same film because they share different codes based on geographic location. Naturally, the total meanings that individual audience members generate in each group will vary, but one might expect to see more resemblance between any two New Yorkers than a New Yorker and an Arizonan. At the same time, the Arizonan, who has adored the previous work of the director of the film, might hate this particular film because it disparages Americans. If this were the case, we might reason that the interpretive strategies based on this person's nationality supersede those based on state residency in this instance. Thus, the fact that people can and do belong to many interpretive communities at once explains the similarity and variation in their interpretive strategies.

Meaning ultimately resides in interpretive communities in Fish's paradigm, and that assertion collapses the distinction between producers and audiences that so many other theorists struggle over. Rather than concentrate on whether power over meaning lies in the producer or the audience, Fish claims that interpretive communities give rise to all producers, texts, and audiences in the first place. The communities that an individual belongs to shape how that person will interpret texts, but the communities that an author/producer/creator belongs to also influence how that individual constructs the text initially. Fish points out that all texts carry with them "a projection on the part of a speaker or author of the moves *he* [sic] would make if confronted by the sounds or marks he is uttering or setting down."[21] Readers and audiences who belong to the same communities as the author/producer will pick up on these projections as directions for understanding the text; those outside of his/her communities will not. Meaning is not inherent in producers, texts, or audiences, but only in the interpretive communities that constitute each.

One of the most notable historical studies dealing with interpretive communities is Janice Radway's analysis of women and meaning in romance novels.[22] In her study, Radway surveyed and interviewed a sizable group of women in the midwestern town of Smithton in order to better understand the meanings they attributed to reading romance novels. All of the women in the study were connected to a central respondent named Dot, who worked at a local bookstore and helped women select novels to read. During the course of her study, Radway found that the women did not passively absorb the conventional meanings of romance novels and instead actively used the romances in order to supplement their needs and desires. Many of Radway's respondents, for example, claimed that they consciously used the novels to escape the emotional demands of their daily life and construct a world of personal meaning and satisfaction. These responses point to the fact that romances do not carry a singular or stable meaning imbued by the novel's author. Meaning comes from interpretation on the part of the audience.

One could speculate that these women belonged to a number of intermingling interpretive communities. Although they differed in their educational levels, family income, and religious conviction, all of the respondents were women, and all lived in the town of Smithton. As a result, Radway discovered that many of the respondents mimicked one another when discussing the meanings of romance novels. Beyond the common theme of escapism, the women in the study also tended to agree on what constitutes a good romance novel:

> A romance is, first and foremost, a story about a woman. That woman, however, may not figure in a larger plot simply as a hero's prize. ... To qualify as a romance, the story must chronicle not merely the events of a courtship but *what it feels like* to be the *object of* one.[23]

This similarity in interpretation speaks to the shared communities of the women in question. Although they disagreed over some aspects of good romances (first-person or third-person narratives, for example), they shared enough reading strategies as women and as romance readers located in Smithton to articulate a common interpretation of quality. The ratio of agreement and disagreement between the women is directly related to the overlapping of interpretive communities between individual women.

Overall, Fish's theory of interpretive communities locates meaning completely in the audience, and it also accounts for similarity and variation among individual audience members. Even textual producers are "audiences" in the sense that they draw from their own experiences and interpretations in creating a text. This is not to say that Fish's approach is the supreme or correct one in relation to media Reception theory, but it is certainly one of the closest to the spirit of ethnographic Reception studies. The best approaches to Reception analysis will consider the work of all of the theorists we have discussed thus far and understand how their various perspectives fit together. Even though Radway's study focused on meaning-making within a particular community, other aspects of the study (such as her discussion of the romance publishing industry) nod to the power relationships found in concepts like encoding/decoding and polysemy. It also provides our first glimpse into the process of ethnographic audience studies in this chapter. The careful designing of surveys, extensive interviewing, and attention to detail we see in Radway's analysis are the hallmarks of the ethnographic process. The remainder of the chapter will further consider the major tenets of this research method.

Ethnographic Research and Memory

Ethnography is a qualitative research method that focuses on understanding a cultural phenomenon from the perspective of the members of that culture. Ethnographers attempt to immerse themselves in a culture as much as possible through observation, interviews, and participation to gain an insider's knowledge of a cultural phenomenon. In theory, this immersion accomplishes two goals (1) it minimizes the researcher's cultural biases by displacing the researcher's own culture as the basis for judgment and (2) it yields additional understanding about how the phenomenon in question functions within the larger, complex practices of a particular cultural group. Because ethnography has developed predominantly in the fields of anthropology and sociology, many people tend to think of ethnic or national cultures when they think of ethnographic research. In reality, almost any "culture" can be analyzed with this method: workplace culture, videogame culture, fan culture, etc. (see Chapter 6 for an extended discussion of different types of cultures).

Although it is central to the application of Reception theory within media studies, ethnography actually began in the larger field of communication as a tool to better understand the link between language and culture. This early approach, which continues to thrive today, is often called the "ethnography of speaking" or the "ethnography of communication." Here ethnographers approach a culture with two basic questions in mind: what does a speaker need to know to communicate appropriately within a particular speech community, and how does he or she learn to do so?[24] In order to answer these questions, ethnographers of communication look at the interaction patterns, power differentials, and identity performances of a given culture/speech community. Understanding the way members of a culture communicate with one another helps explain particular behaviors and beliefs within that culture.

Perhaps the most famous example of an ethnography of communication is Gerry Philipsen's extended analysis in the 1970s of a blue-collar Chicago neighborhood he dubbed Teamsterville.[25] Philipsen observed and talked to residents of Teamsterville for nearly two and a half years in order to gain a nuanced understanding of the neighborhood's communication patterns. He learned that speaking in Teamsterville was intrinsically tied to concepts of gender, ethnicity, and even physical location. Teamsterville men could talk to other men of similar background and social standing, but for men to talk at length to a person with less social power (a child, for example) was not appropriate. "To speak 'like a man' in Teamsterville," Philipsen elaborates, "required knowing when and under what circumstances to speak at all."[26] Similarly, Philipsen discovered that the front porch of Teamsterville homes functioned as an important place for community socialization. One resident even confessed that a man who had recently moved to the neighborhood could never fully acclimatize because he lacked a porch.[27] By observing and interviewing Teamsterville residents in their own environment, Philipsen was able to assess the subtle communication patterns of the neighborhood culture in a way that would be impossible using other methods.

As we noted in Chapter 6, ethnographic research on media audiences grew out of the ideological work of British Cultural studies in the 1970s. Ethnographers interested in media Reception research utilize similar methods as Philipsen to understand how audiences engage media texts. These scholars attempt to immerse themselves in the actual environments of audience media consumption as a way of capturing the intricacies of meaning-making and negotiation. Media ethnographers might, for instance, attend a film society's weekly screenings to discuss what the films mean to the members of the group. By interviewing members of the society and closely monitoring their viewing practices, a media ethnographer would be able to discover the codes, meanings, and complex negotiations that inform how they make sense of the cinema. This method might reveal how the society's conception of film as art (and not passing entertainment) colors their interpretation of the weekly narratives, a conclusion that would be difficult to fully realize without "knowing" the group first. Other media ethnographers could potentially study the regular patrons of a local music store, the fans of an author, or even the participants in an online role-playing game. In short, these scholars use ethnographic methods of participation, observation, and interviewing to understand how an actual group of people makes sense of specific media texts.

The most significant example of ethnographic analysis in media Reception research is David Morley's *Nationwide* audience study of the 1970s.[28] Morley is a British Cultural studies scholar and was one of the first to break away from traditional conceptions of the "duped" audience. Informed by issues of ideology and Hall's model of dominant, negotiated, and oppositional reading, Morley was interested in investigating the degree to which a person's access to cultural codes influenced his/her reception of dominant ideologies in media texts. He disagreed with uses and gratifications theories because they often ignored ideology, and he also rejected Hall's focus on class as a determinant for decoding positions. As a result, his *Nationwide* study was an attempt to look at how audiences with different qualities interpreted ideological messages in the British media.

Nationwide was a popular, weekday evening British news program broadcast by BBC One between 1969 and 1983, which at the time placed special emphasis on representing the various parts of Britain in its reporting. Morley (along with colleague Charlotte Brunsdon) had already catalogued the types of dominant ideologies present in the program in a previous study.[29] With "The *Nationwide* Audience: Structure and Decoding," Morley shifted attention to understanding how different members of British society made sense of these ideological messages through the use of dominant, negotiated, and oppositional codes. The study consisted of two phases. In the first, Morley screened a specific episode of the program that "covered a fairly representative sample of *Nationwide*'s characteristic topics" to 18 different small groups.[30] These groups included apprentice engineers, apprentice electricians, black college students, middle school students, teachers in training, and more, all selected on the basis of factors he assumed were related to decoding practices (sex, race, class, union membership, educational level, political affiliation, etc.). In the second phase, Morley screened an episode focused specifically on the economy to 11 different groups such as bank managers, sociology students, apprentice printers, shop stewards, etc. In each case Morley gained access to the social groups through courses they were taking together at technical/trade schools and universities. In this way, he attempted to use pre-existing groups that were somewhat cohesive in their shared educational pursuits. After each group viewed the program in the context of their classes, Morley led a focused discussion with the group and recorded their answers on tape.

Morley discovered that the particular combination of social factors in each group led to unique understandings of *Nationwide*. This may not seem like a revolutionary conclusion now, but at the time it represented the first real evidence of an active audience who negotiated or resisted meaning in the media. Certain groups, like the apprentices and bank managers, mostly interpreted the program within the dominant code. Others, like the black college students, felt that "the concerns of *Nationwide* are not the concerns of their world," as they rejected the very process of interpretation.[31] Most of the groups exhibited different degrees of negotiated reading, either closer to preferred (teachers) or oppositional (university students) sides of the reading spectrum. Additionally, the study revealed that class was not the determinant factor of reading style as Hall had proposed. The apprentices, shop stewards, and black students all shared a similar class in the study, but they performed widely divergent readings as a result of other social factors like union involvement and racial subcultures.

Morley's landmark study was one of the first to open up room within media scholarship for ethnographic analyses of the actual audience. It reinforced Hall's model by acknowledging the place of both industry ideologies and audience interpretation, but it also dispelled his reliance on class by revealing the multifaceted basis of audience reading strategies. This concentration on audience diversity and variation has become a hallmark of ethnographic analyses ever since.

The *Nationwide* study also provides valuable insight into how media ethnographies can differ significantly from ethnographies of communication. For example, while Morley did attempt to use intact groups in their own educational settings, parts of the study itself resemble more traditional experimental methods. These groups would probably never watch an episode of *Nationwide* in any of their respective classes, much less discuss their personal interpretations of its content. He also spent far less time "in the field" gathering information about audience members than his more anthropologically-minded counterparts. Morley's half-hour interviews with 29 groups hardly compare to Philipsen's two and a half years in Teamsterville. The fact that Morley "set up" the environment and then recorded his findings via interviews seems to downplay the natural qualities of the audience that ethnography seeks to represent. Coupled with a comparatively brief data-collection period, this quasi-experimentation casts doubt on how much the *Nationwide* study could actually be called "ethnography."

More recent scholarship in the field of audience studies, however, has argued for a looser definition of ethnography to accommodate the complex process of media reception. Morley's work certainly falls within what we might call the "contemporary" standards of media ethnography. Media texts and audiences have become increasingly diverse since *Nationwide*, and some scholars have now recognized that "classic ethnographic fieldwork may not be an appropriate method for studying dispersed media audiences."[32] As a loose methodological movement within audience studies, then, media ethnography emphasizes certain ethnographic methods over others as a function of today's media landscape. Media ethnographers today can certainly attempt to capture the interpretations of a widespread audience, but it has also become permissible to consider smaller groups/cultures (even the reading strategies of a single family). Many ethnographic studies of media still focus on the importance of the actual environment in which audiences consume texts, but the amount of time spent observing audiences in these environments is usually far shorter than traditional ethnographic methods require. In this way, media ethnography takes useful aspects of traditional ethnography (a focus on context, allowing people to represent themselves in the research) while discarding parts that often do not fit with the media object of study (lengthy data-gathering periods, extensive immersion in the field). Media ethnography is ethnography in spirit, and "if the means of investigation are not always identical, then the aims of the inquiry can be."[33]

One important method for media research that has developed within these flexible ethnographic standards involves the use of **memory**, or audience members' recollection of their reception histories. Rather than observe audience members in an actual context of media reception, some Reception scholars instead ask audience members about their memories of consuming media at a particular historical moment or in relation to specific objects. This approach is somewhat "ethnographic" in the sense that the audience is often conceived of as a cultural group (held together according to history or around a common object), and the researcher's primary interest is understanding the management of meaning among members of this cultural group, but the individuals included in the study often never interact with one another. The goal of memory-based "ethnographies" is to recreate as much as possible an otherwise inaccessible or lost media reception context. While traditional ethnography might be able to capture the nuances of reception practices in the public or the present, memory studies allow scholars to "observe" reception practices that occur in private or in the past.

One of the most famous reception studies grounded in memory forms the basis of Jackie Stacey's book *Star Gazing: Hollywood Cinema and Female Spectatorship*.[34] Troubled by the overwhelmingly textual approach to studying the role of gender in the structure and reception of classic Hollywood cinema (see discussion of the male gaze in Chapter 7), Stacey set out in the late 1980s to discover how actual audiences, and specifically women, related to images of female stars in mid-century Hollywood films. The most significant portion of Stacey's study involved soliciting letters from "keen cinema-goers" about their memories of film stars of the 1940s and 1950s through four popular women's magazines in Britain. She received more than 350 responses to this request. Twenty of these respondents also agreed to fill out an open-ended questionnaire, which allowed them to discuss their memories further and with minimal direction. Though the individual respondents did not know one another, they were a fairly homogenous cultural group: mostly British, white women who were 50 to 60 years old.

On the basis of these letters and questionnaire responses, Stacey constructs a detailed account of this audience's reception practices which occurred nearly half a century prior. The responses challenge narrow, Psychoanalytic theories of female sexual objectification in film, positioning female stars instead as focal points within rich tapestries of leisure and escapism for the actual women who watched them. Stacey notes that the opulent movie palace was a haven for these viewers from wartime and postwar life in Britain, and many used the cinema to escape the house and its attendant (and often dreary) domestic chores. Viewers remember stars as archetypes and innovators of femininity, as sources of inspiration, and as signifiers of national culture. By accessing actual viewers' memories, then, Stacey was able to uncover significant information about film spectatorship and challenge standing interpretations about film during the time period.

In the third chapter of her book Stacey refers to the women in her study (and those like them) as "the lost audience," largely ignored within film studies in favor of formal or textual approaches. Without the ascent of memory as a tool for ethnographic media studies, they might still be overlooked today. Memory is not perfect recall in the sense that memories are often distorted by time and other factors, but sometimes memories are the only way to learn about reception practices that are inaccessible to more traditional methods of ethnographic observation. The use of memory, then, is in many ways a product of the ethnographic flexibility that has marked media Reception studies from its inception.

Conclusion

This chapter has looked at the role of Reception theory, ethnography, and memory in understanding media from the perspective of the actual audience. Theories of encoding/decoding, polysemy, and interpretive communities allow us to conceive of the audience not as a passive mass ready to absorb singular ideological messages from media texts, but rather as an active group of diverse people who "read" texts according to their social positions and lived experiences. This departure from classic conceptions of the audience shifts the discussion for scholars from media effects to media meanings: Where does meaning in a text come from? How do audiences negotiate meaning? What continues to structure the process of audience meaning-making? Ethnographic research methods are key to answering these questions because they allow scholars to investigate the subtle and otherwise invisible meanings that audiences attribute to the media texts they consume. In many ways these methods are complements to the types of industry and textual analyses outlined in the first two sections of this book. By analyzing actual audience media consumption along with the production of media texts, scholars gain a more complete picture of American media today.

MEDIA LAB 9: DOING RECEPTION ANALYSIS

OBJECTIVE

The aim of this lab is to utilize Reception theories of meaning to understand the role of the media audience. Specifically, students will be reacting to and sharing their personal understandings of a media text.

ACTIVITY

- Divide the class into small groups of 4–5 students each.
- Screen a short music video for the groups. We suggest choosing a popular artist with a long-standing career, such as Madonna, in order to maximize possible responses.
- Have each student individually record his/her reactions to the video in a brief paragraph. Possible prompts for this paragraph include: What is this video about? What is the central message of this video? What do you like or dislike about the video?
- Have students convene in their groups, compare reactions, and answer the following questions.
    1   How did the individual responses in your group vary? Which differences are examples of polysemy, and which are examples of polyvalence?
    2   How did the individual responses in your group converge? Identify possible shared interpretive communities that could explain this similarity.
    3   Which group members used dominant codes for interpreting the video? Negotiated codes? Oppositional codes? How do you know?

SUGGESTED READING

Acosta-Alzuru, C. Tackling the Issues: Meaning-Making in a Telenovela. *Popular Communication* 2003, 1, 193–215.

Allor, M. Relocating the Site of the Audience. *Critical Studies in Mass Communication* 1998, 5, 217–33.

Ang, I. *Living Room Wars: Rethinking Media Audiences for a Postmodern World*. New York: Routledge, 1996.

Bird, S.E. *The Audience in Everyday Life: Living in a Media World*. New York: Routledge, 2003.

Cavicchi, D. *Tramps Like Us: Music and Meaning Among Springsteen Fans*. New York: Oxford University Press, 1998.

D'Acci, J. *Defining Women: Television and the Case of Cagney & Lacey*. Chapel Hill, NC: University of North Carolina Press, 1994.

Feasey, R. Reading *Heat*: the Meanings and Pleasures of Star Fashions and Celebrity Gossip. *Continuum: Journal of Media & Cultural Studies* 2008, 22, 687–99.

Fish, S. *Is There a Text in This Class? The Authority of Interpretive Communities*. Cambridge, MA: Harvard University Press, 1982.

Fiske, J. *Understanding Popular Culture*. New York: Routledge, 1989.

Fiske, J. and Dawson, R. Audiencing Violence: Watching Homeless Men Watch *Die Hard*. In *The Audience and its Landscape*, J. Hay, L. Grossberg, and E. Wartella (eds), pp. 297–316. Boulder, CO: Westview Press, 1996.

Gamson, J. *Claims to Fame: Celebrity in Contemporary America*. Berkeley, CA: University of California Press, 1994.

Hall, S. Encoding/Decoding. In *Media and Cultural Studies: Keyworks*, M.G. Durham and D.M. Kellner (eds), pp. 163–73. Oxford: Blackwell, 2006.

Lowe, M. Colliding Feminisms: Britney Spears, "Tweens," and the Politics of Reception. *Popular Music and Society* 2003, 26, 123–40.

Morley, D. *Television, Audiences & Cultural Studies*. New York: Routledge, 1992.

Press, A. Toward a Qualitative Methodology of Audience Study: Using Ethnography to Study the Popular Culture Audience. In *The Audience and its Landscape*, J. Hay, L. Grossberg, and E. Wartella (eds), pp. 113–30. Boulder, CO: Westview Press, 1996.

Radway, J.A. *Reading the Romance: Women, Patriarchy, and Popular Literature*, 2nd edn. Chapel Hill, NC: University of North Carolina Press, 1991.

Schutten, J.K. Invoking *Practical Magic*: New Social Movements, Hidden Populations, and the Public Screen. *Western Journal of Communication* 2006, 70, 331–54.

Staiger, J. *Perverse Spectators: the Practices of Film Reception*. New York: New York University Press, 2000.

Staiger, J. *Media Reception Studies*. New York: New York University Press, 2005.

Winocur, R. Radio and Everyday Life: Uses and Meanings in the Domestic Sphere. *Television & New Media* 2005, 6, 319–32.

NOTES

1. S. Chbosky, *The Perks of Being a Wallflower* (New York: Pocket Books, 1999), 32–3.
2. W. Iser, The Reading Process: a Phenomenological Approach, in *Reader Response Criticism: from Formalism to Post-Structuralism*, J.P. Tompkins (ed.) (Baltimore: Johns Hopkins University Press, 1980), 51.
3. P.F. Lazarsfeld, B. Berelson, and H. Gaudet, *The People's Choice: How the Voter Makes Up His Mind in a Presidential Campaign* (New York: Columbia Press, 1944).
4. For an excellent summary of cultivation analysis, see G. Gerbner, Cultivation Analysis: an Overview, *Mass Communication and Society* 1998, 1(3/4), 175–94.
5. M.E. McCombs and D.L. Shaw, The Agenda Setting Function of the Mass Media, *Public Opinion Quarterly* 1972, 36(2), 176–87.
6. E. Katz, J.G. Blumler, and M. Gurevitch, Utilization of Mass Communication by the Individual, in *The Uses of Mass Communication: Current Perspectives on Gratification Research* (Beverly Hills, CA: Sage Publications, 1974), 19–32.
7. J. Staiger, *Media Reception Studies* (New York: New York University Press, 2005), 53.
8. S. Hall, Encoding/Decoding, in *Media and Cultural Studies: Keyworks*, M.G. Durham and D.M. Kellner (eds) (Oxford: Blackwell, 2006), 167.
9. Hall, 166.
10. Hall, 173.
11. Hall, 172.
12. J. Fiske, Television: Polysemy and Popularity, in *Critical Perspectives on Media and Society*, R.K. Avery and D. Eason (eds) (New York: The Guilford Press, 1991), 359.
13. J. Fiske, *Television Culture* (New York: Methuen, 1987), 95.
14. C. Condit, The Rhetorical Limits of Polysemy, in *Critical Perspectives on Media and Society*, R.K. Avery and D. Eason (eds) (New York: The Guilford Press, 1991), 365–86.
15. Condit, 373.
16. Condit, 369.
17. L. Ceccarelli, Polysemy: Multiple Meanings in Rhetorical Criticism, *Quarterly Journal of Speech* 1998, 84(4), 395–415.
18. Ceccarelli, 396.
19. S. Fish, Interpreting the *Variorum*, in *Is There a Text in This Class? The Authority of Interpretive Communities* (Cambridge, MA: Harvard University Press, 1982), 168.

20. Fish, 166.

21. Fish, 173.

22. J. Radway, *Reading the Romance: Women, Patriarchy, and Popular Literature*, 2nd edn (Chapel Hill, NC: University of North Carolina Press, 1991).

23. Radway, 64.

24. M. Saville-Troike, *The Ethnography of Communication: an Introduction*, 3rd edn (Oxford: Blackwell, 2003), 2.

25. G. Philipsen, Speaking "Like a Man" in Teamsterville: Culture Patterns of Role Enactment in an Urban Neighborhood, *Quarterly Journal of Speech* 1975, 61, 13–22; G. Philipsen, Places for Speaking in Teamsterville, *Quarterly Journal of Speech* 1976, 62, 15–25.

26. Philipsen, Speaking "Like a Man" in Teamsterville, 20.

27. Philipsen, Places for Speaking.

28. D. Morley, The *Nationwide* Audience: Structure and Decoding, in *The* Nationwide *Television Studies*, D. Morley and C. Brunsdon (eds) (New York: Routledge, 1999), 111–288.

29. C. Brunsdon and D. Morley, Everyday Television: *Nationwide*, in *The* Nationwide *Television Studies*, D. Morley and C. Brunsdon (eds) (New York: Routledge, 1999), 19–110.

30. Morley, 152.

31. Morley, 257.

32. S.E. Bird, Beyond the Audience: Living in a Media World, in *The Audience in Everyday Life: Living in a Media World* (New York: Routledge, 2003), 7.

33. S. Moores, *Interpreting Audiences: the Ethnography of Media Consumption* (Thousand Oaks, CA: Sage Publications, 1993), 4.

34. J. Stacey, *Star Gazing: Hollywood Cinema and Female Spectatorship* (New York: Routledge, 1994).

11   Sociological Analysis

In 2010, AMC's *The Walking Dead* became basic cable's fall breakout hit. The series, which is loosely based on Robert Kirkman's monthly comic book series by the same name, chronicles the struggle of small town sheriff's deputy Rick Grimes (Andrew Lincoln), his family, and others to stay alive following a zombie apocalypse. Each week, Grimes and the other survivors must fend off the latest ravenous horde of flesh-eating "walkers," whose bite transforms the living into the undead. Famous for its creative methods of killing zombies and its gruesome scenes of dismemberment, *The Walking Dead* has garnered substantial critical acclaim. In addition to being named one of the top 10 television programs of 2010 by the American Film Institute, *The Walking Dead* earned a Writers Guild of America nomination for Best New Series and a Golden Globe nomination for Best New Television Series Drama in 2011. The series' success is also evident in its tremendous popularity. In fact, the show's third season premiere drew an audience of 10.9 million viewers, making it the most watched basic cable drama telecast in history.[1]

The show's critical and commercial success is hardly surprising when one considers the recent string of popular films that also story zombie outbreaks such as *Dawn of the Dead* (2004), *I Am Legend* (2007), *28 Weeks Later* (2007), *Zombieland* (2009), *The Dead* (2010), *Resident Evil: Afterlife* (2010), *ParaNorman* (2012), *Warm Bodies* (2013), and *World War Z* (2013). Nor is a fascination with zombies a new

Critical Media Studies: An Introduction, Second Edition. Brian L. Ott and Robert L. Mack.
© 2014 John Wiley & Sons, Inc. Published 2014 by John Wiley & Sons, Inc.

phenomenon. Zombies have been capturing the imagination of American audiences since their 1932 appearance on film in *White Zombie*. But zombies have not always been depicted in the same way, and it was not until the late 1950s that zombies became the insatiable consumers of human flesh we all know and love today.[2] So, what is it about these brain-dead, putrid-smelling, rotting corpses that audiences find so compelling time and time again? One answer, suggested by Doug Gross in an article for CNN, is that zombies "are so darned versatile – helping reflect whatever our greatest fears happen to be at the time."[3] In other words, zombies are a particularly useful vehicle for symbolic action; they are empty vessels that society can pour its deepest anxieties and fears into, and whose destruction will aid in assuaging those fears. At various historical junctures, zombies have symbolically assisted audiences in confronting everything from their anxieties around forced labor to their concerns about conspicuous consumption.

Zombie stories are, of course, but one example of the countless ways that audiences negotiate the challenges, difficulties, and demands of everyday life through the meanings they assign, if only unconsciously, to the images and messages that circulate widely in the media. The repeating theme of incompetent, egocentric, or overly demanding bosses in workplace comedies on television (*The Office*, *30 Rock*, *Scrubs*, etc.) and in theaters (*Office Space*, *In Good Company*, *The Devil Wears Prada*, and *Horrible Bosses*), for instance, assists viewers in making sense of, framing, and coping with related workplace stresses. Being able to identify recurrent patterns in media and how those patterns influence the interactions of people lies at the heart of "sociological criticism."[4] In many ways, this approach extends the Reception approach discussed in the previous chapter. But in addition to trying to understand how audiences assign meanings to messages, Sociological analysis also seeks to understand how audiences take up those meanings in their daily lives. To clarify this approach, this chapter locates the roots of Sociological analysis in the perspective of symbolic interactionism and then explores three contemporary methods of engaging in Sociological analysis: dramaturgy, frame analysis, and equipment for living.

Sociological Theory: an Overview

The theoretical basis for Sociological criticism of the mass media is rooted in the perspective of **symbolic interactionism**, which suggests that the character and conduct of people's social interactions are powerfully shaped by the symbolic meanings they assign to objects, events, other people, and social contexts. This perspective was heavily influenced by the work of the German sociologist Max Weber (1864–1920) and the American sociologist George Herbert Mead (1863–1931), both of whom emphasized that individuals act in accordance with their interpretation of the world – their subjective meanings of the world – and not necessarily the world as it objectively exists. But it was a student of Mead's at the University of Chicago, Herbert Blumer (1900–87), who actually coined the phrase "symbolic interactionism" and explicitly laid out its central tenets. In his 1969 book, *Symbolic Interactionism: Perspective and Method*, Blumer outlined the three core premises of this theory.

According to Blumer, "The first premise is that human beings act toward things on the basis of the meanings that they have for them."[5] While this premise seems simple and straightforward, Blumer suggests that it is often ignored, downplayed, or taken for granted in studies of human behavior. Scholars too often ignore that everything in the world – physical objects, persons, categories, ideals, institutions, activities, events, etc. – carries meaning for humans and, thus, shapes their attitudes and actions. For Blumer, meaning is not only central to all human behavior, but it is also complex. This leads to his second premise, the idea that meaning is "derived from, or arises out of, the social interaction that one has with one's fellows." Meaning, in other words, is rarely simple, neutral, self-evident, and uncontested. Rather, it is contingent and contextual; meaning is negotiated through interactions with others, as well as with social institutions like education, religion, and the media. The third premise of symbolic interactionism is "that these meanings are handled in and modified through, an interpretive process used by the person in dealing with the things he [*sic*] encounters." With this premise, Blumer is pointing to the individual as well as collective character of meaning. Interpretation, in other words, is not "a mere automatic application of established meanings" but a formative process in which each person revises meaning as a guide for action based upon individual experiences and particular context.[6]

Symbolic interactionism seeks, then, to understand and explain how persons interact with one another in society. Since interactionists do this by attending to and analyzing patterns of communication and behavior in relation to specific contexts or aspects of social life rather than by examining broad scale social systems and structures, it is regarded as a micro- rather than macro-level perspective. Historically, interactionism has employed qualitative methods (primarily participant observation and interpretive analysis) as opposed to quantitative methods (empirical analysis) in the execution of its work. It should be noted that as initially formulated, symbolic interactionism was, strictly speaking, a social theory and not a media theory. But as media have come to occupy a more central role in society, the premises of symbolic interactionism have been extended, adapted, and modified, as well as challenged by critical media scholars to help account for the role that media play in our social lives. In the remainder of this chapter, we outline three contemporary perspectives that draw in varying degrees and ways on the tradition of symbolic interactionism to explicate how our interactions with media influence and shape human behavior.

Before turning to our first perspective, dramaturgy, we wish to say a few words about the twin concepts of agency and structure. In sociological literature, (individual) **agency** describes the capacity of human beings to act purposively and according to their own volitions, while (institutional) **structure** refers to any social feature or force that constrains or limits agency. These two concepts, which exist in dialectical tension with one another, are useful for thinking about the relationship between media audiences and media texts. While media audiences exercise agency in both the interpretation and use of media, media texts impose structures that limit how audiences can reasonably interpret and use media. This tension will arise in varying ratios throughout this chapter. While dramaturgy places a great deal of emphasis on individual agency, framing focuses more on structures that limit audience understandings and practices. So, while we have placed this chapter in the section of the book concerned with audiences, our readers should not lose sight of the fact that audiences are always constrained to some extent by the structured invitations of the media texts with which they interact.

Dramaturgy

One contemporary microsociological perspective that is useful in understanding the ways in which media shape human behavior is **dramaturgy**. Dramaturgy is a theory developed by the Canadian-born sociologist Erving Goffman (1922–82) that utilizes the metaphor of theater to explain the character and function of public behavior, especially face-to-face interaction. The foundational assumption of dramaturgy, which Goffman lays out in his 1959 book, *The Presentation of Self in Everyday Life*, is that the self – our sense of who we are – is not a stable, independent entity, but a performed character we are endlessly staging and restaging in the presence of others.[7] Generally speaking, we care about how others perceive us because their perceptions contribute to our own sense of who we are. Identity, in other words, is not inherent or innate, but a product that emerges through social interaction. It would be difficult to regard oneself as an intelligent person, for instance, if others routinely informed you that you were stupid. If someone deeply desires to be perceived as intelligent, she or he will publicly perform "intelligence." Such a performance will involve a host of theatrical devices involving setting, props, costumes, characters, scripted dialog, etc. For example, a person performing intelligence might regularly go to coffee shops, read books, wear reading glasses and a scarf (in the summer!), hang out with others who are perceived as intelligent, and say things like, "I am unconvinced by Derrida's assertion that there is no outside to textuality." Since reading is a solitary activity, when one chooses to read in public, and especially when one chooses to read Derrida in public, one is performing for an audience.

A dramaturgical perspective, then, understands social interactions as performances aimed at impression management. For Goffman, **impression management** is the art of successfully staging a character or "part," of enacting a performance that creates the desired impression of the self – "an idealized self that fits appropriately into the require-ments of the context."[8] Like all theatrical performances, performances of the self entail certain dramatic elements such as stage, setting (or scene), part (or character), and teams (or players). Before discussing these four dramatic elements, we wish to note that this is not a comprehensive list. For Goffman, "a 'performance' may be defined as all the activity of a given participant on a given occasion which serves to influence in any way any of the other participants."[9] Given the breadth of this definition, virtually any aspect of social life could be treated in terms of the theatrical metaphor. But we will concentrate on those that we think are most helpful to media scholars.

1   *Stage* describes a performance's degree of publicness. Goffman distinguishes between the two primary regions in this regard: front stage and back stage. Front stage refers to those performances that occur in full view of an audience, while back stage refers to a place reserved only for the performer. This distinction is significant because behavior varies greatly depending upon whether or not there is an audience. Since the back stage affords performers a safe place to step out of character, people do many things in private or back stage that they would never do in public or front stage. There are few things that disrupt the performance of self more than an audience member suddenly and unexpectedly gaining access to back stage, as anyone who has been caught with their pants down will tell you.

2   *Setting* refers to the scene or situation in which the performance is occurring. For Goffman, the setting includes everything from the actual physical location in which a social interaction takes place to the accoutrements and features of that location such as furniture, décor, physical layout, etc. Because settings are so closely connected to performances, audiences are likely to reject performances that appear to be out of place. You would be unlikely to follow a professor's direction to take your seat and turn to page 34 of your textbook while in the checkout line at the grocery store. Settings or situations, in other words, are never neutral. When we enter a particular setting, we have been socialized to expect and abide by certain rules, rituals, and practices. Behaviors that are acceptable in a dance club would likely get one kicked out of a library, if not arrested. So, settings place powerful limits and constraints on performances of self. Such constraints are often unspoken and unwritten. There are, for instance, implicit codes of accepted behavior in restrooms. While it is acceptable for a man to continue a conversation with someone at a urinal if he entered the restroom with that person, starting up a conversation at the urinal with someone who was already there is generally frowned upon.

3   *Part*, or what Goffman calls "personal front," describes the pattern of actions that define the character being performed. When playing a part, a performer typically tries to convey a particular image of her- or himself through "appearance" (attire, sex, age, race, etc.) and "manner" (speech, gestures, posture, expressions, temperament, etc.). Obviously, some of these elements are more fixed than others, making it more difficult for some people to play certain parts. It would be almost impossible for a 12-year-old to convincingly perform the part of a medical doctor, for instance. For Goffman, appearance informs the audience of things like a performer's social status and current ritual state (i.e., whether the actor is engaged in a social, work-related, or informal activity), while manner highlights the interaction role the performer is likely to play (i.e., whether the actor is expected to be meek, assertive, friendly, standoffish, reserved, outgoing, etc.).[10] Thus, like settings, parts carry heavy social expectations, though the expectations are with regard to ritual and role performances. For example, audiences expect someone playing the part of flight attendant to wear a uniform and to be courteous, attentive, and reassuring. Imagine how shocking, which is to say inappropriate, it would be if you asked a flight attendant for a beverage and were sharply told, "Get it yourself!"

4   *Team* takes into account the troupe or cast of players who share in a performance. While we tend to think about performances of self in individual terms, most performances rely upon a cast of supporting characters. "A team," writes Goffman, "may be defined as a set of individuals whose intimate co-operation is required if a given projected definition of the situation is to be maintained."[11] Take the flight attendant from our previous example. He or she is only able to successfully perform that part in the context of a setting where others are performing roles that complement, support, or reinforce that performance. Flight attendants rely on pilots, gate agents, baggage movers, air traffic controllers, and a host of others to compellingly perform their parts. Imagine a scenario in which a key member of a team is absent. How would you respond to a flight attendant who, even if dressed professionally and behaving courteously, calmly asked you to turn off your electronic devices and fasten your seatbelt low and tight around your waist in preparation for takeoff in an airplane that had no pilot? Without appropriate team support, such a performance would likely cause alarm rather than comfort. Moreover, given the reciprocal dependence of teammates to the success of a public performance, any member of a team can give away the performance through inappropriate conduct.

Having discussed the dramatic elements of stage, setting, part, and teams, it is not difficult to see the utility of a dramaturgical approach to the study of human interaction in online environments, especially with regard to social networking sites like Facebook, Twitter, LinkedIn, MySpace, Google+, etc. Behavior on Facebook offers an excellent example of the explanatory power of dramaturgy since everything a user does (or does not do!) is about impression management. Profile pages, whether one's own or someone else's, constitute the front stage, while private inboxes are more analogous to the back stage. Through the actions of friending (and de-friending), posting, liking, tagging, and joining groups, Facebook users create carefully constructed impressions. They selectively post and tag themselves in images, "like" comments and other postings that reflect their sense of themselves, and favorite books, movies, etc. that they want to be associated with. Meanwhile, on Facebook, one's "friends" serve as the audience for one's performance. We have inscribed "friends" in quotation marks to highlight the fact that many people in one's friend circle are not actually friends; they may be casual acquaintances, former romantic partners, or professional colleagues, but they are not, in fact, friends. A user's actual friends are part of the team performance, which is why a user may delete a wall posting from someone they do not regard as part of the team. On occasion, users also disavow the performances of teammates by untagging themselves from photographs they deem as unflattering and deleting wall postings they regard as inappropriate. Facebook, then, is largely a self-serving performance, which explains why research on social networking sites indicates that users with a large number of friends (a large audience) and frequent self-focused posts and photos (frequent performances) tend to be narcissists.[12]

As useful as dramaturgy is to understanding the dynamics of social networking sites, we are more interested in its capacity to help explain, first, why performers play some parts "in the manner" that they do and, second, why some performers are readily accepted playing some parts and not others. With regard to the former issue, we turn to the matter of romantic relationships. Given the transactional nature of identity, romantic relationships play a crucial role in our sense of self. But where do we learn what to expect out of romantic relationships and how to behave in them? According to Mary-Lou Galician, "From the time we're very young, we're barraged with fairy-tale depictions and hard-to-break stereotypes of sex, love, and romance in … popular culture. … Mass media are very powerful socialization agents that rely on simplification, distortions of reality, and dramatic symbols and stereotypes to communicate their messages."[13] Galician underscores twelve myths perpetuated by the media that lead to dissatisfaction, unhappiness, and unrealistic expectations in romantic couplings, and sometimes even to "serious emotional and physical harm from depression, abuse, and violence."[14] A few of the romantic myths identified by Galician include:

> Your perfect partner is cosmically predestined, so nothing/nobody can ultimately separate you.
> If your partner is truly meant for you, sex is easy and wonderful.
> The love of a good and faithful woman can change a man from a "beast" into a "prince."
> Bickering and fighting a lot mean that a man and a woman really love each other passionately.
> All you really need is love, so it doesn't matter if you and your lover have very different values.[15]

In just 2010, these and the other romantic myths identified by Galician were perpetuated in films such as *Eat, Pray, Love, Leap Year, Letters to Juliet, Love & Other Drugs, The Twilight Saga: Eclipse*, and *When in Rome*, and in songs such as Taylor Swift's "Today Was a Fairy Tale," Katy Perry's "Teenage Dream" and "California Gurls," Ringo Starr's "Mystery of the Night," and Eminem's "Love the Way You Lie."[16]

In addition to contributing to our understanding of how the media impact our performance of roles and rituals in romantic relations, a dramaturgical perspective can also shed light on why society judges certain performances the way it does. While any number of examples could be used to illustrate this point, we briefly consider televisual representations of motherhood. The image of ideal motherhood has evolved significantly over the history of television. In the 1950s, *Leave It to Beaver* imagined June Cleaver, with her perfectly coiffed hair and well-accessorized dresses cooking in the kitchen, as the ideal mom. By the 1970s, an audience favorite like Carol Brady on *The Brady Bunch*, while still confined to the home, was aided by a fulltime housekeeper. Then, in the 1980s, the intelligent and eloquent Clair Huxtable set a new standard for mothers with her job as a lawyer on *The Cosby Show*, though viewers never actually saw her at work. More recently, the *Gilmore Girls*' Lorelai Gilmore has been rated highly on several lists of top TV moms for her ability to strike a careful work–life balance as a single mother. Despite their changing social roles around work and the home over the decades, what each of these highly rated TV moms embodies are the traits of ideal femininity; they are calm, composed, nurturing, sensitive, domestic, and above all attractive.

If there is any question about the deeply embedded cultural values linking ideal motherhood to ideal femininity on television, one need look no further than to lists of TV's worst moms, which includes characters like *Roseanne's* Roseanne Conner, *Married … With Children's* Peg Bundy, *Everybody Loves Raymond's* Marie Barone, and *Malcolm in the Middle's* Lois. What these women share in common are a series of mannerisms; they are loud, bossy, caustic, obnoxious, overbearing, manipulative, inattentive, nagging, narcissistic, crazy, lazy, and just generally unfeminine. Given that these lists of TV's best and worst moms were created by critics and viewers, it appears that audiences have unconsciously internalized the belief that ideal moms must also embody ideal femininity. As we hope this example illustrates, dramaturgy can be a useful tool for media scholars who wish to critically assess why we value some performances and devalue others.

Frame Analysis

A second approach to emerge out of the microsociological tradition and its concern with everyday life is frame analysis. As with dramaturgy, frame analysis owes a major debt to the work of Erving Goffman, whose 1974 book *Frame Analysis: an Essay on the Organization of Experience* was central to its development. But in contrast to dramaturgy, frame analysis is more properly understood as a "structuralist" approach than as an "interactionist" approach. Whereas an interactionist approach is concerned with close observation of the particularities of situations that make up everyday life, a structuralist approach emphasizes the more abstract forms and modes that govern, which is to say structure, the situations of everyday life.[17] This shift in emphasis is detectable in Goffman's description of **frames** as social constructs that organize our experience and, thus, our understanding of a situation based upon how they name or define it. Accordingly, **frame analysis** is, for Goffman, an examination of "the organization of experience."[18]

To appreciate the explanatory force of frames, it is helpful to first consider the contextual or relative character of all action and experience. The behavior of crying, for example, has no inherent, stable meaning. If you were told your friend Eddie was crying, you would not know whether he was joyful or sorrowful without more contextual information. The context would, in other words, frame your interpretation of Eddie's emotional display. This is what Goffman means when he says frames organize our experience; they aid us in interpreting or making sense of social behavior and interaction. Goffman divided the most basic of frames, which he called primary frameworks, into two broad classes: natural and social. *Natural frameworks* describe purely physical occurrences that lie beyond human control such as the weather or biological processes, while *social frameworks* "provide background understanding for events that incorporate the will, aim, and controlling effort of an intelligence, a live agency" such as human beings.[19] Let us assume for a minute that Eddie is crying because he is sad. If Eddie is standing in front of his house, which was recently reduced to rubble by a tornado, then you would interpret his sadness principally through a natural framework. In contrast, if Eddie just ended a phone conversation in which his romantic partner ended their relationship, you would understand his sadness in terms of a social framework or schema.

After Goffman published his account of frames, media scholars were quick to realize the utility of this concept in explaining how the media organize our experience of issues, events, and even our social world. The early work on framing in media studies concentrated almost exclusively on journalism. Building on the work of Goffman, sociologist and media scholar Todd Gitlin defined **media frames** as "*persistent patterns of cognition, interpretation, and presentation, of selection, emphasis, and exclusion, by which symbol-handlers routinely organize discourse, whether verbal or visual*."[20] In his 1980 book, *The Whole World is Watching*, Gitlin examined how the *New York Times* and CBS News covered the activities of the anti-war movement, the New Left, and in particular Students for a Democratic Society (SDS) during the 1960s and early 1970s, arguing that the mainstream news media tend to "frame" oppositional movements in ways that either marginalize their messages or tame them.[21] Such framing has had the effect of blunting progressive reform and maintaining the political status quo. Among the main contributions of Gitlin's study was that it demonstrated frames work by means of the principles of selection, emphasis, and presentation.

1 *Selection*. Frames shape our perceptions of events by including some details and excluding others. In any given situation, there are an infinite number of particulars that could be reported. But because of the time and space restrictions that govern news reporting, as well as the desire to hold audience members' attention, consciously or not, journalists share only select details when reporting a story. Obviously, the details that are left out of a news report could significantly alter or re-frame the audience's understanding of that event. Your perception of someone who is accused of murder, for instance, would almost certainly be more sympathetic if you also knew that the accused was acting in self-defense in response to the burglary of her home.

2 *Emphasis*. In addition to selecting the details to be included and excluded, journalists also give more attention to certain elements in a story than to others. In other words, not all of the details included in a story are given equal weight. A reporter who spends substantially more time describing *where* a crime took place than describing *what* the actual crime was would likely cause the audience to perceive the location of the crime as more significant to the overall story than the crime itself. Thus, by emphasizing some elements or details and minimizing others, news frames direct audiences to draw conclusions about which aspects of an event are the most salient and important.

3 *Presentation.* Finally, there is the matter of presentation, which is probably the most subtle mechanism at work within news frames. After details of an event have been included and excluded, emphasized or de-emphasized, they are presented to the audience through the use of certain linguistic and visual symbols. But since all symbols are value-laden, the use of one set of symbols as opposed to another set of symbols alters, even if only marginally, meaning and perception, thereby communicating a different attitude toward the person or event being described. A criminal defendant who is referred to by a journalist as a "local honor student" is likely to be perceived very differently than a defendant described as a "violent repeat offender" even if they are accused of the same crime.

The importance of the principle of presentation to framing was dramatically illustrated by Kahneman and Tversky in 1984. In their study, the authors presented a focus group with the following scenario:

> Imagine that the U.S. is preparing for the outbreak of an unusual Asian disease, which is expected to kill 600 people. Two alternative programs to combat the disease have been proposed. Assume that the exact scientific estimates of the consequences of the programs are as follows: If Program A is adopted, 200 people will be saved. If Program B is adopted, there is a one-third probability that 600 people will be saved and a two-thirds probability that no people will be saved. Which program do you favor?[22]

In response to this scenario, 72 percent of participants selected Program A, while only 28 percent selected Program B. The researchers then presented a second focus group with the same scenario, but re-framed the outcome in terms of likely deaths rather than likely lives saved: "If Program C is adopted, 400 people will die. If Program D is adopted, there is a one-third probability that nobody will die and a two-thirds probability that 600 people will die."[23] Though the outcomes of Programs C and A are *identical*, as are the outcomes of Programs B and D, in the revised scenario, only 22 percent of the participants selected C (compared with 72 percent who opted for A in the first study), while 78 percent of participants selected D (compared with 28 percent who opted for B in the first study). By changing how the two programs were *presented*, Kahneman and Tversky demonstrated that framing can powerfully influence both audience perception and decision-making.

Since these early studies, scholars have continued to examine and expand upon the notion of framing in the news media. Reflecting on the state of framing research in 1993, Robert Entman concluded that, based upon the guiding principles of *selection* and *salience* (salience essentially combines Gitlin's principles of emphasis and presentation), frames perform four primary functions: (1) naming and defining a problem in a particular way, (2) diagnosing and characterizing the principal causes of the problem, (3) making moral judgments about the actors or agents involved, and (4) offering specific recommendations or remedies.[24] It should be noted that Entman's use of the word "problem" may itself be problematic since frames define situations in ways other than as problems. More recent scholarship on the subject of framing suggests that studies of news framing generally fall into one of two categories: *issue-specific news frames* and *generic news frames*.[25] Studies of issue-specific news frames focus on identifying frames that are unique to a particular story or context, while generic news frames seek to identify recurring frames that, as a consequence of news conventions (see the discussion of informational bias in Chapter 3), extend across stories.

One important study to examine generic news frames is Ott and Aoki's analysis of news media coverage and framing of public traumas. Taking the print media's coverage (from the *New York Times*, *Washington Post*, and *Los Angeles Times*) of the Matthew Shepard murder as their case study, the authors explore the narrative pattern of victimage or scapegoating in ongoing news reports surrounding shocking public events. According to Ott and Aoki, when a public tragedy such as a school shooting first occurs, news reports commonly invite audiences to reflect on social problems, such as inadequate gun control laws, that may have contributed to the disaster. But as the story unfolds, blame is affixed to a specific party (scapegoat) who is then demonized and dehumanized. When the scapegoat is ultimately punished, it promotes a sense of psychological resolution regarding the issue, and the public policy reforms discussed immediately following the tragedy are rarely implemented. "Since tragic frames ultimately alleviate the social guilt associated with a disaster through victimage," Ott and Aoki conclude, "they tend to bring both closure *and* resolution to the larger social issues they raise. As such, tragic frames do not serve the public well as a basis for social and political action."[26]

Though most of the work in critical media studies involving framing has focused on the news media, the concept also has heuristic value for understanding the role of entertainment media in framing public attitudes and opinions. In his 2002 book *Latino Images on Film: Stereotypes, Subversion, and Resistance*, Charles Ramírez Berg investigates the evolving representations and meanings of Aliens in Science Fiction (SF) films. According to Berg, SF films are inevitably about a society's fears and anxieties at a particular historical juncture. The Alien invader in 1950s SF films, for instance, was a personification of the Red Menace, "those hordes of Communists foisted on the American people by such venomous Red-baiters as Joseph McCarthy, Richard Nixon, and Billy Graham."[27] SF films, like news media frames, organize our experience and understanding of a situation, who we hold responsible for it, and how we think it should be resolved.

But by the 1970s and 1980s, the SF Alien had increasingly become "a figure for the alien immigrants who have been entering the country in increasing numbers for the past several decades."[28] Represented as creatures from foreign worlds, Aliens had to be eliminated, either by benevolently helping them return to their home, as seen in films like *Close Encounters of the Third Kind* (1997), *E.T.* (1982), and *Cocoon* (1985), or by violently killing them, as seen in films like *Critters* (1986), *Aliens* (1986), and *Predator* (1987). In subsequent decades, Aliens have progressively been depicted as more and more menacing, as an invading force that threatens our basic freedoms and way of life. Films such as *Independence Day* (1996), *War of the Worlds* (2005), and *Battle: Los Angeles* (2011) depict Aliens who not only come to Earth (read: the USA), but who also want to annihilate us. Conveniently, the Aliens in these films look less human than the benevolent Aliens of earlier eras. Dehumanizing them, of course, works to Other them (see the discussion of Othering in Chapter 6) and to heighten the audience's desire to see them brutally exterminated. Because SF films frame how we see the Alien Other (as welcome visitor, displaced child, less technologically advanced species, or invading force), they also implicitly suggest programs of action for dealing with them. In Berg's book, he traces how changes in US immigration policy over time tend to reflect the changing images of the Alien Other in science fiction films.

Equipment for Living

A third critical approach for evaluating the complex ways in which the media assist us in comprehending, managing, and negotiating our social environment and social relations is equipment for living. The concept of **equipment for living** is based on the premise that messages, media and otherwise, provide individuals with symbolic resources for addressing and resolving the anxieties and difficulties they confront in their everyday lives. Twentieth-century literary scholar and philosopher Kenneth Burke (1897–1993) advanced this idea in an essay titled "Literature as Equipment for Living," which was originally published in the magazine *Direction* in 1938 before being republished in a collection of Burke's essays titled *The Philosophy of Literary Form* in 1941.

Burke begins his famous essay with a discussion of proverbs, noting that proverbs are really just literary devices for naming typical, recurrent situations. A popular proverb like "birds of a feather flock together," for instance, simply names the fact that people who have common or shared tastes frequently associate with one another. But because proverbs describe recurring situations in life, they offer a means for quickly sizing up a "type" of situation and developing a strategy to respond to it. If you attend a party in which a select group of people has congregated in one corner, then invoking the "birds" proverb under your breath provides a way of admonishing the group for having excluded you. Verbally lumping the individuals together and then disparaging them for drinking too much, behaving badly, or dressing poorly is a particularly effective way of resolving the anxiety of having been excluded. For Burke, proverbs were just succinct instances of how literature in general functions as "stylistic medicine" for everyday problems.

Thus, for Burke, various literary forms such as comedy, tragedy, satire, elegy, etc. are themselves ways of naming recurring social situations, thereby providing readers with symbolic resources for addressing those situations in their real lives. The notion that literature, or really any type of discourse for that matter, functions as equipment for living is rooted in the idea of **symbolic action**, which, for Burke, "involve[s] modes of behavior made possible by the acquiring of a conventional, arbitrary symbol system."[29] Burke contrasts symbolic action, or the use of symbols by humans to act in the world, with non-symbolic motion, by which he means the realm of matter or those natural processes that occur without human intervention. This distinction is important for Burke because it suggests that to understand human behavior, as well as human motives, we need to attend carefully to what humans *do* with symbols, to how they use them to act in the world. Sometimes, we engage in an action or behavior as a symbolic substitute for another action or behavior. "The reading of a book on the attaining of success," explains Burke, "is in itself the symbolic attaining of that success,"[30] which is why the reader is unlikely to take any actions to attain success beyond reading the book. Similarly, we may write an angry letter to a person, which we never mail, *instead* of actually confronting the person we are angry at. Writing the letter, nevertheless, helps us resolve our anger.

One of the reasons why literature and other art forms function as equipment for living for audiences is because producers of art create it as a means of dealing with some challenge (i.e. recurring social situation) in everyday life. Authors write books, Burke believed, as a way of "coming to terms" with – of symbolically confronting and resolving – the difficulties in their own lives. Though a prolific writer, Burke wrote only one novel, *Towards a Better Life*, in his lifetime. He wrote the book in 1931, just two years before he married Elizabeth Batterham, the sister of his first wife, Lily Mary Batterham. In the story, Burke's narrator undergoes moments of extreme discomfiture only for the theme of resurgence to be explicitly proclaimed. Perhaps himself aware of the symbolic connection to his own life, years later in the 1965 preface to the second edition, Burke wrote, "Often, a closer look at ... texts will make it appear that, however roundabout, they are modes of symbolic action classifiable as rituals of resurgence, transcendence, rebirth. ... My ... study of various literary texts, viewed as modes of 'symbolic action,' has convinced me that this book is to be classed among the many rituals of rebirth that mark our fiction."[31]

One of the most common recurring situations in the human condition is guilt. According to Burke, every aspect of our lives is governed by values and rules, which he refers to as **hierarchy** or order. **Guilt** is the condition that arises every time we violate hierarchy. Because we all participate in multiple hierarchies, which often have conflicting rules, it is impossible to keep all the rules all the time. Consequently, guilt is ubiquitous. Imagine the following scenario: your best friend is celebrating her twenty-first birthday and wants you to join her for the festivities that evening. But you have an exam the next day that is worth 30 percent of your grade in a class you need to graduate. One set of rules (hierarchy) is telling you to go have fun with your friend, while another set is saying you should stay home and study. Ultimately, you will have to violate one of these hierarchies, which will cause you to feel guilty. Because guilt is profoundly disquieting and discomforting, we have developed an array of symbolic strategies for ridding ourselves of it. Burke calls this process the pollution–purification–redemption cycle (Table 11.1), and it offers three different means of addressing guilt: transcendence, mortification, and victimage.

1   *Transcendence* is not so much a way of resolving guilt as it is a way of avoiding guilt by appealing to a new hierarchy or third perspective in which the two conflicting hierarchies cease to be in opposition.[32] Rather than celebrating with your

Table 11.1   Kenneth Burke's pollution–purification–redemption cycle

	Pollution	Purification	Redemption
Description	The violation of order	The purging or punishment of guilt	The restoration of purity
Symbolic act	Sin→guilt	Transcendence, mortification, or victimage	Absolution→rebirth

friend, you decide to stay in and study after all. You rationalize your decision not by placing the exam ahead of your friend, an action sure to lead to guilt, but by reminding yourself that your friend values family above all else and that your family is struggling to pay your way through school. Poof: your guilt is gone.

2   *Mortification*, a second means of dealing with guilt, requires a symbolical act of atonement such as confession or self-sacrifice.[33] Perhaps you decide to celebrate with your friend instead of studying for your exam, which you subsequently fail. This leads to feelings of guilt about your choice. As a means of relieving your guilt, you punish yourself by swearing off beer, which just so happens to be your favorite beverage in the whole wide world, for an entire year. Though your abstinence lasts only two days, you nevertheless feel as though you have paid a heavy price and your guilt subsides. Self-flagellation is another a form of atonement, though a slightly more masochistic one than confession or sacrifice.

3   *Victimage* offers a third strategy for addressing guilt, and it is the one that most directly concerns us as media scholars. Victimage is a form of scapegoating in which the guilty party transfers his or her guilt onto another party. To the extent that a character in a novel, television show, or film is guilty of a "sin" (i.e. any violation of hierarchy) similar to our own, that character may serve as a surrogate for our own guilt. The resolution of the character's guilt is, through symbolic action, the resolution of our own. Scapegoating can be seen in two archetypical symbolic forms, tragedy and comedy, both of which function as equipment for living. The ways they equip us to resolve guilt vary greatly, however.

Tragedy is a form of drama in which the protagonist or tragic hero experiences a reversal of fortune as a result of some mistake or error in judgment. The tragic hero's inevitable demise, typically in the form of his/her death, serves as symbolic equipment for audiences to the extent that they identify with the hero and his/her error. Herman Melville's classic 1851 novel, *Moby Dick*, is a well-known tragedy, in which the tragic hero, Captain Ahab, dooms both himself and his crew because of his monomaniacal obsession with a whale. Most of us have, at one point or another, been obsessed with someone or something. Imagine that you are so obsessed with playing Angry Birds or watching reality TV, for instance, that you begin to neglect family and friends. Such actions could readily produce feelings of guilt and regret.

Reading *Moby Dick* or watching a film with a character similar to Ahab, who is ultimately punished for his obsessive actions, can function symbolically to purge that guilt. In essence, Ahab's punishment vicariously serves as your punishment.

Comedy, by contrast, traces the buffoonery of its central character, the comic fool, who is reinstated into the community after being shown the error of his/her ways. In the opinion of one of the authors of this text, one of the greatest comic fools in history is Peter Griffin, the crude and dimwitted father of the Griffin family on the television show *Family Guy*. When Peter's doltish behavior inevitably causes things to go horribly awry, he must be taught his error, so that it can be corrected and he may be accepted again by his family and/or friends. Since most of us are not that much brighter than Peter Griffin, we frequently engage in stupid behavior that has negative consequences. If, hypothetically speaking, you recklessly drank too much alcohol one evening and then vomited on the seat of your best friend's car, you would likely feel badly about it ... at least after you sobered up. Peter aids in resolving such guilt by reminding us that we all throw up on someone else's car seat (couch, bed, or pant leg). Who among us, after all, has not done something idiotic? Watching someone else make poor choices and seeing that person corrected serves as our own admonishment to avoid errors like vomiting in the future.[34] Burke viewed comedy as a particularly humane way of resolving guilt because it recognizes that "to err is human" and therefore calls for the tolerant reinstatement of the fool in society, rather than for his or her tragic punishment.[35]

Tragedy and comedy are very broad (generic) forms and subsequently can function as symbolic equipment for a wide variety of situations (types of guilt) over time. But Burke also recognized that societies continuously face social problems that are unique to particular historical moments, and therefore must continually develop new, specialized discursive forms to address them. Noting the contextual character of form, Burke wrote, "the conventional forms of one age are as resolutely shunned by another."[36] Following the end of the Cold War and the collapse of the former Soviet Union, for instance, there was a noticeable decline in films like *Firefox* (1982), *War Games* (1983), *The Day After* (1983), *Red Dawn* (1984), and *Threads* (1984) that addressed anxieties over mutually assured destruction. One aim of sociological criticism, then, is "to identify the modes of discourse enjoying currency in a society and to link discourse to the real situations for which it is symbolic equipment."[37]

An excellent example of this practice in critical media studies is Barry Brummett's study of haunted house (note: not horror) films. Based upon his analysis of *The Shining* (1980), *The Amityville Horror* (1979), *The Hearse* (1980), *The Haunting* (1963), and *The Uninvited* (1944), Brummett argues that haunted house films stage "horrors" that help us cope with real, if unconscious, horrors. Specifically, he maintains that haunted house films help equip us to confront feelings of disorientation, the fear of the unpredictable and shocking, and the idea of death. One of the most interesting and insightful aspects of Brummett's study is that it shows that haunted house films provide symbolic equipment for audiences at the level of medium as well as form and content.[38] Because films are typically viewed in darkened theaters, they are especially well suited for staging symbolic horrors. But the capacity of film to function as equipment for living is not limited to haunted house films. Science fiction films, especially dystopian ones, tell stories about wide scale social anxieties as a means of coping with those anxieties. Fear of human extinction is storied in films like *2012* (2009) and *Melancholia* (2011), concern about government repression underlies films like *Children of Men* (2006) and *The Hunger Games* (2012), and technophobia is at the heart of blockbusters like *I, Robot* (2004) and *Avatar* (2009).

To date, the most sustained study of how media function as equipment for living is Brian Ott's 2007 book, *The Small Screen*. Ott is interested in how people cope with fundamental social change, the kind of change that only occurs following a major technological and/or economic revolution. So, he explores prime-time television programming in the USA during the 1990s, charting the symbolic resources it offers viewers for negotiating the transition from a primarily industrial-based society to a primarily information-based society. In his study, Ott identifies two major symbolic forms that dominated the televisual landscape during that time: *hyperconscious* and *nostalgia* television. Hyperconscious TV is typified by the conventions of eclecticism, intertextuality, and self-reflexivity, while nostalgia TV is defined by the elements of purity, unity, and security. *The Simpsons* is an archetype of the former symbolic form and *Dr. Quinn, Medicine Woman* is an exemplar of the latter. Ott then explores the very different sets of symbolic resources that these two forms offered viewers for confronting and managing the particular social anxieties, such as information overload, identify drift, acceleration, and fragmentation, associated with the rise of the Information Age.[39] In several subsequent studies, Ott has continued to demonstrate how evolving forms of media equip viewers with symbolic resources to deal with paradigmatic social change.[40]

Conclusion

Over the course of this chapter, we have highlighted a few of the ways that audiences not only assign meanings to media texts, but also employ those meanings in the conduct of their daily lives. The first perspective we discussed, dramaturgy, looked at life through the metaphor of theater, exploring both how persons increasingly perform their sense of self in online contexts such as Facebook and how performances of self, whether online or not, are constrained by the social roles and rituals presented in and reinforced by the mass media. The second perspective, framing, pointed to the manner in which news and entertainment media organize our experience of issues, events, and social contexts. It suggested that how situations are framed in the media can play a powerful role in our perceptions of them, our subsequent attitudes toward them, and finally what we regard as appropriate and inappropriate future action. Equipment for living, the third and final perspective, considers how audiences use media to symbolically confront, negotiate, and resolve the trials and tribulations they face in their personal, professional, and public lives. In sum, all three perspectives help to illuminate how our interactions with media actively contribute to the production of everyday life.

MEDIA LAB 10: DOING SOCIOLOGICAL ANALYSIS

OBJECTIVE

The chief aim of this lab is to affirm the principles of Media Ecology by furnishing students with an opportunity to examine the symbolic equipment of a media text and the features and logics of a specific medium.

ACTIVITY

- Divide the class into small groups of 4–5 students each.
- Equipment for Living: show the *South Park* episode, "Over Logging," and then ask students to answer the following questions.
    1   What social anxiety does this episode stage?
    2   Who is the comic fool and how is he shown the error of his ways?
    3   What symbolic resources does the episode provide for confronting the social anxiety it stages?

SUGGESTED READING

Blumer, H. *Symbolic Interactionism: Perspective and Method*. Berkeley, CA: University of California Press, 1986.

Brummett, B. Burke's Representative Anecdote as a Method in Media Criticism. *Critical Studies in Mass Communication* 1984, 1, 161–76.

Brummett, B. Burkean Comedy and Tragedy, Illustrated in Reactions to the Arrest of John Delorean. *Central States Speech Journal* 1984, 35, 217–27.

Brummett, B. Electric Literature as Equipment for Living: Haunted House Films. *Critical Studies in Mass Communication* 1985, 9, 247–61.

Burke, K. *The Philosophy of Literary Form: Studies in Symbolic Action*, pp. 293–304. Baton Rouge, LA: Louisiana State University Press, 1941.

Entman, R.M. Framing: Toward Clarification of a Fractured Paradigm. *Journal of Communication* 1993, 43(4), 51–8.

Gamson, W.A. News as Framing: Comments on Graber. *American Behavioral Scientist* 1989, 33(2), 157–61.

Gitlin, T. *The Whole World is Watching: Mass Media in the Making of the New Left*. Berkeley, CA: University of California Press, 1980.

Goffman, E. *The Presentation of Self in Everyday Life*. New York: Anchor Books, 1959.

Goffman, E. *Frame Analysis: an Essay on the Organization of Experience*. Cambridge, MA: Harvard University Press, 1974.

Ott, B.L. *The Small Screen: How Television Equips Us to Live in the Information Age*. Oxford: Wiley-Blackwell, 2007.

Ott, B.L. (Re)Framing Fear: Equipment for Living in a Post-9/11 World. In *Cylons in America: Critical Studies in* Battlestar Galactica, T. Potter and C.W. Marshall (eds), pp. 13–26. New York: Continuum, 2008.

Ott, B.L. Unnecessary Roughness: ESPN's Construction of Hypermasculine Citizenship in the Penn State Sex Abuse Scandal. *Cultural Studies <=> Critical Methodologies* 2012, 12(4), 332–4.

Ott, B.L. and Aoki, E. The Politics of Negotiating Public Tragedy: Media Framing of the Matthew Shepard Murder. *Rhetoric and Public Affairs* 2002, 5(3), 483–505.

Ott, B.L. and Bonnstetter, B. "We're at Now, Now": *Spaceballs* as Parodic Tourism. *Southern Journal of Communication* 2007, 72(4), 309–27.

Ott, B.L. and Keeling, D.M. Cinema and Choric Connection: *Lost in Translation* as Sensual Experience. *Quarterly Journal of Speech* 2011, 97(4), 363–86.

NOTES

1. J. Hibberd, "Walking Dead" Premiere Gets Fall's Biggest Rating, *Entertainment Weekly*, October 15, 2012, http://insidetv.ew.com/2012/10/15/walking-dead-season-3-premiere-ratings/ (accessed August 21, 2013).

2. J. Gunn and S. Treat, Zombie Trouble: a Propaedeutic on Ideological Subjectification and the Unconscious, *Quarterly Journal of Speech* 2005, 91, 152.

3. D. Gross, Why We Love Those Rotting, Hungry, Putrid Zombies, *CNN.com*, October 2, 2009, http://articles.cnn.com/2009-10-02/entertainment/zombie.love_1_zombie-movie-encyclopedia-white-zombie-peter-dendle?_s=PM:SHOWBIZ (accessed August 21, 2013).

4. K. Burke, Literature as Equipment for Living, in *The Philosophy of Literary Form: Studies in Symbolic Action* (Baton Rouge, LA: Louisiana State University Press, 1941), 301.

5. H. Blumer, *Symbolic Interactionism: Perspective and Method* (Berkeley, CA: University of California Press, 1986), 2.

6. Blumer, 5.

7. E. Goffman, *The Presentation of Self in Everyday Life* (New York: Random House Books, 1959), 252.

8. S. Metts and W.R. Cupach, Face Theory: Goffman's Dramatistic Approach to Interpersonal Interaction, in *Engaging Theories in Interpersonal Communication: Multiple Perspectives*, L.A. Baxter and D.O. Braithwaite (eds) (Thousand Oaks, CA: Sage, 2008), 205.

9. Goffman, *The Presentation*, 15.

10. Goffman, *The Presentation*, 24.

11. Goffman, *The Presentation*, 104.

12. See, for instance, S.M. Bergman, M.E. Fearrington, S.W. Davenport, and J.Z. Bergman, Millennials, Narcissism, and Social Networking: What Narcissists Do on Social Networking Sites and Why, *Personality and Individual Differences* 2001, 50, 706–11; and L.E. Buffardi and W.K. Campbell, Narcissism and Social Networking Web Sites, *Personality and Social Psychology Bulletin* 2008, 34(10), 1303–14. Research also indicates that low self-esteem correlates with a greater amount of time spent on Facebook. See S. Mehdizadeh, Self-Presentation 2.0: Narcissism and Self-Esteem on Facebook, *Cyberpsychology, Behavior, and Social Networking* 2010, 13(4), 357–64. Other research suggests that "Twitter may be the network of choice for narcissists." See B.C. McKinney, L. Kelly, and R.L. Duran, Narcissism or Openness?: College Students' Use of Facebook and Twitter, *Communication Research Reports* 2012, 29(2), 108–18.

13. M.L. Galician, *Sex, Love, and Romance in the Mass Media: Analysis and Criticism of Unrealistic Portrayals and Their Influence* (Mahwah, NJ: Lawrence Erlbaum Associates, 2004), x.

14. M.L. Galician, "*Dis*-illusioning" as Discovery: the Research Basis and Media Literacy Applications of *Dr. FUN's Mass Media Love Quiz©* and *Dr. Galician's Prescriptions©*, in *Critical Thinking about Sex, Love, and Romance in the Mass Media: Media Literacy Applications*, M.L. Galician and D.L. Merskin (eds) (Mahwah, NJ: Lawrence Erlbaum Associates, 2007), 2.

15. Galician, *Sex, Love, and Romance*, ix.

16. M.L Galician, 9th annual *Dr. FUN's Stupid Cupid & Realistic Romance® Awards™*, *RealisticRomance.com*, http://www.realisticromance.com/PDFs/2011SC&RR-Release&AwardsList.pdf (accessed August 21, 2013).

17. For more on this distinction, see G. Gonos, "Situation" versus "Frame": the "Interactionist" and "Structuralist" Analyses of Everyday Life, *American Sociological Review* 1977, 42(6), 854–67.

18. E. Goffman, *Frame Analysis: an Essay on the Organization of Experience* (Cambridge, MA: Harvard University Press, 1974), 11.

19. Goffman, *Frame Analysis*, 22.
20. T. Gitlin, *The Whole World is Watching: Mass Media in the Making of the New Left* (Berkeley, CA: University of California Press, 1980), 7.
21. Gitlin, 290–1.
22. D. Kahneman and A. Tversky, Choice, Values, and Frames, *American Psychologist* 1984, 39, 343.
23. Kahneman and Tversky, 343.
24. R.M. Entman, Framing: Toward Clarification of a Fractured Paradigm, *Journal of Communication* 1993, 43(4), 52.
25. Vreese, C.H. de, New Framing: Theory and Typology, *Information Design Journal* 2005, 13(1), 55.
26. B.L. Ott and E. Aoki, The Politics of Negotiating Public Tragedy: Media Framing of the Matthew Shepard Murder, *Rhetoric and Public Affairs* 2002, 5(3), 498.
27. C.M. Berg, *Latino Images in Film: Stereotypes, Subversion, and Resistance* (Austin, TX: University of Texas Press, 2002), 154.
28. Quoted in Berg, 154.
29. K. Burke, (Nonsymbolic) Motion/(Symbolic) Action, *Critical Inquiry* 1978, 4(4), 809.
30. Burke, Literature as Equipment, 299.
31. K. Burke, *Towards a Better Life: Being a Series of Epistles or Declamations* (Berkeley, CA: University of California Press, 1966), vii, vi.
32. K. Burke, *Attitudes Toward History*, 3rd edn (Berkeley, CA: University of California Press, 1984), 336.
33. M.P. Moore, To Execute Capital Punishment: the Mortification and Scapegoating of Illinois Governor George Ryan, *Western Journal of Communication* 2006, 70, 312. In Burke's words, "Mortification is the scrupulous and deliberate clamping of limitation upon the self." See K. Burke, *Permanence and Change: an Anatomy of Purpose*, revised edn (Los Altos, CA: Hermes Publications, 1954), 289.
34. Burke, *Attitudes*, 41.
35. B. Brummett, Burkean Comedy and Tragedy, Illustrated in Reactions to the Arrest of John Delorean, *Central States Speech Journal* 1984, 35, 220.
36. K. Burke, *Counter-Statement* (Los Altos, CA: Hermes Publications, 1931), 139.
37. B. Brummett, Burke's Representative Anecdote as a Method in Media Criticism, *Critical Studies in Mass Communication* 1984, 1, 161.
38. B. Brummett, Electric Literature as Equipment for Living: Haunted House Films, *Critical Studies in Mass Communication* 1985, 2, 247–61.
39. B.L. Ott, *The Small Screen: How Television Equips Us to Live in the Information Age* (Oxford: Wiley-Blackwell, 2007), 47–56.
40. See, for instance, B.L. Ott and B. Bonnstetter, "We're at Now, Now": *Spaceballs* as Parodic Tourism, *Southern Journal of Communication* 2007, 72(4), 309–27; and B.L. Ott and D.M. Keeling, Cinema and Choric Connection: *Lost in Translation* as Sensual Experience, *Quarterly Journal of Speech* 2011, 97(4), 363–86.

12 Erotic Analysis

KEY CONCEPTS

CARNIVALESQUE
CULTURAL PRODUCTION
FANDOM
GROTESQUE REALISM
INTERPRETIVE PLAY
INTERTEXTUALITY
JOUISSANCE
MEDIA EROTICS
PLAISIR
POLYPHONY
PRODUCTIVE
READERLY TEXT
TRANSGRESSION
USER PARTICIPATION
USER-CREATED CONTENT
WRITERLY TEXT

… Spike is coming, spurting onto both their chests, and it's enough to send Xander over the edge, emptying himself into Spike with a gasp of completion. He collapses bonelessly onto the vampire and they['re] still. Lifting his head slowly, Xander blinks, feeling like he has just woken up, but it was no dream, because Spike is still there, smiling tentatively at him, reaching out to brush a sweaty lock of hair out of Xander's eyes. His body shaking only a little, Xander disentangles himself from his vampire lover. With a final, lingering kiss, and a mutual groan of loss as he pulls out of Spike's body, he slumps to the side and they lie, side by side. [He] grins when he realises that he now actually *has* a vampire lover.[1]

For casual viewers of *Buffy the Vampire Slayer*, the preceding story fragment, which recounts a sexual encounter between Spike and Xander – two of the series' popular male characters – probably seems strange and unfamiliar, and perhaps even a little unsettling. But for serious fans of Buffyverse (Josh Whedon's fictional universe about teen vampire slayer Buffy Summers and her friends),[2] it is just one of the hundreds of stories – each written by fans – in which Spike and Xander engage in sexual relations. It typifies a type of fan writing known as slash fiction, which we will discuss in more detail later in this chapter. But what is important to note at this point is that, thanks to the internet, it is just one of the many ways media audiences create and circulate their own media content today.

Critical Media Studies: An Introduction, Second Edition. Brian L. Ott and Robert L. Mack.
© 2014 John Wiley & Sons, Inc. Published 2014 by John Wiley & Sons, Inc.

From fan fiction websites like Fanfiction.net, which boasts "more than 87,000 stories about the boy wizard Harry Potter" alone,[3] to the widely popular image-sharing website, Instagram, to the exponentially expanding "broadcast yourself" video website, YouTube, media *consumers* are increasingly becoming media *producers* as well. The decentralizing power of digital technologies has shattered the conventional understanding of media audiences as "inert vessels waiting to be activated by injunctions to ... consume,"[4] and in the process generated a need for new ways of understanding audiences and their interactions with media. As we demonstrate in this chapter, the key to understanding much audience activity – activity that positions audiences as, at once, consumers *and* producers (i.e. "prosumers"[5]) – is pleasure. Thus, this chapter unfolds in four parts. First, we review what media scholars have had to say about pleasure and, in particular, transgressive pleasures. Second, we look at the pleasures associated with transgressive texts. Third, we consider the pleasures that arise from the transgressive practices of audiences. Finally, we conclude by reflecting on transgressive pleasure as a subject of study in the field of critical media studies.

Theories of Pleasure: an Overview

Historically, media scholars have avoided the topic of pleasure, deeming it unworthy of serious attention. On those rare occasions when media scholars have directly addressed it, they have forcefully condemned it. Perhaps the most famous academic assault on pleasure comes from the Frankfurt School scholars Max Horkheimer and Theodor W. Adorno, who in 1972 wrote, "Pleasure always means not to think about anything, to forget suffering even when it is shown. Basically it is helplessness. It is flight; not, as is asserted, flight from a wretched reality, but from the last remaining thought of resistance."[6] Nor were Horkheimer and Adorno the last media scholars to criticize pleasure so vigorously. Just three years later, Feminist film critic Laura Mulvey, in her famous essay titled "Visual Pleasure and Narrative Cinema," set out to "destroy" the pleasure afforded by Hollywood cinema.[7] Initially, then, pleasure – as both an audience experience and an academic pursuit – was ignored or damned.

It was not until the 1980s – when media scholars began to attend carefully to audiences – that pleasure emerged as a subject of sustained inquiry.[8] Challenging the view that pleasure is simple and uncomplicated, media critic Ien Ang argued:

> Both in common sense and in more theoretical ways of thinking, entertainment is usually associated with simple, uncomplicated pleasure – hence the phrase, for example, "mere entertainment". This is to evade the obligation to investigate which mechanisms lie at the basis of that pleasure, how that pleasure is produced and how it works – as though that pleasure were something natural and automatic. Nothing is less true, however. Any form of pleasure is constructed and functions in a specific social and historical context.[9]

Though the study of pleasure became increasingly common, pleasure itself continued to be disparaged. The nearly universal condemnation of pleasure was rooted in the widespread belief that "pleasures were 'complicit' with a dominant ideology" and therefore subjugation.[10] More recently, however, scholars have begun to recognize that pleasure need not necessarily serve dominant or hegemonic interests, for there is more than one type of pleasure.

In his 1975 book, *The Pleasure of the Text*, the French semiotician Roland Barthes made an important distinction between two types of pleasure: *plaisir* and *jouissance*. While these two types of pleasure both arise out of audience–text interactions, they involve very different modes of approaching or interacting with texts and, thus, function in very different ways. For Barthes, **plaisir** describes a comfortable and comforting pleasure that emerges from a passive interaction with the text. Because *plaisir* is gener-ated when audiences willingly submit to the structured invitations of the text such as its narrative form (see Chapter 5), its stereotypical images (Chapter 6), or its activation of the male gaze (see Chapter 7), it works to preserve the ideological status quo, making it an essentially conservative and hegemonic pleasure. Often, *plaisir* is associated with the pleasure of consumption because it accepts the text on its own terms, treating it as fin-ished and finalized, a ready-made product to simply be consumed. As there is nothing especially creative or productive about this mode of audience–text interaction, the American media scholar John Fiske argues that the resulting pleasure, *plaisir*, affirms the "dominant ideology and the subjectivity it proposes."[11]

In contrast to *plaisir*, **jouissance** – which is often translated into English as "bliss, ecstasy, or orgasm"[12] – is an ecstatic and disruptive pleasure that emerges from an active engagement with the text. Instead of submitting to the text, audiences rework and remake the text to serve their own needs and desires. *Jouissance* is typically associated with the pleasure of production because the interaction of audience and text creates something novel and inventive in its wake. Consequently, *jouissance* typically functions as a transgressive or counter-hegemonic pleasure. Elaborating on this point, Fiske explains that *jouissance* involves a temporary breakdown of subjectivity, a momentary release from the social order, and an evasion of ideology.[13] To further clarify the distinc-tion between *plaisir* and *jouissance*, consider the different types of pleasures that one might derive from passively "watching" a film and actively "playing" a video game. The pleasure of the former is one of comfort and reassurance that derives from identifying with the protagonist and being led along step-by-step by the story. The pleasure of the latter is one of involvement and interactivity, of directing and controlling the action, of "losing oneself" in the game: "the ultimate 'eroticism of the text'."[14]

It is Barthes's second mode of pleasure, *jouissance*, that concerns us most directly in this chapter. Barthes employs an array of sexual metaphors to explain *jouissance*, a mode of audience–text interaction other scholars have referred to as an "erotics of reading."[15] The use of the term erotics seems especially fitting to us, for it captures the dual character and function of *jouissance*: transgression and production. Consequently, we have dubbed the critical approach that animates this chapter, media erotics. For us, **media erotics** reflects a concern with the sensuous, transgressive, and productive ways audiences inter-act with texts. Since erotics may seem like a strange descriptor to portray an approach to media, it is worth looking closer at its etymology. The term *erotic* derives from *Eros*, the Greek god of primordial lust, sublimated impulses, creative urges, and fertility. Like *Eros*, erotics or eroticism has two principle traits or dimensions, one involving prohibition,

Figure 12.1   A piece of street art by Banksy in Los Angeles. This one depicts a drunk Mickey Mouse along with a coked out Minnie Mouse partying with a skinny model on a giant billboard. The piece was named "LiViN THE DREAM," and is located on a billboard in front of the Directors Guild of America Building on Sunset Blvd. © TED SOQUI/CORBIS.

taboo, and transgression and the other involving expenditure, dissemination, and production.[16] Thus, eroticism is, at once, transgressive (of the status quo or established order) and productive (of something new), which is why *Eros* was also known to the Greeks by the epithet *Eleutherios*, which means "the liberator."

But in what contexts might interaction with media be understood as erotic or liberating, which is to say both transgressive and productive? To answer this question, it is worthwhile to reflect on what is meant by these two concepts. **Transgression** refers to an action or artistic practice that breaks with the prevailing cultural codes and conventions of society (i.e. those codes and conventions that function to sustain the ideological status quo in a particular place and time). When we speak of transgression in relationship to the media, many people think of high-profile acts involving the political appropriation and alteration of media icons such as when the British graffiti artist Banksy painted an image of a drunken Mickey Mouse fondling a scantily clad woman on a Los Angeles billboard advertisement in 2011 (Figure 12.1). But transgressive practices are typically not so public or dramatic. Audiences engage in a wide range of transgressive behaviors every day, including the practice of "oppositional reading" discussed in Chapter 10 or the writing of fan fiction like that which opens this chapter. Nor is transgression limited to political activists and media audiences. On occasion, even mainstream media texts possess transgressive or resistive elements. Indeed, as we will see shortly, certain kinds of texts possess strong transgressive potential.

In addition to their transgressive quality, erotic interactions with media are **productive**, by which we mean generative of alternative pleasures, meanings, and identities. When audiences take up media in creative, inventive, and novel ways, adapting and altering it to serve purposes other than what it was intended for, their activities – whether interpretive, participatory, or material – can be understood as productive. In contrast to consumptive practices, which involve deferring to the text and its dominant pleasures, productive practices co-create the text, facilitating new habits of seeing, thinking, and being in the world and, by extension, counter-pleasures that trouble and disturb the status quo. Erotic analysis provides critics with a set of critical tools for understanding the transgressive and productive practices of audiences, practices that are unique to human beings, as is evident in the difference between animal and human sexual activity. Whereas the sexual behavior of animals is purely instinctual, serving the purpose of procreation, human sexual activity is something more, involving what Georges Bataille calls "an immediate aspect of inner experience."[17] In other words, eroticism concerns subjective desires and not simply an innate urge to reproduce. It is because eroticism is unique to human sexual activity that they alone can experience shame, as well as profound enjoyment, in the transgression of taboos.[18] In the next two sections, we will adopt an Erotic perspective to more fully understand both transgressive texts and the transgressive practices of audiences.

Transgressive Texts

As we have seen throughout *Critical Media Studies*, much of the popular media produced in the Western world works to reaffirm dominant ideologies concerning gender, race, class, and sexuality. This has to do with how the media industry is organized (Chapter 2), how media workers are professionalized (Chapter 3), and how deeply embedded cultural ideologies and psychic structures unconsciously seep into and are reproduced by media products (Chapters 6–9). But not all media products or texts – even mainstream media texts – are hegemonic or, at least, not exclusively hegemonic. Though no media text is inherently transgressive (since what is transgressive in one context may not be in another context), certain kinds of texts are more likely to function transgressively than others because of the way they engage audiences. In this section, we examine two kinds of texts with strong potential for facilitating transgression: writerly texts and carnivalesque texts.

The writerly text

In addition to his distinction between *plaisir* and *jouissance*, Roland Barthes made a crucial distinction between readerly (*lisible*) and writerly (*scriptible*) texts.[19] For Barthes, the **readerly text** is one whose meaning is relatively clear and settled and, therefore, asks very little of the audience. The readerly text is designed to be passively consumed. A classic example of a readerly text would be Steven Spielberg's 1975 film *Jaws*, which is designed to elicit a precise set of emotional responses in a very particular sequence. It is difficult to watch this film and not be swept along by its story. So successful was *Jaws* at eliciting a particular response (fear) that many viewers were scared to swim in the ocean afterwards. Alternatively, the **writerly text** is more unfinished and unsettled and, thus, invites the audience to co-create its meaning. The writerly text favors the active involvement and interpretation of the audience. In fact, if the audience fails to invest in making their own meanings and connections, then it is likely their experience of the text will be unfulfilling and perhaps even boring. The 2012 film *Cloud Atlas* affords a good example of a writerly text, for it resists simple description and explanation; its meaning depends to a great extent on what audiences bring to and do with the text.

Barthes's distinction between readerly and writerly texts closely parallels the Italian scholar Umberto Eco's differentiation between closed and open texts. Though Barthes's and Eco's classification of texts are very similar, it is worth exploring how Eco describes the difference between closed and open texts. Whereas the closed text aims "at eliciting a sort of 'obedient' cooperation," the open text, according to Eco, "not only calls for the cooperation of its own reader, but also wants this reader to make a series of interpretive choices."[20] In other words, while the closed text invites a limited and predetermined response from the audience, the open text actively involves the audience in the production of interpretation as part of the generative process of the text.[21] Adopting the language from the previous chapter regarding polysemy, we might say that closed and open texts vary in their degree of strategic polysemy. Closed texts tend to be less polysemous and open texts tend to be more polysemous. But regardless of which terminology we adopt, scholars agree that texts encourage different levels and types of audience interaction, and vary in the degree to which they constrain or empower audience interpretations. Though the writerly text can be "open" in a wide variety of ways, we wish to highlight two features common to many writerly texts: intertextuality and polyphony.

Intertextuality concerns the ways that texts gesture or refer to other texts. In some cases, intertextual gestures are intentional, meaning that the producer of the text deliberately made reference to another text. This mode of intertextuality might be described as *strategic* because it exists by design. In contrast to strategic intertextuality, we would add *tactical intertextuality*. In this instance, the reference to an outside text is initiated by an audience member rather than by the producer of the text; the gesture is unplanned and unintentional. Tactical intertextuality could be as simple as someone being reminded of a favorite song by something they heard a character say on television even though the character did not explicitly reference that song. The intertextual gesture in this example is initiated entirely by the audience member. We will return to tactical intertextuality later in this chapter when discussing the topic of interpretive play. But for the moment we are concerned with strategic or planned intertextuality, which Ott and Walter have classified into three types.[22]

1   *Parodic allusion* describes a type of intertextuality in which the primary text incorporates a caricature or parody of another text. This is a common device on television programs like *The Simpsons* or *Family Guy*, which frequently mimic or imitate well-known scenes, plot devices, or characters from other

media texts.[23] Parodic allusion is commonly used for comedic effect, mocking or poking fun at the text it is mimicking.

2   *Creative appropriation* refers to a stylistic device in which the primary text incorporates an actual portion or segment of another text. Rather than imitating or mimicking another text, creative appropriation weaves a whole or part of another text into its very fabric. The inclusion of another text is usually done for artistic or creative reasons. The most obvious example would be hip-hop music, which frequently samples the beats of other songs.

3   *Self-reflexive reference* reflects an intertextual strategy in which the primary text gestures to external discourses or events in a manner that demonstrates a self-awareness of its own cultural status or production history. It is often the most subtle and difficult to detect of the three types of strategic intertextuality, as it relies on "insider" or fan-based knowledge. Self-reflexive references generally function as knowing winks or inside jokes to fans. An example would be when the dialog between two characters also comments on something that recently happened in the personal life of one of the actors.

This taxonomy of strategic intertextuality, while by no means comprehensive, does begin to highlight the diverse ways that texts might elicit the active participation of audiences. With all three types of intertextuality, the audience is invited to co-create the meaning of the primary text by "opening" it to dialog with other texts. While strategic intertexuality is not inherently transgressive, it does activate a mode of audience–text interaction that through dialog increases the text's "polysemic potential."[24]

Whereas intertextuality places the text in dialog with other texts, polyphony places the text in dialog with itself. **Polyphony**, which refers to the "many-voicedness" of a text, was coined by the Russian literary scholar Mikhail Bakhtin to explain the dialogic quality of some novels such as those of Dostoevsky.[25] A *dialogic text* is one that stages an unending conversation between Self and Other and, thus, is perpetually open and unfinished. But how is such dialog possible? Intertextuality is, as we have seen, one answer and polyphony is another. The latter has to do with the relation between the characters, narrator, and author. In a polyphonic text, the characters' voices are autonomous, meaning that they exist on the same plane or level as the narrator and have equal authority to speak. In other words, the narrator does not speak *for* the characters, but *to* and *with* the characters, each of whom also has a voice and is interacting dialogically both with other characters and with themselves (i.e. internal dialog). In Bakhtin's words, "*The polyphonic novel is dialogic through and through.* Dialogic relationships exist among all elements of novelistic structure.... ultimately, dialogue penetrates within, into every word of the novel, making it double-voiced."[26] Because all voices or utterances occur on an equal level, notes Sue Vice, "The polyphonic novel is a democratic one."[27] While Bakhtin's concern was exclusively with the novel, polyphony can also be used to assess the dialogic potential of other media such as films and massively multiplayer online games.[28]

The carnivalesque text

In the previous section, we explored the writerly text, a type of text that lends itself to a mode of audience–text interaction that is erotic, meaning that it is both transgressive and productive. In this section, we explore the carnivalesque text, a second type of text that is well suited to an erotic mode of audience–text interaction. Like polyphony, the notion of the carnivalesque was developed by Mikhail Bakhtin to account for a certain tendency in some literature. Writing in a repressive and suffocating political climate, much of Bakhtin's scholarship was concerned with literary forms that challenged the hierarchies of "official" culture and disrupted the monologic (singular) voice of authority. He found one of these forms in François Rabelais' sixteenth-century novel *Gargantua and Pantagruel*. According to Bakhtin, Rabelais' novel was characterized by traits common to medieval carnival. *Carnival* refers to the popular feasts, festivals, and revelries of the Middle Ages, though it is rooted in the Dionysian celebrations of the Greeks and the Saturnalia of the Romans. According to Bakhtin, "carnival celebrated temporary liberation from the prevailing truth and from the established order; it marked the suspension of all hierarchical rank, privileges, norms, and prohibitions. ... It was hostile to all that was immortalized and completed."[29] The **carnivalesque**, then, describes those texts that embrace and embody the spirit of medieval carnival.

Carnival was, for Bakhtin, dominated by two elements: folk humor, which was opposed to the serious tone and official authority of both church (ecclesiastical culture) and state (feudal culture); and laughter, which was "a special kind of universal laughter, a cosmic gaiety that is directed at everyone, including the carnival's participants."[30] Bakhtin divided folk humor into three main forms: (1) *ritual spectacles*, which included carnival pageants and comic shows in the marketplace; (2) *comic verbal compositions*, which were typified by written and oral parodies, as well as inversions and travesties; and (3) *genres of billingsgate*, which involved curses, profanities, insults, and invective. Perhaps the closest thing to this kind of folk humor in contemporary society would be sporting spectacles like professional wrestling, though sketch comedy shows like *Saturday Night Live* and *Chappelle's Show*, and daytime and late night talk shows like *The Jerry Springer Show* and *Conan* also share some common elements. Central to carnival's three major forms is **grotesque realism**, an aesthetic of degradation or debasement, "the lowering of all that is high, spiritual, ideal, abstract."[31] Through grotesque imagery and language, lofty things are brought down to a material, earthly level, while lowly or less privileged things are valued and celebrated. In the remainder of this section, we explore four common and intertwined tropes used in grotesque realism: the grotesque body, abjection, uncrowning, and ambivalence.

1   *The grotesque body.* Images of the body play a central role in the aesthetic of grotesque realism. But these images privilege a particular type of body: one that is unruly and unfinished, polluted and mutable, and disfigured and deformed; one that privileges the lower bodily stratum and its excremental excesses (feces, urine,

sperm, and menstrual blood). The grotesque body – in contrast to the docile and finished, sterile and settled, and refined and beautiful *classical body* (think of marble Greek sculptures) – is a leaky body; it concerns openings and orifices, celebrating that which is socially taboo. The grotesque body is common to the horror, slasher, and zombie film genres. But it is also featured on reality-based television shows such as AMC's *Freakshow*, where the dominant norms and conventions of the classical body are called into question. Though NBC's *The Biggest Loser* also features grotesque bodies, the show is not especially transgressive because it is specifically about disciplining corpulent and excessive bodies and bringing them more in line with the ideal of the classical body.

2   *Abjection.* In *Powers of Horror*, Julia Kristeva defines abjection as "what disturbs identity, system, order. What does not respect borders, positions, rules."[32] Abjection arises from the crossing of cultural boundaries and the pollution/defilement of social categories. By dividing the world into internal and external, the body establishes an ideal boundary for staging the abject. Hence, that which is discharged or expelled from the body (i.e. menstrual blood, spittle, sweat, urine, feces, mucus) evokes disgust and revolt. For some, the frequent images of and discourses about excrement on *South Park* may give rise to the abject. Commenting on the abject in this series, Brian Ott writes, "If something can come out of or go into someone's anus, it probably has on *South Park*."[33] The pleasure of abjection lies within its very transgressions, which captivate as well as revolt, attract as well as repel, fascinate as well as disgust. Abjection desires the very things it casts out. Like the compulsion to stare at a horrific traffic accident, the abject registers and appeals at an affective, bodily level.

3   *Uncrowning.* In contradistinction to the grotesque body and abjection, which exalt that which is considered lowly and taboo, the trope of uncrowning degrades and debases that which is lofty or high. Uncrowning utilizes mockery or ridicule to bring down to earth governing figures or controlling institutions. In the process, it fosters *symbolic inversion* or a world-upside-down perspective. Uncrowning or social inversion is also a familiar trope on the television show *South Park*, where adults and celebrities are frequently derided. In the episode, "Stupid Spoiled Whore Video Playset," for instance, Paris Hilton is depicted as an unintelligent, selfish "whore." The pleasure involved in inverting existing cultural hierarchies – of bringing adults and celebrities down to earth, and elevating children as superior in insight – is carnivalesque, "for it is the pleasure of the subordinate escaping from the rules and conventions that are the agents of social control."[34] Uncrowning is also a common element in television programs like *The Daily Show with Jon Stewart* and *The Colbert Report*, which mercilessly mock politicians and expose their human foibles.

4   *Ambivalence.* Perhaps the most challenging of the four tropes Bakhtin associates with an aesthetic of grotesque realism is that of ambivalence. Carnivalesque texts are, for Bakhtin, inherently ambivalent because they contain contradictory feelings and impulses like fear and elation, seriousness and humor, praise and abuse, crowning and uncrowning, order and chaos, certainty and uncertainty,

and familiarity and unfamiliarity. But the ambivalent dimension of the carnivalesque – and the universal laughter at its heart – fuels the very possibility of social change, for it is fundamentally dialogic in character, an exchange between Self and Other. As Shanti Elliot explains, "In the narrative, song, and ritual of many traditions [and media], ambivalence creates a flexible realm of meaning that holds socially transformative potential."[35] In the conversations it stages between high and low, life and death, carnivalesque texts generate new ways of seeing, thinking, and being in the world. And therein lies their erotic force, their capacity to combine transgression and production.

Before turning from transgressive texts to the transgressive practices of audiences, we wish to briefly reflect on how critics might utilize an Erotic perspective. One option available to the Erotic critic is to study the audience–text interaction facilitated by writerly and carnivalesque texts, assessing their capacity to elicit disruptive and productive pleasures. Examining textual traits such as intertextuality, polyphony, and/or grotesque realism, the critic evaluates the level and nature of audience interaction, along with the pleasures and meanings that interaction evokes.

Transgressive Practices

Just as texts vary in their degree of openness (readerly vs. writerly), audiences vary in their degree of activeness. As audience activity increases, so too does the erotic *potential* of the audience–text interaction. But it is important to remember that no audience activity, like no text, is inherently transgressive. What practices count as transgression always depends upon the particular social and historical context in which the practices occur. Moreover, audience activity can be measured and evaluated in a number of different ways. In this portion of the chapter, we will focus on three types of audience activity in particular: interpretive play, user participation and user-created content, and fandom and cultural production.

Interpretive play

The first type of erotic activity or practice engaged in by audiences is interpretive play. By **interpretive play**, we mean an improvisational mode of audience–text interaction that ignores dominant interpretive codes in favor of interpretive codes that fulfill personal needs or desires. If we were to chart the interpretive activity of audiences on a continuum, it would range from highly passive (a *vessel* waiting to be filled with received cultural meaning) to highly active (a *bricoleur* who constructs their own meaning out of the raw semiotic materials found in texts). Interpretive play aligns with the highly active end of the continuum and may arise out of one of the following three interpretive practices:

1   *Cruising.* When audiences engage with texts, it is often for the purpose of sense-making; they simply wish to understand what the text means and, thus, proceed to interpret signs consistent with dominant codes and conventions. But sometimes, audiences do not care about the prescribed meaning of the text and they are driven less by a desire to understand it intellectually and more by a desire to experience it sensually. In this context, according to Harms and Dickens, "images and communications are not rationally interpreted for their meaning, but received somatically as bodily intensities."[36] Barthes terms this interpretive practice "cruising," adding that "the body is in a state of alert, on the lookout for its own desire."[37] As an interpretive practice, cruising is about surface rather than depth, about getting caught up in the material pleasure of sensation. If you have ever found yourself so mesmerized by the colors of a film that you stopped paying attention to its plot or dialog, you were cruising the text. "The pleasure [*jouissance*] of the text," elaborates Barthes, "is that moment when my body pursues its own ideas – for my body does not have the same ideas I do."[38] Because such bodily pleasure is always singular and fleeting, it destabilizes – if only momentarily – socially constructed meanings and subjectivities.[39]

2   *Drifting.* To understand the interpretive practice of drifting, it is helpful to think of the activity of reading a book. "Has it never happened, as you were reading a book," queries Barthes, "that you kept stopping as you read, not because you weren't interested, but because you were: because of a flow of ideas, stimuli, associations? In a word, haven't you ever happened *to read while looking up from your book?*"[40] Drifting involves audiences generating highly personal associations to other texts, a practice we defined earlier in this chapter as tactical intertextuality. Tactical intertextuality arises not from the text, but from the audience reading practice: drifting. Rather than following the text, the text follows the reader as she or he makes individualized connections and links. Drifting is not daydreaming; it does not arise out of boredom or a lack of interest in the text, but from a deep focus on elements within the text. When one reads with this sort of intensity, one does not *recognize* associations so much as one *creates* them. When you are reading for a class and you suddenly connect that reading with some personal event or experience in your life, you are drifting.

3   *Skimming.* A third interpretive practice that possesses erotic potential is skimming. If cruising is reading sensually and drifting is reading intertextually, then skimming is reading purposefully. It is typically undertaken with a specific aim, often to identify the main concepts or themes in a message as quickly as possible. Skimming allows the reader to form an overall impression of the text without investing the time required to attend to every word or sign. Skimming is transgressive inasmuch as it does not respect the whole, thus challenging the authority of the text's producer to delimit the meanings of the text. As an interpretive practice, skimming is about both surface and depth; the reader scans the surface of the text until she finds an important point or nugget, at which point she dips into the text, taking greater care and time to interact with it. Skimming is an

interpretive practice that nearly every college student has engaged in while cramming for a quiz or text and one that, when performed successfully, is almost certainly a site of pleasure.

These three modes of interpretive play are neither comprehensive nor mutually exclusive. Indeed, they often work in tandem, as one can move in and out of different interpretive practices. The common link between them, as well as others we might add to the list, is the notion of *play*. Commenting on the importance of play in our everyday lives, Henry Bial observes,

> We play to escape, to step out of everyday existence, if only for a moment, and to observe a different set of rules. We play to explore, to learn about ourselves and the world around us.... [P]lay is ... the force of uncertainty which counter-balances the structure provided by ritual. Where ritual depends on repetition, play stresses innovation and creativity. Where ritual is predictable, play is contingent.[41]

Play, especially as children engage in it, is a highly creative and inventive activity. Objects are utilized for undesignated and illegitimate purposes (e.g. a large box becomes a fort) and rules are created, modified, and often discarded as desire dictates. Impulsive and loosely structured, children's play models what we mean by interpretive play. To approach a media text in this fashion is to take, quoting Michel de Certeau, "neither the position of the author nor an author's position," but to detach it from its origin, to invent in the text something different than was intended, and to create something unknown from its fragments.[42]

User participation and user-created content

In addition to generating their own pleasures, meanings, and identities through interpretive play, audiences can also potentially generate erotic experiences through direct involvement in the co-production or production of the text. Co-production arises from **user participation**, by which we mean an audience-text interaction that requires the audience – through the aid of an interface device – to directly engage with the text in a manner that alters the experience of the text. Digital video games are the most obvious example, but there are others. With the aid of a remote control, user participation is also possible in relationship to television viewing, for instance. While most viewers watch television according to strict programming schedules, a viewer may surf through many channels for an extended period of time without ever settling on a single program. The itinerant viewer is still having a meaningful and presumably pleasurable experience, but he or she is actively influencing the contours and texture of that experience. The activity of channel surfing, which is admittedly less common in the era of digital TV (because one need not change the channel to learn what is on other channels), generates a text unique to the individual user.

But let us return to video games, which began to garner serious academic attention in the 1980s due to interest in their *interactive* quality. Unlike more traditional communication technologies such as print, radio, and film, which allow for only limited user participation, digital video games require direct and frequent inputs from users. Simply put, digital games oblige users to "play" them. Recently, scholars have begun to chart the specific pleasures that users derive from playing video games.[43] The three principal pleasures suggested by research in this arena are control, immersion, and performance.

1 *Control.* In 1990, psychologist Mihaly Csikszentmihalyi introduced the concept of *flow* to describe moments of optimal experience in life.[44] For Csikszentmihalyi, certain activities in life produce heightened states of enjoyment because they strike a delicate balance between being too easy (boredom) and being too difficult (anxiety). Basically, people achieve flow, an intense feeling of joy and creativity, when they feel challenged – pushed to their limits – by an activity, but not frustrated by it. Put another way, the experience of flow involves the paradox of control. One must feel that one has sufficient control to obtain an objective, but never so much control that the activity stops being challenging. Digital games operate according to this same principle. They present an opportunity for the gamer to experience control (quite literally concretized through a controller or joystick) without ever ceding complete control. Digital games are designed so that the better one becomes at playing them, the more challenging the task becomes; as soon as a player masters a skill, she or he advances to the "next level." By employing the paradox of control, digital games continuously produce extreme enjoyment.

2 *Immersion.* Given the frustrations and burdens of everyday life, we often evince a desire to escape from the "real" world into a land of pure wish fulfillment: a fact that partially accounts for the popularity of amusement and theme parks. Because of their interactive quality, digital games are especially effective at fostering elaborately simulated places in which we can forget our troubles and lose ourselves. When one becomes fully immersed in a digital game, the external world vanishes and the distinction between game and player fades away. The combined experience of total immersion and flow is frequently described by players as *being* "in the zone." If you have ever attempted to speak to a player when he or she is in the zone, you know how futile it is. Digital games are not, of course, the only media that allow for immersion. Recent research on the iPod, for instance, suggests that it creates a sonorous envelope in which one loses one's self in the sensorial enjoyment of music (*jouissance*).[45] Again, this is why people listening to their iPods in public appear to be in a different world.

3 *Performance.* Immersion in simulated worlds allows for yet another type of pleasure, the "experimentation with alternative identities.... The pleasure of leaving one's identity behind and taking on someone else's."[46] Role-playing digital games necessitate the creation of avatars (i.e. computer users' unique representations of themselves) and, thus, allow users to inhabit bodies or characters, if only virtually,

and to adopt personas that may be drastically different from their non-gaming selves.[47] This type of "identity play" creates opportunities for users to escape the social structures that routinely discipline them (i.e. keep them in line) according to their gender, race, sexuality, and the way they look, sound, or dress. For some, this means not only trying out or experimenting with unfamiliar subjectivities, but also expressing actual desires and aspects of themselves that may not be accepted or acceptable in everyday life. The pleasure of performance lies in its inventive, creative, and productive character. Unlike so much of our mediated environment, which by positioning us as (passive) consumers tells us both who to be and how to be, role-play games (RPGs) foster imagination and self-creation. We tell them who and what we want to be.

User participation is hardly limited to just video games, however, especially as new media technologies become more and more interactive. Devices such as smart phones, tablets, and other computing technologies all demand user participation. Though such devices were used primarily for sending and receiving messages or for storing and retrieving data early on, advances in wireless connectivity have created novel opportunities for interactive play and engagement. Mobile games such as *I Like Frank*, for instance, use mobile devices equipped with Global Positioning System (GPS) technology to allow players in the real city of Adelaide to interact with players in a virtual city who log on from around the world. The game, which interrogates the boundaries between "real" and "virtual" by requiring street players and online players to swap information, was created by Blast Theory, a London-based artists' group that mixes interactive media, art, and performance "to ask questions about the ideologies present in the information that envelops us."[48] While new media technologies increasingly require user participation, the content – be it in the form of virtual environments or navigational maps – is still principally (though certainly not exclusively) produced and distributed by large media conglomerates. Consequently, there are definite limits to the range of meanings and pleasures users can generate.

In contrast to user participation, which involves the co-creation of the text, **user-created content** (UCC) places production of texts exclusively in the hands of the masses. But before looking at few specific examples of UCC and the personal and social functions it serves, it is useful to chart its chief characteristics. A report prepared for the Organisation for Economic Co-operation and Development (OECD) by Sacha Wunsch-Vincent and Graham Vickery of the Directorate for Science, Technology and Industry identifies three central characteristics of UCC: the material must (1) be "published in some context" that is publicly available, (2) demonstrate "creative effort" through the production of original content or the sufficient adaptation of existing content, and (3) be "created outside of professional routines and practices."[49] This definition is designed to include diverse media formats (i.e. text, image, audio, video) across a variety of platforms, including blogs, wikis (Wikipedia), podcasting, social networking sites (Facebook, Twitter, LinkedIn, Pinterest), digital video (YouTube, Vimeo, Dailymotion) and photo-sharing sites (Flickr, Photobucket, Instagram), digital message boards and forums, and online feedback, while excluding email, bilateral instant messages, and commercial market material. Since it is impractical to discuss all of the UCC platforms mentioned above, we have chosen to limit our discussion to blogs.

Short for web log, a *blog* is an online site maintained by an individual or group that features time-dated postings of commentary and other material such as graphics, video, and links. Though blogs did not appear until the late 1990s, current estimates put the total number of "active" English language blogs at about 450 million. Blogs typically fall into one of two categories: issue-oriented or personal diary. Issue-oriented blogs, explains alternative media scholar Chris Atton, "democratize what has long been the providence of the accredited expert (such as the professional politician and the journalist) by enabling the 'ordinary' contributions of people outside the elite groups that usually form the pool for opinion and comment" on the political and social concerns of the day.[50] Bloggers draw their authority not from professional credentials or expertise, but from their own personal, subjective experience with issues. Thus, they often tell stories using language and examples that relate to and resonate with their audience. Moreover, since issue-oriented blogs are largely opinion-driven and do not face the same organizational constraints as media institutions, they can tackle topics and issues often considered taboo in mainstream journalism.

Not surprisingly, personal diary blogs, unlike issue-oriented blogs, tend to be about the person who writes them. In some cases, such blogs are mostly a means of promoting one's own artistic and creative activities. Consider Jenna Mourey (aka Jenna Marbles), who after graduating from college with a B.S. in psychology, began regularly vlogging (video blogging) on YouTube. As of March 2013, Jenna had 7.9 million subscribers, the third most of any person on YouTube. Jenna's most well-known video, "How to Trick People into Thinking You're Good Looking," accounts for 50 million of the more than one billion views of her videos. Jenna's popularity, as well as that of other online celebrities, is significant, for as Atton explains, "Participatory, amateur media production contests the concentration of institutional and professional media power and challenges the media monopoly on producing symbolic forms."[51] Though Jenna's vlogs focus on self-promotion, some personal diary blogs focus on self-expression through autobiographical writing. A study of an erotic story (available via the *Sehakia* website) by Al Kawthar, a self-identified Muslim lesbian from Algeria, concluded that autobiographical writing can create "a space for agency within which counterhegemonic sexualities are asserted, and transgressive normative possibilities enacted."[52] These examples, though limited to blogs, reinforce previous research, which has concluded that user-created content "leads to three cross-sectional trends: increased user autonomy, increased participation, and increased diversity."[53]

Fandom and cultural production

All of us are fans of something: a sports team, an actor or actress, a musical group, or perhaps, like Carrie Bradshaw, Manolo Blahnik shoes. Fans are audiences who possess a special affinity for and loyalty to a particular media or cultural text; they are, in a word, enthusiasts. One of the authors of this book is a committed fan of Fox's *So You Think You Can Dance*. He views the show religiously, reads online blogs about it, cheers for his favorite dancers, analyzes it (at length) with other friends who are also fans, and occasionally goes to see the live tour. The show is, to say the least, quite meaningful to him. The other author is a diehard fan of the sandwiches made at a little shop in Boulder, Colorado, called Snarf's. He would eat their sandwiches, which he often describes as orgasmic, every day if he could (but it is a 45-minute drive). Obviously, they are a source of great pleasure for him. These examples suggest that fans do not merely receive media texts, but rework them "into an intensely pleasurable, intensely satisfying popular culture."[54] In this section, we will examine the multitude of ways that fans actively make meanings, derive pleasures, and fashion senses of self through media.

The study of **fandom** – organized communities or subcultures comprised of persons who share a special affinity for or attachment to a media text, which they, in turn, express through their participation in communal practices (fan fiction, etc.) and events (conventions) – began in the 1980s. At that time, fans were often derided by the media and non-fans as fanatics, obsessive nut jobs, and just plain weird. The first wave of scholars to study fandom, which included figures such as John Fiske, Henry Jenkins, Camille Bacon-Smith, and Constance Penley, was very much interested in challenging this stereotype. For them, fandom involved interpretive communities whose creative and productive activities empowered fans and challenged the hegemonic culture. Contemporary fan scholar Jonathan Gray has dubbed this period and type of scholarship "Fandom is Beautiful"[55] because of its overly romantic view of fans and the counter-hegemonic potential of fan culture. In spite of this limitation, it nevertheless established several important categories for understanding and evaluating fandom. The first generation of fan scholars recognized that what most separates fans from other audiences is the degree to which they engage in **cultural production** or the generation of semiotic, enunciative, and textual materials related to a specific media artifact.[56]

1   *Semiotic productivity* refers to the way fans use the semiotic (i.e. symbolic) resources in media texts to enhance the meaningfulness of their everyday lives. In the previous chapter, for instance, we discussed Janice Radway's study of romance novels, whose female readers often select only those stories and attend to only those themes that reaffirm feelings of self-worth.[57] Similarly, in her study of online fandom surrounding television soap operas, Nancy Baym found that *personalization* is among the chief interpretive practices of fans:

> One core practice in interpreting the soap is personalization, whereby viewers make the shows personally meaningful. They do this by putting themselves in the drama and identifying with its situations and characters. They also bring the drama into their own lives, making sense of the story in terms of the norms by which they make sense of their own experiences. This referencing from the world of the drama to the lives of viewers is the overriding way in which viewers relate to soaps.[58]

Henry Jenkins, drawing upon the work of Michel de Certeau, refers to this process of selective personalization by fans as *textual poaching*. Based on his study of science fiction fandoms, he too argues that fans promote their own meanings over those of producers as a way of drawing texts closer to the realm of lived experience.[59] Textual poaching should not be confused with Stuart Hall's notion of oppositional decoding explained in Chapter 10. Whereas oppositional reading adopts a reactionary stance to the text's preferred ideology, poaching is far more fluid and arises from fans asserting interpretive authority: their own right to make textual meanings. "For the fan," explains Jenkins, "reading becomes a kind of play, responsive only to its loosely structured rules and generating its own kind of pleasure."[60]

In addition to the notion of textual poaching, Jenkins is also interested in *rereading*, or the fact that fans repeatedly return to the same text again and again. Once a story's resolution is fully known, the reader no longer bears the same relation to that text. Instead of being motivated by form and the desire to resolve narrative mysteries, the reader may turn his or her attention to other interests, such as specific themes and characters.[61] The opportunity to focus so intensely on characters – to get to know them – allows for the development of *parasocial* relationships, in which fans form intimate bonds with media characters or personalities that, though inevitably one-sided, can produce outcomes similar to actual social relationships. Rereading, then, is an intensely personal mode of textual poaching that allows fans to build (parasocial) relationships with media characters or celebrities. Though, at first glance, this behavior may seem "fanatical," it is quite common today. Increasingly, Facebook users invite musicians, athletes, and other famous people to be their "friends." Some users go a step further, and leave personal messages on these celebrities' Facebook pages.

2 *Enunciative productivity*, in contrast to the primarily internal and personal character of semiotic productivity, is public and communal. Fans are rarely fans in isolation. Rather, they discuss and debate their shared interest in a media text at length. This can occur in person (i.e. face-to-face) through participation in local clubs and fan conventions, or it can occur remotely (i.e. virtually) through online chatrooms, listservs, and other electronic forums. Regardless of how participants "come together," they engage in similar (though certainly not identical) communication rituals or practices. Among the most common types of enunciative productivity or fan talk is *exegesis*: the careful attention to textual minutiae and hyper-detailed analysis of characters, themes, and plot developments. Close textual analysis can include a wide variety of interpretive activities such as judging the quality or emotional realism of a text, commenting on surprising plot twists, pointing out narrative and character inconsistencies or visual continuity goofs, highlighting seemingly trivial actions or events that have deeper meaning or relevance, and speculating about what will happen next. Exegetical energy is particularly high around texts with lengthy, complex storylines such as soaps or with mysterious, seemingly inexplicable phenomena such as *Twin Peaks*, *The X-Files*, or *Lost*. Regardless of text, however, analysis is designed to demonstrate textual mastery

and fan knowledge, which in an informational economy such as a fan community, translates into prestige, reputation, and thus influence.[62]

Another way fans demonstrate textual knowledge and mastery, thereby heightening their cultural capital within a fan community, is by being the first to report "insider" information such as production schedules, future narrative events or arcs (termed *spoilers* by fans), actor contract disputes, and the like. Fan communities are often very hierarchical, and consequently newcomers or *neophytes* to a particular fandom may be verbally disciplined if they fail to follow communal norms or demonstrate proper respect for fan elders. Alternatively, the newbie–elder relationship may function in a more apprentice–mentor capacity, whereby the newcomer is initiated into the community by being taught its codes and customs. In her largely auto-ethnographic account of *Star Trek* fandom, Camille Bacon-Smith discusses the relatively structured phases of initiation she underwent, including being greeted by the *Star Trek* Welcommittee, meeting and getting to know members personally, and learning about fan-produced texts. It is to this third category that we now turn our attention.

3   *Textual productivity*, the third category of fan production, refers to the vast array of artistic, literary, educational, and entertaining cultural products that fans create. Games, character biographies, episode guides (for television shows), artwork, short films, fanzines, and fan fiction represent just a few of the fan-produced products common to fandom. In many ways, the products created by fans resemble the products generated by the mainstream media, fashion, and culture industries. The principal difference is that, while media texts are produced for profit, most fan texts are produced for pleasure, albeit often at considerable effort and financial expense to the fan. Though it is tempting to consider fan-produced media as simple, amateur, or childish, especially since fans rarely have access to state-of-the-art equipment to produce their products, it can rival and even exceed mainstream media products in creativity, originality, aesthetic quality, and overall production values. In his study of online *South Park* fandom, for instance, Ott noted the sophistication of *Babylon Park*, an animated spoof that combined the elaborate storylines of *Babylon 5* with the fart jokes, general character style, and stop-motion technique of *South Park*.[63] Ott also mentions the 3D images produced by a fan at sweeet.com, many of which were parodies of movie posters involving *South Park* characters, as an example of creative fan artwork (Figure 12.2). A more recent type of fan art – referred to simply as "vids" – entails the splicing together of clips from films and television shows to create video montages, which tell stories that differ in theme or perspective from the original text. The fans, known as "vidders," who produce these montages demonstrate their creative and artistic abilities through audio and video editing rather than filming. "Experienced vidders," notes Mazar, "hold formal and informal workshops to help others learn these skills," allowing more and more fans to become cultural producers.[64]

Perhaps the most studied form of fans' textual productivity is fan fiction. *Fan fiction*, or fanfic for short, is a literary genre in which fans write unauthorized stories that

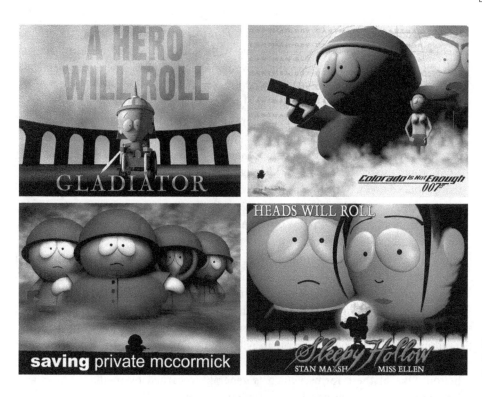

Figure 12.2 Fan artwork: South Park movie poster parodies.

expand upon the storyworld (characters or setting) of a mainstream media text, such as a novel, film, or television show.[65] "Writing stories about characters of a favorite television program," explains Rhiannon Bury, "is a means of extending the meanings and pleasures of the primary text."[66] Fan fiction is typically written by women and often revolves around science fiction texts such as *Blake's 7*, *Dr Who*, *Smallville*, *Heroes*, *Battlestar Galactica*, or *Stargate: SG-1*. Since fan fiction is not sanctioned by the companies that hold the copyrights to the media texts used as the basis for its stories, and it is commonly published online or in fan magazines, most fanfic is illegal. Despite clear copyright infringement, fan fiction tends to be ignored or, at least, tolerated by media companies, however. They recognize that it is produced by their most loyal fans, a group they do not want to alienate. The transgressive character of fan fiction, then, has less to do with its legal status and more to do with how it is specifically functioning for the fans who write it. Fans appropriate and rework media texts they love as a way of making those texts better address their own needs and social agenda.[67] To illustrate this process, we briefly examine two popular subcategories of fan fiction, Mary Sue and slash.

Mary Sue is a sub-genre of fan fiction in which the author/fan inserts herself as a character into the storyworld of a popular media text. Such stories are referred to as "Mary Sues" because it was the name of the central female character in Paula Smith's famous parody of this sub-genre titled, "A Trekkie's Tale."[68] Though the content of Mary Sue fan fiction is infinitely diverse, the underlying form of the stories is overwhelmingly predictable. With few exceptions, Mary Sue characters are adolescents, who are either related to or romantically involved with one of the principal characters from the original media text. An author/fan of a Mary Sue writing about the storyworld of *Stargate Atlantis*, for instance, might introduce a young female character who is romantically involved with Col. John Sheppard. In addition to being closely linked to one of the primary characters, Mary Sues are almost always beautiful, beloved by the other characters, and extremely intelligent. They are also central to the narrative action, and usually save the day before meeting an untimely death at the story's end. Mary Sues are, for most fan writers, the first fan fictions they write. Because they are seen as beginning attempts at fan writing, they are widely denigrated even within the fan communities that produced them. But, nonetheless, they serve an important cultural function for the women who write them.

According to fandom scholar Camille Bacon-Smith, Mary Sue stories are a way for their authors to confront the painful memories and experiences of adolescence, when they were teased for interests (i.e. science fiction and action adventure) and behaviors (i.e. non-seductive fashion and non-subordinate attitudes) deemed too "masculine." Mary Sue stories rewrite and hence recode childhood experiences by creating "perfect" female characters that are both competent *and* well liked, intelligent *and* desirable. They fulfill an emotional need for their authors by creating a cultural model of the ideal woman with which fans can identify.[69] Often, as fan writers "mature," they stop writing Mary Sues and begin writing other forms of fan fiction. One of these forms, which is generally regarded by media scholars as a far more subversive sub-genre of fan fiction, is known as slash.

Slash, like Mary Sue fan fiction, appropriates the characters and storyworld of a popular (and, historically, often science fiction) text for personal ends. But in contrast to Mary Sues, slash fan fiction does not insert the author as a character in the story. It does, however, feature two or more of the main characters from a popular media text in a romantic and often explicitly sexual relationship that they do not, in fact, have in the original (or "canon") text. This sub-genre is referred to as *slash* because the stories are identified by the first name or initial of each of the paired lovers, separated by a "/." Slash fiction centers exclusively on the relationship between same-sex (usually male) characters.[70] It emerged in the 1970s when *Star Trek* fans began writing erotic stories about the relationship between Captain Kirk and his first officer, Mr. Spock. Although slash fiction was dominated by Kirk/Spock stories early on, it has greatly diversified over the years. A few popular pairings today include Edward Cullen and Jacob Black (*Twilight*), Harry Potter and Draco Malfoy (*Harry Potter*), Xena and Gabrielle (*Xena: Warrior Princess*), and Frodo Baggins and Samwise Gamgee (*Lord of the Rings*). Slash stories are commonly accompanied by fan art, such as the Edward/Jacob and Frodo/Sam images seen in Figures 12.3 and 12.4.

For the mostly heterosexual women who write it, slash fiction furnishes a vital outlet to envision, explore, and tell stories about romantic and sexual relationships in which the partners are powerful equals.[71] It is, notes Constance Penley, "an exemplary case of female appropriation of, resistance to, and negotiation with massproduced culture."[72] In the specific case of *Buffy the Vampire Slayer* slash, like the snippet of Spike/Xander slash that begins this chapter, the figure of the vampire

Figure 12.3 Fan artwork: Slash image of Edward and Jacob. Randy Owen, Edward and Jacob, 2009. Graphite on paper, 7" × 12" (17.8 cm × 30.5 cm), private collection. (www.facebook.com/randyowencreations). Randy Owen.

Figure 12.4 Hand-drawn fan slash image. © Solarfall.

offers an additional "vehicle through which to encode subversive pleasures of sexuality and desire."[73] Because vampires, as with the central characters in many other science fiction texts, are not quite human, slash writers have even more freedom to "imagine something akin to the liberating transgression of gender hierarchy John Stoltenberg describes: a refusal of fixed-object choices in favor of a fluidity of erotic identification."[74] In other words, fan fiction is not simply about producing alternate meanings and interpretations; it is also about experimenting with and producing alternate identities, about exploring the limits of who one is and what one can become.

Reflections on Transgression

The study of pleasure, transgression, and their intersection is extraordinarily challenging. Since the experience of pleasure is intensely personal, it is difficult to measure and quantify. Despite this difficulty, critics operating from an Erotic perspective can investigate both (1) particular kinds of texts and the pleasures they afford and (2) the interpretive, participatory, and material practices of audiences and the pleasures associated with those practices. But even if the critic is able to isolate the pleasures in audience–text interactions, it raises the question of whether or not those pleasures function transgressively and productively. In other words, what difference do they make in the world? Though a comprehensive answer to this question is beyond the scope of this chapter, we would like to briefly reflect on the relationship between transgression and social change. Transgression is one form of social resistance; other forms include subversion, disruption, and rebellion.[75] But in contrast to these forms, which are either collective or coordinated, transgression is individual and improvisational. Transgression is not undertaken with the intent of bringing about social change.

That transgression is not strategically designed to promote social change does not mean that it cannot contribute to such change, however. Over time, many individual transgressive acts can accumulate and have an aggregative effect. So, while an isolated act of transgression may seem innocuous and insignificant, numerous such acts can, collectively, participate in processes of social change. Hence, critics should be careful not to judge the character and significance of transgressive texts or practices according to their immediate social effects. It is far more important to study how transgressive texts and practices are personally productive, how they allow audiences to invent their own meanings, pleasures, and identities, and how they contribute, in the words of Michel de Certeau, to "making do" in a world where most media are created for corporate profit not social benefit.[76] Further, because its effects are cumulative, transgression rarely results in rapid social change. Unlike rebellion, which brings about social change suddenly and often violently, transgression promotes change incrementally, remaking social norms and conventions slowly and subtly.

While transgression can and does participate in processes of social change, then, students do need to be cautious about its uncritical celebration. There is a propensity to romanticize the role of transgressive texts and practices in society, thereby underestimating hegemony and its capacity to co-opt and commodify transgression and to re-interpellate subjects. There is also a tendency after studying the topic of media erotics to see transgression in everything; such a move greatly weakens the force of the concept along with the transformative potential it holds. So, the key to studying media erotics involves striking a careful balance between appreciating the transgressive pleasures of audiences and recognizing their contextual character.

Conclusion

This chapter approached media from the newly emerging and still developing perspective of media erotics, a perspective that seeks to understand the counter-hegemonic pleasures (both transgressive and productive) made possible by some audience–text interactions. The chapter began by charting two kinds of texts – writerly and carnivalesque – that possess qualities with strong potential for generating erotic pleasures. We then turned to the transgressive practices of audiences, highlighting how interpretive play, user participation and user-created content, and fandom and cultural production all hold out the promise of erotic pleasure. The final portion of the chapter situated the study of transgression within the topic of cultural resistance more broadly, showing how transgression may contribute to broader cultural change, but also cautioning students about romanticizing transgressive pleasures.

MEDIA LAB 11: DOING EROTIC ANALYSIS

OBJECTIVE

The purpose of this lab is to heighten students' understanding of Media Erotics by having them produce a fan text. The hope is that students will not merely describe or give an account of a transgressive pleasure, but experience such a pleasure.

ACTIVITY

- Divide the class into small groups of 4–5 students each.
- Ask students to select a popular media text, and write a short fan fiction involving canon characters **or** select one character and develop an extended biography about that character and how he or she ended up where he or she is in the canon universe.
- After writing the fan fiction or bio, students should answer the following questions.
    1   In what ways, if any, was the act of cultural production pleasurable?
    2   How does fan fiction wrest control away from the original author in favor of the fan?
    3   In what ways does being a fan/cultural producer alter one's relationship to media?
    4   Do you think YouTube is a common site of resistive pleasures? Why or why not? Give several examples to support your position.

SUGGESTED READING

Bacon-Smith, C. *Enterprising Women: Television Fandom and the Creation of Popular Myth*. Philadelphia, PA: University of Pennsylvania Press, 1992.

Bakhtin, M. *Rabelais and His World*, trans. H. Iswolsky. Bloomington, IN: Indiana University Press, 1984.

Barthes, R. *The Pleasure of the Text*, trans. R. Miller. New York: Hill and Wang, 1975.

Bataille, G. *Erotism: Death and Sensuality*, trans. M. Dalwood. San Francisco, CA: City Lights Books, 1962.

Bonstetter, B.E. and Ott, B.L. (Re)Writing Mary Sue: *Écriture Féminine* and the Performance of Subjectivity. *Text and Performance Quarterly* 2011, 31, 342–67.

Brooker, W. *Using the Force: Creativity, Community and* Star Wars *Fans*. New York: Continuum, 2002.

Butler, C. The Pleasures of the Experimental Text. In *Criticism and Critical Theory*, J. Hawthorn (ed.), pp. 129–39. London: Edward Arnold, 1984.

de Certeau, M. *The Practice of Everyday Life*, trans. S. Rendall. Berkeley, CA: University of California Press, 1984.

Dhaenens, F., Van Bauwel, S., and Biltereyst, D. Slashing the Fiction of Queer Theory: Slash Fiction, Queer Reading, and Transgressing the Boundaries of Screen Studies, Representations, and Audiences. *Journal of Communication Inquiry* 2008, 32, 335–47.

Fiske, J. *Understanding Popular Culture*. Boston, MA: Unwin Hyman, 1989.

Gray, J., Sandvoss, C., and Harrington, C.L. (eds) *Fandom: Identities and Communities in a Mediated World*. New York: New York University Press, 2007.

Hills, M. *Fan Cultures*. New York: Routledge, 2002.

Jenkins, H. *Textual Poachers: Television Fans & Participatory Culture*. New York: Routledge, 1992.

Jenkins, H. *Fans, Bloggers and Gamers: Exploring Participatory Culture*. New York: New York University Press, 2006.

Keft-Kennedy, V. Fantasising Masculinity in *Buffyverse* Slash Fiction: Sexuality, Violence, and the Vampire. *Nordic Journal of English Studies* 2008, 7, 49–80.

Kerr, A., Kücklich, J., and Brereton, P. New Media – New Pleasures? *International Journal of Cultural Studies* 2006, 9, 63–82.

Kristeva, J. *Powers of Horror: an Essay on Abjection*, trans. L.S. Roudiez. New York: Columbia University Press, 1982.

Lewis, L.A. (ed.) *The Adoring Audience: Fan Culture and Popular Media*. New York: Routledge, 1992.

O'Connor, B. and Klaus, E. Pleasure and Meaningful Discourse: an Overview of Research Ideas. *International Journal of Cultural Studies* 2000, 3, 369–87.

Ott, B.L. (Re)Locating Pleasure in Media Studies: Toward an Erotics of Reading. *Communication and Critical/Cultural Studies* 2004, 1, 194–212.

Ott, B.L. Television as Lover, Part I: Writing Dirty Theory. *Cultural Studies <–> Critical Methodologies* 2007, 7, 26–47.

Ott, B.L. Television as Lover, Part II: Doing Auto[Erotic]Ethnography. *Cultural Studies <–> Critical Methodologies* 2007, 7, 294–307.

Ott, B.L. The Pleasures of *South Park* (an Experiment in Media Erotics). In *Taking* South Park *Seriously*, J. Weinstock (ed.), pp. 39–58. Albany, NY: State University of New York Press, 2008.

Scodari, C. Resistance Re-examined: Gender, Fan Practices, and Science Fiction Television. *Popular Communication* 2003, 1, 111–30.

Stallybrass, P. and White, A. *The Politics and Poetics of Transgression*. Ithaca, NY: Cornell University Press, 1986.

Stam, R. *Subversive Pleasure: Bakhtin, Cultural Criticism, and Film*. Baltimore, MD: The Johns Hopkins University Press, 1989.

Taylor, T.L. Multiple Pleasures: Women and Online Gaming. *Convergence: the International Journal of Research into New Media Technologies* 2003, 9, 21–46.

Vice, S. *Introducing Bakhtin*. New York: Manchester University Press, 1997.

NOTES

1. This is a brief excerpt from a *Buffy the Vampire*-inspired slash (Spike/Xander) story. Spurglie, Joined at the Hip, *All About Spike: Fanfiction that Explores Spike's Ambiguities*, www.allaboutspike.com/fic.html?id=497 (accessed December 14, 2008).

2. V. Keft-Kennedy, Fantasising Masculinity in *Buffyverse* Slash Fiction: Sexuality, Violence, and the Vampire, *Nordic Journal of English Studies* 7, 2008, 50.

3. R. Mazar, Slash Fiction/Fanfiction, in *The International Handbook of Virtual Learning Environments*, J. Weiss, J. Hunsinger, J. Nolan, and P.P. Trifonas (eds) (Dordrecht: Springer, 2006), 1141.

4. A. Ruddock, Media Audiences 2.0? Binge Drinking and Why Audiences Still Matter, *Sociology Compass* 2008, 2, 8.

5. A. Toffler, *The Third Wave* (New York: William Morrow and Company, 1980), 282–305.

6. M. Horkheimer and T.W. Adorno, *Dialectic of Enlightenment*, trans. J. Cumming (New York: Continuum, 2001), 144. Originally published by Querido of Amsterdam in 1947, the first English translation did not appear until 1972.

7. L. Mulvey, Visual Pleasure and Narrative Cinema, in *Feminism and Film Theory*, C. Penley (ed.) (New York: Routledge, 1988), 59. This essay was originally published in the autumn 1975 issue of the film journal *Screen*.

8. B. O'Connor and E. Klaus, Pleasure and Meaningful Discourse: an Overview of Research Ideas, *International Journal of Cultural Studies* 2000, 3, 370.

9. I. Ang, *Watching Dallas: Soap Opera and the Melodramatic Imagination* (New York: Routledge, 1985), 19.

10. O'Connor and Klaus, 375.

11. J. Fiske, *Understanding Popular Culture* (Boston, MA: Unwin Hyman, 1989), 54.

12. Fiske, *Understanding*, 50.

13. Fiske, *Understanding*, 50–1.

14. J. Fiske, *Reading the Popular* (New York: Routledge, 1989), 93.

15. R. Barthes, *The Grain of the Voice: Interviews 1962–1980*, trans. L. Coverdale (Berkeley, CA: University of California Press), 175. B.L. Ott, (Re)locating Pleasure in Media Studies: Toward an Erotics of Reading, *Communication and Critical/Cultural Studies* 2004, 1, 194–212.

16. G. Mayné, *Eroticism in Georges Bataille and Henry Miller* (Birmingham, AL: Summa Publications 1993), 13.

17. G. Bataille, *Erotism: Death and Sensuality* (San Francisco, CA: City Lights Books, 1962), 29.

18. Bataille, 29–31; see also Mayné, 3.

19. R. Barthes, *S/Z: An Essay*, trans. R. Miller (New York: Hill and Wang, 1974), 5.

20. U. Eco, *The Role of the Reader: Explorations in the Semiotics of Texts* (Bloomington, IN: Indiana University Press, 1979), 7, 4.

21. B.L. Ott, Television as Lover, Part I: Writing Dirty Theory, *Cultural Studies < – > Critical Methodologies* 2007, 7, 29.

22. B. Ott and C. Walter, Intertextuality: Interpretive Practice and Textual Strategy, *Critical Studies in Media Communication* 2000, 17, 435.

23. H. Gray, *Watching with The Simpsons: Television, Parody, and Intertextuality* (New York: Routledge, 2006).

24. J. Fiske, *Television Culture*, 2nd edn (New York: Routledge), 128.

25. M. Holquist, *Dialogism: Bakhtin and His World*, 2nd edn (New York: Routledge, 2002), 33–4.

26. M. Bakhtin, *Problems of Dostoevsky's Poetics*, trans. C. Emerson (Minneapolis, MN: University of Minnesota Press, 1984), 40.

27. S. Vice, *Introducing Bakhtin* (New York: Manchester University Press, 1997), 112.

28. M. Flanagan, *Bakhtin and the Movies: New Ways of Understanding Hollywood Film* (New York: Palgrave Macmillan, 2009); R. Stam, Bakhtin, Polyphony, and Ethnic/Racial Representation, in *Unspeakable Images: Ethnicity and American Cinema*, L.D. Friedman (ed.) (Urbana, IL: University of Illinois Press, 1991), 251–76.

29. M. Bakhtin, *Rabelais and His World*, trans. H. Iswolsky (Cambridge, MA: MIT Press), 10.

30. R. Stam, *Subversive Pleasures: Bakhtin, Cultural Criticism, and Film* (Baltimore: The Johns Hopkins University Press, 1989), 87.

31. Bakhtin, *Rabelais and His World*, 19.

32. J. Kristeva, *Powers of Horror: an Essay on Abjection*, trans. L.S. Roudiez (New York: Columbia University Press, 1982), 4.

33. B.L. Ott, The Pleasures of *South Park* (An Experiment in Media Erotics) in *Taking* South Park *Seriously*, J. Weinstock (ed.) (Albany, NY: State University of New York Press, 2008), 41.

34. J. Fiske, *Television Culture* (London: Methuen, 1987), 243.

35. S. Elliot, Carnival and Dialogue in Bakhtin's Poetics of Folklore, *Folklore Forum* 1999, 30, 129.

36. J.B. Harms and D.R. Dickens, Postmodern Media Studies: Analysis or Symptom?, *Critical Studies in Mass Communication* 13, 1996, 222.

37. Barthes, *The Grain of the Voice*, 231.

38. R. Barthes, *The Pleasure of the Text*, trans. R. Miller (New York: Hill and Wang, 1975), 17.

39. Fiske, *Understanding*, 51.

40. R. Barthes, *The Rustle of Language*, trans. R. Howard (Berkeley, CA: University of California Press, 1989), 29.

41. H. Bial, Play, in *The Performance Studies Reader*, H. Bial (ed.) (New York: Routledge, 2004), 115.

42. M. de Certeau, *The Practice of Everyday Life*, trans. S. Rendall (Berkeley, CA: University of California Press, 1984), 169.

43. A. Kerr, J. Kucklich, and P. Brereton, New Media – New Pleasures?, *International Journal of Cultural Studies* 2006, 9, 63–82.

44. M. Csikszentmihalyi, *Flow: the Psychology of Optimal Experience* (New York: Harper & Row, 1990).

45. J. Gunn and M.M. Hall, Stick it in Your Ear: the Psychodynamics of iPod Enjoyment, *Communication and Critical/Cultural Studies* 2008, 5, 135–57.

46. Kerr *et al.*, 74.

47. T.L. Taylor, Multiple Pleasures: Women and Online Gaming, *Convergence* 2003, 9, 26; see also S. Turkle, *Life on Screen: Identity in the Age of the Internet* (New York: Touchstone, 1995), 177–96.

48. Blast Theory, *About Blast Theory*, www.blasttheory.co.uk/bt/about.html (accessed December 14, 2008).

49. Working Party on the Information Economy, *Participative Web: User-Created Content* (2007), 8, www.oecd.org/dataoecd/57/14/38393115.pdf (accessed December 14, 2008).

50. C. Atton, Current Issues in Alternative Media Research, *Sociology Compass* 2007, 7, 21; see also H. Hewitt, *Blog: Understanding the Information Reformation That's Changing Your World* (Nashville, TN: Thomas Nelson, 2005), 71.

51. Atton, 21.

52. N. Zukic, Webbing Sexual/Textual Agency in Autobiographical Narratives of Pleasure, *Text and Performance Quarterly* 2008, 28, 397.

53. Working Party on the Information Economy, *Participative Web: User-Created Content* (2007), 35, www.oecd.org/dataoecd/57/14/38393115.pdf (accessed December 14, 2008).

54. J. Fiske, The Cultural Economy of Fandom, in *The Adoring Audience: Fan Culture and Popular Media*, L.A. Lewis (ed.) (New York: Routledge, 1992), 30.

55. J. Gray (ed.), *Fandom: Identities and Communities in a Mediated World* (New York: New York University Press, 2007), 1.

56. Fiske, The Cultural Economy of Fandom, 37.

57. J.A. Radway, *Reading the Romance: Women, Patriarchy, and Popular Literature* (Chapel Hill, NC: University of North Carolina Press, 1984), 184.

58. N.K. Baym, *Tune In, Log On: Soaps, Fandom, and Online Community* (Thousand Oaks, CA: Sage Publications), 71.

59. H. Jenkins, *Textual Poachers: Television Fans & Participatory Culture* (New York: Routledge, 1992), 18, 34, 53.

60. H. Jenkins, Star Trek Rerun, Reread, Rewritten, in *Fans, Bloggers, Gamers: Exploring Participatory Culture* (New York: New York University Press, 2006), 39.

61. Jenkins, *Textual Poachers*, 67.

62. H. Jenkins, "Do You Enjoy Making the Rest of Us Feel Stupid?": alt.tv.twinpeaks, the Trickster Author, and Viewer Master, in *Full of Secrets: Critical Approaches to Twin Peaks*, D. Lavery (ed.) (Detroit, MI: Wayne State University Press, 1995), 59.

63. B.L. Ott, "Oh My God, They Digitized Kenny!" Travels in the *South Park* Cybercommunity v4.0, in *Prime Time Animation: Television Animation and American Culture*, C.A. Stabile and M. Harrison (eds) (New York: Routledge, 2003), 228–9.

64. Mazar, 1148.

65. Mazar, 1141.

66. R. Bury, A Critical Eye for the Queer Text: Reading and Writing Slash Fiction on (the) Line, in *The International Handbook of Virtual Learning Environments*, J. Weiss, J. Hunsinger, J. Nolan, and P.P. Trifonas (eds) (Dordrecht: Springer, 2006), 1152.

67. Jenkins, *Textual Poachers*, 102.

68. C. Bacon-Smith, *Enterprising Women: Television Fandom and the Creation of Popular Myth* (Philadelphia, PA: University of Pennsylvania Press, 1992), 94.

69. Bacon-Smith, 102.

70. Keft-Kennedy, 49; see also Mazar, 1147.

71. Bacon-Smith, 249.

72. C. Penley, Feminism, Psychoanalysis, and the Study of Popular Culture, in *Cultural Studies*, L. Grossberg, C. Nelson, and P. Treichler (eds) (New York: Routledge, 1992), 492.

73. Keft-Kennedy, 50.

74. Jenkins, *Textual Poachers*, 189.

75. B.L. Ott, Review Essay: Rhetorics of Social Resistance, *Quarterly Journal of Speech* 2011, 97, 335.

76. de Certeau, 30–1.

13 Ecological Analysis

KEY CONCEPTS

ACOUSTIC SPACE
COOL MEDIUM
HOT MEDIUM
LITERACY
MEDIUM THEORY

ORALITY
PARADIGM SHIFT
SPACE-BIASED MEDIA
TIME-BIASED MEDIA
VISUAL SPACE

In October of 1999, as a way of ushering in the new millennium, *Biography*, a television show on the Arts and Entertainment (A&E) cable channel, counted down the 100 most influential people of the past 1,000 years. To create the remarkable list for the program's four-hour world premiere, A&E polled 360 noted scholars, scientists, and artists. Their responses, along with individual ballots cast through *Biography*'s website, were evaluated by A&E's editorial board, who eventually settled on a rank-ordered list. Sitting atop the list as the single most influential person in the past 1,000 years was Johannes Gutenberg, the inventor of moveable type mechanical printing. Gutenberg, who edged out such legendary historical figures as Sir Isaac Newton, Charles Darwin, William Shakespeare, Karl Marx, Leonardo da Vinci, and Mahatma Gandhi, was awarded top honors because the printing press was felt to have more profoundly transformed the world than any other invention, discovery, or action by a world leader. The invention of the printing press was, after all, one of those pivotal events in history when, in the words of philosopher Mark Taylor, "technological innovation triggers massive social and cultural transformation."[1]

With the advent of Gutenberg's printing press, the flow of information was no longer limited to individual transmission. For the first time in human history, it was now possible to circulate messages to large, anonymous, and distant audiences. The world had its first mass communication technology. As more and more people had access to the printed word, literacy spread, forever transforming the spheres of science, politics, and religion. Scientists had greater access to the insights of others, allowing them to build upon previous discoveries. Literary and political figures could more easily disseminate their ideas, shaping beliefs and understandings. And while

Critical Media Studies: An Introduction, Second Edition. Brian L. Ott and Robert L. Mack.
© 2014 John Wiley & Sons, Inc. Published 2014 by John Wiley & Sons, Inc.

religions could also share their doctrines more widely, they could no longer exercise such strict control over the interpretation of their religious texts. Today, the development of the printing press is credited with everything from the rise of rationality to the Industrial Revolution. In altering how information was created, distributed, and circulated, Gutenberg's invention initiated a massive **paradigm shift** – a fundamental transformation in how persons know and perceive the world.

The printing press's revolutionary impact on society offers a particularly clear example of the centrality of communication technologies (i.e. media) to our lives. For many, it points to an underlying truth about social life, namely that media or communication technologies are not merely something *in* our social environment so much as they *are* our social environment. This perspective, known broadly as media ecology, highlights that social environments are, first and foremost, communication environments, which, in turn, are dominated by certain communication technologies at particular historical moments. Thus, the central goal of media ecology, according to Neil Postman, is to:

> study the interaction between people and their communications technology. More particularly, media ecology looks into the matter of how media of communication affect human perception, understanding, feeling, and value; and how our interaction with media facilitates or impedes our chances of survival. The word ecology suggests the study of environments: their structure, content, and impact on people in their daily lives.[2]

In this chapter, we will unpack the perspective of media ecology, or what we have dubbed Ecological Analysis, by explaining the central tenets of medium theory, exploring the work of several well-known medium theorists, and reflecting on our current digital environment.

Medium Theory: an Overview

The basis for doing media ecology is **medium theory** – a research tradition that considers the *technology* or individual *medium* of communication to be equally important to, or even more important than, the content of media to understanding our social environment. To clarify this distinction and why it matters, we can think of "sending a package" as a metaphor for communication. In this metaphor, the contents of the package would represent the *message*, the shape and size of the packaging would represent the *form*, and the means by which it was delivered would represent the *medium*. Historically, media scholars have focused far more on the message and its form than on the medium. What difference, after all, does it make if the package was delivered by a horse or a truck? Seemingly little. But what if the message (the contents) happened to be fresh fruit, the packaging a mesh bag, and it was being delivered from thousands of miles away? In that case, assuming that the truck is refrigerated, the medium makes a world of difference (at least to one's taste buds). Medium theory posits that the technology of communication *always* makes a world of difference, or, to adopt Marshall McLuhan's famous aphorism, "the medium *is* the message." Medium theorists are quick to point out that studying the specific medium of communication is important precisely because we do not typically think about it, which means that we are largely oblivious to its influence and effects.

The three central premises of medium theory are: (1) that each medium of communication has a relatively unique and fixed set of characteristics, (2) that those characteristics produce a particular type of communication environment, and (3) that the communication environment has consequences for human consciousness and social organization. Thus, medium theorists seek to identify the characteristics of a medium – what senses it appeals to, its directionality, speed of dissemination, structure, mode of use, size and location of audience, etc. – that distinguish it psychologically and socially from other media.[3] Medium theory can be utilized at either a micro- (single-situation) or macro-level (social). At a micro-level, medium theory might ask, for instance, what are the consequences of breaking up with your significant other in person versus via text message? Even if the message was identical (e.g. "I can't stand you. I never want to see you again. And you smell funny!"), the medium would matter. By contrast, macro-level medium theory asks what type of human relations and social structures emerge in a particular communication environment.

Most media ecologists are interested in medium theory at the macro level, which despite their very different approaches has produced a remarkably clear and consistent picture of the history of civilization – one that, broadly speaking, connects three phases of civilization to three modes of communication.[4] As Table 13.1 illustrates, medium theorists generally divide civilization into traditional oral society societies, modern print societies, and contemporary electronic or digital societies.

The information in Table 13.1 offers only broad brush strokes, however. For a more nuanced and complex picture of communication technologies or mediums and the particular types of communication environments that they create, we turn to the work of medium theory's leading proponents: Harold Innis, Marshall McLuhan, and Walter Ong.

Harold A. Innis (1894–1952)

Harold Adams Innis was a professor of political economy at the University of Toronto, where his interest in economic monopolies would eventually lead to the study of information monopolies. The exercise of political power within society, Innis argued, is influenced by the unique character of the communication media that dominate the dissemination of information. Hence, information monopolies can be diffused or reconfigured by the development and spread of new media. The printing press, for instance, is regarded as having had a democratizing effect because it diminished the privileged position held by religious scribes and undermined the medieval Church's

Table 13.1   History of civilization from a medium-theory perspective

	Oral societies	Print societies	Electronic societies
Technology	speech	paper	light and sound
Sensory experience	multisensory (balances the senses)	visual (privileges sight)	visual + aural (combines sight and hearing)
Scope	tribal	national	global
Directionality	bidirectional	unidirectional	multidirectional
Speed of dissemination	slow (face-to-face)	medium (tied to transportation)	instantaneous (wires and waves)
Audience	local and small	distant and mass	decentered and niche
Intellectual process oriented toward	*preservation* of existing knowledge	*discovery* of new knowledge	*access* to/*retrieval* of abundant knowledge
Knowledge sites	living memory	libraries and museums	digital archives
Logic and thought (mode)	rhythmic and instinctual (cyclical)	causal and rational (linear/sequential)	associational and affective (networked)
Social world (ideology)	communal (collectivist)	segmented (individualistic)	connected (coalitional)

monopoly over religious information and ultimately over salvation.[5] Even though the content of the scriptures had not changed, the change in medium – from an elite class of scribes that painstakingly reproduced scripture by hand to the efficient mass reproduction of scripture by the printing press – fundamentally altered the public's relation to the Bible. As the scriptures became widely available and literacy spread among the masses, they no longer relied as heavily upon the Church to interpret religious doctrine for them.

Innis's interest in the relation among monopolies of knowledge, political power, and technologies of communication in society is most fully explored in his 1950 book, *Empire and Communications*, which was based on a series of lectures he delivered at Oxford University in 1948. It was here that Innis introduced his now famous distinction between time-biased and space-biased media, arguing that most communication media are inclined (i.e. biased) toward either enduring for long historical periods or moving easily across vast distances.[6] "Media that emphasize time," according to Innis, "are those that are durable in character, such as parchment, clay, and stone."[7] **Time-biased media** are characteristic of tribal or oral civilizations. Because their production utilizes heavy materials and is frequently labor-intensive (e.g. carving and hand-writing), they reach only a limited audience. Politically and organizationally, civilizations based on such media are usually decentralized and hierarchical.[8] Since time-biased media do not allow for efficient

Table 13.2   Time-biased vs. space-biased media

	Time-biased (binding)	Space-biased (binding)
Medium	Stone, clay, parchment, and speech	Papyrus, paper, and electronic media (radio and television)
Character	Durable, heavy, static	Ephemeral, light, mutable
Biased toward	The *preservation* of knowledge; endures for a long time	The *dissemination* of knowledge; reaches large audiences
Favors	Stability, continuity, community, religion, tradition	Rapid change, individualism, secularism
Institutions	Decentralization, hierarchical	Centralization, less hierarchical
Social organization	Religious control	Political control
Knowledge	Moral	Scientific/technical
Systems of writing	Complex (hieroglyphics, cuneiform script)	Relatively simple/flexible (Phoenician alphabet)

or easy communication over great distances, the various communities that comprise such civilizations tend to be relatively independent and autonomous. As it is difficult for a leader located in one tribal area to communicate with other tribal areas, it is also more difficult to exert direct political influence and control. Meanwhile, leadership *within* a particular tribal region or community is exceedingly hierarchical because knowledge is tied to tradition, which is preserved by community elders or religious figures.

Whereas time-biased media favor religion and political stability, **space-biased media** are inclined toward secularism, materialism, and rapid social change. They are typically lighter in character, less durable, and more ephemeral than time-biased media.[9] Space-biased media such as papyrus, paper, television, radio, and newspapers can reach many people over long distances, and thus support centralized systems of government that are less hierarchical. Because societies built upon space-biased media can communicate easily over great distances, it is easier for a government located in one place (i.e. highly centralized) to govern far-away places. At the same time, because knowledge is not controlled by a select few, the structure of government itself is more egalitarian, which in turn fosters rational deliberation and democratic debate. The fundamental differences between time-biased and space-biased media are summarized in Table 13.2.

Innis's interest in the bias of media informed his analysis of the Egyptian, Babylonian, Greek, and Roman empires in *Empire and Communications*. Since empires are characterized by rule over large areas for long periods of time,

Innis believed that empires had to strike a careful balance between media biased toward space and time. He wrote:

> Large-scale political organizations such as empires must be considered from the standpoint of two dimensions, those of space and time, and persist by overcoming the bias of media which over-emphasize either direction. They have tended to flourish under conditions in which civilization reflects the influence of more than one medium and in which the bias of one medium towards decentralization is offset by the bias of another medium towards centralization.[10]

To more fully understand this process, it is helpful to look at his specific analysis of a particular empire. We have selected his discussion of the Egyptian empire, as it furnishes a fertile example.

Innis begins his discussion of the ebb and flow of the Egyptian empire by reflecting on the importance of the Nile, and its role in agricultural production and trade. Though this may seem like an odd place to begin an analysis of the relation between media and empire, Innis's discussion of the Nile moves quickly from the water itself to the necessity of creating a calendar that could accurately predict the river's annual floods. The first such calendar, which relied upon astronomy to reconcile the lunar calendar with the solar year, imposed Ra – the Sun god – as the supreme author of the universe. From roughly 2895 to 2540 BC, this "divinely inspired" calendar affirmed an absolute monarchy in which the Pharaoh – by controlling knowledge associated with the calendar – was elevated to the status of a god. The rigidly hierarchical character of society at this time was reflected in the dominant communication medium, pictorial hieroglyphic writing on stone. These sacred engravings functioned to consolidate power, allowing the Pharaoh to establish authority and control over all arable land. This authority was perhaps most evident in the construction of the pyramids and elaborate burial rites of the Pharaohs, which "suggested that the people expected the same miracles from the dead as from the living king."[11]

Over time, difficulties in the sidereal year created irregularities in the calendar, which the priests exploited to challenge the authority of the Pharaoh, who was lowered in status from an individual godhead to the Son of Ra. Eventually, the absolute monarch was replaced by a royal family when the clergy of Heliopolis established a more contemporary calendar and imposed it on Egypt.[12] This shift in power led to the development of a more feudal society that ceded authority to local administrators and clergy. "The profound disturbances in Egyptian civilization involved in the shift from absolute monarchy to a more democratic organization," Innis noted, "coincides with a shift in emphasis on stone as a medium of communication or as a basis of prestige, as shown in the pyramids, to an emphasis on papyrus."[13] As power was increasingly decentralized, the necessity for administrative communications increased. This led to the development of new forms of writing that were more secular and less like the sacred symbols used in hieroglyphics, a development that broadened literacy and brought even more change. In an effort to resist this change and re-centralize power, the scribes were elevated to the upper classes, which included priests and nobility.

Though this re-centralization was successful in re-monopolizing knowledge over writing and thus accurate predictions about the Nile, it caused problems for ruling over a space that had grown quite large. Consequently, Innis argued, the new monopoly over writing defeated efforts to solve the problem of space and gradually cost Egypt its empire.[14] The ideas introduced by Innis in *Empire and Communications* would eventually be extended by a fellow professor at the University of Toronto, Marshall McLuhan.

Marshall McLuhan (1911–80)

Herbert Marshall McLuhan began his academic career teaching English at St. Louis University in 1937. He continued teaching there even as he worked on his graduate degrees at the University of Cambridge, England. McLuhan earned his PhD in 1942 after completing his dissertation on the historical development of the verbal arts or *trivium* (rhetoric, dialectic, and grammar). Prior to leaving St. Louis University for a position at a Canadian institution in 1944, McLuhan would direct Walter Ong's Master's thesis and introduce him to the topic on which he would later write his doctoral dissertation under Perry Miller's direction.[15] A few years later, McLuhan took up residence in Toronto, where he was influenced by Harold Innis, and served for several years as chairperson for the Ford Foundation Seminar on Culture and Communication. During that time, McLuhan published his first book, a broad-ranging study of popular culture titled *The Mechanical Bride: Folklore of Industrial Man*. But it was his 1962 book, *The Gutenberg Galaxy: the Making of Typographic Man*, that established McLuhan as a major scholar of media.

The Gutenberg Galaxy is a sustained study of the printing press's influence not only on European culture, but also on human consciousness itself. According to McLuhan, technologies create unique social environments that modify our "*forms of thought* and the organization of experience in society and politics."[16] For McLuhan, moveable-type printing constituted a decisive break from the oral societies of the past and produced "Gutenberg man:" a subject who was characterized by rational, linear thought processes. The cognitive reorganization of humans was accompanied by an equally dramatic social reorganization, not the least of which included the creation of *publics*. Prior to the development of mass printing, there was no way to create publics on a national scale, and indeed, what we call "nations" could not, McLuhan argues, have preceded Gutenberg's invention. For both individuals and publics, the printing press fostered a visually oriented self-consciousness, which isolated the visual faculty from the other senses and affirmed the principles of uniformity and continuity. Linking technologies to specific senses was one of McLuhan's key contributions to media studies. In his view, each medium is an extension of human senses, limbs, or processes, and therefore of ourselves.[17]

Since different communication technologies privilege different senses, the prevalence of certain technologies at any given historical moment contributes to our overall *sensory balance*. Based on the idea of sensory balance, McLuhan argues all of human history can be divided into three major epochs or periods: oral, writing/ print, and electronic. In each of these periods, what matters is not the content delivered by media, but the character of the medium itself. To illustrate this point, McLuhan adopts the example of electric light in chapter one of his most famous book, *Understanding Media: the Extensions of Man* (1964). He explains:

> The electric light is pure information. It is a medium without a message, as it were[.] ... Whether the light is being used for brain surgery or night baseball is a matter of indifference. It could be argued that these activities are in some way the "content" of the electric light, since they could not exist without the electric light. This fact merely underlines the point that "the medium is the message" because it is the medium that shapes and controls the scale and form of human association and action.[18]

In the remainder of the book, McLuhan proceeds to identify the unique characteristics of various media using his distinction between hot and cool media as a broad template.

A **hot medium** is one that "extends a single sense in 'high definition,'" while a **cool medium** is "low definition" because it is "high in participation or completion by the audience."[19] For McLuhan, the distinction is not so much an either/or, as it is a spectrum for evaluating the degree to which media are low or high in participation. Media such as radio, photographs, film, and the phonetic alphabet are relatively hot, while media such as television, telephones, speech, and cartoons are comparatively cool. This distinction can be a confusing one, especially if one is encountering it for the first time. To underscore the point McLuhan is making, it is helpful to consider his inspiration. Paul Levinson offers this insightful history:

> McLuhan's invocation of hot and cool derived from jazz slang for brassy, big band music that overpowers and intoxicates the soul (hot) versus wispy, tinkly stretches of sound that intrigue and seduce the psyche (cool). The brassiness of the big band bounces off us, knocks us out – we neither embrace it nor are immersed in it – in contrast to the cool tones that breeze through us and bid our senses to follow like the Pied Piper.[20]

So, whereas hot media fully satiate the senses (at least those that they engage), cool media have less clarity, depth, and vividness, and therefore invite our involvement; they ask us to fill in the details. McLuhan regarded film as a hot medium because it asks very little from us, supplying all the necessary input. Television (at least, analog television), by contrast, is cool because it is incomplete, less overwhelming than cinema, and more fleeting. But McLuhan also recognized that mediums change over time, thereby altering their relative degree of hot or coolness. The advent of high definition television has almost certainly, for instance, made TV a less cool medium than when McLuhan was writing.

Near the end of his life, McLuhan began working on updating *Understanding Media* with his son Eric. The result of that effort was the posthumous publication of *Laws of Media: the New Science* in 1988. Many of McLuhan's most mature ideas can

Table 13.3 Acoustic space vs. visual space

Acoustic (pre- and post-Euclidean) space	Visual (Euclidean) space
Orality and electronic media	Writing and print media
Multisensory (hearing, touch, etc.) interplay	A single sense (vision) detached from others
Dynamic, spherical, and discontinuous	Static, linear, and continuous
Heterogeneous and multidimensional	Homogenous and uniform
Open, boundless, and creative	Enclosed, contained, and controlled
Experiential, resonant, and sensual	Abstracted, rational, and mental
Participatory, cool	Detached, hot
Primeval, natural, environmental form	Civilized, artificial, human-made artifact
Amorphic, undirected, and simultaneous	Geometric, directed, and sequential
Figure and ground continually transform one another	Abstract figure minus a ground

be found in that book, though we will concentrate our attention on just two: (1) the distinction between acoustic and visual space, and (2) the four laws of media. McLuhan's interest in how human senses (sight, hearing, touch, taste, and smell) and their interactions produce different experiences of space dates all the way back to the 1950s,[21] though it did not gain much intellectual traction until a few decades later. The first chapter of *Laws of Media* is dedicated to distinguishing between acoustic and visual space. For McLuhan, **acoustic space** characterized the world as it was experienced during primary orality. At this time, space involved the interplay of multiple senses; it was "spherical, discontinuous, non-homogenous, resonant, and dynamic."[22] But the invention of the alphabet, McLuhan argued, ushered in a new kind of space, which was later extended and intensified by the technologies of print.[23] This new space, **visual space**, detaches sight from the other senses; it is "an infinite container, linear and continuous, homogenous and uniform."[24] While visual space would dominate society for centuries, McLuhan believed that electronic media had reinvigorated and retuned us to acoustic space. Table 13.3 highlights a number of key distinctions between acoustic and visual space.

To appreciation McLuhan's distinction between acoustic and visual space, consider the difference between having a conversation with a friend and reading a book. When you are chatting with a friend in a public place, all of your senses are engaged. You see, smell, and hear your surrounding environment. In addition to your friend's voice, you hear the voices of others in the background, perhaps birds chirping, or an automobile passing by. You feel a cool breeze on your neck. You take in everything from multiple directions all at once. And since the stimuli activating your senses keep changing, the space itself is in a constant state of flux. This is acoustic space. But when you read a book (even when you read in a public place), you focus your attention in one direction and largely block out your other senses. Indeed, if you are unable to do so, you probably will not get much out of what you are reading. This is visual space. As this example illustrates, different communication technologies produce different *experiences* of space.

McLuhan's distinction between acoustic and visual space, as well as that between hot and cool media, was an attempt on his part to understand the effects of a medium upon other media, the environment, individual users, and society as a whole. As valuable as these analyses were, they did not establish a general blueprint for conducting this kind of analysis. So McLuhan set out to identify the basic functions, or what he called laws, of all media. These laws, he argued, had to be provable or disprovable through direct observation. Ultimately, McLuhan concluded that media perform four basic functions: extension, closure, retrieval, and reversal. These form the basis of McLuhan's four laws of media, which he posed as questions.[25]

1   *Extension* describes McLuhan's belief that every technology extends or amplifies some organ, sense, or faculty of the user. So, he proposed that medium theorists begin by asking: What does a medium enhance or intensify or make possible or accelerate?
2   *Closure* refers to his belief that as a technology amplifies or extends one aspect of experience, it must necessarily diminish or push aside others. This led to the question: What does a medium erode or obsolesce?
3   *Retrieval* takes into account McLuhan's conviction that all media recast and remake previous media, bringing back into play earlier experiences. Thus, he queried: What does a medium retrieve that has been earlier obsolesced?
4   *Reversal* is rooted in the notion that a medium, when taken to its extreme, will reverse certain of its characteristics. His fourth and final question, then, is: What does a medium flip when pushed to the limits of its potential?

McLuhan believed that his four laws, or tetrad, could be applied to virtually anything, and in the glossary to *The Global Village* he employs it to assess 44 different mediums. Keeping in mind that McLuhan understood media to be "any extension of ourselves,"[26] here is what he had to say about the medium of the "crowd:" It intensifies the desire to grow; it obsolesces individual identity; it retrieves paranoia; and it reverts into violence at the fear of decrease.[27] As interesting and provocative as McLuhan's ideas were, it was a student of his, Walter Ong, who was perhaps most responsible for bringing medium theory into the mainstream of academic study.

Walter J. Ong (1912–2003)

While McLuhan's work is characterized by its breadth and generalizations, Walter J. Ong's work is defined by its historical depth and specificity. A Jesuit Catholic priest, Ong spent most of his academic career at St. Louis University as Professor of

Humanities in Psychiatry and then as William E. Haren Professor of English. He had earned his doctorate degree in English from Harvard University in 1955 after completing his dissertation on the French logician Peter Ramus. Ong's dissertation would lead the publication of *Ramus, Method, and the Decay of Dialogue: From the Art of Discourse to the Art of Reason* in 1958 in which he argued that the emergence of a visualist print culture enabled a new, mathematical state of mind in the Middle Ages. In his 1967 *The Presence of the Word: Some Prolegomena for Cultural and Religious History*, which was based upon the Terry Lectures he delivered at Yale in 1964, Ong turns to the "word" – humans' primary medium of communication – and its successive stages or transformations: (1) oral or oral–aural, (2) script (alphabet and print), and (3) electronic.[28] In that work, Ong explores the phenomenon of sound, and specifically the spoken word, arguing that it "is more real or existential than other sense objects [such as images]" because it occurs in time and, thus, produces a feeling of liveliness.[29]

But Ong's most famous study of the word and its transformation over time comes in his 1982 book, *Orality and Literacy: the Technologizing of the Word*. The most popular of Ong's writings, *Orality and Literacy* has been translated into more than 10 languages. It explores the critical changes to society and human consciousness that accompanied the shift from orality to literacy in the ancient world. For Ong, **orality** refers to "thought and its verbal expression."[30] Primary orality describes those cultures that have no known literate modes of communication. In contrast, **literacy** refers to the technologies of writing and print. Literacy is reflected in both *chirographic* (writing) and *typographic* (print) cultures. While oral, writing, and print cultures all rely upon *words* as the basis of communication, they conceptualize words in fundamentally different ways. In primary oral cultures, the word is an *event* – something that is experienced only in the moment of its utterance.[31] Because sound is evanescent or fleeting, one had to be physically present at the time of speaking to experience the word in a world before writing. But writing and print transformed the word from an event into an *object* or *thing* that could be preserved and widely distributed.[32] Suddenly, one could see, rather than simply hear, words. As an image, the word was understood spatially, *where* it appeared, as opposed to temporally, *when* it was heard.

The transformation of the word from (aural) event into (visual) object, Ong argued, altered the character of human thought and expression. Accordingly, Ong's main objective in *Orality and Literacy* was to chart the specific modes of thought and expression (i.e. psychodynamics) that characterize oral, writing, and print cultures. Ong identified nine deeply interconnected psychodynamics of orally-based thought and expression: [33]

1   *Additive rather than subordinative.* Oral expression piles ideas one upon the next, often using words like *and* or *next*, rather than organizing ideas according to the reasoned, analytic subordination typical of the printed word. Notice how the information in this chapter, for instance, is structured according to headings and subheadings, rather than presented as one continuous flow of uninterrupted ideas.
2   *Aggregative rather than analytic.* Oral expression employs clusters of words to aid in recall and memory that are generally frowned upon in writing as

cumbersome and unnecessary. For example, orality prefers the "beautiful princess" to the "princess" and the "courageous knight" to the "knight."

3   *Redundant or "copious."* Because the word is fleeting in oral expression, the speaker relies upon repetition and redundancy to keep the listener oriented. In print, such redundancy is unnecessary because if readers lose their place, they can simply back up a few sentences and reread them.

4   *Conservative or traditionalist.* Since knowledge that is not repeated aloud vanishes quickly in primary orality, "oral societies must invest great energy in saying over and over again what has been arduously learned over the ages."[34] Oral expression is conservative in the sense that it values the retention of existing knowledge (through repetition) over the production of new knowledge. Print, by contrast, is all about the production of the new.

5   *Close to the human lifeworld.* Since abstractions are not easily recalled, oral expression depends upon linking information and ideas closely to lived experience. This explains, in part, why oral cultures rely so heavily on storytelling as opposed to analytic categorization to convey information.

6   *Agonistically toned.* Oral expression favors a combative engagement both in terms of style and characters (villains and heroes) so as to encourage intellectual combat and the testing of ideas. Literary works, by contrast, often locate such tensions internally, as something an individual character wrestles with psychologically.

7   *Empathic and participatory rather than objectively distanced.* While writing and reading are solitary activities seen as distanced, objective, and rational, oral expression is a shared experience that fosters communal identification. It depends much more on connection and active participation.

8   *Homeostatic.* In contrast to writing and print cultures, oral societies are concerned with the present more than the past. To maintain equilibrium or homeostasis, there is a willingness to let go of memories and meanings that no longer have relevance to the present moment. Print culture, alternatively, carefully records, catalogues, and stores outdated and obsolete information.

9   *Situational rather than abstract.* Since memory is biased toward that which is concrete, oral expression tends to employ concepts in situational, operational frames of reference so that they remain close to the living human lifeworld. Homer applied the epithet or byname of *amymōn* to Aegisthus, which means not the simple abstraction "blameless," as it is often (mis)translated, but "beautiful-in-the-way-warrior-ready-to-fight-is-beautiful." Hence, the concept supplies the listener with the necessary contextual framing.

As a consequence of these psychodynamics, people in oral cultures do not know history in the same way that people in literate and electronic cultures do. In oral cultures, one is constantly losing contact with the past because of the fleeting character of speech. Since nothing is recorded or written down in primary orality, there is no way to look anything up. Thus, the only way to learn something other than through direct experience is to ask another living person. If there is no living person who experienced or can recall what another wishes to know, then that information or knowledge is lost. This is, of course, quite different than in literature cultures, where technologies of writing and print allow for the storage and retrieval of knowledge (in the form of libraries and museums). The transition from orality to literacy also shifted our sensory experience of the social world from predominantly one of sound, which is group-oriented, to one of sight, which is individually-oriented. Reading is, after all, an inward, isolated, introverted practice. Memory also decreased in importance with the rise of literacy, as events could now be recorded for posterity.

The rise of print had an array of other consequences as well. Because print can reproduce with complete accuracy and in any quantity extremely complex information, it made possible the rise of modern science, which builds upon the findings of others to advance knowledge. Print also favors a fixed point of view. While you may disagree with that last statement, this book is entirely unresponsive to your objections. The printed word presents its point of view and is generally unaltered by its reception; it is a product to be consumed. Additionally, print contributed to the romantic notions of "originality" and "creativity," which fostered a sense of the private ownership of words, which is reflected in modern copyright laws. Similarly, print fueled the notion of individuality and personal privacy by allowing persons to withdraw or escape into their own mental states through the solitary acts of writing and reading. The whole concept of a *private* diary, for example, is a modern invention, since an oral diary would by necessity be public. Interestingly, as we have moved from a print-dominated society to an increasingly electronic one, the concept of a *public* diary has been revived through blogging and social networking.

The connection we have just made between blogging and orality is not an isolated one. Electronic media such as motion pictures, radio, television, and computers all contribute to what Ong calls "secondary orality," by restoring the strong group sense associated with the spoken word. He did not regard secondary orality as identical to primary orality, though, noting that "secondary orality generates a sense for groups immeasurably larger than those of primary oral culture: McLuhan's 'global village.'"[35] Ong stopped short of identifying the psychodynamics of secondary orality and its impact on human consciousness, as the electronic revolution was still in its infancy.[36] Drawing on the work of recent medium theorists, our aim in the final section is to chart the key features and logics of secondary orality.

Charting the Third Wave

There is, as of yet, no consensus on precisely what to call contemporary culture. It has variously been referred to as postmodern, electronic, digital, secondary orality, and the *third wave*. We have settled on the last of these phrases, which was coined by futurologist Alvin Toffler in 1980,[37] because despite the varying terminological preferences of medium theorists, they all seem to agree that if history is measured according to communication technologies, then we now inhabit the third stage of human history. Furthermore, as a dramatic swelling or disturbance that moves through space and time, and ends with the transfer of energy, the "wave" metaphor is especially apt. For most scholars, the social changes that characterize the transition from print culture to third-wave culture are no less striking and significant than those marking the shift from orality to literacy. The changes wrought by the rise of computer-mediated communication technologies are nothing short of paradigmatic. In this section, we begin by identifying the central features of third-wave media, and then consider how repeated exposure to those features fosters a unique way of perceiving, knowing, and being.

Characteristics of third-wave media

Third wave media, alternatively referred to as "new media," describes those communication mediums that employ computing technology to create, store, and distribute data. This is an admittedly broad definition that includes everything from websites and computer games to DVDs and MP3 files. As such, it is difficult to identify a set of fixed characteristics shared by these varying formats of communication. So, our list will be necessarily broad. We take the defining characteristics of "new media" to be digitality, variability, interactivity, connectivity, and virtuality.

1   *Digitality.* All new media are digital, meaning they exists as *bits* or strings of numerical information typically in the form of binary code (1s and 0s). Whereas digital media are composed of bits, traditional print media like books, newspapers, and magazines are made up of matter and, thus, *atoms*. The significance of this distinction is discussed by Nicholas Negroponte in his 1995 book, *Being Digital*. Unlike an atom, a "bit has no color, size, or weight, and it can travel at the speed of light."[38] Because bits are just numerical codes, they are easy and inexpensive to replicate. Anyone who has ever made a digital copy of a text, sound, or image file on their computer has replicated bits. This process, which costs nothing if you own or have access to a computer, is virtually instantaneous and the "copy" is indistinguishable from the "original." The ways that bits differ from atoms is causing us to rethink everything from intellectual property to the concepts of authorship, authenticity, originality, and creativity.

2   *Variability.* A second key characteristic of new media is its variability; this refers both to (a) the fluidity or manipulability of its content and (b) to the flexibility of user navigation. New media tend to be fluid and dynamic because digital information is easily alterable. It is fast and simple to update one's blog, change one's status on Facebook, or edit a digital photograph before posting it online. "A new media object," explains Lev Manovich, "is not something fixed once and for all, but something that can exist in different, potentially infinite versions."[39] The printed word, by contrast, is relatively static, making it difficult, time-consuming, and expensive to update or revise. Nor is new media's variability strictly limited to its content, for even when the content does not change, users have great flexibility in *where* they enter (and exit) a new media object and in *how* they navigate it. While printed books have a fixed and usually linear organizational structure designed to be followed in a particular manner, it is not at all uncommon to randomly "shuffle"

the songs on one's MP3 player or to surf the web according to one's personal desires and taste. Indeed, the decentered and hypertextual character of the internet make it particularly amenable to flexible navigation.

3   *Interactivity.* While print media involve the dissemination of single-authored messages to more or less passive receivers, third-wave media demand active involvement. Perhaps the most obvious example of this capacity is video games, which as we saw in the previous chapter require user participation; they necessitate that the user engage directly with the new media object, continuously making choices and/or taking actions. Other new media require interaction as well, though perhaps in less obvious ways. The technologies of texting, surfing, blogging, Tweeting, and Skyping all depend upon responding to content produced by others. Indeed, interface devices such as touch screens, joysticks, keyboards, motion sensors, and voice activation software are designed precisely to facilitate direct user interaction. New media are interactive not just because they involve participation, but because such participation is also an act of co-creation or collaborative production. Hence, new media have begun to collapse the old boundaries between producer and consumer, sender and receiver, author and reader. To engage with third-wave media is itself an act of invention and authorship.

4   *Connectivity.* We live in an increasingly connected world. Nearly all of the digital media we use are connected by cable, fiber, or wireless technology to the vast and continuously expanding network of data and information stored on computer servers around the globe. Those few digital media devices that are not connected, like the stand-alone MP3 player, are rapidly becoming obsolete. Due to the decreasing cost of computing technology and the convergence of media, a process we discussed in Chapter 1, an astronomical amount and array of media content is available almost anywhere and at any time … at least if you are willing to pay for it. But new media technologies are linking us to each other as well as to media content. Smart phones and social networking sites allow us to easily stay in touch or contact with family, friends, and even acquaintances. But *connectivity* should not be confused with a strong sense of community, commitment, and connection. Even as digital media allow for heightened connectivity, they may also be alienating us and undermining the depth of connection we once felt with others.[40] This is due, in part, to the fifth and final characteristic of new media: virtuality.

5   *Virtuality.* New media create and foster intensely engrossing, virtual environments. In using the term virtual, we do not mean to suggest that those environments are in any way fake or unreal. While the digital image of a giraffe on one's computer screen is not an *actual* giraffe, it is nevertheless a very *real* image of a giraffe. In much the same way that a digital image of a giraffe is real, virtual spaces generate real sensations and experiences. When you are speaking with a friend on your smart phone, for instance, the person on the other end of the phone is virtually (though not actually) present. In other words, it *feels* like she or he is there. The simulated, virtual worlds or environments of third-wave media can generate intense sensations and feelings that are every bit as real and consequential as actuality. But since a virtual world is not bound by the constraints of the actual world, new media have

the potential to create virtual experiences that are not possible in the actual world. There are countless examples today where individuals form real relationships with virtual people – people who do not actually exist.

The five characteristics of new media we have just discussed, though radically different than those of modern print media, extend and intensify some dimensions of non-digital electronic media like film, radio, and analog television. We highlight this point because it suggests that the transition from one communication paradigm to another may involve intermediary steps or technologies. Just as chirographic culture served as a bridge between primary orality and modern print culture, televisual culture may have been a bridge between modern print culture and the global network culture of new media.

Logics of third-wave media

The characteristics of digitality, variability, interactivity, connectivity, and virtuality serve to distinguish third-wave media from the print-based media of modernity. The rise of new media and corresponding decline of print media have resulted in a series of seismic social and cultural changes. In the remainder of this chapter, we consider how third-wave media are remaking human consciousness by examining four key logics that underlie new media technologies.

1 *Associational.* The highly linear character of print media favors a mode of information processing rooted in causality and temporality. It invites us to make sense of our world in terms of scientific rationalism, where actions have direct and measurable consequences. Indeed, the scientific method is designed to allow scientists to conduct experiments that determine causality (such as how objects move) in the physical world. In contrast to traditional print media, third-wave media favor non-linear networks, which invite lateral connections and favor an *associational* logic.[41] In a linear system, moving from point A to point C demands passage through point B. But in a dynamic, non-linear system, there are multiple channels or pathways for moving from point A to point C, many of which do not involve point B at all (see Figure 13.1).

  Repeated exposure to non-linear systems such as third-wave media trains the mind to perceive the world spatially rather than temporally: to see the connection among

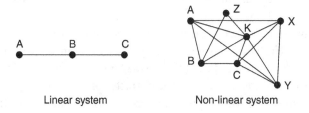

Linear system   Non-linear system

Figure 13.1   Linear and non-linear systems.

individual nodal points as relational, rather than causal. According to Mark Taylor, linear systems produce grids, while non-linear systems produce networks.[42] The difference between the two is evident in the architecture that employs these concepts (see Figures 13.2 and 13.3). In grids, there are borders, straight lines, and a geometric sense of space; in networks, there are flows, curves, and an amorphous sense of space.

The non-linear, relational, associative logic of third-wave media is evident in the practice of *surfing*. One can surf channels on television, surf stations on radio, and surf the internet online. With each generation, surfing becomes an increasingly common way of navigating media and the world. Studies of remote control use, for instance, have found that young viewers are far more likely than older viewers are to "zap:" to switch from one channel to another during a program.[43] Fundamentally, surfing is about "gap jumping" rather than following a straight line. Thanks to the hypertextual structure of the internet, one can jump directly to required information by using a search engine like Google instead of following an outdated linear structure like the Dewey Decimal System.[44] In *Playing the Future*, media guru Douglas Rushkoff argues that the emergence of snowboarding and digital media at about the same time is not coincidental. Snowboarders have internalized the logic of surfing, which they literally embody as they speed down the mountain. For Rushkoff, skiing reflects the old linear logic of print and snowboarding the new non-linear logic of third-wave media.[45]

2   *Contingent.* A second logic promoted by third-wave media is contingent and conditional thinking. This is a rejection of the essentialist and absolutist thinking of modernity. In the modern era, happenings in the world were thought to be governed by a set of immutable laws and universal truths. The printed word had a way of making matters seem settled and beyond dispute. Books, after all, did not readily invite disagreement. If one did disagree with what she or he had read, it was not easy to circulate a counter viewpoint. Even at the start of the broadcast era, the world seemed somehow more certain. Walter Cronkite's famous nightly sign off, "And that's the way it was," indicated a strong belief in the objectivity of "facts." Due to the digitality, variability, and virtuality of new media, however, the world looks far less certain today than it once did. In a Twitter-verse and Wiki-world, where information and data are constantly being updated, extended, contested, and edited, "truth" is viewed as more subjective, situational, and contextual. New media have also contributed to contingent and conditional thinking by collapsing physical distance, thereby exposing audiences to multiple perspectives and points of view. It is increasingly difficult in a global network society to cling to the idea that one has access to ultimate truth because one regularly confronts the conflicting truths of a situation. The contingent logic of new media is evident not just in everyday life, but also in the rise of anti-foundational philosophy, which rejects correspondence theories of truth.[46]

3   *Prosumptive.* The term "prosumer" was first used by Alvin Toffler in 1980 to describe audiences who, thanks to interactive media, are producers as well as consumers.[47] While the closed, static, and directive character of print media privilege a logic of consumption or passive reception, the open, variable, and interactive qualities of new media promote a logic of production or active creation. Instead of consuming

Figure 13.2   Seagram Building and grid architecture. PHILIP GENDREAU/BETTMANN/CORBIS.

Figure 13.3
Guggenheim
Museum and
network architecture.
© Ian Dagnal/Alamy.

media in a uniform manner as intended by the author, users of new media become active co-creators of meanings, texts, and experiences. Though audiences have long been central to the interpretive process, third-wave media make users central not just to the production of meaning, but also to the production of the text – to its direction, development, and duration – and, thus, to experience itself. The digitality of new media further contribute to a prosumptive logic by encouraging users to treat media objects not as fixed and finished, but as mutable bits to be edited, altered, and manipulated. There are countless examples on YouTube today in which users have taken images, music videos, movie clips, and other media and creatively recombined and refashioned them into something unique.

4   *Affective*. While print media rely predominantly on the sense of sight and favor linear, visual space, new media generally appeal to multiple senses (often sound and touch), creating a spherical, acoustic space more like that of orality. But whereas the acoustic space of primary orality was highly communal, the acoustic space of new media tends to be intimate and personal. If you have ever been walking across campus and seen someone walk into another person, tree, or pond while texting, you have witnessed how new media create personal bubbles, or sensual environments, around their users. People listening to their iPods while on public transportation often occupy a private sonic bubble, utterly unaware of their physical surroundings. The interactivity and virtuality of new media create this unusual version of personal acoustic space. Unlike personal visual space, which is exceedingly cognitive, the acoustic space of new media is filled with *affect* or intensities and sensations that work directly on the body. Because we occupy virtual spaces more and more, we are increasingly making sense of the world in embodied, affective ways. In other words, our judgments about the world have less to do with what we *think* about something and more with how we *feel* about something.

Trying to give an account of new media and the ways they restructure human consciousness is a sort of like describing water to fish; it is completely invisible to them, not because it does not exist, but because it *is* their very environment and not merely something in their environment … that and, of course, fish do not understand speech. Nonetheless, to fully appreciate just how profoundly thought is dominated by associative, contingent, prosumptive, and affective modes of knowing today requires careful historical comparison to technologies of the past, and that is the work of medium theorists.

Conclusion

The conclusion to our final perspective, Ecological analysis, offers in many ways a fitting conclusion to the book as a whole. Media Ecology is, after all, about seeing the big picture, about understanding the way that media shape and influence how we process and make sense of our social world. Medium theory has, for many years, been criticized as deterministic, as suggesting too strong a link between communication technologies and the character of human thought and the structure of society. But it is precisely these relationships that medium theory seeks to understand, not uncritically accept. Medium theory does not claim the social changes fueled by communication technologies are causal or unidirectional. It simply insists that the underlying technologies of our social environment are as consequential as its messages. And just as society cannot be reduced exclusively to form or content, nor can critical media studies be reduced to a solitary, universal perspective. We hope the many perspectives presented here affirm that.

MEDIA LAB 12: DOING ECOLOGICAL ANALYSIS

OBJECTIVE

The chief aim of this lab is affirm the principles of Media Ecology by furnishing students with an opportunity to consider the defining characteristics of a media and to inquire into the types of thought reflected by those characteristics.

ACTIVITY

- Divide the class into small groups of 4–5 students each.
- Invite students to select a contemporary communication technology such as the smart phone and then answer the following questions.
    1   What are the key characteristics of this technology?
    2   What "logics" do those characteristics foster?
    3   How has this technology changed or altered society?

SUGGESTED READING

Altheide, D.L. and Snow, R.P. *Media Worlds in the Postjournalism Era*. New York: Aldine de Gruyter, 1991.

Angus, I. *Primal Scenes of Communication: Communication, Consumerism, and Social Movements*. Albany, NY: State University of New York Press, 2000.

Castells, M., Fernández-Ardèvol, M., Qiu, J.L., and Sey, A. *Mobile Communication and Society: a Global Perspective*. Cambridge, MA: The MIT Press, 2007.

Chesebro, J.W. and Bertelsen, D.A. *Analyzing Media: Communication Technologies as Symbolic and Cognitive Systems*. New York: Guildford Press, 1996.

Gronbeck, B.E., Farrell, T.J., and Soukup, P.A. (eds) *Media Consciousness, and Culture: Explorations of Walter Ong's Thought*. Newbury Park, CA: Sage Publications, 1991.

Havelock, E.A. *Preface to Plato*. Cambridge, MA: Harvard University Press, 1982.

Havelock, E.A. *The Muse Learns to Write: Reflections on Orality and Literacy from Antiquity to the Present*. New Haven, CT: Yale University Press, 1988.

Innis, H.A. *The Bias of Communication*. Toronto: University of Toronto Press, 1964.

Innis, H.A. *Empire and Communications*. Toronto: University of Toronto Press, 1972.

Levinson, P. *The Soft Edge: a Natural History and Future of the Information Revolution*. New York: Routledge, 1997.

Levinson, P. *Digital McLuhan: a Guide to the Information Millennium*. New York: Routledge, 1999.

Manovich, L. *The Language of New Media*. Cambridge, MA: The MIT Press, 2001.

McLuhan, M. *The Gutenberg Galaxy: the Making of Typographic Man*. Toronto: University of Toronto Press, 1962.

McLuhan, M. *Understanding Media: The Extensions of Man*. New York: McGraw-Hill Book Company, 1964.

McLuhan, M. and Powers, B.R. *The Global Village: Transformations in World Life and Media in the 21st Century*. New York: Oxford University Press, 1989.

Meyrowitz, J. *No Sense of Place: the Impact of Electronic Media on Social Behavior*. New York: Oxford University Press, 1985.

Meyrowitz, J. Medium Theory. In *Communication Theory Today*, D. Crowley and D. Mitchell (eds), pp. 50–77. Stanford, CA: Stanford University Press, 1994.

Meyrowitz, J. Taking McLuhan and "Medium Theory" Seriously: Technological Change and the Evolution of Education. In *Technology and the Future of Schooling: Ninety-fifth Yearbook of the National Society for the Study of Education. Part II*, S.T. Kerr (ed.), pp. 73–110. Chicago, IL: University of Chicago Press, 1996.

Meyrowitz, J. Multiple Media Literacies. *Journal of Communication* 1998, 48, 96–108.

Ong, W.J. *Orality and Literacy: the Technologizing of the Word*. New York: Routledge, 1982.

Ong, W.J. *The Presence of the Word: Some Prolegomena for Cultural and Religious History*. Binghamton, NY: Global Publications, 2000.

Postman, N. The Reformed English Curriculum. In *High School 1980: the Shape of the Future in American Secondary Education*, A.C. Eurich (ed.), pp. 160–8. New York: Pitman Publishing Corporation, 1970.

Postman, N. *The Disappearance of Childhood*. New York: Vintage Books, 1982.

Postman, N. *Technopoly: the Surrender of Culture to Technology*. New York: Alfred A. Knopf, 1992.

Stephens, M. *The Rise of the Image the Fall of the Word*. New York: Oxford University Press, 1998.

NOTES

1. M.C. Taylor, *The Moment of Complexity: Emerging Network Culture* (Chicago: University of Chicago Press, 2001), 19.

2. N. Postman, The Reformed English Curriculum, in *High School 1980: The Shape of the Future in American Secondary Education*, A.C. Eurich (ed.) (New York: Pitman Publishing Corporation, 1970), 161.

3. J. Meyrowitz, Medium Theory, in *Communication Theory Today*, D. Crowley and D. Mitchell (eds) (Stanford, CA: Stanford University Press, 1994), 50.

4. Meyrowitz, Medium Theory, 53.

5. Meyrowitz, Medium Theory, 51.

6. Meyrowitz, Medium Theory, 52.

7. H.A. Innis, *Empire and Communications* (Toronto: University of Toronto Press, 1972), 7.

8. I. Angus, *Primal Scenes of Communication: Communication, Consumerism, and Social Movement* (Albany, NY: State University of New York Press, 2000), 20.

9. Innis, 7.

10. Innis, 7.

11. Innis, 14.

12. Innis, 15.

13. Innis, 15.

14. Innis, 25.

15. T.J. Farrell, An Overview of Walter Ong's Work, in *Media, Consciousness, and Culture: Explorations of Walter Ong's Thought*, B.E. Gronbeck, T.J. Farrell, and P.A. Soukup (eds) (Newbury Park, CA: Sage Publications, 1991), 27.

16. M. McLuhan, *The Gutenberg Galaxy: the Making of Typographic Man* (Toronto: University of Toronto Press, 1962), 1.

17. Meyrowitz, Medium Theory, 52.

18. M. McLuhan, *Understanding Media: the Extensions of Man* (New York: McGraw-Hill Book Company, 1964), 8–9.

19. McLuhan, *Understanding Media*, 22–3.

20. P. Levinson, *Digital McLuhan: a Guide to the Information Millennium* (New York: Routledge, 1999), 106.

21. E. Carpenter and M. McLuhan, Acoustic Space, *Explorations in Communication*, E. Carpenter and M. McLuhan (eds) (Boston: Beacon Press, 1960), 65–70.

22. M. McLuhan and E. McLuhan, *Laws of Media: the New Science* (Toronto: University of Toronto Press, 1988), 33.

23. McLuhan and McLuhan, 33.

24. McLuhan and McLuhan, 33.

25. McLuhan and McLuhan, viii, 98–9.

26. McLuhan, *Understanding Media*, 7.

27. M. McLuhan and B.R. Powers, *The Global Village: Transformations in World Life and Media in the 21st Century* (New York: Oxford University Press, 1989), 171.

28. W.J. Ong, *The Presence of the Word: Some Prolegomena for Cultural and Religious History* (Binghamton, NY: Global Publications, 2000), 17.

29. Ong, *The Presence*, 111.

30. W.J. Ong, *Orality and Literacy: the Technologizing of the Word* (New York: Routledge, 1982), 1.

31. Ong, *Orality*, 32.

32. Ong, *Orality*, 33.

33. Ong, *Orality*, 37–57.

34. Ong, *Orality*, 41.

35. Ong, *Orality*, 136.

36. B.E. Gronbeck, The Rhetorical Studies Tradition and Walter J. Ong: Oral-Literacy Theories of Mediation, Culture, and Consciousness, in *Media, Consciousness, and Culture: Explorations of Walter Ong's Thought*, B.E. Gronbeck, T.J. Farrell, and P.A. Soukup (eds) (Newbury Park, CA: Sage Publications, 1991), 15.

37. A. Toffler, *The Third Wave* (New York: William Morrow and Company, 1980).

38. N. Negroponte, *Being Digital* (New York: Vintage Books, 1995), 14.

39. L. Manovich, *The Language of New Media* (Cambridge, MA: The MIT Press, 2001), 36.

40. See S. Turkle, *Alone Together: Why We Expect More from Technology and Less from Each Other* (New York: Basic Books, 2011).

41. D.D. Cali, The Logic of the Link: the Associative Paradigm in Communication Criticism, *Critical Studies in Media Communication* 2000, 17, 401.

42. M.C. Taylor, *The Moment of Complexity: Emerging Network Culture* (Chicago, IL: University of Chicago Press, 2001), 19–46.

43. R.V. Bellamy Jr and J.R. Walker, *Television and the Remote Control: Grazing on a Vast Wasteland* (New York: Guilford Press, 1996), 97; see also J.W. Chesebro and D.A. Bertelsen, *Analyzing Media: Communication Technologies as Symbolic and Cognitive Systems* (New York: Guildford Press, 1996), 134.

44. On this point, see M. Heim, *The Metaphysics of Virtual Reality* (Oxford: Oxford University Press, 1993), 34–9.

45. D. Rushkoff, *Playing the Future: How Kids' Culture Can Teach Us to Thrive in an Age of Chaos* (New York: HarperCollins, 1996), 15–16.

46. R. Rorty, *Contingency, Irony, and Solidarity* (New York: Cambridge University Press, 1989), 5.

47. Toffler, 406.

14 Conclusion: the Partial Pachyderm

KEY CONCEPTS

CULTURE JAMMING
MEDIA LITERACY
MEDIA REFORM

We begin with a rather obscure American poet: John Godfrey Saxe. Saxe was born in Vermont in 1816 and worked throughout his life as a lawyer and newspaper editor in addition to writing poetry. His most famous rhyme (indeed, his only famous piece of work at all) is a poem titled "The Blind Men and the Elephant," a retelling of a classic Indian fable. The poem opens in India with six blind men approaching an elephant in order to better understand what the animal looks like as a whole. The fact that these men, presumably, have lived their entire lives in India but have never encountered an elephant prior to this occasion is not addressed. The first man approaches the elephant and, feeling the side of the creature with his hands, proclaims to the others that the elephant is best understood as something like a living wall: rough, hard, and very large. The second man, eager to join the first, happens to grasp onto the elephant's tusk instead of its side. As a result, he loudly disputes the first man's claim and says that the elephant is *really* more like a spear: smooth, pointy, and sharp. Each of the other four men approach the elephant in succession, and each provides his own interpretation of what an elephant *really* looks like: a snake (when grasping the animal's trunk), a tree (when touching its legs), a fan (when caressing its large ears), and a rope (when holding onto its tail). An argument ensues. Saxe concludes the poem by imparting a moral to the reader regarding the pitfalls of perception:

> So oft in theologic wars,
> The disputants, I ween,
> Rail on in utter ignorance
> At what each other mean,
> *And prate about an Elephant*
> *Not one of them have seen!*[1]

Critical Media Studies: An Introduction, Second Edition. Brian L. Ott and Robert L. Mack.
© 2014 John Wiley & Sons, Inc. Published 2014 by John Wiley & Sons, Inc.

At this point you may be asking, what does an elephant have to do with approaches to critical media studies? Beyond the fact that both can, in certain circumstances, crush an eager individual new to the field, Saxe's poem provides an important allegory for a metatheoretical approach to media studies. If we replace the word "theologic" with "theoretical" in Saxe's concluding stanza, we arrive at a fairly useful warning for anyone engaging in the critical study of contemporary media. Despite what the individual theorists addressed in this book may think, no single approach covered in these pages is the correct or best interpretation of this strange creature we call the media. Instead, each represents one way of grasping the media to better understand a certain part. Marxist analysis, Rhetorical analysis, and Reception analysis can each only tell us so much about the role of the media in society, and confusing any individual part for the whole only closes down inquiry, misrepresents phenomena, and stunts the growth of the field overall.

Thus, we conclude this theoretical adventure by looking again at the widely disparate approaches to media studies in an attempt to synthesize them into an entire "elephant." The fact that each approach "discovers" a different part of the mass media does not mean that they are all distinct or mutually exclusive. We contend that a critical understanding of the media is useful to the extent that it recognizes the interconnectedness of the various approaches and traditions represented here. Useful knowledge comes from the understanding that all of the parts of the media, from tusk to tail, are deeply intertwined and influence one another. Only by recognizing this fact can we begin to think of ways to apply the critique of media to issues of media reform. Toward this end, the first part of this concluding chapter provides a critical overview of the different approaches discussed in this book, with particular attention to their intersections and various combinations. The second extends these critical ideas to the ways in which individuals are transforming how we interact with the mass media through pedagogy, activism, and new media outlets.

Critical Media Studies: an Overview

We opened this textbook by considering the very basic function of the media as a source of knowledge for human beings. Much of what we know about the world we live in comes to us in mediated forms, rather than through the direct experience of different phenomena. At this point, if you have read through our entire book (or even if you only poached from select chapters), you now know something about the mass media that you did not know before. An understanding of Sociological analysis, for example, came to you not by ruminating on a bodily response you had to media text, but *through* the medium of this very book. In an image-saturated society like our own, the acquisition of knowledge through the media is becoming more and more common. As such, it is important to understand the multiple, often conflicting ways of analyzing the mass media. We divided this analysis into three parts: theories of media industries, media messages, and media audiences.

Approaches to media industries

If pressed to identify the legs of our mass media elephant, we would be tempted to offer the various theoretical approaches to media industries as a possible answer. As the oldest and longest-standing strand of critical media studies (dating back to the work of the Frankfurt School in 1923), approaches to media industries are often the base of the traditions that followed them, if only as implied and "incorrect" perspectives to which more recent traditions respond and critique. To say that these approaches are the base of critical media studies is not to imply that they are any more or less correct than the other approaches. Instead, approaches to media industries represent the first time scholars and theorists took the mass media as a serious and important force in everyday life. As such, these perspectives inaugurated the discipline of critical media studies and deserve to be called the base of contemporary critique and analysis. We divided the study of industries into three different approaches: Marxist analysis, Organizational analysis, and Pragmatic analysis.

Marxist analysis. The section on media industries began with Marxist analysis, or a focus on the role of economic exchange and the profit-motive on the structure of the media industry and the content that mass outlets produce. Following the canonical work of Karl Marx, Marxist scholars look at the ways in which the economic base of a society influences – or, in classic/vulgar Marxism, actually determines – the make-up of its cultural superstructure. Marxist media critics contend that those who control the means of media production (the Big Six corporations that own the vast majority of media outlets) shape the look and form of media content to secure their continued profit and economic domination. In addition to this ever-present goal, carried out through strategies of profit maximization like joint ventures and the logic of safety, the capitalist profit-motive and the media content it inspires have important consequences for our daily lives. Marxist scholars reveal how the economic logic of media industries, in turn, restricts the possibility of variation and diversity in media content. This is a vital connection between Marxist scholars and the ideological work of Cultural analysis (Chapter 6). Though Marxist critics disagree with their Cultural counterparts over the *source* and primacy of ideological power, or the ability to enforce one's personal interpretation as the standard for "reality," both camps agree that the concept of ideology is an important lens of interpretation when it comes to studying the mass media.

Organizational analysis. The next chapter in the media industries section, Organizational analysis, concentrated on the ways that the matrix of hierarchies and relationships present in any media industry influences the production of its content. In other words, Organizational media scholars contend that the economy is but one factor in a larger nexus of interconnected pieces that make up a media industry. The chapter undertook an in-depth case study of contemporary news organizations as a way of understanding this perspective. The news, far from standing as an objective account of the most important events happening on any given day, is in fact shaped by the norms and practices of the organization that produces it. The fact that a newspaper must fill its pages every day regardless of the day's actual events, or the fact that a journalist covers and reports on a particular beat even if nothing really happens in that sphere of society, begins to point out how issues of process and professionalization color the supposedly factual news. Organizational analysis is an important extension of Marxist analysis because it reveals how an industry, though based in economic necessity, can begin to run on its own cultural conventions somewhat divorced from the capitalist profit-motive.

Pragmatic analysis. We concluded the section on media industries with Pragmatic analysis, an original perspective by which to assess federal and self-regulation of these industries. While many authors consider this very important area of analysis through the lenses of politics or history, we feel that the philosophy of pragmatism and its focus on consequences and contingencies is a more appropriate and fruitful lens of assessment. By evaluating a media regulation – be it the US Telecommunications Act of 1996 or the broadcast of indecent content – through pragmatic standards of truth or "goodness," scholars can come to a better understanding of quality media control in contemporary life. This chapter also considered the always-current debate over violence in the media as an important case study in Pragmatic analysis, especially because so much of the debate relies upon the perceived effect of mediated violence on children. Though the debate is long from over, we hope that other scholars find our particular application of Pragmatic philosophy to be a productive springboard for the way we understand media regulation in the years to come.

Approaches to media messages

The next content section, on media messages, could be likened to the *body* of our theoretical elephant. When people refer to "the mass media" in casual conversation, they are often referring to the variety and circulation of media messages and images: in a word, texts. Textual analysis has represented the bulk of critical media studies throughout its history in academic institutions around the world, but the project of understanding how the mass media paint reality is a complicated one, housing many different theoretical perspectives. Thus, while a close inspection of our creature's hide reveals a rough, bumpy, and diverse surface, these peaks and valleys are unified in their approach to analyzing issues of media representation and its subsequent influence. We divided our study of messages into five different approaches: Rhetorical analysis, Cultural analysis, Psychoanalytic analysis, Feminist analysis, and Queer analysis.

Rhetorical analysis. The first approach we considered in understanding media messages is Rhetorical analysis, the study of how the artful and purposeful combination of signs works to move audiences toward particular ends. In their most basic form, all texts can be conceived of as an association of signifying words and images. By understanding their specific combination, as well as noticing what signs are *not* present in the text, Rhetorical critics reveal how a text functions to persuade audiences to feel certain ways or to undertake particular actions. Although this approach dates back to the ancient Greek art of oratory, this chapter presented a number of different ways to understand the association between signs: clusters, form, genre, narrative, and affect.

The textual "building block" approach of Rhetorical analysis outlined in this chapter is its key contribution to other areas of media studies. Assessing original audience meanings in Reception analysis, for example, would not be possible without first understanding *how* a text comes to signify meaning at all.

Cultural analysis. One of the longest-standing traditions of media analysis is the study of how texts embody and transmit ideology, the primary focus of Cultural analysis and the academic "interdiscipline" of Cultural studies. Ideology and the various forms it takes – myth, doxa, and hegemony – are implicit in any culture, and media texts are a primary site of ideological construction and reinforcement. Cultural studies scholars, in turn, deconstruct texts for the ways that they normalize relations of power between ideological subjects, which marks Cultural studies as the first of the many political approaches to media texts we cover in this book. This chapter focused primarily on the media representation of class and race as a way of practically understanding this approach, but in reality Cultural studies is interested in media representations associated with any axis of social power: race, class, gender, sexuality, age, disability, etc. In this way, the Cultural studies focus on the textual negotiation of power between social groups becomes a crucial framework in both Feminist and Queer analysis (Chapters 8 and 9, respectively). In addition, Cultural studies' tendency to elevate subordinate groups also becomes an important way to center media audiences, a project fully developed in Reception analysis (Chapter 10). Because of these various connections with other traditions, Cultural analysis and Cultural studies are virtual juggernauts in the field of critical media studies.

Psychoanalytic analysis. The midpoint in our discussion of media messages delved into the esoteric world of Psychoanalysis and its special convergence with film. Like Marxist analyses of the media, Psychoanalytic analysis adapts theory from an outside discipline to the realm of critical media studies. The developmental theories of Sigmund Freud and Jacques Lacan help media scholars understand how issues of human drive and desire manifest in relation to the movie theater and the cinematic image, as well as to other forms of media in certain instances. Though perhaps the most theoretically obtuse of all the approaches discussed in this section, Psychoanalytic analysis provides a truly unique perspective on the role of desire and bodily pleasures in the consumption of media. As a result, this chapter diverged from other perspectives by de-emphasizing the meaning of symbols and instead concentrating on the unconscious appeal of texts through notions of regression, scopophilia, and fantasy. We can, then, see echoes of psychoanalysis in Erotic analysis (Chapter 12) and its own focus on the audience's very somatic response to the media.

Feminist analysis. The next approach we considered in our understanding of media messages was Feminist analysis. A Feminist approach to media concentrates on how texts can frame ideological categories of gender as biological or natural constants. Feminists seek to disrupt systems of sexism and patriarchal power that reify gender roles and privilege the needs, desires, and interests of men in society to the detriment of women. "Feminism" is a historically fluid term often contested and demonized in the popular consciousness, and this chapter demonstrates the complexity of Feminist analysis through its consideration of stereotypical media representations of both femininity *and* masculinity, as well as the role of the postfeminist sensibility in contemporary media. These two concepts are important to a general Feminist analysis of media, but the various specific strands of feminist theory not discussed here (including Womanism, Ecofeminism, and Power Feminism, among others) provide an arsenal of critical tools for media scholars. Like Cultural analysis and Queer analysis (Chapters 6 and 9), Feminist analysis reminds us that mass mediated images are often partial or biased in some way. This is an important quality to remember when engaging in Sociological analysis (Chapter 11) or other approaches concerned with the actions audiences take on the basis of media representations.

Queer analysis. The final chapter in the section on media messages looked at the approach of Queer analysis. Like Feminists with gender, Queer theorists analyze the ways in which media texts represent and normalize issues of sexuality as a basis for critique and social transformation. The political project of Queer theory intentionally eschews easy definition. It is the embodiment of a disruptive and elusive ambiguity that shatters social binaries and the ideological powers they maintain; "queerness" is a radical rejection of categories in relation to sexuality. This chapter looked at the notion of queerness in two different ways. The first considered stereotypical representations of heterosexuality and homosexuality in the media, looking at how each supported systems of heteronormativity that, in turn, render the categories coherent. The second considered the role of camp and the fourth persona in investing media texts with queer (if typically hidden) experiences. Taken together, these two sections give some form to a purposefully formless approach, and in them we can see the critical overlap between Queer analysis and other political projects (Cultural and Feminist analysis most notably).

Approaches to media audiences

Recalling our elephant metaphor again, approaches to understanding media audiences would likely form the various appendages of our theoretical beast. Widespread, serious studies of the audience did not really begin in earnest until the 1970s, and in many ways these approaches represent the most shifting and mutable areas of study today. In fact, the final two chapters in this section represent our own syntheses of widely disparate theories into coherent traditions of audience studies. This indicates that approaches to media audiences are more fluid and ill-defined than their industry or textual counterparts. At the same time, we contend that audience studies are more uniquely communicative than either industry- or message-based approaches because they bring to the fore all of the classic aspects of human communication: signs and symbols, of course, but also feedback, perception, and environment. This is the reason we associate audience approaches with the ears, tail, and trunk of our elephant: these are the dynamic, shifting appendages that mark the elephant as a unique creature. We divided our study of audiences into four different approaches: Reception analysis, Sociological analysis, Erotic analysis, and Ecological analysis.

Reception analysis. Our first approach to the audience was Reception analysis, a tradition that takes the audience as the primary site of meaning-making in relation to the media. Rather than analyze the economic underpinnings of a media text or investigate the power relations it reinscribes, Reception scholars seek to understand the meanings that actual individuals make out of the media texts they consume every day. They recognize that media producers may intend a text to mean something in particular, but they also point out that audiences may come to understand it in a radically different way. This chapter addressed many different theories of meaning – including the encoding/decoding process, polysemy/polyvalence, and interpretive communities – before looking at observational ethnography and memory as two primary means of gathering data regarding audience perception. Reception theorists and ethnographers both challenge the traditional understanding of the audiences as a passive, vulnerable mass at the whims of the media, and they lay a foundation for the type of work on individual pleasure central to Erotic analysis (Chapter 12).

Sociological analysis. Close in spirit to Reception analysis, our chapter on Sociological analysis considered not only the meanings that audiences create in relation to the mass media, but also how audiences utilize media to help manage interactions with others and negotiate aspects of their daily lives. These include dramaturgy (where media function as avenues of public presentation and offer different social roles to "try on"), frame analysis (where media offer selective interpretations of events that guide perceptions of collective experience), and equipment for living (where media provide tools for the symbolic resolution of guilt and other conflicts inherent to social interaction). Most importantly, the undercurrent of symbolic interactionism in Sociological analysis reminds us that people act toward a thing on the basis of meanings assigned to it, *not* on what the thing is actually. Media are increasingly common outlets to which audiences turn in order to make meaning today, and as a result Sociological analysis illuminates how the ideological concerns of Marxist and Cultural analysis (Chapters 2 and 6) might be activated and enacted on a micro-level.

Erotic analysis. The third approach to the audience we considered, and one that is original to this book, is called Erotic analysis. Erotic analysis takes the twin notions of pleasure and resistance as central components in attempting to understand how audiences consume media. Positioning themselves in opposition to Marxist approaches to media, scholars employing an Erotic perspective understand pleasure as a transient but powerful force on the part of media consumers. This chapter discussed two ways that transgressive pleasure may appear in relation to the media. The first is the transgressive text, where "writerly" and carnivalesque texts grant audiences experiences and abilities otherwise uncommon in mainstream media. The second is the transgressive practices of audience, where audiences rework mainstream media texts to various degrees through interpretative play, user participation, and cultural production. Erotic engagements of the media provide a form of resistance that, while often highly individual and fleeting, allows users to escape the system of meaning and power outlined by all of the other critical perspectives. As such, Erotic analysis is a comment upon and important derivation from classic conceptions of the audience and the entire field of media studies.

Ecological analysis. We concluded the section on media audiences with a largely epochal perspective called Ecological analysis. More than an analysis of how the media function as important aspects of our contemporary environment, Media Ecology considers how the media *are* our environment, effectively creating the world in which people live. Work collectively known as Medium theory (represented here by Innis, McLuhan, and Ong) reveals how changes in communication technology have historically altered the ways people interact and interpret reality. In contrast to previous ages ushered in by technologies of orality and literacy, today's digital and electronic technologies have created a largely connected and interactive globe, one that endorses logics of association over linearity and contingency over absolutism. Moreover, the necessarily wide scope of Ecological analysis provides a novel way of reflecting on issues surrounding media industry and representation. While a Marxist may claim, for example, that economic factors largely shape the look of the media, a media ecologist would counter that the very structure of the state (and therefore the economy) is a result of the media technology of the age. Media, then, create the look and logic of each historical moment.

Applied Media Studies

As we have just reviewed, this textbook outlines twelve different approaches to the critical study of media. Now it is finally time to see what we can *do* with them. We have seen inklings of application in the media labs at the end of every chapter, but, really, what can we do in the world outside of the classroom with these theories? Why do they matter, and what is the point of a class on critical media studies anyway? This section, on the translation of media studies into social action, addresses three possible "things" to do with media theory: education, resistance, and reform. Each course of action grounds the abstract understanding of media theory in political struggles for meaning and change. As the novelist and poet Edith Wharton famously wrote, "There are two ways of spreading light: to be the candle or the mirror that reflects it."[2] If we consider the theoretical traditions outlined in these pages as the candles of critical media studies (and the light our own understanding of media), then the following three projects are the various ways of potentially acting as mirrors.

Media literacy

A difficult concept to pin down, **media literacy** broadly refers to any learning opportunity that increases an individual's understanding of how the mass media function. W. James Potter frames media literacy as a source of individual empowerment:

> Becoming more media literate gives you a much clearer perspective to see the border between your real world and the world manufactured by the media. When you are

media literate, you have clear maps to help you navigate better in the media world so that you can get to those experiences and information you want without becoming distracted by those things that are harmful to you.[3]

To be media literate, then, is to possess the dual understandings of how the mass media function *and* how those modes of operation have bearing on one's daily life. As society relies more and more on media to transmit information or share values, a critical awareness of the media – as well as the interaction between individuals and wider cultural contexts – is becoming increasingly important.

In reviewing current literature in the field, two major themes or conceptions of media literacy become apparent. The first is an emphasis on media *production* as a way of learning about how mass media generate and circulate messages. This interpretation of media literacy often takes the form of adolescent educational programs that allow young adults to record their own media messages. In creating their own media texts, adolescents learn about the kinds of decisions which all media creators face: how to tell a story, how to represent an idea, how to attract an audience, etc. The experience, especially if supplemented with critical inquiry or reflection, educates young people about the constraints of media production and its subsequent influence on representation and reception. A school's morning announcements or radio station can serve as an important learning site for understanding how to prioritize newsworthy information or build a station identity.[4] Classroom video projects reveal to young film makers how processes like editing change the ways audiences interpret messages.[5] Whatever the medium, this type of media literacy encourages young people to view the media as an active, participatory social outlet rather than as a distant, confusing network beyond their control. It also supplies them with a cursory understanding of how the media operate as a symbolic or cultural form.

Such an understanding of the symbolic codes, logics, and powers present in the media is central to the second major approach to media literacy. From this vantage, media literacy represents the acquisition of explicitly critical tools in relation to aspects of media production, circulation, and reception. This textbook is firmly in line with this second strand of media literacy. By equipping you with different perspectives regarding power in the media (economic, ideological, or otherwise), this book increases your ability to understand the media in all its various forms and functions. You are now, in some ways, media literate: congratulations! Moreover, you are probably reading this text because you are enrolled in a college class organized around the theme of the media. Classes like your own are becoming increasingly common around the world and show much success in teaching students to carefully discern the structures and effects of contemporary media.[6] Likewise, recent studies show that general audience instruction in these critical perspectives can influence perceptions of race and gender stereotypes, as well as impressions of violence.[7] In short, then, this type of media literacy, inside or outside of the classroom, focuses on teaching the ideas one might conceive of as the "critical media tradition" in higher education.

Although this second approach to literacy is perhaps more cerebral or scholarly than the concurrent, "hands-on" focus of the production route, both interpretations represent the real-world application of critical media theories in appropriate contexts. The original generation of media content and the creation of college media courses are both productive responses to theoretical understandings of the media. Both represent important nodes of convergence between knowledge of the media and the *dissemination* of knowledge of the media. Overall, it may be best to understand media literacy projects as the distillation of abstract theory into concrete, localized activities and seminars, educating individuals on why the media matters (or should matter) to them.

Culture jamming

Near the end of his most widely known work, *Society of the Spectacle*, Guy Debord makes a curious statement on the role of plagiarism in contemporary culture:

> Ideas improve. The meaning of words participates in the involvement. Plagiarism is necessary. Progress implies it. It embraces an author's phrase, makes use of his expressions, erases a false idea, and replaces it with the right idea.[8]

Debord's interpretation of plagiarism as the appropriation and refashioning of pre-existing signs into the "right idea" is at the heart of the second area of media application we consider: culture jamming. **Culture jamming** is the use of familiar media symbols and channels to reveal and overturn the consumerist or capitalist ideologies they embody. Like media literacy, culture jamming is difficult to describe succinctly, and many scholars conceive of it in different ways. For example, Michael R. Solomon positions it as a strategy "that aims to disrupt efforts by the corporate world to dominate our cultural landscape."[9] Tim Jordan calls jamming "an attempt to reverse and transgress the meaning of cultural codes whose primary aim is to persuade us to buy something or be someone," a sort of "semiotic terrorism."[10] In all cases, culture jamming refers to the individual or organized effort to turn mass media messages against the media itself.

The organization Adbusters is perhaps the most visible example of culture jamming. A self-proclaimed "global network of artists, activists, writers, pranksters, students, educators and entrepreneurs" whose aim it is to "topple existing power structures and forge a major shift in the way we live in the 21st century,"[11] the Canadian-based Adbusters culture jams primarily through advertisement parody. For example, in the "Spoof Ads" section on the organization's website, users can browse a variety of images which call into question the social importance or benevolence of corporations. One features a runner in fluorescent Nike apparel sipping on a large convenience-store soda. The accompanying tagline, following the curve of a huge day-glo Nike "swoosh," reads "Just Douche It." Another ad depicts a hospital operating room with a patient open on the table. In the foreground of the ad, a heart monitor reveals the familiar McDonald's Golden Arches imbedded in the jagged cardiac line. These "subvertisments," as the organization sometimes calls them, refashion familiar media codes and symbols to criticize big business practices.

In her 2004 article, "Pranking Rhetoric: 'Culture Jamming' as Media Activism," however, Christine Harold questions the effectiveness of parody as a jamming form.[12] Pointing out that parody "perpetuates a commitment to rhetorical binaries [and] the hierarchical form it supposedly wants to upset,"[13] she instead proposes "pranking" as an effective form of culture jamming. Media pranking, or actions that "playfully and provocatively [fold] existing cultural forms in on themselves,"[14] disrupts the *original/commentary* dichotomy that parody relies upon and inspires a deeper reflection in those who witness it. Harold cites the famous Barbie/G.I. Joe computer chip switch as an example of pranking. Just before the winter holiday shopping season of 1989, media pranksters referring to themselves the Barbie Liberation Organization purchased hundreds of electronic "talking" Barbie and G.I. Joe dolls. Members of the BLO spent weeks removing the talking computer chips from the figures and switching them so that the Barbie dolls played messages of death and destruction while the G.I. Joes discussed shopping and fashion. The group then proceeded to return every doll to the stores, causing a very confusing Christmas morning for thousands of American children. To make sure their prank reached the maximum number of audiences, the BLO included messages inside the packing of each returned doll that urged consumers to contact their local media about the switch. The organization also prepared news packages about their work and intentions and disseminated them to local news outlets when the prank broke. Harold contends that this kind of pranking, whose coherent message' only comes later and with much reflection, serves to subvert media resources far more effectively than exercises in parody.

At the same time, some scholars continue to see parody as an important form of culture jamming, especially in relation to "jamming" other forms of culture like the political sphere. In her 2007 article, "Political Culture Jamming: the Dissident Humor of *The Daily Show with Jon Stewart*," Jamie Warner argues that the satirical form of Comedy Central's *The Daily Show* jams the branding practices inherent to US politics.[15] Because politicians have begun to employ the same kinds of marketing and image-management strategies of corporate advertisers, Warner contends that culture jamming can be equally applied to the political landscape as an effective means of critique. Jon Stewart's "fake" news program uses the same production conventions as "real" news programs (graphic montages, interviews, and packaged stories with correspondents), but it juxtaposes this form with humorous and scathingly critical interpretations of global politics. This creates a sense of incongruity between form and content, an important platform from which viewers can understand the conflation of marketing and politics in contemporary society. Drawing upon the work of Cultural studies scholar Stuart Hall, Warner claims that any type of incongruity is powerful because it represents danger, taboo, and threats to the cultural order. In essence, parody *is* powerful because it taps into and challenges our unquestioned ideas about the symbolic world in which we live.

Obviously, the debate over the power of parody in relation to culture jamming is ongoing. What is important to glean from these examples for the purposes of this chapter is the very *active* nature of culture jamming itself. If approaches to media theory provide the ability to critique mass media industries, texts, and reception practices, then culture jamming is the messy and living fusion of all these perspectives into real-world activism and action. Culture jamming efforts, especially widespread ones like the Barbie prank or *The Daily Show*, which reach many people, extend the highly academic work of media scholars into the public sphere and daily life. Though far less organized or sanctioned (or even, in some instances, legal) than media literacy programs, culture jamming is also far more visible, dynamic, and exciting in most instances. Culture jamming is an important link between the realm of ideas and the realm of action, and it represents some of the most vibrant phenomena in media studies today.

Media reform

The summer of 2003 will go down in history as host to one of the most significant examples of widespread citizen involvement in governmental media policy ever.[16] Alarmed by Federal Communications Commission (FCC) deregulatory policies and galvanized by watchdog groups like Free Press and MoveOn.org (in addition to publicly dissenting members of the FCC itself), millions of Americans opposed what they saw as reckless and dangerous moves by the FCC to promote increased monopoly ownership of media industries. Journalists and Hollywood union members also voiced their discontent with the FCC's free-market logic, claiming that journalistic integrity and media content suffer when fewer companies own more media outlets. In many cases the FCC, which had anticipated an easy fight for deregulation against a largely apathetic public, found themselves ducking out of public meetings and avoiding an increasingly angry citizenry. Responding to this sudden spike in policy interests among everyday individuals, the Senate overturned the FCC's rules changes in September 2003 by a 55:40 vote. In late June 2004, the Third Circuit Court of Appeals in Philadelphia reinforced the Senate's position when it soundly rejected the FCC's attempts to deregulate the industry.[17]

The events of 2003 represent a fairly recent example of a growing citizen interest in media reform. **Media reform** refers to any efforts by citizens and citizens' interest groups to effect change in the structure and operation of mass media industries. Although the issues involved in media reform are wide, they usually concentrate on increased transparency of media operation and increased accountability of industries to matters of public interest (see Chapter 4, Pragmatic analysis, for a discussion of the role of public interest in the media). In the words of Robert W. McChesney, President of Free Press and vehement supporter of media reform, once people understand "media as a policy issue…all bets are off. Organized people can defeat organized money."[18] Thus, media reform represents something of a median between practices of media literacy and culture jamming. It blends together the structured and organized channels of media literacy with the radical zeal and spirit of culture jamming.

One of the most apparent manifestations of contemporary media reform is the current increase of alternative media outlets. For example, the growing Indymedia movement represents more than 150 global and fairly autonomous Independent Media Centers networked though a central online hub, all of which operate community-based newspapers and other sources of alternative information.[19] In relying on contemporary media technologies like the internet, the Indymedia network "enables activists to appropriate the technologies of globalization to promote access to citizen-produced content."[20] At the same time, the rise of "citizen journalism," or the increase of blogs and other online resources where citizens directly report to other citizens about the state of their world, signals growing dissatisfaction with traditional media outlets and the impulse toward more democratic forms of media.

The focus on media policy, however, is still central to many media reform movements. Rather than attempt to catalog all of the important policy battles in the last 30 years, we will briefly consider the fight over low-power radio (low-power FM, LPFM) as a representative case study of this kind of work. Throughout the 1990s the broadcast of (sometimes pirate) community-based radio programs over short distances on LPFM frequencies became a point of tension between individual citizens and the commercial radio industry, especially after the Telecommunications Act of 1996 increased industry control over radio.[21] In an effort to diffuse this tension and reduce the amount of unlicensed broadcasting by citizens, William Kennard, the chair of the FCC, approved a program in January 2000 that would extend broadcasting licenses for 1,000 LPFM stations to non-profit groups throughout the nation. Many community broadcasters jumped at this opportunity, and more than 3,000 had applied for LPFM licensure by the fall of 2003.[22]

Unfortunately, commercial radio heavyweights like Clear Channel Communications quickly lobbied Congress to block this emerging LPFM movement, claiming that such a proliferation of community radio signals would jam their own high-power signals. Congress responded to these concerns sympathetically and passed the Radio Preservation Act of 2000. The act limited the FCC's ability to license LPFM stations by reducing the number of available frequencies; under the law no LPFM station could legally broadcast within three frequencies of a high-power station. Although a Congressional study found that industry claims of signal jamming were questionable, and despite the lobbying efforts of grassroots media campaigns like the Prometheus Radio Project of Philadelphia,[23] commercial interests ultimately prevailed here, blocking most of the FM spectrum from community use over the following decade. Additionally, FCC content restrictions on the few LPFM stations that remained – such as a ban on supporting political candidates or a 36-hour per week broadcast requirement – forced the structure of community radio "into highly rationalized forms" that in many ways further preserved the "commercial dominance of radio broadcasting."[24] In short, rather than adapting to the needs and preferences of their local audiences, those LPFM stations that survived Congressional intervention ended up looking much like their higher-powered, national counterparts.

These legislative set-backs, however, did not stop lobbying efforts from continuing to fight for citizens' access to LPFM, and throughout the 2000s Congressional representatives sponsored at least three bills attempting to relax restrictions on the format. These efforts finally paid off when President Obama signed the Local Community Radio Act into law in December 2010.[25] The act stipulates that the FCC shall again make LPFM licenses available to non-profit or other community groups, and it allowed the FCC to modify the existing three-frequency distance rule in order to open more of the FM broadcast spectrum to low-power stations. In response to the passage of the act, and for the first time in a decade, the FCC began accepting applications for LPFM broadcast licenses in late 2013.

The struggle over LPFM reveals that media reform movements in the name of citizen access or public interest often face heavy opposition from industry representatives, but by no means is the goal of reform impossible. By inaugurating alternative media or challenging entrenched media policies through legal battles and awareness campaigns, media reformers represent perhaps the most ambitious application of critical media theory. The efforts of media reformists teach us all that the media is not some overwhelming system impossible to comprehend, but rather a complex field of interests and needs which we can engage creatively and persistently in order to build a better tomorrow. Drawing upon media education programs and the "semiotic terrorism" of culture jammers, media reformers are applying their nuanced understanding of media to utterly transform the mediated world in which all of us live. Theirs is a battle over symbols *and* the wires that transmit them, representations *and* the laws that shape them.

As a result, we can see in media reform the point that underlies any application of media theory (and, indeed, the purpose of this concluding chapter): everything in a mediated world is deeply, profoundly interconnected. Knowledge, activism, understanding, and participation are all facets of living in an image-saturated world that cannot afford to ignore one another. Only by understanding the links that exist between nodes in the mediascape, as well as the intersections that *can be made* with the proper training, can any of us hope to begin to talk about this creature we call the media. Only by understanding each part of our elephant as necessarily incomplete but ultimately important can we train the animal to serve our needs during the twenty-first century.

SUGGESTED READING

Carducci, V. Culture Jamming: a Sociological Perspective. *Journal of Consumer Culture* 6, 2006, 116–38.

Gibson, T.A. WARNING—The Existing Media System May Be Toxic to Your Health: Health Communication and the Politics of Media Reform. *Journal of Applied Communication Research* 35, 2007, 125–32.

Gray, J. Television Teaching: Parody, *The Simpsons*, and Media Literacy Education. *Critical Studies in Media Communication* 22, 2005, 223–38.

Harold, C. *OurSpace: Resisting the Corporate Control of Culture*. Minneapolis, MN: University of Minnesota Press, 2009.

Jeong, S., Cho, H., and Hwang, Y. Media Literacy Interventions: a Meta-Analytic Review. *Journal of Communication* 62, 2012, 454–72.

Koltay, T. The Media and the Literacies: Media Literacy, Information Literacy, Digital Literacy. *Media, Culture & Society* 33, 2011, 211–21.

Lasn, K. *Culture Jam.* New York: Quill, 2000.

Livingstone, S. Engaging With Media – a Matter of Literacy? *Communication, Culture & Critique* 1, 2008, 51–62.

Martens, H. Evaluating Media Literacy Education: Concepts, Theories and Future Directions. *Journal of Media Literacy Education* 2, 2010, 1–22.

McChesney, R.W. *Communication Revolution: Critical Junctures and the Future of Media.* New York: The New Press, 2007.

McChesney, R.W., Newman, R., and Scott, B. (eds) *The Future of Media: Resistance and Reform in the 21st Century.* New York: Seven Stories Press, 2005.

McChesney, R.W. and Nichols, J. *The Death and Life of American Journalism: the Media Revolution that Will Begin the World Again.* Philadelphia, PA: Nation Books, 2010.

Potter, W.J. *Media Literacy,* 4th edn. Thousand Oaks, CA: Sage Publications, 2008.

Stengrim, L.A. Negotiating Postmodern Democracy, Political Activism, and Knowledge Production: Indymedia's Grassroots and e-Savvy Answer to Media Oligopoly. *Communication and Critical/Cultural Studies* 2, 2005, 281–304.

Teurlings, J. Media Literacy and the Challenges of Contemporary Media Culture: on Savvy Viewers and Critical Apathy. *European Journal of Cultural Studies* 13, 2010, 359–73.

NOTES

1. J.G. Saxe, The Blind Men and the Elephant: a Hindoo Fable, in *The Poetical Works of John Godfrey Saxe, Household Edition* (New York: Houghton, Mifflin and Company, 1882), 112.

2. E. Wharton, Vesalius in Zante, in *Artemis to Actaeon and Other Verse* (New York: Charles Scribner's Sons, 1909), 23.

3. W.J. Potter, *Media Literacy,* 4th edn (Thousand Oaks, CA: Sage Publications, 2008), 9.

4. For other literacy strategies in relation to radio, see L. Burton, I Heard it on the Radio: Broadcasting in the Classroom, *Screen Education* 50, 2008, 68–73; J. Braman and J. Goldberg, Traditional and Youth Media Education: Collaborating and Capitalizing on Digital Storytelling, *Youth Media Reporter* 5, 2009, 162–5.

5. For other literacy strategies in relation to video, see S. Sobers, Consequences and Coincidences: a Case Study of Experimental Play in Media Literacy, *Journal of Media Practice* 9, 2008, 53–66; L. Charmaraman, Congregating to Create for Social Change: Urban Youth Media Production and Sense of Community, *Learning, Media & Technology* 38, 2013, 102–15.

6. See R.L. Duran, B. Yousman, K.M. Walsh, and M.A. Longshore, Holistic Media Education: as Assessment of the Effectiveness of a College Course in Media Literacy, *Communication Quarterly* 56, 2008, 49–68.

7. S. Ramasubramanian, Media-Based Strategies to Reduce Racial Stereotypes Activated by News Stories, *Journalism & Mass Communication Quarterly* 84, 2007, 249–64; T. Reichert, M.S. LaTour, J.J. Lambiase, and M. Adkins, A Test of Media Literacy Effects and Sexual Objectification in Advertising, *Journal of Current Issues and Research in Advertising* 29, 2007, 81–92; B.E. Pinkleton, E.W. Austin, Y. Chen, and M. Cohen, The Role of Media Literacy in Shaping Adolescents' Understanding of and Responses to Sexual Portrayals in Mass Media, *Journal of Health Communication* 17, 2012, 460–76; T. Webb and K. Martin, Evaluation of a US School-Based Media Literacy Violence Prevention Curriculum on Changes in Knowledge and Critical Thinking Among Adolescents, *Journal of Children and Media* 6, 2012, 430–49.

8. G. Debord, *Society of the Spectacle*, trans. unknown (Detroit, MI: Black and Red, 1983), 207.

9. M.R. Solomon, *Conquering Consumerspace: Marketing Strategies for a Branded World* (New York: American Management Association, 2003), 208.

10. T. Jordan, *Activism! Direct Action, Hacktivism and the Future of Society* (London: Reaktion Books, 2002), 102.

11. About Adbusters, *Adbusters*, www.adbusters.org/about/adbusters (accessed March 1, 2013).

12. C. Harold, Pranking Rhetoric: "Culture Jamming" as Media Activism, *Critical Studies in Media Communication* 21, 2004, 189–211.

13. Harold, 191.

14. Harold, 191.

15. J. Warner, Political Culture Jamming: the Dissident Humor of *The Daily Show with John Stewart, Popular Communication* 5, 2007, 17–36.

16. For an excellent comprehensive summary of the events surrounding citizen involvement in media policy in 2003, see R.W. McChesney, Media Policy Goes to Main Street: the Uprising of 2003, *The Communication Review* 7, 2004, 223–58.

17. S. Labaton, Court Orders FCC to Rethink New Rules on Growth of Media, *The New York Times*, June 25, 2004, A1.

18. R.W. McChesney, The Emerging Struggle for a Free Press, in *The Future of Media: Resistance and Reform in the 21st Century*, R.W. McChesney, R. Newman, and B. Scott (eds), 9–20 (New York: Seven Stories Press, 2005), 19.

19. L.A Stengrim, Negotiating Postmodern Democracy, Political Activism, and Knowledge Production: Indymedia's Grassroots and e-Savvy Answer to Media Oligopoly, *Communication and Critical/Cultural Studies* 2, 2005, 281–304.

20. Stengrim, 283.

21. J. Hamilton, Rationalizing Dissent? Challenging Conditions of Low-Power FM Radio, *Critical Studies in Media Communication* 21, 2004, 44–63.

22. M. Connors, A High Powered Battle, *The News Media and the Law* 27, 2003, 44–5.

23. See McChesney, Media Policy Goes to Main Street, as well as the organization's website, http://www.prometheusradio.org/ (accessed March 22, 2013).

24. Hamilton, 50.

25. See K. Murphy, Power to Low-Power FM, *The Nation*, January 10, 2011, 5. The full text of the Act may be accessed though the Government Printing Office at http://www.gpo.gov/fdsys/pkg/PLAW-111publ371/html/PLAW-111publ371.htm (accessed March 22, 2013).

Appendix: Sample Student Essays

Marxist Analysis

Ian T. Dawe

The Entertainment and Sports Programming Network, better known as ESPN, debuted in 1979 and has, over the course of the last thirty years, become the de facto voice for sports and sports information in the United States, reaching more than 97 million households. According to its website, ESPN provides its viewers with live game footage, roundtable discussions of games and future game-related events, pre- and post-game analysis, and coverage of all major and minor US sports. Reporting on major US sports is the job of *SportsCenter*, ESPN's flagship program. The hour-long program has, since its introduction, gone from airing only once a day to as many as ten times a day. *SportsCenter* is just one element in the ESPN empire, whose online, print, radio, and film arms also have enormous reach. Like its parent company Disney, ESPN is integrated both horizontally and vertically, which means that it has the ability to produce and distribute content across these multiple mediums. As a result of this integration, ESPN has a virtual monopoly in the sports media marketplace, making it a powerful socializing force. ESPN's dominance in sports entertainment furnishes a useful case study for examining the consequences of contemporary patterns of media ownership. In this paper, I argue that the programming on ESPN is governed by three interrelated strategies for profit maximization: the logic of safety, niche marketing/advertising, and synergy.

The logic of safety, or a practice of risk avoidance that focuses on the replication of previously successful formats or ideas (Ott & Mack, 2014, p. 40), is a regular feature of ESPN content. As indicated above, ESPN's flagship program *SportsCenter* now airs as many as ten times a day, allowing viewers to watch spectacular highlights of the day's top plays at almost any hour. The logic here is fairly straightforward. If *SportsCenter* is the network's most popular program, then playing it ten times a day is a safe bet because the repetition ensures that the network will almost always be disseminating something desirable to its viewers. Playing anything else during these slots would be wasting space on something less popular.

Additionally, the majority of ESPN's non-*SportsCenter* televised programming resembles this ubiquitous highlight show. For example, over the course of the day

Critical Media Studies: An Introduction, Second Edition. Brian L. Ott and Robert L. Mack.
© 2014 John Wiley & Sons, Inc. Published 2014 by John Wiley & Sons, Inc.

on both their online and televised platforms, ESPN opinion-editorial programs like *Pardon the Interruption, Morning Call, Around the Horn,* and *By the Numbers* utilize the same highlights from *SportsCenter* while providing additional analysis that their flagship program is unable to include. These programs effectively function as little more than extensions of *SportsCenter*, which means that ESPN generates much of its additional content on the basis of what they know audiences already enjoy about the network. The inclusion of the same in-game highlights across their televised, digital, and filmic programming further exemplifies their "logic of safety" in content development.

A second strategy of profit maximization, niche marketing, also illustrates the impact of ownership on ESPN content. Niche marketing refers to targeting content at "a specific segment of the public that shares particular, but known demographic traits such as age, sex, [or] income" in order to charge a premium to advertisers (Ott & Mack, 2014, p. 48). Because the operative goal of Disney is to return a profit to its shareholders, the practice of developing content that speaks to unique and lucrative audiences is crucial to this end. ESPN attracts a very specific demographic: 71 percent of their viewers are men between the ages of 18 and 54. For advertisers, this audience is a valuable demographic due to the perception of its immense purchasing power. Older men often have higher levels of income compared to other demographic groups, and younger men often have high levels of "disposable" income for entertainment and athletics.

In order to attract this demographic for advertisers and charge a consequently higher price, ESPN produces content that would likely appeal specifically to them. For example, ESPN has developed a highly successful *30 for 30* documentary series in which it highlights notable sports stories over the last thirty years in a filmic format. The series includes films like *The Fab Five*, concerning the legacy of the first all freshman starting five NCAA men's college basketball program, and *Survive and Advance*, the story of the underdog 1983 North Carolina State University NCAA basketball champions, coached by Jim Valvano. Although it is impossible to know who exactly watches these documentaries, it is safe to guess that they are designed for older men who lived through these sports events and younger men who want to learn more about them.

Because ESPN consistently delivers a fairly specific audience to advertisers, and because advertisers have to pay more for space as a result, many advertisements for essentially non-athletic products also take on an athletic angle to increase the appeal and economic return of the promotion. For example, during the content breaks of *Survive and Advance*, viewers are presented with advertisements for many products somehow tied to ESPN or that reference sports and/or sports personalities: the "Miami Project to Cure Paralysis" with Marc and Nick Buoniconti (of The Citadel and Miami Dolphins, respectively); the Bank of America Cash Rewards card that can be used to obtain cash back when buying and attending sporting events; a DirecTV advertisement for "soccer moms"; Mayhem, of Allstate Insurance, laying on the ground after crashing a basketball rim on top of a car after a serious slam dunk; and former NBA Finals MVP (and fifteen-time

All Star) Shaquille O'Neal promoting Gold Bond Men's Ultimate lotion and encouraging viewers to "man up." The advertisements that fill the gaps between other programs also feature typically "masculine" products like Chevrolet vehicles, Nike athletic products, and Coors Light beer. Essentially, the design of "narrowcast" content in turn shapes the look of other content on the network, and ESPN is able to generate a large amount of revenue despite its aim at a very specific section of the market.

Further highlighting the role of the profit motive on ESPN content is the concept of synergy. Synergy refers to "the involvement of multiple subsidiary companies in the cross-development, production, and distribution of a media brand" (Ott & Mack, 2014, p. 37). Due to its horizontal and vertical integration, ESPN is able to promote itself and ensure brand loyalty across many platforms quite effectively. For example, during commercial breaks ESPN television viewers are constantly encouraged to visit ESPN.com and encounter advertisements for programming on additional ESPN platforms (ESPN2, ESPNU, and ESPN Deportes). ESPN's website further refers users to additional platforms such as ESPN podcasts (by notable contributors Bill Simmons and Rick Reilly) and to their highly successful ESPN radio programming featuring programs like *Mike and Mike in the Morning*, *The Herd with Colin Cowherd*, and the *SVP & Russillo* show. When viewed in conjunction with the logic of safety and niche marketing, ESPN's cross-promotional appeals provide a clear example of the impact ownership can have on developed programming. Confusingly, sometimes the content of the network and its various platforms is simply the network and its platforms.

In conclusion, through the use of concepts like the logic of safety, niche marketing, and synergy, an analysis of ESPN illustrates the problematic influence of the profit-motive on developed content. As ESPN and *SportsCenter* primarily highlight the major US American sports for the niche market and bombard these viewers with the same images/stories, a diverse representation of what counts as sport and who can participate in that sport is drastically reduced. ESPN, then, functions as a gatekeeper, specifically selecting what to share with its immense (if narrowed) audience. This process, unfortunately, excludes many other voices and perspectives on contemporary athletics. In addition, given its reach across so many platforms, ESPN's framing of issues significant to collegiate and professional sports today works to socialize audiences into seeing sport-specific issues in certain ways and not others. There are simply few other outlets for news that are as pervasive and accessible as ESPN. In the end, then, ESPN may not just be the de facto voice for sports today, but a voice for exactly what is wrong with contemporary sports programming.

REFERENCES

Ott, B.L. & Mack, R.L. (2014) *Critical Media Studies: an Introduction*, 2nd edn. Malden, MA: Wiley-Blackwell.

Rhetorical Analysis

Mirissa Price

In direct response to the pervasive televised campaigns that now define the United States electoral process (Price, 2011, p. 20), the American public has voiced an increasing distaste for the pugnacious and scantly informative nature of televised political campaigns. At the same time, those advertisements targeted as the source of increasing political cynicism have resulted in an increase in voter turnout and political participation (Fu, Mou, Miller, & Jalette, 2011, p. 47), which suggests that they successfully function at a seemingly unrecognized or affective level. An affective engagement of the United States public was the very tactic employed in the 2012 Barack Obama presidential campaign, best highlighted in his brief, 60-second commercial, "The Choice." In it, President Obama introduces the topic of the upcoming election and outlines opponent Mitt Romney's propositions. Then, with coinciding images depicting education, employment, and green energy development, President Obama explains his own plan for our nation, ultimately positioning the audience as the agent of change for the United States (Organizing for Action, 2012).

However, there are some critical dimensions of the commercial beyond its seemingly informative nature. Through the use of tools like focus and zoom, rapidly paced cuts, second-person narration, and a calming soundtrack, "The Choice" craftily invites the passive viewer into a stimulating experience that awakens a political drive despite any particular ideological affiliation. In fact, in accordance with the rhetorical ideas of progressive form and clustering, one can trace the heightened affective engagement of the viewer through three steps: (1) a simple greeting, to (2) an association of political signs, to (3) a concluding call to action.

Following Kenneth Burke, Ott and Mack (2014) define progressive form as "the way a story advances step by step, each step following logically from the previous step" (p. 119). Because audiences are socialized to enjoy presentations with a clear and interrelated beginning, middle, and end, presentations that embody such a progressive form have a much better chance of appealing to viewers. Providing an audience a beginning and middle whets their appetite for the most logical end. Each section of this progressive form may also be further structured by clusters, or ways in which "individual signs are associated with and dissociated from one another" (p. 117) in a text. By clustering together specific signs or objects in the beginning, middle, and end of a presentation, and also by purposefully leaving out signs and objects in these sections, a person who generates a presentation can greatly influence the audience's perception of its subject matter.

When "The Choice" begins, President Obama is seated in a living room. Although viewers know that he is speaking to them from a distance, the rhetorical artistry of camera focus and zoom makes for a far more intimate presence. A soft focus here selectively directs the viewer's attention to the President. This technique directly manipulates the viewer's emotional or affective state, as the loss of focus inspires a longing to remove the frame and simply view the President clearly. As if responding to such a request and assuming the viewer's perspective, the camera gradually zooms inward toward the President at an eye-level view that appears to place the viewer in the direct company of the President's image. A soothing blue background and an instrumental, non-intrusive soundtrack lend a sense of tranquility to the scene. Therefore, in the beginning of the commercial, the clustering of the President's intimate image, the blue background, and the music transform him into a figure of tranquility and transition the viewer to a state of feeling both calm and connected.

Quickly, though, the middle of the commercial heightens to a tempo that awakens a political vigor in the viewer. As an interesting disassociation from the calming first part of the advertisement, the transitions between shots grow increasingly rapid in accordance with the President's growing excitement for his message here: the foreseen progress of the United States upon his re-election. This pacing alone, though, could not enliven the same reaction in every viewer. Rather, to enliven viewers specifically with political *fervor* – and ideally, to encourage them to donate money to the Democratic party in alignment with the President, the man with whom the audience just experienced an intimate connection – the commercial associates the rapid pacing with a cluster of signs that each invoke an image of idealistic progress in the United States. The visual nature of these signs augments the awakened excitement, as the nationally idyllic "visual messages give the first impression before a person engages his/her [political party specific] logic" (Price, 2011, p. 21). Thus, as these signs each possess a significance that relates to topics of the political debate, the advertisement skillfully excites the viewer regarding American ideals while simultaneously, if only subconsciously, aligning the viewer with the political ideology responsible for screening such progress.

Finally, after establishing a connection between the viewer and the President and politically invigorating the viewer in alignment with the President's portrayed ambitions, the advertisement achieves a climactic "call to action" (Creamer, 2012) at its end. Although returning to the initial image of President Obama seated in a living room, the soundtrack is much more invigorating. The music no longer fades into the background, but rather, at an unmistakable crescendo in the score, it fuses message and feeling, clustering the President's ambitions with the excitement and connection the viewer has established in only a one-minute duration. Moreover, the second-person narration by the President becomes more prominent than ever before as the camera does not hesitate to draw "you," the viewer, within a medium close-up distance from the President during his appeal for the audience to assume their civic responsibility – again, one assumes, in his favor. Thus, as the "choice [the viewer faces] ... couldn't be bigger" (Organizing for Action, 2012), the advertisement's ability to enliven political excitement and connect the viewer with the President, if only at an affective level, couldn't be more persuasive.

Certainly, the contemporary population of the United States anticipates political advertising with a cynicism grounded in the belligerent rhetoric of political media campaigns (Price, 2011, p. 20), and the individual viewer always witnesses such media appeals with certain attachment to his/her own political viewpoints. To overcome these hurdles and engage the audience at an affective rather than purely cognitive level, President Obama's 2012 re-election advertisement, "The Choice," uses progressive form and clustering to connect viewers with the President, align them with his political visions, and have them identify with the climactic excitement those goals entail. Although this affective appeal is seductive, the advertisement is really too brief to stir anything but an immediate emotional response, and many viewers may readily discount it in place of more enduring, pre-existing beliefs once the commercial has concluded. In fact, political advertisements are characterized by their only transient influence on the voting populace (Sides, 2012), prompting the increasing use of other means, such as social media (Franz & Ridout, 2010, p. 321), in order to influence public opinion effectively (Creamer, 2012). In accordance with constitutional rights, such affective advertisements are certainly legally admissible (Federal Election Commission, 2006). However, given their typically limited influence, perhaps critics should focus instead on how they encourage more reflection of media campaign ethics, especially in the proper role of emotion in the form of contemporary campaigns.

REFERENCES

Creamer, M. (2012, November) Designing for Obama. *Advertising Age*, 83 (41).

Federal Election Commission (2006, October) *Special Notices on Political Ads and Solicitations*. Retrieved from http://www.fec.gov/pages/brochures/notices.shtml (accessed August 23, 2013).

Franz, M.M. & Ridout, T.N. (2010) Political Advertising and Persuasion in the 2004 and 2008 Presidential Elections. *American Politics Research*, 38, 303–29. doi: 10.1177/1532673X09353507.

Fu, H., Mou, Y., Miller, M.J. & Jalette, G. (2011) Reconsidering Political Cynicism and Political Involvement: a Test of Antecedents. *American Communication Journal*, 13, 44–6.

Ott, B.L. & Mack, R.L. (2014) *Critical Media Studies: an Introduction*, 2nd edn. Malden, MA: Wiley-Blackwell.

Organizing for Action (2012, July 23) "The Choice" – Obama for America TV Ad [video file]. Retrieved from http://www.youtube.com/watch?v=FBorRZnqtMo (accessed August 23, 2013).

Price, C.J. (2011) Using Visual Theories to Analyze Advertising. *Visual Communication Quarterly*, 18, 18–30. doi: 10.1080/15551393.2011.548725.

Sides, J. (2012, December 29) Where Obama's Early Ads Really the Game Changer? *The New York Times*.

Cultural Analysis

Michael Lechuga

La Mission (2009), directed by Peter Bratt and starring his brother Benjamin Bratt, tells the tale of negotiating multiple identities in the Mission District of San Francisco. The district, known for its significant contributions to the Chicano movement of the late 1960s and 1970s, is rich with Chicano pride, serving as the backdrop for a number of cultural performances. *La Mission* can be viewed as a popular media text that uses ideas of cultural and gender identity to critique themes of race and gender dominance. The film's main character, Che Rivera (Benjamin Bratt), is a working-class Chicano, who must balance his own cultural attachments with the news of his son's coming out. However, while this film may highlight some issues of gender within the Mexican American community, in this essay I look at the ways in which it overwhelmingly reinforces stereotypes of its Mexican American characters and weaves a narrative of assimilation through their development. As a result, the film supports an ideal American dream that continues to portray success from a white, middle-class perspective.

According to Ott and Mack (2014), mainstream media texts tend to reinforce dominant ideologies or understandings of social groups defined by their race, gender, and class. This means that these texts work as an important tool of hegemony, or "the process by which one ideology subverts other, competing ideologies and gains cultural dominance through the won consent of the governed" (p. 142). If the public did not regularly see "normal" representations of these groups in the media, or if they did not perceive any benefits from believing in or enacting these norms, then the public would be more likely to challenge them and upset the existing distribution of power in society. In media texts these norms are often communicated through stereotypes, or "misleading and reductionist representations" (Ott & Mack, 2014, p. 152) of social groups. However, even texts that appear to be accurately representing social groups may not always be doing so, as in the case of assimilation, where texts portray social groups positively while "simultaneously dehistoricizing or stripping them of their cultural identities" (Ott & Mack, 2014, p. 153). *La Mission* falls into this second category of text.

The film opens with images of the heavily Mexican-influenced Mission district. Aztec dancers and drummers perform ancient dances in the street, street art adorning the alleys depicts Indigenous and Chicano icons, and people of many colors shop at an outdoor *mercado*. Che, the protagonist, walks through these scenes on his way to work as a bus driver. He has tattoos down both of his arms and his neck, his hair is slicked back, and he wears a pair of plastic sunglasses that stretch across his face. In the first narrative scene, Che abruptly stops his bus and walks to the back where two young Latinos, dressed in baggy clothing and carrying a boom box, have boarded playing loud music. He confronts them, threatens them, and then kicks them off the bus. From the outset, the film situates the hyper-masculine stereotype of Mexican American men in order to provide contrast for the narrative of Jes (Jeremy Ray Valdez). Jes is a high school student in the Mission, and coming out to his father as gay challenges Che's homophobic, hyper-masculine attitudes.

This conflict is set into motion when Jes tells Che that he won't be joining him for a low-rider cruise, a passion that Che invests most of his spare time in. The film's narrative is closely woven in to the low-riding tradition, and this too becomes a platform for masculinity. Lying to his father, Jes meets his boyfriend Jordan (Max Rosenak) at a gay nightclub in the Castro district, another community in San Francisco. While embracing shirtless, someone snaps a photo of the two men, and when Jes returns home, he casually leaves the photo on the nightstand. Che discovers the picture, and while confronting Jes about it the following day, Che verbally and physically assaults his son. While perhaps this scene is meant to criticize the persistence of hateful attitudes towards the gay community, it also places these attitudes within *Che's* performance of violence, supporting the stereotype that Mexican American men are homophobic, violent, and abusive. When we find out that Che is a former convict and a recovering alcoholic, it further perpetuates these negative stereotypes of Mexican American men. Jes goes to live with his uncle, Che's brother, and continues studying to reach his goal of making it into UCLA. However, the film isn't about Jes. It's about Che and how he comes to deal with these changes in his life.

The ways in which the producers of *La Mission* center the plot on Che continue the reductive representation of Mexican American men in the USA, particularly in relation to masculinity. The film concentrates heavily on Che and his struggles with his relationship to his son; it does not really center on the one character who directly challenges the attitudes attributed to Mexican Americans – Jes. For example, soon after their fight, Che invites Jes to come back home. This period is marked with strain and discomfort, but Che is shown coping well with the changes. He even continues work on a low-rider that he hopes to give Jes as a graduation gift. The film seems to show his attitudes progressing until he slips, gets angry with Jes, and goes out. That night, after almost being hit by a car, Che reaches in the window and punches the driver five times. In the next scene, the young Latino, the same one that Che kicked off the bus, pulls up in a low-rider and opens fire on Jes and Jordan, critically injuring Jes. In both of these scenes, we see how Mexican American men are unable to control their anger toward gay men, and therefore, act out violently. The severity of the violence perpetuates a stereotype of criminality in the Mexican American community without equally reflecting on how Jes and Jordan might challenge these stereotypes. A final depiction of violence drives this point home. When Che arrives at the hospital and approaches Jes's hospital room, he sees Jordan and Jes embracing, and this, again, drives Che into a rage. He violently confronts Jordan, choking him and pushing him against the wall. It seems like Che will always be the stereotypical Mexican American male who is hyper-masculine, violent, and unable to deal with people who challenge prescribed gender roles.

The film ends with Jes moving in with Jordan and his parents in an upper-class, beach-view property. Here Jes is essentially saved from the violent and hyper-masculine Mission district by his white boyfriend; assimilating into this white family becomes the mode by which Jes can reach his goal of attending college. So, while the film makers attempt to challenge hateful attitudes toward gender within the Mexican American community, they actually ultimately weave a narrative of assimilation. As a parallel to the gender performances in the film, there are clear class performances as well. Che and his community are working class. Even when a new neighbor moves in upstairs, Che criticizes her for contributing to the gentrification of the neighborhood. Che, then, is a static character: he begins as a violent, homophobic, working-class individual and ends the same way. The only change he does achieve is the alienation of his son, Jes, who chooses the comforts of a white, middle-class life and assimilates out of the Mission district and into UCLA.

In this essay, I have considered how *La Mission* at times challenges the unequal treatment and attitudes of gay men in the Mexican American community, but to do so, the film relies on classic stereotypes of Mexican American men and reaffirms whiteness as desirable through a narrative of assimilation. In many ways, the film's characters are all performing the (white) American dream, where they strive to reach a level of success and happiness through work. While *La Mission* introduces many cultural elements that may not have been widely accepted, the film still "boils down all of the complications of modern life into a simple equation (hard work = success), and it symbolically erases real issues of social inequality, class struggle, profit motive, and others that may provide barriers toward success" (Ott & Mack, 2014, p. 148). In other words, the film uses class and racial stereotypes and a narrative of assimilation to challenge gender norms, and this reduced portrayal of the Mexican American community supports the notion that the white, middle class is an ideal goal for everyone. Texts like *La Mission* are often seen as cultural artifacts that depict critical issues in culture. However, my analysis suggests that we need to be critical of these texts as well, especially because they can also perpetuate stereotypes and class ideologies that can be harmful to cultural groups.

REFERENCES

Ott, B.L. & Mack, R.L. (2014) *Critical Media Studies: an Introduction*, 2nd edn. Malden, MA: Wiley-Blackwell.

Psychoanalytic Analysis

Mary Domenico

In the symbolic economy of Western phallocentrism, woman's prescribed roles as virgin, bride, wife, and anima leave her few choices beyond masochistic acceptance or suffering rebellion (Kristeva, 1986). Given her unsatisfactory archetypal foundation, it is hardly surprising that woman's plight continues to be a source of anxiety in the collective sphere. As a "picture of the collective unconscious," cinema has a unique ability to animate the unresolved tensions between the feminine place in the patriarchy and contemporary woman's desire for individuality and wholeness (Rushing & Frentz, 1995, p. 47). In this essay, I argue that Lars von Trier's *Melancholia* (2011), through a juxtaposition of formalistic and realistic styles that portray inner and outer worlds and stir affect, wrestles with the status of contemporary woman by exploring what happens when she refuses the symbolic roles that have been allotted to her. Based on a psychoanalytic critique of the film grounded in Sigmund Freud's theory of the death drive, I propose that *Melancholia* may be a collective attempt to restore equilibrium to an unbalanced and unresolved social situation (Grenell, 2008). My essay proceeds through a brief plot synopsis, a discussion of the death drive, and descriptions of four key scenes as they relate to Freud's theory. I end with a reflection concerning how the film's ending enables contemplation of a new feminine symbolic role in the collective.

The plot of *Melancholia* weaves together two catastrophes that feature Kirsten Dunst as the protagonist Justine – a failed wedding and the collision of earth with the rogue planet Melancholia. The wedding narrative revolves around the lavish reception that Justine's sister Claire and her husband John host for Justine and her groom, a party that deteriorates as Justine's initial, supposed contentment decomposes and she refuses her role as wife. The wedding fails to be consummated, her new husband abandons her, and Justine succumbs to an almost catatonic depression. In the second plot line, the planet Melancholia has escaped its sun and hurtles through space toward earth. Scientists and John predict that the planets will not collide, but their optimism proves incorrect, and, as people begin to fall apart – John commits suicide and Claire rushes about in a futile panic – Justine alone becomes calm and competent while the earth explodes.

These plot lines – a wedding and an apocalyptic explosion – provoke reflection on two key parts of Freud's psychoanalytic theory: the drives and the unconscious. Freud proposed that humans have two basic drives: the sexual drive and the death drive. The drives are unconscious motivators that, when unfulfilled, become conscious through symbolic expression in dreams. The sexual drive, *Eros*, motivates an individual toward self-preservation, connection with others, sex, and reproduction; the death drive, *Thanatos*, motivates an individual toward division from others, aggression, and destruction (Ott & Mack, 2014, p. 166). This destructive impulse can be directed toward self and/or toward others. These two motivating drives constitute an ever-present dialectical tension within every person, but during trauma, the death instinct becomes predominant. Under the pressure of "disturbing external forces" when a person experiences an overload of sensations and emotions beyond their ability to cope, the death drive motivates a return to an earlier state of calm and stillness (Mills, 2006, p. 378). This motivation for quiescence can manifest as the urge to sleep, depression (melancholia), or, in extreme cases, suicide or homicide. The narrative arc in *Melancholia* can be understood through four key scenes that I read through Freud's drive and unconscious concepts.

The movie opens with a prolonged, formalistic montage that portrays Justine's internal, unconscious state. Among the cinematic techniques used to create this context are slow motion, jump cuts, a non-diegetic score, a stylized *mise-en-scène*, and fantastical images (Boeck, 2007). The slow motion and time-disrupting jump cuts signal dream time; Wagner's operatic score from *Tristan and Isolde* conveys inner turmoil; Dali-esque, saturated colors and surreal landscapes reinforce the internal, dreamy motif. Throughout the scene, Justine, floating Ophelia-like in a stream or struggling in her wedding gown against root-like organic tendrils that threaten to submerge her, is juxtaposed with shots of the two planets, Earth and Melancholia, drawing near until they collide. The scene is affectively depressed and hopeless, a dark foreshadowing of what is to come – the choice Justine faces between accepting her status as bride or suffering the consequences of refusal.

The next scene, the traumatic wedding feast, is shot with a hand-held camera, long takes, deep focus, pans and tilts, and framing that favors content over style to give the illusion of representing reality (Boeck, 2007). The hand-held camera yields the jumpy, grainy, in-and-out of focus feel of an amateur documentary or family movie. Long takes in deep focus do not linger on any particular detail, leaving the viewer free – as in a real situation – to choose where to focus. The pans and tilts cut off heads, shoot the ceiling and floor, and weave about from one person to another, contributing to a chaotic and anxious atmosphere. Justine, hemmed in by people making demands on her to be happy, becomes by degrees angry, sullen, and withdrawn. By morning, her disappointed husband has left, she has had meaningless sex with her boss's nephew, she loses her job, and, due to emotional overload, she falls into a state of classic melancholy – depressed, uninterested in the world, and almost catatonic (Freud, 1917). Affectively, the scene is relentlessly tense and sad. By refusing her patriarchal role, Justine pays the price of what Kristeva calls "submission to the father," a state that is experienced as "punishment, pain, and suffering" (1986, p. 148). Kristeva says that refusing prescribed roles costs a woman her identity within the patriarchal order and results in her feeling unable to sustain her own life, so that death takes over. This profound loss of *Eros*, and the ascendancy of the death drive, is portrayed in *Melancholia* by Justine's inability to stay awake, eat, or even lift her leg into the bath.

The third key scene returns to a formalistic style to portray Justine's inner dream life. Again, a montage of jump cuts from Justine to the two planets, with fantastical images and non-diegetic music, serves to draw the viewer into her inner world. Awakened in the middle of the night by Melancholia's unearthly glow, Justine leaves her bed and, as if in a trance, wanders to a rocky hill where she lies naked and, bathed in the planet's soft light, makes love to herself. On a symbolic level, the glowing round planet can be seen as a mandala, a symbol of wholeness. Here, in natural surroundings, separate from patriarchal structures and demands, Justine undergoes a transformation back to life. Importantly, the scene suggests that woman's own nature has the power to defeat the death drive and empower the sexual, or life, drive. The montage ends the following morning, with Justine smiling serenely and drinking a cup of coffee as the ascendancy of *Eros* over *Thanatos* results in the transformation of melancholy into a state of calm and well-being.

The fourth key scene, a return to a realistic cinematic style, is again shot with a hand-held camera in an attitude of spontaneity and directness. The pans and tilts follow Justine, her sister, and her nephew to a forest clearing where they prepare for the planets' collision by building a ritual hut of branches. Here, in nature, the figures are in and out of focus, and the weaving camera gives the scene an unedited, urgent appeal. The three enter the hut, hold hands, close their eyes, and the planets collide in an apocalyptic explosion. The scene is affectively complex, both terrifying from the perspective of Justine's sister and calm from Justine's perspective. The viewer is reminded of Justine's earlier words: "The earth is evil; we don't need to grieve for it." Symbolically, this scene seems to indicate that for woman to be whole, the current way of life – where woman can be only virgin, wife, mother, and anima – will have to end. When woman's capacity for individuality and wholeness – the feminine *Eros* in its full power – confronts the patriarchy, there will be something like a massive explosion that will transform relationships with self and other. From a feminine viewpoint, this scene conveys a satisfying symbolic resolution. Escape from the patriarchy does not have to be met with the ascent of the death drive; woman has a mechanism – her own *Eros* force – that is powerful enough to prevail.

Melancholia's juxtaposition of formalistic and realistic styles initiates an affective means of contemplating contemporary woman's symbolic plight. Viewers are part of Justine's trajectory from depression to wholeness – from *Thanatos* to *Eros* – as they participate in her refusal to become the symbolic bride, her melancholy as she withdraws from others, and her eventual transformation. While many contemporary films suggest that woman's dilemma may be resolved only by her assumption of hyper-masculinity or a male-oriented sexuality, *Melancholia* offers a different corrective. By dwelling within her own nature, she may be able to defeat the death drive and destroy the way of life that traditionally has destroyed her. *Melancholia* hopefully suggests that, while corrective elements that can liberate the feminine from her prescribed symbolic roles may not be widespread, they do exist in our collective unconscious.

REFERENCES

Boeck, R. (2007) Ways of Seeing in *American Beauty*. *Film and Text*, 10, 181–7.

Freud, S. (1917) Mourning and Melancholia. In *The Standard Edition of the Complete Psychological Works of Sigmund Freud, Volume XIV: On the History of the Psycho-Analytic Movement* (pp. 237–58).

Grenell, G. (2008) Affect Integration in Dreams and Dreaming. *Journal of the American Psychological Association*, 56(1), 223–51. doi: 10.1177/0003065108315694.

Kristeva, J. (1986) About Chinese Women. In T. Moi (ed.), *The Kristeva Reader* (pp. 138–59). Oxford: Blackwell Publishing.

Mills, J. (2006) Reflections on the Death Drive. *Psychoanalytic Psychology*, 23(2), 373–82.

Ott, B.L. & Mack, R.L. (2014) *Critical Media Studies: an Introduction*, 2nd edn. Malden, MA: Wiley-Blackwell.

Rushing, J.A. & Frentz, T.S. (1995) *Projecting the Shadow: the Cyborg Hero in American Film*. Chicago, IL: University of Chicago Press.

Feminist Analysis

Cassie Schoon

While anti-drug campaigns have been a fixture in the American cultural landscape for decades, the "Not Even Once" campaign against methamphetamine use broke new ground with its unflinchingly graphic depictions of the effects of meth addiction. The print, online, billboard, and television campaign, featuring commercials directed by *Requiem for a Dream*'s Darren Aronofsky, is an extension of the Meth Project Foundation founded in Montana in 2005. The Project has since been rolled out in several mountain-Western and Midwestern American states, specifically in response to the growing and deadly epidemic of methamphetamine use among teenagers in those regions.

Since its inception the campaign has garnered the attention of criminology and health scholars, who have published papers questioning the campaign's (self-reported) effectiveness in reducing meth use (Anderson, 2010; Erceg-Hurn, 2008). However, the project has so far garnered only limited attention from rhetorical critics. Within this slim body of literature is the work of Elizabeth A. Dickinson, who has studied the project extensively. In "Limitations of Drug Prevention Messages," Dickinson (2009a) criticizes the campaign for its presentation of meth use as an individual choice, unrelated to societal or environmental context. Dickinson (2009b) has also proposed the campaign as a teachable artifact for instructors who wish to apply Burke's "dramatistic pentad" to issues of motive, dominant relationships, and agency utilized in the advertisements.

This essay extends the analysis of the campaign's symbolism, especially as it relates to gender, or the "culturally constructed differences between men and women: tastes, roles, activities, and more" (Ott & Mack, 2014, p. 194). While a large amount of advertising is aimed at persuading individuals *to obtain* a product or *to take* an action in order to perform social roles in a satisfactory manner, the "Not Even Once" campaign, like other anti-drug initiatives, is an example of negative persuasion. The campaign is directed at encouraging individuals *not to* participate in an action or to *refrain from* consumption of a product. Since the days of *Reefer Madness*, anti-drug messages have provided such encouragement by depicting the many failures that result from drug use, and within this rhetoric lurks an implicit message of how each failure relates to the audience's culturally-dictated performance of self. More specifically, because the "Not Even Once" campaign is directed at both young men and young women, these PSAs appeal directly to expectations associated with preferred cultural performances of masculinity and femininity. The campaign, I argue, features messages regarding the violation of sexual purity, attractiveness, and familial obligation, effectively utilizing fears of culturally incorrect gender performance in each to persuade teens to avoid meth. By frequently alluding to how meth use corrupts gender norms, the campaign brings these norms into relief and reinforces their desirability.

According to the Meth Project's website, 71 percent of those surveyed reported that one of the negative associations they now have with meth use is "Having sex with someone they don't want to." This statistic makes sense in light of the campaign's heavy use of sexual imagery to reinforce the idea that prostitution is part of meth addiction for both male and female users. In both cases, the campaign uses fears associated with violating gendered, sexual purity to stop teens from using meth. The boys who engage in sex work in these ads, or who are violated sexually due to their addiction, are either portrayed briefly before a scene fades or represented only implicitly, such as in the case of the "romantic evening" alluded to in a print ad's image of a jail cell. Still, in light of the uniformly male assailants depicted throughout the campaign, these ads strongly imply that the victim is having submissive/receptive sex with another man. Such acts feminize the male victim, scaring potential male meth users away by depicting a reverse of the "pure" or culturally normalized act of masculine penetration.

In contrast, young girls engaging in prostitution are depicted more often and in more graphic detail, and the issue of sexual purity is that much more evident as a result. In a print ad, a young, dead-eyed girl is pinned down by a man, accompanied by the words "15 dollars for sex isn't normal. But on meth it is." In another, a girl in panties and a bra cries dark mascara tears down her face as her boyfriend, who has just exchanged money with her john outside their motel room door, lights the meth pipe. A final ad depicts an overdosed young girl who lies with bare legs spread on a bed as her little sister tells the camera, "I'll only smoke meth once." The immediate and vivid representations of female prostitution and sexual abuse here suggest that meth leads girls to violate culturally prized feminine traits of virginity and waiting for sex until adulthood or marriage. The more graphic depictions of females, coupled with stronger cultural associations between femininity and sexual purity, make the campaign's potential effect on teen girls who view it that much stronger.

The physical ravages of meth use are another frequent trope in the "Not Even Once" campaign, primarily in print advertisements and on billboards. Again, though the genders are depicted differently here, what binds them together is the notion of meth as the gateway to disobeying gender norms. Girls feature in the majority of the ads that depict the connection between meth use and physical ruin. In one, a topless girl with sunken eyes and visible ribs looks at herself in the mirror. The ad asks, "Will meth change the way I look?" A close-up of an example of "meth mouth" (extreme tooth decay and skin eruptions) includes the text "You'll never worry about lipstick on your teeth again." The sole ad featuring a boy shows a face destroyed by scabs and advanced dental decay, and the text, "Actually, meth won't make it easier to hook up." Radio ads also feature girls more frequently than boys discussing the effects of meth on physical appearance. In the campaign's 30-second radio spots, former users tell their stories. "Jayden" describes becoming skeletally underweight, her skin and hair becoming "gross" due to meth use. "Elizabeth" talks about how meth use "tears apart your looks." Taken together, the ads relay the classic gendered binary that positions girls as beautiful sexual objects and boys as virile, sexual subjects (Ott & Mack, 2014, p. 202).

While perhaps not as psychologically gruesome as the ads depicting sexual victimization, the ads graphically depicting models made-up to look like "meth-heads" are a jarring foil to the typical image of young people in all advertising contexts. Each cracked, chapped mouth, each blackened tooth, and each sunken eye socket is in direct contradiction to the airbrushed, fresh-faced, bright-eyed models whom teens are expected to idolize. Thus, the campaign scares boys away from meth by showing how the drug threatens their ability to perform sexually at culturally-expected levels (like a "real man"), and it scares girls away from the drug by showing how meth will stop them from achieving cultural standards and expectations of beauty. Here again women seem to bear the overwhelming brunt of these expectations. While the boy appears to have lost his ability to relate to or conquer others, the many girls seem to have lost the very thing that gives them worth at all.

Finally, the campaign depicts both male and female addicts failing to enact gendered, familial roles in different but highly normalized ways. Young men are primarily shown as acting out violently, physically abusing parents or siblings. In other words, the ads depict "normal" masculine aggression taken much too far. Young girls violate the feminine ideal of sisterly collegiality as they abandon, disappoint, and (literally) sell out siblings in return for drugs. Mothers grieve daughters lost to prostitution, while accompanying images depict (now shattered) dreams of high-school graduation and success. The campaign's most intense portrayal of meth's negative effect on domestic obligation is that of an unintended pregnancy. This consequence of meth use disrupts two significant cultural expectations for female gender performance: sexual purity and the preferred mode of motherhood. A video ad depicting the "meth baby" (premature, underweight, crying alone in her NICU incubator) confronts the viewer with the ultimate filial disaster for a young woman: the failure of a daughter to delay childbearing until marriage (or at least, adulthood), and the failure of a mother to provide a healthy, stable life for her child. Yet again, then, the campaign attempts to scare boys and girls away from meth use through images that validate culturally sanctioned understandings of what each gender is "supposed" to contribute to the family, but the most developed and heart-wrenching images seem reserved for women.

The "Not Even Once" campaign employs graphic depictions of the consequences of meth use in order to elicit fear in the viewer. Much of the fear that the campaign images evoke is deeply rooted in cultural expectations of gender performance, underscoring the desirability of these limiting norms even as it attempts to achieve a very pro-social goal. Given its reliance on these gender norms, it is not entirely surprising that women are the subject of more graphic and extreme messages in the campaign; though individuals of both genders suffer under the expectations of patriarchy, women typically experience a disproportionate amount (Ott & Mack, 2014). As a result, while the effectiveness of "Not Even Once" is the subject of debate among scholars across disciplines, the campaign, as it appeals to broadly-held cultural fears associated with a failure to meet gender performances, remains a valuable artifact to understand the cultural expectations placed on young men and women. If "Not Even Once" is any indication, anti-drug rhetoric remains a study of victimhood, choices and consequences dictated as "good" or "bad" by dominant cultural norms. Perhaps we're not so far removed from *Reefer Madness* after all.

REFERENCES

Anderson, D. (2010) Does Information Matter? The Effect of the Meth Project on Meth Use among Youths. *Journal of Health Economics*, 29(5), 732–42.

Dickinson, E.A. (2009a) Limitations of Drug Prevention Messages. *Communication Currents*, 4(4), 1–2.

Dickinson, E.A. (2009b) The Montana Meth Project: Applying Burke's Dramatistic Pentad to a Persuasive Anti-Drug Media Campaign. *Communication Teacher*, 23(3), 126–31.

Erceg-Hurn, D.M. (2008) Drugs, Money, and Graphic Ads: a Critical Review of the Montana Meth Project. *Prevention Science*, 9(4), 256–63.

Ott, B.L. & Mack, R.L. (2014) *Critical Media Studies: an Introduction*, 2nd edn. Malden, MA: Wiley-Blackwell.

Queer Analysis

Michael Alley

In a recent television advertisement for J.P. Morgan Chase, two middle-aged, white male business owners reflect on how the Ink card made possible their dream of owning a restaurant. The ad depicts the men performing an array of tasks related to their business as they comment on the importance of the card. On first glance, this ad, which is titled "The Meatball Shop TV Spot," may seem rather unremarkable. But to the trained critic, it raises interesting questions about how a single media text can simultaneously address and appeal to diverse audiences. To help explain this process, I turn to the concept of the "textual wink" as developed by queer studies scholars. Ott & Mack (2014) define the textual wink as the subtle codes of a text that speak to a hidden or veiled audience even as the text explicitly addresses another audience who does not have access to these codes (p. 235). Specifically, I contend that J.P. Morgan Chase's "Meatball Shop" television advertisement employs the textual wink to market its product successfully to both heteronormative and queer audiences. This essay advances in two parts: First, I define and explain the textual wink and its attendant concepts, showing how they manifest in "The Meatball Shop." Then, I reflect on the broader social and political implications of my analysis.

The textual wink is a sophisticated concept that requires an understanding of the first, second, third, and fourth personas. The first persona, though in many ways the least relevant to this study, refers to the implied author of a message (Ott & Mack, 2014, p. 235), which in this instance is J.P. Morgan Chase. The second persona, by contrast, describes the text's implied audience, which I argue is a mainstream or heteronormative one based upon the explicit codes in the text. For example, the ad portrays the two men in a typically masculine ownership/leadership role, especially when giving instructions to a subordinate female (0:06). The various customers within the restaurant also appear to perform gender in a normal manner, and a man and women who appear together enact a traditionally gendered interaction (0:17). Because heterosexuality is often unconsciously associated with "normal" gender expression (Ott & Mack, 2014), we can say with some confidence that this ad is attempting to reflect the conventions of its intended, heterosexual audience. Moreover, it is likely that members of a larger, heteronormative audience would see the central two men as straight based on these cues.

While appealing to one audience, the cues already identified also exclude certain audiences. The excluded audience constitute the third persona within a text. To target a specific audience effectively, authors of a text must necessarily exclude certain groups, and the marked fragmentation of society often restricts texts from addressing everyone. The excluded audience of "Meatball Shop" includes many different social groups, including people of color, adolescents, and the elderly. There are many ways that a director may capture a restaurant scene, so the fairly uniform race and age of those present in the commercial are not incorporated by accident. This advertisement could just as easily have prioritized the Asian population with different actors and a slight manipulation of the surroundings.

However, even as they ignore certain audiences, some texts manage to speak to veiled or hidden audiences in addition to their implied, mainstream audience. Such veiled audiences constitute the text's fourth persona, hailed by codes or cues in the text largely invisible to the implied audience. Charles E. Morris III (2002) associates this process with passing, or the act of masking oneself as member of a group to which one does not really belong, and much current research focuses on the queer community as a "passing" or veiled audience. As Morris notes, a "particular ideological bent, presumably one who is sexually marginalized, understands the dangers of homophobia, acknowledges the rationale for the closet, and possesses an intuition that renders a pass transparent" (p. 230).

A queer audience certainly comprises the fourth persona in the advertisement under analysis. The "untrained" eye may never think twice about this advertisement, but a few specific cues or "winks" call attention to this veiled audience. First, the playful nudge from one actor to the other is one cue that may be picked up by queer viewers (0:02). While nudging does not necessarily denote homosexuality, the smile on each of the men's faces increases the likelihood of such a reading. Also, the way the men are dressed serves as a subtle cue. Of course, heterosexual men can just as easily dress in snugly fitting clothing like the two men in the advertisements, but they are less likely to fold up their pant legs (0:10). This attire does not define either of the men as gay, but it does potentially signal as much to someone who has access to non-heteronormative codes.

The ambiguity expressed when the men are speaking acts as the most salient wink in the advertisement. Both the beginning and the end of the ad features a headshot of the men standing together. While these scenes appear conventional, as a skeptical viewer, one cannot determine where the arms and hands of each man lie (0:00 and 0:25). Whereas the more explicit cue here suggests that the men are simply standing next to one another, the veiled cue suggests that their arms are positioned on or around the other's torso. This cue is amplified through the discourse at the end of the advertisement. The men explain that owning a restaurant is something they both have always wanted to do (0:24). This shared dream, especially surrounded by the other cues, can be interpreted by a queer audience as something only two men in a romantic relationship would do. At the same time, however, the heteronormative community may view the two men simply as brothers or friends.

Additional cues are likely to surface upon further analysis, but the cues addressed in this essay thus far certainly contribute to the interpretation of the men as a homosexual couple and, as a result, speak to a queer community. It is hard to ignore this veiled audience once the codes are acknowledged, but a person lacking these codes from the outset would probably be unable to notice what the veiled audience sees easily. There are a number of lessons this essay can impart about the role of the textual wink in media. First, the United States is currently undergoing a substantial shift toward equal rights for the homosexual population, and advertisements that speak to both heteronormative and queer audiences straddle both sides of this political struggle. The textual wink may be an important way for the media to reflect political change. Additionally, appealing to multiple audiences at the same time allows the mass media to further their economic successes, and incorporating the textual wink into advertisements may prove extremely valuable if done correctly. Finally, the ability to prioritize multiple audiences while remaining discrete in the process solidifies the fragmentation of media viewers through "narrowcasting" (Ott & Mack, 2014), which appears to provide members of society with individuality and a "choice." The textual wink in some ways demonstrates that these choices are mainly a top-down construction, and that consumers are not necessarily in control of which niche audience they belong to.

In the midst of a social movement, such as the current struggle for rights by the homosexual community, being acknowledged by the mass media is a victory in itself. Although homosexuality has been identified in past media, it was often done in a mocking tone or through the inclusion of damaging stereotypes. Texts like J.P. Morgan Chase's "Meatball Shop" portray the homosexual population in a more complex way. Since the media contribute to the ideologies that are available for us to adopt, removing the stereotypes of homosexuality in media may be a critical move to attaining equal rights. Further, because the actions of the mass media drive and reflect social norms and values, the rise of the textual wink may ultimately be a progressive reflection of the larger social movements occurring today.

REFERENCES

Ink from Chase (2012, October 25) *TMS: The Meatball Shop TV Spot*. Retrieved August 23, 2013, from http://www.youtube.com/watch?v=qIzDQntRG0A

Morris III, C.E. (2002) Pink Herring & the Fourth Persona: J. Edgar Hoover's Sex Crime Panic. *Quarterly Journal of Speech*, 88(2), 228–44.

Ott, B.L. & Mack, R.L. (2014) *Critical Media Studies: an Introduction*, 2nd edn. Malden, MA: Wiley-Blackwell.

Sociological Analysis

Samuel M. Jay

The US financial market is a paradox. On the one hand, it is defined by the never-ending fluctuation of security, commodity, and bond prices. On the other, the stock market as a system cannot function without some sense of order. Because the market reacts unpredictably to historical moments of anxiety or uncertainty, investors shy away from high-risk stocks, put their money in bonds, and disrupt the natural processes of the market, limiting profitability. This remains so until order is re-established. Financial journalism, from cable news networks like CNBC and monthly magazines like *Money* to websites like *Morningstar* and iPhone applications like LearnVest, is the messenger of such order.

This essay argues that financial journalism functions as "equipment for living" (Burke, 1941), providing stakeholders in the American financial market with symbolic resources for addressing and resolving the ambiguity of market activity and its attendant anxieties. Kenneth Burke uses the term "guilt" to signify all of the anxieties associated with violating established rules, patterns, and systems of order, so as representative of a system defined by its volatility, finance journalism provides a primary means for negotiating constant guilt. However, in supplying "stylistic medicine" for working through chaos, finance journalism establishes order without ever really questioning the hierarchy or the nature of the market system itself. Below I examine three financial news stories to show how transcendence, mortification, and victimage offer stakeholders means for addressing and dealing with market disorder.

The US financial market is fickle. It changes minute-by-minute on trading days, and when investors are not sure of what will happen in the long term, they cease investing, hindering the natural processes of the market. The market is especially fickle in the months leading up to presidential elections, as the future of the country remains uncertain until someone is voted into the Oval Office. This was the case during the 2012 presidential election when the battle between Barack Obama and Mitt Romney caused the Standard & Poor's 500 and the Dow Jones Industrial Average – two market indexes that provide an overall reading of financial activity – to fluctuate significantly for several weeks.

Following Burke, Ott and Mack (2014) suggest that transcendence, as a strategy for dealing with disorder and the feelings of guilt it can produce, avoids these feelings completely by denying the disorder (p. 278). Thus, when the markets were going haywire from September 2012 to the beginning of November, finance journalism offered no solution to the problem and avoided critiquing many internal market issues, including the tendency among publicly traded companies like Facebook and Apple to provide little guidance and contribute to investor uncertainty. This lack of comment helped frame the volatility as a natural product of the election season, something that *had* to happen every two or four years. Through an appeal to transcendence, financial news encouraged investors to turn away from the social hierarchy of economics and toward a new hierarchy – that of politics – for encouragement. As a result, the market appeared less volatile and order was re-established after President Obama was re-elected. However, the use of transcendence here also discouraged any actual reflection on the inherent fragility of the market. Rather than examining and critiquing any internal issues that may have led to market uncertainty, financial journalism outlets ignored them.

The bursting of the housing bubble in 2008 and the US financial market crisis that followed was a textbook example of an established hierarchy falling into disarray. Institutions that were once great bastions of order, such as Wall Street investment banks, mutual fund companies, and the Federal Reserve, suddenly offered no guidance. Instead, with the country in the middle of a "Great Recession," financial journalism once again supplied frames for making sense of the disorder. Different methods for working through guilt were employed at different moments during the crisis, but mortification was often called upon as a frame for making sense of one specific element of the crisis: the dip in consumer spending.

Mortification is a means of dealing with disorder and guilt that requires a symbolic act of atonement, such as confession of sins or self-sacrifice (Ott & Mack, 2014, p. 279). In response to the housing crisis, consumer spending diminished from the middle of 2008 until the early months of 2011. Rather than freely spending their money, people saved up in fear of another financial meltdown. Financial journalism turned to mortification as a framework to help make sense of this thrift, explaining that American consumers "tightened their belts" and embodied the responsibility of the recession by penalizing themselves, or by denying themselves the items they bought when times were good (*The Economist*, 2011). This frame importantly implied that atonement had been made and consumers could soon return to normal levels of spending, which in fact happened in the months following the intervention. However, as consumers symbolically took on all of the blame and "abstained" from luxuries, financial journalism provided a sense-making device that glossed over the internal weaknesses of the market. When the market returned to normalcy, it did so without much discussion of other possible systemic fissures.

"Sequestration," or across-the-board spending cuts to various governmental agencies, was a heavily debated political issue in the middle of February 2013. When it became clear that these cuts would go into effect at the beginning of March, investors were uncertain as to what would happen in their aftermath. This uncertainty sent the market into disorder, and this time financial journalism looked for someone or something to blame for the problem. Victimage or scapegoating is a final strategy for addressing guilt where afflicted parties target a "vessel" and symbolically transform it into the source of all problems, effectively "filling" the vessel with their guilt (Ott & Mack, 2014, p. 279). Criticizing, punishing, or destroying the vessel resolves negative feelings and helps restore order. Interestingly, to purge guilt during "sequestration" coverage, financial journalism outlets blamed various targets for the problem. For example, these outlets often blamed Congress for failing to work with President Obama and find a middle ground on spending cuts. The President was also blamed for wanting to take a macro-level approach, cutting spending across the board rather than picking and choosing specific programs that could be cut entirely. However, by providing these localized targets for blame, financial journalism never problematized the financial market system as a whole. Rather than critiquing the relationship between market activity and governmental policy, order was re-established by placing blame on a select few parties and purging guilt by criticizing them.

In conclusion, this essay argued that financial journalism functions as "equipment for living" because it offers symbolic sensing-making frames for working through guilt and re-establishing order in times of disarray. By looking at examples of transcendence, mortification, and victimage in financial news, it is clear that people can use language to restore order without forcing a re-evaluation or critique of systemic issues that may have caused disorder in the first place. Because the US financial market is so volatile, frames are very important for keeping the system working and for getting investors to act. However, this gives a great deal of power to media outlets that are often owned by publicly traded companies with vested interests in the market and the news it creates.

REFERENCES

Burke, K. (1941) Literature as Equipment for Living. In *The Philosophy of Literary Form: Studies in Symbolic Action* (pp. 293–304). Baton Rouge, LA: Louisiana State University Press.
Ott, B.L. & Mack, R.L. (2014) *Critical Media Studies: an Introduction*, 2nd edn. Malden, MA: Wiley-Blackwell.
The Economist (2011, October 25) Hard Times. Retrieved from http://www.economist.com/blogs/dailychart/2011/10/us-consumer-spending (accessed August 23, 2013).

Erotic Analysis

Rachael Thompson

Reality television programs provide viewers the opportunity to peek into the lives of strangers, an activity that can be irresistible. In recent years, a subset of reality television programs that focus on mental illnesses such as obsessive compulsive disorder, substance abuse, and bizarre appetites and compulsions have appeared on several cable networks. One mental illness that is the subject of programs on two different networks is hoarding. *Hoarding: Buried Alive* (which airs on TLC) and *Hoarders* (which airs on A&E) both profile individuals and families who are struggling with hoarding, or a compulsion to collect and hold on to often worthless items. In this essay I argue that these programs provide access to the resistive pleasures of abjection, the carnivalesque, and liminal space, pleasures which are elusive in most other media texts. Through close examination of several episodes available on A&E's website of *Hoarders*, I will illustrate how these pleasures are accessible to audience members.

Hoarders first aired on A&E in 2009. The program was nominated for a 2011 Emmy Award for Outstanding Reality Program, and it began airing a sixth season in early 2013. Each episode profiles two hoarders and their struggles to clean their house. The show begins with interviews of hoarders and their friends and family members, intercut with shots of the hoarders' messy homes. During the opening sequence, hoarders typically identify a traumatic loss that was the impetus for their hoarding. Their family members also have an opportunity to express their feelings about hoarding. Shots of the hoard are typically closely framed and cut together quickly. The camera tends to focus on the most repulsive objects in the collection like rotten food, animal or human feces, and garbage. After the introduction of the main characters, the narrative arc follows a general pattern: identification of an imminent crisis, introduction of the helpers (a psychologist and organizer), the cleaning process, and a conclusion.

The first resistive pleasure *Hoarders* provides to viewers is abjection. Abjection is found in subject matter that which disturbs order through "crossing of cultural boundaries and pollution/defilement of social categories" (Ott & Mack, 2010, p. 247). In *Hoarders*, cultural boundaries become polluted through the hoarders' accumulation of trash throughout their living spaces. In season 1, episode 0, Steven, a 48-year-old man, has filled his small apartment with empty food containers, newspapers, and, in his bathroom, a layer of bundles that the viewer is informed are filled with human excrement. The professional organizer who is assisting Steven informs the viewer that the bathroom is disgusting as well as very embarrassing for Steven. She has a mask tied over her face and heavy gloves on as she shovels out the bathroom. The camera lingers on the bundles that cover the floor. There isn't an explanation for the piles of feces such as broken plumbing or health issue and Steven never addresses the issue.

While excrement is a common motif in abjection, spoiled food also represents a violation of boundaries. Food is a nourishing and life-sustaining substance, but when it is spoiled it represents the threat of death from biologic organisms like botulism toxin and molds. It is also suggestive of vomiting and gag reflexes. In season 1, episode 4, the viewer is introduced to Jill, a 60-year-old woman who hoards food. Her entire home is filled with food in various stages of decay. The psychologist who is assigned to help Jill asks her to identify what food is too rotten to keep, but Jill does not recognize that the food is spoiled. The camera lingers on the obvious spoilage and then cuts to a shot that shows several fly strips hanging from the ceiling that are loaded with dead flies. Jill refuses to throw out puffed up cans of food, blackened produce, and meat with green spots. The most telling incident is when the psychologist uncovers a liquefied pumpkin in Jill's living room. When confronted with the pumpkin, Jill recalls when she got the pumpkin, how beautiful the pumpkin was and what she intended to do with the pumpkin. Even when the cleaners are scooping up the pile of goo, Jill cannot let go; she takes a few seeds to save so she can grow more pumpkins.

Hoarders also provides pleasure through the presentation of the carnivalesque. The carnivalesque involves the reversal or debasement of all that is high or ideal (Ott & Mack, 2010, p. 247). Parents, particularly mothers, are often the subjects of

Hoarders. The mothers profiled in *Hoarders* are typically not able to properly perform their roles as caretakers and heads of families, which is an inversion of typical social ideals. In fact, children must usually confront their parents and are often the ones to model appropriate behavior in regards to their parent's hoarding. Linda, one of the featured subjects in season 1, episode 0, is living alone in a house she has filled with possessions. Interviews with her children reveal the anger they feel because their mother has replaced them with her possessions. During the cleaning process, Linda has a breakdown when she finds her children's baby clothes. While she is not successful caring for her actual children, she cares deeply about the possessions that represent her mothering role. However, she is not able to respond to her children's concern for the quality of her living space.

Likewise, Jennifer and Ron, a couple profiled in season 1, episode 4, are at risk of losing custody of their three young children due to the unsafe condition of their home. Their house is filled with possessions, dirty clothes, toys, and spilled Cheerios. Jennifer and the psychologist helping her focus on a pile of Cheerios on the children's room floor as evidence of her failure as a mother. Cheerios, typically a symbol of childhood nourishment, do not serve their intended purpose but are instead debased here as one more item that fills the house. Additionally, Jennifer expresses how overwhelmed she is with the amount of laundry that needs to be washed, dried, and put away. Their home is literally being filled up with evidence that Jennifer cannot perform her proper role of mother. An important aspect of carnivalesque pleasure is the knowledge that social order will eventually return (Ott & Mack, 2010), and this is certainly the case on *Hoarders*. The psychologists and organizers that assist the hoarding individuals instruct these dethroned mothers on how to get back to their rightful place as head of household. Many of the most pleasurable episodes are ones in which the parent's home is restored to a comfortable center of family activity.

The final pleasure available to viewers is the presentation of liminal spaces. While abjection relates to the crossing of social or cultural boundaries, liminality relates to the dissolving of these boundaries (Ott & Mack, 2010, p. 248). There are two ways liminality is expressed in *Hoarders*: the hoarder exists somewhere between human and animal, and the defined boundaries within the home are dissolved. A common remark from family members of the hoarder is that the hoarder is living like an animal. For example, during the opening sequence of season 6, episode 80, the subject's sister is hysterical because her sister sleeps in a pile of garbage in the middle of the room "like an animal." In addition to houses on these programs existing somewhere between acceptable human living spaces and animal dens, the individual rooms within the houses are not typically used for their intended purposes. Hoarders and their family members are usually embarrassed and appalled if the hoarder is not using their rooms properly, such as sleeping in a room other than the bedroom. Other common disappointments include not being able to cook in the kitchen or use the bathroom for self-hygiene. In each case, the conventionally established boundaries between rooms become permeable as the hoarder performs vital tasks wherever there happens to be space. Although helpers on the program typically display strong positive emotions when rooms are restored to their intended purposes at the end of some episodes, viewers may gain pleasure from watching the temporary collapse of rigid social definitions of domestic space.

The pleasures of abjection, the carnivalesque, and liminal spaces are available to audience members of *Hoarders* through the presentation of human and animal waste, rotten food, parents failing to perform their rightful roles, and domestic spaces being improperly utilized. While *Hoarders* does not explicitly invite viewers to experience these pleasures, individual viewers may choose to read the program with attention to their own transgressive and bodily reactions. Of course, the final question of intention is a good one: Is *Hoarders* relying on the audience to experience such transgressive pleasures in order to make the program successful? This analysis clues us into the fact that the otherwise resistive potential of affect in the media may sometimes be appropriated by companies looking to make a program appealing.

REFERENCES

A&E Television Networks (2013) About Hoarders. Retrieved from http://www.aetv.com/hoarders/about/ (accessed August 23, 2013).

Chan, M., Severson, D., & Kelly, M. (Executive Producers) (2009–13) *Hoarders* [television series]. Seattle, WA: Screaming Flea Productions.

Ott, B.L. & Mack, R.L. (2010) *Critical Media Studies: an Introduction*. Malden, MA: Wiley-Blackwell.

Glossary

acoustic space—Space that is spherical, discontinuous, resonant, and dynamic.

advertising—A form of communication and marketing designed to persuade audiences to feel and/or behave a certain way toward a product, service, or corporate brand.

aesthetics—Those qualities of an artwork that, while asignifying, generate sensual experiences and evoke affective responses from audiences; the meaningfulness of art (and life) as apprehended through the senses; the beauty of art and the sensual enjoyment it engenders.

affect—An intensity registered directly by the body that operates on a non-representational or asignifying register.

agency—The capacity of human beings to act purposively and according to their own volitions.

agenda-setting—The capacity of the news media to establish what issues and events are considered significant.

aggressor effect—The hypothesis that repeated exposure to representations of violence increases aggressive behavior on the part of audiences.

American Dream—The unquestioned assumption that hard work leads to success, and that success is measured in terms of economic wealth.

apparatus theory—An early psychoanalytic approach to film that claims the actual environment and machinery of the cinema activates a number of desires within spectators.

assimilation—The process of "white washing" ethnic diversity by de-historicizing cultural difference.

base (in Marxist theory)—The underlying economic and material conditions of society.

bystander effect—The hypothesis that repeated exposure to representations of violence promotes increased callousness about violence directed at others.

camp—A collection of stylistic elements that, as they happen to converge around and/or within a specific media text, resonate with the experiences of queer individuals living within a heteronormative social system.

carnivalesque—A characteristic of texts that embrace and embody the subversive spirit of medieval carnival.

catharsis effect—The hypothesis that repeated exposure to representations of violence functions as an outlet for pent-up aggressive drives in the individual.

celebrity—A cultural phenomenon that celebrates famous or well-known personalities.

closed text—A text that is structured to elicit a particular, usually singular, response from audiences.

clusters—The way individual signs are associated and dissociated with one another.

code—A set of rules that govern the use of visual and linguistic signs within a culture.

code of ethics—A self-imposed set of rules that outline the ethical strivings of a particular media outlet.

concentration—An organizational state in which the ownership and control of an entire industry, such as the mass media, is dominated by just a few companies; an oligopoly.

conglomeration—The corporate practice of accumulating multiple, though not necessarily media, companies and businesses through startups, mergers, buyouts, and takeovers.

connotation—The cultural meaning of a text; second-order signification.

consequences (in regulation)—The clear effects of a given regulatory action.

conspicuous consumption—The belief that one can attain the kind of happiness or completeness often conceived of as upper class through the purchase of material goods and services.

Critical Media Studies: An Introduction, Second Edition. Brian L. Ott and Robert L. Mack.
© 2014 John Wiley & Sons, Inc. Published 2014 by John Wiley & Sons, Inc.

content—The informational component of a message; the specific details, facts, ideas, and opinions communicated through mass media.

contingencies (in regulation)—The unique contextual and historical factors that influence regulatory action.

conventions—The norms that govern the technical and creative choices made by workers in the execution of their duties, art, or craft.

convergence—The tendency of formerly diverse media to share a common, integrated platform.

cool medium—Low-definition communication technologies that are high in audience participation or completion (e.g. television, telephone, cartoons).

copyright—The legal granting of exclusive control of a creative work to that work's creator.

critical media studies—An umbrella term used to describe an array of theoretical perspectives on the media, which – though diverse – are united by their skeptical attitude, humanistic approach, political assessment, and commitment to social justice.

cruising—The interpretive practice of reading with one's body.

cultural imperialism—The imposition of one set of cultural values on other cultures; the exporting of cultural values and ideologies around the globe, usually to the detriment of local culture and national sovereignty.

cultural production—The generation of semiotic, enunciative, and textual materials related to a specific media artifact by fans of that artifact.

Cultural studies—An interdisciplinary approach to the study of culture that seeks to understand how relations of power are enacted, reified, and challenged.

culture—The collection of artifacts, practices, and beliefs of a particular group of people at a particular historical moment, supported by symbolic systems and directed by ideology.

culture jamming—The use of familiar media symbols and channels to reveal and overturn the consumerist, capitalist ideologies they embody.

decoding—The process of using a code to decipher a message and assess meaning.

denotation—The literal meaning of a text; first-order signification.

desire—The unquenchable yearning for love or recognition that no one else can ever perfectly or absolutely fill.

dialogic text—A text that stages an unending conversation between Self and Other and, thus, is perpetually open and unfinished.

difference—The depiction of others who are subordinate to, but a source of pleasure for, Western tourists and consumers.

digital rights management—Any software program that media industries employ to control the distribution and use of digital intellectual property.

discursive construction—A social construction made invisible, natural, normal, and indeed "biological" by its discursive aspects.

doxa—Cultural knowledge that is accepted as common sense; the realm of the taken-for-granted.

dramaturgy—A microsociological perspective that utilizes the metaphor of theater to explain the character and function of public behavior, especially face-to-face interaction.

drives—Motivating forces that arise when biological needs register within the mind and seek gratification through objects in external reality.

encoding—The process of creating a meaningful message according to a particular code.

encryption—The digital scrambling of a message such that it can only be read by using an appropriately correlated decoding program.

enculturation—The process by which persons internalize the values of an organization or culture.

equipment for living—The idea that public discourse provides audiences with symbolic resources for confronting the anxieties and difficulties of their own lives.

essentialism—The belief that cultural distinctions such as masculinity and femininity are inherent, universal, and natural.

ethnography—A qualitative research method that employs observation to understand cultural phenomena from the perspective of the members of that culture.

exclusion—The symbolical annihilation of various cultural groups through erasure or under-representation.

exoticism—Images of foreign lands and bodies that romanticize or mystify other cultures.

false consciousness—The belief that the masses are duped into blindly accepting the prevailing ideology.

fandom—Organized communities or subcultures comprised of persons who share a special affinity for or attachment to a media text, which they, in turn, express through their participation in communal practices (fan fiction, etc.) and events (conventions).

fantasy—A mental representation of conscious or unconscious wish fulfillment.

feminism—A political project that explores the diverse ways men and women are socially empowered or disempowered.

fetishism—The psychic structuring of an object or person as a source of sexual pleasure.

forces of production (in Marxist theory)—The land, natural resources, and technology needed to produce material goods.

form—(1) The overall structure or configuration of a message; (2) the creation and satisfaction of desire.

fourth persona—A projection or impression of the author(s), indicated though textual features, that is only available to select audience members who possess the necessary interpretive codes.

fragmentation—A splintering of the consuming public into ever more specialized taste cultures.

frame analysis—The examination of how media organize experience.

frames—Social constructs that organize our experience and, thus, our understanding of a situation based upon how they name or define it.

gatekeeping—The ability to control access to the public.

gender—The culturally constructed differences (tastes, roles, activities, etc.) between men and women.

gender performativity—The idea that gender, rather than a coherent component of identity incorporated through socialization, is in fact a bodily performance of discourse that exists only because people believe it is significant.

genre—A class or constellation of messages that share discernible stylistic (syntactic), substantive (semantic), and situational (pragmatic) characteristics.

glass ceiling—Informal, gendered workplace policies that allow women to progress only so far in promotion.

globalization—A complex set of social, political, and economic processes in which the physical boundaries and structural policies that previously reinforced the autonomy of the nation state are collapsing in favor of instantaneous and flexible worldwide social relations.

grotesque realism—An aesthetic of degradation or debasement that emphasizes the lower bodily stratum.

guilt—The emotional condition that arises when we violate hierarchy.

habit—Mental "shortcut" or established tendency that directs future thought and action along predictable paths.

hegemony—Spontaneous consent; the process by which one ideology subverts other competing ideologies and gains cultural dominance.

hermeneutic depth—The critical recognition of multiple meanings in a text as the source of its overall meaning.

heteronormativity—A system of inequality that perpetuates a binary understanding of heterosexuality and homosexuality in which heterosexuality is privileged.

hierarchy—The social rules by which we play.

historical materialism—The underlying method of Marxism; a perspective that regards the character of social life to be a reflection of the material conditions that exist at a particular historical juncture.

historical violence—Representations of violence that invite self-reflection and social consciousness.

homogenization—The reduction or erasure of diversity.

hot medium—High-definition communication technologies that are low in audience participation (e.g. radio, photographs, and films).

hyper-real violence—Highly stylized representations of violence that are absent of any critical reflexivity.

iconic sign—A sign that structurally resembles the object for which it stands.

idealism—A philosophy which holds that ideas, not material conditions, determine social existence.

ideology—A prison for the mind; a wide-scale system of ideas that unconsciously shapes and constrains our beliefs and behaviors; the ruling ideas of society.

Imaginary—A primary developmental space in which the child learns to make demands; it is the realm of chaotic images and sensory impressions into which the child is born.

impression management—The art of successfully staging a character or "part," of enacting a performance that creates the desired impression of the self.

indecency—Material that is morally unfit for general distribution or broadcast.

indexical sign—A sign that conveys meaning through cause or association.

informational bias—The journalistic predisposition that governs how a story is structured and told; four common informational biases are *dramatization, personalization, fragmentation*, and *authority–disorder*.

integration—An ownership pattern in which the subsidiary companies or branches within a corporation are strategically interrelated; integration can be *vertical* (within a media industry) or *horizontal* (across media industries).

interpellation—The process by which individuals are turned into ideological subjects.

interpretive communities—Groups who interpret texts similarly because they share similar social positions and experiences.

interpretive play—An improvisational mode of audience–text interaction that ignores dominant interpretive codes in favor of interpretive codes that fulfill personal needs or desires.

intertextuality—The ways that texts gesture or refer to other texts; three common types of intertextuality include parodic allusion, creative appropriation, and self-reflexive reference.

ironism—A commitment to seeing the world in terms of contingent historical descriptions (and *not* in terms of an unchanging essence).

joint venture—A business practice in which two or more companies split the costs of a new venture so that no single company has to bear the full financial burden should the venture fail.

jouissance—A radically disruptive pleasure that destabilizes culture and subjectivity; an elusive and ecstatic pleasure that emerges from an active engagement with the text.

journalistic beats—The places and institutions where news is regularly expected to occur.

lack—In psychoanalysis, the unquenchable quality of desire that references the difference between the Imaginary and Symbolic orders.

langue—A linguistic system.

libel—Printed statements that falsely impugn or defame a person's character.

literacy—The technologies of writing and print.

logic of safety—A strategy of profit maximization rooted in risk avoidance and the logic of sequels, remakes, and spin-offs.

male gaze—The cinema's frequent positioning of women as objects coded for strong visual and erotic impact.

Marxism—A theory and social movement rooted in the idea that "society is the history of class struggles."

mass media—Communication technologies that have the potential to reach large, distant and anonymous audiences.

media ecology—An approach that views communication technologies as environments.

media erotics—An approach that reflects a concern with the sensuous, transgressive, and productive ways audiences interact with texts.

media frames—Persistent patterns (either stylistic or substantive) of discourse in media.

media literacy—Any learning opportunity that increases an individual's understanding of how the mass media function.

media reform—Any effort by citizens and citizens' interest groups to effect change in the structure and operation of mass media industries.

medium—A particular communication technology through which information is communicated; the term means "middle" or that which comes between two things.

medium theory—A research tradition that considers the *technology* or individual *medium* of communication to be equally important to, or even more important than, the content of media to understanding our social environment.

meliorism—The pragmatic belief that people can correct social problems through proper identification and applied effort.

memory—Audience members' recollection of their reception histories.

mobility—The capacity of an object to be moved from place to place with ease.

mortification—A means of resolving guilt that requires a symbolic act of atonement such as confession or self-sacrifice.

multinationalism—A corporate presence in multiple countries, allowing for the production and distribution of media products on a global scale.

myth—A sacred story or "type of speech" that reaffirms and reproduces ideology in relation to an object.

narrative—The visual or verbal retelling of a series of events, real or fictitious, that occur in (often chronological) succession.

narrowcasting—The practice of targeting niche audiences.

news—The product produced by the organizational structures and practices of journalism.

news agencies—Corporations that produce and sell stories to other news providers or non-profit cooperatives, which work with large media companies to generate news centrally and distribute it locally.

objectivity—The reporting of facts in an impartial manner.

obscenity—Illegal, sexually explicit material that lacks literary, artistic, political, or scientific value.

Oedipus complex—A developmental moment where drives/desires are prohibited, granting the child access to the Symbolic order and/or "normal" subjectivity formation.

open text—A text that is structured to call for the active participation of audiences in the production of meaning.

orality—Thought and its verbal expression.

organization—A system (or network) of ordered relationships and coordinated activities directed toward specific goals.

organizational culture—The set(s) of norms and customs, artifacts and events, and values and assumptions that emerge as a consequence of organizational members' communicative practices.

othering—The process of marginalizing minorities by defining them in relationship to the majority, which is assumed to be the norm.

paradigm shift—A fundamental transformation in how persons know and perceive the world.

parole—Individual speech acts or utterances.

participatory media—Communication technologies that necessitate either *direct-user interaction* (DUI) or *user-created content* (UCC) to function.

patriarchy—A system of social relationships in which women's interests are subordinated to those of men.

performance—Expressive displays that carry symbolic significance in a particular context.

phallocentrism—A social condition in which images or representations of the penis carry connotations of power and dominance.

plaisir—A hegemonic pleasure; a comfortable and comforting pleasure that reproduces dominant culture/subjectivity.

planned obsolescence—A business strategy whereby the obsolescence of a product is built into it from the start.

pleasure principle—The tendency for motivating drives to seek satisfaction, as well as the effect of this tendency on an individual's actions.

polyphony—The "many-voicedness" of a text.

polysemy—The notion that a text has many meanings or is open to multiple interpretations.

polyvalence—The notion that a text has a relatively unified meaning that is valued differently by different audiences.

postfeminism—A conceptual shift within the popular understanding of feminism from an emphasis on the systemic oppression of all women to the empowerment of individual women.

postmodernity—The historical epoch that began to emerge in the 1960s as the economic mode of production in most Western societies slowly shifted from goods-based manufacturing to information-based services.

Pragmatism—A branch of philosophy that assesses truth in terms of effect, outcome, and practicality.

press release—A strategically prepared written or recorded statement produced for news organizations to announce something that claims to be newsworthy.

product placement—The (paid) inclusion of a product, service, or brand in a media text.

productive—Something that is generative of alternative pleasures, meanings, and identities.

profanity—An utterance that is abusive, irreverent, or vulgar.

professional culture—The set(s) of norms and customs, artifacts and events, and values and assumptions that emerge as a consequence of formal training (i.e. education, apprenticeships, internships, etc.), membership and participation (i.e. professional associations, conferences, workshops, licenses, etc.), and recognition (i.e. industry awards and honors) within a profession.

professionalization—The socialization of workers to produce certain kinds of work; the process by which an individual with free will and choice is transformed (i.e. socialized) into an ideological subject (i.e. professional) whose behaviors and actions reaffirm his/her status as a professional.

professionals—Persons who possess expertise in a particular area or field that allows them to accomplish the distinctive tasks of their position.

profit-motive—The continuous desire to increase capital.

punditry—News that is pre-packaged by politicians and their communication consultants (i.e. press advisors and public relations managers) to promote a favorable image of a politician and her or his specific policy initiatives.

Queer theory—An interdisciplinary perspective that seeks to disrupt socially constructed systems of meaning surrounding human sexuality.

readerly text—A text whose meaning is relatively clear and settled and, therefore, asks very little of the audience.

reality principle—The constant curbing of drive according to possibility, law, or social convention.

Reception theory—A diverse body of work that stresses audience interpretation as a primary site of meaning-making.

relations of production (in Marxist theory)—Labor practices and ownership (of property, company shares, or the ways goods are distributed).

relativism—The belief that diverse approaches and theories related to a given subject are all equally correct.

representation—The manner in which various social and cultural groups are depicted in the media.

repression—The process of mentally containing drives beneath conscious recognition or expression.

resistance—Any symbolic or material practice that challenges, subverts, or suspends the cultural codes, rules, or norms, which through their everyday operation create, sustain, and naturalize the prevailing social structure in a particular space and time.

resistive reading—The active, audience-based creation of textual meaning that is contrary to the meaning intended by the text's author, creator, or producer.

rhetoric—The ancient art of persuasion; the use of symbols by humans to influence and move other humans.

ritualistic violence—Representations of violence that are spectacular, gory, exaggerated, hyper-masculine, and adrenaline-pumping.

scopophilia—The pleasure that comes from the process of looking.

semiology—Ferdinand de Saussure's approach to the study of signs.

semiotic—Charles Sanders Peirce's quasi-scientific approach to the study of signs.

sex—The innate, biological differentiation (anatomy, reproduction, hormones, etc.) between men and women.

sexism—Discrimination based upon a person's biological sex.

sexual othering—The process of stigmatizing homosexuality (or really any non-heterosexual practice) as abnormal.

sexuality—An enduring emotional, romantic, or sexual attraction toward others based upon their gender or sex.

sign—Something that invites someone to think of something other than itself.

signified—The mental concept evoked by the signifier.

signifier—The material form (sound-image) of a sign as perceived by the senses.

signifying system—Roland Barthes's approach to the study of signs.

simulation—An implosion of the image (i.e. representations) and the real.

slander—Speech that falsely impugns or defames a person's character.

socialization—The process by which persons – both individually and collectively – learn, adopt, and internalize the prevailing cultural beliefs, values, and norms of a society.

soft news—News that is high in entertainment value, but low in educational value.

space-biased media—Ephemeral media such as paper and television that are inclined toward secularism, materialism, and rapid social change.

spectacle—An obsession with the sensational and arresting, scandalous and shocking dimensions of a situation or context.

stereotype—A misleading and reductionistic representation of a cultural group.

strategic ambiguity—The intentional decision to craft a vague, semantically rich text that is purposefully open to multiple interpretations.

structuralism—The view, largely popularized by the anthropologist Claude Lévi-Strauss, that each element in a cultural system derives its meaning in relation to other elements in that system.

structure—Any social feature or force that constrains or limits agency.

structure of feeling—The sum of the subtle and nuanced aspects of a historical culture, those aspects not obviously or completely captured in the artifacts of a society.

superstructure (in Marxist theory)—Social consciousness, as encoded in institutions such as culture (art and media), religion, education, politics, and the judicial system.

symbol—A sign that is linked to its corresponding object purely by social convention or agreement.

Symbolic—The cultural order of meaning maintained through words and symbols.

symbolic action—The notion that symbol use by humans not only *means* something, but also *does* something; the idea that language and images are tools for doing things.

symbolic interactionism—A theoretical perspective which suggests that the character and conduct of people's social interactions are powerfully shaped by the symbolic meanings they assign to objects, events, other people, and social contexts.

synergy—The cross-development, production, and distribution of a media brand for the purpose of increasing profits.

text—A set of signs working together to produce a relatively unified effect.

textual wink—A feature of the text which only the "clairvoyants" will find meaningful based upon their similarity to the author.

theory—An "optic" or way of seeing, explaining, and interpreting; an explanatory and interpretive tool that simultaneously enables and limits our understanding of the particular social product, practice, or process under investigation.

time-biased media—Durable media such as stone or clay.

token—An exception to a social rule that affirms the correctness of an ideology.

transcendence—A means of resolving or avoiding guilt by appealing to a new hierarchy (or third perspective) in which the two conflicting hierarchies cease to be in opposition.

transgression—An action or artistic practice that breaks with the prevailing cultural codes and conventions of society.

unconscious—A "mental screen" that shields repressed drives from the conscious mind even as they attempt to make themselves known; aspects of the self that cannot be known or expressed in the Symbolic order.

user-created content—Media content that is produced by individuals rather than corporations.

user participation—An audience–text interaction that requires the audience – through the aid of an interface device – to directly engage with the text in a manner that alters the experience of the text.

victim effect—The hypothesis that repeated exposure to representations of violence promotes increased fearfulness of violence.

victimage—A means of resolving guilt that entails scapegoating or the transfer of guilt to a third party.

visibility—The degree to which various social or cultural groups are present in the media.

visual space—Space that is linear, continuous, homogenous, and uniform.

voyeurism—The process of experiencing pleasure by watching a desired object or person from a distance.

writerly text—A text whose meaning is relatively unfinished and unsettled and, thus, invites the audience to co-create its meaning.

yellow journalism—A style of news that lacks any sense of social responsibility and privileges sensational and even fabricated stories and photos.

Index